Principles of Economics

Unabridged Eighth Edition

ALFRED MARSHALL

COSIMO CLASSICS

NEW YORK

Principles of Economics: Unabridged Eighth Edition
Cover Copyright © 2009 by Cosimo, Inc.

Principles of Economics: Unabridged Eighth Edition was originally
published in 1890.

For information, address:
P.O. Box 416, Old Chelsea Station
New York, NY 10011

or visit our website at:
www.cosimobooks.com

Ordering Information:
Cosimo publications are available at online bookstores. They may
also be purchased for educational, business or promotional use:
- *Bulk orders:* special discounts are available on bulk orders for reading
groups, organizations, businesses, and others. For details contact
Cosimo Special Sales at the address above or at info@cosimobooks.com.
- *Custom-label orders:* we can prepare selected books with your cover or
logo of choice. For more information, please contact Cosimo at
info@cosimobooks.com.

Cover Design by www.popshopstudio.com

ISBN: 978-1-60520-801-5

The *raison d'être* of economics as a separate science is that it deals chiefly with that part of man's action which is most under the control of measurable motives; and which therefore lends itself better than any other to systematic reasoning and analysis.

-from Chapter IV

PREFACE TO THE FIRST EDITION

ECONOMIC conditions are constantly changing, and each generation looks at its own problems in its own way. In England, as well as on the Continent and in America, Economic studies are being more vigorously pursued now than ever before; but all this activity has only shown the more clearly that Economic science is, and must be, one of slow and continuous growth. Some of the best work of the present generation has indeed appeared at first sight to be antagonistic to that of earlier writers; but when it has had time to settle down into its proper place, and its rough edges have been worn away, it has been found to involve no real breach of continuity in the development of the science. The new doctrines have supplemented the older, have extended, developed, and sometimes corrected them, and often have given them a different tone by a new distribution of emphasis; but very seldom have subverted them.

The present treatise is an attempt to present a modern version of old doctrines with the aid of the new work, and with reference to the new problems, of our own age. Its general scope and purpose are indicated in Book I; at the end of which a short account is given of what are taken to be the chief subjects of economic inquiry, and the chief practical issues on which that inquiry has a bearing. In accordance with English traditions, it is held that the function of the science is to collect, arrange and analyse economic facts, and to apply the knowledge, gained by observation and experience, in determining what are likely to be the immediate and ultimate effects of various groups of causes; and it is held that the Laws of Economics are statements of tendencies expressed in the indicative mood, and not ethical precepts in the imperative. Economic laws and reasonings in fact are merely a part of the material which Conscience and Common-sense have to turn to account in solving practical problems, and in laying down rules which may be a guide in life.

But ethical forces are among those of which the economist has to take account. Attempts have indeed been made to construct an abstract science with regard to the actions of an " economic man," who is under no ethical influences and who pursues pecuniary gain warily and energetically, but mechanically and selfishly. But they have not been successful, nor even thoroughly carried out. For they have never really treated the economic man as perfectly selfish : no one could be relied on better to endure toil and sacrifice with the unselfish desire to make provision for his family; and his normal motives have always been tacitly assumed to include the family affections. But if they include these, why should they not include all other altruistic motives the action of which is so far uniform in any class at any time and place, that it can be reduced to general rule ? There seems to be no reason; and in the present book normal action is taken to be that which may be expected, under certain conditions, from the members of an industrial group; and no attempt is made to exclude the influence of any motives, the action of which is regular, merely because they are altruistic. If the book has any special character of its own, that may perhaps be said to lie in the prominence which it gives to this and other applications of the Principle of Continuity.

This principle is applied not only to the ethical quality of the motives by which a man may be influenced in choosing his ends, but also to the sagacity, the energy and the enterprise with which he pursues those ends. Thus stress is laid on the fact that there is a continuous gradation from the actions of " city men," which are based on deliberate and far-reaching calculations, and are executed with vigour and ability, to those of ordinary people who have neither the power nor the will to conduct their affairs in a business-like way. The normal willingness to save, the normal willingness to undergo a certain exertion for a certain pecuniary reward, or the normal alertness to seek the best markets in which to buy and sell, or to search out the most advantageous occupation for oneself or for one's children—all these and similar phrases must be relative to the members of a particular class at a given place and time : but, when that is once understood, the theory of normal value is applicable to the actions of the unbusiness-like classes in the same way, though not with the same precision of detail, as to those of the merchant or banker.

And as there is no sharp line of division between conduct which is normal, and that which has to be provisionally neglected as abnormal, so there is none between normal values and " current " or " market " or " occasional " values. The latter are those values in which the accidents of the moment exert a preponderating influence; while normal values are those which would be ultimately attained, if the economic conditions under view had time to work out undisturbed their full effect. But there is no impassable gulf between these two; they shade into one another by continuous gradations. The values which we may regard as normal if we are thinking of the changes from hour to hour on a Produce Exchange, do but indicate current variations with regard to the year's history : and the normal values with reference to the year's history are but current values with reference to the history of the century. For the element of Time, which is the centre of the chief difficulty of almost every economic problem, is itself absolutely continuous : Nature knows no absolute partition of time into long periods and short; but the two shade into one another by imperceptible gradations, and what is a short period for one problem, is a long period for another.

Thus for instance the greater part, though not the whole, of the distinction between Rent and Interest on capital turns on the length of the period which we have in view. That which is rightly regarded as interest on " free " or " floating " capital, or on new investments of capital, is more properly treated as a sort of rent—a *Quasi-rent* it is called below—on old investments of capital. And there is no sharp line of division between floating capital and that which has been " sunk " for a special branch of production, nor between new and old investments of capital; each group shades into the other gradually. And thus even the rent of land is seen, not as a thing by itself, but as the leading species of a large genus; though indeed it has peculiarities of its own which are of vital importance from the point of view of theory as well as of practice.

Again, though there is a sharp line of division between man himself and the appliances which he uses; and though the supply of, and the demand for, human efforts and sacrifices have peculiarities of their own, which do not attach to the supply of, and the demand for, material goods; yet, after all, these material goods are themselves generally the result of human efforts and sacrifices. The theories of the values of labour, and of the things made by it, cannot be separated : they are parts of one great whole; and what differences there are between them even in matters of detail, turn out on inquiry to be, for the most part, differences of degree rather than of kind. As, in spite of the great differences in form between birds and quadrupeds, there is one Fundamental Idea running through all their frames, so the general theory of the equilibrium of demand and supply is a Fundamental Idea running through the frames of all the various parts of the central problem of Distribution and Exchange.[1]

---

[1] In the *Economics of Industry* published by my wife and myself in 1879 an endeavour was made to show the nature of this fundamental unity. A short provisional account of the relations of demand and supply was given before the theory of Distribution; and then this one scheme of general reasoning was applied in succession to the earnings of labour, the interest on capital and the Earnings of Management. But the drift of this arrangement was not made sufficiently clear; and on Professor Nicholson's suggestion, more prominence has been given to it in the present volume.

Another application of the Principle of Continuity is to the use of terms. There has always been a temptation to classify economic goods in clearly defined groups, about which a number of short and sharp propositions could be made, to gratify at once the student's desire for logical precision, and the popular liking for dogmas that have the air of being profound and are yet easily handled. But great mischief seems to have been done by yielding to this temptation, and drawing broad artificial lines of division where Nature has made none. The more simple and absolute an economic doctrine is, the greater will be the confusion which it brings into attempts to apply economic doctrines to practice, if the dividing lines to which it refers cannot be found in real life. There is not in real life a clear line of division between things that are and are not Capital, or that are and are not Necessaries, or again between labour that is and is not Productive.

The notion of continuity with regard to development is common to all modern schools of economic thought, whether the chief influences acting on them are those of biology, as represented by the writings of Herbert Spencer; or of history and philosophy, as represented by Hegel's *Philosophy of History*, and by more recent ethico-historical studies on the Continent and elsewhere. These two kinds of influences have affected, more than any other, the substance of the views expressed in the present book; but their form has been most affected by mathematical conceptions of continuity, as represented in Cournot's *Principes Mathématiques de la Théorie des Richesses*. He taught that it is necessary to face the difficulty of regarding the various elements of an economic problem,—not as determining one another in a chain of causation, A determining B, B determining C, and so on—but as all mutually determining one another. Nature's action is complex: and nothing is gained in the long run by pretending that it is simple, and trying to describe it in a series of elementary propositions.

Under the guidance of Cournot, and in a less degree of von Thünen, I was led to attach great importance to the fact that our observations of nature, in the moral as in the physical world, relate not so much to aggregate quantities, as to increments of quantities, and that in particular the demand for a thing is a continuous function, of which the " marginal " [1] increment is, in stable equilibrium, balanced against the corresponding increment of its cost of

---

[1] The term " marginal " increment I borrowed from von Thünen's *Der isolirte Staat*, 1826–63, and it is now commonly used by German economists. When Jevons' Theory appeared, I adopted his word " final "; but I have been gradually convinced that " marginal " is the better.

production. It is not easy to get a clear full view of continuity in this aspect without the aid either of mathematical symbols or of diagrams. The use of the latter requires no special knowledge, and they often express the conditions of economic life more accurately, as well as more easily, than do mathematical symbols; and therefore they have been applied as supplementary illustrations in the footnotes of the present volume. The argument in the text is never dependent on them; and they may be omitted; but experience seems to show that they give a firmer grasp of many important principles than can be got without their aid; and that there are many problems of pure theory, which no one who has once learnt to use diagrams will willingly handle in any other way.

The chief use of pure mathematics in economic questions seems to be in helping a person to write down quickly, shortly and exactly, some of his thoughts for his own use : and to make sure that he has enough, and only enough, premisses for his conclusions (i.e. that his equations are neither more nor less in number than his unknowns). But when a great many symbols have to be used, they become very laborious to any one but the writer himself. And though Cournot's genius must give a new mental activity to everyone who passes through his hands, and mathematicians of calibre similar to his may use their favourite weapons in clearing a way for themselves to the centre of some of those difficult problems of economic theory, of which only the outer fringe has yet been touched; yet it seems doubtful whether any one spends his time well in reading lengthy translations of economic doctrines into mathematics, that have not been made by himself. A few specimens of those applications of mathematical language which have proved most useful for my own purposes have, however, been added in an Appendix.

September 1890.

PREFACE TO THE EIGHTH EDITION

THIS edition is a reprint of the seventh, which was almost a reprint of the sixth, the only changes being in small matters of detail : the Preface is almost the same as in the seventh edition.

It is now thirty years since the first edition of this volume implied a promise that a second volume, completing the treatise, would appear within a reasonable time. But I had laid my plan on too large a scale; and its scope widened, especially on the realistic side, with every pulse of that Industrial Revolution of the present generation, which has far outdone the changes of a century ago, in both rapidity and breadth of movement. So ere long I was compelled to abandon my hope of completing the work in two volumes. My subsequent plans were changed more than once; partly by the course of events, partly by my other engagements, and the decline of my strength.

Industry and Trade, published in 1919, is in effect a continuation of the present volume. A third (on Trade, Finance and the Industrial Future) is far advanced. The three volumes are designed to deal with all the chief problems of economics, so far as the writer's power extends.

The present volume therefore remains as a general introduction to the study of economic science; similar in some respects, though not in all, to that of volumes on *Foundations* (*Grundlagen*), which Roscher and some other economists have put in the forefront of groups of semi-independent volumes on economics. It avoids such special topics as currency and the organization of markets : and, in regard to such matters as the structure of industry, employment, and the problem of wages, it deals mainly with normal conditions.

Economic evolution is gradual. Its progress is sometimes arrested or reversed by political catastrophes : but its forward movements are never sudden; for even in the Western world and in Japan it is based on habit, partly conscious, partly unconscious. And though an inventor, or an organizer, or a financier of genius may seem to have modified the economic structure of a people almost at a stroke; yet that part of his influence, which has not been merely superficial and transitory, is found on inquiry to have done little more than bring to a head a broad constructive movement which had long been in preparation. Those manifestations of nature which occur most frequently, and are so orderly that they can be closely watched and narrowly studied, are the basis of economic as of most other scientific work; while those which are spasmodic, infrequent, and difficult of observation, are commonly reserved for special examination at a later stage : and the motto *Natura non facit saltum* is specially appropriate to a volume on Economic Foundations.

An illustration of this contrast may be taken from the distribution of the study of large businesses between the present volume and that on *Industry and Trade*. When any branch of industry offers an open field for new firms which rise to the first rank, and perhaps after a time decay, the normal cost of production in it can be estimated with reference to " a representative firm," which enjoys a fair share both of those internal economies which belong to a well-organized individual business, and of those general or external economies which arise out of the collective organization of the district as a whole. A study of such a firm belongs properly to a volume on Foundations. So also does a study of the principles on which a firmly established monopoly, in the hands of a Government department or a large railway, regulates its prices with main reference indeed to its own revenue; but also with more or less consideration for the wellbeing of its customers.

But normal action falls into the background, when Trusts are striving for the mastery of a large market; when communities of interest are being made and unmade; and, above all, when the policy of any particular establishment is likely to be governed, not with a single eye to its own business success, but in subordination to some large stock-exchange manoeuvre, or some campaign for the control of markets. Such matters cannot be fitly discussed in a volume on Foundations : they belong to a volume dealing with some part of the Superstructure.

The Mecca of the economist lies in economic biology rather than in economic dynamics. But biological conceptions are more complex than those of mechanics; a volume on Foundations must therefore give a relatively large place to mechanical analogies; and frequent use is made of the term " equilibrium," which suggests something of statical analogy. This fact, combined with the predominant attention paid in the present volume to the normal conditions of life in the modern age, has suggested the notion that its central idea is " statical," rather than " dynamical." But in fact it is concerned throughout with the forces that cause movement: and its key-note is that of dynamics, rather than statics.

The forces to be dealt with are however so numerous, that it is best to take a few at a time; and to work out a number of partial solutions as auxiliaries to our main study. Thus we begin by isolating the primary relations of supply, demand and price in regard to a particular commodity. We reduce to inaction all other forces by the phrase " other things being equal ": we do not suppose that they are inert, but for the time we ignore their activity. This scientific device is a great deal older than science : it is the method by which, consciously or unconsciously, sensible men have dealt from time immemorial with every difficult problem of ordinary life.

In the second stage more forces are released from the hypothetical slumber that had been imposed on them : changes in the conditions of demand for and supply of particular groups of commodities come into play; and their complex mutual interactions begin to be observed. Gradually the area of the dynamical problem becomes larger; the area covered by provisional statical assumptions becomes smaller; and at last is reached the great central problem of the Distribution of the National Dividend among a vast number of different agents of production. Meanwhile the dynamical principle of " Substitution " is seen ever at work, causing the demand for, and the supply of, any one set of agents of production to be influenced through indirect channels by the movements of demand and supply in relation to other agents, even though situated in far remote fields of industry.

The main concern of economics is thus with human beings who are impelled, for good and evil, to change and progress. Fragmentary statical hypotheses are used as temporary auxiliaries to dynamical—or rather biological—conceptions : but the central idea of economics, even when its Foundations alone are under discussion, must be that of living force and movement.

There have been stages in social history in which the special features of the income yielded by the ownership of land have dominated human relations : and perhaps they may again assert a pre-eminence. But in the present age, the opening out of new countries, aided by low transport charges on land and sea, has almost suspended the tendency to Diminishing Return, in that sense in which the term was used by Malthus and Ricardo, when the English labourers' weekly wages were often less than the price of half a bushel of good wheat. And yet, if the growth of population should continue for very long even at a quarter of its present rate, the aggregate rental values of land for all its uses (assumed to be as free as now from restraint by public authority) may again exceed the aggregate of incomes derived from all other forms of material property; even though that may then embody twenty times as much labour as now.

Increasing stress has been laid in successive editions up to the present on these facts; and also on the correlated fact that in every branch of production and trade there is a margin, up to which an increased application of any agent will be profitable under given conditions; but beyond which its further application will yield a diminishing return unless there be some increase of demand accompanied by an appropriate increase of other agents of production needed to co-operate with it. And a similar increasing stress has been laid on the complementary fact that this notion of a margin is not uniform and absolute: it varies with the conditions of the problem in hand, and in particular with the period of time to which reference is being made. The rules are universal that, (1) marginal costs do not govern price; (2) it is only at the margin that the action of those forces which do govern price can be made to stand out in clear light; and (3) the margin, which must be studied in reference to long periods and enduring results, differs in character as well as in extent from that which must be studied in reference to short periods and to passing fluctuations.

Variations in the nature of marginal costs are indeed largely responsible for the well-known fact that those effects of an economic cause, which are not easily traced, are frequently more important than, and in the opposite direction to, those which lie on the surface and attract the eye of the casual observer. This is one of those fundamental difficulties which have underlain and troubled the economic analysis of past times; its full significance is perhaps not yet generally recognized, and much more work may need to be done before it is fully mastered.

The new analysis is endeavouring gradually and tentatively to bring over into economics, as far as the widely different nature of the material will allow, those methods of the science of small increments (commonly called the differential calculus) to which man owes directly or indirectly the greater part of the control that he has obtained in recent times over physical nature. It is still in its infancy; it has no dogmas, and no standard of orthodoxy. It has not yet had time to obtain a perfectly settled terminology; and some differences as to the best use of terms and other subordinate matters are but a sign of healthy life. In fact however there is a remarkable harmony and agreement on essentials among those who are working constructively by the new method; and especially among such of them as have served an apprenticeship in the simpler and more definite, and therefore more advanced, problems of physics. Ere another generation has passed, its dominion over that limited but important field of economic inquiry to which it is appropriate will probably be no longer in dispute.

My wife has aided and advised me at every stage of successive editions of this volume. Each one of them owes a great deal to her suggestions, her care, and her judgment. Dr Keynes and Mr L. L. Price read through the proofs of the first edition and helped me greatly; and Mr A. W. Flux also has done much for me. Among the many who have helped me on special points, in some cases in regard to more than one edition, I would specially mention Professors Ashley, Cannan, Edgeworth, Haverfield, Pigou and Taussig; Dr Berry, Mr C. R. Fay, and the late Professor Sidgwick.

BALLIOL CROFT,
  6 MADINGLEY ROAD, CAMBRIDGE.
    October 1920.

CONTENTS

BOOK I

PRELIMINARY SURVEY

BOOK IV.

THE AGENTS OF PRODUCTION

LAND, LABOUR, CAPITAL AND ORGANIZATION

BOOK V

GENERAL RELATIONS OF DEMAND, SUPPLY, AND VALUE

BOOK VI

THE DISTRIBUTION OF THE NATIONAL INCOME

Appendix F. Barter. The uncertainties of market bargaining are greater in barter than where money is used; partly because a man can generally give out, or take in, a given *quantum* (not a given percentage) of value in the form of money without greatly altering its marginal utility to him, than he can in the form of any single commodity   .   .   .   .   .   **pp. 652–654**

Appendix G. The incidence of local rates, with some suggestions as to policy. § 1. The ultimate incidence of a rate varies greatly according as the population is or is not migratory, and as the rate is Onerous or Beneficial. Rapid changes in conditions make clear foresight impossible. § 2. The "building value " of a property together with its site value combine to make its whole value, provided the building is appropriate to the site : but not otherwise. § 3. Onerous taxes on site values fall mainly on owners : or, if unforeseen, on lessees. § 4. But such onerous taxes on building values, as are uniform all over the country, fall mainly on the occupier. Exceptionally heavy local onerous rates are however largely paid by owner (or lessee), even in so far as assessed on building values. § 5. The distribution of the burden of old rates and taxes is but little affected by their being collected from the occupier : but a sudden increase of onerous rates is a grievous burden to the occupier, especially if a shopkeeper, under the present system of collection. § 6. Assessment of vacant building sites on the basis of their capital value, and a partial transference of assessments from building to site values generally, might be beneficial, provided they were gradual, and accompanied by stringent bylaws as to the relation between the heights of buildings and the free spaces in front and back. § 7. Some further observations on rural rates. §§ 8, 9. Some practical suggestions. The permanent limitations in the supply of land, and the large share which collective action has in its present value, require it to be classed in a separate category for the purposes of taxation.

pp. 655–663

Appendix H. Limitations of the use of statical assumptions in regard to increasing return. §§ 1–4. The hypothesis of a rigid supply schedule leads to the possibility of multiple positions of equilibrium, stable and unstable. But this hypothesis diverges so far from actual conditions, in regard to increasing return, that it can be applied only tentatively and within a narrow scope. Caution in regard to the use of the term Normal Supply-price in this connection   .   .   .   .   .   .   **pp. 664–669**

Appendix I. Ricardo's theory of value. §§ 1–3. Though obscurely expressed, it anticipated more of the modern doctrine of the relations between cost, utility and value, than has been recognized by Jevons and some other critics   .   .   .   .   **pp. 670–676**

Appendix J. The doctrine of the wages-fund. § 1. The scarcity of capital a century ago inclined economists to lay excessive stress on the part played by the supply of capital in governing wages. §§ 2, 3. This exaggeration is found in the discussion of wages in Mill's Second Book, which preceded his study of Value ; but not in the later discussion of Distribution in his Fourth

BOOK I

PRELIMINARY SURVEY

CHAPTER I

INTRODUCTION

§ 1. POLITICAL ECONOMY or ECONOMICS is a study of mankind in the ordinary business of life; it examines that part of individual and social action which is most closely connected with the attainment and with the use of the material requisites of wellbeing.

I, I, 1.

Thus it is on the one side a study of wealth; and on the other, and more important side, a part of the study of man. For man's character has been moulded by his every-day work, and the material resources which he thereby procures, more than by any other influence unless it be that of his religious ideals; and the two great forming agencies of the world's history have been the religious and the economic. Here and there the ardour of the military or the artistic spirit has been for a while predominant: but religious and economic influences have nowhere been displaced from the front rank even for a time; and they have nearly always been more important than all others put together. Religious motives are more intense than economic, but their direct action seldom extends over so large a part of life. For the business by which a person earns his livelihood generally fills his thoughts during by far the greater part of those hours in which his mind is at its best; during them his character is being formed by the way in which he uses his faculties in his work, by the thoughts and the feelings which it suggests, and by his relations to his associates in work, his employers or his employees.

Economics is a study of wealth and a part of the study of man.

Man's character formed by his daily work.

And very often the influence exerted on a person's character by the amount of his income is hardly less, if it is less, than that exerted by the way in which it is earned. It may make little difference to the fulness of life of a family whether its yearly income is £1000 or £5000; but it makes a very great difference whether the income is £30 or £150: for with £150 the family has, with £30 it has not, the material conditions of a complete life. It is true that in religion, in

Poverty causes degradation.

B

the family affections and in friendship, even the poor may find scope for many of those faculties which are the source of the highest happiness. But the conditions which surround extreme poverty, especially in densely crowded places, tend to deaden the higher faculties. Those who have been called the Residuum of our large towns have little opportunity for friendship; they know nothing of the decencies and the quiet, and very little even of the unity of family life; and religion often fails to reach them. No doubt their physical, mental, and moral ill-health is partly due to other causes than poverty : but this is the chief cause.

And, in addition to the Residuum, there are vast numbers of people both in town and country who are brought up with insufficient food, clothing, and house-room; whose education is broken off early in order that they may go to work for wages; who thenceforth are engaged during long hours in exhausting toil with imperfectly nourished bodies, and have therefore no chance of developing their higher mental faculties. Their life is not necessarily unhealthy or unhappy. Rejoicing in their affections towards God and man, and perhaps even possessing some natural refinement of feeling, they may lead lives that are far less incomplete than those of many, who have more material wealth. But, for all that, their poverty is a great and almost unmixed evil to them. Even when they are well, their weariness often amounts to pain, while their pleasures are few; and when sickness comes, the suffering caused by poverty increases tenfold. And, though a contented spirit may go far towards reconciling them to these evils, there are others to which it ought not to reconcile them. Overworked and undertaught, weary and careworn, without quiet and without leisure, they have no chance of making the best of their mental faculties.

May we not outgrow the belief that poverty is necessary ? Although then some of the evils which commonly go with poverty are not its necessary consequences; yet, broadly speaking, " the destruction of the poor is their poverty," and the study of the causes of poverty is the study of the causes of the degradation of a large part of mankind.

§ 2. Slavery was regarded by Aristotle as an ordinance of nature, and so probably was it by the slaves themselves in olden time. The dignity of man was proclaimed by the Christian religion : it has been asserted with increasing vehemence during the last hundred years : but, only through the spread of education during quite recent times, are we beginning to feel the full import of the phrase. Now at last we are setting ourselves seriously to inquire whether it is necessary that there should be any so-called " lower classes " at all : that is, whether there need be large numbers of people doomed from their birth to hard work in order to provide for others the requisites of a refined and cultured life; while they themselves are prevented by their poverty and toil from having any share or part in that life.

The hope that poverty and ignorance may gradually be extinguished, derives indeed much support from the steady progress of the working classes during the nineteenth century. The steam-engine has relieved them of much exhausting and degrading toil; wages have risen; education has been improved and become more general; the railway and the printing-press have enabled members of the same trade in different parts of the country to communicate easily with one another, and to undertake and carry out broad and far-seeing lines of policy; while the growing demand for intelligent work has caused the artisan classes to increase so rapidly that they now outnumber those whose labour is entirely unskilled. A great part of the artisans have ceased to belong to the " lower classes " in the sense in which the term was originally used; and some of them already lead a more refined and noble life than did the majority of the upper classes even a century ago.

This progress had done more than anything else to give practical interest to the question whether it is really impossible that all should start in the world with a fair chance of leading a cultured life, free from the pains of poverty and the stagnating influences of excessive mechanical toil; and this question is being pressed to the front by the growing earnestness of the age.

The question cannot be fully answered by economic science. For the answer depends partly on the moral and political capabilities of human nature, and on these matters the economist has no special means of information : he must do as others do, and guess as best he can. But the answer depends in a great measure upon facts and inferences, which are within the province of economics; and this it is which gives to economic studies their chief and their highest interest.

§ 3. It might have been expected that a science, which deals with questions so vital for the wellbeing of mankind, would have engaged the attention of many of the ablest thinkers of every age, and be now well advanced towards maturity. But the fact is that the number of scientific economists has always been small relatively to the difficulty of the work to be done; so that the science is still almost in its infancy. One cause of this is that the bearing of economics on the higher wellbeing of man has been overlooked. Indeed, a science which has wealth for its subject-matters, is often repugnant at first sight to many students; for those who do most to

I, I, 4. advance the boundaries of knowledge, seldom care much about the
possession of wealth for its own sake.

Changeful-   But a more important cause is that many of those conditions of
ness of
economic   industrial life, and of those methods of production, distribution and
conditions. consumption, with which modern economic science is concerned, are
themselves only of recent date.   It is indeed true that the change in
substance is in some respects not so great as the change in outward
form; and much more of modern economic theory, than at first
appears, can be adapted to the conditions of backward races.   But
unity in substance, underlying many varieties of form, is not easy to
detect; and changes in form have had the effect of making writers
in all ages profit less than they otherwise might have done by the
work of their predecessors.

The economic conditions of modern life, though more complex,
are in many ways more definite than those of earlier times.   Business
is more clearly marked off from other concerns; the rights of
individuals as against others and as against the community are more
sharply defined; and above all the emancipation from custom, and
the growth of free activity, of constant forethought and restless
enterprise, have given a new precision and a new prominence to the
causes that govern the relative values of different things and different
kinds of labour.

The funda-   § 4. It is often said that the modern forms of industrial life are
mental cha-
racteristic distinguished from the earlier by being more competitive.   But this
of modern   account is not quite satisfactory.   The strict meaning of competition
industrial
life is   seems to be the racing of one person against another, with special
not com-   reference to bidding for the sale or purchase of anything.   This kind
petition,
of racing is no doubt both more intense and more widely extended
than it used to be : but it is only a secondary, and one might almost
say, an accidental consequence from the fundamental characteristics
of modern industrial life.

but self-   There is no one term that will express these characteristics
reliance,
inde-   adequately.   They are, as we shall presently see, a certain independence,   pendence and habit of choosing one's own course for oneself, a self-
deliberate
choice and   reliance; a deliberation and yet a promptness of choice and judg-
fore-   ment, and a habit of forecasting the future and of shaping one's
thought.
course with reference to distant aims.   They may and often do cause
people to compete with one another; but on the other hand they may
tend, and just now indeed they are tending, in the direction of co-
operation and combination of all kinds good and evil.   But these
tendencies towards collective ownership and collective action are
quite different from those of earlier times, because they are the result

not of custom, not of any passive drifting into association with one's neighbours, but of free choice by each individual of that line of conduct which after careful deliberation seems to him the best suited for attaining his ends, whether they are selfish or unselfish.

The term " competition " has gathered about it evil savour, and has come to imply a certain selfishness and indifference to the well-being of others. Now it is true that there is less deliberate selfishness in early than in modern forms of industry; but there is also less deliberate unselfishness. It is deliberateness, and not selfishness, that is the characteristic of the modern age.

For instance, while custom in a primitive society extends the limits of the family, and prescribes certain duties to one's neighbours which fall into disuse in a later civilization, it also prescribes an attitude of hostility to strangers. In a modern society the obligations of family kindness become more intense, though they are concentrated on a narrower area; and neighbours are put more nearly on the same footing with strangers. In ordinary dealings with both of them the standard of fairness and honesty is lower than in some of the dealings of a primitive people with their neighbours : but it is much higher than in their dealings with strangers. Thus it is the ties of neighbourhood alone that have been relaxed : the ties of family are in many ways stronger than before, family affection leads to much more self-sacrifice and devotion than it used to do; and sympathy with those who are strangers to us is a growing source of a kind of deliberate unselfishness, that never existed before the modern age. That country which is the birthplace of modern competition devotes a larger part of its income than any other to charitable uses, and spent twenty millions on purchasing the freedom of the slaves in the West Indies.

In every age poets and social reformers have tried to stimulate the people of their own time to a nobler life by enchanting stories of the virtues of the heroes of old. But neither the records of history nor the contemporary observation of backward races, when carefully studied, give any support to the doctrine that man is on the whole harder and harsher than he was; or that he was ever more willing than he is now to sacrifice his own happiness for the benefit of others in cases where custom and law have left him free to choose his own course. Among races, whose intellectual capacity seems not to have developed in any other direction, and who have none of the originating power of the modern business man, there will be found many who show an evil sagacity in driving a hard bargain in a market even with their neighbours. No traders are more unscrupulous in taking advantage

I, I, 4.

"Competition" implies too much as well as too little. Man is not more selfish than he was.

of the necessities of the unfortunate than are the corn-dealers and money-lenders of the East.

Man is not more dishonest than he was.

Again, the modern era has undoubtedly given new openings for dishonesty in trade. The advance of knowledge has discovered new ways of making things appear other than they are, and has rendered possible many new forms of adulteration. The producer is now far removed from the ultimate consumer; and his wrong-doings are not visited with the prompt and sharp punishment which falls on the head of a person who, being bound to live and die in his native village, plays a dishonest trick on one of his neighbours. The opportunities for knavery are certainly more numerous than they were; but there is no reason for thinking that people avail themselves of a larger proportion of such opportunities than they used to do. On the contrary, modern methods of trade imply habits of trustfulness on the one side and a power of resisting temptation to dishonesty on the other, which do not exist among a backward people. Instances of simple truth and personal fidelity are met with under all social conditions : but those who have tried to establish a business of modern type in a backward country find that they can scarcely ever depend on the native population for filling posts of trust. It is even more difficult to dispense with imported assistance for work, which calls for a strong moral character, than for that which requires great skill and mental ability. Adulteration and fraud in trade were rampant in the middle ages to an extent that is very astonishing, when we consider the difficulties of wrong-doing without detection at that time.

Dreams of a past GoldenAge are beautiful but misleading.

In every stage of civilization, in which the power of money has been prominent, poets in verse and prose have delighted to depict a past truly " Golden Age," before the pressure of mere material gold had been felt. Their idyllic pictures have been beautiful, and have stimulated noble imaginations and resolves; but they have had very little historical truth. Small communities with simple wants for which the bounty of nature has made abundant provisions, have indeed sometimes been nearly free from care about their material needs, and have not been tempted to sordid ambitions. But whenever we can penetrate to the inner life of a crowded population under primitive conditions in our own time, we find more want, more narrowness, and more hardness than was manifest at a distance : and we never find a more widely diffused comfort alloyed by less suffering than exists in the western world to-day. We ought therefore not to brand the forces, which have made modern civilization, by a name which suggests evil.

It is perhaps not reasonable that such a suggestion should attach to the term "competition"; but in fact it does. In fact, when competition is arraigned, its anti-social forms are made prominent; and care is seldom taken to inquire whether there are not other forms of it, which are so essential to the maintenance of energy and spontaneity, that their cessation might probably be injurious on the balance to social wellbeing. The traders or producers, who find that a rival is offering goods at a lower price than will yield them a good profit, are angered at his intrusion, and complain of being wronged; even though it may be true that those who buy the cheaper goods are in greater need than themselves, and that the energy and resourcefulness of their rival is a social gain. In many cases the "regulation of competition" is a misleading term, that veils the formation of a privileged class of producers, who often use their combined force to frustrate the attempts of an able man to rise from a lower class than their own. Under the pretext of repressing anti-social competition, they deprive him of the liberty of carving out for himself a new career, where the services rendered by him to the consumers of the commodity would be greater than the injuries, that he inflicts on the relatively small group which objects to his competition.

If competition is contrasted with energetic co-operation in unselfish work for the public good, then even the best forms of competition are relatively evil; while its harsher and meaner forms are hateful. And in a world in which all men were perfectly virtuous, competition would be out of place; but so also would be private property and every form of private right. Men would think only of their duties; and no one would desire to have a larger share of the comforts and luxuries of life than his neighbours. Strong producers could easily bear a touch of hardship; so they would wish that their weaker neighbours, while producing less should consume more. Happy in this thought, they would work for the general good with all the energy, the inventiveness, and the eager initiative that belonged to them; and mankind would be victorious in contests with nature at every turn. Such is the Golden Age to which poets and dreamers may look forward. But in the responsible conduct of affairs, it is worse than folly to ignore the imperfections which still cling to human nature.

History in general, and especially the history of socialistic ventures, shows that ordinary men are seldom capable of pure ideal altruism for any considerable time together; and that the exceptions are to be found only when the masterful fervour of a small band of

I, i, 4.

Modern competition is of two kinds,

constructive and destructive.

Even constructive competition is less beneficent than ideal altruistic co-operation.

I, ɪ, 5.   religious enthusiasts makes material concerns to count for nothing in comparison with the higher faith.

No doubt men, even now, are capable of much more unselfish service than they generally render : and the supreme aim of the economist is to discover how this latent social asset can be developed most quickly, and turned to account most wisely. But he must not decry competition in general, without analysis : he is bound to retain a neutral attitude towards any particular manifestation of it until he is sure that, human nature being what it is, the restraint of competition would not be more anti-social in its working than the competition itself.

We may conclude then that the term " competition " is not well suited to describe the special characteristics of industrial life in the modern age. We need a term that does not imply any moral qualities, whether good or evil, but which indicates the undisputed fact that modern business and industry are characterized by more self-reliant habits, more forethought, more deliberate and free choice.

Economic Freedom.

There is not any one term adequate for this purpose : but *Freedom of Industry and Enterprise*, or more shortly, *Economic Freedom*, points in the right direction ; and it may be used in the absence of a better. Of course this deliberate and free choice may lead to a certain departure from individual freedom when co-operation or combination seems to offer the best route to the desired end. The questions how far these deliberate forms of association are likely to destroy the freedom in which they had their origin and how far they are likely to be conducive to the public weal, lie beyond the scope of the present volume.[1]

Rough sketches of the growth of economic freedom and of economic science are transferred from this Book to Appendices A and B.

§ 5. This introductory chapter was followed in earlier editions by two short sketches : the one related to the growth of free enterprise and generally of economic freedom, and the other to the growth of economic science. They have no claim to be systematic histories, however compressed ; they aim only at indicating some landmarks on the routes by which economic structure and economic thought have travelled to their present position. They are now transferred to Appendices A and B at the end of this volume, partly because their full drift can best be seen after some acquaintance has been made with the subject-matter of economics ; and partly because in the twenty years, which have elapsed since they were first written, public opinion as to the position which the study of economic and social science should hold in a liberal education has greatly developed. There is less need

[1] They occupy a considerable place in the forthcoming volumes on *Industry and Trade*.

now than formerly to insist that the economic problems of the present I, I, 5.
generation derive much of their subject-matter from technical and
social changes that are of recent date, and that their form as well as
their urgency assume throughout the effective economic freedom of
the mass of the people.

The relations of many ancient Greeks and Romans with the *The
slaves of their households were genial and humane. But even in *growth of
economic*
Attica the physical and moral wellbeing of the great body of the *freedom.*
inhabitants was not accepted as a chief aim of the citizen. Ideals
of life were high, but they concerned only a few : and the doctrine
of value, which is full of complexities in the modern age, could then
have been worked out on a plan ; such as could be conceived to-day,
only if nearly all manual work were superseded by automatic
machines which required merely a definite allowance of steam-power
and materials, and had no concern with the requirements of a full
citizen's life. Much of modern economics might indeed have been
anticipated in the towns of the Middle Ages, in which an intelligent
and daring spirit was for the first time combined with patient
industry. But they were not left to work out their career in peace ;
and the world had to wait for the dawn of the new economic era till a
whole nation was ready for the ordeal of economic freedom.

England especially was gradually prepared for the task ; but *The early
towards the end of the eighteenth century, the changes, which had *roughness
of eco-*
so far been slow and gradual, suddenly became rapid and violent. *nomic freedom in
Mechanical inventions, the concentration of industries, and a system *England.*
of manufacturing on a large scale for distant markets broke up the
old traditions of industry, and left everyone to bargain for himself as
best he might ; and at the same time they stimulated an increase of
population for which no provision had been made beyond standing-
room in factories and workshops. Thus free competition, or rather,
freedom of industry and enterprise, was set loose to run, like a huge
untrained monster, its wayward course. The abuse of their new
power by able but uncultured business men led to evils on every
side ; it unfitted mothers for their duties, it weighed down children
with overwork and disease ; and in many places it degraded the race.
Meanwhile the kindly meant recklessness of the poor law did even
more to lower the moral and physical energy of Englishmen than the
hard-hearted recklessness of the manufacturing discipline : for by
depriving the people of those qualities which would fit them for the
new order of things, it increased the evil and diminished the good *The
caused by the advent of free enterprise. *growth of
economic*
And yet the time at which free enterprise was showing itself in *science.*

an unnaturally harsh form, was the very time in which economists were most lavish in their praises of it. This was partly because they saw clearly, what we of this generation have in a great measure forgotten, the cruelty of the yoke of custom and rigid ordinance which it had displaced; and partly because the general tendency of Englishmen at the time was to hold that freedom in all matters, political and social, was worth having at every cost except the loss of security. But partly also it was that the productive forces which free enterprise was giving to the nation, were the only means by which it could offer a successful resistance to Napoleon. Economists therefore treated free enterprise not indeed as an unmixed good, but as a less evil than such regulation as was practicable at the time.

Adhering to the lines of thought that had been started chiefly by mediæval traders, and continued by French and English philosophers in the latter half of the eighteenth century, Ricardo and his followers developed a theory of the action of free enterprise (or, as they said, free competition), which contained many truths, that will be probably important so long as the world exists. Their work was wonderfully complete within the narrow area which it covered. But much of the best of it consists of problems relating to rent and the value of corn :—problems on the solution of which the fate of England just then seemed to depend; but many of which, in the particular form in which they were worked out by Ricardo, have very little direct bearing on the present state of things.

A good deal of the rest of their work was narrowed by its regarding too exclusively the peculiar condition of England at that time; and this narrowness has caused a reaction. So that now, when more experience, more leisure, and greater material resources have enabled us to bring free enterprise somewhat under control, to diminish its power of doing evil and increase its power of doing good, there is growing up among many economists a sort of spite against it. Some even incline to exaggerate its evils, and attribute to it the ignorance and suffering, which are the results either of tyranny and oppression in past ages, or of the misunderstanding and mismanagement of economic freedom.

Intermediate between these two extremes are the great body of economists who, working on parallel lines in many different countries, are bringing to their studies an unbiassed desire to ascertain the truth, and a willingness to go through with the long and heavy work by which alone scientific results of any value can be obtained. Varieties of mind, of temper, of training and of opportunities lead them to work in different ways, and to give their chief attention to different parts of the problem. All are bound more or less to collect I, I, 5. and arrange facts and statistics relating to past and present times; and all are bound to occupy themselves more or less with analysis and reasoning on the basis of those facts which are ready at hand : but some find the former task the more attractive and absorbing, and others the latter. This division of labour, however, implies not opposition, but harmony of purpose. The work of all adds something or other to that knowledge, which enables us to understand the influences exerted on the quality and tone of man's life by the manner in which he earns his livelihood, and by the character of that livelihood.

CHAPTER II

THE SUBSTANCE OF ECONOMICS

I, II, 1.
he chief
ιotives of
usiness
fe can be
ιeasured
ιdirectly
ι money.

§ 1. ECONOMICS is a study of men as they live and move and think in the ordinary business of life. But it concerns itself chiefly with those motives which affect, most powerfully and most steadily, man's conduct in the business part of his life. Everyone who is worth anything carries his higher nature with him into business; and, there as elsewhere, he is influenced by his personal affections, by his conceptions of duty and his reverence for high ideals. And it is true that the best energies of the ablest inventors and organizers of improved methods and appliances are stimulated by a noble emulation more than by any love of wealth for its own sake. But, for all that, the steadiest motive to ordinary business work is the desire for the pay which is the material reward of work. The pay may be on its way to be spent selfishly or unselfishly, for noble or base ends; and here the variety of human nature comes into play. But the motive is supplied by a definite amount of money : and it is this definite and exact money measurement of the steadiest motives in business life, which has enabled economics far to outrun every other branch of the study of man. Just as the chemist's fine balance has made chemistry more exact than most other physical sciences; so this economist's balance, rough and imperfect as it is, has made economics more exact than any other branch of social science. But of course economics cannot be compared with the exact physical sciences : for it deals with the ever changing and subtle forces of human nature.[1]

The advantage which economics has over other branches of social science appears then to arise from the fact that its special field of work gives rather larger opportunities for exact methods than any other branch. It concerns itself chiefly with those desires, aspirations and other affections of human nature, the outward manifestations of which appear as incentives to action in such a form that the force or quantity of the incentives can be estimated and measured with some approach to accuracy; and which therefore are in some

[1] Some remarks on the relation of economics to the sum total of social science will be found in Appendix C, 1, 2.

degree amenable to treatment by scientific machinery. An opening I, II, 1.
is made for the methods and the tests of science as soon as the force
of a person's motives—*not* the motives themselves—can be approximately measured by the sum of money, which he will just give up in
order to secure a desired satisfaction; or again by the sum which is
just required to induce him to undergo a certain fatigue.

It is essential to note that the economist does not claim to *Even*
measure any affection of the mind in itself, or directly; but only *common
pleasures*
indirectly through its effect. No one can compare and measure *and pains
can be*
accurately against one another even his own mental states at different *compared*
times : and no one can measure the mental states of another at all *only
through*
except indirectly and conjecturally by their effects. Of course *the
strength*
various affections belong to man's higher nature and others to his *of the*
lower, and are thus different in kind. But, even if we confine our *incentives
which*
attention to mere physical pleasures and pains of the same kind, we *they sup-*
find that they can only be compared indirectly by their effects. In *ply to
action,*
fact, even this comparison is necessarily to some extent conjectural,
unless they occur to the same person at the same time.

For instance the pleasures which two persons derive from
smoking cannot be directly compared : nor can even those which
the same person derives from it at different times. But if we find a
man in doubt whether to spend a few pence on a cigar, or a cup of
tea, or on riding home instead of walking home, then we may follow
ordinary usage, and say that he expects from them equal pleasures.

If then we wish to compare even physical gratifications, we must
do it not directly, but indirectly by the incentives which they afford
to action. If the desires to secure either of two pleasures will
induce people in similar circumstances each to do just an hour's
extra work, or will induce men in the same rank of life and with the
same means each to pay a shilling for it; we then may say that
those pleasures are equal for our purposes, because the desires for
them are equally strong incentives to action for persons under
similar conditions.

Thus measuring a mental state, as men do in ordinary life, by its *and this
indirect*
motor-force or the incentive which it affords to action, no new *compari-*
difficulty is introduced by the fact that some of the motives of which *son can be
applied to*
we have to take account belong to man's higher nature, and others *all classes*
to his lower. *of desire.*

For suppose that the person, whom we saw doubting between
several little gratifications for himself, had thought after a while of a
poor invalid whom he would pass on his way home; and had spent
some time in making up his mind whether he would choose a physical

I, ɪɪ, 1. gratification for himself, or would do a kindly act and rejoice in
another's joy. As his desires turned now towards the one, now the
other, there would be change in the quality of his mental states; and
the philosopher is bound to study the nature of the change.

Economics
ollows the
ractice of
rdinary
liscourse.

But the economist studies mental states rather through their
manifestations than in themselves; and if he finds they afford
evenly balanced incentives to action, he treats them *prima facie*
as for his purpose equal. He follows indeed in a more patient and
thoughtful way, and with greater precautions, what everybody is
always doing every day in ordinary life. He does not attempt to
weigh the real value of the higher affections of our nature against
those of our lower : he does not balance the love for virtue against
the desire for agreeable food. He estimates the incentives to action
by their effects just in the same way as people do in common life.
He follows the course of ordinary conversation, differing from it only
in taking more precautions to make clear the limits of his knowledge
as he goes. He reaches his provisional conclusions by observations of
men in general under given conditions without attempting to
fathom the mental and spiritual characteristics of individuals. But
he does not ignore the mental and spiritual side of life. On the
contrary, even for the narrower uses of economic studies, it is
important to know whether the desires which prevail are such as will
help to build up a strong and righteous character. And in the
broader uses of those studies, when they are being applied to
practical problems, the economist, like every one else, must concern
himself with the ultimate aims of man, and take account of differences in real value between gratifications that are equally powerful
incentives to action and have therefore equal economic measures.
A study of these measures is only the starting-point of economics :
but it is the starting-point.[1]

[1] The objections raised by some philosophers to speaking of two pleasures as equal,
under any circumstances, seem to apply only to uses of the phrase other than those
with which the economist is concerned. It has however unfortunately happened that
the customary uses of economic terms have sometimes suggested the belief that
economists are adherents of the philosophical system of Hedonism or of Utilitarianism.
For, while they have generally taken for granted that the greatest pleasures are those
which come with the endeavour to do one's duty, they have spoken of " pleasures "
and " pains " as supplying the motives to all action; and they have thus brought
themselves under the censure of those philosophers, with whom it is a matter of
principle to insist that the desire to do one's duty is a different thing from a desire for
the pleasure which, if one happens to think of the matter at all, one may expect from
doing it; though perhaps it may be not incorrectly described as a desire for " self
satisfaction " or " the satisfaction of the permanent self." (See for instance T. H.
Green, *Prolegomena to Ethics*, pp. 165–6.)

It is clearly not the part of economics to appear to take a side in ethical controversy : and since there is a general agreement that all incentives to action, in so far as
they are conscious desires at all, may without impropriety be spoken of shortly as
desires for " satisfaction," it may perhaps be well to use this word instead of "pleasure,"
when occasion arises for referring to the aims of all desires, whether appertaining to

§ 2. There are several other limitations of the measurement of motive by money to be discussed. The first of these arises from the necessity of taking account of the variations in the amount of pleasure, or other satisfaction, represented by the same sum of money to different persons and under different circumstances.

A shilling may measure a greater pleasure (or other satisfaction) at one time than at another even for the same person; because money may be more plentiful with him, or because his sensibility may vary.[1] And persons whose antecedents are similar, and who are outwardly like one another, are often affected in very different ways by similar events. When, for instance, a band of city school children are sent out for a day's holiday in the country, it is probable that no two of them derive from it enjoyment exactly the same in kind, or equal in intensity. The same surgical operation causes different amounts of pain to different people. Of two parents who are, so far as we can tell, equally affectionate, one will suffer much more than the other from the loss of a favourite son. Some who are not very sensitive generally are yet specially susceptible to particular kinds of pleasure and pain; while differences in nature and education make one man's total capacity for pleasure or pain much greater than another's.

The same price measures different satisfactions even to persons with equal incomes;

It would therefore not be safe to say that any two men with the same income derive equal benefit from its use; or that they would suffer equal pain from the same diminution of it. Although when a tax of £1 is taken from each of two persons having an income of £300 a-year, each will give up that £1 worth of pleasure (or other satisfaction) which he can most easily part with, i.e. each will give up what is measured to him by just £1; yet the intensities of the satisfaction given up may not be nearly equal.

Nevertheless, if we take averages sufficiently broad to cause the personal peculiarities of individuals to counterbalance one another, the money which people of equal incomes will give to obtain a benefit

but these differences may generally be

---

man's higher or lower nature. The simple antithesis to satisfaction is " dissatisfaction " : but perhaps it may be well to use the shorter and equally colourless word " detriment " in its place.

It may however be noted that some followers of Bentham (though perhaps not Bentham himself) made this large use of " pain and pleasure " serve as a bridge by which to pass from individualistic Hedonism to a complete ethical creed, without recognizing the necessity for the introduction of an independent major premiss; and for such a premiss the necessity would appear to be absolute, although opinions will perhaps always differ as to its form. Some will regard it as the Categorical Imperative; while others will regard it as a simple belief that, whatever be the origin of our moral instincts, their indications are borne out by a verdict of the experience of mankind to the effect that true happiness is not to be had without self-respect, and that self-respect is to be had only on the condition of endeavouring so to live as to promote the progress of the human race.

[1] Compare Edgeworth's *Mathematical Psychics.*

I, II, 2.

ₑglected
hen we
ₙsider
ₑ aver-
ₑ of
rge num-
ₑrs of
ₑₒple.

or avoid an injury is a good measure of the benefit or injury. If there are a thousand persons living in Sheffield, and another thousand in Leeds, each with about £100 a-year, and a tax of £1 is levied on all of them; we may be sure that the loss of pleasure or other injury which the tax will cause in Sheffield is of about equal importance with that which it will cause in Leeds : and anything that increased all the incomes by £1 would give command over equivalent pleasures and other benefits in the two towns. This probability becomes greater still if all of them are adult males engaged in the same trade; and therefore presumably somewhat similar in sensibility and temperament, in taste and education. Nor is the probability much diminished, if we take the family as our unit, and compare the loss of pleasure that results from diminishing by £1 the income of each of a thousand families with incomes of £100 a-year in the two places.

he sig-
ificance
ₜ a given
rice is
reater for
ₑe poor
ₘan the
ch.

Next we must take account of the fact that a stronger incentive will be required to induce a person to pay a given price for anything if he is poor than if he is rich. A shilling is the measure of less pleasure, or satisfaction of any kind, to a rich man than to a poor one. A rich man in doubt whether to spend a shilling on a single cigar, is weighing against one another smaller pleasures than a poor man, who is doubting whether to spend a shilling on a supply of tobacco that will last him for a month. The clerk with £100 a-year will walk to business in a much heavier rain than the clerk with £300 a-year; for the cost of a ride by tram or omnibus measures a greater benefit to the poorer man than to the richer. If the poorer man spends the money, he will suffer more from the want of it afterwards than the richer would. The benefit that is measured in the poorer man's mind by the cost is greater than that measured by it in the richer man's mind.

ₗut this
ₗ not im-
ortant in
ₒmparing
ₓo groups
ₒmposed
f rich and
ₒor in
ke pro-
ortions.

But this source of error also is lessened when we are able to consider the actions and the motives of large groups of people. If we know, for instance, that a bank failure has taken £200,000 from the people of Leeds and £100,000 from those of Sheffield, we may fairly assume that the suffering caused in Leeds has been about twice as great as in Sheffield; unless indeed we have some special reason for believing that the shareholders of the bank in the one town were a richer class than those in the other; or that the loss of employment caused by it pressed in uneven proportions on the working classes in the two towns.

ₙcrease of
ₘaterial
ₘeans
ₒmetimes

By far the greater number of the events with which economics deals affect in about equal proportions all the different classes of society; so that if the money measures of the happiness caused by two events are equal, it is reasonable and in accordance with common usage to regard the amounts of the happiness in the two cases as equivalent. And, further, as money is likely to be turned to the higher uses of life in about equal proportions, by any two large groups of people taken without special bias from any two parts of the western world, there is even some *primâ facie* probability that equal additions to their material resources will make about equal additions to the fulness of life, and the true progress of the human race.

I, п, 3.
a fair measure of real progress.

§ 3. To pass to another point. When we speak of the measurement of desire by the action to which it forms the incentive, it is not to be supposed that we assume every action to be deliberate, and the outcome of calculation. For in this, as in every other respect, economics takes man just as he is in ordinary life : and in ordinary life people do not weigh beforehand the results of every action, whether the impulses to it come from their higher nature or their lower.[1]

Action is largely ruled by habit.

Now the side of life with which economics is specially concerned is that in which man's conduct is most deliberate, and in which he most often reckons up the advantages and disadvantages of any particular action before he enters on it. And further it is that side of his life in which, when he does follow habit and custom, and proceeds for the moment without calculation, the habits and customs themselves are most nearly sure to have arisen from a close and careful watching the advantages and disadvantages of different courses of conduct. There will not in general have been any formal reckoning up of two sides of a balance-sheet : but men going home from their day's work, or in their social meetings, will have said to one another, " It did not answer to do this, it would have been better to do that," and so on. What makes one course answer better than another, will not necessarily be a selfish gain, nor any material gain ; and it will often have been argued that " though this or that plan saved a little trouble or a little money, yet it was not fair to others," and " it made one look mean," or " it made one feel mean."

especially as regards business conduct.

[1] This is specially true of that group of gratifications, which is sometimes named " the pleasures of the chase." They include not only the light-hearted emulation of games and pastimes, of hunts and steeplechases, but the more serious contests of professional and business life : and they will occupy a good deal of our attention in discussions of the causes that govern wages and profits, and forms of industrial organization.

Some people are of wayward temperament, and give no good account even to themselves of the motives of their action. But if a man is steadfast and thoughtful, even his impulses are the products of habits which he has adopted more or less deliberately. And, whether these impulses are an expression of his higher nature or not ; whether they spring from mandates of his conscience, the pressure of social connection, or the claims of his bodily wants, he yields a certain relative precedence to them without reflection now, because on previous occasions he has decided deliberately to yield that relative precedence. The predominant attractiveness of one course of action over others, even when not the result of calculation at the time, is the product of more or less deliberate decisions made by him before in somewhat similar cases.

I, II, 4.   It is true that when a habit or a custom, which has grown up under one set of conditions, influences action under other conditions, there is so far no exact relation between the effort and the end which is attained by it. In backward countries there are still many habits and customs similar to those that lead a beaver in confinement to build himself a dam; they are full of suggestiveness to the historian, and must be reckoned with by the legislator. But in business matters in the modern world such habits quickly die away.

Thus then the most systematic part of people's lives is generally that by which they earn their living. The work of all those engaged in any one occupation can be carefully observed; general statements can be made about it, and tested by comparison with the results of other observations; and numerical estimates can be framed as to the amount of money or general purchasing power that is required to supply a sufficient motive for them.

The unwillingness to postpone enjoyment, and thus to save for future use, is measured by the interest on accumulated wealth which just affords a sufficient incentive to save for the future. This measurement presents however some special difficulties, the study of which must be postponed.

The motives that lead to the pursuit of money may themselves be noble.

§ 4. Here, as elsewhere, we must bear in mind that the desire to make money does not itself necessarily proceed from motives of a low order, even when it is to be spent on oneself. Money is a means towards ends, and if the ends are noble, the desire for the means is not ignoble. The lad who works hard and saves all he can, in order to be able to pay his way afterwards at a University, is eager for money; but his eagerness is not ignoble. In short, money is general purchasing power, and is sought as a means to all kinds of ends, high as well as low, spiritual as well as material.[1]

And there is no truth in the common opinion that economics regards man as absorbed in a selfish pursuit of wealth.

Thus though it is true that " money " or " general purchasing power " or " command over material wealth," is the centre around which economic science clusters; this is so, not because money or material wealth is regarded as the main aim of human effort, nor even as affording the main subject-matter for the study of the economist, but because in this world of ours it is the one convenient means of measuring human motive on a large scale. If the older economists had made this clear, they would have escaped many

---

[1] See an admirable essay by Cliffe Leslie on *The Love of Money*. We do indeed hear of people who pursue money for its own sake without caring for what it will purchase, especially at the end of a long life spent in business : but in this as in other cases the habit of doing a thing is kept up after the purpose for which it was originally done has ceased to exist. The possession of wealth gives such people a feeling of power over their fellow-creatures, and insures them a sort of envious respect in which they find a bitter but strong pleasure.

grievous misrepresentations; and the splendid teachings of Carlyle *I, II, 5.* and Ruskin as to the right aims of human endeavour and the right uses of wealth, would not then have been marred by bitter attacks on economics, based on the mistaken belief that that science had no concern with any motive except the selfish desire for wealth, or even that it inculcated a policy of sordid selfishness.[1]

Again, when the motive to a man's action is spoken of as supplied *The desire* by the money which he will earn, it is not meant that his mind is *for money does not* closed to all other considerations save those of gain. For even the *exclude* most purely business relations of life assume honesty and good faith; *fluences;* while many of them take for granted, if not generosity, yet at least the absence of meanness, and the pride which every honest man takes in acquitting himself well. Again, much of the work by which *such as the* people earn their living is pleasurable in itself; and there is truth in *pleasure afforded* the contention of socialists that more of it might be made so. *by the* Indeed even business work, that seems at first sight unattractive, *work itself and the* often yields a great pleasure by offering scope for the exercise of *instinct of power.* men's faculties, and for their instincts of emulation and of power. For just as a racehorse or an athlete strains every nerve to get in advance of his competitors, and delights in the strain; so a manufacturer or a trader is often stimulated much more by the hope of victory over his rivals than by the desire to add something to his fortune.[2]

§ 5. It has indeed always been the practice of economists to take *Econo-* careful account of all the advantages which attract people generally *mists have always* towards an occupation, whether they appear in a money form or not. *reckoned* Other things being equal, people will prefer an occupation in which *for advantages of an* they do not need to soil their hands, in which they enjoy a good social *occupation* position, and so on; and since these advantages affect, not indeed *other than material* every one exactly in the same way, but most people in nearly the *gain;* same way, their attractive force can be estimated and measured by the money wages to which they are regarded as equivalent.

Again, the desire to earn the approval, to avoid the contempt of *and they* those around one is a stimulus to action which often works with some *have allowed for* sort of uniformity in any class of persons at a given time and place; *class sym-* though local and temporary conditions influence greatly not only the *pathies,* intensity of the desire for approval, but also the range of persons whose approval is desired. A professional man, for instance, or an artisan will be very sensitive to the approval or disapproval of those

---

[1] In fact a world can be conceived in which there is a science of economics very much like our own, but in it there is no money of any sort. See Appendices B, 8 and D, 2.
[2] Some remarks on the large scope of economics as conceived in Germany will be found in Appendix D, 3.

in the same occupation, and care little for that of other people; and there are many economic problems, the discussion of which would be altogether unreal, if care were not taken to watch the direction and to estimate pretty closely the force of motives such as these.

and family affections.

As there may be a taint of selfishness in a man's desire to do what seems likely to benefit his fellow-workers, so there may be an element of personal pride in his desire that his family should prosper during his life and after it. But still the family affections generally are so pure a form of altruism, that their action might have shown little semblance of regularity, had it not been for the uniformity in the family relations themselves. As it is, their action is fairly regular; and it has always been fully reckoned with by economists, especially in relation to the distribution of the family income between its various members, the expenses of preparing children for their future career, and the accumulation of wealth to be enjoyed after the death of him by whom it has been earned.

It is then not the want of will but the want of power, that prevents economists from reckoning in the action of motives such as these; and they welcome the fact that some kinds of philanthropic action can be described in statistical returns, and can to a certain extent be reduced to law, if sufficiently broad averages are taken. For indeed there is scarcely any motive so fitful and irregular, but that some law with regard to it can be detected by the aid of wide and patient observation. It would perhaps be possible even now to predict with tolerable closeness the subscriptions that a population of a hundred thousand Englishmen of average wealth will give to support hospitals and chapels and missions; and, in so far as this can be done, there is a basis for an economic discussion of supply and demand with reference to the services of hospital nurses, missionaries and other religious ministers. It will however probably be always true that the greater part of those actions, which are due to a feeling of duty and love of one's neighbour, cannot be classed, reduced to law and measured; and it is for this reason, and not because they are not based on self-interest, that the machinery of economics cannot be brought to bear on them.

The motives to collective action are of great and growing importance.

§ 6. Perhaps the earlier English economists confined their attention too much to the motives of individual action. But in fact economists, like all other students of social science, are concerned with individuals chiefly as members of the social organism. As a cathedral is something more than the stones of which it is made, as a person is something more than a series of thoughts and feelings, so the life of society is something more than the sum of the lives of its

individual members. It is true that the action of the whole is made I, II, 7.
up of that of its constituent parts; and that in most economic
problems the best starting-point is to be found in the motives that
affect the individual, regarded not indeed as an isolated atom, but as
a member of some particular trade or industrial group; but it is also
true, as German writers have well urged, that economics has a great
and an increasing concern in motives connected with the collective
ownership of property, and the collective pursuit of important aims.
The growing earnestness of the age, the growing intelligence of the
mass of the people, and the growing power of the telegraph, the press,
and other means of communication are ever widening the scope of
collective action for the public good; and these changes, together
with the spread of the co-operative movement, and other kinds of
voluntary association are growing up under the influence of various
motives besides that of pecuniary gain : they are ever opening to the
economist new opportunities of measuring motives whose action it
had seemed impossible to reduce to any sort of law.

But in fact the variety of motives, the difficulties of measuring
them, and the manner of overcoming those difficulties are among the
chief subjects with which we shall be occupied in this treatise.
Almost every point touched in the present chapter will need to be
discussed in fuller detail with reference to some one or more of the
leading problems of economics.

§ 7. To conclude provisionally : economists study the actions of Econo-
individuals, but study them in relation to social rather than individual mists
study the
life; and therefore concern themselves but little with personal individual
peculiarities of temper and character. They watch carefully the as a member of an
conduct of a whole class of people, sometimes the whole of a nation, industrial
sometimes only those living in a certain district, more often those group;
engaged in some particular trade at some time and place : and by the
aid of statistics, or in other ways, they ascertain how much money
on the average the members of the particular group, they are
watching, are just willing to pay as the price of a certain thing which
they desire, or how much must be offered to them to induce them to
undergo a certain effort or abstinence that they dislike. The
measurement of motive thus obtained is not indeed perfectly
accurate; for if it were, economics would rank with the most
advanced of the physical sciences; and not, as it actually does, with
the least advanced.

But yet the measurement is accurate enough to enable experi- and mea-
enced persons to forecast fairly well the extent of the results that will sure the
play of
follow from changes in which motives of this kind are chiefly concerned. motives in

demand
and sup-
ply at first
in simple
cases,

Thus, for instance, they can estimate very closely the payment that will be required to produce an adequate supply of labour of any grade, from the lowest to the highest, for a new trade which it is proposed to start in any place. When they visit a factory of a kind that they have never seen before, they can tell within a shilling or two a week what any particular worker is earning, by merely observing how far his is a skilled occupation and what strain it involves on his physical, mental and moral faculties. And they can predict with tolerable certainty what rise of price will result from a given diminution of the supply of a certain thing, and how that increased price will react on the supply.

and
afterwards
in more
complex
cases.

And, starting from simple considerations of this kind, economists go on to analyse the causes which govern the local distribution of different kinds of industry, the terms on which people living in distant places exchange their goods with one another, and so on : and they can explain and predict the ways in which fluctuations of credit will affect foreign trade; or again the extent to which the burden of a tax will be shifted from those on whom it is levied, on to those for whose wants they cater; and so on.

They deal
mainly
with one
side of
man's life,
but it is
always the
life of a
real man
not of a
fictitious
being.

In all this they deal with man as he is : not with an abstract or "economic" man; but a man of flesh and blood. They deal with a man who is largely influenced by egoistic motives in his business life to a great extent with reference to them; but who is also neither above vanity and recklessness, nor below delight in doing his work well for its own sake, or in sacrificing himself for the good of his family, his neighbours, or his country; a man who is not below the love of a virtuous life for its own sake. They deal with man as he is : but being concerned chiefly with those aspects of life in which the action of motive is so regular that it can be predicted, and the estimate of the motor-forces can be verified by results, they have established their work on a scientific basis.

The
claims of
economics
to be a
science,
are its
power of
appeal to
definite
external
tests, and
its internal
homo-
geneity.

For in the first place, they deal with facts which can be observed, and quantities which can be measured and recorded; so that when differences of opinion arise with regard to them, the differences can be brought to the test of public and well-established records; and thus science obtains a solid basis on which to work. In the second place, the problems, which are grouped as economic, because they relate specially to man's conduct under the influence of motives that are measurable by a money price, are found to make a fairly homogeneous group. Of course they have a great deal of subject-matter in common : that is obvious from the nature of the case. But, though not so obvious à priori, it will also be found to be true that there is a fundamental unity of form underlying all the chief of them; I, II, 7. and that in consequence, by studying them together, the same kind of economy is gained, as by sending a single postman to deliver all the letters in a certain street, instead of each one entrusting his letters to a separate messenger. For the analyses and organized processes of reasoning that are wanted for any one group of them, will be found generally useful for other groups.

The less then we trouble ourselves with scholastic inquiries as to whether a certain consideration comes within the scope of economics, the better. If the matter is important let us take account of it as far as we can. If it is one as to which there exist divergent opinions, such as cannot be brought to the test of exact and well-ascertained knowledge; if it is one on which the general machinery of economic analysis and reasoning cannot get any grip, then let us leave it aside in our purely economic studies. But let us do so simply because the attempt to include it would lessen the certainty and the exactness of our economic knowledge without any commensurate gain; and remembering always that some sort of account of it must be taken by our ethical instincts and our common sense, when they as ultimate arbiters come to apply to practical issues the knowledge obtained and arranged by economics and other sciences.

CHAPTER III

ECONOMIC GENERALIZATIONS OR LAWS

§ 1. It is the business of economics, as of almost every other science, to collect facts, to arrange and interpret them, and to draw inferences from them. " Observation and description, definition and classification are the preparatory activities. But what we desire to reach thereby is a knowledge of the interdependence of economic phenomena. . . . Induction and deduction are both needed for scientific thought as the left and right foot are both needed for walking." [1] The methods required for this twofold work are not peculiar to economics; they are the common property of all sciences. All the devices for the discovery of the relations between cause and effect, which are described in treatises on scientific method, have to be used in their turn by the economist : there is not any one method of investigation which can properly be called the method of economics; but every method must be made serviceable in its proper place, either singly or in combination with others. And as the number of combinations that can be made on the chess-board is so great that probably no two games exactly alike were ever played; so no two games which the student plays with nature to wrest from her her hidden truths, which were worth playing at all, ever made use of quite the same methods in quite the same way.

But in some branches of economic inquiry and for some purposes, it is more urgent to ascertain new facts, than to trouble ourselves with the mutual relations and explanations of those which we already have. While in other branches there is still so much uncertainty as to whether those causes of any event which lie on the surface and suggest themselves at first are both *true* causes of it and the *only* causes of it, that it is even more urgently needed to scrutinize our reasoning about facts which we already know, than to seek for more facts.

For this and other reasons, there always has been and there probably always will be a need for the existence side by side of workers with different aptitudes and different aims, some of whom

Marginal notes:
I, III, 1.
Economics uses both induction and deduction,

but in different proportions for different purposes.

Analytical and historical schools

---

[1] Schmoller in the article on *Volkswirtschaft* in Conrad's *Handwörterbuch.*

give their chief attention to the ascertainment of facts, while others give their chief attention to scientific analysis; that is taking to pieces complex facts, and studying the relations of the several parts to one another and to cognate facts. It is to be hoped that these two schools will always exist; each doing its own work thoroughly, and each making use of the work of the other. Thus best may we obtain sound generalizations as to the past and trustworthy guidance from it for the future.

I, III, 3.

are both needed and supplement

§ 2. Those physical sciences, which have progressed most beyond the points to which they were brought by the brilliant genius of the Greeks, are not all of them strictly speaking " exact sciences." But they all aim at exactness. That is they all aim at precipitating the result of a multitude of observations into provisional statements, which are sufficiently definite to be brought under test by other observations of nature. These statements, when first put forth, seldom claim a high authority. But after they have been tested by many independent observations, and especially after they have been applied successfully in the prediction of coming events, or of the results of new experiments, they graduate as *laws*. A science progresses by increasing the number and exactness of its laws; by submitting them to tests of ever increasing severity; and by enlarging their scope till a single broad law contains and supersedes a number of narrower laws, which have been shown to be special instances of it.

Imagination acting on organized study of facts frames general statements; and some of these are selected for the title of "laws."

In so far as this is done by any science, a student of it can in certain cases say with authority greater than his own (greater perhaps than that of any thinker, however able, who relies on his own resources and neglects the results obtained by previous workers), what results are to be expected from certain conditions, or what are the true causes of a certain known event.

Although the subject-matter of some progressive physical sciences is not, at present at least, capable of perfectly exact measurement; yet their progress depends on the multitudinous co-operation of armies of workers. They measure their facts and define their statements as closely as they can : so that each investigator may start as nearly as possible where those before him left off. Economics aspires to a place in this group of sciences : because though its measurements are seldom exact, and are never final; yet it is ever working to make them more exact, and thus to enlarge the range of matters on which the individual student may speak with the authority of his science.

§ 3. Let us then consider more closely the nature of economic

I, III, 3.

Nearly all laws of science are statements of tendencies.

laws, and their limitations. Every cause has a tendency to produce some definite result if nothing occurs to hinder it. Thus gravitation tends to make things fall to the ground : but when a balloon is full of gas lighter than air, the pressure of the air will make it rise in spite of the tendency of gravitation to make it fall. The law of gravitation states how any two things attract one another; how they tend to move towards one another, and will move towards one another if nothing interferes to prevent them. The law of gravitation is therefore a statement of tendencies.

The exact laws of simple sciences.

It is a very exact statement—so exact that mathematicians can calculate a Nautical Almanac, which will show the moments at which each satellite of Jupiter will hide itself behind Jupiter. They make this calculation for many years beforehand; and navigators take it to sea, and use it in finding out where they are. Now there are no economic tendencies which act as steadily and can be measured as exactly as gravitation can : and consequently there are no laws of economics which can be compared for precision with the law of gravitation.

The inexact laws of complex sciences.

But let us look at a science less exact than astronomy. The science of the tides explains how the tide rises and falls twice a day under the action of the sun and the moon : how there are strong tides at new and full moon, and weak tides at the moon's first and third quarter; and how the tide running up into a closed channel, like that of the Severn, will be very high; and so on. Thus, having studied the lie of the land and the water all round the British isles, people can calculate beforehand when the tide will *probably* be at its highest on any day at London Bridge or at Gloucester; and how high it will be there. They have to use the word *probably*, which the astronomers do not need to use when talking about the eclipses of Jupiter's satellites. For, though many forces act upon Jupiter and his satellites, each one of them acts in a definite manner which can be predicted beforehand : but no one knows enough about the weather to be able to say beforehand how it will act. A heavy downpour of rain in the upper Thames valley, or a strong north-east wind in the German Ocean, may make the tides at London Bridge differ a good deal from what had been expected.

The science of man is complex and its laws are inexact.

The laws of economics are to be compared with the laws of the tides, rather than with the simple and exact law of gravitation. For the actions of men are so various and uncertain, that the best statement of tendencies, which we can make in a science of human conduct, must needs be inexact and faulty. This might be urged as a reason against making any statements at all on the subject; but that would be almost to abandon life.   Life is human conduct, and the thoughts and emotions that grow up around it.   By the fundamental impulses of our nature we all—high and low, learned and unlearned—are in our several degrees constantly striving to understand the courses of human action, and to shape them for our purposes, whether selfish or unselfish, whether noble or ignoble.   And since we *must* form to ourselves some notions of the tendencies of human action, our choice is between forming those notions carelessly and forming them carefully.   The harder the task, the greater the need for steady patient inquiry; for turning to account the experience, that has been reaped by the more advanced physical sciences; and for framing as best we can well thought-out estimates, or provisional laws, of the tendencies of human action.

§ 4.   The term " law " means then nothing more than a general proposition or statement of tendencies, more or less certain, more or less definite.   Many such statements are made in every science : but we do not, indeed we cannot, give to all of them a formal character and name them as laws.   We must select; and the selection is directed less by purely scientific considerations than by practical convenience.   If there is any general statement which we want to bring to bear so often, that the trouble of quoting it at length, when needed, is greater than that of burdening the discussion with an additional formal statement and an additional technical name, then it receives a special name, otherwise not.[1]

Thus a law of social science, or a *Social Law*, is a statement of social tendencies; that is, a statement that a certain course of action may be expected under certain conditions from the members of a social group.   *Definition of law social,*

Economic laws, or statements of economic tendencies, are those social laws which relate to branches of conduct in which the strength of the motives chiefly concerned can be measured by a money price.   *and economic*

There is thus no hard and sharp line of division between those social laws which are, and those which are not, to be regarded also as economic laws.   For there is a continuous gradation from social laws concerned almost exclusively with motives that can be measured by price, to social laws in which such motives have little place; and which are therefore generally as much less precise and exact than economic laws, as those are than the laws of the more exact physical sciences.

---

[1] The relation of " natural and economic laws," is exhaustively discussed by Neumann (*Zeitschrift für die gesamte Staatswissenschaft*, 1892) who concludes (p. 464) that there is no other word than Law (*Gesetz*) to express those statements of tendency, which play so important a part in natural as well as economic science.   See also Wagner (*Grundlegung*, §§ 86–91).

I, III, 4.

Corresponding to the substantive " law " is the adjective " legal." But this term is used only in connection with " law " in the sense of an ordinance of government; not in connection with " law " the sense of a statement of relation between cause and effect. The adjective used for this purpose is derived from " norma," a term which is nearly equivalent to " law," and might perhaps with advantage be substituted for it in scientific discussions. And following our definition of an economic law, we may say that the course of action which may be expected *under certain conditions* from the members of an industrial group is the *normal action* of the members of that group relatively to those conditions.

Definition of *normal* economic action.

This use of the term Normal has been misunderstood; and it may be well to say something as to the unity in difference which underlies various uses of the term. When we talk of a Good man or a Strong man, we refer to excellence or strength of those particular physical mental or moral qualities which are indicated in the context. A strong judge has seldom the same qualities as a strong rower; a good jockey is not always of exceptional virtue. In the same way every use of the term normal implies the predominance of certain tendencies which appear likely to be more or less steadfast and persistent in their action over those which are relatively exceptional and intermittent. Illness is an abnormal condition of man : but a long life passed without any illness is abnormal. During the melting of the snows, the Rhine rises above its normal level : but in a cold dry spring when it is less than usual above that normal level, it may be said to be abnormally low (for that time of year). In all these cases normal results are those which may be expected as the outcome of those tendencies which the context suggests; or, in other words, which are in accordance with those " statements of tendency," those Laws or Norms, which are appropriate to the context.

The term *Normal* implies harmony with whatever conditions happen to be under discussion.

This is the point of view from which it is said that normal economic action is that which may be expected in the long run under certain conditions (provided those conditions are persistent) from the members of an industrial group. It is normal that bricklayers in most parts of England are willing to work for 10*d*. an hour, but refuse to work for 7*d*. In Johannesburg it may be normal that a bricklayer should refuse work at much less than £1 a day. The normal price of *bona fide* fresh laid eggs may be taken to be a penny when nothing is said as to the time of the year : and yet threepence may be the normal price in town during January; and twopence may be an abnormally low price then, caused by " unseasonable " warmth.

Thus normal conditions may imply high wages or low wages;

Another misunderstanding to be guarded against arises from the notion that only those economic results are normal, which are due to the undisturbed action of free competition. But the term has often to be applied to conditions in which perfectly free competition does not exist, and can hardly even be supposed to exist; and even where free competition is most dominant, the normal conditions of every fact and tendency will include vital elements that are not a part of competition nor even akin to it. Thus, for instance, the normal arrangement of many transactions in retail and wholesale trade, and on Stock and Cotton Exchanges, rests on the assumption that verbal contracts, made without witnesses, will be honourably discharged; and in countries in which this assumption cannot legitimately be made, some parts of the Western doctrine of normal value are inapplicable. Again, the prices of various Stock Exchange securities are affected "normally" by the patriotic feelings not only of the ordinary purchasers, but of the brokers themselves : and so on.

I, III, 4.
——
they may
imply the
presence
or the
absence
of eager
compe-
tition.

Lastly it is sometimes erroneously supposed that normal action in economics is that which is right morally. But that is to be understood only when the context implies that the action is being judged from the ethical point of view. When we are considering the facts of the world, as they are, and not as they ought to be, we shall have to regard as " normal " to the circumstances in view, much action which we should use our utmost efforts to stop. For instance, the normal condition of many of the very poorest inhabitants of a large town is to be devoid of enterprise, and unwilling to avail themselves of the opportunities that may offer for a healthier and less squalid life elsewhere; they have not the strength, physical, mental and moral, required for working their way out of their miserable surroundings. The existence of a considerable supply of labour ready to make match-boxes at a very low rate is normal in the same way that a contortion of the limbs is a normal result of taking strychnine. It is one result, a deplorable result, of those tendencies the laws of which we have to study. This illustrates one peculiarity which economics shares with a few other sciences, the nature of the material of which can be modified by human effort. Science may suggest a moral or practical precept to modify that nature and thus modify the action of laws of nature. For instance, economics may suggest practical means of substituting capable workers for those who can only do such work as match-box making; as physiology may suggest measures for so modifying the breeds of cattle that they mature early, and carry much flesh on light frames. The laws of the fluctuation

Normal
action is
not always
right
action.

I, III, 5.
——

of credit and prices have been much altered by increased powers of prediction.

Again when "normal" prices are contrasted with temporary or market prices, the term refers to the dominance in the long run of certain tendencies under given conditions. But this raises some difficult questions which may be postponed.[1]

All scientific doctrines tacitly or implicitly assume certain conditions and are in this sense hypothetical.

§ 5. It is sometimes said that the laws of economics are "hypothetical." Of course, like every other science, it undertakes to study the effects which will be produced by certain causes, not absolutely, but subject to the condition that *other things are equal*, and that the causes are able to work out their effects undisturbed. Almost every scientific doctrine, when carefully and formally stated, will be found to contain some proviso to the effect that other things are equal : the action of the causes in question is supposed to be isolated; certain effects are attributed to them, but only *on the hypothesis* that no cause is permitted to enter except those distinctly allowed for. It is true however that the condition that time must be allowed for causes to produce their effects is a source of great difficulty in economics. For meanwhile the material on which they work, and perhaps even the causes themselves, may have changed; and the tendencies which are being described will not have a sufficiently "long run" in which to work themselves out fully. This difficulty will occupy our attention later on.

But in economics the implied conditions must be emphasized.

The conditioning clauses implied in a law are not continually repeated, but the common sense of the reader supplies them for himself. In economics it is necessary to repeat them oftener than elsewhere, because its doctrines are more apt than those of any other science to be quoted by persons who have had no scientific training, and who perhaps have heard them only at second hand, and without their context. One reason why ordinary conversation is simpler in form than a scientific treatise, is that in conversation we can safely omit conditioning clauses; because, if the hearer does not supply them for himself, we quickly detect the misunderstanding, and set it right. Adam Smith and many of the earlier writers on economics attained seeming simplicity by following the usages of conversation, and omitting conditioning clauses. But this has caused them to be constantly misunderstood, and has led to much waste of time and trouble in profitless controversy; they purchased apparent ease at too great a cost even for that gain.[2]

Though economic analysis and general reasoning are of wide

---

[1] They are discussed in Book V, especially chapters III and V.
[2] Compare Book II, chapter I.

application, yet every age and every country has its own problems; and every change in social conditions is likely to require a new development of economic doctrines.[1]

[1] Some parts of economics are relatively abstract or *pure*, because they are concerned mainly with broad general propositions : for, in order that a proposition may be of broad application it must necessarily contain few details : it cannot adapt itself to particular cases; and if it points to any prediction, that must be governed by a strong conditioning clause in which a very large meaning is given to the phrase " other things being equal."

Other parts are relatively *applied*, because they deal with narrower questions more in detail; they take more account of local and temporary elements; and they consider economic conditions in fuller and closer relation to other conditions of life. Thus there is but a short step from the applied science of banking in its more general sense, to broad rules or precepts of the general Art of banking : while the step from a particular local problem of the applied science of banking to the corresponding rule of practice or precept of Art may be shorter still.

CHAPTER IV

THE ORDER AND AIMS OF ECONOMIC STUDIES

I, iv, 1.
———
Summary
of chap·
ters II
and III.

§ **1.** WE have seen that the economist must be greedy of facts; but that facts by themselves teach nothing. History tells of sequences and coincidences; but reason alone can interpret and draw lessons from them. The work to be done is so various that much of it must be left to be dealt with by trained common sense, which is the ultimate arbiter in every practical problem. Economic science is but the working of common sense aided by appliances of organized analysis and general reasoning, which facilitate the task of collecting, arranging, and drawing inferences from particular facts. Though its scope is always limited, though its work without the aid of common sense is vain, yet it enables common sense to go further in difficult problems than would otherwise be possible.

Economic laws are statements with regard to the tendencies of man's action under certain conditions. They are hypothetical only in the same sense as are the laws of the physical sciences : for those laws also contain or imply conditions. But there is more difficulty in making the conditions clear, and more danger in any failure to do so, in economics than in physics. The laws of human action are not indeed as simple, as definite or as clearly ascertainable as the law of gravitation; but many of them may rank with the laws of those natural sciences which deal with complex subject-matter.

The *raison d'être* of economics as a separate science is that it deals chiefly with that part of man's action which is most under the control of measurable motives; and which therefore lends itself better than any other to systematic reasoning and analysis. We cannot indeed measure motives of any kind, whether high or low, as they are in themselves : we can measure only their moving force. Money is never a perfect measure of that force; and it is not even a tolerably good measure unless careful account is taken of the general conditions under which it works, and especially of the riches or poverty of those whose action is under discussion. But with careful precautions money affords a fairly good measure of the moving force of a great part of the motives by which men's lives are fashioned.

The study of theory must go hand in hand with that of facts :

and for dealing with most modern problems it is modern facts that are of the greatest use. For the economic records of the distant past are in some respects slight and untrustworthy; and the economic conditions of early times are wholly unlike those of free enterprise, of general education, of true democracy, of steam, of the cheap press and the telegraph.

§ 2. Economics has then as its purpose firstly to acquire knowledge for its own sake, and secondly to throw light on practical issues. But though we are bound, before entering on any study, to consider carefully what are its uses, we should not plan out our work with reference to them. For by so doing we are tempted to break off each line of thought as soon as it ceases to have an immediate bearing on that particular aim which we have in view at the time : the direct pursuit of practical aims leads us to group together bits of all sorts of knowledge, which have no connection with one another except for the immediate purposes of the moment; and which throw but little light on one another. Our mental energy is spent in going from one to another; nothing is thoroughly thought out; no real progress is made.

I, IV, 2, 3.

Scientific inquiries are to be arranged with reference not to the practical aims which they subserve, but to the nature of the subjects with which they are concerned.

The best grouping, therefore, for the purposes of science is that which collects together all those facts and reasonings which are similar to one another in nature : so that the study of each may throw light on its neighbour. By working thus for a long time at one set of considerations, we get gradually nearer to those fundamental unities which are called nature's laws : we trace their action first singly, and then in combination; and thus make progress slowly but surely. The practical uses of economic studies should never be out of the mind of the economist, but his special business is to study and interpret facts and to find out what are the effects of different causes acting singly and in combination.

§ 3. This may be illustrated by enumerating some of the chief questions to which the economist addresses himself. He inquires :—

Questions investigated by the economist.

What are the causes which, especially in the modern world, affect the consumption and production, the distribution and exchange of wealth; the organization of industry and trade; the money market; wholesale and retail dealing; foreign trade, and the relations between employers and employed? How do all these movements act and react upon one another? How do their ultimate differ from their immediate tendencies?

Subject to what limitations is the price of anything a measure of its desirability? What increase of wellbeing is *primâ facie* likely to result from a given increase in the wealth of any class of society?

c

I, IV, 4. How far is the industrial efficiency of any class impaired by the
insufficiency of its income? How far would an increase of the
income of any class, if once effected, be likely to sustain itself through
its effects in increasing their efficiency and earning power?

How far does, as a matter of fact, the influence of economic
freedom reach (or how far has it reached at any particular time) in
any place, in any rank of society, or in any particular branch of
industry? What other influences are most powerful there; and how
is the action of all these influences combined? In particular, how
far does economic freedom tend of its own action to build up combinations and monopolies, and what are their effects? How are the
various classes of society likely to be affected by its action in the long
run; what will be the intermediate effects while its ultimate results
are being worked out; and, account being taken of the time over
which they will spread, what is the relative importance of these two
classes of ultimate and intermediate effects? What will be the
incidence of any system of taxes? What burdens will it impose on
the community, and what revenue will it afford to the State?

Practical
issues
which
stimulate
the
inquiries
of the
English
economist
at the
present
time,
though
they do
not lie
wholly
within the
range of
his science.
§ 4. The above are the main questions with which economic
science has to deal directly, and with reference to which its main
work of collecting facts, of analysing them and reasoning about them
should be arranged. The practical issues which, though lying for the
greater part outside the range of economic science, yet supply a chief
motive in the background to the work of the economist, vary from time
to time, and from place to place, even more than do the economic facts
and conditions which form the material of his studies. The following
problems seem to be of special urgency now in our own country :—

How should we act so as to increase the good and diminish the
evil influences of economic freedom, both in its ultimate results and
in the course of its progress? If the first are good and the latter evil,
but those who suffer the evil, do not reap the good; how far is it
right that they should suffer for the benefit of others?

Taking it for granted that a more equal distribution of wealth is
to be desired, how far would this justify changes in the institutions
of property, or limitations of free enterprise even when they would
be likely to diminish the aggregate of wealth? In other words, how
far should an increase in the income of the poorer classes and a
diminution of their work be aimed at, even if it involved some
lessening of national material wealth? How far could this be done
without injustice, and without slackening the energies of the leaders
of progress? How ought the burdens of taxation to be distributed
among the different classes of society?

I, IV, 4.

Ought we to rest content with the existing forms of division of labour? Is it necessary that large numbers of the people should be exclusively occupied with work that has no elevating character? Is it possible to educate gradually among the great mass of workers a new capacity for the higher kinds of work; and in particular for undertaking co-operatively the management of the business in which they are themselves employed?

What are the proper relations of individual and collective action in a stage of civilization such as ours? How far ought voluntary association in its various forms, old and new, to be left to supply collective action for those purposes for which such action has special advantages? What business affairs should be undertaken by society itself acting through its government, imperial or local? Have we, for instance, carried as far as we should the plan of collective ownership and use of open spaces, of works of art, of the means of instruction and amusement, as well as of those material requisites of a civilized life, the supply of which requires united action, such as gas and water, and railways?

When government does not itself directly intervene, how far should it allow individuals and corporations to conduct their own affairs as they please? How far should it regulate the management of railways and other concerns which are to some extent in a position of monopoly, and again of land and other things the quantity of which cannot be increased by man? Is it necessary to retain in their full force all the existing rights of property; or have the original necessities for which they were meant to provide, in some measure passed away?

Are the prevailing methods of using wealth entirely justifiable? What scope is there for the moral pressure of social opinion in constraining and directing individual action in those economic relations in which the rigidity and violence of government interference would be likely to do more harm than good? In what respect do the duties of one nation to another in economic matters differ from those of members of the same nation to one another?

Economics is thus taken to mean a study of the economic aspects and conditions of man's political, social and private life; but more especially of his social life. The aims of the study are to gain knowledge for its own sake, and to obtain guidance in the practical conduct of life, and especially of social life. The need for such guidance was never so urgent as now; a later generation may have more abundant leisure than we for researches that throw light

The dominant aim of economics in the present generation is to contribute to a solution of social problems.

I, IV, 5. on obscure points in abstract speculation, or in the history of past
times, but do not afford immediate aid in present difficulties.

But though thus largely directed by practical needs, economics
avoids as far as possible the discussion of those exigencies of party
organization, and those diplomacies of home and foreign politics of
which the statesman is bound to take account in deciding what
measures that he can propose will bring him nearest to the end that
he desires to secure for his country. It aims indeed at helping him to
determine not only what that end should be, but also what are the best
methods of a broad policy devoted to that end. But it shuns many
political issues, which the practical man cannot ignore : and it is therefore a science, pure and applied, rather than a science and an art. And
it is better described by the broad term " Economics " than by the
narrower term " Political Economy."

The
functions
of percep-
tion,
imagina-
tion and
reason in
economics.
§ 5. The economist needs the three great intellectual faculties,
perception, imagination and reason : and most of all he needs
imagination, to put him on the track of those causes of visible
events which are remote or lie below the surface, and of those effects
of visible causes which are remote or lie below the surface.

The natural sciences and especially the physical group of them
have this great advantage as a discipline over all studies of man's
action, that in them the investigator is called on for exact conclusions
which can be verified by subsequent observation or experiment.
His fault is soon detected if he contents himself with such causes and
such effects as lie on the surface; or again if he ignores the mutual
interaction of the forces of nature, wherein every movement modifies
and is modified by all that surround it. Nor does the thorough
student of physics rest satisfied with a mere general analysis ; he is
ever striving to make it quantitative; and to assign its proper proportion to each element in his problem.

An
external
standard of
measure-
ment to
steady the
judgment
is in some
measure
attainable
by the
economist.
In sciences that relate to man exactness is less attainable. The
path of least resistance is sometimes the only one open : it is always
alluring; and though it is also always treacherous, the temptation is
great to follow it even when a more thorough way can be fought out
by resolute work. The scientific student of history is hampered by
his inability to experiment and even more by the absence of any
objective standard to which his estimates of relative proportion can
be referred. Such estimates are latent in almost every stage of his
argument : he cannot conclude that one cause or group of causes has
been overridden by another without making some implicit estimate
of their relative weights. And yet it is only by a great effort that he
perceives how dependent he is on his own subjective impressions.

The economist also is hampered by this difficulty, but in a less degree than other students of man's action; for indeed he has some share in those advantages which give precision and objectivity to the work of the physicist. So long, at all events, as he is concerned with current and recent events, many of his facts group themselves under classes as to which statements can be made that are definite, and often were approximately accurate numerically : and thus he is at some advantage in seeking for causes and for results which lie below the surface, and are not easily seen; and in analyzing complex conditions into their elements and in reconstructing a whole out of many elements.

In smaller matters, indeed, simple experience will suggest the unseen. It will, for instance, put people in the way of looking for the harm to strength of character and to family life that comes from ill-considered aid to the thriftless; even though what is seen on the surface is almost sheer gain. But greater effort, a larger range of view, a more powerful exercise of the imagination are needed in tracking the true results of, for instance, many plausible schemes for increasing steadiness of employment. For that purpose it is necessary to have learnt how closely connected are changes in credit, in domestic trade, in foreign trade competition, in harvests, in prices; and how all of these affect steadiness of employment for good and for evil. It is necessary to watch how almost every considerable economic event in any part of the Western world affects employment in some trades at least in almost every other part. If we deal only with those causes of unemployment which are near at hand, we are likely to make no good cure of the evils we see; and we are likely to cause evils, that we do not see. And if we are to look for those which are far off and weigh them in the balance, then the work before us is a high discipline for the mind.

Again, when by a " standard rule " or any other device wages are kept specially high in any trade, imagination set agoing will try to track the lives of those who are prevented by the standard rule from doing work, of which they are capable, at a price that people are willing to pay for it. Are they pushed up, or are they pushed down? If some are pushed up and some pushed down, as commonly happens, is it the many that are pushed up and the few that are pushed down, or the other way about? If we look at surface results, we may suppose that it is the many who are pushed up. But if, by the scientific use of the imagination, we think out all the ways in which prohibitions, whether on Trade Union authority or any other, prevent people from doing their best and earning their best,

But his main reliance must be on disciplined imagination;

I, IV, 6. we shall often conclude that it is the many who have been pushed down, and the few who have been pushed up. Partly under English influence, some Australasian colonies are making bold ventures, which hold out specious promise of greater immediate comfort and ease to the workers. Australasia has indeed a great reserve of borrowing power in her vast landed property : and should the proposed short cuts issue in some industrial decadence, the fall may be slight and temporary. But it is already being urged that England should move on similar lines : and a fall for her would be more serious. What is needed, and what we may hope is coming in the near future, is a larger study of such schemes of the same kind and by the same order of minds as are applied to judging a new design for a battleship with reference to her stability in bad weather.

and he needs active sympathy. In such problems as this it is the purely intellectual, and sometimes even the critical faculties, which are most in demand. But economic studies call for and develop the faculty of sympathy, and especially that rare sympathy which enables people to put themselves in the place, not only of their comrades, but also of other classes. This class sympathy is, for instance, strongly developed by inquiries, which are becoming every day more urgent, of the reciprocal influences which character and earnings, methods of employment and habits of expenditure exert on one another; of the ways in which the efficiency of a nation is strengthened by and strengthens the confidences and affections which hold together the members of each economic group—the family, employers and employees in the same business, citizens of the same country; of the good and evil that are mingled in the individual unselfishness and the class selfishness of professional etiquette and of trade union customs; and of movements by which our growing wealth and opportunities may best be turned to account for the wellbeing of the present and coming generations.[1]

Caution is demanded by an increasing recognition of the limitation of our knowledge and the uncertain perman- § 6. The economist needs imagination especially in order that he may develop his ideals. But most of all he needs caution and reserve in order that his advocacy of ideals may not outrun his grasp of the future.

After many more generations have passed, our present ideals and methods may seem to belong to the infancy, rather than to the maturity of man. One definite advance has already been made. We have learnt that every one until proved to be hopelessly weak or

---

[1] This Section is reproduced from a *Plea for the creation of a curriculum in economics and associated branches of political science* addressed to the University of Cambridge in 1902, and conceded in the following year.

base is worthy of full economic freedom : but we are not in a position to guess confidently to what goal the advance thus begun will ultimately lead. In the later Middle Ages a rough beginning was made of the study of the industrial organism, regarded as embracing all humanity. Each successive generation has seen further growths of that organism; but none has seen so large a growth as our own. The eagerness with which it has been studied has grown with its growth; and no parallel can be found in earlier times to the breadth and variety of the efforts that have been made to comprehend it. But the chief outcome of recent studies is to make us recognize more fully, than could be done by any previous generation, how little we know of the causes by which progress is being fashioned, and how little we can forecast the ultimate destiny of the industrial organism.

Some harsh employers and politicians, defending exclusive class privileges early in last century, found it convenient to claim the authority of political economy on their side; and they often spoke of themselves as "economists." And even in our own time, that title has been assumed by opponents of generous expenditure on the education of the masses of the people, in spite of the fact that living economists with one consent maintain that such expenditure is a true economy, and that to refuse it is both wrong and bad business from a national point of view. But Carlyle and Ruskin, followed by many other writers who had no part in their brilliant and ennobling poetical visions, have without examination held the great economists responsible for sayings and deeds to which they were really averse; and in consequence there has grown up a popular misconception of their thoughts and character.

The fact is that nearly all the founders of modern economics were men of gentle and sympathetic temper, touched with the enthusiasm of humanity. They cared little for wealth for themselves; they cared much for its wide diffusion among the masses of the people. They opposed antisocial monopolies however powerful. In their several generations they supported the movement against the class legislation which denied to trade unions privileges that were open to associations of employers; or they worked for a remedy against the poison which the old Poor Law was instilling into the hearts and homes of the agricultural and other labourers; or they supported the factory acts, in spite of the strenuous opposition of some politicians and employers who claimed to speak in their name. They were without exception devoted to the doctrine that the well-being of the whole people should be the ultimate goal of all private effort and all public policy. But they were strong in courage and

Marginal notes:

I, IV, 6.
—ence of our present social ideals.

Popular misconceptions of the character of the founders of modern economics.

I, IV, 6. caution; they appeared cold, because they would not assume the responsibility of advocating rapid advances on untried paths, for the safety of which the only guarantees offered were the confident hopes of men whose imaginations were eager, but not steadied by knowledge nor disciplined by hard thought.

Biology has given new hopes as to the future of the human race.

Their caution was perhaps a little greater than necessary: for the range of vision even of the great seers of that age was in some respects narrower than is that of most educated men in the present time; when, partly through the suggestions of biological study, the influence of circumstances in fashioning character is generally recognized as the dominant fact in social science. Economists have accordingly now learnt to take a larger and more hopeful view of the possibilities of human progress. They have learnt to trust that the human will, guided by careful thought, can so modify circumstances as largely to modify character; and thus to bring about new conditions of life still more favourable to character; and therefore to the economic, as well as the moral, wellbeing of the masses of the people. Now as ever it is their duty to oppose all plausible short cuts to that great end, which would sap the springs of energy and initiative.

But it is still true that short cuts are dangerous: progress must be cautious and tentative.

The rights of property, as such, have not been venerated by those master minds who have built up economic science; but the authority of the science has been wrongly assumed by some who have pushed the claims of vested rights to extreme and antisocial uses. It may be well therefore to note that the tendency of careful economic study is to base the rights of private property not on any abstract principle, but on the observation that in the past they have been inseparable from solid progress; and that therefore it is the part of responsible men to proceed cautiously and tentatively in abrogating or modifying even such rights as may seem to be inappropriate to the ideal conditions of social life.

BOOK II

SOME FUNDAMENTAL NOTIONS

CHAPTER I

INTRODUCTORY

§ 1. WE have seen that economics is, on the one side, a Science of Wealth; and, on the other, that part of the Social Science of man's action in society, which deals with his Efforts to satisfy his Wants, in so far as the efforts and wants are capable of being measured in terms of wealth, or its general representative, *i.e.* money. We shall be occupied during the greater part of this volume with these wants and efforts; and with the causes by which the prices that measure the wants are brought into equilibrium with those that measure the efforts. For this purpose we shall have to study in Book III wealth in relation to the diversity of man's wants, which it has to satisfy; and in Book IV wealth in relation to the diversity of man's efforts by which it is produced. II, I, 1.
Economics regards wealth as satisfying Wants and as the result of Efforts.

But in the present Book, we have to inquire which of all the things that are the result of man's efforts, and are capable of satisfying man's wants, are to be counted as Wealth; and into what groups or classes these are to be divided. For there is a compact group of terms connected with Wealth itself, and with Capital, the study of each of which throws light on the others; while the study of the whole together is a direct continuation, and in some respects a completion, of that inquiry as to the scope and methods of economics on which we have just been engaged. And, therefore, instead of taking what may seem the more natural course of starting with an analysis of wants, and of wealth in direct relation to them, it seems on the whole best to deal with this group of terms at once. But it is best to make a preliminary study of wealth itself.

In doing this we shall of course have to take some account of the variety of wants and efforts; but we shall not want to assume anything that is not obvious and a matter of common knowledge. The real difficulty of our task lies in another direction; being the result of the need under which economics, alone among sciences, lies of

II, I, 2.   making shift with a few terms in common use to express a great
——   number of subtle distinctions.

Principles   § 2. As Mill says [1] :—" The ends of scientific classification are
of classifi- best answered when the objects are formed into groups respecting
cation.
             which a greater number of general propositions can be made, and
             those propositions more important, than those which could be made
             respecting any other groups into which the same things could be
             distributed." But we meet at starting with the difficulty that those
             propositions which are the most important in one stage of economic
             development, are not unlikely to be among the least important in
             another, if indeed they apply at all.

The diffi-   In this matter economists have much to learn from the recent
culties of   experiences of biology : and Darwin's profound discussion of the
classifying
things   question [2] throws a strong light on the difficulties before us. He
which are   points out that those parts of the structure which determine the
changing
their   habits of life and the general place of each being in the economy of
characters   nature, are as a rule not those which throw most light on its origin,
and their
uses.   but those which throw least. The qualities which a breeder or a
             gardener notices as eminently adapted to enable an animal or a plant
             to thrive in its environment, are for that very reason likely to have
             been developed in comparatively recent times. And in like manner
             those properties of an economic institution which play the most
             important part in fitting it for the work which it has to do now, are
             for that very reason likely to be in a great measure of recent growth.

                 Instances are found in many of the relations between employer
             and employed, between middleman and producer, between bankers
             and their two classes of clients, those from whom they borrow and
             those to whom they lend. The substitution of the term " interest "
             for " usury " corresponds to a general change in the character of
             loans, which has given an entirely new key-note to our analysis and
             classification of the different elements into which the cost of pro-
             duction of a commodity may be resolved. Again, the general
             scheme of division of labour into skilled and unskilled is undergoing
             a gradual change; the scope of the term " rent " is being broadened
             in some directions and narrowed in others; and so on.

                 But on the other hand we must keep constantly in mind the
             history of the terms which we use. For, to begin with, this history
             is important for its own sake; and because it throws side-lights on
             the history of the economic development of society. And further,
             even if the sole purpose of our study of economics were to obtain

----

[1] *Logic*, Bk. iv. ch. vii. Par. 2.
[2] *Origin of Species*, ch. xiv.

knowledge that would guide us in the attainment of immediate practical ends, we should yet be bound to keep our use of terms as much as possible in harmony with the traditions of the past; in order that we might be quick to perceive the indirect hints and the subtle and subdued warnings, which the experiences of our ancestors offer for our instruction.

§ 3. Our task is difficult. In physical sciences indeed, whenever it is seen that a group of things have a certain set of qualities in common, and will often be spoken of together, they are formed into a class with a special name; and as soon as a new notion emerges, a new technical term is invented to represent it. But economics cannot venture to follow this example. Its reasonings must be expressed in language that is intelligible to the general public; it must therefore endeavour to conform itself to the familiar terms of everyday life, and so far as possible must use them as they are commonly used.

In its use of terms economics must follow as closely as possible the practice of everyday life.

In common use almost every word has many shades of meaning, and therefore needs to be interpreted by the context. And, as Bagehot has pointed out, even the most formal writers on economic science are compelled to follow this course; for otherwise they would not have enough words at their disposal. But unfortunately they do not always avow that they are taking this freedom; sometimes perhaps they are scarcely even aware of the fact themselves. The bold and rigid definitions, with which their expositions of the science begin, lull the reader into a false security. Not being warned that he must often look to the context for a special interpretation clause, he ascribes to what he reads a meaning different from that which the writers had in their own minds; and perhaps misrepresents them and accuses them of folly of which they had not been guilty.[1]

But that is not always consistent,

Again, most of the chief distinctions marked by economic terms

definite.

[1] We ought " to write more as we do in common life, where the context is a sort of unexpressed ' interpretation clause '; only as in Political Economy we have more difficult things to speak of than in ordinary conversation, we must take more care, give more warning of any change; and at times write out ' the interpretation clause ' for that page or discussion lest there should be any mistake. I know that this is difficult and delicate work; and all that I have to say in defence of it is that in practice it is safer than the competing plan of inflexible definitions. Any one who tries to express various meanings on complex things with a scanty vocabulary of fastened senses, will find that his style grows cumbrous without being accurate, that he has to use long periphrases for common thoughts, and that after all he does not come out right, for he is half the time falling back into the senses which fit the case in hand best, and these are sometimes one, sometimes another, and almost always different from his ' hard and fast ' sense. In such discussions we should learn to vary our definitions as we want, just as we say ' let x, y, z, mean ' now this, and now that, in different problems; and this, though they do not always avow it, is really the practice of the clearest and most effective writers." (Bagehot's *Postulates of English Political Economy*, pp. 78, 9.) Cairnes also (*Logical Method of Political Economy*, Lect. VI.) combats " the assumption that the attribute on which a definition turns ought to be one which does not admit of degrees "; and argues that " to admit of degrees is the character of all natural facts."

II, I, 4.

are differences not of kind but of degree. At first sight they appear to be differences of kind, and to have sharp outlines which can be clearly marked out; but a more careful study has shown that there is no real breach of continuity. It is a remarkable fact that the progress of economics has discovered hardly any new real differences in kind, while it is continually resolving apparent differences in kind into differences in degree. We shall meet with many instances of the evil that may be done by attempting to draw broad, hard and fast lines of division, and to formulate definite propositions with regard to differences between things which nature has not separated by any such lines.

It is necessary that notions should be clearly defined, but not that the use of terms should be rigid.

§ 4. We must then analyse carefully the real characteristics of the various things with which we have to deal; and we shall thus generally find that there is some use of each term which has distinctly greater claims than any other to be called its leading use, on the ground that it represents a distinction that is more important for the purposes of modern science than any other that is in harmony with ordinary usage. This may be laid down as the meaning to be given to the term whenever nothing to the contrary is stated or implied by the context. When the term is wanted to be used in any other sense, whether broader or narrower, the change must be indicated.

Even among the most careful thinkers there will always remain differences of opinion as to the exact places in which some at least of the lines of definition should be drawn. The questions at issue must in general be solved by judgments as to the practical convenience of different courses; and such judgments cannot always be established or overthrown by scientific reasoning : there must remain a margin of debatable ground. But there is no such margin in the analysis itself : if two people differ with regard to that, they cannot both be right. And the progress of the science may be expected gradually to establish this analysis on an impregnable basis.[1]

---

[1] When it is wanted to narrow the meaning of a term (that is, in logical language, to diminish its extension by increasing its intension), a qualifying adjective will generally suffice, but a change in the opposite direction cannot as a rule be so simply made. Contests as to definitions are often of this kind :—A and B are qualities common to a great number of things, many of these things have in addition the quality C, and again many the quality D, while some have both C and D. It may then be argued that on the whole it will be best to define a term so as to include all things which have the qualities A and B, or only those which have the qualities A, B, C, or only those which have the qualities A, B, D; or only those which have A, B, C, D. The decision between these various courses must rest on considerations of practical convenience, and is a matter of far less importance than a careful study of the qualities A, B, C, D, and of their mutual relations. But unfortunately this study has occupied a much smaller space in English economics than controversies as to definitions; which have indeed occasionally led indirectly to the discovery of scientific truth, but always by roundabout routes, and with much waste of time and labour.

CHAPTER II

WEALTH

§ 1. ALL wealth consists of desirable things; that is, things II, II, 1. which satisfy human wants directly or indirectly : but not all *Wealth* desirable things are reckoned as wealth. The affection of friends, *consists of* for instance, is an important element of wellbeing, but it is not *things or* reckoned as wealth, except by a poetic licence. Let us then begin by *Goods.* classifying desirable things, and then consider which of them should be accounted as elements of wealth.

In the absence of any short term in common use to represent all desirable things, or things that satisfy human wants, we may use the term *Goods* for that purpose.

Desirable things or goods are Material, or Personal and Im- *Material* material. *Material goods* consist of useful material things, and of all *goods.* rights to hold, or use, or derive benefits from material things, or to receive them at a future time. Thus they include the physical gifts of nature, land and water, air and climate; the products of agriculture, mining, fishing, and manufacture; buildings, machinery, and implements; mortgages and other bonds; shares in public and private companies, all kinds of monopolies, patent-rights, copyrights; also rights of way and other rights of usage. Lastly, opportunities of travel, access to good scenery, museums, etc., are the embodiment of material facilities, external to a man; though the faculty of appreciating them is internal and personal.

A man's *non-material* goods fall into two classes. One consists of *External* his own qualities and faculties for action and for enjoyment; such *and* for instance as business ability, professional skill, or the faculty of *goods.* deriving recreation from reading or music. All these lie within him-self and are called *internal*. The second class are called *external* because they consist of relations beneficial to him with other people. Such, for instance, were the labour dues and personal services of various kinds which the ruling classes used to require from their serfs and other dependents. But these have passed away; and the chief instances of such relations beneficial to their owner now-a-days

II, II, 2. are to be found in the good will and business connection of traders
and professional men.[1]

*Transfer-
able* and
*non-trans-
ferable
goods.*

Again, goods may be *transferable* or *non-transferable*.   Among the
latter are to be classed a person's qualities and faculties for action
and enjoyment (*i.e.* his internal goods); also such part of his business
connection as depends on personal trust in him and cannot be transferred, as part of his vendible good will; also the advantages of
climate, light, air, and his privileges of citizenship and rights and
opportunities of making use of public property.[2]

Free goods

Those goods are *free*, which are not appropriated and are afforded
by Nature without requiring the effort of man.   The land in its
original state was a free gift of nature.   But in settled countries it is
not a free good from the point of view of the individual.   Wood is
still free in some Brazilian forests.   The fish of the sea are free
generally : but some sea fisheries are jealously guarded for the
exclusive use of members of a certain nation, and may be classed as
national property.   Oyster beds that have been planted by man are
not free in any sense; those that have grown naturally are free in
every sense if they are not appropriated; if they are private property
they are still free gifts from the point of view of the nation.   But,
since the nation has allowed its rights in them to become vested in
private persons, they are not free from the point of view of the
individual; and the same is true of private rights of fishing in rivers.
But wheat grown on free land and the fish that have been landed from
free fisheries are not free : for they have been acquired by labour.

*A person's
wealth*

§ 2. We may now pass to the question which classes of a man's
goods are to be reckoned as part of his wealth.   The question is one
as to which there is some difference of opinion, but the balance of
argument as well as of authority seems clearly to incline in favour of
the following answer :—

---

[1] For, in the words in which Hermann begins his masterly analysis of wealth,
" Some Goods are *internal*, others *external*, to the individual.   An internal good is that
which he finds in himself given to him by nature, or which he educates in himself by
his own free action, such as muscular strength, health, mental attainments.   Everything that the outer world offers for the satisfaction of his wants is an external good
to him."

[2] The above classification of goods may be expressed thus :—

$$\text{Goods are} \begin{cases} \text{external} \begin{cases} \text{material} \begin{cases} \text{transferable} \\ \text{non-transferable} \end{cases} \\ \text{personal} \begin{cases} \text{transferable} \\ \text{non-transferable} \end{cases} \end{cases} \\ \text{internal-personal-non-transferable.} \end{cases}$$

Another arrangement is more convenient for some purposes :—

$$\text{Goods are} \begin{cases} \text{material-external} \begin{cases} \text{transferable} \\ \text{non-transferable} \end{cases} \\ \text{personal} \begin{cases} \text{external} \begin{cases} \text{transferable} \\ \text{non-transferable} \end{cases} \\ \text{internal-non-transferable.} \end{cases} \end{cases}$$

When a man's *wealth* is spoken of simply, and without any interpretation clause in the context, it is to be taken to be his stock of
two classes of goods.

In the first class are those material goods to which he has (by law
or custom) private rights of property, and which are therefore transferable and exchangeable. These it will be remembered include not
only such things as land and houses, furniture and machinery, and
other material things which may be in his single private ownership,
but also any shares in public companies, debenture bonds, mortgages
and other obligations which he may hold requiring others to pay
money or goods to him. On the other hand, the debts which he
owes to others may be regarded as negative wealth; and they must
be subtracted from his gross possessions before his true net wealth
can be found.

Services and other goods, which pass out of existence in the same
instant that they come into it, are, of course, not part of the stock of
wealth.[1]

In the second class are those immaterial goods which belong to
him, are external to him, and serve directly as the means of enabling
him to acquire material goods. Thus it excludes all his own personal
qualities and faculties, even those which enable him to earn his living;
because they are Internal. And it excludes his personal friendships,
in so far as they have no direct business value. But it includes his
business and professional connections, the organization of his
business, and—where such things exist—his property in slaves, in
labour dues, etc.

This use of the term Wealth is in harmony with the usage of
ordinary life : and, at the same time, it includes those goods, and
only those, which come clearly within the scope of economic science,
as defined in Book I; and which may therefore be called *economic
goods*. For it includes all those things, external to a man, which (i)
belong to him, and do not belong equally to his neighbours, and therefore are distinctly his ; and which (ii) are directly capable of a money
measure,—a measure that represents on the one side the efforts and
sacrifices by which they have been called into existence, and, on the
other, the wants which they satisfy.[2]

II, ii, 2.
———
is his stock
of two
classes of
goods,
material
goods,

and such
immaterial
external
goods as
are used
to obtain
material
goods.

The two
classes
together
constitute
*economic
goods.*

---

[1] That part of the value of the share in a trading company which is due to the
personal reputation and connection of those who conduct its affairs ought properly
to come under the next head as external personal goods. But this point is not of
much practical importance.

[2] It is not implied that the owner of transferable goods, if he transferred them,
could always realize the whole money value, which they have for him. A well-fitting
coat, for instance, may be worth the price charged for it by an expensive tailor to its
owner, because he wants it and cannot get it made for less : but he could not sell it for

II, II, 3, 4.

A broader use of the term *wealth* is sometimes required.

Personal wealth.

A broad term to include all forms of private wealth.

But we still have to take account of the individual's share of the common wealth.

§ 3. A broader view of wealth may indeed be taken for some purposes; but then recourse must be had to a special interpretation clause, to prevent confusion. Thus, for instance, the carpenter's skill is as direct a means of enabling him to satisfy other people's material wants, and therefore indirectly his own, as are the tools in his work-basket; and perhaps it may be convenient to have a term which will include it as part of wealth in a broader use. Pursuing the lines indicated by Adam Smith,[1] and followed by most continental economists, we may define *personal wealth* so as to include all those energies, faculties, and habits which directly contribute to making people industrially efficient; together with those business connections and associations of any kind, which we have already reckoned as part of wealth in the narrower use of the term. Industrial faculties have a further claim to be regarded as economic in the fact that their value is as a rule capable of some sort of indirect measurement.[2]

The question whether it is ever worth while to speak of them as wealth is merely one of convenience, though it has been much discussed as if it were one of principle.

Confusion would certainly be caused by using the term " wealth " by itself when we desire to include a person's industrial qualities. " Wealth " simply should always mean external wealth only. But little harm, and some good seems likely to arise from the occasional use of the phrase " material and personal wealth."

§ 4. But we still have to take account of those material goods which are common to him with his neighbours; and which therefore it would be a needless trouble to mention when comparing his wealth with theirs; though they may be important for some purposes, and especially for comparisons between the economic conditions of distant places or distant times.

These goods consist of the benefits which he derives from living in a certain place at a certain time, and being a member of a certain

---

half that sum. The successful financier who has spent £50,000 on having a house and grounds made to suit his own special fancy, is from one point of view right in reckoning them in the inventory of his property at their cost price : but, should he fail, they will not form an asset to his creditors of anything like that value.

And in the same way from one point of view we may count the business connection of the solicitor or physician, the merchant or the manufacturer, at the full equivalent of the income he would lose if he were deprived of it; while yet we must recognize that its exchange value, *i.e.* the value which he could get for it by selling it, is much less than that.

[1] Comp. *Wealth of Nations*, Bk. II. ch. II.

[2] " The bodies of men are without doubt the most valuable treasure of a country," said Davenant in the seventeenth century; and similar phrases have been common whenever the trend of political development has made men anxious that the population should increase fast.

state or community; they include civil and military security, and II, II, 5.
the right and opportunity to make use of public property and
institutions of all kinds, such as roads, gaslight, etc., and rights to
justice or to a free education. The townsman and the countryman
have each of them for nothing many advantages which the other
either cannot get at all, or can get only at great expense. Other
things being equal, one person has more real wealth in its broadest
sense than another, if the place in which the former lives has a better
climate, better roads, better water, more wholesome. drainage;
and again better newspapers, books, and places of amusement and
instruction. House-room, food and clothing, which would be
insufficient in a cold climate, may be abundant in a warm climate :
on the other hand, that warmth which lessens men's physical needs,
and makes them rich with but a slight provision of material wealth,
makes them poor in the energy that procures wealth.

Many of these things are *collective goods*; *i.e.* goods which are not *Collective*
in private ownership. And this brings us to consider wealth from *goods.*
the social, as opposed to the individual point of view.

§ 5. Let us then look at those elements of the wealth of a nation In a broad
which are commonly ignored when estimating the wealth of the view of
national
individuals composing it. The most obvious forms of such wealth wealth
are public material property of all kinds, such as roads and canals,
buildings and parks, gasworks and waterworks; though unfortunately many of them have been secured not by public savings,
but by public borrowings, and there is the heavy " negative "
wealth of a large debt to be set against them.

But the Thames has added more to the wealth of England than account
all its canals, and perhaps even than all its railroads. And though must be
taken of
the Thames is a free gift of nature (except in so far as its navigation free goods
has been improved), while the canal is the work of man, yet we and of
ought for many purposes to reckon the Thames a part of England's
wealth.

German economists often lay stress on the non-material elements the organi-
of national wealth; and it is right to do this in some problems zation of
society or
relating to national wealth, but not in all. Scientific knowledge the State.
indeed, wherever discovered, soon becomes the property of the whole
civilized world, and may be considered as cosmopolitan rather than
as specially national wealth. The same is true of mechanical
inventions and of many other improvements in the arts of production; and it is true of music. But those kinds of literature
which lose their force by translation, may be regarded as in a
special sense the wealth of those nations in whose language they are

II, n, 5. written. And the organization of a free and well-ordered State is to be regarded for some purposes as an important element of national wealth.

But national wealth includes the individual as well as the collective property of its members. And in estimating the aggregate sum of their individual wealth, we may save some trouble by omitting all debts and other obligations due to one member of a nation from another. For instance, so far as the English national debt and the bonds of an English railway are owned within the nation, we can adopt the simple plan of counting the railway itself as part of the national wealth, and neglecting railway and government bonds altogether. But we still have to deduct for those bonds etc. issued by the English Government or by private Englishmen, and held by foreigners; and to add for those foreign bonds etc. held by Englishmen.[1]

Debts from one member of a nation to another may be omitted.

Cosmopolitan wealth differs from national wealth much as that differs from individual wealth. In reckoning it, debts due from members of one nation to those of another may conveniently be omitted from both sides of the account. Again, just as rivers are important elements of national wealth, the ocean is one of the most valuable properties of the world. The notion of cosmopolitan wealth

Cosmopolitan wealth.

---

[1] The value of a business may be to some extent due to its having a monopoly, either a complete monopoly, secured perhaps by a patent; or a partial monopoly, owing to its wares being better known than others which are really equally good; and in so far as this is the case the business does not add to the real wealth of the nation. If the monopoly were broken down, the diminution of national wealth due to the disappearance of its value would generally be more than made up, partly by the increased value of rival businesses, and partly by the increased purchasing power of the money representing the wealth of other members of the community. (It should, however, be added that in some exceptional cases, the price of a commodity may be lowered in consequence of its production being monopolized : but such cases are very rare, and may be neglected for the present.)

Again, business connections and trade reputations add to the national wealth, only in so far as they bring purchasers into relation with those producers who will meet their real wants most fully for a given price; or in other words, only in so far as they increase the extent to which the efforts of the community as a whole meet the wants of the community as a whole. Nevertheless when we are estimating national wealth, not indirectly as the aggregate of individual wealth, we must allow for these businesses at their full value, even though this partly consists of a monopoly which is not used for the public benefit. For the injury they do to rival producers was allowed for in counting up the values of the businesses of those rivals; and the injury done to consumers by raising the price of the produce, which they buy, was allowed for in reckoning the purchasing power of their means, so far as this particular commodity is concerned.

A special case of this is the organization of credit. It increases the efficiency of production in the country, and thus adds to national wealth. And the power of obtaining credit is a valuable asset to any individual trader. If, however, any accident should drive him out of business, the injury to national wealth is something less than the whole value of that asset; because some part at least of the business, which he would have done, will now be done by others with the aid of some part at least of the capital which he would have borrowed.

There are similar difficulties as to how far money is to be reckoned as part of national wealth; but to treat them thoroughly would require us to anticipate a good deal of the theory of money.

is indeed nothing more than that of national wealth extended over II, II, 6
the whole area of the globe.

Individual and national rights to wealth rest on the basis of civil The
and international law, or at least of custom that has the force of law. juridical
An exhaustive investigation of the economic conditions of any time rights to
and place requires therefore an inquiry into law and custom; and wealth.
economics owes much to those who have worked in this direction.
But its boundaries are already wide; and the historical and juridical
bases of the conceptions of property are vast subjects which may best
be discussed in separate treatises.

§ 6. The notion of *Value* is intimately connected with that of *Value.*
Wealth; and a little may be said about it here. " The word *value*," Price is
says Adam Smith, " has two different meanings, and sometimes visionally
expresses the utility of some particular object and sometimes the sent
power of purchasing other goods which the possession of that object general
conveys." But experience has shown that it is not well to use the power.
word in the former sense.

The value, that is the exchange value, of one thing in terms of
another at any place and time, is the amount of that second thing
which can be got there and then in exchange for the first. Thus the
term value is relative, and expresses the relation between two things
at a particular place and time.

Civilized countries generally adopt gold or silver or both as
money. Instead of expressing the values of lead and tin, and wood,
and corn and other things in terms of one another, we express them
in terms of money in the first instance; and call the value of each
thing thus expressed its *price.* If we know that a ton of lead will
exchange for fifteen sovereigns at any place and time, while a ton of
tin will exchange for ninety sovereigns, we say that their prices then
and there are £15 and £90 respectively, and we know that the value
of a ton of tin in terms of lead is six tons then and there.

The price of every thing rises and falls from time to time and
place to place; and with every such change the purchasing power of
money changes so far as that thing goes. If the purchasing power of
money rises with regard to some things, and at the same time falls
equally with regard to equally important things, its general purchasing power (or its power of purchasing things in general) has
remained stationary. This phrase conceals some difficulties, which
we must study later on. But meanwhile we may take it in its
popular sense, which is sufficiently clear; and we may throughout
this volume neglect possible changes in the general purchasing power
of money. Thus the price of anything will be taken as representative

II, II, 6. of its exchange value relatively to things in general, or in other words as representative of its general purchasing power.[1]

But if inventions have increased man's power over nature very much, then the real value of money is better measured for some purposes in labour than in commodities. This difficulty however will not much affect our work in the present volume, which is only a study of the " Foundations " of economics.

[1] As Cournot points out (*Principes Mathématiques de la Théorie des Richesses*, ch. II.), we get the same sort of convenience from assuming the existence of a standard of uniform purchasing power by which to measure value, that astronomers do by assuming that there is a " mean sun " which crosses the meridian at uniform intervals, so that the clock can keep pace with it; whereas the actual sun crosses the meridian sometimes before and sometimes after noon as shown by the clock.

CHAPTER III

PRODUCTION. CONSUMPTION. LABOUR. NECESSARIES

§ 1. MAN cannot create material things. In the mental and
moral world indeed he may produce new ideas; but when he is said Man cannot produce matter, but only utilities inherent in matter.
to produce material things, he really only produces utilities; or in
other words, his efforts and sacrifices result in changing the form or
arrangement of matter to adapt it better for the satisfaction of wants.
All that he can do in the physical world is either to readjust matter so
as to make it more useful, as when he makes a log of wood into a
table; or to put it in the way of being made more useful by nature,
as when he puts seed where the forces of nature will make it burst out
into life.[1]

It is sometimes said that traders do not produce : that while the The trader produces utilities.
cabinet-maker produces furniture, the furniture-dealer merely sells
what is already produced. But there is no scientific foundation for
this distinction. They both produce utilities, and neither of them
can do more : the furniture-dealer moves and rearranges matter so
as to make it more serviceable than it was before, and the carpenter
does nothing more. The sailor or the railway-man who carries coal
above ground produces it, just as much as the miner who carries it
underground; the dealer in fish helps to move on fish from where it is
of comparatively little use to where it is of greater use, and the
fisherman does no more. It is true that there are often more traders
than are necessary; and that, whenever that is the case, there is a
waste. But there is also waste if there are two men to a plough
which can be well worked by one man; in both cases all those who are
at work produce, though they may produce but little. Some
writers have revived the mediæval attacks on trade on the ground
that it does not produce. But they have not aimed at the right
mark. They should have attacked the imperfect organization of
trade, particularly of retail trade.[2]

Consumption may be regarded as negative production. Just as

---

[1] Bacon, *Novum Organum* IV., says " Ad opera nil aliud potest homo quam ut
corpora naturalia admoveat et amoveat, reliqua natura intus agit" (quoted by Bonar,
Philosophy and Political Economy, p. 249).
[2] Production, in the narrow sense, changes the form and nature of products.
Trade and transport change their external relations.

II, III, 2.

Man can consume, as he can produce, only utilities.

man can produce only utilities, so he can consume nothing more. He can produce services and other immaterial products, and he can consume them. But as his production of material products is really nothing more than a rearrangement of matter which gives it new utilities; so his consumption of them is nothing more than a disarrangement of matter, which diminishes or destroys its utilities. Often indeed when he is said to consume things, he does nothing more than to hold them for his use, while, as Senior says, they " are destroyed by those numerous gradual agents which we call collectively time." [1] As the " producer " of wheat is he who puts seed where nature will make it grow, so the " consumer " of pictures, of curtains, and even of a house or a yacht does little to wear them out himself; but he uses them while time wastes them.

Consumers' and producers' goods.

Another distinction to which some prominence has been given, but which is vague and perhaps not of much practical use, is that between *consumers' goods* (called also *consumption goods*, or again *goods of the first order*), such as food, clothes, etc., which satisfy wants *directly* on the one hand; and, on the other hand, *producers' goods* (called also *production goods*, or again *instrumental*, or again *intermediate goods*), such as ploughs and looms and raw cotton, which satisfy wants *indirectly* by contributing towards the production of the first class of goods. [2]

Nearly all labour is in some sense productive.

§ 2. All labour is directed towards producing some effect. For though some exertions are taken merely for their own sake, as when a game is played for amusement, they are not counted as labour. We may define *labour* as any exertion of mind or body undergone partly or wholly with a view to some good other than the pleasure derived directly from the work. [3] And if we had to make a fresh start it would be best to regard all labour as productive except that

---

[1] *Political Economy*, p. 54. Senior would like to substitute the verb " to use " for the verb " to consume."

[2] Thus flour to be made into a cake when already in the house of the consumer, is treated by some as a consumers' good; while not only the flour, but the cake itself is treated as a producers' good when in the hand of the confectioner. Carl Menger (*Volkswirthschaftslehre*, ch. I. § 2) says bread belongs to the first order, flour to the second, a flour mill to the third order and so on. It appears that if a railway train carries people on a pleasure excursion, also some tins of biscuits, and milling machinery and some machinery that is used for making milling machinery; then the train is at one and the same time a good of the first, second, third and fourth orders.

[3] This is Jevons' definition (*Theory of Political Economy*, ch. v.), except that he includes only painful exertions. But he himself points out how painful idleness often is. Most people work more than they would if they considered only the direct pleasure resulting from the work; but in a healthy state, pleasure predominates over pain in a great part even of the work that is done for hire. Of course the definition is elastic; an agricultural labourer working in his garden in the evening thinks chiefly of the fruit of his labours; a mechanic returning home after a day of sedentary toil finds positive pleasure in his garden work, but he too cares a good deal about the fruit of his labour; while a rich man working in like manner, though he may take a pride in doing it well, will probably care little for any pecuniary saving that he effects by it.

which failed to promote the aim towards which it was directed, and
so produced no utility. But in all the many changes which the
meaning of the word " productive " has undergone, it has had
special reference to stored-up wealth, to the comparative neglect and
sometimes even to the exclusion of immediate and transitory
enjoyment; [1] and an almost unbroken tradition compels us to
regard the central notion of the word as relating to the provision for
the wants of the future rather than those of the present. It is true
that all wholesome enjoyments, whether luxurious or not, are legitimate ends of action both public and private; and it is true that the
enjoyment of luxuries affords an incentive to exertion, and promotes
progress in many ways. But if the efficiency and energy of industry
are the same, the true interest of a country is generally advanced by
the subordination of the desire for transient luxuries to the attainment of those more solid and lasting resources which will assist
industry in its future work, and will in various ways tend to make life
larger. This general idea has been in solution, as it were, in all
stages of economic theory; and has been precipitated by different
writers into various hard and fast distinctions by which certain
trades have been marked off as productive and certain others as
unproductive.

For instance, many writers even of recent times have adhered to
Adam Smith's plan of classing domestic servants as unproductive.
There is doubtless in many large houses a superabundance of servants,
some of whose energies might with advantage to the community be
transferred to other uses : but the same is true of the greater part of
those who earn their livelihood by distilling whisky; and yet no
economist has proposed to call them unproductive. There is no
distinction in character between the work of the baker who provides
bread for a family, and that of the cook who boils potatoes. If the
baker should be a confectioner, or fancy baker, it is probable that he
spends at least as much of his time as the domestic cook does, on

Marginal notes:

II, III, 2.

But that labour is generally said to be specially productive which provides for the wants of the future rather than the present.

The work of domestic servants is not necessarily unproductive.

---

[1] Thus the Mercantilists who regarded the precious metals, partly because they
were imperishable, as wealth in a fuller sense than anything else, regarded as unproductive or " sterile " all labour that was not directed to producing goods for exportation in exchange for gold and silver. The Physiocrats thought all labour sterile which
consumed an equal value to that which it produced ; and regarded the agriculturist
as the only productive worker, because his labour alone (as they thought) left it a net
surplus of stored-up wealth. Adam Smith softened down the Physiocratic definition ;
but still he considered that agricultural labour was more productive than any other.
His followers discarded this distinction ; but they have generally adhered, though with
many differences in points of detail, to the notion that productive labour is that which
tends to increase accumulated wealth ; a notion which is implied rather than stated in
the celebrated chapter of The Wealth of Nations which bears the title, "On the Accumulation of Capital, or on Productive and Unproductive Labour." (Comp. Travers
Twiss, Progress of Political Economy, Sect. VI., and the discussions on the word Productive in J. S. Mill's Essays, and in his Principles of Political Economy.)

II, III, 3. labour that is unproductive in the popular sense of providing unnecessary enjoyments.

Provisional definition of *productive*. Whenever we use the word *Productive* by itself, it is to be understood to mean *productive of the means of production, and of durable sources of enjoyment*. But it is a slippery term, and should not be used where precision is needed.[1]

If ever we want to use it in a different sense, we must say so : for instance we may speak of labour as *productive of necessaries, etc.*

Productive consumption. *Productive consumption*, when employed as a technical term, is commonly defined as the use of wealth in the production of further wealth; and it should properly include not all the consumption of productive workers, but only that which is necessary for their efficiency. The term may perhaps be useful in studies of the accumulation of material wealth. But it is apt to mislead. For consumption is the end of production; and all wholesome consumption is productive of benefits, many of the most worthy of which do not directly contribute to the production of material wealth.[2]

Necessaries are things which meet wants that *must* be satisfied. But this account is ambiguous. § 3. This brings us to consider the term Necessaries. It is common to distinguish necessaries, comforts, and luxuries; the first class including all things required to meet wants which *must* be satisfied, while the latter consist of things that meet wants of a less urgent character. But here again there is a troublesome ambiguity. When we say that a want *must* be satisfied, what are the consequences

[1] Among the means of production are included the necessaries of labour but not ephemeral luxuries; and the maker of ices is thus classed as unproductive whether he is working for a pastry-cook, or as a private servant in a country house. But a bricklayer engaged in building a theatre is classed as productive. No doubt the division between permanent and ephemeral sources of enjoyment is vague and unsubstantial. But this difficulty exists in the nature of things and cannot be completely evaded by any device of words. We can speak of an increase of tall men relatively to short, without deciding whether all those above five feet nine inches are to be classed as tall, or only those above five feet ten. And we can speak of the increase of productive labour at the expense of unproductive without fixing on any rigid, and therefore arbitrary line of division between them. If such an artificial line is required for any particular purpose, it must be drawn explicitly for the occasion. But in fact such occasions seldom or never occur.

[2] All the distinctions in which the word Productive is used are very thin and have a certain air of unreality. It would hardly be worth while to introduce them now : but they have a long history; and it is probably better that they should dwindle gradually out of use, rather than be suddenly discarded.

The attempt to draw a hard and fast line of distinction where there is no real discontinuity in nature has often done more mischief, but has perhaps never led to more quaint results, than in the rigid definitions which have been sometimes given of this term Productive. Some of them for instance lead to the conclusion that a singer in an opera is unproductive, that the printer of the tickets of admission to the opera is productive; while the usher who shows people to their places is unproductive, unless he happens to sell programmes, and then he is productive. Senior points out that " a cook is not said to *make* roast meat but to *dress* it; but he is said to *make* a pudding. . . . A tailor is said to *make* cloth into a coat, a dyer is not said to *make* undyed cloth into dyed cloth. The change produced by the dyer is perhaps greater than that produced by the tailor, but the cloth in passing through the tailor's hands changes its name; in passing through the dyer's it does not : the dyer has not produced a *new name*, nor consequently a *new thing*." *Pol. Econ.* pp. 51, 2.

which we have in view if it is not satisfied ?   Do they include death ?
Or do they extend only to the loss of strength and vigour ?   In other
words, are necessaries the things which are necessary for life, or those
which are necessary for efficiency ?

The term Necessaries, like the term Productive, has been used *The term Neces-saries is elliptical.*
elliptically, the subject to which it refers being left to be supplied by
the reader; and since the implied subject has varied, the reader has
often supplied one which the writer did not intend, and thus misunderstood his drift.   In this, as in the preceding case, the chief
source of confusion can be removed by supplying explicitly in every
critical place that which the reader is intended to understand.

The older use of the term Necessaries was limited to those things *Neces-saries for existence and for efficiency.*
which were sufficient to enable the labourers, taken one with another,
to support themselves and their families.   Adam Smith and the
more careful of his followers observed indeed variations in the
standard of comfort and " decency " : and they recognized that
differences of climate and differences of custom make things necessary
in some cases, which are superfluous in others.[1]   But Adam Smith
was influenced by reasonings of the Physiocrats : they were based
on the condition of the French people in the eighteenth century,
most of whom had no notion of any necessaries beyond those which
were required for mere existence.   In happier times, however, a
more careful analysis has made it evident that there is for each rank
of industry, at any time and place, a more or less clearly defined
income which is necessary for merely sustaining its members; while
there is another and larger income which is necessary for keeping it in
full efficiency.[2]

It may be true that the wages of any industrial class might have *Account must be taken of the conditions of place and time and of the habits of living.*
sufficed to maintain a higher efficiency, if they had been spent with
perfect wisdom.   But every estimate of necessaries must be relative
to a given place and time; and unless there be a special interpretation clause to the contrary, it may be assumed that the wages will
be spent with just that amount of wisdom, forethought, and unselfish-

[1] Compare Carver, *Principles of Political Economy*, p. 474 ; which called my attention to Adam Smith's observation that customary decencies are in effect necessaries.
[2] Thus in the South of England population has increased during the last hundred years
at a fair rate, allowance being made for migration.   But the efficiency of labour, which
in earlier times was as high as that in the North of England, has sunk relatively to the
North ; so that the low-waged labour of the South is often dearer than the more highly-
paid labour of the North.   We cannot thus say whether the labourers in the South have
been supplied with necessaries, unless we know in which of these two senses the word is
used.   They have had the bare necessaries for existence and the increase of numbers,
but apparently they have not had the necessaries for efficiency.   It must however be
remembered that the strongest labourers in the South have constantly migrated to the
North ; and that the energies of those in the North have been raised by their larger
share of economic freedom and of the hope of rising to a higher position.   See Mackay
in *Charity Organization Journal*, Feb. 1891.

II, III, 4.

Neces-saries.

ness, which prevails in fact among the industrial class under discussion. With this understanding we may say that the income of any class in the ranks of industry is below its *necessary* level, when any increase in their income would in the course of time produce a more than proportionate increase in their efficiency. Consumption may be economized by a change of habits, but any stinting of necessaries is wasteful.[1]

Illustration. Necessaries of unskilled labour.

§ 4. Some detailed study of the necessaries for efficiency of different classes of workers will have to be made, when we come to inquire into the causes that determine the supply of efficient labour. But it will serve to give some definiteness to our ideas, if we consider here what are the necessaries for the efficiency of an ordinary agricultural or of an unskilled town labourer and his family, in England, in this generation. They may be said to consist of a well-drained dwelling with several rooms, warm clothing, with some changes of underclothing, pure water, a plentiful supply of cereal food, with a moderate allowance of meat and milk, and a little tea, etc., some education and some recreation, and lastly, sufficient freedom for his wife from other work to enable her to perform properly her maternal and her household duties. If in any district unskilled labour is deprived of any of these things, its efficiency will

There is waste when any one consumes less than is necessary. Conventional necessaries.

suffer in the same way as that of a horse that is not properly tended, or a steam-engine that has an inadequate supply of coals. All consumption up to this limit is strictly productive consumption : any stinting of this consumption is not economical, but wasteful.

In addition, perhaps, some consumption of alcohol and tobacco, and some indulgence in fashionable dress are in many places so habitual, that they may be said to be *conventionally necessary*, since in order to obtain them the average man and woman will sacrifice some things which are necessary for efficiency. Their wages are therefore less than are practically necessary for efficiency, unless they provide not only for what is strictly necessary consumption, but include also a certain amount of conventional necessaries.[2]

[1] If we considered an individual of exceptional abilities we should have to take account of the fact that there is not likely to be the same close correspondence beween the real value of his work for the community and the income which he earns by it, that there is in the case of an ordinary member of any industrial class. And we should have to say that all his consumption is strictly productive and necessary, so long as by cutting off any part of it he would diminish his efficiency by an amount that is of more real value to him or the rest of the world than he saved from his consumption. If a Newton or a Watt could have added a hundredth part to his efficiency by doubling his personal expenditure, the increase in his consumption would have been truly productive. As we shall see later on, such a case is analogous to additional cultivation of rich land that bears a high rent : it may be profitable though the return to it is less than in proportion to the previous outlay.

[2] Compare the distinction between " Physical and Political Necessaries " in James Steuart's *Inquiry*, A.D. 1767, II, XXI.

The consumption of conventional necessaries by productive workers is commonly classed as productive consumption; but strictly speaking it ought not to be; and in critical passages a special interpretation clause should be added to say whether or not they are included.

It should however be noticed that many things which are rightly described as superfluous luxuries, do yet, to some extent, take the place of necessaries; and to that extent their consumption is productive when they are consumed by producers.[1]

[1] Thus a dish of green peas in March, costing perhaps ten shillings, is a superfluous luxury : but yet it is wholesome food, and does the work perhaps of three pennyworth of cabbage; or even, since variety undoubtedly conduces to health, a little more than that. So it may be entered perhaps at the value of fourpence under the head of necessaries, and at that of nine shillings and eightpence under that of superfluities; and its consumption may be regarded as strictly productive to the extent of one-fortieth. In exceptional cases, as for instance when the peas are given to an invalid, the whole ten shillings may be well spent, and reproduce their own value.

For the sake of giving definiteness to the ideas it may be well to venture on estimates of necessaries, rough and random as they must be. Perhaps at present prices the strict necessaries for an average agricultural family are covered by fifteen or eighteen shillings a week, the conventional necessaries by about five shillings more. For the unskilled labourer in the town a few shillings must be added to the strict necessaries. For the family of the skilled workman living in a town we may take twenty-five or thirty shillings for strict necessaries, and ten shillings for conventional necessaries. For a man whose brain has to undergo great continuous strain the strict necessaries are perhaps two hundred or two hundred and fifty pounds a year if he is a bachelor : but more than twice as much if he has an expensive family to educate. His conventional necessaries depend on the nature of his calling.

CHAPTER IV

INCOME. CAPITAL

Income in its broad use.

§ 1. In a primitive community each family is nearly self-sufficing, and provides most of its own food and clothing and even household furniture. Only a very small part of the income, or comings in, of the family is in the form of money; when one thinks of their income at all, one reckons in the benefits which they get from their cooking utensils, just as much as those which they get from their plough : one draws no distinction between their capital and the rest of their accumulated stock, to which the cooking utensils and the plough alike belong.[1]

Corresponding to money-income,

But with the growth of a money economy there has been a strong tendency to confine the notion of income to those incomings which are in the form of money; including " payments in kind " (such as the free use of a house, free coals, gas, water), which are given as part of an employee's remuneration, and in lieu of money payments.

we have trade capital.

In harmony with this meaning of Income, the language of the market-place commonly regards a man's capital as that part of his wealth which he devotes to acquiring an income in the form of money; or, more generally, to acquisition (*Erwerbung*) by means of trade. It may be convenient sometimes to speak of this as his *trade capital*; which may be defined to consist of those external goods which a person uses in his trade, either holding them to be sold for money or applying them to produce things that are to be sold for money. Among its conspicuous elements are such things as the factory and the business plant of a manufacturer; that is, his machinery, his raw material, any food, clothing, and house-room that he may hold for the use of his employees, and the goodwill of his business.

Its most conspicuous elements.

To the things in his possession must be added those to which he

---

[1] This and similar facts have led some people to suppose not only that some parts of the modern analysis of distribution and exchange are inapplicable to a primitive community; which is true : but also that there are no important parts of it that are applicable; which is not true. This is a striking instance of the dangers that arise from allowing ourselves to become the servants of words, avoiding the hard work that is required for discovering unity of substance underlying variety of form.

has a right and from which he is drawing income : including lo**a**ns II, IV, 2.
which he has made on mortgage or in other ways, and all the
command over capital which he may hold under the complex forms
of the modern " money market." On the other hand debts owed by
him must be deduced from his capital.

This definition of capital from the individual or business point of
view is firmly established in ordinary usage; and it will be assumed
throughout the present treatise whenever we are discussing problems
relating to business in general, and in particular to the supply of any
particular group of commodities for sale in open market. Income
and capital will be discussed from the point of view of private
business in the first half of the chapter; and afterwards the social
point of view will be considered.

§ 2. If a person is engaged in business, he is sure to have to incur *Net*
certain outgoings for raw material, the hire of labour, etc. And, in *income.*
that case, his true or *net income* is found by deducting from his gross
income " the outgoings that belong to its production." [1]

Anything which a person does for which he is paid directly or
indirectly in money, swells his nominal income; while no services
that he performs for himself are commonly reckoned as adding to his
nominal income. But, though it is best generally to neglect them
when they are trivial, account should for consistency be taken of
them, when they are of a kind which people commonly pay for
having done for them. Thus a woman who makes her own clothes or
a man who digs in his own garden or repairs his own house, is earning
income; just as would the dressmaker, gardener or carpenter who
might be hired to do the work.

In this connection we may introduce a term of which we shall *Pro-*
have to make frequent use hereafter. The need for it arises from the *visional*
definition
fact that every occupation involves other disadvantages besides the *of net ad-*
fatigue of the work required in it, and every occupation offers other *vantages.*
advantages besides the receipt of money wages. The true reward
which an occupation offers to labour has to be calculated by deducting the money value of all its disadvantages from that of all its
advantages; and we may describe this true reward as the *net
advantages* of the occupation.

The payment made by a borrower for the use of a loan for, say, a *Interest of*
year is expressed as the ratio which that payment bears to the loan, *capital.*
and is called *interest*. And this term is also used more broadly to
represent the money equivalent of the whole income which is derived
from capital. It is commonly expressed as a certain percentage on

[1] See a report of a Committee of the British Association. 1878. on the Income Tax.

II, IV, 2. the " capital " sum of the loan. Whenever this is done the capital must not be regarded as a stock of things in general. It must be regarded as a stock of one particular thing, money, which is taken to represent them. Thus £100 may be lent at four per cent., that is for an interest of £4 yearly. And, if a man employs in business a capital stock of goods of various kinds which are estimated as worth £10,000 in all; then £400 a year may be said to represent interest at the rate of four per cent. on that capital, on the supposition that the aggregate money value of the things which constitute it has remained unchanged. He would not, however, be willing to continue the business unless he expected his total net gains from it to *Profits.* exceed interest on his capital at the current rate. These gains are called *profits.*

Free or floating capital. The command over goods to a given money value, which can be applied to any purpose, is often described as " free " or " floating " capital.[1]

Earnings of management. When a man is engaged in business, his profits for the year are the excess of his receipts from his business during the year over his outlay for his business. The difference between the value of his stock of plant, material, etc. at the end and at the beginning of the year is taken as part of his receipts or as part of his outlay, according as there has been an increase or decrease of value. What remains of his profits after deducting interest on his capital at the current rate (allowing, where necessary, for insurance) is generally called his *earnings of undertaking* or *management.* The ratio in which his profits for the year stand to his capital is spoken of as his *rate of profits.* But this phrase, like the corresponding phrase with regard to interest, assumes that the money value of the things which constitute his capital has been estimated : and such an estimate is often found to involve great difficulties.

Rents and Quasi-rents. When any particular thing, as a house, a piano, or a sewing machine is lent out, the payment for it is often called *Rent.* And economists may follow this practice without inconvenience when they are regarding the income from the point of view of the individual trader. But, as will be argued presently, the balance of advantage seems to lie in favour of reserving the term Rent for the income derived from the free gifts of nature, whenever the discussion of business affairs passes from the point of view of the individual to that

[1] Professor Clark has made the suggestion to distinguish between *Pure Capital* and *Capital Goods* : the former is to correspond to a waterfall which remains stationary; while Capital Goods are the particular things which enter and leave the business, as particular drops pass through the waterfall. He would of course connect interest with pure capital, not with capital goods.

of society at large. And for that reason, the term *Quasi-rent* will be II, iv, 3.
used in the present volume for the income derived from machines ——
and other appliances for production made by man. That is to say,
any particular machine may yield an income which is of the nature of
a rent, and which is sometimes called a Rent; though on the whole,
there seems to be some advantage in calling it a Quasi-rent. But we
cannot properly speak of the interest yielded by a machine. If we
use the term " interest " at all, it must be in relation not to the
machine itself, but to its money *value*. For instance if the work
done by a machine which cost £100 is worth £4 a year net, that
machine is yielding a quasi-rent of £4 which is equivalent to interest
at four per cent. on its original cost : but if the machine is worth only
£80 now, it is yielding five per cent. on its present value. This
however raises some difficult questions of principle, which will be
discussed in Book V.

§ 3. Next to consider some details relating to capital. It has
been classed as Consumption capital, and Auxiliary or Instrumental
capital : and though no clear distinction can be drawn between the
two classes, it may sometimes be convenient to use the terms, with
the understanding that they are vague. Where definiteness is
necessary, the terms should be avoided; and explicit enumerations
should be given. The general notion of the distinction which the
terms are designed to suggest, can be gathered from the following
approximate definitions.

Consumption capital consists of goods in a form to satisfy wants *Con-*
directly; that is, goods which afford a direct sustenance to the *sumption
capital.*
workers, such as food, clothes, house-room, etc.

Auxiliary, or *instrumental*, *capital* is so called because it consists *Auxiliary
or instru-
mental
capital.*
of all the goods that aid labour in production. Under this head
come tools, machines, factories, railways, docks, ships, etc.; and
raw materials of all kinds.

But of course a man's clothes assist him in his work and are
instrumental in keeping him warm; and he derives a direct benefit
from the shelter of his factory as he does from the shelter of his
house.[1]

We may follow Mill in distinguishing *circulating capital* " which *Circulating* and
*fixed
capital.*
fulfils the whole of its office in the production in which it is engaged,
by a single use," from *fixed capital* " which exists in a durable shape
and the return to which is spread over a period of corresponding
duration." [2]

[1] See above II, III. 1.
[2] Adam Smith's distinction between fixed and circulating capital turned on the
question whether the goods "yield a profit without changing masters " or not.

II, IV, 4.

Transition to the social point of view of income.

§ 4. The customary point of view of the business man is that which is most convenient for the economist to adopt when discussing the production of goods for a market, and the causes which govern their exchange value. But there is a broader point of view which the business man, no less than the economist, must adopt when he studies the causes which govern the material wellbeing of the community as a whole. Ordinary conversation may pass from one point of view to another without any formal note of the change : for if a misunderstanding arises it soon becomes manifest; and confusion is cut short by a question or by a volunteered explanation. But the economist may take no risks of that sort : he must make prominent any change in his point of view or in his uses of terms. His path might have seemed smoother for the time, if he had passed silently from one use to another : but in the long run better progress is made by a clear indication of the meaning attached to each term in every doubtful case.[1]

Let us then during the remainder of this chapter deliberately adopt the *social*, in contrast with the individual point of view : let us look at the production of the community as a whole, and at its total net income available for all purposes. That is, let us revert nearly to the point of view of a primitive people, who are chiefly concerned with the production of desirable things, and with their direct uses; and who are little concerned with exchange and marketing.

In practical matters theoretical completeness may be purchased at too great a cost.

From this point of view income is regarded as including all the benefits which mankind derive at any time from their efforts, in the present and in the past, to turn nature's resources to their best account. The pleasure derived from the beauties of the rainbow, or the sweet taste of the fresh morning air, are left out of the reckoning, not because they are unimportant, nor because the estimate would in any way be vitiated by including them; but solely because reckoning them in would serve no good purpose, while it would add greatly to the length of our sentences and the prolixity of our discussions. For a similar reason it is not worth while to take separate account of the simple services which nearly every one renders to himself, such as putting on his clothes; though there are a few persons who choose to pay others to do such things for them. Their exclusion involves no principle; and time spent by some con-

---

Ricardo made it turn on whether they are " of slow consumption or require to be frequently reproduced "; but he truly remarks that this is " a division not essential, and in which the line of demarcation cannot be accurately drawn." Mill's modification is generally accepted by modern economists.

[1] Compare above II. I. 3.

troversial writers on discussing it has been wasted. It simply follows the maxim *De minimis non curat lex.* A driver who, not noticing a pool in his way, splashes a passer by is not held to have done him legal injury; though there is no distinction in principle between his act and that of another, who by a similar lack of attention, did serious harm to someone else.

A man's present labour yields him income directly, when devoted to his own use; and he looks to be paid for it in some form or another if he devotes it as a matter of business to the service of others. Similarly any useful thing which he has made or acquired in the past, or which has been handed down to him, under the existing institutions of property, by others who have so made or acquired it, is generally a source of material benefit to him directly or indirectly. If he applies it in business, this income generally appears in the form of money. But a broader use of this term is occasionally needed, which embraces the whole income of benefits of every sort which a person derives from the ownership of property however applied : it includes for instance the benefits which he gets from the use of his own piano, equally with those which a piano dealer would win by letting out a piano on hire. The language of common life while averse to so broad a use of the term Income as this even when discussing social problems, yet habitually includes a certain number of forms of income, other than money income.

The Income Tax Commissioners count a dwelling-house inhabited by its owner as a source of taxable income, though it yields its income of comfort directly. They do this, not on any abstract principle; but partly because of the practical importance of house-room, partly because the ownership of a house is commonly treated in a business fashion, and partly because the real income accruing from it can easily be separated off and estimated. They do not claim to establish any absolute distinction in kind between the things which their rule includes, and those which it excludes.

Jevons, regarding the problem from a purely mathematical point of view, was justified in classing all commodities in the hands of consumers as capital. But some writers, while developing this suggestion with great ingenuity, have treated it as a great principle; and that appears to be an error in judgment. A true sense of proportion requires us not to burden our work with the incessant enumeration of details of secondary importance, of which no account is taken in customary discourse, and which cannot even be described without offending against popular conventions.

D

II, IV, 5.

The corre-
lation of
income
and
capital.

§ 5. This brings us to consider the use of the term *capital* from the point of view of inquiries into the material wellbeing of society as a whole. Adam Smith said that a person's capital is *that part of his stock from which he expects to derive an income*. And almost every use of the term capital, which is known to history, has corresponded more or less closely to a parallel use of the term Income : in almost every use, capital has been that part of a man's stock from which he expects to derive an income.

By far the most important use of the term Capital in general, *i.e.* from the social point of view, is in the inquiry how the three agents of production, land (that is, natural agents), labour and capital, contribute to producing the national income (or the national dividend, as it will be called later on); and how that income is distributed among the three agents. And this is an additional reason for making the terms Capital and Income correlative from the social, as we did from the individual point of view.

Meaning
in this
treatise of
the terms
Capital
and *Land*
from the
social
point of
view.

Accordingly it is proposed in this treatise to count as part of capital from the social point of view all things other than land, which yield income that is generally reckoned as such in common discourse; together with similar things in public ownership, such as government factories : the term Land being taken to include all free gifts of nature, such as mines, fisheries, etc., which yield income.

Thus it will include all things held for trade purposes, whether machinery, raw material or finished goods; theatres and hotels; home farms and houses : but not furniture or clothes owned by those who use them. For the former are and the latter are not commonly regarded as yielding income by the world at large, as is shown by the practice of the income tax commissioners.

This usage of the term is in harmony with the common practice of economists of treating social problems in broad outline to start with, and reserving minor details for later consideration : it is in harmony also with their common practice of taking Labour to include those activities, and those only, which are regarded as the source of income in this broader use of the term. Labour together with capital and land thus defined are the sources of all that income of which account is commonly taken in reckoning up the National Income.[1]

---

[1] Just as for practical purposes it is better not to encumber ourselves with specifying the " income " of benefit which a man derives from the labour of brushing his hat in the morning, so it is better to ignore the element of capital vested in his brush. But no such consideration arises in a merely abstract discussion : and therefore the logical simplicity of Jevons' dictum that commodities in the hands of consumers are capital has some advantages and no disadvantages for mathematical versions of economic doctrines.

§ 6. Social income may be estimated by adding together the incomes of the individuals in the society in question, whether it be a nation or any other group of persons. We must however not count the same thing twice. If we have counted a carpet at its full value, we have already counted the values of the yarn and the labour that were used in making it; and these must not be counted again. And further, if the carpet was made of wool that was in stock at the beginning of the year, the value of that wool must be deducted from the value of the carpet before the net income of the year is reached; while similar deduction must be made for the wear and tear of machinery and other plant used in making it. This is required by the general rule, with which we started, that true or net income is found by deducting from gross income the outgoings that belong to its production.

II, IV, 6.
Elements
of social
income
that are
in danger
of being
counted
twice or
of being
omitted.

But if the carpet is cleaned by domestic servants or at steam scouring works, the value of the labour spent in cleaning it must be counted in separately; for otherwise the results of this labour would be altogether omitted from the inventory of those newly-produced commodities and conveniences which constitute the real income of the country. The work of domestic servants is always classed as " labour " in the technical sense; and since it can be assessed *en bloc* at the value of their remuneration in money and in kind without being enumerated in detail, its inclusion raises no great statistical difficulty. There is however some inconsistency in omitting the heavy domestic work which is done by women and other members of the household, where no servants are kept.

Again, suppose a landowner with an annual income of £10,000 hires a private secretary at a salary of £500, who hires a servant at wages of £50. It may seem that if the incomes of all these three persons are counted in as part of the net income of the country, some of it will be counted twice over, and some three times. But this is not the case. The landlord transfers to his secretary, in return for his assistance, part of the purchasing power derived from the produce of land; and the secretary again transfers part of this to his servant in return for his assistance. The farm produce the value of which goes as rent to the landlord, the assistance which the landlord derives from the work of the secretary, and that which the secretary derives from the work of the servant are independent parts of the real net income of the country; and therefore the £10,000 and the £500 and the £50 which are their money measures, must all be counted in when we are estimating the income of the country. But if the landlord makes an allowance of £500 a year to his son, that must

II, IV, 7, 8. not be counted as an independent income; because no services are
rendered for it.   And it would not be assessed to the Income tax.
As the *net* payments on account of interest etc. due to an
individual—*net, i.e.* after deducting those due from him to others—
are part of his income, so the money and other things received *net*
by a nation from other countries are part of its income.

National § 7. The money income, or inflow, of wealth gives a measure of a
income is nation's prosperity, which, untrustworthy as it is, is yet in some
a better
measure respects better than that afforded by the money value of its stock of
of general
economic wealth.
prosperity For income consists chiefly of commodities in a form to give
than
national pleasure directly; while the greater part of national wealth consists
wealth. of the means of production, which are of service to the nation only
in so far as they contribute to producing commodities ready for
consumption.   And further, though this is a minor point, con-
sumable commodities, being more portable, have more nearly
uniform prices all the world over than the things used in producing
them : the prices of an acre of good land in Manitoba and Kent
differ more than those of a bushel of wheat in the two places.

But if we look chiefly at the income of a country we must allow
for the depreciation of the sources from which it is derived.   More
must be deducted from the income derived from a house if it is made
of wood, than if it is made of stone; a stone house counts for more
towards the real richness of a country than a wooden house which
gives equally good accommodation.   Again, a mine may yield for a
time a large income, but be exhausted in a few years : in that case,
it must be counted as equivalent to a field, or a fishery, which yields
a much smaller annual income, but will yield that income
permanently.

Prospec- § 8. In purely abstract, and especially in mathematical, reasoning
tiveness the terms Capital and Wealth are used as synonymous almost
and
produc- perforce, except that " land " proper may for some purposes be
tiveness
control the omitted from Capital.   But there is a clear tradition that we should
demand speak of Capital when considering things as agents of production;
for capital
and the and that we should speak of Wealth when considering them as results
supply of production, as subjects of consumption and as yielding pleasures
of it.
of possession.   Thus the chief *demand* for capital arises from its
productiveness, from the services which it renders, for instance, in
enabling wool to be spun and woven more easily than by the unaided
hand, or in causing water to flow freely wherever it is wanted
instead of being carried laboriously in pails; (though there are
other uses of capital, as for instance when it is lent to a spendthrift,

which cannot easily be brought under this head).   On the other hand II, IV, 8.
the *supply* of capital is controlled by the fact that, in order to
accumulate it, men must act prospectively : they must " wait "
and " save," they must sacrifice the present to the future.

At the beginning of this Book it was argued that the economist
must forego the aid of a complete set of technical terms.   He must
make the terms in common use serve his purpose in the expression of
precise thought, by the aid of qualifying adjectives or other indications in the context.   If he arbitrarily assigns a rigid exact use to a
word which has several more or less vague uses in the market-place,
he confuses business men, and he is in some danger of committing
himself to untenable positions.   The selection of a normal use for
such terms as Income and Capital must therefore be tested by
actually working with it.[1]

[1] A short forecast of some of this work may be given here.   It will be seen how
Capital needs to be considered in regard *both* to the embodied aggregate of the benefits
derivable from its use, *and* to the embodied aggregate of the costs of the efforts and of
the saving needed for its production : and it will be shown how these two aggregates
tend to balance.   Thus in V. IV., which may be taken as in some sense a continuation
of the present chapter, they will be seen balancing directly in the forecasts of an
individual Robinson Crusoe ; and—for the greater part at least—in terms of money
in the forecasts of a modern business man.   In either case both sides of the account
must be referred to the same date of time ; those that come after that date being " discounted " back to it ; and those that come before being " accumulated " up to it.
A similar balancing in regard to the benefits and the costs of capital at large
will be found to be a chief corner stone of social economy : although it is true that in
consequence of the unequal distribution of wealth, accounts cannot be made up
from the social point of view with that clearness of outline that is attainable in the case
of an individual, whether a Robinson Crusoe, or a modern business man.
In every part of our discussion of the causes that govern the accumulation and the
application of productive resources, it will appear that there is no universal rule
that the use of roundabout methods of production is more efficient than direct
methods ; that there are some conditions under which the investment of effort in
obtaining machinery and in making costly provision against future wants is economical
in the long run, and others in which it is not : and that capital is accumulated in proportion to the prospectiveness of man on the one hand, and on the other to the absorption
of capital by those roundabout methods, which are sufficiently productive to remunerate their adoption.   See especially IV. VII. 8 ; V. IV. ; VI. I. 8 ; and VI. VI. 1.
The broader forces, that govern the production of capital in general and its contribution to the national income, are discussed in IV. VII. IX.–XI. : the imperfect
adjustments of the money measures of benefits and costs to their real volume are
discussed chiefly in III. III.–V. ; IV. VII. ; and VI. III.–VIII. ; the resulting share in
the total product of labour and capital, aided by natural resources, which goes to
capital, is discussed chiefly in VI. I. II. VI.–VIII. XI. XII.
Some of the chief incidents in the history of the definitions of Capital are given in
Appendix E.

BOOK III

ON WANTS AND THEIR SATISFACTION

CHAPTER I

INTRODUCTORY

§ 1. THE older definitions of economics described it as the science which is concerned with the production, the distribution, the exchange, and the consumption of wealth. Later experience has shown that the problems of distribution and exchange are so closely connected, that it is doubtful whether anything is to be gained by the attempt to keep them separate. There is however a good deal of general reasoning with regard to the relation of demand and supply which is required as a basis for the practical problems of value, and which acts as an underlying backbone, giving unity and consistency to the main body of economic reasoning. Its very breadth and generality mark it off from the more concrete problems of distribution and exchange to which it is subservient; and therefore it is put together in Book V on "The General Theory of Demand and Supply" which prepares the way for "Distribution and Exchange, or Value."

But first comes the present Book III, a study of Wants and their satisfaction, *i.e.* of demand and consumption : and then Book IV, a study of the agents of production, that is, the agents by whose means wants are satisfied, including man himself, the chief agent and the sole aim of production. Book IV corresponds in general character to that discussion of production to which a large place has been given in nearly all English treatises on general economics during the last two generations; although its relation to the problems of demand and supply has not been made sufficiently clear.

§ 2. Until recently the subject of demand or consumption has been somewhat neglected. For important as is the inquiry how to turn our resources to the best account, it is not one which lends itself, so far as the expenditure of private individuals is concerned, to the methods of economics. The common sense of a person who

has had a large experience of life will give him more guidance in such III, 1, 2.
a matter than he can gain from subtle economic analyses; and
until recently economists said little on the subject, because they
really had not much to say that was not the common property of all
sensible people.   But recently several causes have combined to give
the subject a greater prominence in economic discussions.

The first of these is the growing belief that harm was done by The first
Ricardo's habit of laying disproportionate stress on the side of cost cause.
of production, when analysing the causes that determine exchange
value.   For although he and his chief followers were aware that the
conditions of demand played as important a part as those of supply
in determining value, yet they did not express their meaning with
sufficient clearness, and they have been misunderstood by all but the
most careful readers.

Secondly, the growth of exact habits of thought in economics is The second
making people more careful to state distinctly the premises on which cause.
they reason.   This increased care is partly due to the application
by some writers of mathematical language and mathematical habits
of thought.   It is indeed doubtful whether much has been gained
by the use of complex mathematical formulæ.   But the application
of mathematical habits of thought has been of great service; for it
has led people to refuse to consider a problem until they are quite
sure what the problem is; and to insist on knowing what is, and what
is not intended to be assumed before proceeding further.

This has in its turn compelled a more careful analysis of all the
leading conceptions of economics, and especially of demand; for
the mere attempt to state clearly how the demand for a thing is to
be measured opens up new aspects of the main problems of economics.
And though the theory of demand is yet in its infancy, we can
already see that it may be possible to collect and arrange statistics
of consumption in such a way as to throw light on difficult questions
of great importance to public wellbeing.

Lastly, the spirit of the age induces a closer attention to the The third
question whether our increasing wealth may not be made to go cause.
further than it does in promoting the general wellbeing; and this
again compels us to examine how far the exchange value of any
element of wealth, whether in collective or individual use, represents
accurately the addition which it makes to happiness and wellbeing.

We will begin this Book with a short study of the variety of We will
human wants, considered in their relation to human efforts and begin with
activities.   For the progressive nature of man is one whole.   It is a study of
wants in
only temporarily and provisionally that we can with profit isolate for relation to
efforts.

III, 1, 2. study the economic side of his life ; and we ought to be careful to take together in one view the whole of that side.   There is a special need to insist on this just now, because the reaction against the comparative neglect of the study of wants by Ricardo and his followers shows signs of being carried to the opposite extreme.   It is important still to assert the great truth on which they dwelt somewhat too exclusively; viz. that while wants are the rulers of life among the lower animals, it is to changes in the forms of efforts and activities that we must turn when in search for the keynotes of the history of mankind.

CHAPTER II

WANTS IN RELATION TO ACTIVITIES

§ 1. HUMAN wants and desires are countless in number and very various in kind : but they are generally limited and capable of being satisfied. The uncivilized man indeed has not many more than the brute animal; but every step in his progress upwards increases the variety of his needs together with the variety in his methods of satisfying them. He desires not merely larger *quantities* of the things he has been accustomed to consume, but better qualities of those things; he desires a greater choice of things, and things that will satisfy new wants growing up in him.

III., II, 1.
The wants of the savage are few;

Thus though the brute and the savage alike have their preferences for choice morsels, neither of them cares much for variety for its own sake. As, however, man rises in civilization, as his mind becomes developed, and even his animal passions begin to associate themselves with mental activities, his wants become rapidly more subtle and more various; and in the minor details of life he begins to desire change for the sake of change, long before he has consciously escaped from the yoke of custom. The first great step in this direction comes with the art of making a fire : gradually he gets to accustom himself to many different kinds of food and drink cooked in many different ways; and before long monotony begins to become irksome to him, and he finds it a great hardship when accident compels him to live for a long time exclusively on one or two kinds of food.

but civilization brings with it a desire for variety for its own sake.

As a man's riches increase, his food and drink become more various and costly; but his appetite is limited by nature, and when his expenditure on food is extravagant it is more often to gratify the desires of hospitality and display than to indulge his own senses.

Man's capacity for food is limited,

This brings us to remark with Senior that " Strong as is the desire for variety, it is weak compared with the desire for distinction : a feeling which if we consider its universality, and its constancy, that it affects all men and at all times, that it comes with us from the cradle and never leaves us till we go into the grave, may be pronounced to be the most powerful of human passions." This

but not his craving for distinction:

III, II, 2, 3. great half-truth is well illustrated by a comparison of the desire for choice and various food with that for choice and various dress.

which is a chief source of the desire for costly dress.

§ 2. That need for dress which is the result of natural causes varies with the climate and the season of year, and a little with the nature of a person's occupations. But in dress conventional wants overshadow those which are natural. Thus in many of the earlier stages of civilization the sumptuary mandates of Law and Custom have rigidly prescribed to the members of each caste or industrial grade, the style and the standard of expense up to which their dress must reach and beyond which they may not go; and part of the substance of these mandates remains now, though subject to rapid change. In Scotland, for instance, in Adam Smith's time many persons were allowed by custom to go abroad without shoes and stockings who may not do so now; and many may still do it in Scotland who might not in England. Again, in England now a well-to-do labourer is expected to appear on Sunday in a black coat and, in some places, in a silk hat; though these would have subjected him to ridicule but a short time ago. There is a constant increase both in that variety and expensiveness which custom requires as a minimum, and in that which it tolerates as a maximum; and the efforts to obtain distinction by dress are extending themselves throughout the lower grades of English society.

But in the upper grades, though the dress of women is still various and costly, that of men is simple and inexpensive as compared with what it was in Europe not long ago, and is to-day in the East. For those men who are most truly distinguished on their own account, have a natural dislike to seem to claim attention by their dress; and they have set the fashion.[1]

House room.

§ 3. House room satisfies the imperative need for shelter from the weather : but that need plays very little part in the effective demand for house room. For though a small but well-built cabin gives excellent shelter, its stifling atmosphere, its necessary uncleanliness, and its want of the decencies and the quiet of life are great evils. It is not so much that they cause physical discomfort as that

---

[1] A woman may display wealth, but she may not display only her wealth, by her dress; or else she defeats her ends. She must also suggest some distinction of character as well as of wealth; for though her dress may owe more to her dressmaker than to herself, yet there is a traditional assumption that, being less busy than man with external affairs, she can give more time to taking thought as to her dress. Even under the sway of modern fashions, to be " well dressed "—not " expensively dressed "—is a reasonable minor aim for those who desire to be distinguished for their faculties and abilities; and this will be still more the case if the evil dominion of the wanton vagaries of fashion should pass away. For to arrange costumes beautiful in themselves, various and well-adapted to their purposes, is an object worthy of high endeavour; it belongs to the same class, though not to the same rank in that class, as the painting of a good picture.

they tend to stunt the faculties, and limit people's higher activities. III, II, 4.
With every increase in these activities the demand for larger house
room becomes more urgent.[1]

And therefore relatively large and well-appointed house room is,
even in the lowest social ranks, at once a " necessary for efficiency," [2]
and the most convenient and obvious way of advancing a material
claim to social distinction. And even in those grades in which
everyone has house room sufficient for the higher activities of
himself and his family, a yet further and almost unlimited increase
is desired as a requisite for the exercise of many of the higher social
activities.

§ 4. It is, again, the desire for the exercise and development of
activities, spreading through every rank of society, which leads not
only to the pursuit of science, literature and art for their own
sake, but to the rapidly increasing demand for the work of those
who pursue them as professions. Leisure is used less and less
as an opportunity for mere stagnation; and there is a growing
desire for those amusements, such as athletic games and travelling, which develop activities rather than indulge any sensuous
craving.[3]

For indeed the desire for excellence for its own sake, is almost as
wide in its range as the lower desire for distinction. Just as the
desire for distinction graduates down from the ambition of those who
may hope that their names will be in men's mouths in distant lands
and in distant times, to the hope of the country lass that the new
ribbon she puts on for Easter may not pass unnoticed by her neighbours; so the desire for excellence for its own sake graduates down
from that of a Newton, or a Stradivarius, to that of the fisherman
who, even when no one is looking and he is not in a hurry, delights in
handling his craft well, and in the fact that she is well built and
responds promptly to his guidance. Desires of this kind exert a
great influence on the supply of the highest faculties and the greatest
inventions; and they are not unimportant on the side of demand.
For a large part of the demand for the most highly skilled professional services and the best work of the mechanical artisan, arises
from the delight that people have in the training of their own faculties,

*Wants
resulting
from
activities.*

*Gradations
of the
desire for
excellence.*

---

[1] It is true that many active-minded working men prefer cramped lodgings in a
town to a roomy cottage in the country ; but that is because they have a strong taste
for those activities for which a country life offers little scope.

[2] See Book II. ch. III. § 3.

[3] As a minor point it may be noticed that those drinks which stimulate the mental
activities are largely displacing those which merely gratify the senses. The consumption of tea is increasing very fast, while that of alcohol is stationary ; and there is in
all ranks of society a diminishing demand for the grosser and more immediately
stupefying forms of alcohol.

III, II, 4.   and in exercising them by aid of the most delicately adjusted and responsive implements.

In a healthy state new activities pioneer the way for new wants.

Speaking broadly therefore, although it is man's wants in the earliest stages of his development that give rise to his activities, yet afterwards each new step upwards is to be regarded as the development of new activities giving rise to new wants, rather than of new wants giving rise to new activities.

We see this clearly if we look away from healthy conditions of life, where new activities are constantly being developed; and watch the West Indian negro, using his new freedom and wealth not to get the means of satisfying new wants, but in idle stagnation that is not rest; or again look at that rapidly lessening part of the English working classes, who have no ambition and no pride or delight in the growth of their faculties and activities, and spend on drink whatever surplus their wages afford over the bare necessaries of a squalid life.

The theory of wants can claim no supremacy over the theory of efforts.

It is not true therefore that "the Theory of Consumption is the scientific basis of economics." [1] For much that is of chief interest in the science of wants, is borrowed from the science of efforts and activities. These two supplement one another; either is incomplete without the other. But if either, more than the other, may claim to be the interpreter of the history of man, whether on the economic side or any other, it is the science of activities and not that of wants; and McCulloch indicated their true relations when, discussing "the progressive nature of man," [2] he said :—" The gratification of a want or a desire is merely a step to some new pursuit. In every stage of his progress he is destined to contrive and invent, to engage in new undertakings; and when these are accomplished to enter with fresh energy upon others."

From this it follows that such a discussion of demand as is possible at this stage of our work, must be confined to an elementary analysis of an almost purely formal kind. The higher study of consumption must come after, and not before, the main body of economic analysis; and, though it may have its beginning within the proper domain of

---

[1] This doctrine is laid down by Banfield, and adopted by Jevons as the key of his position. It is unfortunate that here as elsewhere Jevons' delight in stating his case strongly has led him to a conclusion, which not only is inaccurate, but does mischief by implying that the older economists were more at fault than they really were. Banfield says "the first proposition of the theory of consumption is that the satisfaction of every lower want in the scale creates a desire of a higher character." And if this were true, the above doctrine, which he bases on it, would be true also. But, as Jevons points out (*Theory*, 2nd Ed. p. 59), it is not true : and he substitutes for it the statement that the satisfaction of a lower want permits a higher want to manifest itself. That is a true and indeed an identical proposition : but it affords no support to the claims of the Theory of Consumption to supremacy.

[2] *Political Economy*, ch. II.

economics, it cannot find its conclusion there, but must extend far III, II, 4.
beyond.[1]

[1] The formal classification of Wants is a task not without interest; but it is
not needed for our purposes. The basis of most modern work in this direction is
to be found in Hermann's *Staatswirthschaftliche Untersuchungen*, Ch. II., where
wants are classified as "absolute and relative, higher and lower, urgent and capable
of postponement, positive and negative, direct and indirect, general and particular,
constant and interrupted, permanent and temporary, ordinary and extraordinary,
present and future, individual and collective, private and public."

Some analysis of wants and desires is to be found in the great majority of French
and other Continental treatises on economics even of the last generation; but the rigid
boundary which English writers have ascribed to their science has excluded such discussions. And it is a characteristic fact that there is no allusion to them in Bentham's
Manual of Political Economy, although his profound analysis of them in the *Principles
of Morals and Legislation* and in the *Table of the Springs of Human Action* has exercised
a wide-spread influence. Hermann has studied Bentham; and on the other hand
Banfield, whose lectures were perhaps the first ever given in an English University
that owed much directly to German economic thought, acknowledges special obligations to Hermann. In England the way was prepared for Jevons' excellent work on
the theory of wants, by Bentham himself; by Senior, whose short remarks on the
subject are pregnant with far-reaching hints; by Banfield, and by the Australian
Hearn. Hearn's *Plutology or Theory of the Efforts to satisfy Human Wants* is at once
simple and profound : it affords an admirable example of the way in which detailed
analysis may be applied to afford a training of a very high order for the young, and
to give them an intelligent acquaintance with the economic conditions of life, without
forcing upon them any particular solution of those more difficult problems on which
they are not yet able to form an independent judgment. At about the same time as
Jevons' *Theory* appeared, Carl Menger gave a great impetus to the subtle and interesting
studies of wants and utilities by the Austrian school of economists : they had already
been initiated by von Thünen, as is indicated in the Preface to this Volume.

CHAPTER III

GRADATIONS OF CONSUMERS' DEMAND

III, III, 1.

The consumers' demand governs traders' demand.

§ 1. WHEN a trader or a manufacturer buys anything to be used in production, or be sold again, his demand is based on his anticipations of the profits which he can derive from it. These profits depend at any time on speculative risks and on other causes, which will need to be considered later on. But in the long run the price which a trader or manufacturer can afford to pay for a thing depends on the prices which consumers will pay for it, or for the things made by aid of it. The ultimate regulator of all demand is therefore consumers' demand. And it is with that almost exclusively that we shall be concerned in the present Book.

Utility and Want are used as correlative terms, having no ethical or prudential connotations.

Utility is taken to be correlative to Desire or Want. It has been already argued that desires cannot be measured directly, but only indirectly by the outward phenomena to which they give rise : and that in those cases with which economics is chiefly concerned the measure is found in the price which a person is willing to pay for the fulfilment or satisfaction of his desire. He may have desires and aspirations which are not consciously set for any satisfaction : but for the present we are concerned chiefly with those which do so aim ; and we assume that the resulting satisfaction corresponds in general fairly well to that which was anticipated when the purchase was made.[1]

The law of satiable wants or diminishing utility.

There is an endless variety of wants, but there is a limit to each separate want. This familiar and fundamental tendency of human nature may be stated in the *law of satiable wants* or *of diminishing utility* thus :—The *total utility* of a thing to anyone (that is, the total

---

[1] It cannot be too much insisted that to measure directly, or *per se*, either desires or the satisfaction which results from their fulfilment is impossible, if not inconceivable. If we could, we should have two accounts to make up, one of desires, and the other of realized satisfactions. And the two might differ considerably. For, to say nothing of higher aspirations, some of those desires with which economics is chiefly concerned, and especially those connected with emulation, are impulsive ; many result from the force of habit ; some are morbid and lead only to hurt ; and many are based on expectations that are never fulfilled. (See above I. II. 3, 4.) Of course many satisfactions are not common pleasures, but belong to the development of a man's higher nature, or to use a good old word, to his *beatification* ; and some may even partly result from self-abnegation. (See I. II. 1.) The two direct measurements then might differ. But as neither of them is possible, we fall back on the measurement which economics supplies, of the motive or moving force to action : and we make it serve, with all its faults, *both* for the desires which prompt activities and for the satisfactions that result from them. (Compare " Some remarks on Utility " by Prof. Pigou in the *Economic Journal* for March, 1903.)

pleasure or other benefit it yields him) increases with every increase III, III, 2.
in his stock of it, but not as fast as his stock increases. If his stock $\frac{Total}{utility.}$
of it increases at a uniform rate the benefit derived from it increases
at a diminishing rate. In other words, the additional benefit which
a person derives from a given increase of his stock of a thing,
diminishes with every increase in the stock that he already has.

That part of the thing which he is only just induced to purchase
may be called his *marginal purchase*, because he is on the margin of *Marginal purchase.*
doubt whether it is worth his while to incur the outlay required to
obtain it. And the utility of his marginal purchase may be called the
marginal utility of the thing to him. Or, if instead of buying it, he *Marginal utility.*
makes the thing himself, then its marginal utility is the utility of that
part which he thinks it only just worth his while to make. And thus
the law just given may be worded :—

The marginal utility of a thing to anyone diminishes with every
increase in the amount of it he already has.[1]

There is however an implicit condition in this law which should It is
be made clear. It is that we do not suppose time to be allowed for implied
that the
any alteration in the character or tastes of the man himself. It is consumer's
therefore no exception to the law that the more good music a man character
is un-
hears, the stronger is his taste for it likely to become; that avarice changed.
and ambition are often insatiable; or that the virtue of cleanliness
and the vice of drunkenness alike grow on what they feed upon.
For in such cases our observations range over some period of time;
and the man is not the same at the beginning as at the end of it. If
we take a man as he is, without allowing time for any change in his
character, the marginal utility of a thing to him diminishes steadily
with every increase in his supply of it.[2]

§ 2. Now let us translate this law of diminishing utility into terms Transla-
of price. Let us take an illustration from the case of a commodity tion of the
law into

[1] See Note I in the Mathematical Appendix at the end of the Volume. This
law holds a priority of position to the *law of diminishing return* from land; which
however has the priority in time; since it was the first to be subjected to a rigid
analysis of a semi-mathematical character. And if by anticipation we borrow some
of its terms, we may say that the *return* of pleasure which a person gets from each
additional *dose* of a commodity diminishes till at last a margin is reached at which it
is no longer worth his while to acquire any more of it.
The term *marginal utility* (*Grenz-nutz*) was first used in this connection by the
Austrian Wieser. It has been adopted by Prof. Wicksteed. It corresponds to the
term *Final* used by Jevons, to whom Wieser makes his acknowledgments in the
Preface (p. xxiii, of the English edition). His list of anticipators of his doctrine is
headed by Gossen, 1854.

[2] It may be noticed here, though the fact is of but little practical importance,
that a small quantity of a commodity may be insufficient to meet a certain special
want; and then there will be a more than proportionate increase of pleasure when
the consumer gets enough of it to enable him to attain the desired end. Thus,
for instance, anyone would derive less pleasure in proportion from ten pieces of
wall-paper than from twelve, if the latter would, and the former would not, cover
the whole of the walls of his room. Or again a very short concert or a holiday may fail

III, III, 3.

terms of price.

such as tea, which is in constant demand and which can be purchased in small quantities. Suppose, for instance, that tea of a certain quality is to be had at 2s. per lb. A person might be willing to give 10s. for a single pound once a year rather than go without it altogether; while if he could have any amount of it for nothing he would perhaps not care to use more than 30 lbs. in the year. But as it is, he buys perhaps 10 lbs. in the year; that is to say, the difference between the satisfaction which he gets from buying 9 lbs. and 10 lbs. is enough for him to be willing to pay 2s. for it : while the fact that he does not buy an eleventh pound, shows that he does not think that it would be worth an extra 2s. to him. That is, 2s. a pound measures the utility to him of the tea which lies at the margin or terminus or end of his purchases; it measures the marginal utility to him. If the price which he is just willing to pay for any pound be

Marginal demand price.

called his *demand price*, then 2s. is his *marginal demand price*. And our law may be worded :—

The larger the amount of a thing that a person has the less, other things being equal (*i.e.* the purchasing power of money, and the amount of money at his command being equal), will be the price which he will pay for a little more of it : or in other words his marginal demand price for it diminishes.

His demand becomes *efficient*, only when the price which he is willing to offer reaches that at which others are willing to sell.

This last sentence reminds us that we have as yet taken no account of changes in the marginal utility of money, or general purchasing power. At one and the same time, a person's material resources being unchanged, the marginal utility of money to him is a fixed quantity, so that the prices he is just willing to pay for two commodities are to one another in the same ratio as the utility of those two commodities.

The marginal utility of money is greater for the poor than the rich.

§ 3. A greater utility will be required to induce him to buy a thing if he is poor than if he is rich. We have seen how the clerk with £100 a year will walk to business in a heavier rain than the clerk with £300 a year.[1] But although the utility, or the benefit, that is measured in the poorer man's mind by twopence is greater than that measured by it in the richer man's mind; yet if the richer man rides a hundred times in the year and the poorer man twenty times, then

of its purpose of soothing and recreating : and one of double length might be of more than double total utility. This case corresponds to the fact, which we shall have to study in connection with the tendency to diminishing return, that the capital and labour already applied to any piece of land may be so inadequate for the development of its full powers, that some further expenditure on it even with the existing arts of agriculture would give a more than proportionate return; and in the fact that an improvement in the arts of agriculture may resist that tendency, we shall find an analogy to the condition just mentioned in the text as implied in the law of diminishing utility.

[1] See I. II. 2.

III, III, 4.

the utility of the hundredth ride which the richer man is only just induced to take is measured to him by twopence; and the utility of the twentieth ride which the poorer man is only just induced to take is measured to him by twopence. For each of them the marginal utility is measured by twopence; but this marginal utility is greater in the case of the poorer man than in that of the richer.

In other words, the richer a man becomes the less is the marginal utility of money to him; every increase in his resources increases the price which he is willing to pay for any given benefit. And in the same way every diminution of his resources increases the marginal utility of money to him, and diminishes the price that he is willing to pay for any benefit.[1]

§ 4. To obtain complete knowledge of demand for anything, we should have to ascertain how much of it he would be willing to purchase at each of the prices at which it is likely to be offered; and the circumstance of his demand for, say, tea can be best expressed by a list of the prices which he is willing to pay; that is, by his several demand prices for different amounts of it. (This list may be called his *demand schedule*.) A more definite expression for the demand of an individual.

Thus for instance we may find that he would buy

6 lbs. at 50*d*. per lb.   10 lbs. at 24*d*. per lb.
7 „ 40 „   11 „ 21 „
7 „ 33 „   12 „ 19 „
9 „ 28 „   13 „ 17 „

If corresponding prices were filled in for all intermediate amounts we should have an exact statement of his demand.[2] We

---

[1] See note II. in the Mathematical Appendix.

[2] Such a demand schedule may be translated, on a plan now coming into familiar use, into a curve that may be called his *demand curve*. Let Ox and Oy be drawn the one horizontally, the other vertically. Let an inch measured along Ox represent 10 lbs. of tea, and an inch measured along Oy represent 40*d*.

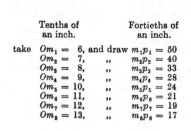

Tenths of
an inch.

Fortieths of
an inch.

take $Om_1 = 6$, and draw $m_1p_1 = 50$
$Om_2 = 7$, „ $m_2p_2 = 40$
$Om_3 = 8$, „ $m_3p_3 = 33$
$Om_4 = 9$, „ $m_4p_4 = 28$
$Om_5 = 10$, „ $m_5p_5 = 24$
$Om_6 = 11$, „ $m_6p_6 = 21$
$Om_7 = 12$, „ $m_7p_7 = 19$
$Om_8 = 13$, „ $m_8p_8 = 17$

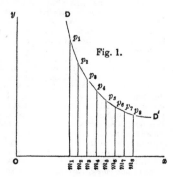

Fig. 1.

III, III, 5. cannot express a person's demand for a thing by the " amount he is

The mean-
ing of the
term
increase of
demand.

willing to buy," or by the "intensity of his eagerness to buy a certain amount," without reference to the prices at which he would buy that amount and other amounts. We can represent it exactly only by lists of the prices at which he is willing to buy different amounts.[1]

When we say that a person's demand for anything increases, we mean that he will buy more of it than he would before at the same price, and that he will buy as much of it as before at a higher price. A general increase in his demand is an increase throughout the whole list of prices at which he is willing to purchase different amounts of it, and not merely that he is willing to buy more of it at the current prices.[2]

Transition
to the
demand of
a group of
persons, or
market.

§ 5. So far we have looked at the demand of a single individual. And in the particular case of such a thing as tea, the demand of a single person is fairly representative of the general demand of a whole market : for the demand for tea is a constant one ; and, since it can be purchased in small quantities, every variation in its price is likely to affect the amount which he will buy. But even among those things which are in constant use, there are many for

---

m_1 being on Ox and m_1p_1 being drawn vertically from m_1; and so for the others. Then $p_1p_2....p_8$ are points on his demand curve for tea ; or as we may say *demand points.* If we could find demand points in the same manner for every possible quantity of tea, we should get the whole continuous curve DD' as shown in the figure. This account of the demand schedule and curve is provisional ; several difficulties connected with it are deferred to chapter v.

[1] Thus Mill says that we must " mean by the word demand, the quantity demanded, and remember that this is not a fixed quantity, but in general varies according to the value." (*Principles*, III. II. 4.) This account is scientific in substance ; but it is not clearly expressed and it has been much misunderstood. Cairnes prefers to represent " demand as the desire for commodities and services, seeking its end by an offer of general purchasing power, and supply as the desire for general purchasing power, seeking its end by an offer of specific commodities or services." He does this in order that he may be able to speak of a ratio, or equality, of demand and supply. But the quantities of two desires on the part of two different persons cannot be compared directly ; their measures may be compared, but not they themselves. And in fact Cairnes is himself driven to speak of supply as " limited by the quantity of specific commodities offered for sale, and demand by the quantity of purchasing power offered for their purchase." But sellers have not a fixed quantity of commodities which they offer for sale unconditionally at whatever price they can get : buyers have not a fixed quantity of purchasing power which they are ready to spend on the specific commodities, however much they pay for them. Account must then be taken in either case of the relation between quantity and price, in order to complete Cairnes' account, and when this is done it is brought back to the lines followed by Mill. He says, indeed, that " Demand, as defined by Mill, is to be understood as measured, not, as my definition would require, by the quantity of purchasing power offered in support of the desire for commodities, but by the quantity of commodities for which such purchasing power is offered." It is true that there is a great difference between the statements, " I will buy twelve eggs," and " I will buy a shilling's worth of eggs." But there is no substantive difference between the statement, " I will buy twelve eggs at a penny each, but only six at three-halfpence each," and the statement, "I will spend a shilling on eggs at a penny each, but if they cost three-halfpence each I will spend ninepence on them." But while Cairnes' account when completed becomes substantially the same as Mill's, its present form is even more misleading. (See an article by the present writer on *Mill's Theory of Value* in the *Fortnightly Review* for April, 1876.)

[2] We may sometimes find it convenient to speak of this as *a raising of his demand schedule*. Geometrically it is represented by raising his demand curve, or, what comes to the same thing, moving it to the right, with perhaps some modification of its shape.

which the demand on the part of any single individual cannot vary continuously with every small change in price, but can move only by great leaps.   For instance, a small fall in the price of hats or watches will not affect the action of every one; but it will induce a few persons, who were in doubt whether or not to get a new hat or a new watch, to decide in favour of doing so.

 There are many classes of things the need for which on the part of any individual is inconstant, fitful, and irregular.   There can be no list of individual demand prices for wedding-cakes, or the services of an expert surgeon.   But the economist has little concern with particular incidents in the lives of individuals.   He studies rather "the course of action that may be expected under certain conditions from the members of an industrial group," in so far as the motives of that action are measurable by a money price; and in these broad results the variety and the fickleness of individual action are merged in the comparatively regular aggregate of the action of many.

 In large markets, then—where rich and poor, old and young, men and women, persons of all varieties of tastes, temperaments and occupations are mingled together,—the peculiarities in the wants of individuals will compensate one another in a comparatively regular gradation of total demand.   Every fall, however slight in the price of a commodity in general use, will, other things being equal, increase the total sales of it;   just as an unhealthy autumn increases the mortality of a large town, though many persons are uninjured by it.   And therefore if we had the requisite knowledge, we could make a list of prices at which each amount of it could find purchasers in a given place during, say, a year.

 The total demand in the place for, say, tea, is the sum of the demands of all the individuals there.   Some will be richer and some poorer than the individual consumer whose demand we have just written down; some will have a greater and others a smaller liking for tea than he has. Let us suppose that there are in the place a million purchasers of tea, and that their average consumption is equal to his at each several price. Then the demand of that place is represented by the same list of prices as before, if we write a million pounds of tea instead of one pound.[1]

Margin notes: III, III, 5. The demand on the part of any individual for some things is discontinuous.

But the aggregate demand of many persons shows a fall of demand price for every increase in quantity.

[1] The demand is represented by the same curve as before, only an inch measured along Ox now represents ten million pounds instead of ten pounds. And a formal definition of the demand curve for a market may be given thus :—The demand curve for any commodity in a market during any given unit of time is the locus of demand points for it. That is to say, it is a curve such that if from any point P on it, a straight line PM be drawn perpendicular to Ox, PM represents the price at which purchasers will be forthcoming for an amount of the commodity represented by OM.

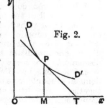

Fig. 2.

III, III, 6.

The
law of
demand.

There is then one general *law of demand* :—The greater the amount to be sold, the smaller must be the price at which it is offered in order that it may find purchasers; or, in other words, the amount demanded increases with a fall in price, and diminishes with a rise in price. There will not be any uniform relation between the fall in price and the increase of demand. A fall of one-tenth in the price may increase the sales by a twentieth or by a quarter, or it may double them. But as the numbers in the left-hand column of the demand schedule increase, those in the right-hand column will always diminish.[1]

The price will measure the marginal utility of the commodity to each purchaser individually : we cannot speak of price as measuring marginal utility in general, because the wants and circumstances of different people are different.

The in-
fluence on
demand of
the growth
of a rival
com-
modity.

§ 6. The demand prices in our list are those at which various quantities of a thing can be sold in a market *during a given time and under given conditions*. If the conditions vary in any respect the prices will probably require to be changed; and this has constantly to be done when the desire for anything is materially altered by a variation of custom, or by a cheapening of the supply of a rival commodity, or by the invention of a new one. For instance, the list of demand prices for tea is drawn out on the assumption that the price of coffee is known; but a failure of the coffee harvest would raise the prices for tea. The demand for gas is liable to be reduced by an improvement in electric lighting; and in the same way a fall in the price of a particular kind of tea may cause it to be substituted for an inferior but cheaper variety.[2]

---

[1] That is, if a point moves along the curve away from Oy it will constantly approach Ox. Therefore if a straight line PT be drawn touching the curve at P and meeting Ox in T, the angle PTx is an obtuse angle. It will be found convenient to have a short way of expressing this fact; which may be done by saying that PT is *inclined negatively*. Thus the one universal rule to which the demand curve conforms is that it is *inclined negatively* throughout the whole of its length.

It will of course be understood that " the law of demand " does not apply to the demand in a campaign between groups of speculators. A group, which desires to unload a great quantity of a thing on to the market, often begins by buying some of it openly. When it has thus raised the price of the thing, it arranges to sell a great deal quietly, and through unaccustomed channels. See an article by Professor Taussig in the *Quarterly Journal of Economics* (May, 1921, p. 402).

[2] It is even conceivable, though not probable, that a simultaneous and proportionate fall in the price of all teas may diminish the demand for some particular kind of it; if it happens that those whom the increased cheapness of tea leads to substitute a superior kind for it are more numerous than those who are led to take it in the place of an inferior kind. The question where the lines of division between different commodities should be drawn must be settled by convenience of the particular discussion. For some purposes it may be best to regard Chinese and Indian teas, or even Souchong and Pekoe teas, as different commodities; and to have a separate demand schedule for each of them. While for other purposes it may be best to group together commodities as distinct as beef and mutton, or even as tea and coffee, and to have a single list to represent the demand for the two combined; but in such a case of

Our next step will be to consider the general character of demand III, III, 6.
in the cases of some important commodities ready for immediate
consumption. We shall thus be continuing the inquiry made in the
preceding chapter as to the variety and satiability of wants; but we
shall be treating it from a rather different point of view, viz. that of
price-statistics.[1]

Relation of the following to the preceding chapter.

---

course some convention must be made as to the number of ounces of tea which are taken as equivalent to a pound of coffee.

Again, a commodity may be simultaneously demanded for several uses (for instance there may be a " composite demand " for leather for making shoes and portmanteaus); the demand for a thing may be conditional on there being a supply of some other thing without which it would not be of much service (thus there may be a " joint demand " for raw cotton and cotton-spinners' labour). Again, the demand for a commodity on the part of dealers who buy it only with the purpose of selling it again, though governed by the demand of the ultimate consumers in the background, has some peculiarities of its own. But all such points may best be discussed at a later stage.

[1] A great change in the manner of economic thought has been brought about during the present generation by the general adoption of semi-mathematical language for expressing the relation between small increments of a commodity on the one hand, and on the other hand small increments in the aggregate price that will be paid for it : and by formally describing these small increments of price as measuring corresponding small increments of pleasure. The former, and by far the more important, step was taken by Cournot (*Recherches sur les Principes Mathématiques de la Théorie des Richesses*, 1838); the latter by Dupuit (*De la Mesure d'utilité des travaux publics* in the *Annales des Ponts et Chaussées*, 1844), and by Gossen (*Entwickelung der Gesetze des menschlichen Verkehrs*, 1854). But their work was forgotten; part of it was done over again, developed and published almost simultaneously by Jevons and by Carl Menger in 1871, and by Walras a little later. Jevons almost at once arrested public attention by his brilliant lucidity and interesting style. He applied the new name *final utility* so ingeniously as to enable people who knew nothing of mathematical science to get clear ideas of the general relations between the small increments of two things that are gradually changing in causal connection with one another. His success was aided even by his faults. For under the honest belief that Ricardo and his followers had rendered their account of the causes that determine value hopelessly wrong by omitting to lay stress on the law of satiable wants, he led many to think he was correcting great errors; whereas he was really only adding very important explanations. He did excellent work in insisting on a fact which is none the less important, because his predecessors, and even Cournot, thought it too obvious to be explicitly mentioned, viz. that the diminution in the amount of a thing demanded in a market indicates a diminution in the intensity of the desire for it on the part of individual consumers, whose wants are becoming satiated. But he has led many of his readers into a confusion between the provinces of Hedonics and Economics, by exaggerating the applications of his favourite phrases, and speaking (*Theory*, 2nd Edn. p. 105) without qualification of the price of a thing as measuring its final utility not only to an individual, which it can do, but also to " a trading body," which it cannot do. These points are developed later on in Appendix I. on Ricardo's Theory of value. It should be added that Prof. Seligman has shown (*Economic Journal*, 1903, pp. 356–363) that a long-forgotten Lecture, delivered by Prof. W. F. Lloyd at Oxford in 1833, anticipated many of the central ideas of the present doctrine of utility.

An excellent bibliography of Mathematical Economics is given by Prof. Fisher as an appendix to Bacon's translation of Cournot's *Researches*, to which the reader may be referred for a more detailed account of the earlier mathematical writings on economics, as well as of those by Edgeworth, Pareto, Wicksteed, Auspitz, Lieben and others. Pantaleoni's *Pure Economics*, amid much excellent matter, makes generally accessible for the first time the profoundly original and vigorous, if somewhat abstract, reasonings of Gossen.

CHAPTER IV

THE ELASTICITY OF WANTS

§ 1. WE have seen that the only universal law as to a person's desire for a commodity is that it diminishes, other things being equal, with every increase in his supply of that commodity. But this diminution may be slow or rapid. If it is slow the price that he will give for the commodity will not fall much in consequence of a considerable increase in his supply of it; and a small fall in price will cause a comparatively large increase in his purchases. But if it is rapid, a small fall in price will cause only a very small increase in his purchases. In the former case his willingness to purchase the thing stretches itself out a great deal under the action of a small inducement : the elasticity of his wants, we may say, is great. In the latter case the extra inducement given by the fall in price causes hardly any extension of his desire to purchase : the elasticity of his demand is small. If a fall in price from say 16*d.* to 15*d.* per lb. of tea would much increase his purchases, then a rise in price from 15*d.* to 16*d.* would much diminish them. That is, when the demand is elastic for a fall in price, it is elastic also for a rise.

And as with the demand of one person so with that of a whole market. And we may say generally :—The *elasticity* (or *responsiveness*) *of demand* in a market is great or small according as the amount demanded increases much or little for a given fall in price, and diminishes much or little for a given rise in price.[1]

[1] We may say that the elasticity of demand is one, if a small fall in price will cause an equal proportionate increase in the amount demanded : or as we may say roughly, if a fall of one per cent. in price will increase the sales by one per cent.; that it is two or a half, if a fall of one per cent. in price makes an increase of two or one half per cent. respectively in the amount demanded; and so on. (This statement is rough; because 98 does not bear exactly the same proportion to 100 that 100 does to 102.) The elasticity of demand can be best traced in the demand curve with the aid of the following rule. Let a straight line touching the curve at any point P meet O*x* in T and O*y* in *t*, then *the measure of elasticity at the point P is the ratio of PT to Pt.*

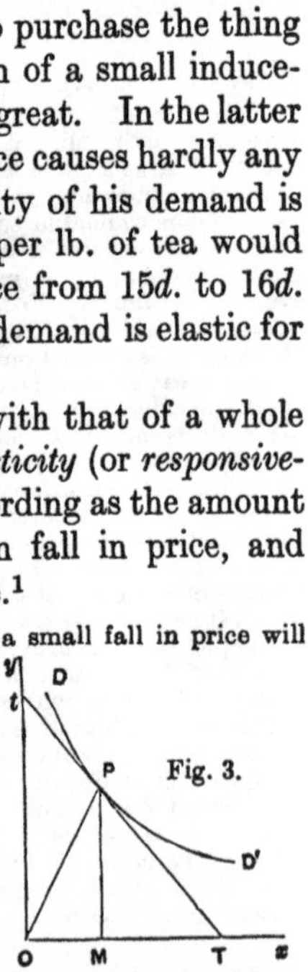

Fig. 3.

If PT were twice P*t*, a fall of 1 per cent. in price would cause an increase of 2 per cent., in the amount demanded; the elasticity of demand would be two. If PT were one-third of P*t*, a fall of 1 per cent. in price would cause an increase of ⅓ per cent. in the amount demanded; the elasticity of demand would be one-third; and so on. Another way of looking at the same result is this :—the elasticity at the point P is measured by the ratio of PT to P*t*, that is of MT to MO (PM being drawn perpen-

§ 2. The price which is so high relatively to the poor man as to be almost prohibitive, may be scarcely felt by the rich; the poor man, for instance, never tastes wine, but the very rich man may drink as much of it as he has a fancy for, without giving himself a thought of its cost. We shall therefore get the clearest notion of the law of the elasticity of demand by considering one class of society at a time. Of course there are many degrees of richness among the rich, and of poverty among the poor; but for the present we may neglect these minor subdivisions.

III, IV, 2, 3.

The gene-ral law of variation of the elasticity of demand, and its consequent responsive-ness to changes of price.

When the price of a thing is very high relatively to any class, they will buy but little of it; and in some cases custom and habit may prevent them from using it freely even after its price has fallen a good deal. It may still remain set apart for a limited number of special occasions, or for use in extreme illness, etc. But such cases, though not infrequent, do not form the general rule; and anyhow as soon as it has been taken into common use, any considerable fall in its price causes a great increase in the demand for it. The elasticity of demand is great for high prices, and great, or at least considerable, for medium prices; but it declines as the price falls; and gradually fades away if the fall goes so far that satiety level is reached.

This rule appears to hold with regard to nearly all commodities and with regard to the demand of every class; save only that the level at which high prices end and low prices begin, is different for different classes; and so again is the level at which low prices end and very low prices begin. There are however many varieties in detail; arising chiefly from the fact that there are some commodities with which people are easily satiated, and others—chiefly things used for display—for which their desire is almost unlimited. For the latter the elasticity of demand remains considerable, however low the price may fall, while for the former the demand loses nearly all its elasticity as soon as a low price has once been reached.[1]

§ 3. There are some things the current prices of which in this country are very low relatively even to the poorer classes; such are for instance salt, and many kinds of savours and flavours, and also cheap medicines. It is doubtful whether any fall in price would induce a considerable increase in the consumption of these.

Illustra-tions drawn from the demand for par-ticular commo-dities.

---

dicular to *Om*); and therefore *the elasticity is equal to one when the angle TPM is equal to the angle OPM; and it always increases when the angle TPM increases relatively to the angle OPM, and vice versâ*. See Note III. in the Mathematical Appendix.

[1] Let us illustrate by the case of the demand for, say, green peas in a town in which all vegetables are bought and sold in one market. Early in the season perhaps

III, IV, 3.   The current prices of meat, milk and butter, wool, tobacco, imported fruits, and of ordinary medical attendance, are such that every variation in price makes a great change in the consumption of them by the working classes, and the lower half of the middle classes; but the rich would not much increase their own personal consumption of them however cheaply they were to be had. In other words, the direct demand for these commodities is very elastic on the part of the working and lower middle classes, though not on the part of the rich. But the working class is so numerous that their consumption of such things as are well within their reach is much greater than that of the

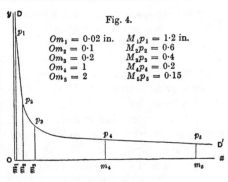

100 lb. a day will be brought to market and sold at 1s. per lb., later on 500 lb. will be brought and sold at 6d., later on 1,000 lb. at 4d., later still 5,000 at 2d., and later still 10,000 at $1\frac{1}{2}d$. Thus demand is represented in fig. 4, an inch along Ox representing 5,000 lbs. and an inch along Oy representing 10d. Then a curve through $p_1p_2...p_5$, found as shown above, will be the total demand curve. But this total demand will be made up of the demands of the rich, the middle class and the poor. The amounts that they will severally demand may perhaps be represented by the following schedules :—

Fig. 4.

$Om_1 = 0.02$ in. $M_1p_1 = 1.2$ in.
$Om_2 = 0.1$ $M_2p_2 = 0.6$
$Om_3 = 0.2$ $M_3p_3 = 0.4$
$Om_4 = 1$ $M_4p_4 = 0.2$
$Om_5 = 2$ $M_5p_5 = 0.15$

At price in pence per lb.	Number of lbs. bought by—			
	Rich.	Middle class.	Poor.	Total.
12	100	0	0	100
6	300	200	0	500
4	500	400	100	1,000
2	800	2,500	1,700	5,000
$1\frac{1}{2}$	1,000	4,000	5,000	10,000

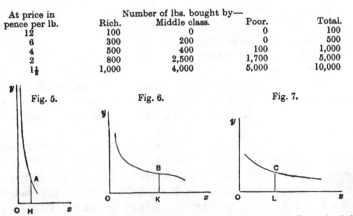

These schedules are translated into curves figs. 5, 6, 7, showing the demands of the rich, the middle class and the poor represented on the same scale as fig. 4. Thus for instance AH, BK and CL each represents a price of 2d. and is ·2 inches in length; $OH = ·16$ in. representing 800 lb., $OK = ·5$ in. representing 2,500 lb. and $OL = ·34$ in. representing 1,700 lb., while $OH + OK + OL = 1$ inch, i.e. $= Om_4$ in fig. 4 as they should do. This may serve as an example of the way in which several partial demand curves, drawn to the same scale, can be superimposed horizontally on one another to make the total demand curve representing the aggregate of the partial demand.

rich; and therefore the aggregate demand for all things of the kind is III, IV, 4. very elastic. A little while ago sugar belonged to this group of commodities : but its price in England has now fallen so far as to be low relatively even to the working classes, and the demand for it is therefore not elastic.[1]

The current prices of wall-fruit, of the better kinds of fish, and other moderately expensive luxuries are such as to make the consumption of them by the middle class increase much with every fall in price; in other words, the middle class demand for them is very elastic : while the demand on the part of the rich and on the part of the working class is much less elastic, the former because it is already nearly satiated, the latter because the price is still too high.

The current prices of such things as rare wines, fruit out of season, highly skilled medical and legal assistance, are so high that there is but little demand for them except from the rich : but what demand there is, often has considerable elasticity. Part of the demand for the more expensive kinds of food is really a demand for the means of obtaining social distinction, and is almost insatiable.[2]

§ 4. The case of necessaries is exceptional. When the price of *The demand for neces-saries.* wheat is very high, and again when it is very low, the demand has very little elasticity : at all events if we assume that wheat, even when scarce, is the cheapest food for man; and that, even when most plentiful, it is not consumed in any other way. We know that a fall in the price of the quartern loaf from 6d. to 4d. has scarcely any effect in increasing the consumption of bread. With regard to the other end of the scale it is more difficult to speak with certainty, because there has been no approach to a scarcity in England since the repeal of the corn laws. But, availing ourselves of the experience of a less happy time, we may suppose that deficits in the supply of 1, 2, 3, 4, or 5 tenths would cause a rise in price of 3, 8, 16, 28, or 45 tenths

---

[1] We must however remember that the character of the demand schedule for any commodity depends in a great measure on whether the prices of its rivals are taken to be fixed or to alter with it. If we separated the demand for beef from that for mutton, and supposed the price of mutton to be held fixed while that for beef was raised, then the demand for beef would become extremely elastic. For any slight fall in the price of beef would cause it to be used largely in the place of mutton and thus lead to a very great increase of its consumption : while on the other hand even a small rise in price would cause many people to eat mutton to the almost entire exclusion of beef. But the demand schedule for all kinds of fresh meat taken together, their prices being supposed to retain always about the same relation to one another, and to be not very different from those now prevailing in England, shows only a moderate elasticity. And similar remarks apply to beet-root and cane-sugar. Compare the note on p. 84.

[2] See above ch. II. § 1. In April 1894, for instance, six plovers' eggs, the first of the season, were sold in London at 10s. 6d. each. The following day there were more, and the price fell to 5s.; the next day to 3s. each; and a week later to 4d.

III, IV, 4.
——

respectively.[1] Much greater variations in prices indeed than this have not been uncommon. Thus wheat sold in London for ten shillings a bushel in 1335, but in the following year it sold for ten-pence.[2]

Commodities some part of the consumption of which is necessary.

There may be even more violent changes than this in the price of a thing which is not necessary, if it is perishable and the demand for it is inelastic : thus fish may be very dear one day, and sold for manure two or three days later.

Water is one of the few things the consumption of which we are able to observe at all prices, from the very highest down to nothing at all. At moderate prices the demand for it is very elastic. But the uses to which it can be put are capable of being completely filled : and as its price sinks towards zero the demand for it loses its elasticity. Nearly the same may be said of salt. Its price in England is so low that the demand for it as an article of food is very inelastic : but in India the price is comparatively high and the demand is comparatively elastic.

The price of house room, on the other hand, has never fallen very low except when a locality is being deserted by its inhabitants. Where the condition of society is healthy, and there is no check to general prosperity, there seems always to be an elastic demand for house room, on account both of the real conveniences and the social distinction which it affords. The desire for those kinds of clothing which are not used for the purpose of display, is satiable : when their price is low the demand for them has scarcely any elasticity.

Influence of sensibility and acquired tastes and distastes.

The demand for things of a higher quality depends much on sensibility : some people care little for a refined flavour in their wine provided they can get plenty of it : others crave a high quality, but are easily satiated. In the ordinary working class districts the inferior and the better joints are sold at nearly the same price : but

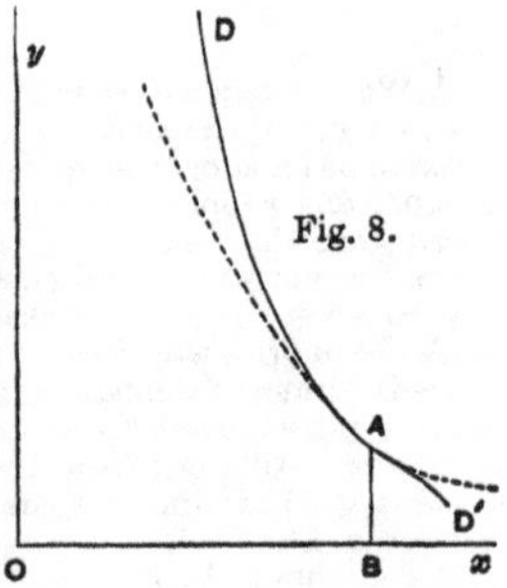

Fig. 8.

[1] This estimate is commonly attributed to Gregory King. Its bearing on the law of demand is admirably discussed by Lord Lauderdale (*Inquiry*, pp. 51-3). It is represented in fig. 8 by the curve DD', the point A corresponding to the ordinary price. If we take account of the fact that where the price of wheat is very low, it may be used, as it was for instance in 1834, for feeding cattle and sheep and pigs and for brewing and distilling, the lower part of the curve would take a shape somewhat like that of the dotted line in the figure. And if we assume that when the price is very high, cheaper substitutes can be got for it, the upper part of the curve would take a shape similar to that of the upper dotted line.

[2] *Chronicon Preciosum* (A.D. 1745) says that the price of wheat in London was as low as 2s. a quarter in 1336 : and that at Leicester it sold at 40s. on a Saturday, and at 14s. on the following Friday.

some well-paid artisans in the north of England have developed a III, IV, 4.
liking for the best meat, and will pay for it nearly as high a price as
can be got in the west end of London, where the price is kept artificially high by the necessity of sending the inferior joints away for
sale elsewhere.   Use also gives rise to acquired distastes as well as to
acquired tastes.   Illustrations which make a book attractive to many
readers, will repel those whose familiarity with better work has
rendered them fastidious.   A person of high musical sensibility in a
large town will avoid bad concerts : though he might go to them
gladly if he lived in a small town, where no good concerts are to be
heard, because there are not enough persons willing to pay the high
price required to cover their expenses.   The effective demand for
first-rate music is elastic only in large towns; for second-rate music
it is elastic both in large and small towns.

Generally speaking those things have the most elastic demand, Influence
which are capable of being applied to many different uses.   Water of variety
for instance is needed first as food, then for cooking, then for washing of uses.
of various kinds and so on.   When there is no special drought, but
water is sold by the pailful, the price may be low enough to enable
even the poorer classes to drink as much of it as they are inclined,
while for cooking they sometimes use the same water twice over, and
they apply it very scantily in washing.   The middle classes will perhaps not use any of it twice for cooking; but they will make a pail of
water go a good deal further for washing purposes than if they had an
unlimited supply at command.   When water is supplied by pipes,
and charged at a very low rate by meter, many people use as much of
it even for washing as they feel at all inclined to do; and when the
water is supplied not by meter but at a fixed annual charge, and is
laid on in every place where it is wanted, the use of it for every purpose is carried to the full satiety limit.[1]

On the other hand, demand is, generally speaking, very inelastic, Inelastic
firstly, for absolute necessaries (as distinguished from conventional demand.
necessaries and necessaries for efficiency); and secondly, for some

[1] Thus the general demand of any one person for such a thing as water is the
aggregate (or *compound*, see V. VI. 3) of his demand for it for each use; in the same way
as the demand of a group of people of different orders of wealth for a commodity,
which is serviceable in only one use, is the aggregate of the demands of each member of
the group.   Again, just as the demand of the rich for peas is considerable even at a
very high price, but loses all elasticity at a price that is still high relatively to the consumption of the poor; so the demand of the individual for water to drink is considerable even at a very high price, but loses all elasticity at a price that is still high
relatively to his demand for it for the purpose of cleaning up the house.   And as the
aggregate of a number of demands on the part of different classes of people for peas
retains elasticity over a larger range of price than will that of any one class, so the
demand of an individual for water for many uses retains elasticity over a larger range of
prices than his demand for it for any one use.   Compare an article by J. B. Clark on *A
Universal Law of Economic Variation* in the *Harvard Journal of Economics* Vol. VIII.

III,IV,5,6. of those luxuries of the rich which do not absorb much of their income.

Difficulties of the statistical study; The element of Time.
§ 5. So far we have taken no account of the difficulties of getting exact lists of demand prices, and interpreting them correctly. The first which we have to consider arises from the element of *time*, the source of many of the greatest difficulties in economics.

Thus while a list of demand prices represents the changes in the price at which a commodity can be sold consequent on changes in the amount offered for sale, *other things being equal*; yet other things seldom are equal in fact over periods of time sufficiently long for the collection of full and trustworthy statistics. There are always occurring disturbing causes whose effects are commingled with, and cannot easily be separated from, the effects of that particular cause which we desire to isolate. This difficulty is aggravated by the fact that in economics the full effects of a cause seldom come at once, but often spread themselves out after it has ceased to exist.

Changes in the purchasing power of money,
To begin with, the purchasing power of money is continually changing, and rendering necessary a correction of the results obtained on our assumption that money retains a uniform value. This difficulty can however be overcome fairly well, since we can ascertain with tolerable accuracy the broader changes in the purchasing power of money.

whether permanent, or temporary.
Next come the changes in the general prosperity and in the total purchasing power at the disposal of the community at large. The influence of these changes is important, but perhaps less so than is generally supposed. For when the wave of prosperity is descending, prices fall, and this increases the resources of those with fixed incomes at the expense of those whose incomes depend on the profits of business. The downward fluctuation of prosperity is popularly measured almost entirely by the conspicuous losses of this last class; but the statistics of the total consumption of such commodities as tea, sugar, butter, wool, etc. prove that the total purchasing power of the people does not meanwhile fall very fast. Still there is a fall, and the allowance to be made for it must be ascertained by comparing the prices and the consumption of as many things as possible.

Next come the changes due to the gradual growth of population and wealth. For these an easy numerical correction can be made when the facts are known.[1]

§ 6. Next, allowance must be made for changes in fashion, and

---

[1] When a statistical table shows the gradual growth of the consumption of a commodity over a long series of years, we may want to compare the percentage by which it increases in different years. This can be done pretty easily with a little practice. But when the figures are expressed in the form of a statistical diagram, it cannot easily be done, without translating the diagram back into figures; and this

taste and habit,[1] for the opening out of new uses of a commodity, for the discovery or improvement or cheapening of other things that can be applied to the same uses with it.   In all these cases there is great difficulty in allowing for the time that elapses between the economic cause and its effect.   For time is required to enable a rise in the price of a commodity to exert its full influence on consumption.   Time is required for consumers to become familiar with substitutes that can be used instead of it, and perhaps for producers to get into the habit of producing them in sufficient quantities.   Time may be also wanted for the growth of habits of familiarity with the new commodities and the discovery of methods of economizing them.

III, IV, 6.

Gradual changes in habits and in the familiarity with new things and new ways of using them.

For instance when wood and charcoal became dear in England, familiarity with coal as a fuel grew slowly, fireplaces were but slowly adapted to its use, and an organized traffic in it did not spring up quickly even to places to which it could be easily carried by water : the invention of processes by which it could be used as a substitute for charcoal in manufacture went even more slowly, and is indeed hardly yet complete.   Again, when in recent years the price of coal became very high, a great stimulus was given to the invention of economies in its use, especially in the production of iron and steam; but few of these inventions bore much practical fruit till after the high price had passed away.   Again, when a new tramway or suburban railway is opened, even those who live near the line do not get into the habit of making the most of its assistance at once; and a good deal more time elapses before many of those whose places of business are near one end of the line change their homes so as to live near the other end.   Again, when petroleum first became plentiful few people were ready to use it freely; gradually petroleum and petroleum lamps have become familiar to all classes of society : too much influence

Illus- trations.

is a cause of the disfavour in which many statisticians hold the graphic method.   But by the knowledge of one simple rule the balance can be turned, so far as this point goes, in favour of the graphic method.   The rule is as follows :—Let the quantity of a commodity consumed (or of trade carried, or of tax levied etc.) be measured by horizontal lines parallel to Ox, fig. 9, while the corresponding years are in the usual manner ticked off in descending order at equal distances along Oy.   To measure the rate of growth at any point P, put a ruler to touch the curve at P.   Let it meet Oy in t, and let N be the point on Oy at the same vertical height as P; then the number of years marked off along Oy by the distance Nt is the inverse of the fraction by which the amount is increasing.

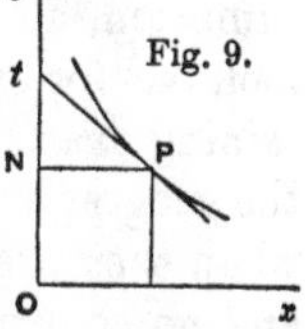

Fig. 9.

That is, if Nt is 20 years, the amount is increasing at the rate of $\frac{1}{20}$, i.e. of 5 per cent. annually; if Nt is 25 years, the increase is $\frac{1}{25}$ or 4 per cent. annually; and so on.   See a paper by the present writer in the Jubilee number of the *Journal of the London Statistical Society*, June 1885; also Note IV. in the Mathematical Appendix.

[1] For illustrations of the influence of fashion see articles by Miss Foley in the *Economic Journal*, Vol. III., and Miss Heather Bigg in the *Nineteenth Century*, Vol. XXIII.

III, IV, 7. would therefore be attributed to the fall in price which has occurred since then, if it were credited with all the increase of consumption.

Some demands can be more easily postponed than others.   Another difficulty of the same kind arises from the fact that there are many purchases which can easily be put off for a short time, but not for a long time. This is often the case with regard to clothes and other things which are worn out gradually, and which can be made to serve a little longer than usual under the pressure of high prices. For instance, at the beginning of the cotton famine the recorded consumption of cotton in England was very small. This was partly because retail dealers reduced their stock, but chiefly because people generally made shift to do as long as they could without buying new cotton goods. In 1864 however many found themselves unable to wait longer; and a good deal more cotton was entered for home consumption in that year, though the price was then much higher than in either of the preceding years. For commodities of this kind then a sudden scarcity does not immediately raise the price fully up to the level, which properly corresponds to the reduced supply. Similarly after the great commercial depression in the United States in 1873 it was noticed that the boot trade revived before the general clothing trade; because there is a great deal of reserve wear in the coats and hats that are thrown aside in prosperous times as worn out, but not so much in the boots.

Imperfections of statistics.   § 7. The above difficulties are fundamental : but there are others which do not lie deeper than the more or less inevitable faults of our statistical returns.

We desire to obtain, if possible, a series of prices at which different amounts of a commodity can find purchasers during a given time in a market. A perfect market is a district, small or large, in which there are many buyers and many sellers all so keenly on the alert and so well acquainted with one another's affairs that the price of a commodity is always practically the same for the whole of the district. But independently of the fact that those who buy for their own consumption, and not for the purposes of trade, are not always on the look out for every change in the market, there is no means of ascertaining exactly what prices are paid in many transactions. Again, the geographical limits of a market are seldom clearly drawn, except when they are marked out by the sea or by custom-house barriers; and no country has accurate statistics of commodities produced in it for home consumption.

Increase of dealers' stocks mistaken   Again, there is generally some ambiguity even in such statistics as are to be had. They commonly show goods as entered for consumption as soon as they pass into the hands of dealers; and consequently an increase of dealers' stocks cannot easily be distinguished from an increase of consumption. But the two are governed by different causes. A rise of prices tends to check consumption; but if the rise is expected to continue, it will probably, as has already been noticed, lead dealers to increase their stocks.[1]

Next it is difficult to insure that the commodities referred to are always of the same quality. After a dry summer what wheat there is, is exceptionally good; and the prices for the next harvest year appear to be higher than they really are. It is possible to make allowance for this, particularly now that dry Californian wheat affords a standard. But it is almost impossible to allow properly for the changes in quality of many kinds of manufactured goods. This difficulty occurs even in the case of such a thing as tea : the substitution in recent years of the stronger Indian tea for the weaker Chinese tea has made the real increase of consumption greater than that which is shown by the statistics.

Marginal notes: III, IV, 8. for increase of consumption.
Changes of quality.

NOTE ON STATISTICS OF CONSUMPTION.

§ 8. General Statistics of consumption are published by many Governments with regard to certain classes of commodities. But partly for the reasons just indicated they are of very little service in helping us to trace either a causal connection between variations in prices and variations in the amounts which people will buy, or in the distribution of different kinds of consumption among the different classes of the community.

As regards the first of these objects, viz. the discovery of the laws connecting variations in consumption consequent on variations in price, there seems much to be gained by working out a hint given by Jevons (*Theory*, pp. 11, 12) with regard to shopkeepers' books. A shopkeeper, or the manager of a co-operative store, in the working man's quarter of a manufacturing town has often the means of ascertaining with tolerable accuracy the financial position of the great body of his customers. He can find out how many factories are at work, and for how many hours in the week, and he can hear about all the important changes in the rate of wages : in fact he makes it his business to do so. And as a rule his customers are quick in finding out changes in the price of things which they commonly use. He will therefore often find cases in which an increased consumption of a commodity is brought about by a fall in its price, the cause acting quickly, and acting alone without any admixture of disturbing causes. Even where disturbing causes are present, he will

Marginal notes: Inductive study of demand is difficult; but traders could further it much by analysing their own accounts.

---

[1] In examining the effects of taxation, it is customary to compare the amounts entered for consumption just before and just after the imposition of the tax. But this is untrustworthy. For dealers anticipating the tax lay in large stocks just before it is imposed, and need to buy very little for some time afterwards. And *vice versâ* when a tax is lowered. Again, high taxes lead to false returns. For instance, the nominal importation of molasses into Boston increased fiftyfold in consequence of the tax being lowered by the Rockingham Ministry in 1766, from 6*d*. to 1*d*. per gallon. But this was chiefly due to the fact that with the tax at 1*d*., it was cheaper to pay the duty than to smuggle.

III, IV, 8. often be able to allow for their influence. For instance, he will know that as the winter comes on, the prices of butter and vegetables rise; but the cold weather makes people desire butter more and vegetables less than before : and therefore when the prices of both vegetables and butter rise towards the winter, he will expect a greater falling off of consumption in the case of vegetables than should properly be attributed to the rise in price taken alone, but a less falling off in the case of butter. If however in two neighbouring winters his customers have been about equally numerous, and in receipt of about the same rate of wages; and if in the one the price of butter was a good deal higher than in the other, then a comparison of his books for the two winters will afford a very accurate indication of the influence of changes in price on consumption. Shopkeepers who supply other classes of society must occasionally be in a position to furnish similar facts relating to the consumption of their customers.

Consumption by the poor of cheap things may suggest the probable variations in its consumption by the rich if it became very dear. If a sufficient number of tables of demand by different sections of society could be obtained, they would afford the means of estimating indirectly the variations in total demand that would result from extreme variations in price, and thus attaining an end which is inaccessible by any other route. For, as a general rule, the price of a commodity fluctuates within but narrow limits; and therefore statistics afford us no direct means of guessing what the consumption of it would be, if its price were either fivefold or a fifth part of what it actually is. But we know that its consumption would be confined almost entirely to the rich if its price were very high; and that, if its price were very low, the great body of its consumption would in most cases be among the working classes. If then the present price is very high relatively to the middle or to the working classes, we may be able to infer from the laws of their demand at the present prices what would be the demand of the rich if the price were so raised so as to be very high relatively even to their means. On the other hand, if the present price is moderate relatively to the means of the rich, we may be able to infer from their demand what would be the demand of the working classes if the price were to fall to a level which is moderate relatively to their means. It is only by thus piecing together fragmentary laws of demand that we can hope to get any approach to an accurate law relating to widely different prices. (That is to say, the general demand curve for a commodity cannot be drawn with confidence except in the immediate neighbourhood of the current price, until we are able to piece it together out of the fragmentary demand curves of different classes of society. Compare the Second Section of this Chapter.)

When some progress has been made in reducing to definite law the demand for commodities that are destined for immediate consumption, then, but not till then, will there be use in attempting a similar task with regard to those secondary demands which are dependent on these—the demands namely for the labour of artisans and others who take part in the production of things for sale; and again the demand for machines, factories, railway material and other instruments of production. The demand for the work of medical men, of domestic servants and of all those whose services are rendered direct to the consumer is similar in character to the demand for commodities for immediate consumption, and its laws may be investigated in the same manner.

Another method is to collect budgets of individuals in different classes. It is a very important, but also difficult task to ascertain the proportions in which the different classes of society distribute their expenditure between necessaries, comforts and luxuries; between things that provide only present pleasure, and those that build up stores of physical and moral strength; and lastly between those which gratify the lower wants and those which stimulate and educate the higher wants. Several endeavours have been made in this direction on the Continent during the last fifty years; and latterly the

subject has been investigated with increasing vigour not only there but also III, IV, 8.
in America and in England.[1]

[1] A single table made out by the great statistician Engel for the consumption of the
lower, middle and working classes in Saxony in 1857, may be quoted here; because it
has acted as a guide and a standard of comparison to later inquiries.   It is as follows :—

Items of expenditure.	Proportions of the expenditure of the family of—		
	1 Workman with an income of £45 to £60 a year.	2 Workman with an income of £90 to £120 a year.	3 Middle-class person with an income of £150 to £200 a year.
1. Food only . . .	62·0 per cent.	55·0 per cent.	50·0 per cent.
2. Clothing . . .	16·0 ,,	18·0 ,,	18·0 ,,
3. Lodging . . .	12·0 ,,	12·0 ,,	12·0 ,,
4. Light and fuel . .	5·0 ,,	5·0 ,,	5·0 ,,
5. Education . . .	2·0 ,,	3·5 ,,	5·5 ,,
6. Legal protection . .	1·0 ,,	2·0 ,,	3·0 ,,
7. Care of health . .	1·0 ,,	2·0 ,,	3·0 ,,
8. Comfort and recreation .	1·0 ,,	2·5 ,,	3·5 ,,
Total . . .	100·0 per cent.	100·0 per cent.	100·0 per cent.

Working-men's budgets have often been collected and compared.   But like all
other figures of the kind they suffer from the facts that those who will take the trouble
to make such returns voluntarily are not average men, that those who keep careful
accounts are not average men ; and that when accounts have to be supplemented by
the memory, the memory is apt to be biassed by notions as to how the money ought to
have been spent, especially when the accounts are put together specially for another's
eye.   This border ground between the provinces of domestic and public economy is one
in which excellent work may be done by many who are disinclined for more general and
abstract speculations.

Information bearing on the subject was collected long ago by Harrison, Petty,
Cantillon (whose lost Supplement seems to have contained some workmen's budgets),
Arthur Young, Malthus and others.   Working-men's budgets were collected by Eden
at the end of the last century ; and there is much miscellaneous information on the
expenditure of the working classes in subsequent Reports of Commissions on Poor-
relief, Factories, etc.   Indeed almost every year sees some important addition from
public or private sources to our information on these subjects.

It may be noted that the method of le Play's monumental *Les Ouvriers Européens*
is the *intensive* study of all the details of the domestic life of a few carefully chosen
families.   To work it well requires a rare combination of judgment in selecting cases,
and of insight and sympathy in interpreting them.   At its best, it is the best of all :
but in ordinary hands it is likely to suggest more untrustworthy general conclusions,
than those obtained by the *extensive* method of collecting more rapidly very numerous
observations, reducing them as far as possible to statistical form, and obtaining broad
averages in which inaccuracies and idiosyncrasies may be trusted to counteract one
another to some extent.

E

CHAPTER V

CHOICE BETWEEN DIFFERENT USES OF THE SAME THING. IMMEDIATE AND DEFERRED USES

§ 1. THE primitive housewife finding that she has a limited number of hanks of yarn from the year's shearing, considers all the domestic wants for clothing and tries to distribute the yarn between them in such a way as to contribute as much as possible to the family wellbeing. She will think she has failed if, when it is done, she has reason to regret that she did not apply more to making, say, socks, and less to vests. That would mean that she had miscalculated the points at which to suspend the making of socks and vests respectively; that she had gone too far in the case of vests, and not far enough in that of socks; and that therefore at the points at which she actually did stop, the utility of yarn turned into socks was greater than that of yarn turned into vests. But if, on the other hand, she hit on the right points to stop at, then she made just so many socks and vests that she got an equal amount of good out of the last bundle of yarn that she applied to socks, and the last she applied to vests. This illustrates a general principle, which may be expressed thus :—

If a person has a thing which he can put to several uses, he will distribute it among these uses in such a way that it has the same marginal utility in all. For if it had a greater marginal utility in one use than another, he would gain by taking away some of it from the second use and applying it to the first.[1]

One great disadvantage of a primitive economy, in which there is but little free exchange, is that a person may easily have so much of one thing, say wool, that when he has applied it to every possible use, its marginal utility in each use is low : and at the same time he may have so little of some other thing, say wood, that its marginal utility for him is very high. Meanwhile some of his neighbours may be in great need of wool, and have more wood than they can turn to good account. If each gives up that which has for him the lower

---

[1] Our illustration belongs indeed properly to domestic production rather than to domestic consumption. But that was almost inevitable; for there are very few things ready for immediate consumption which are available for many different uses. And the doctrine of the distribution of means between different uses has less important and less interesting applications in the science of demand than in that of supply. See e.g. V. III. 3.

utility and receives that which has the higher, each will gain by the exchange. But to make such an adjustment by barter, would be tedious and difficult.

The difficulty of barter is indeed not so very great where there are but a few simple commodities each capable of being adapted by domestic work to several uses; the weaving wife and the spinster daughters adjusting rightly the marginal utilities of the different uses of the wool, while the husband and the sons do the same for the wood.

> Barter is a partial remedy.

§ 2. But when commodities have become very numerous and highly specialized, there is an urgent need for the free use of money, or general purchasing power; for that alone can be applied easily in an unlimited variety of purchases. And in a money-economy, good management is shown by so adjusting the margins of suspense on each line of expenditure that the marginal utility of a shilling's worth of goods on each line shall be the same. And this result each one will attain by constantly watching to see whether there is anything on which he is spending so much that he would gain by taking a little away from that line of expenditure and putting it on some other line.

> Money can be distributed so as to have equal marginal utilities in each use.

Thus, for instance, the clerk who is in doubt whether to ride to town, or to walk and have some little extra indulgence at his lunch, is weighing against one another the (marginal) utilities of two different modes of spending his money. And when an experienced house-keeper urges on a young couple the importance of keeping accounts carefully; a chief motive of the advice is that they may avoid spending impulsively a great deal of money on furniture and other things; for, though some quantity of these is really needful, yet when bought lavishly they do not give high (marginal) utilities in proportion to their cost. And when the young pair look over their year's budget at the end of the year, and find perhaps that it is necessary to curtail their expenditure somewhere, they compare the (marginal) utilities of different items, weighing the loss of utility that would result from taking away a pound's expenditure here, with that which they would lose by taking it away there : they strive to adjust their parings down so that the aggregate loss of utility may be a minimum, and the aggregate of utility that remains to them may be a maximum.[1]

> Illustrations.

> A chief use of domestic accounts.

[1] The working-class budgets which were mentioned in Ch. IV, § 8 may render most important services in helping people to distribute their resources wisely between different uses, so that the marginal utility for each purpose shall be the same. But the vital problems of domestic economy relate as much to wise action as to wise spending. The English and the American housewife make limited means go a less way towards satisfying wants than the French housewife does, not because they do not know how to buy, but because they cannot produce as good finished commodities out of the raw material of inexpensive joints, vegetables etc., as she can. Domestic economy is

III, v, 3.

The balancing of future benefits against present.

§ 3. The different uses between which a commodity is distributed need not all be present uses; some may be present and some future. A prudent person will endeavour to distribute his means between all their several uses, present and future, in such a way that they will have in each the same marginal utility. But in estimating the present marginal utility of a distant source of pleasure a twofold allowance must be made; firstly, for its uncertainty (this is an *objective* property which all well-informed persons would estimate in the same way); and secondly, for the difference in the value to them of a distant as compared with a present pleasure (this is a *subjective* property which different people would estimate in different ways according to their individual characters, and their circumstances at the time).

Future benefits are "discounted," at different rates.

If people regarded future benefits as equally desirable with similar benefits at the present time, they would probably endeavour to distribute their pleasures and other satisfactions evenly throughout their lives. They would therefore generally be willing to give up a present pleasure for the sake of an equal pleasure in the future, provided they could be certain of having it. But in fact human nature is so constituted that in estimating the " present value " of a future benefit most people generally make a second deduction from its future value, in the form of what we may call a " discount," that increases with the period for which the benefit is deferred. One will reckon a distant benefit at nearly the same value which it would have for him if it were present; while another who has less power of realizing the future, less patience and self-control, will care comparatively little for any benefit that is not near at hand. And the same person will vary in his mood, being at one time impatient, and greedy for present enjoyment; while at another his mind dwells on the future, and he is willing to postpone all enjoyments that can conveniently be made to wait. Sometimes he is in a mood to care little for anything else : sometimes he is like the children who pick the plums out of their pudding to eat them at once, sometimes like those who put them aside to be eaten last. And, in any case, when calculating the rate at which a future benefit is discounted, we must be careful to make allowance for the pleasures of expectation.

Desire for lasting sources of

The rates at which different people discount the future affect not only their tendency to save, as the term is ordinarily understood, but also their tendency to buy things which will be a lasting source of

---

often spoken of as belonging to the science of consumption : but that is only half true. The greatest faults in domestic economy, among the sober portion of the Anglo-Saxon working-classes at all events, are faults of production rather than of consumption.

pleasure rather than those which give a stronger but more transient enjoyment; to buy a new coat rather than to indulge in a drinking bout, or to choose simple furniture that will wear well, rather than showy furniture that will soon fall to pieces.

It is in regard to these things especially that the pleasure of possession makes itself felt. Many people derive from the mere feeling of ownership a stronger satisfaction than they derive from ordinary pleasures in the narrower sense of the term : for example, the delight in the possession of land will often induce people to pay for it so high a price that it yields them but a very poor return on their investment. There is a delight in ownership for its own sake; and there is a delight in ownership on account of the distinction it yields. Sometimes the latter is stronger than the former, sometimes weaker; and perhaps no one knows himself or other people well enough to be able to draw the line quite certainly between the two.

§ 4. As has already been urged, we cannot compare the *quantities* of two benefits, which are enjoyed at different times even by the same person. When a person postpones a pleasure-giving event he does not postpone the pleasure; but he gives up a present pleasure and takes in its place another, or an expectation of getting another at a future date : and we cannot tell whether he expects the future pleasure to be greater than the one which he is giving up, unless we know all the circumstances of the case. And therefore, even though we know the rate at which he discounts future pleasurable events, such as spending £1 on immediate gratifications, we yet do not know the rate at which he discounts future pleasures.[1]

We can however get an artificial measure of the rate at which he

---

[1] In classifying some pleasures as more *urgent* than others, it is often forgotten that the postponement of a pleasurable event may alter the circumstances under which it occurs, and therefore alter the character of the pleasure itself. For instance it may be said that a young man discounts at a very high rate the pleasure of the Alpine tours which he hopes to be able to afford himself when he has made his fortune. He would much rather have them now, partly because they would give him much greater pleasure now.

Again, it may happen that the postponement of a pleasurable event involves an unequal distribution in Time of a certain good, and that the Law of Diminution of Marginal Utility acts strongly in the case of this particular good. For instance, it is sometimes said that the pleasures of eating are specially urgent; and it is undoubtedly true that if a man goes dinnerless for six days in the week and eats seven dinners on the seventh, he loses very much; because when postponing six dinners, he does not postpone the pleasures of eating six separate dinners, but substitutes for them the pleasure of one day's excessive eating. Again, when a person puts away eggs for the winter he does not expect that they will be better flavoured then than now; he expects that they will be scarce, and that therefore their utility will be higher than now. This shows the importance of drawing a clear distinction between discounting a future pleasure, and discounting the pleasure derived from the future enjoyment of a certain amount of a commodity. For in the latter case we must make separate allowance for differences between the marginal utilities of the commodity at the two times : but in the former this has been allowed for once in estimating the amount of the pleasure; and it must not be allowed for again.

III, v, 4.

An artificial measure of the rate of discount of future benefits.

discounts future benefits by making two assumptions. These are, firstly, that he expects to be about as rich at the future date as he is now; and secondly, that his capacity for deriving benefit from the things which money will buy will on the whole remain unchanged, though it may have increased in some directions and diminished in others. On these assumptions, if he is willing, but only just willing, to spare a pound from his expenditure now with the certainty of having (for the disposal of himself or his heirs) a guinea one year hence, we may fairly say that he discounts future benefits that are perfectly secure (subject only to the conditions of human mortality) at the rate of five per cent. per annum. And on these assumptions the rate at which he discounts future (certain) benefits, will be the rate at which he can discount money in the money market.[1]

Future pleasures expected from the ownership of durable commodities.

So far we have considered each pleasure singly; but a great many of the things which people buy are durable, *i.e.* are not consumed in a single use; a durable good, such as a piano, is the probable source of many pleasures, more or less remote; and its value to a purchaser is the aggregate of the usance, or worth to him of all these pleasures, allowance being made for their uncertainty and for their distance.[2]

[1] It is important to remember that, except on these assumptions, there is no direct connection between the rate of discount on the loan of money, and the rate at which future pleasures are discounted. A man may be so impatient of delay that a certain promise of a pleasure ten years hence will not induce him to give up one close at hand which he regards as a quarter as great. And yet if he should fear that ten years hence money may be so scarce with him (and its marginal utility therefore so high) that half-a-crown then may give him more pleasure or save him more pain than a pound now, he will save something for the future even though he have to hoard it, on the same principle that he might store eggs for the winter. But we are here straying into questions that are more closely connected with Supply than with Demand. We shall have to consider them again from different points of view in connection with the Accumulation of Wealth, and later again in connection with the causes that determine the Rate of Interest.

We may however consider here how to measure numerically the present value of a future pleasure, on the supposition that we know, (i) its amount, (ii) the date at which it will come, if it comes at all, (iii) the chance that it will come, and (iv) the rate at which the person in question discounts future pleasures.

If the probability that a pleasure will be enjoyed is three to one, so that three chances out of four are in its favour, the value of its expectation is three-fourths of what it would be if it were certain : if the probability that it will be enjoyed were only seven to five, so that only seven chances out of twelve are in its favour, the value of its expectation is only seven-twelfths of what it would be if the event were certain, and so on. [This is its actuarial value : but further allowance may have to be made for the fact that the true value to anyone of an uncertain gain is generally less than its actuarial value (see the note on p. 174).] If the anticipated pleasure is both uncertain and distant, we have a twofold deduction to make from its full value. We will suppose, for instance, that a person would give 10s. for a gratification if it were present and certain, but that it is due a year hence, and the probability of its happening then is three to one. Suppose also that he discounts the future at the rate of twenty per cent. per annum. Then the value to him of the anticipation of it is $\frac{3}{4} \times \frac{100}{100} \times 10s.$ *i.e.* 6s. Compare the Introductory chapter of Jevons' *Theory of Political Economy*.

[2] Of course this estimate is formed by a rough instinct; and in any attempt to reduce it to numerical accuracy (see Note V in the Mathematical Appendix), we must recollect what has been said, in this and the preceding Section, as to the impossibility of comparing accurately pleasures or other satisfactions that do not occur at the same time; and also as to the assumption of uniformity involved in supposing the discount of future pleasures to obey the exponential law.

CHAPTER VI

VALUE AND UTILITY

§ 1. WE may now turn to consider how far the price which is actually paid for a thing represents the benefit that arises from its possession. This is a wide subject on which economic science has very little to say, but that little is of some importance.

We have already seen that the price which a person pays for a thing can never exceed, and seldom comes up to that which he would be willing to pay rather than go without it : so that the satisfaction which he gets from its purchase generally exceeds that which he gives up in paying away its price ; and he thus derives from the purchase a surplus of satisfaction. The excess of the price which he would be willing to pay rather than go without the thing, over that which he actually does pay, is the economic measure of this surplus satisfaction. It may be called *consumer's surplus*.

It is obvious that the consumer's surpluses derived from some commodities are much greater than from others. There are many comforts and luxuries of which the prices are very much below those which many people would pay rather than go entirely without them ; and which therefore afford a very great consumer's surplus. Good instances are matches, salt, a penny newspaper, or a postage-stamp.

This benefit, which he gets from purchasing at a low price things for which he would rather pay a high price than go without them, may be called the benefit which he derives from his *opportunities*, or from his *environment*; or, to recur to a word that was in common use a few generations ago, from his *conjuncture*. Our aim in the present chapter is to apply the notion of consumer's surplus as an aid in estimating roughly some of the benefits which a person derives from his environment or his conjuncture.[1]

---

[1] This term is a familiar one in German economics, and meets a need which is much felt in English economics. For " opportunity " and " environment," the only available substitutes for it, are sometimes rather misleading. By *Conjunctur*, says Wagner (*Grundlegung*. Ed. III. p. 387), " we understand the sum total of the technical, economic, social and legal conditions ; which, in a mode of national life (*Volkswirthschaft*) resting upon division of labour and private property,—especially private property in land and other material means of production—determine the demand for and supply of goods, and therefore their exchange value : this determination being as a rule, or at least in the main, *independent* of the will of the owner, of his activity and his remissness."

III, vi, 2.

——

Con-
sumer's
surplus in
relation to
the de-
mand
of an in-
dividual.

§ 2. In order to give definiteness to our notions, let us consider the case of tea purchased for domestic consumption. Let us take the case of a man, who, if the price of tea were 20s. a pound, would just be induced to buy one pound annually; who would just be induced to buy two pounds if the price were 14s., three pounds if the price were 10s., four pounds if the price were 6s., five pounds if the price were 4s., six pounds if the price were 3s., and who, the price being actually 2s., does purchase seven pounds. We have to investigate the consumer's surplus which he derives from his power of purchasing tea at 2s. a pound.

The fact that he would just be induced to purchase one pound if the price were 20s., proves that the total enjoyment or satisfaction which he derives from that pound is as great as that which he could obtain by spending 20s. on other things. When the price falls to 14s., he could, if he chose, continue to buy only one pound. He would then get for 14s. what was worth to him at least 20s.; and he will obtain a surplus satisfaction worth to him at least 6s., or in other words a consumer's surplus of at least 6s. But in fact he buys a second pound of his own free choice, thus showing that he regards it as worth to him at least 14s., and that this represents the *additional* utility of the second pound to him. He obtains for 28s. what is worth to him at least 20s. + 14s.; i.e. 34s. His surplus satisfaction is at all events not diminished by buying it, but remains worth at least 6s. to him. The total utility of the two pounds is worth at least 34s., his consumer's surplus is at least 6s.[1] The fact that each

---

[1] Some further explanations may be given of this statement; though in fact they do little more than repeat in other words what has already been said. The significance of the condition in the text that he buys the second pound of his own free choice is shown by the consideration that if the price of 14s. had been offered to him on the condition that he took two pounds, he would then have to elect between taking one pound for 20s. or two pounds for 28s.: and then his taking two pounds would not have proved that he thought the second pound worth more than 8s. to him. But as it is, he takes a second pound paying 14s. unconditionally for it; and that proves that it is worth at least 14s. to him. (If he can get buns at a penny each, but seven for sixpence; and he elects to buy seven, we know that he is willing to give up his sixth penny for the sake of the sixth and the seventh buns: but we cannot tell how much he would pay rather than go without the seventh bun only.)

It is sometimes objected that as he increases his purchases, the urgency of his need for his earlier purchases is diminished, and their utility falls; therefore we ought to continually redraw the earlier parts of our list of demand prices at a lower level, as we pass along it towards lower prices (*i.e.* to redraw at a lower level our demand curve as we pass along it to the right). But this misconceives the plan on which the list of prices is made out. The objection would have been valid, if the demand price set against each number of pounds of tea represented the *average* utility of that number. For it is true that, if he would pay just 20s. for one pound, and just 14s. for a second, then he would pay just 34s. for the two; *i.e.* 17s. each on the average. And if our list had had reference to the *average* prices he would pay, and had set 17s. against the second pound; then no doubt we should have had to redraw the list as we passed on. For when he has bought a third pound the average utility to him of each of the three will be less than that of 17s.; being in fact 14s. 8d. if, as we go on to assume, he would pay just 10s. for a third pound. But this difficulty is entirely avoided on the plan of making out demand prices which is here adopted; according to which his second pound is credited,

additional purchase reacts upon the utility of the purchases which he had previously decided to make *has already been allowed for in making out the schedule and must not be counted a second time.*

When the price falls to 10s., he might, if he chose, continue to buy only two pounds; and obtain for 20s. what was worth to him at least 34s., and derive a surplus satisfaction worth at least 14s. But in fact he prefers to buy a third pound : and as he does this freely, we know that he does not diminish his surplus satisfaction by doing it. He now gets for 30s. three pounds; of which the first is worth to him at least 20s., the second at least 14s., and the third at least 10s. The total utility of the three is worth at least 44s., his consumer's surplus is at least 14s., and so on.

When at last the price has fallen to 2s. he buys seven pounds, which are severally worth to him not less than 20, 14, 10, 6, 4, 3, and 2s. or 59s. in all. This sum measures their total utility to him, and his consumer's surplus is (at least) the excess of this sum over the 14s. he actually does pay for them, *i.e.* 45s. This is the excess value of the satisfaction he gets from buying the tea over that which he could have got by spending the 14s. in extending a little his purchase of other commodities, of which he had just not thought it worth while to buy more at their current prices; and any further purchases of which at those prices would not yield him any consumer's surplus. In other words, he derives this 45s. worth of surplus enjoyment from his conjuncture, from the adaptation of the environment to his wants in the particular matter of tea. If that adaptation ceased, and tea could not be had at any price, he would have incurred a loss of satisfaction at least equal to that which he could have got by spending 45s. more on extra supplies of things that were worth to him only just what he paid for them.[1]

---

not with the 17s. which represents the average value per pound of the two pounds; but with the 14s., which represents the *additional* utility which a second pound has for him. For that remains unchanged when he has bought a third pound, of which the additional utility is measured by 10s.

The first pound was probably worth to him more than 20s. All that we know is that it was not worth less to him. He probably got some small surplus even on that. Again, the second pound was probably worth more than 14s. to him. All that we know is that it was worth at least 14s. and not worth 20s. to him. He would get therefore at this stage a surplus satisfaction of at least 6s., probably a little more. A ragged edge of this kind, as mathematicians are aware, always exists when we watch the effects of considerable changes, as that from 20s. to 14s. a pound. If we had begun with a very high price, had descended by practically infinitesimal changes of a farthing per pound, and watched infinitesimal variations in his consumption of a small fraction of a pound at a time, this ragged edge would have disappeared.

[1] Prof. Nicholson (*Principles of Political Economy*, Vol. I and *Economic Journal*, Vol. IV.) has raised objections to the notion of consumers' surplus, which have been answered by Prof. Edgeworth in the same Journal. Prof. Nicholson says : —" Of what avail is it to say that the utility of an income of (say) £100 a year is worth (say) £1000 a year ? " There would be no avail in saying that. But there might be use, when comparing life in Central Africa with life in England, in saying that, though the

III, VI, 3.   § 3. In the same way if we were to neglect for the moment the
———   fact that the same sum of money represents different amounts of
Demand of
a market.   pleasure to different people, we might measure the surplus satisfaction which the sale of tea affords, say, in the London market, by the
aggregate of the sums by which the prices shown in a complete list
of demand prices for tea exceeds its selling price.[1]

things which money will buy in Central Africa may on the average be as cheap there as
here, yet there are so many things which cannot be bought there at all, that a person
with a thousand a year there is not so well off as a person with three or four hundred a
year here. If a man pays 1d. toll on a bridge, which saves him an additional drive that
would cost a shilling, we do not say that the penny is worth a shilling, but that the
penny together with the advantage offered him by the bridge (the part it plays in his
conjuncture) is worth a shilling for that day. Were the bridge swept away on a day
on which he needed it, he would be in at least as bad a position as if he had been
deprived of eleven pence.

   [1] Let us then consider the demand curve DD' for tea in any large market.
   Let OH be the amount which is sold there at the price
HA annually, a year being taken as our unit of time.
Taking any point M in OH let us draw MP vertically upwards to meet the curve in P and cut a horizontal line
through A in R. We will suppose the several lbs. numbered
in the order of the eagerness of the several purchasers : the
eagerness of the purchaser of any lb. being measured by
the price he is just willing to pay for that lb. The figure
informs us that OM can be sold at the price PM ; but that
at any higher price not quite so many lbs. can be sold.
There must be then some individual who will buy more at
the price PM, than he will at any higher price ; and we
are to regard the OMth lb. as sold to this individual.

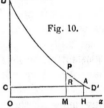

Fig. 10.

Suppose for instance that PM represents 4s., and that OM represents a million lbs.
The purchaser described in the text is just willing to buy his fifth lb. of tea at the
price 4s., and the OMth or millionth lb, may be said to be sold to him. If AH and
therefore RM represents 2s., the consumers' surplus derived from the OMth lb. is
the excess of PM or 4s. which the purchaser of that lb. would have been willing to
pay for it over RM the 2s. which he actually does pay for it. Let us suppose that
a very thin vertical parallelogram is drawn of which the height is PM and of which
the base is the distance along Ox that measures the single unit or lb. of tea. It
will be convenient henceforward to regard price as measured not by a mathematical
straight line without thickness, as PM ; but by a very thin parallelogram, or as it may
be called a thick straight line, of which the breadth is in every case equal to the
distance along Ox which measures a unit or lb. of tea. Thus we should say that the
total satisfaction derived from the OMth lb. of tea is represented (or, on the assumption
made in the last paragraph of the text, is measured) by the thick straight line MP ;
that the price paid for this lb. is represented by the thick straight line MR and the
consumers' surplus derived from this lb. by the thick straight line RP. Now let us
suppose that such thin parallelograms, or thick straight lines, are drawn from all
positions of M between O and H, one for each lb. of tea. The thick straight lines thus
drawn, as MP is, from Ox up to the demand curve will each represent the aggregate of
the satisfaction derived from a lb. of tea ; and taken together thus occupy and exactly
fill up the whole area DOHA. Therefore we may say that the area DOHA represents
the aggregate of the satisfaction derived from the consumption of tea. Again, each
of the straight lines drawn, as MR is, from Ox upwards as far as AC represents the
price that actually is paid for a lb. of tea. These straight lines together make up the
area COHA ; and therefore this area represents the total price paid for tea. Finally
each of the straight lines drawn as RP is from AC upwards as far as the demand curve,
represents the consumers' surplus derived from the corresponding lb. of tea. These
straight lines together make up the area DCA ; and therefore this area represents the
total consumers' surplus that is derived from tea when the price is AH. But it must
be repeated that this geometrical measurement is only an aggregate of the measures of
benefits which are not all measured on the same scale except on the assumption just
made in the text. Unless that assumption is made the area only represents an
aggregate of satisfactions, the several amounts of which are not exactly measured. On
that assumption only, its area measures the volume of the total net satisfaction derived
from the tea by its various purchasers.

This analysis, with its new names and elaborate machinery, appears at first sight laboured and unreal.   On closer study it will be found to introduce no new difficulties and to make no new assumptions; but only to bring to light difficulties and assumptions that are latent in the common language of the market-place.   For in this, as in other cases, the apparent simplicity of popular phrases veils a real complexity, and it is the duty of science to bring out that latent complexity; to face it; and to reduce it as far as possible : so that, in later stages we may handle firmly difficulties that could not be grasped with a good grip by the vague thought and language of ordinary life.

III, VI, 3.

This analysis aims only at giving definite expression to familiar notions.

It is a common saying in ordinary life that the real worth of things to a man is not gauged by the price he pays for them : that though he spends for instance much more on tea than on salt, yet salt is of greater real worth to him; and that this would be clearly seen if he were entirely deprived of it.   This line of argument is but thrown into precise technical form when it is said that we cannot trust the marginal utility of a commodity to indicate its total utility. If some shipwrecked men, expecting to wait a year before they were rescued, had a few pounds of tea and the same number of pounds of salt to divide between them, the salt would be the more highly prized; because the marginal utility of an ounce of salt, when a person expects to get only a few of them in the year, is greater than that of tea under like circumstances.   But, under ordinary circumstances, the price of salt being low, every one buys so much of it that an additional pound would bring him little additional satisfaction : the total utility of salt to him is very great indeed, and yet its marginal utility is low.   On the other hand, since tea is costly, most people use less of it and let the water stay on it rather longer than they would, if it could be got at nearly as low a price as salt can.   Their desire for it is far from being satiated : its marginal utility remains high, and they may be willing to pay as much for an additional ounce of it as they would for an additional pound of salt.   The common saying of ordinary life with which we began suggests all this : but not in an exact and definite form, such as is needed for a statement which will often be applied in later work.   The use of technical terms at starting adds nothing to knowledge : but it puts familiar knowledge in a firm compact shape, ready to serve as the basis for further study.[1]

[1] Harris On Coins 1757, says " Things in general are valued, not according to their real uses in supplying the necessities of men; but rather in proportion to the land, labour and skill that are requisite to produce them.   It is according to this proportion nearly, that things or commodities are exchanged one for another; and

III, vi, 3.   Or the real worth of a thing might be discussed with reference not

In regard   to a single person but to people in general; and thus it would
to different naturally be assumed that a shilling's worth of gratification to one
people
allowance   Englishman might be taken as equivalent with a shilling's worth to
may have   another, "to start with," and "until cause to the contrary were
to be made
where   shown." But everyone would know that this was a reasonable
necessary   course only on the supposition that the consumers of tea and those of
for differ-
ences of   salt belonged to the same classes of people; and included people of
sensibility   every variety of temperament.[1]

and for   This involves the consideration that a pound's worth of satisfac-
differences
of wealth :   tion to an ordinary poor man is a much greater thing than a pound's
worth of satisfaction to an ordinary rich man : and if instead of comparing tea and salt, which are both used largely by all classes, we
compared either of them with champagne or pineapples, the correction to be made on this account would be more than important : it
would change the whole character of the estimate. In earlier
generations many statesmen, and even some economists, neglected to
make adequate allowance for considerations of this class, especially
when constructing schemes of taxation; and their words or deeds
seemed to imply a want of sympathy with the sufferings of the poor;
though more often they were due simply to want of thought.

On the whole however it happens that by far the greater number

but it is   of the events with which economics deals, affect in about equal pro-
seldom
needed in   portions all the different classes of society; so that if the money
consider-   measures of the happiness caused by two events are equal, there is
ing large
groups of   not in general any very great difference between the amounts of the
people.   happiness in the two cases. And it is on account of this fact that the
exact measurement of the consumers' surplus in a market has already
much theoretical interest, and may become of high practical
importance.

It will be noted however that the demand prices of each com-

---

it is by the said scale, that the intrinsic values of most things are chiefly estimated.
Water is of great use, and yet ordinarily of little or no value; because in most places,
water flows spontaneously in such great plenty, as not to be withheld within the
limits of private property; but all may have enough, without other expense than
that of bringing or conducting it, when the case so requires. On the other hand,
diamonds being very scarce, have upon that account a great value, though they are but
little use."

[1] There might conceivably be persons of high sensibility who would suffer specially
from the want of either salt or tea : or who were generally sensitive, and would
suffer more from the loss of a certain part of their income than others in the same
station of life. But it would be assumed that such differences between individuals
might be neglected, since we were considering in either case the average of large
numbers of people; though of course it might be necessary to consider whether there
were some special reason for believing, say, that those who laid most store by tea were
a specially sensitive class of people. If it could, then a separate allowance for this
would have to be made before applying the results of economical analysis to practical
problems of ethics or politics.

modity, on which our estimates of its total utility and consumers' surplus are based, assume that *other things remain equal*, while its price rises to scarcity value : and when the total utilities of two commodities which contribute to the same purpose are calculated on this plan, we cannot say that the total utility of the two together is equal to the sum of the total utilities of each separately.[1]

§ 4. The substance of our argument would not be affected if we took account of the fact that, the more a person spends on anything the less power he retains of purchasing more of it or of other things, and the greater is the value of money to him (in technical language every fresh expenditure increases the marginal value of money to him). But though its substance would not be altered, its form would be made more intricate without any corresponding gain; for there are very few practical problems, in which the corrections to be made under this head would be of any importance.[2]

There are however some exceptions. For instance, as Sir R. Giffen has pointed out, a rise in the price of bread makes so large a drain on the resources of the poorer labouring families and raises so

Margin note: III, vi, 4. It is seldom necessary to take account of changes in the purchaser's command of money.

---

[1] Some ambiguous phrases in earlier editions appear to have suggested to some readers the opposite opinion. But the task of adding together the total utilities of all commodities, so as to obtain the aggregate of the total utility of all wealth, is beyond the range of any but the most elaborate mathematical formulæ. An attempt to treat it by them some years ago convinced the present writer that even if the task be theoretically feasible, the result would be encumbered by so many hypotheses as to be practically useless.

Attention has already (pp. 84 n.[2], 89 n.[1]) been called to the fact that for some purposes such things as tea and coffee must be grouped together as one commodity : and it is obvious that, if tea were inaccessible, people would increase their consumption of coffee, and *vice versa*. The loss that people would suffer from being deprived of both of tea and coffee would be greater than the sum of their losses from being deprived of either alone : and therefore the total utility of tea and coffee is greater than the sum of the total utility of tea calculated on the supposition that people can have recourse to coffee, and that of coffee calculated on a like supposition as to tea. This difficulty can be theoretically evaded by grouping the two " rival " commodities together under a common demand schedule. On the other hand, if we have calculated the total utility of fuel with reference to the fact that without it we could not obtain hot water to obtain the beverage tea from tea leaves, we should count something twice over if we added to that utility the total utility of tea leaves, reckoned on a similar plan. Again the total utility of agricultural produce includes that of ploughs ; and the two may not be added together ; though the total utility of ploughs may be discussed in connection with one problem, and that of wheat in connection with another. Other aspects of these two difficulties are examined in V. vi.

Prof. Patten has insisted on the latter of them in some able and suggestive writings. But his attempt to express the aggregate utility of all forms of wealth seems to overlook many difficulties.

[2] In mathematical language the neglected elements would generally belong to the second order of small quantities; and the legitimacy of the familiar scientific method by which they are neglected would have seemed beyond question, had not Prof. Nicholson challenged it. A short reply to him has been given by Prof. Edgeworth in the *Economic Journal* for March 1894; and a fuller reply by Prof. Barone in the *Giornale degli Economisti* for Sept. 1894; of which some account is given by Mr. Sanger in the *Economic Journal* for March 1895.

As is indicated in Note VI in the Mathematical Appendix, formal account could be taken of changes in the marginal utility of money, if it were desired to do so. If we attempted to add together the total utilities of all commodities, we should be bound to do so : that task is however impracticable.

III, vi, 5. much the marginal utility of money to them, that they are forced to curtail their consumption of meat and the more expensive farinaceous foods : and, bread being still the cheapest food which they can get and will take, they consume more, and not less of it. But such cases are rare; when they are met with, each must be treated on its own merits.

We can seldom obtain a complete list of demand prices : nor do we often need them. It has already been remarked that we cannot guess at all accurately how much of anything people would buy at prices very different from those which they are accustomed to pay for it : or in other words, what the demand prices for it would be for amounts very different from those which are commonly sold. Our list of demand prices is therefore highly conjectural except in the neighbourhood of the customary price; and the best estimates we can form of the whole amount of the utility of anything are liable to large error. But this difficulty is not important practically. For the chief applications of the doctrine of consumers' surplus are concerned with such changes in it as would accompany changes in the price of the commodity in question in the neighbourhood of the customary price : that is, they require us to use only that information with which we are fairly well supplied. These remarks apply with special force to necessaries.[1]

Elements of collective wealth are apt to be overlooked. § 5. There remains another class of considerations which are apt to be overlooked in estimating the dependence of wellbeing upon material wealth. Not only does a person's happiness often depend more on his own physical, mental and moral health than on his

---

[1] The notion of consumers' surplus may help us a little now; and, when our statistical knowledge is further advanced, it may help us a great deal to decide how much injury would be done to the public by an additional tax of 6d. a pound on tea, or by an addition of ten per cent. to the freight charges of a railway : and the value of the notion is but little diminished by the fact that it would not help us much to estimate the loss that would be caused by a tax of 30s. a pound on tea, or a tenfold rise in freight charges.

Reverting to our last diagram, we may express this by saying that, if A is the point on the curve corresponding to the amount that is wont to be sold in the market, data can be obtained sufficient for drawing the curve with tolerable correctness for some distance on either side of A ; though the curve can seldom be drawn with any approach to accuracy right up to D. But this is practically unimportant, because in the chief practical applications of the theory of value we should seldom make any use of a knowledge of the whole shape of the demand curve if we had it. We need just what we can get, that is, a fairly correct knowledge of its shape in the neighbourhood of A. We seldom require to ascertain the total area DCA ; it is sufficient for most of our purposes to know the changes in this area that would be occasioned by moving A through small distances along the curve in either direction. Nevertheless it will save trouble to assume provisionally, as in pure theory we are at liberty to do, that the curve is completely drawn.

There is however a special difficulty in estimating the whole of the utility of commodities some supply of which is necessary for life. If any attempt is made to do it, the best plan is perhaps to take that necessary supply for granted, and estimate the total utility only of that part of the commodity which is in excess of this amount. But we must recollect that the desire for anything is much dependent on the difficulty of getting substitutes for it. (See Note VI in the Mathematical Appendix.)

external conditions : but even among these conditions many that III, VI, 6.
are of chief importance for his real happiness are apt to be omitted
from an inventory of his wealth. Some are free gifts of nature; and
these might indeed be neglected without great harm if they were
always the same for everybody; but in fact they vary much from
place to place. More of them however are elements of collective
wealth which are often omitted from the reckoning of individual
wealth; but which become important when we compare different
parts of the modern civilized world, and even more important when
we compare our own age with earlier times.

Collective action for the purpose of securing common wellbeing, *So-called*
as for instance in lighting and watering the streets, will occupy us *consumers'*
much towards the end of our inquiries. Co-operative associations *tions*
for the purchase of things for personal consumption have made more *the subject*
progress in England than elsewhere : but those for purchasing the *of Pro-*
things wanted for trade purposes by farmers and others, have until *duction.*
lately been backward in England. Both kinds are sometimes
described as Consumers' associations; but they are really associations for economizing effort in certain branches of business, and
belong to the subject of Production rather than Consumption.

§ 6. When we speak of the dependence of wellbeing on material *We are*
wealth, we refer to the flow or stream of wellbeing as measured by *here con-*
the flow or stream of incoming wealth and the consequent power of *with large*
using and consuming it. A person's stock of wealth yields by its *rather*
usance and in other ways an income of happiness, among which of *than large*
course are to be counted the pleasures of possession : but there is *sions.*
little direct connection between the aggregate amount of that stock
and his aggregate happiness. And it is for that reason that we have
throughout this and preceding chapters spoken of the rich, the middle
classes and the poor as having respectively large, medium and small
incomes—not possessions.[1]

In accordance with a suggestion made by Daniel Bernoulli, we *Ber-*
may regard the satisfaction which a person derives from his income *noulli's*
as commencing when he has enough to support life, and afterwards as *tion.*
increasing by equal amounts with every equal successive percentage
that is added to his income; and *vice versa* for loss of income.[2]

---

[1] See Note VII in the Appendix.

[2] That is to say, if £30 represent necessaries, a person's satisfaction from his
income will begin at that point; and when it has reached £40, an additional £1
will add a tenth to the £10 which represents its happiness-yielding power. But if
his income were £100, that is £70 above the level of necessaries, an additional £7
would be required to add as much to his happiness as £1 if his income were £40 :
while if his income were £10,000, an additional £1000 would be needed to produce
an equal effect (compare Note VIII in the Appendix). Of course such estimates
are very much at random, and unable to adapt themselves to the varying circum-

III, vi, 6.   But after a time new riches often lose a great part of their charms.
Partly this is the result of familiarity; which makes people cease to
derive much pleasure from accustomed comforts and luxuries,
though they suffer greater pain from their loss. Partly it is due to
the fact that with increased riches there often comes either the weariness of age, or at least an increase of nervous strain; and perhaps
even habits of living that lower physical vitality, and diminish the
capacity for pleasure.

The edge of enjoyment is blunted by familiarity.

      In every civilized country there have been some followers of the
Buddhist doctrine that a placid serenity is the highest ideal of life;
that it is the part of the wise man to root out of his nature as many
wants and desires as he can; that real riches consist not in the
abundance of goods but in the paucity of wants. At the other
extreme are those who maintain that the growth of new wants and
desires is always beneficial because it stimulates people to increased
exertions. They seem to have made the mistake, as Herbert Spencer
says, of supposing that life is for working, instead of working for life.[1]

The value of leisure and rest.

      The truth seems to be that as human nature is constituted, man
rapidly degenerates unless he has some hard work to do, some
difficulties to overcome; and that some strenuous exertion is
necessary for physical and moral health. The fulness of life lies in
the development and activity of as many and as high faculties as
possible. There is intense pleasure in the ardent pursuit of any aim,
whether it be success in business, the advancement of art and science,
or the improvement of the condition of one's fellow-beings. The

The excellence of a moderate income obtained by moderate work.

---

stances of individual life. As we shall see later, the systems of taxation which are
now most widely prevalent follow generally on the lines of Bernoulli's suggestion.
Earlier systems took from the poor very much more than would be in accordance with
that plan; while the systems of graduated taxation, which are being foreshadowed
in several countries, are in some measure based on the assumption that the addition
of one per cent. to a very large income adds less to the wellbeing of its owner than an
addition of one per cent. to smaller incomes would, even after Bernoulli's correction
for necessaries has been made.

It may be mentioned in passing that from the general law that the utility to
anyone of an additional £1 diminishes with the number of pounds he already has,
there follow two important practical principles. The first is that gambling involves
an economic loss, even when conducted on perfectly fair and even terms. For instance,
a man who having £600 makes a fair even bet of £100, has now an expectation of
happiness equal to half that derived from £700, and half that derived from £500;
and this is less than the certain expectation of the happiness derived from £600,
because by hypothesis the difference between the happiness got from £600 and £500 is
greater than the difference between the happiness got from £700 and £600. (Compare
Note IX in the Appendix and Jevons, *l.c.* Ch. iv.) The second principle, the direct
converse of the first, is that a theoretically fair insurance against risks is always an
economic gain. But of course every insurance office, after calculating what is a
theoretically fair premium, has to share in addition to it enough to pay profits on its
own capital, and to cover its own expenses of working, among which are often to be
reckoned very heavy items for advertising and for losses by fraud. The question
whether it is advisable to pay the premium which insurance offices practically do
charge, is one that must be decided for each case on its own merits.

[1] See his lecture on *The Gospel of Relaxation.*

highest constructive work of all kinds must often alternate between periods of over-strain and periods of lassitude and stagnation; but for ordinary people, for those who have no strong ambitions, whether of a lower or a higher kind, a moderate income earned by moderate and fairly steady work offers the best opportunity for the growth of those habits of body, mind, and spirit in which alone there is true happiness.

There is some misuse of wealth in all ranks of society. And though, speaking generally, we may say that every increase in the wealth of the working classes adds to the fulness and nobility of human life, because it is used chiefly in the satisfaction of real wants; yet even among the artisans in England, and perhaps still more in new countries, there are signs of the growth of that unwholesome desire for wealth as a means of display which has been the chief bane of the well-to-do classes in every civilized country. Laws against luxury have been futile; but it would be a gain if the moral sentiment of the community could induce people to avoid all sorts of display of individual wealth. There are indeed true and worthy pleasures to be got from wisely ordered magnificence : but they are at their best when free from any taint of personal vanity on the one side and envy on the other; as they are when they centre round public buildings, public parks, public collections of the fine arts, and public games and amusements. So long as wealth is applied to provide for every family the necessaries of life and culture, and an abundance of the higher forms of enjoyment for collective use, so long the pursuit of wealth is a noble aim; and the pleasures which it brings are likely to increase with the growth of those higher activities which it is used to promote.

When the necessaries of life are once provided, everyone should seek to increase the beauty of things in his possession rather than their number or their magnificence. An improvement in the artistic character of furniture and clothing trains the higher faculties of those who make them, and is a source of growing happiness to those who use them. But if instead of seeking for a higher standard of beauty, we spend our growing resources on increasing the complexity and intricacy of our domestic goods, we gain thereby no true benefit, no lasting happiness. The world would go much better if everyone would buy fewer and simpler things, and would take trouble in selecting them for their real beauty; being careful of course to get good value in return for his outlay, but preferring to buy a few things made well by highly paid labour rather than many made badly by low paid labour.

III, vi, 6.

Expenditure for the sake of display.

The superior nobility of the collective over the private use of wealth.

The tasteful purchaser educates the producer. We thus approach the fringe of broad inquiries, which must be deferred.

But we are exceeding the proper scope of the present Book; the discussion of the influence on general wellbeing which is exerted by the mode in which each individual spends his income is one of the more important of those applications of economic science to the art of living.

BOOK IV

THE AGENTS OF PRODUCTION
LAND, LABOUR, CAPITAL AND ORGANIZATION

CHAPTER I

INTRODUCTORY

§ 1. THE agents of production are commonly classed as Land, Labour and Capital. By Land is meant the material and the forces which Nature gives freely for man's aid, in land and water, in air and light and heat. By Labour is meant the economic work of man, whether with the hand or the head.[1] By Capital is meant all stored-up provision for the production of material goods, and for the attainment of those benefits which are commonly reckoned as part of income. It is the main stock of wealth regarded as an agent of production rather than as a direct source of gratification.

Capital consists in a great part of knowledge and organization : and of this some part is private property and other part is not. Knowledge is our most powerful engine of production; it enables us to subdue Nature and force her to satisfy our wants. Organization aids knowledge; it has many forms, e.g. that of a single business, that of various businesses in the same trade, that of various trades relatively to one another, and that of the State providing security for all and help for many. The distinction between public and private property in knowledge and organization is of great and growing importance : in some respects of more importance than that between public and private property in material things; and partly for that reason it seems best sometimes to reckon Organization apart as a distinct agent of production. It cannot be fully examined till a much later stage in our inquiry; but something has to be said of it in the present Book.

---

[1] Labour is classed as economic when it is "undergone partly or wholly with a view to some good other than the pleasure directly derived from it." See p. 54 and footnote. Such labour with the head as does not tend directly or indirectly to promote material production, as for instance the work of the schoolboy at his tasks, is left out of account, so long as we are confining our attention to production in the ordinary sense of the term. From some points of view, but not from all, the phrase Land, Labour, Capital would be more symmetrical if labour were interpreted to mean the labourers, i.e. mankind. See Walras, *Économie Politique Pure*, Leçon 17, and Prof. Fisher, *Economic Journal*, VI. p. 529.

but for
some
purposes
under two.

Man both
the end
and an
agent of
produc-
tion.

Pro-
visional
antithesis
of demand
and
supply,

ordinary
labour
being
selected
for illus-
tration.

In a sense there are only two agents of production, nature and man. Capital and organization are the result of the work of man aided by nature, and directed by his power of forecasting the future and his willingness to make provision for it. If the character and powers of nature and of man be given, the growth of wealth and knowledge and organization follow from them as effect from cause. But on the other hand man is himself largely formed by his surroundings, in which nature plays a great part : and thus from every point of view man is the centre of the problem of production as well as that of consumption; and also of that further problem of the relations between the two, which goes by the twofold name of Distribution and Exchange.

The growth of mankind in numbers, in health and strength, in knowledge, ability, and in richness of character is the end of all our studies : but it is an aim to which economics can do no more than contribute some important elements. In its broader aspects therefore the study of this growth belongs to the end, if to any part of a treatise on economics : but does not properly belong even there. Meanwhile we cannot avoid taking account of the direct agency of man in production, and of the conditions which govern his efficiency as a producer. And on the whole it is perhaps the most convenient course, as it certainly is that most in accordance with English tradition, to include some account of the growth of population in numbers and character as a part of the general discussion of production.

§ 2. It is not possible at this stage to do more than indicate very slightly the general relations between demand and supply, between consumption and production. But it may be well, while the discussion of utility and value is fresh in our minds, to take a short glance at the relations between value and the disutility or discommodity that has to be overcome in order to obtain those goods which have value because they are at once desirable and difficult of attainment. All that can be said now must be provisional; and may even seem rather to raise difficulties than to solve them : and there will be an advantage in having before us a map, in however slight and broken outline, of the ground to be covered.

While demand is based on the desire to obtain commodities, supply depends mainly on the overcoming of the unwillingness to undergo "discommodities." These fall generally under two heads :—labour, and the sacrifice involved in putting off consumption. It must suffice here to give a sketch of the part played by ordinary labour in supply. It will be seen hereafter that remarks similar, though not quite the same, might have been made about the work of management and the sacrifice which is involved (sometimes, but not always) in that waiting which is involved in accumulating the means of production.

The discommodity of labour may arise from bodily or mental fatigue, or from its being carried on in unhealthy surroundings, or with unwelcome associates, or from its occupying time that is wanted for recreation, or for social or intellectual pursuits. But whatever be the form of the discommodity, its intensity nearly always increases with the severity and the duration of labour.

Of course much exertion is undergone for its own sake, as for instance in mountaineering, in playing games and in the pursuit of literature, of art, and of science; and much hard work is done under the influence of a desire to benefit others.[1] But the chief motive to most labour, in our use of the term, is the desire to obtain some material advantage; which in the present state of the world appears generally in the form of the gain of a certain amount of money. It is true that even when a man is working for hire he often finds pleasure in his work: but he generally gets so far tired before it is done that he is glad when the hour for stopping arrives. Perhaps after he has been out of work for some time, he might, as far as his immediate comfort is concerned, rather work for nothing than not work at all; but he will probably prefer not to spoil his market, any more than a manufacturer would, by offering what he has for sale much below its normal price. On this matter much will need to be said in another volume.

In technical phrase this may be called the *marginal disutility* of labour. For, as with every increase in the amount of a commodity its marginal utility falls; and as with every fall in that desirableness, there is a fall in the price that can be got for the whole of the commodity, and not for the last part only; so the marginal disutility of labour generally increases with every increase in its amount.

---

[1] We have seen (p. 103) that, if a person makes the whole of his purchases at the price which he would be just willing to pay for his last purchases, he gains a surplus of satisfaction on his earlier purchases; since he gets them for less than he would have paid rather than go without them. So, if the price paid to him for doing any work is an adequate reward for that part which he does most unwillingly; and if, as generally happens, the same payment is given for that part of the work which he does less unwillingly and at less real cost to himself; then from that part he obtains a producer's surplus. Some difficulties connected with this notion are considered in Appendix K.

The labourer's unwillingness to sell his labour for less than its normal price resembles the unwillingness of manufacturers to spoil their market by pushing goods for sale at a low price; even though, so far as the particular transaction is concerned, they would rather take the low price than let their works stand idle.

Though
much work
is pleasur-
able,

The unwillingness of anyone already in an occupation to increase his exertions depends, under ordinary circumstances, on fundamental principles of human nature which economists have to accept as ultimate facts. As Jevons remarks,[1] there is often some resistance to be overcome before setting to work. Some little painful effort is often involved at starting; but this gradually diminishes to zero, and is succeeded by pleasure; which increases for a while until it attains a certain low maximum; after which it diminishes to zero, and is succeeded by increasing weariness and craving for relaxation and change. In intellectual work, however, the pleasure and excitement, after they have once set in, often go on increasing till progress is stopped of necessity or by prudence. Everyone in health has a certain store of energy on which he can draw, but which can only be replaced by rest; so that if his expenditure exceed his income for long, his health becomes bankrupt; and employers often find that in cases of great need a temporary increase of pay will induce their workmen to do an amount of work which they cannot long keep up, whatever they are paid for it. One reason of this is that the need for relaxation becomes more urgent with every increase in the hours of labour beyond a certain limit. The disagreeableness of additional work increases; partly because, as the time left for rest and other activities diminishes, the agreeableness of additional free time increases.

yet on
certain
supposi-
tions the
willingness
to do it is
governed
by the
price to be
got for it.

Supply
price.

Subject to these and some other qualifications, it is broadly true that the exertions which any set of workers will make, rise or fall with a rise or fall in the remuneration which is offered to them. As the price required to attract purchasers for any given amount of a commodity, was called the demand price for that amount during a year or any other given time; so the price required to call forth the exertion necessary for producing any given amount of a commodity, may be called the *supply price* for that amount during the same time. And if for the moment we assumed that production depended solely upon the exertions of a certain number of workers, already in existence and trained for their work, we should get a list of supply prices corresponding to the list of demand prices which we have already considered. This list would set forth theoretically in one column of figures various amounts of exertion and therefore of production; and in a parallel column the prices which must be paid to induce the available workers to put forth these amounts of exertion.[2]

But this simple method of treating the supply of work of any

[1] *Theory of Political Economy*, Ch. v. This doctrine has been emphasized and developed in much detail by Austrian and American economists.
[2] See above III. III. 4.

kind, and consequently the supply of goods made by that work, assumes that the number of those who are qualified for it is fixed; and that assumption can be made only for short periods of time. The total numbers of the people change under the action of many causes. Of these causes only some are economic; but among them the average earnings of labour take a prominent place; though their influence on the growth of numbers is fitful and irregular.

But the distribution of the population between different trades is more subject to the influence of economic causes. In the long run the supply of labour in any trade is adapted more or less closely to the demand for it : thoughtful parents bring up their children to the most advantageous occupations to which they have access; that is to those that offer the best reward, in wages and other advantages, in return for labour that is not too severe in quantity or character, and for skill that is not too hard to be acquired. This adjustment between demand and supply can however never be perfect; fluctuations of demand may make it much greater or much less for a while, even for many years, than would have been just sufficient to induce parents to select for their children that trade rather than some other of the same class. Although therefore the reward to be had for any kind of work at any time does stand in some relation to the difficulty of acquiring the necessary skill combined with the exertion, the disagreeableness, the waste of leisure, etc. involved in the work itself; yet this correspondence is liable to great disturbances. The study of these disturbances is a difficult task; and it will occupy us much in later stages of our work. But the present Book is mainly descriptive and raises few difficult problems.

IV, I, 2.

Forecast of the difficulty of this problem in real life.

CHAPTER II

THE FERTILITY OF LAND

§ 1. THE requisites of production are commonly spoken of as land, labour and capital: those material things which owe their usefulness to human labour being classed under capital, and those which owe nothing to it being classed as land. The distinction is obviously a loose one: for bricks are but pieces of earth slightly worked up; and the soil of old settled countries has for the greater part been worked over many times by man, and owes to him its present form. There is however a scientific principle underlying the distinction. While man has no power of creating matter, he creates utilities by putting things into a useful form; [1] and the utilities made by him can be increased in supply if there is an increased demand for them: they have a supply price. But there are other utilities over the supply of which he has no control; they are given as a fixed quantity by nature and have therefore no supply price. The term "land" has been extended by economists so as to include the permanent sources of these utilities; [2] whether they are found in land, as the term is commonly used, or in seas and rivers, in sunshine and rain, in winds and waterfalls.

When we have inquired what it is that marks off land from those material things which we regard as products of the land, we shall find that the fundamental attribute of land is its extension. The right to use a piece of land gives command over a certain space—a certain part of the earth's surface. The area of the earth is fixed: the geometric relations in which any particular part of it stands to other parts are fixed. Man has no control over them; they are wholly unaffected by demand; they have no cost of production, there is no supply price at which they can be produced.

The use of a certain area of the earth's surface is a primary condition of anything that man can do; it gives him room for his

The notion that land is a free gift of nature while the produce of land is due to man's work is a loose one: but there is a truth underlying it.

[1] See Book II. Chapter iii.

[2] In Ricardo's famous phrase "the original and indestructible powers of the soil." Von Thünen, in a noteworthy discussion of the basis of the theory of rent, and of the positions which Adam Smith and Ricardo took with regard to it, speaks of "Der Boden an sich"; a phrase which unfortunately cannot be translated, but which means the soil as it would be by itself, if not altered by the action of man (*Der Isolirte Staat*, i. i. 5).

own actions, with the enjoyment of the heat and the light, the air
and the rain which nature assigns to that area; and it determines
his distance from, and in a great measure his relations to, other
things and other persons. We shall find that it is this property of
" land " which, though as yet insufficient prominence has been given
to it, is the ultimate cause of the distinction which all writers on
economics are compelled to make between land and other things.
It is the foundation of much that is most interesting and most
difficult in economic science.

Some parts of the earth's surface contribute to production
chiefly by the services which they render to the navigator : others
are of chief value to the miner; others—though this selection is
made by man rather than by nature—to the builder. But when
the productiveness of land is spoken of our first thoughts turn to
its agricultural use.

§ 2. To the agriculturist an area of land is the means of supporting a certain amount of vegetable, and perhaps ultimately of animal,
life. For this purpose the soil must have certain mechanical and
chemical qualities.

Mechanically, it must be so far yielding that the fine roots of
plants can push their way freely in it; and yet it must be firm enough
to give them a good hold. It must not err as some sandy soils do
by affording water too free a passage : for then it will often be
dry, and the plant food will be washed away almost as soon as it is
formed in the soil or put into it. Nor must it err, as stiff clays do,
by not allowing the water a fairly free passage. For constant
supplies of fresh water, and of the air that it brings with it in its
journey through the soil, are essential : they convert into plant food
the minerals and gases that otherwise would be useless or even
poisonous. The action of fresh air and water and of frosts are
nature's tillage of the soil; and even unaided they will in time make
almost any part of the earth's surface fairly fertile if the soil that
they form can rest where it is, and is not torn away down-hill by
rain and torrents as soon as it is formed. But man gives great aid
in this mechanical preparation of the soil. The chief purpose of his
tillage is to help nature to enable the soil to hold plant roots gently
but firmly, and to enable the air and water to move about freely in
it. And farmyard manure subdivides clay soils and makes them
lighter and more open; while to sandy soils it gives a much needed
firmness of texture, and helps them, mechanically as well as chemically, to hold the materials of plant food which would otherwise be
quickly washed out of them.

IV, ii, 3.
———
Chemical
conditions
of fertility.

Chemically the soil must have the inorganic elements that the plant wants in a form palatable to it; and in some cases man can make a great change with but little labour. For he can then turn a barren into a very fertile soil by adding a small quantity of just those things that are needed; using in most cases either lime in some of its many forms, or those artificial manures which modern chemical science has provided in great variety: and he is now calling in the aid of bacteria to help him in this work.

Man's
power of
altering
the cha-
racter of
the soil.

§ 3. By all these means the fertility of the soil can be brought under man's control. He can by sufficient labour make almost any land bear large crops. He can prepare the soil mechanically and chemically for whatever crops he intends to grow next. He can adapt his crops to the nature of the soil and to one another; selecting such a rotation that each will leave the land in such a state, and at such a time of year, that it can be worked up easily and without loss of time into a suitable seed bed for the coming crop. He can even permanently alter the nature of the soil by draining it, or by mixing with it other soil that will supplement its deficiencies. Hitherto this has been done only on a small scale; chalk and lime, clay and marl have been but thinly spread over the fields; a completely new soil has seldom been made except in gardens and other favoured spots. But it is possible, and even as some think probable, that at some future time the mechanical agencies used in making railways and other great earthworks may be applied on a large scale to creating a rich soil by mixing two poor soils with opposite faults.

All these changes are likely to be carried out more extensively and thoroughly in the future than in the past. But even now the greater part of the soil in old countries owes much of its character to human action; all that lies just below the surface has in it a large element of capital, the produce of man's past labour. Those free gifts of nature which Ricardo classed as the " inherent " and " indestructible " properties of the soil, have been largely modified; partly impoverished and partly enriched by the work of many generations of men.

But it is different with that which is above the surface. Every acre has given to it by nature an annual income of heat and light, of air and moisture; and over these man has but little control. He may indeed alter the climate a little by extensive drainage works or by planting forests, or cutting them down. But, on the whole, the action of the sun and the wind and the rain are an annuity fixed by nature for each plot of land. Ownership of the land gives possession of this annuity : and it also gives the space required for the life and action of vegetables and animals; the value of this space being much affected by its geographical position.

We may then continue to use the ordinary distinction between the original or inherent properties, which the land derives from nature, and the artificial properties which it owes to human action; provided we remember that the first include the space-relations of the plot in question, and the annuity that nature has given it of sunlight and air and rain; and that in many cases these are the chief of the inherent properties of the soil. It is chiefly from them that the ownership of agricultural land derives its peculiar significance, and the Theory of Rent its special character.

§ 4. But the question how far the fertility of any soil is due to the original properties given to it by nature, and how far to the changes in it made by man, cannot be fully discussed without taking account of the kind of produce raised from it. Human agency can do much more to promote the growth of some crops than of others. At one end of the scale are forest trees; an oak well planted and with plenty of room has very little to gain from man's aid : there is no way of applying labour to it so as to obtain any considerable return. Nearly the same may be said of the grass on some rich river bottoms which are endowed with a rich soil and good natural drainage; wild animals feeding off this grass without man's care will farm it nearly as well as he does; and much of the richest farm land in England (paying a rent of £6 an acre and upwards) would give to unaided nature almost as great a return as is got from it now. Next comes land which, though not quite so rich, is still kept in permanent pasture; and after this comes arable land on which man does not trust to nature's sowing, but prepares for each crop a seed bed to suit its special wants, sows the seed himself and weeds away the rivals to it. The seeds which he sows are selected for their habit of quickly maturing and fully developing just those parts which are most useful to him; and though the habit of making this selection carefully is only quite modern, and is even now far from general, yet the continued work of thousands of years has given him plants that have but little resemblance to their wild ancestors. Lastly, the kinds of produce which owe most to man's labour and care are the choicer kinds of fruits, flowers and vegetables, and of animals, particularly those which are used for improving their own breeds. For while nature left to herself would select those that are best able to take care of themselves and their offspring, man selects those which will provide him most quickly with the largest supplies

IV, II, 4.

of the things he most wants; and many of the choicest products could not hold their own at all without his care.

In any case the extra return to additional capital and labour diminishes sooner or later.

Thus various then are the parts which man plays in aiding nature to raise the different kinds of agricultural produce. In each case he works on till the extra *return* got by extra capital and labour has so far *diminished* that it will no longer remunerate him for applying them. Where this limit is soon reached he leaves nature to do nearly all the work; where his share in the production has been great, it is because he has been able to work far without reaching this limit. We are thus brought to consider the law of diminishing return.

The return is here measured by the quantity of the produce, not by its value.

It is important to note that the return to capital and labour now under discussion is measured by the *amount* of the produce raised independently of any changes that may meanwhile take place in the exchange value or price of produce; such, for instance, as might occur if a new railway had been made in the neighbourhood, or the population of the county had increased much, while agricultural produce could not be imported easily. Such changes will be of vital importance when we come to draw inferences from the law of diminishing return, and particularly when we discuss the pressure of increasing population on the means of subsistence. But they have no bearing on the law itself, because that has to do not with the value of the produce raised, but only with its amount.[1]

[1] But see the latter part of IV. III. 8; also IV. XIII. 2.

CHAPTER III

THE FERTILITY OF LAND, CONTINUED. THE TENDENCY TO DIMINISHING RETURN

§ 1. *THE law of* or *statement of tendency to Diminishing Return* may be provisionally worded thus :

IV, III, 1.

Pro-visional statement of the tendency to diminishing return.

An increase in the capital and labour applied in the cultivation of land causes *in general* a less than proportionate increase in the amount of produce raised, unless it happens to coincide with an improvement in the arts of agriculture.

We learn from history and by observation that every agriculturist in every age and clime desires to have the use of a good deal of land; and that when he cannot get it freely, he will pay for it, if he has the means. If he thought that he would get as good results by applying all his capital and labour to a very small piece, he would not pay for any but a very small piece.

When land that requires no clearing is to be had for nothing, everyone uses just that quantity which he thinks will give his capital and labour the largest return. His cultivation is " extensive," not " intensive." He does not aim at getting many bushels of corn from any one acre, for then he would cultivate only a few acres. His purpose is to get as large a total crop as possible with a given expenditure of seed and labour; and therefore he sows as many acres as he can manage to bring under a light cultivation. Of course he may go too far : he may spread his work over so large an area that he would gain by concentrating his capital and labour on a smaller space; and under these circumstances if he could get command over more capital and labour so as to apply more to each acre, the land would give him an *Increasing Return*; that is, an extra return larger in proportion than it gives to his present expenditure. But if he has made his calculations rightly, he is using just so much ground as will give him the highest return; and he would lose by concentrating his capital and labour on a smaller area. If he had command over more capital and labour and were to apply more to his present land, he would gain less than he would by taking up more land; he would get a *Diminishing Return*, that is, an extra return smaller in proportion than he gets

Land may be under-cultivated, and then extra capital and labour will give an increasing return until a maximum rate has been reached, after which it will diminish again.

IV, III, 1. for the last applications of capital and labour that he now makes, provided of course that there is meanwhile no perceptible improvement in his agricultural skill. As his sons grow up they will have more capital and labour to apply to land; and in order to avoid obtaining a diminishing return, they will want to cultivate more land. But perhaps by this time all the neighbouring land is already taken up, and in order to get more they must buy it or pay a rent for the use of it, or migrate where they can get it for nothing.[1]

Were it otherwise every farmer would save most of his rent by applying all his capital and labour to a small part of his land.

This tendency to a diminishing return was the cause of Abraham's parting from Lot,[2] and of most of the migrations of which history tells. And wherever the right to cultivate land is much in request, we may be sure that the tendency to a diminishing return is in full operation. Were it not for this tendency every farmer could save nearly the whole of his rent by giving up all but a small piece of his land, and bestowing all his capital and labour on that. If all the capital and labour which he would in that case apply to it, gave as good a return in proportion as that which he now applies to it, he would get from that plot as large a produce as he now gets from his whole farm; and he would make a net gain of all his rent save that of the little plot that he retained.

It may be conceded that the ambition of farmers often leads them to take more land than they can properly manage : and indeed almost every great authority on agriculture, from Arthur Young downwards, has inveighed against this mistake. But when they tell a farmer that he would gain by applying his capital and labour to a smaller area, they do not necessarily mean that he would get a larger gross produce. It is sufficient for their argument that the saving in rent would more than counterbalance any probable diminution of the total returns that he got from the land. If a farmer pays a fourth of his produce as rent, he would gain by concentrating his capital and labour on less land, provided the extra capital and labour applied to each acre gave anything more than three-fourths as good a return in proportion, as he got from his earlier expenditure.

Improved methods may enable more

Again, it may be granted that much land, even in a country as advanced as England, is so unskilfully cultivated that it could be made to give more than double its present gross produce if twice

---

[1] Increasing return in the earlier stages arises partly from economy of organization, similar to that which gives an advantage to manufacture on a large scale. But it is also partly due to the fact that where land is very slightly cultivated the farmer's crops are apt to be smothered by nature's crops of weeds. The relation between Diminishing and Increasing Return is discussed further in the last chapter of this Book.

[2] " The land was not able to bear them, that they might dwell together : for their substance was great, so that they could not dwell together." Genesis xiii. 6.

the present capital and labour were applied to it skilfully. Very likely those are right who maintain that if all English farmers were as able, wise and energetic as the best are, they might profitably apply twice the capital and labour that is now applied. Assuming rent to be one-fourth of the present produce, they might get seven hundredweight of produce for every four that they now get : it is conceivable that with still more improved methods they might get eight hundredweight, or even more. But this does not prove that, *as things are*, further capital and labour could obtain from land an increasing return. The fact remains that, taking farmers as they are with the skill and energy which they actually have, we find as the result of universal observation that there is not open to them a short road to riches by giving up a great part of their land, by concentrating all their capital and labour on the remainder, and saving for their own pockets the rent of all but that remainder. The reason why they cannot do this is told in the law of diminishing return; that return being measured, as has already been said by its quantity, not its exchange value.

We may now state distinctly the limitations which were implied under the words " in general " in our provisional wording of the law. The law is a statement of a tendency which may indeed be held in check for a time by improvements in the arts of production and by the fitful course of the development of the full powers of the soil; but which must ultimately become irresistible if the demand for produce should increase without limit. Our final statement of the tendency may then be divided into two parts, thus :—

Although an improvement in the arts of agriculture may raise the rate of return which land generally affords to any given amount of capital and labour; and although the capital and labour already applied to any piece of land may have been so inadequate for the development of its full powers, that some further expenditure on it even with the existing arts of agriculture would give a more than proportionate return; yet these conditions are rare in an old country : and, except when they are present, the application of increased capital and labour to land will add a less than proportionate amount to the produce raised, unless there be meanwhile an increase in the skill of the individual cultivator. Secondly, whatever may be the future developments of the arts of agriculture, a continued increase in the application of capital and labour to land must ultimately result in a diminution of the extra produce which can be obtained by a given extra amount of capital and labour.

§ 2. Making use of a term suggested by James Mill, we may

IV, III, 2.

capital and labour to be profitably applied.

Final statement of the tendency to diminishing return.

IV, III, 2.

A *dose* of capital and labour.

regard the capital and labour applied to land as consisting of equal successive *doses*.[1] As we have seen, the return to the first few doses may perhaps be small and a greater number of doses may get a larger proportionate return; the return to successive doses may even in exceptional cases alternately rise and fall. But our law states that sooner or later (it being always supposed that there is meanwhile no change in the arts of cultivation) a point will be reached after which all further doses will obtain a less proportionate return than the preceding doses. The dose is always a combined dose of labour and capital, whether it is applied by a peasant owner working unaided on his own land, or at the charges of a capitalist farmer who does no manual labour himself. But in the latter case the main body of the outlay presents itself in the form of money; and when discussing the business economy of farming in relation to English conditions, it is often convenient to consider the labour converted at its market value into a money equivalent, and to speak of doses of capital simply, rather than of doses of labour and capital.

Marginal dose, marginal return, margin of cultivation.

The dose which only just remunerates the cultivator may be said to be the *marginal dose*, and the return to it the *marginal return*. If there happens to be in the neighbourhood land that is cultivated but only just pays its expenses, and so gives no surplus for rent, we may suppose this dose applied to it. We can then say that the dose applied to it is applied to land on the *margin of cultivation*, and this way of speaking has the advantage of simplicity. But it is not necessary for the argument to suppose that there is any such land : what we want to fix our minds on is the return to the marginal dose; whether it happens to be applied to poor land or to rich does not matter; all that is necessary is that it should be the last dose which can profitably be applied to that land.[2]

The marginal dose is not necessarily the last in time.

When we speak of the marginal, or the " last " dose applied to the land, we do not mean the last in time, we mean that dose which is on the margin of profitable expenditure; that is, which is applied so as just to give the ordinary returns to the capital and labour of the cultivator, without affording any surplus. To take a concrete instance, we may suppose a farmer to be thinking of sending the hoers over a field once more; and after a little hesitation he decides that it is worth his while, but only just worth his while to do it. The dose of capital and labour spent on doing it, is then the last dose in our present sense, though there are many doses still to be applied

---

[1] As to this term see the Note at the end of the chapter.
[2] Ricardo was well aware of this : though he did not emphasize it enough. Those opponents of his doctrine who have supposed that it has no application to places where all the land pays a rent, have mistaken the nature of his argument.

in reaping the crop. Of course the return to this last dose cannot be separated from the others; but we ascribe to it all that part of the produce which we believe would not have been produced if the farmer had decided against the extra hoeing.[1]

Since the return to the dose on the margin of cultivation just remunerates the cultivator, it follows that he will be just remunerated for the whole of his capital and labour by as many times the marginal return as he has applied doses in all. Whatever he gets in excess of this is the *surplus produce* of the land. This surplus is retained by the cultivator if he owns the land himself.[2]

Surplus produce.

It is important to note that this description of the nature of

[1] An illustration from recorded experiments may help to make clearer the notion of the return to a marginal dose of capital and labour. The Arkansas experimental station (see *The Times*, 18 Nov. 1889) reported that four plots of an acre each were treated exactly alike except in the matter of ploughing and harrowing, with the following result :—

Plot.	Cultivation.	Crop yields, bushels per acre.
1	Ploughed once	16
2	Ploughed once and harrowed once	18½
3	Ploughed twice and harrowed once	21¾
4	Ploughed twice and harrowed twice	23¼

This would show that the dose of capital and labour applied in harrowing a second time an acre which had already been ploughed twice gave a return of 1⁷⁄₁₂ bushels. And if the value of these bushels, after allowing for expenses of harvesting, etc. *just* replaced that dose with profits, then that dose was a *marginal* one; even though it was not the last in point of time, since those spent on harvesting must needs come later.

[2] Let us seek a graphical illustration. It is to be remembered that graphical illustrations are not proofs. They are merely pictures corresponding very roughly to the main conditions of certain real problems. They obtain clearness of outline, by leaving out of account many considerations which vary from one practical problem to another, and of which the farmer must take full account in his own special case. If on any given field there were expended a capital of £50, a certain amount of produce would be raised from it : a certain amount larger than the former would be raised if there were expended on it a capital of £51. The difference between these two amounts may be regarded as the produce due to the fifty-first pound ; and if we suppose the capital to be applied in successive doses of £1 each we may speak of this difference as the produce due to the fifty-first dose. Let the doses be represented in order by successive equal divisions of the line *OD*. Let there now be drawn from the division of this line representing the fifty-first dose *M*, a line *MP* at right angles to *OD*, in thickness equal to the length of one of the divisions, and such that its length represents the amount of the produce due to the fifty-first dose. Suppose this done for each separate division up to that corresponding to the last dose which it is found profitable to put on the land. Let this last dose be the 110th at *D*, and *DC* the corresponding return that only just remunerates the farmer. The extremities of such lines will lie on a curve *APC*. The gross produce will be represented by the sum of these lines : *i.e.*, since the thickness of each line is equal to the length of the division on which it stands, by the area *ODCA*. Let *CGH* be drawn parallel to *DO*, cutting *PM* in *G* ; then *MG* is equal to *CD* ; and since *DC* just remunerates the farmer for one dose, *MG* will just remunerate him for another : and so for all the portions of the thick vertical lines cut off between *OD* and *HC*. Therefore the sum of these, that is, the area *ODCH*, represents the share of the produce that is required to remunerate him ; while the remainder, *AHGCPA*, is the surplus produce, which under certain conditions becomes the rent.

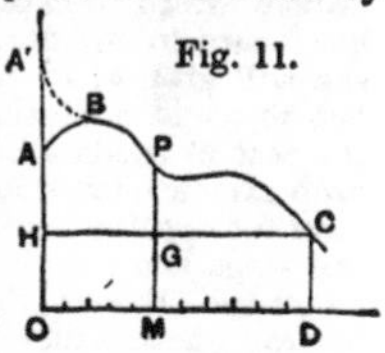

Fig. 11.

F

IV, III, 3.

This description of surplus produce is not a theory of rent.

surplus produce is *not* a theory of rent: we shall not be ready for that till a much later stage. All that can be said here, is that this surplus produce may, *under certain conditions*, become the rent which the owner of the land can exact from the tenant for its use. But, as we shall see hereafter, the full rent of a farm in an old country is made up of three elements: the first being due to the value of the soil as it was made by nature; the second to improvements made in it by man; and the third, which is often the most important of all, to the growth of a dense and rich population, and to facilities of communication by public roads, railroads, etc.

Ricardo confined his attention to the circumstances of an old country.

It is to be noted also that in an old country it is impossible to discover what was the original state of the land before it was first cultivated. The results of some of man's work are for good and evil fixed in the land, and cannot be distinguished from those of nature's work: the line of division is blurred, and must be drawn more or less arbitrarily. But for most purposes it is best to regard the first difficulties of coping with nature as pretty well conquered before we begin to reckon the farmer's cultivation. Thus the returns that we count as due to the first doses of capital and labour are generally the largest of all, and the tendency of the return to diminish shows itself at once. Having English agriculture chiefly in view, we may fairly take, as Ricardo did, this as the typical case.[1]

The elasticity of nature's return to

§ 3. Let us next inquire on what depends the *rate* of diminution or of increase of the returns to successive doses of capital and labour. We have seen that there are great variations in the share of the

---

[1] That is, we may substitute (fig. 11) the dotted line *BA′* for *BA* and regard *A′BPC* as the typical curve for the return to capital and labour applied in English agriculture. No doubt crops of wheat and some other annuals cannot be raised at all without some considerable labour. But natural grasses which sow themselves will yield a good return of rough cattle to scarcely any labour.

It has already been noticed (Book III. ch. III. § 1), the law of diminishing return bears a close analogy to the law of demand. The return which land gives to a dose of capital and labour may be regarded as the price which land offers for that dose. Land's return to capital and labour is, so to speak, her effective demand for them: her return to any dose is her demand price for that dose, and the list of returns that she will give to successive doses may thus be regarded as her demand schedule: but to avoid confusion we shall call it her "Return Schedule." Corresponding to the case of the land in the text is that of a man who may be willing to pay a larger proportionate price for a paper that would cover the whole of the walls of his room than for one that would go only half way; and then his demand schedule would at one stage show an increase and not a diminution of demand price for an increased quantity. But in the aggregate demand of many individuals these unevennesses destroy one another; so that the aggregate demand schedule of a group of people always shows the demand price as falling steadily with every increase in the amount offered. In the same way, by grouping together many pieces of land we might obtain a return schedule that would show a constant diminution for every increase of capital and labour applied. But it is more easy to ascertain, and in some ways more important to take note of, the variations of individual demand in the case of plots of land than in the case of people. And therefore our typical return schedule is not drawn out so as to show as even and uniform a diminution of return as our typical demand schedule does of demand price.

produce which man may claim as the additional result of his own
work over what unaided nature would have produced; and that
man's share is much larger with some crops and soils and methods
of cultivation than with others.   Thus broadly speaking it increases
as we pass from forest to pasture land, from pasture to arable, and
from plough land to spade land; and this is because the rate of
diminution of the return is as a rule greatest in forests, rather less
in pasture, still less in arable land, and least of all in spade land.

IV, III, 3.

capital and
labour
varies with
soil and
crops.

There is no absolute measure of the richness or fertility of land.
Even if there be no change in the arts of production, a mere increase
in the demand for produce may invert the order in which two
adjacent pieces of land rank as regards fertility.   The one which
gives the smaller produce, when both are uncultivated, or when the
cultivation of both is equally slight, may rise above the other and
justly rank as the more fertile when both are cultivated with equal
thoroughness.   In other words, many of those lands which are the
least fertile when cultivation is merely extensive, become among
the most fertile when cultivation is intensive.   For instance, self-
drained pasture land may give a return large in proportion to a very
slight expenditure of capital and labour, but a rapidly diminishing
return to further expenditure: as population increases it may
gradually become profitable to break up some of the pasture and
introduce a mixed cultivation of roots and grains and grasses; and
then the return to further doses of capital and labour may diminish
less quickly.

The
relative
fertility of
two fields
may
change
with
circum-
stances.

Other land makes poor pasture, but will give more or less liberal
returns to a great deal of capital and labour applied in tilling and
in manuring it; its returns to the early doses are not very high, but
they diminish slowly.

Again, other land is marshy.   It may, as did the fens of east
England, produce little but osiers and wild fowl.   Or, as is the case
in many tropical districts, it may be prolific of vegetation, but so
shrouded with malaria that it is difficult for man to live there, and
still more to work there.   In such cases the returns to capital and
labour are at first small, but as drainage progresses, they increase;
afterwards perhaps they again fall off.[1]

---

[1] This case may be represented by diagrams.   If the produce rises in real value
in the ratio of OH' to OH (so that the amount required to remunerate the farmer
for a dose of capital and labour has fallen from OH to OH'), the surplus produce rises
only to $AH'C'$, which is not very much greater than its old amount AHC, fig. 12,
representing the first case.   The second case is represented in fig. 13, where a similar
change in the price of produce makes the new surplus produce $AH'C'$ about three
times as large as the old surplus, AHC; and the third in fig. 14.   The earliest doses
of capital and labour applied to the land give so poor a return, that it would not be
worth while to apply them unless it were intended to carry the cultivation further.

IV, III, 3.   But when improvements of this kind have once been made, the
capital invested in the soil cannot be removed; the early history
of the cultivation is not repeated; and the produce due to further
applications of capital and labour shows a tendency to diminishing
return.[1]

Similar though less conspicuous changes may occur on land
already well cultivated. For instance, without being marshy, it
may be in need of a little drainage to take off the stagnant water
from it, and to enable fresh water and air to stream through it.
Or the subsoil may happen to be naturally richer than the soil at the
surface : or again, though not itself rich, it may have just those
properties in which the surface soil is deficient, and then a thorough
system of deep steam-ploughing may permanently change the
character of the land.

Thus we need not suppose that when the return to extra capital
and labour has begun to diminish, it will always continue to do so.
Improvements in the arts of production may, it has always been
understood, raise generally the return which can be got by any
amount of capital and labour; but this is not what is meant here.
The point is that, independently of any increase in his knowledge,
and using only those methods with which he has long been familiar,
a farmer finding extra capital and labour at his command, may

---

But later doses give an increasing return which culminates at P, and afterwards
diminishes. If the price to be got for produce is so low that an amount OH'' is
required to remunerate the cultivator for a dose of capital and labour, it will then
be only just profitable to cultivate the land. For then cultivation will be carried as
far as D''; there will be a deficit on the earlier doses represented by the area $H''AE''$,
and a surplus on the later doses represented by the area $E''PC''$: and as these two

Fig. 12.   Fig. 13.   Fig. 14.

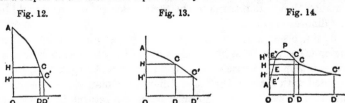

are about equal, the cultivation of the land so far will only just pay its way. But if
the price of produce rises till OH is sufficient to remunerate the cultivator for a dose
of capital and labour, the deficit on the earlier doses will sink to HAE, and the surplus
on the later doses will rise to EPC : the net surplus (the true rent in case the land is
hired out) will be the excess of EPC over HAE. Should the price rise further till
OH' is sufficient to remunerate the cultivator for a dose of capital and labour, this
net surplus will rise to the very large amount represented by the excess of $E'PC'$
over $H'AE'$.

[1] In such a case as this the earlier doses are pretty sure to be sunk in the land ;
and the actual rent paid, if the land is hired out, will then include profits on them
in addition to the surplus produce or true rent thus shown. Provision can easily be
made in the diagrams for the returns due to the landlord's capital.

sometimes obtain an increasing return even at a late stage in his IV, III, 3.
cultivation.[1]

It has been well said that as the strength of a chain is that of its
weakest link, so fertility is limited by that element in which it is
most deficient. Those who are in a hurry, will reject a chain which
has one or two very weak links, however strong the rest may be :
and prefer to it a much slighter chain that has no flaw. But if
there is heavy work to be done, and they have time to make repairs,
they will set the larger chain in order, and then its strength will
exceed that of the other. In this we find the explanation of much
that is apparently strange in agricultural history.

The first settlers in a new country generally avoid land which
does not lend itself to immediate cultivation. They are often
repelled by the very luxuriance of natural vegetation, if it happens
to be of a kind that they do not want. They do not care to plough
land that is at all heavy, however rich it might become if thoroughly
worked. They will have nothing to do with water-logged land.
They generally select light land which can easily be worked with a
double plough, and then they sow their seed broadly, so that the
plants when they grow up may have plenty of light and air, and
may collect their food from a wide area.

Early
settlers
often
rightly
avoid the
land
which an
English
farmer
would be
apt to
select.

When America was first settled, many farming operations that
are now done by horse machinery were still done by hand; and
though now the farmers have a strong preference for flat prairie
land, free from stumps and stones, where their machines can work
easily and without risk, they had then no great objection to a hill-
side. Their crops were light in proportion to their acreage, but
heavy in proportion to the capital and labour expended in raising
them.

We cannot then call one piece of land more fertile than another
until we know something about the skill and enterprise of its cultivators, and the amount of capital and labour at their disposal;
and till we know whether the demand for produce is such as to
make intensive cultivation profitable with the resources at their
disposal. If it is, those lands will be the most fertile which give the
highest average returns to a large expenditure of capital and labour;
but if not, those will be the most fertile which give the best returns
to the first few doses. The term fertility has no meaning except

Fertility
is not
absolute
but rela-
tive to
place and
time.

---

[1] Of course his return may diminish and then increase and
then diminish again; and yet again increase when he is in a
position to carry out some further extensive change, as was
represented by fig. 11. But more extreme instances, of the
kind represented by fig. 15, are not very rare.

Fig. 15.

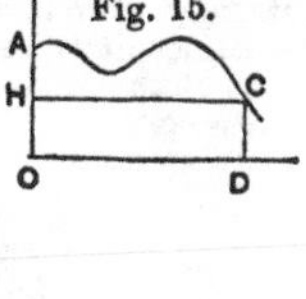

IV, III, 4. with reference to the special circumstances of a particular time and place.

But even when so limited there is some uncertainty as to the usage of the term. Sometimes attention is directed chiefly to the power which land has of giving adequate returns to intensive cultivation and so bearing a large total produce per acre; and sometimes to its power of yielding a large surplus produce or rent, even though its gross produce is not very large : thus in England now rich arable land is very fertile in the former sense, rich meadow in the latter. For many purposes it does not matter which of these senses of the term is understood : in the few cases in which it does matter, an interpretation clause must be supplied in the context.[1]

Other causes of change in the relative values of different pieces of land.

§ 4. But further, the order of fertility of different soils is liable to be changed by changes in the methods of cultivation and in the relative values of different crops. Thus when at the end of last century Mr. Coke showed how to grow wheat well on light soils by preparing the way with clover, they rose relatively to clay soils; and now though they are still sometimes called from old custom "poor," some of them have a higher value, and are really more fertile, than much of the land that used to be carefully cultivated while they were left in a state of nature.

Again, the increasing demand in central Europe for wood to be used as fuel and for building purposes, has raised the value of the pine-covered mountain slopes relatively to almost every other kind of land. But in England this rise has been prevented by the substitution of coal for wood as fuel, and of iron for wood as a material for shipbuilding, and lastly by England's special facilities for importing wood. Again, the cultivation of rice and jute often gives a very high value to lands that are too much covered with water to bear most other crops. And again, since the repeal of the Corn Laws the prices of meat and dairy produce have risen in England relatively to that of corn. Those arable soils that would grow rich forage crops in rotation with corn, rose relatively to the cold clay soils; and permanent pasture recovered part of that great fall in

[1] If the price of produce is such that an amount of it OH (figs. 12, 13, 14) is required to pay the cultivator for one dose of capital and labour, the cultivation will be carried as far as D; and the produce raised, $AODC$, will be greatest in fig. 12, next greatest in fig. 13, and least in fig. 14. But if the demand for agricultural produce so rises that OH' is enough to repay the cultivator for a dose, the cultivation will be carried as far as D', and the produce raised will be $AOD'C'$, which is greatest in fig. 14, next in fig. 13, and least in fig. 12. The contrast would have been even stronger if we had considered the surplus produce which remains after deducting what is sufficient to repay the cultivator, and which becomes under some conditions the rent of the land. For this is AHC in figs. 12 and 13 in the first case and $AH'C'$ in the second; while in fig. 14 it is in the first case the excess of $AODCPA$ over $ODCH$, i.e. the excess of PEC over AHE; and in the second case the excess of $PE'C'$ over $AH'E'$.

value relatively to arable land, which had resulted from the growth IV, III, 4.
of population.[1]

Independently of any change in the suitability of the prevailing Poorer
crops and methods of cultivation for special soils, there is a constant soils rise in relative
tendency towards equality in the value of different soils. In the value
absence of any special cause to the contrary, the growth of popula- as the pressure of
tion and wealth will make the poorer soils gain on the richer. Land population increases.
that was at one time entirely neglected is made by much labour to
raise rich crops; its annual income of light and heat and air, is
probably as good as those of richer soils : while its faults can be
much lessened by labour.[2]

As there is no absolute standard for fertility, so there is none of There is no absolute
good cultivation. The best cultivation in the richest parts of the standard
Channel Islands, for instance, involves a lavish expenditure of of good cultiva-
capital and labour on each acre : for they are near good markets tion.
and have a monopoly of an equable and early climate. If left to
nature the land would not be very fertile, for though it has many
virtues, it has two weak links (being deficient in phosphoric acid and
potash). But, partly by the aid of the abundant seaweed on its
shores, these links can be strengthened, and the chain thus becomes
exceptionally strong. Intense, or as it is ordinarily called in England " good " cultivation, will thus raise £100 worth of early potatoes

---

[1] Rogers (*Six Centuries of Work and Wages*, p. 73) calculates that rich meadow
had about the same value, estimated in grain, five or six centuries ago as it has now;
but that the value of arable land, similarly estimated, has increased about fivefold in
the same time. This is partly due to the great importance of hay at a time when
roots and other modern kinds of winter food for cattle were unknown.

[2] Thus we may compare two pieces of land represented in figs. 16 and 17, with
regard to which the law of diminishing
returns acts in a similar way, so that
their produce curves have similar
shapes, but the former has a higher
fertility than the other for all degrees
of intensity of cultivation. The value
of the land may generally be represented by its surplus produce or rent,
which is in each case represented by

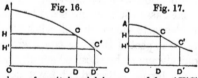

Fig. 16.   Fig. 17.

AHC when *OH* is required to repay a dose of capital and labour ; and by *AH'C'*
when the growth of numbers and wealth have made *OH'* sufficient. It is clear that
AH'C' in fig. 17 bears a more favourable comparison with *AH'C'* in fig. 16 than does
AHC in fig. 17 with *AHC* in fig. 16.   In the same way, though not to the same extent,
the total produce *AOD'C'* in fig. 17 bears a more favourable comparison with *AOD'C'*
in fig. 16, than does *AODC* in fig. 17 with *AODC* in fig. 16.   (It is ingeniously argued
in Wicksteed's *Coordinates of Laws of Distribution*, pp. 51, 2 that rent may be negative.
Of course taxes may absorb rent : but land which will not reward the plough will
grow trees or rough grass. See above, pp. 130, 1.)

Leroy Beaulieu (*Répartition des Richesses*, chap. II.) has collected several facts
illustrating this tendency of poor lands to rise in value relatively to rich. He quotes
the following figures, showing the rental in francs per hectare (2¼ acres) of five classes
of land in several communes of the Départements de l'Eure et de l'Oise in 1829 and
1852 respectively :—

	Class I.	Class II.	Class III.	Class IV.	Class V.
A.D. 1829 . . .	58	48	34	20	8
A.D. 1852 . . .	80	78	60	50	40

IV, III, 5. from a single acre. But an equal expenditure per acre by the
farmer in Western America would ruin him; relatively to his circumstances it would not be good, but bad cultivation.

Ricardo's
wording
of the law
was in-
accurate.

§ 5. Ricardo's wording of the law of diminishing return was
inexact. It is however probable that the inaccuracy was due not
to careless thinking but only to careless writing. In any case he
would have been justified in thinking that these conditions were not
of great importance in the peculiar circumstances of England at the
time at which he wrote, and for the special purposes of the particular
practical problems he had in view. Of course he could not anticipate
the great series of inventions which were about to open up new
sources of supply, and, with the aid of free trade, to revolutionize
English agriculture; but the agricultural history of England and
other countries might have led him to lay greater stress on the
probability of a change.[1]

Ricardo
said that
the richest
lands were
cultivated
first; this
is true in
the sense
in which he
meant it :

He stated that the first settlers in a new country invariably
chose the richest lands, and that as population increased, poorer
and poorer soils were gradually brought under cultivation, speaking
carelessly as though there were an absolute standard of fertility.
But as we have already seen, where land is free, everyone chooses
that which is best adapted for his own purpose, and that which will
give him, all things considered, the best return for his capital and
labour. He looks out, therefore, for land that can be cultivated at
once, and passes by land that has any weak links in the chain of its
elements of fertility, however strong it may be in some other links.
But besides having to avoid malaria, he must think of his communication with his markets and the base of his resources; and in
some cases the need for security against the attacks of enemies and
wild beasts outweighs all other considerations. It is therefore not
to be expected that the lands which were first chosen, should turn
out always to be those which ultimately come to be regarded as the
most fertile. Ricardo did not consider this point, and thus laid
himself open to attacks by Carey and others, which, though for the
greater part based on a misinterpretation of his position, have yet
some solid substance in them.

but it is
apt to be
misunder-
stood, as it

The fact that, in new countries, soils which an English farmer
would regard as poor, are sometimes cultivated before neighbouring
soils which he would regard as rich, is not inconsistent, as some

---

[1] As Roscher says (*Political Economy*, Sect. CLV.), " In judging Ricardo, it must
not be forgotten that it was not his intention to write a text-book on the science of
Political Economy, but only to communicate to those versed in it the result of his
researches in as brief a manner as possible. Hence he writes so frequently making
certain assumptions, and his words are to be extended to other cases only after due
consideration, or rather re-written to suit the changed case."

foreign writers have supposed, with the general tenor of Ricardo's doctrines. Its practical importance is in relation to the conditions under which the growth of population tends to cause increased pressure on the means of subsistence : it shifts the centre of interest from the mere amount of the farmer's produce to its exchange *value* in terms of the things which the industrial population in his neighbourhood will offer for it.[1]

IV, III, 6.
was by Carey.

§ 6. Ricardo, and the economists of his time generally were too hasty in deducing this inference from the law of diminishing return; and they did not allow enough for the increase of strength that comes from organization. But in fact every farmer is aided by the presence of neighbours whether agriculturists or townspeople.[2] Even if most of them are engaged like himself in agriculture, they gradually supply him with good roads, and other means of communication : they give him a market in which he can buy at reasonable terms what he wants, necessaries, comforts and luxuries for himself and his family, and all the various requisites for his farm work : they surround him with knowledge : medical aid, instruction and amusement are brought to his door; his mind becomes wider, and his efficiency is in many ways increased. And if the neighbouring market town expands into a large industrial centre, his gain is much greater. All his produce is worth more; some things which he used to throw away fetch a good price. He finds new openings in dairy farming and market gardening, and with a larger range of produce he makes use of rotations that keep his land always active without denuding it of any one of the elements that are necessary for its fertility.

But Carey has shown that Ricardo underrated the indirect advantages which a dense population offers to agriculture.

[1] Carey claims to have proved that " in every quarter of the world cultivation has commenced on the sides of the hills where the soil was poorest, and where the natural advantages of situation were the least. With the growth of wealth and population, men have been seen descending from the high lands bounding the valley on either side, and coming together at its feet." (*Principles of Social Science*, chap. IV. § 4.) He has even argued that whenever a thickly peopled country is laid waste, " whenever population, wealth, and the power of association decline, it is the rich soil that is abandoned by men who fly again to the poor ones " (*Ib.* ch. v. § 3); the rich soils being rendered difficult and dangerous by the rapid growth of jungles which harbour wild beasts and banditti, and perhaps by malaria. The experience of more recent settlers in South Africa and elsewhere does not however generally support his conclusions, which are indeed based largely on facts relating to warm countries. But much of the apparent attractiveness of tropical countries is delusive : they would give a very rich return to hard work : but hard work in them is impossible at present, though some change in this respect may be made by the progress of medical and especially bacteriological science. A cool refreshing breeze is as much a necessary of vigorous life as food itself. Land that offers plenty of food but whose climate destroys energy, is not more productive of the raw material of human wellbeing, than land that supplies less food but has an invigorating climate.
The late Duke of Argyll described the influence of insecurity and poverty in compelling the cultivation of the hills before that of the valleys of the Highlands was feasible, *Scotland as it is and was*, II. 74, 5.

[2] In a new country an important form of this assistance is to enable him to venture on rich land that he would have otherwise shunned, through fear of enemies or of malaria.

IV, III, 7.   Further, as we shall see later on, an increase of population tends to develop the organization of trade and industry; and therefore the law of diminishing return does not apply to the total capital and labour spent in a district as sharply as to that on a single farm. Even when cultivation has reached a stage after which each successive dose applied to a field would get a less return than the preceding dose, it may be possible for an increase in the population to cause a more than proportional increase in the means of subsistence. It is true that the evil day is only deferred: but it is deferred. The growth of population, if not checked by other causes, must ultimately be checked by the difficulty of obtaining raw produce; but in spite of the law of diminishing return, the pressure of population on the means of subsistence may be restrained for a long time to come by the opening up of new fields of supply, by the cheapening of railway and steamship communication, and by the growth of organization and knowledge.

The value of fresh air, light, water, and beautiful scenery.   Against this must be set the growing difficulty of getting fresh air and light, and in some cases fresh water, in densely peopled places. The natural beauties of a place of fashionable resort have a direct money value which cannot be overlooked; but it requires some effort to realize the true value to men, women and children of being able to stroll amid beautiful and varied scenery.

The fertility of fisheries.   § 7. As has already been said the land in economic phrase includes rivers and the sea. In river-fisheries, the extra return to additional applications of capital and labour shows a rapid diminution. As to the sea, opinions differ. Its volume is vast, and fish are very prolific; and some think that a practically unlimited supply can be drawn from the sea by man without appreciably affecting the numbers that remain there; or in other words, that the law of diminishing return scarcely applies at all to sea-fisheries: while others think that experience shows a falling-off in the productiveness of those fisheries that have been vigorously worked, especially by steam trawlers. The question is important, for the future population of the world will be appreciably affected as regards both quantity and quality, by the available supply of fish.

A mine does not give a diminishing return in the same sense as a farm does.   The produce of mines again, among which may be reckoned quarries and brickfields, is said to conform to the law of diminishing return; but this statement is misleading. It is true that we find continually increasing difficulty in obtaining a further supply of minerals, except in so far as we obtain increased power over nature's stores through improvements in the arts of mining, and through better knowledge of the contents of the earth's crust; and there is

no doubt that, other things being equal, the continued application
of capital and labour to mines will result in a diminishing rate of
yield. But this yield is not a *net* yield, like the return of which we
speak in the law of diminishing return. That return is part of a
constantly recurring income, while the produce of mines is merely a
giving up of their stored-up treasures. The produce of the field
is something other than the soil; for the field, properly cultivated,
retains its fertility. But the produce of the mine is part of the mine
itself.

To put the same thing in another way, the supply of agricultural
produce and of fish is a perennial stream; mines are as it were
nature's reservoir. The more nearly a reservoir is exhausted, the
greater is the labour of pumping from it; but if one man could pump
it out in ten days, ten men could pump it out in one day : and when
once empty, it would yield no more. So the mines that are being
opened this year might just as easily have been opened many years
ago : if the plans had been properly laid in advance, and the requisite
specialized capital and skill got ready for the work, ten years'
supply of coal might have been raised in one year without any
increased difficulty; and when a vein had once given up its treasure,
it could produce no more. This difference is illustrated by the fact
that the rent of a mine is calculated on a different principle from
that of a farm. The farmer contracts to give back the land as rich
as he found it : a mining company cannot do this; and while the
farmer's rent is reckoned by the year, mining rent consists chiefly
of " royalties " which are levied in proportion to the stores that are
taken out of nature's storehouse.[1]

On the other hand, services which land renders to man, in giving
him space and light and air in which to live and work, do conform
strictly to the law of diminishing return. It is advantageous to
apply a constantly increasing capital to land that has any special
advantages of situation, natural or acquired. Buildings tower up
towards the sky; natural light and ventilation are supplemented by
artificial means, and the steam lift reduces the disadvantages of the
highest floors; and for this expenditure there is a return of extra
convenience, but it is a diminishing return. However great the
ground rent may be, a limit is at last reached after which it is better

But building land does give a diminishing return of convenience as increased capital is spent on it.

---

[1] As Ricardo says (*Principles*, chap. II.) : " The compensation given (by the lessee)
for the mine or quarry is paid for the value of the coal or stone which can be removed
from them, and has no connection with the original or indestructible powers of the
land." But both he and others seem sometimes to lose sight of these distinctions in
discussing the law of diminishing return in its application to mines. Especially is
this the case in Ricardo's criticism of Adam Smith's theory of rent (*Principles*, chap.
XXIV.).

IV, III, 8.
———

to pay more ground rent for a larger area than to go on piling up storey on storey any further; just as the farmer finds that at last a stage is reached at which more intensive cultivation will not pay its expenses, and it is better to pay more rent for extra land, than to face the diminution in the return which he would get by applying more capital and labour to his old land.[1] From this it results that the theory of ground rents is substantially the same as that of farm rents. This and similar facts will presently enable us to simplify and extend the theory of value as given by Ricardo and Mill.

The elasticity of the notions of diminishing return and rent foreshadowed.

And what is true of building land is true of many other things. If a manufacturer has, say, three planing machines there is a certain amount of work which he can get out of them easily. If he wants to get more work from them he must laboriously economize every minute of their time during the ordinary hours, and perhaps work overtime. Thus after they are once well employed, every successive application of effort to them bring him a diminishing return. At last the net return is so small that he finds it cheaper to buy a fourth machine than to force so much work out of his old machines : just as a farmer who has already cultivated his land highly finds it cheaper to take in more land than to force more produce from his present land. Indeed there are points of view from which the income derived from machinery partakes of the nature of rent : as will be shown in Book V.

NOTE ON THE LAW OF DIMINISHING RETURN.

The elasticity of the notion of diminishing return further considered.

§ 8. The elasticity of the notion of diminishing return cannot be fully considered here; for it is but an important detail of that large general problem of the economic distribution of resources in the investment of capital, which is the pivot of the main argument of Book V and indeed of a great part of the whole Volume. But a few words about it seem now to be called for in this place, because much stress has recently been laid on it under the able and suggestive leadership of Professor Carver.[2]

If a manufacturer expends an inappropriately large amount of his resources on machinery, so that a considerable part of it is habitually idle; or on buildings, so that a considerable part of his space is not well filled; or on his office staff, so that he has to employ some of them on work that it is not worth what it costs; then his excessive expenditure in that particular direction will not be as remunerative as his previous expenditure had been : and it may be

---

[1] Of course the return to capital spent in building increases for the earlier doses. Even where land can be had for almost nothing, it is cheaper to build houses two stories high than one; and hitherto it has been thought cheapest to build factories about four stories high. But a belief is growing up in America, that where land is not very dear factories should be only two stories high, partly in order to avoid the evil effects of vibration, and of the expensive foundations and walls required to prevent it in a high building : that is, it is found that the return of accommodation diminishes perceptibly after the capital and labour required to raise two stories have been spent on the land.

[2] See also the writings of Professors Bullock and Landry.

said to yield him a " diminishing return." But this use of the phrase, though strictly correct, is apt to mislead unless used with caution. For when the tendency to a diminishing return from increased labour and capital applied to land is regarded as a special instance of the general tendency to diminishing return from any agent of production, applied in excessive proportion to the other agents, one is apt to take it for granted that the supply of the other factors can be increased. That is to say, one is apt to deny the existence of that condition—the fixedness of the whole stock of cultivable land in an old country—which was the main foundation of those great classical discussions of the law of diminishing return, which we have just been considering. Even the individual farmer may not always be able to get an additional ten or fifty acres adjoining his own farm, just when he wants them, save at a prohibitive price. And in that respect land differs from most other agents of production even from the individual point of view. This difference may indeed be regarded as of little account in regard to the individual farmer. But from the social point of view, from the point of view of the following chapters on population it is vital. Let us look into this.

In every phase of any branch of production there is some distribution of resources between various expenditures which yields a better result than any other. The abler the man in control of any business, the nearer he will approach to the ideally perfect distribution; just as the abler the primitive housewife in control of a family's stock of wool, the nearer she will approach to an ideal distribution of wool between the different needs of the family.[1]

If his business extends he will extend his uses of each requisite of production in *due* proportion; but not, as has sometimes been said, proportionately; for instance the proportion of manual work to machine work which would be appropriate in a small furniture factory would not be appropriate in a large one. If he makes the best possible apportionment of his resources, he gets the greatest (marginal) return from each appliance of production of which his business is capable. If he uses too much of any one he gets a diminishing return from it; because the others are not able to back it up properly. And this diminishing return is analogous to that which a farmer obtains, when he cultivates land so intensively that he obtains a diminishing return from it. If the farmer can get more land at the same rent as he has paid for the old, he will take more land, or else lie open to the imputation of being a bad business man : and this illustrates the fact that land from the point of view of the individual cultivator is simply one form of capital.

But when the older economists spoke of the Law of Diminishing Return they were looking at the problems of agriculture not only from the point of view of the individual cultivator but also from that of the nation as a whole. Now if the nation *as a whole* finds its stock of planing machines or ploughs inappropriately large or inappropriately small, it can redistribute its resources. It can obtain more of that in which it is deficient, while gradually lessening its stock of such things as are superabundant : *but it cannot do that in regard to land* : it can cultivate its land more intensively, but it cannot get any more. And for that reason the older economists rightly insisted that, from the social point of view, land is not on exactly the same footing as those implements of production which man can increase without limit.

A diminishing return results generally from an inappropriate apportionment of appliances for production.

But the national agriculture of a densely peopled country is dominated by the fixity of the total stock of

[1] In this he will make large use of what is called below the " Substitution " of more for less appropriate means. Discussions bearing directly on this paragraph will be found in III. v. 1—3 : IV. VII. 8; and XIII. 2 : V. III. 3; IV. 1—4; v. 6—8; VIII. 1—5; x. 3; VI. I. 7; and II. 5.

The tendencies of diminishing utility and of diminishing return have their roots, the one in qualities of human nature, the other in the technical conditions of industry. But the distributions of resources, to which they point, are governed by exactly similar laws. In mathematical phrase, the problems in *maxima* and *minima* to which they give rise are expressed by the same general equations; as may be seen by reference to Mathematical Note XIV.

IV,, III. 8.
_____
one of
the chief
appliances.

No doubt in a new country where there is an abundance of rich land not yet brought under cultivation, this fixedness of the total stock of land is not operative. American economists often speak of the value, or rent, of land as varying with the land's distance from good markets, rather than with its fertility; because even now there is a great deal of rich land in their country which is not fully cultivated. And in like manner they lay but little stress on the fact that the diminishing return to labour and capital in general applied to the land by discreet farmers, in such a country as England, is not exactly on the same footing as the diminishing return to an inappropriate investment of their resources by indiscreet farmers or manufacturers in a disproportionately large number of ploughs or planing machines.

Difficulty
of measur-
ing off a
dose of
labour and
capital,

It is true that when the tendency to diminishing return is generalized, the return is apt to be expressed in terms of value, and not of quantity. It must however be conceded that the older method of measuring return in terms of quantity often jostled against the difficulty of rightly interpreting a dose of labour and capital without the aid of a money measure : and that, though helpful for a broad preliminary survey, it cannot be carried very far.

But even the recourse to money fails us, if we want to bring to a common standard the productiveness of lands in distant times or places; and we must then fall back on rough, and more or less arbitrary modes of measurement, which make no aim at numerical precision, but will yet suffice for the broader purposes of history. We have to take account of the facts that there are great variations in the relative amounts of labour and capital in a dose : and that interest on capital is generally a much less important item in backward than in advanced stages of agriculture, in spite of the fact that the rate of interest is generally much lower in the latter. For most purposes it is probably best to take as a common standard a day's unskilled labour of given efficiency : we thus regard the dose as made up of so much labour of different kinds, and such charges for the use and replacement of capital, as will together make up the value of, say, ten days' such labour; the relative proportions of these elements and their several values in terms of such labour being fixed according to the special circumstances of each problem.[1]

and of
reducing
various
produce to
a common
unit.

A similar difficulty is found in comparing the returns obtained by labour and capital applied under different circumstances. So long as the crops are of the same kind, the quantity of one return can be measured off against that of another : but, when they are of different kinds, they cannot be compared till they are reduced to a common measure of value. When, for instance, it is said that land would give better returns to the capital and labour expended on it with one crop or rotation of crops than with another, the statement must be understood to hold only the basis of the prices at the time. In such a case we must take the whole period of rotation together, assuming the land to be in the same condition at the beginning and the end of the rotation; and counting on the one hand all the labour and capital applied during the whole period, and on the other the aggregate returns of all the crops.

Different
methods of
book-keep-
ing may
class the
same thing
as capital
or produce;
but each
must be
consistent
with itself.

It must be remembered that the return due to a dose of labour and capital is not here taken to include the value of the capital itself. For instance, if part of the capital on a farm consists of two-year-old oxen, then the returns to a year's labour and capital will include not the full weight of these oxen at the end of the year, but only the addition that has been made to it during the year. Again, when a farmer is said to work with a capital of £10 to the acre, this includes the value of everything that he has on the farm; but the total volume of the doses of labour and capital applied to a farm during, say, a year, does not include the whole value of the fixed capital, such as machinery and horses, but only the value of their use after allowing for interest, deprecia-

_____
[1] The labour-part of the dose is of course current agricultural labour; the capital-part is itself also the product of labour in past times rendered by workers of many kinds and degrees, accompanied by " waiting."

tion and repairs; though it does include the whole value of the circulating capital, such as seed.

The above is the method of measuring capital generally adopted, and it is to be taken for granted if nothing is said to the contrary; but another method is more suitable occasionally.   Sometimes it is convenient to speak as though all the capital applied were circulating capital applied at the beginning of the year or during it : and in that case everything that is on the farm at the end of the year is part of the produce.   Thus, young cattle are regarded as a sort of raw material which is worked up in the course of time into fat cattle ready for the butcher.   The farm implements may even be treated in the same way, their value at the beginning of the year being taken as so much circulating capital applied to the farm, and at the end of the year as so much produce. This plan enables us to avoid a good deal of repetition of conditioning clauses as to depreciation, etc., and to save the use of words in many ways.   It is often the best plan for general reasonings of an abstract character, particularly if they are expressed in a mathematical form.

The law of diminishing return must have occupied thoughtful men in every densely peopled country.   It was first stated clearly by Turgot (*Œuvres*, ed. Daire, I. pp. 420, 1), as Prof. Cannan has shown; and its chief applications were developed by Ricardo.

CHAPTER IV

THE GROWTH OF POPULATION

Population and production.

§ 1. THE production of wealth is but a means to the sustenance of man; to the satisfaction of his wants; and to the development of his activities, physical, mental, and moral. But man himself is the chief means of the production of that wealth of which he is the ultimate aim: [1] and this and the two following chapters will be given to some study of the supply of labour; *i.e.* of the growth of population in numbers, in strength, in knowledge, and in character.

The growth of numbers among animals is governed by present conditions; among men it is affected by traditions of the past and forecasts of the future.

In the animal and vegetable world the growth of numbers is governed by the tendency of individuals to propagate their species on the one hand, and on the other hand by the struggle for life which thins out the young before they arrive at maturity. In the human race alone the conflict of these two opposing forces is complicated by other influences. On the one hand regard for the future induces many individuals to control their natural impulses; sometimes with the purpose of worthily discharging their duties as parents; sometimes, as for instance at Rome under the Empire, for mean motives. And on the other hand society exercises pressure on the individual by religious, moral and legal sanctions, sometimes with the object of quickening, and sometimes with that of retarding, the growth of population.

The problems of population are older than civilization.

The study of the growth of population is often spoken of as though it were a modern one. But in a more or less vague form it has occupied the attention of thoughtful men in all ages of the world. To its influence, often unavowed, sometimes not even clearly recognized, we can trace a great part of the rules, customs and ceremonies that have been enjoined in the Eastern and Western world by law-givers, by moralists, and those nameless thinkers, whose far-seeing wisdom has left its impress on national habits. Among vigorous races, and in times of great military conflict, they aimed at increasing the supply of males capable of bearing arms; and in the higher stages of progress they have inculcated a great respect for the sanctity of human life; but in the lower stages, they have encouraged and even compelled the ruthless slaughter of the infirm

[1] See IV. I. 1.

and the aged, and sometimes of a certain proportion of the female IV, IV, 1, children.

In ancient Greece and Rome, with the safety-valve of the power of planting colonies, and in the presence of constant war, an increase in the number of citizens was regarded as a source of public strength; and marriage was encouraged by public opinion, and in many cases even by legislation : though thoughtful men were even then aware that action in the contrary sense might be necessary if the responsibilities of parentage should ever cease to be burdensome.[1]   In later times there may be observed, as Roscher says,[2] a regular ebb and flow of the opinion that the State should encourage the growth of numbers.   It was in full flow in England under the first two Tudors, but in the course of the sixteenth century it slackened and turned; and it began to ebb, when the abolition of the celibacy of the religious orders, and the more settled state of the country had had time to give a perceptible impetus to population; the effective demand for labour having meanwhile been diminished by the increase of sheep runs, and by the collapse of that part of the industrial system which had been organized by the monastic establishments.   Later on the growth of population was checked by that rise in the standard of comfort which took effect in the general adoption of wheat as the staple food of Englishmen during the first half of the eighteenth century.   At that time there were even fears, which later inquiries showed to be unfounded, that the population was actually diminishing.   Petty[3] had forestalled some of Carey's and Wakefield's arguments as to the advantages of a dense population.   Child had argued that " whatever tends to the depopulating of a country tends to the impoverishment of it "; and that " most nations in the civilized parts of the world are more or less rich or poor proportionably to the paucity or plenty of their people, and not to the sterility or fruitfulness of their land." [4]   And by the time that the world-struggle with France had attained its height, when the demands for

Fluctuations of opinion on State encouragement of large families.

[1] Thus Aristotle (*Politics*, II. 6) objects to Plato's scheme for equalizing property and abolishing poverty on the ground that it would be unworkable unless the State exercised a firm control over the growth of numbers.   And as Jowett points out, Plato himself was aware of this (see *Laws*, v. 740 : also Aristotle, *Politics*, VII. 16). The opinion formerly held that the population of Greece declined from the seventh century B.C., and that of Rome from the third, has recently been called in question, see " Die Bevölkerung des Altertums " by Edouard Meyer in the *Handwörterbuch der Staatswissenschaften*.

[2] *Political Economy*, § 254.

[3] He argues that Holland is richer than it appears to be relatively to France, because its people have access to many advantages that cannot be had by those who live on poorer land, and are therefore more scattered.   " Rich land is better than coarse land of the same Rent."   *Political Arithmetick*, ch. I.

[4] *Discourses on Trade*, ch. X.   Harris, Essay on *Coins*, pp. 32, 3, argues to a similar effect, and proposes to " encourage matrimony among the lower classes by giving some privileges to those who have children," etc.

IV, IV, 2. more and more troops were ever growing, and when manufacturers were wanting more men for their new machinery; the bias of the ruling classes was strongly flowing in favour of an increase of population. So far did this movement of opinion reach that in 1796 Pitt declared that a man who had enriched his country with a number of children had a claim on its assistance. An Act, passed amid the military anxieties of 1806, which granted exemptions from taxes to the fathers of more than two children born in wedlock, was repealed as soon as Napoleon had been safely lodged in St. Helena.[1]

The doctrines of recent economists. The Physiocrats.

§ 2. But during all this time there had been a growing feeling among those who thought most seriously on social problems, that an inordinate increase of numbers, whether it strengthened the State or not, must necessarily cause great misery : and that the rulers of the State had no right to subordinate individual happiness to the aggrandizement of the State. In France in particular a reaction was caused, as we have seen, by the cynical selfishness with which the Court and its adherents sacrificed the wellbeing of the people for the sake of their own luxury and military glory. If the humane sympathies of the Physiocrats had been able to overcome the frivolity and harshness of the privileged classes of France, the eighteenth century would probably not have ended in tumult and bloodshed, the march of freedom in England would not have been arrested, and the dial of progress would have been more forward than it is by the space of at least a generation. As it was, but little attention was paid to Quesnay's guarded but forcible protest :—
" one should aim less at augmenting the population than at increasing the national income, for the condition of greater comfort which is derived from a good income, is preferable to that in which a population exceeds its income and is ever in urgent need of the means of subsistence." [2]

---

[1] " Let us," said Pitt, " make relief, in cases where there are a large number of children, a matter of right and an honour, instead of a ground for opprobrium and contempt. This will make a large family a blessing and not a curse, and this will draw a proper line of distinction between those who are able to provide for themselves by labour, and those who after having enriched their country with a number of children have a claim on its assistance for their support." Of course he desired " to discourage relief where it was not wanted." Napoleon the First had offered to take under his own charge one member of any family which contained seven male children; and Louis XIV., his predecessor in the slaughter of men, had exempted from public taxes all those who married before the age of 20 or had more than ten legitimate children. A comparison of the rapid increase in the population of Germany with that of France was a chief motive of the order of the French Chamber in 1885 that education and board should be provided at the public expense for every seventh child in necessitous families : and in 1913 a law was passed giving bounties under certain conditions to parents of large families. The British Budget Bill of 1909 allowed a small abatement of income tax for fathers of families.

[2] The Physiocratic doctrine with regard to the tendency of population to increase up to the margin of subsistence may be given in Turgot's words :—the employer

Adam Smith said but little on the question of population, for IV, IV, 2.
indeed he wrote at one of the culminating points of the prosperity ——
of the English working classes; but what he does say is wise and Adam
Smith.
well balanced and modern in tone. Accepting the physiocratic
doctrine as his basis, he corrected it by insisting that the necessaries
of life are not a fixed and determined quantity, but have varied
much from place to place and time to time; and may vary
more.[1] But he did not work out this hint fully. And there was
nothing to lead him to anticipate the second great limitation
of the Physiocratic doctrine, which has been made prominent
in our time by the carriage of wheat from the centre of America to
Liverpool for less than what had been the cost of its carriage across
England.

The eighteenth century wore on to its close and the next century The
began; year by year the condition of the working classes in England eighteenth
century
became more gloomy. An astonishing series of bad harvests,[2] a ended
most exhausting war,[3] and a change in the methods of industry that and the
nineteenth
dislocated old ties, combined with an injudicious poor law to bring began in
the working classes into the greatest misery they have ever suffered, gloom.
at all events since the beginning of trustworthy records of English
social history.[4] And to crown all, well-meaning enthusiasts, chiefly
under French influence, were proposing communistic schemes which

---

" since he always has his choice of a great number of working men, will choose that
one who will work most cheaply. Thus then the workers are compelled by mutual
competition to lower their price; and with regard to every kind of labour the result is
bound to be reached—and it is reached as a matter of fact—that the wages of the
worker are limited to that which is necessary to procure his subsistence." (*Sur la
formation et la distribution des richesses*, § VI.)

Similarly Sir James Steuart says (*Inquiry*, Bk. I. ch. III.), " The generative faculty
resembles a spring loaded with a weight, which always exerts itself in proportion to
the diminution of resistance : when food has remained some time without augmenta-
tion or diminution, generation will carry numbers as high as possible; if then food
comes to be diminished the spring is overpowered; the force of it becomes less than
nothing, inhabitants will diminish at least in proportion to the overcharge. If, on
the other hand, food be increased, the spring which stood at 0, will begin to exert
itself in proportion as the resistance diminishes; people will begin to be better fed;
they will multiply, and in proportion as they increase in numbers the food will become
scarce again." Sir James Steuart was much under the influence of the Physiocrats,
and was indeed in some respects imbued with Continental rather than English notions
of government: and his artificial schemes for regulating population seem very far
off from us now. See his *Inquiry*, Bk. I. ch. XII., "*Of the great advantage of combining
a well-digested Theory and a perfect Knowledge of Facts with the Practical Part of Government in order to make a People multiply.*"

[1] See *Wealth of Nations*, Bk. I. ch. VIII. and Bk. V. ch. II. See also *supra*, Bk. II.
ch. IV.

[2] The average price of wheat in the decade 1771-1780 in which Adam Smith
wrote was 34s. 7d.; in 1781-1790 it was 37s. 1d.; in 1791-1800 it was 63s. 6d.;
in 1801-1810 it was 83s. 11d.; and in 1811-1820 it was 87s. 6d.

[3] Early in the last century the Imperial taxes—for the greater part war taxes—
amounted to one-fifth of the whole income of the country; whereas now they are not
much more than a twentieth, and even of this a great part is spent on education and
other benefits which Government did not then afford.

[4] See below § 7 and above Bk. I. ch. III. §§ 5, 6.

IV, IV, 3. would enable people to throw on society the whole responsibility for
——   rearing their children.[1]

Thus while the recruiting sergeant and the employer of labour
were calling for measures tending to increase the growth of population, more far-seeing men began to inquire whether the race could
escape degradation if the numbers continued long to increase as they

Malthus.   were then doing.   Of these inquirers the chief was Malthus, and his
Essay on the Principle of Population is the starting-point of all modern
speculations on the subject.

His
argument   § **3.** Malthus' reasoning consists of three parts, which must be
has three   kept distinct.   The first relates to the supply of labour.   By a care-
stages.   ful study of facts he proves that every people, of whose history we
The first. have a trustworthy record, has been so prolific that the growth of
its numbers would have been rapid and continuous if it had not
been checked either by a scarcity of the necessaries of life, or some
other cause, that is, by disease, by war, by infanticide, or lastly by
voluntary restraint.

The   His second position relates to the demand for labour.   Like the
second.   first it is supported by facts, but by a different set of facts.   He
shows that up to the time at which he wrote no country (as distinguished from a city, such as Rome or Venice) had been able to obtain
an abundant supply of the necessaries of life after its territory had
become very thickly peopled.   The produce which Nature returns
to the work of man is her effective demand for population : and he
shows that up to this time a rapid increase in population when
already thick had not led to a proportionate increase in this
demand.[2]

The third. Thirdly, he draws the conclusion that what had been in the past,
was likely to be in the future; and that the growth of population
would be checked by poverty or some other cause of suffering unless
it were checked by voluntary restraint.   He therefore urges people

---

[1] Especially Godwin in his *Inquiry concerning Political Justice* (1792). It is interesting to compare Malthus' criticism of this Essay (Bk. III. ch. II.) with Aristotle's
comments on Plato's *Republic* (see especially *Politics*, II. 6).

[2] But many of his critics suppose him to have stated his position much less un-
reservedly than he did; they have forgotten such passages as this :—" From a
review of the state of society in former periods compared with the present I should
certainly say that the evils resulting from the principle of population have rather
diminished than increased, even under the disadvantage of an almost total ignorance
of their real cause.   And if we can indulge the hope that this ignorance will be gradually dissipated, it does not seem unreasonable to hope that they will be still further
diminished.   The increase of absolute population, which will of course take place,
will evidently tend but little to weaken this expectation, as everything depends on
the relative proportions between population and food, and not on the absolute number
of the people.   In the former part of this work it appeared that the countries which
possessed the fewest people often suffered the most from the effects of the principle of
population." *Essay*, Bk. IV. ch. XII.

to use this restraint, and, while leading lives of moral purity, to IV, IV, 3.
abstain from very early marriages.[1]

His position with regard to the supply of population, with which
alone we are directly concerned in this chapter, remains substantially
valid. The changes which the course of events has introduced into
the doctrine of population relate chiefly to the second and third steps
of his reasoning. We have already noticed that the English economists of the earlier half of last century overrated the tendency of
an increasing population to press upon the means of subsistence;
and it was not Malthus' fault that he could not foresee the great
developments of steam transport by land and by sea, which have
enabled Englishmen of the present generation to obtain the
products of the richest lands of the earth at comparatively small
cost.

But the fact that he did not foresee these changes makes the
second and third steps of his argument antiquated in form; though
they are still in a great measure valid in substance. It remains true
that unless the checks on the growth of population in force at the
end of the nineteenth century are on the whole increased (they are

Margin note: Later events affect the validity of his second and third stages, but not of his first.

[1] In the first edition of his essay, 1798, Malthus gave his argument without any
detailed statement of facts, though from the first he regarded it as needing to be
treated in direct connection with a study of facts; as is shown by his having told
Pryme (who afterwards became the first Professor of Political Economy at Cambridge)
" that his theory was first suggested to his mind in an argumentative conversation
which he had with his father on the state of some other countries " (Pryme's *Recollec-
tions*, p. 66). American experience showed that population if unchecked would double
at least once in twenty-five years. He argued that a doubled population might,
even in a country as thickly populated as England was with its seven million inhabitants, conceivably though not probably double the subsistence raised from the English
soil : but that labour doubled again would not suffice to double the produce again.
" Let us then take this for our rule, though certainly far beyond the truth; and
allow that the whole produce of the island might be increased every twenty-five years
[that is with every doubling of the population] by a quantity of subsistence equal to
that which it at present produces "; or in other words, in an arithmetical progression.
His desire to make himself clearly understood made him, as Wagner says in his
excellent introduction to the study of Population (*Grundlegung*, Ed. 3, p. 453), " put
too sharp a point on his doctrine, and formulate it too absolutely." Thus he got into
the habit of speaking of production as capable of increasing in an arithmetical ratio :
and many writers think that he attached importance to the phrase itself : whereas
it was really only a short way of stating the utmost that he thought any reasonable
person could ask him to concede. What he meant, stated in modern language, was
that the tendency to diminishing return, which is assumed throughout his argument,
would begin to operate sharply after the produce of the island had been doubled.
Doubled labour might give doubled produce : but quadrupled labour would hardly
treble it : octupled labour would not quadruple it.

In the second edition, 1803, he based himself on so wide and careful a statement of
facts as to claim a place among the founders of historical economics; he softened
and explained away many of the " sharp points " of his old doctrine, though he did
not abandon (as was implied in earlier editions of this work) the use of the phrase
" arithmetical ratio." In particular he took a less despondent view of the future
of the human race; and dwelt on the hope that moral restraint might hold population
in check, and that " vice and misery," the old checks, might thus be kept in abeyance.
Francis Place, who was not blind to his many faults, wrote in 1822 an apology for
him, excellent in tone and judgment. Good accounts of his work are given in Bonar's
Malthus and his Work, Cannan's *Production and Distribution*, 1776–1848, and Nicholson's *Political Economy*, Bk. I. ch. XII.

IV, iv, 4.   certain to change their form in places that are as yet imperfectly civilized) it will be impossible for the habits of comfort prevailing in Western Europe to spread themselves over the whole world and maintain themselves for many hundred years. But of this more hereafter.[1]

Natural Increase.

§ 4. The growth in numbers of a people depends firstly on the *Natural Increase*, that is, the excess of their births over their deaths; and secondly on migration.

The number of births depends chiefly on habits relating to marriage, the early history of which is full of instruction; but we must confine ourselves here to the conditions of marriage in modern civilized countries.

Marriage affected by the climate,

The age of marriage varies with the climate. In warm climates where childbearing begins early, it ends early, in colder climates it begins later and ends later; [2] but in every case the longer marriages are postponed beyond the age that is natural to the country, the smaller is the birth-rate; the age of the wife being of course much more important in this respect than that of the husband.[3] Given the climate, the average age of marriage depends chiefly on the ease with which young people can establish themselves, and support a family according to the standard of comfort that prevails among their friends and acquaintances; and therefore it is different in different stations of life.

and the difficulty of supporting a family.

Middle classes marry late and unskilled labourers early.

In the middle classes a man's income seldom reaches its maximum till he is forty or fifty years old; and the expense of bringing up his children is heavy and lasts for many years. The artisan earns nearly as much at twenty-one as he ever does, unless he rises

---

[1] Taking the present population of the world at one and a half thousand millions; and assuming that its present rate of increase (about 8 per 1000 annually, see Ravenstein's paper before the British Association in 1890) will continue, we find that in less than two hundred years it will amount to six thousand millions; or at the rate of about 200 to the square mile of fairly fertile land (Ravenstein reckons 28 million square miles of fairly fertile land, and 14 millions of poor grass lands. The first estimate is thought by many to be too high : but, allowing for this, if the less fertile land be reckoned in for what it is worth, the result will be about thirty million square miles as assumed above). Meanwhile there will probably be great improvements in the arts of agriculture; and, if so, the pressure of population on the means of subsistence may be held in check for about two hundred years, but not longer.

[2] Of course the length of a generation has itself some influence on the growth of population. If it is 25 years in one place and 20 in another; and if in each place population doubles once in two generations during a thousand years, the increase will be a million-fold in the first place, but thirty million-fold in the second.

[3] Dr. Ogle (*Statistical Journal*, Vol. 53) calculates that if the average age of marriage of women in England were postponed five years, the number of children to a marriage, which is now 4·2 would fall to 3·1. Korösi, basing himself on the facts of the relatively warm climate of Buda Pest, finds 18–20 the most prolific age for women, 24–26 that for men. But he concludes that a slight postponement of weddings beyond these ages is advisable mainly on the ground that the vitality of the children of women under 20 is generally small. See *Proceedings of Congress of Hygiene and Demography*, London 1892, and *Statistical Journal*, Vol. 57.

to a responsible post, but he does not earn much before he is twenty- IV, IV, 4.
one : his children are likely to be a considerable expense to him till
about the age of fifteen; unless they are sent into a factory, where
they may pay their way at a very early age; and lastly the labourer
earns nearly full wages at eighteen, while his children begin to pay
their own expenses very early. In consequence, the average age
at marriage is highest among the middle classes : it is low among
the artisans and lower still among the unskilled labourers.[1]

Unskilled labourers, when not so poor as to suffer actual want
and not restrained by any external cause, have seldom, if ever,
shown a lower power of increase than that of doubling in thirty
years; that is, of multiplying a million-fold in six hundred years, a
billion-fold in twelve hundred : and hence it might be inferred
a priori that their increase has never gone on without restraint for
any considerable time. This inference is confirmed by the teaching
of all history. Throughout Europe during the Middle Ages, and in
some parts of it even up to the present time, unmarried labourers
have usually slept in the farmhouse or with their parents; while a
married pair have generally required a house for themselves : when
a village has as many hands as it can well employ, the number of
houses is not increased, and young people have to wait as best they
can.

There are many parts of Europe even now in which custom exer- Hindrances
cising the force of law prevents more than one son in each family to early marriage
from marrying; he is generally the eldest, but in some places the in station.

---

[1] The term marriage in the text must be taken in a wide sense so as to include
not only legal marriages, but all those informal unions which are sufficiently permanent in character to involve for several years at least the practical responsibilities of
married life. They are often contracted at an early age, and not unfrequently lead
up to legal marriages after the lapse of some years. For this reason the average age
at marriage in the broad sense of the term, with which alone we are here concerned,
is below the average age at legal marriage. The allowance to be made on this head for
the whole of the working classes is probably considerable; but it is very much greater
in the case of unskilled labourers than of any other class. The following statistics
must be interpreted in the light of this remark, and of the fact that all English industrial statistics are vitiated by the want of sufficient care in the classification of the
working classes in our official returns. The Registrar-General's forty-ninth Annual
Report states that in certain selected districts the returns of marriages for 1884–5
were examined with the following results; the number after each occupation being
the average age of bachelors in it at marriage, and the following number, in brackets,
being the average age of spinsters who married men of that occupation :—Miners
24·06 (22·46); Textile hands 24·38 (23·43); Shoemakers, Tailors 24·92 (24·31); Artisans
25·35 (23·70); Labourers 25·56 (23·66); Commercial Clerks 26·25 (24·43); Shopkeepers,
Shopmen 26·67 (24·22); Farmers and sons 29·23 (26·91); Professional and Independent Class 31·22 (26·40).

Dr. Ogle, in the paper already referred to, shows that the marriage-rate is greatest
generally in those parts of England in which the percentage of those women between
15 and 25 years of age who are industrially occupied is the greatest. This is no doubt
due, as he suggests, partly to the willingness of men to have their money incomes
supplemented by those of their wives; but it may be partly due also to an excess of
women of a marriageable age in those districts.

youngest : if any other son marries he must leave the village. When great material prosperity and the absence of all extreme poverty are found in old-fashioned corners of the Old World, the explanation generally lies in some such custom as this with all its evils and hardships.[1] It is true that the severity of this custom may be tempered by the power of migration; but in the Middle Ages the free movement of the people was hindered by stern regulations. The free towns indeed often encouraged immigration from the country : but the rules of the gilds were in some respects almost as cruel to people who tried to escape from their old homes as were those enforced by the feudal lords themselves.[2]

The
birth-rate
is often
low among
peasant
proprie-
tors,
§ 5. In this respect the position of the hired agricultural labourer has changed very much. The towns are now always open to him and his children; and if he betakes himself to the New World he is likely to succeed better than any other class of emigrants. But on the other hand the gradual rise in the value of land and its growing scarcity is tending to check the increase of population in some districts in which the system of peasant properties prevails, in which there is not much enterprise for opening out new trades or for emigration, and parents feel that the social position of their children will depend on the amount of their land. They incline to limit artificially the size of their families and to treat marriage very much as a business contract, seeking always to marry their sons to heiresses. Francis Galton pointed out that, though the families of English peers are generally large, the habits of marrying the eldest son to an heiress who is presumably not of a fertile stock, and sometimes dissuading younger sons from marriage, have led to the extinction of many peerages. Similar habits among French peasants, combined with their preference for small families, keep their numbers almost stationary.

On the other hand there seem to be no conditions more favourable to the rapid growth of numbers than those of the agricultural districts of new countries. Land is to be had in abundance, railways and steamships carry away the produce of the land and bring back in exchange implements of advanced types, and many of the comforts and luxuries of life. The " farmer," as the peasant pro-

---

[1] Thus a visit to the valley Jachenau in the Bavarian Alps about 1880 found this custom still in full force. Aided by a great recent rise in the value of their woods, with regard to which they had pursued a farseeing policy, the inhabitants lived prosperously in large houses, the younger brothers and sisters acting as servants in their old homes or elsewhere. They were of a different race from the workpeople in the neighbouring valleys, who lived poor and hard lives, but seemed to think that the Jachenau purchased its material prosperity at too great a cost.

[2] See e.g. Rogers, Six Centuries, pp. 106, 7.

prietor is called in America, finds therefore that a large family is not IV, IV, 5.
a burden, but an assistance to him. He and they live healthy out-
of-door lives; there is nothing to check but everything to stimulate
the growth of numbers. The natural increase is aided by immigration; and thus, in spite of the fact that some classes of the inhabitants of large cities in America are, it is said, reluctant to have many
children, the population has increased sixteen-fold in the last hundred
years.[1]

On the whole it seems proved that the birth-rate is generally General
lower among the well-to-do than among those who make little conclusion

[1] The extreme prudence of peasant proprietors under stationary conditions was
noticed by Malthus; see his account of Switzerland (*Essay*, Bk. II. ch. v). Adam
Smith remarked that poor Highland women frequently had twenty children of whom
not more than two reached maturity (*Wealth of Nations*, Bk. I. ch. VIII.); and the
notion that want stimulated fertility was insisted on by Doubleday, *True Law of
Population*. See also Sadler, *Law of Population*. Herbert Spencer seemed to think
it probable that the progress of civilization will of itself hold the growth of population
completely in check. But Malthus' remark, that the reproductive power is less in
barbarous than in civilized races, has been extended by Darwin to the animal and
vegetable kingdom generally.

Mr. Charles Booth (*Statistical Journal*, 1893) has divided London into 27 districts
(chiefly Registration districts); and arranged them in order of poverty, of over-crowd-
ing, of high birth-rate and of high death-rate. He finds that the four orders are
generally the same. The excess of birth-rate over death-rate is lowest in the very
rich and the very poor districts.

The birth-rate in England and Wales is nominally diminishing at about an equal
rate in both town and country. But the continuous migration of young persons from
rural to industrial areas has considerably depleted the ranks of young married women
in the rural districts; and, when allowance is made for this fact, we find that the percentage of births to women of childbearing ages is much higher in them than in the
towns : as is shown in the following table published by the Registrar-General in 1907.

Mean Annual Birth-rates in Urban and Rural Areas.

Period.	Urban (20 large towns, with an aggregate population of 9,742,404 persons at the date of the Census of 1901).			
	Calculated on the total population.		Calculated on the female population, aged 15–45 years.	
	Rate per 1000.	Compared with rate in 1870–72 taken as 100.	Rate per 1000.	Compared with rate in 1870–72 taken as 100.
1870–72 .	36·7	100·0	143·1	100·0
1880–82 .	35·7	97·3	140·6	98·3
1890–92 .	32·0	87·2	124·6	87·1
1900–1902	29·8	81·2	111·4	77·8

Rural
(112 entirely rural registration districts, with an aggregate population
of 1,330,319 persons at the date of the Census of 1901).

Period.	Rate per 1000.	Compared	Rate per 1000.	Compared
1870–72 .	31·6	100·0	158·9	100·0
1880–82 .	30·3	95·9	153·5	96·6
1890–92 .	27·8	88·0	135·6	85·3
1900–1902	26·0	82·3	120·7	76·0

IV, IV, 6.
———

expensive provision for the future of themselves and their families, and who live an active life : and that fecundity is diminished by luxurious habits of living. Probably it is also diminished by severe mental strain; that is to say, given the natural strength of the parents, their expectation of a large family is diminished by a great increase of mental strain. Of course those who do high mental work, have as a class more than the average of constitutional and nervous strength; and Galton has shown that they are not as a class unprolific. But they commonly marry late.

Population in England.

§ 6. The growth of population in England has a more clearly defined history than that in the United Kingdom, and we shall find some interest in noticing its chief movements.

The Middle Ages.

The restraints on the increase of numbers during the Middle Ages were the same in England as elsewhere. In England as elsewhere the religious orders were a refuge to those for whom no establishment in marriage could be provided; and religious celibacy, while undoubtedly acting in some measure as an independent check on the growth of population, is in the main to be regarded rather as a method in which the broad natural forces tending to restrain population expressed themselves, than as an addition to them. Infectious and contagious diseases, both endemic and epidemic, were caused by dirty habits of life which were even worse in England than in the South of Europe; and famines by the failures of good harvests and the difficulties of communication; though this evil was less in England than elsewhere.

Country life was, as elsewhere, rigid in its habits; young people

---

The movements of the population of France have been studied with exceptional care : and the great work on the subject by Levasseur, *La Population Française*, is a mine of valuable information as regard other nations besides France. Montesquieu, reasoning perhaps rather *a priori*, accused the law of primogeniture which ruled in his time in France of reducing the number of children in a family : and le Play brought the same charge against the law of compulsory division. Levasseur (*l.c.* Vol. III. pp. 171–7) calls attention to the contrast; and remarks that Malthus' expectations of the effect of the Civil Code on population were in harmony with Montesquieu's rather than le Play's diagnosis. But in fact the birth-rate varies much from one part of France to another. It is generally lower where a large part of the population owns land than where it does not. If however the Departments of France be arranged in groups in ascending order of the property left at death (*valeurs successorales par tête d'habitant*), the corresponding birth-rate descends almost uniformly, being 23 per hundred married women between 15 and 50 years for the ten Departments in which the property left is 48–57 fr.; and 13·2 for the Seine, where it is 412 fr. And in Paris itself the arrondissements inhabited by the well-to-do show a smaller percentage of families with more than two children than the poorer arrondissements show. There is much interest in the careful analysis which Levasseur gives of the connection between economic conditions and birth-rate; his general conclusion being that it is not direct but indirect, through the mutual influence of the two on manners and the habit of life (*mœurs*). He appears to hold that, however much the decline in the numbers of the French relatively to surrounding nations may be regretted from the political and military points of view, there is much good mixed with the evil in its influences on material comfort and even social progress.

found it difficult to establish themselves until some other married IV, IV, 6.
pair had passed from the scene and made a vacancy in their own
parish; for migration to another parish was seldom thought of by
an agricultural labourer under ordinary circumstances. Consequently whenever plague or war or famine thinned the population,
there were always many waiting to be married, who filled the vacant
places; and, being perhaps younger and stronger than the average
of newly married couples, had larger families.[1]

There was however some movement even of agricultural labourers
towards districts which had been struck more heavily than their
neighbours by pestilence, by famine or the sword. Moreover
artisans were often more or less on the move, and this was especially
the case with those who were engaged in the building trades, and
those who worked in metal and wood; though no doubt the " wander
years " were chiefly those of youth, and after these were over the
wanderer was likely to settle down in the place in which he was
born. Again, there seems to have been a good deal of migration on
the part of the retainers of the landed gentry, especially of the
greater barons who had seats in several parts of the country. And
lastly, in spite of the selfish exclusiveness which the gilds developed
as years went on, the towns offered in England as elsewhere a
refuge to many who could get no good openings for work and for
marriage in their own homes. In these various ways some elasticity
was introduced into the rigid system of mediæval economy; and
population was able to avail itself in some measure of the increased
demand for labour which came gradually with the growth of knowledge, the establishment of law and order, and the development of
oceanic trade.[2]

In the latter half of the seventeenth and the first half of the Settlement
eighteenth century the central government exerted itself to hinder laws.

---

[1] Thus we are told that after the Black Death of 1349 most marriages were very
fertile (Rogers, *History of Agriculture and Prices*, Vol. I. p. 301).
[2] There is no certain knowledge to be had as to the density of population in England before the eighteenth century; but the following estimates, reproduced from
Steffen (*Geschichte der englischen Lohn-arbeiter*, I. pp. 463 ff.), are probably the best
as yet available. *Domesday Book* suggests that in 1086 the population of England
was between two and two-and-a-half millions. Just before the Black Death (1348)
it may have been between three-and-a-half and four-and-a-half millions; and just
afterwards two-and-a-half millions. It began to recover quickly; but made slow
progress between 1400 and 1550: it increased rather fast in the next hundred years,
and reached five-and-a-half millions in 1700.
If we are to trust Harrison (*Description of England*, Bk. II. ch. XVI.), the muster
of men able for service in 1574 amounted to 1,172,674.
The Black Death was England's only very great calamity. She was not, like the
rest of Europe, liable to devastating wars, such as the Thirty Years' War, which
destroyed more than half the population of Germany, a loss which it required a full
century to recover. (See Rümelin's instructive article on *Bevölkerungslehre* in
Schönberg's *Handbuch*.)

IV, IV, 6.
—

Slow growth of population and rise in the standard of living in the first half of the eighteenth century;

the adjustment of the supply of population in different parts of the country to the demand for it by Settlement laws, which made any one chargeable to a parish who had resided there forty days, but ordered that he might be sent home by force at any time within that period.[1] Landlords and farmers were so eager to prevent people from getting a " settlement " in their parish that they put great difficulties in the way of building cottages, and sometimes even razed them to the ground. In consequence the agricultural population of England was stationary during the hundred years ending with 1760; while the manufactures were not yet sufficiently developed to absorb large numbers. This retardation in the growth of numbers was partly caused by, and partly a cause of, a rise in the standard of living; a chief element of which was an increased use of wheat in the place of inferior grains as the food of the common people.[2]

changes in the second half.

From 1760 onwards those who could not establish themselves at home found little difficulty in getting employment in the new manufacturing or mining districts, where the demand for workers often kept the local authorities from enforcing the removal clauses of the Settlement Act. To these districts young people resorted freely, and the birth-rate in them became exceptionally high; but so did the death-rate also; the net result being a fairly rapid growth of population. At the end of the century, when Malthus wrote, the Poor Law again began to influence the age of marriage; but this time in the direction of making it unduly early. The sufferings of the working classes caused by a series of famines and by the French War made some measure of relief necessary; and the need of large bodies of recruits for the army and navy was an additional inducement to tender-hearted people to be somewhat liberal in their allowances to a large family, with the practical effect of making the father of many children often able to procure more indulgences for himself without working than he could have got by hard work if he had

---

[1] Adam Smith is justly indignant at this. (See *Wealth of Nations*, Bk. I. ch. X. Part II. and Book, IV. ch. II.) The Act recites (14 Charles II. c. 12, A.D. 1662) that " by reason of some defects in the law, poor people are not restrained from going from one parish to another, and thereby do endeavour to settle themselves in those parishes where there is the best stock, the largest wastes or commons to build cottages, and the most woods for them to burn and destroy : etc." and it is therefore ordered " that upon complaint made . . . within forty days after any such person or persons coming, so as to settle as aforesaid, in any tenement under the yearly value of ten pounds . . . it shall be lawful for any two justices of the Peace . . . to remove and convey such person or persons to such parish where he or they were last legally settled." Several Acts purporting to soften its harshness had been passed before Adam Smith's time; but they had been ineffective. In 1795 however it was ordered that no one should be removed until he became actually chargeable.

[2] Some interesting remarks on this subject are made by Eden, *History of the Poor*, I. pp. 560–4.

been unmarried or had only a small family. Those who availed IV, IV, 7.
themselves most of this bounty were naturally the laziest and
meanest of the people, those with least self-respect and enterprise.
So although there was in the manufacturing towns a fearful mortality, particularly of infants, the quantity of the people increased
fast; but its quality improved little, if at all, till the passing of the
New Poor Law in 1834. Since that time the rapid growth of the Since the
town population has, as we shall see in the next chapter, tended to reform of
increase mortality, but this has been counteracted by the growth of laws the
temperance, of medical knowledge, of sanitation and of general growth of
cleanliness. Emigration has increased, the age of marriage has has been
been slightly raised and a somewhat less proportion of the whole steady.
population are married; but, on the other hand, the ratio of births
to a marriage has risen; [1] with the result that population has been
growing very nearly steadily.[2] Let us examine the course of recent
changes a little more closely.

§ 7. Early in this century, when wages were low and wheat was In the
dear, the working classes generally spent more than half their income earlier part
on bread : and consequently a rise in the price of wheat diminished century
marriages very much among them : that is, it diminished very much the
marriage-

---

[1] But this increase in the figures shown is partly due to improved registration of
births. (Farr, *Vital Statistics*, p. 97.)

[2] The following tables show the growth of the population of England and Wales
from the beginning of the eighteenth century. The figures before 1801 are computed
from the registers of births and deaths, and the poll and hearth tax returns : those
since 1801 from Census returns. It will be noticed that the numbers increased nearly
as much in the twenty years following 1760 as in the preceding sixty years. The
pressure of the great war and the high price of corn is shown in the slow growth between 1790 and 1801; and the effects of indiscriminate poor law allowances, in spite
of greater pressure, is shown by the rapid increase in the next ten years, and the still
greater increase when that pressure was removed in the decade ending 1821. The
third column shows the percentage which the increase during the preceding decade
was of the population at the beginning of that decade.

Year.	Population (000's omitted).	Increase per cent.	Year.	Population (000's omitted).	Increase per cent.
1700	5,475	—	1801	8,892	2·5
1710	5,240	−4·9 *	1811	10,164	14·3
1720	5,565	6·2	1821	12,000	18·1
1730	5,796	4·1	1831	13,897	15·8
1740	6,064	4·6	1841	15,909	14·5
1750	6,467	6·6	1851	17,928	12·7
1760	6,736	4·1	1861	20,066	11·9
1770	7,428	10·3	1871	22,712	13·2
1780	7,953	7·1	1881	25,974	14·4
1790	8,675	9·1	1891	29,002	11·7
			1901	32,527	11·7

* Decrease; but these early figures are untrustworthy.

The great growth of emigration during recent years makes it important to correct
the figures for the last three decades so as to show the " natural increase," viz. that
due to the excess of births over deaths. The net emigration from the United Kingdom
during the decades 1871–81 and 1881–91 was 1,480,000, and 1,747,000 respectively.

IV, IV, 7.

rate varied
with the
goodness
of the
harvest.
Later
on the
influence
of com-
mercial
fluctua-
tions pre-
dominated.

the number of marriages by banns. But it raised the income of many members of the well-to-do classes, and therefore often increased the number of marriages by licence.[1] Since however these were but a small part of the whole, the net effect was to lower the marriage-rate.[2] But as time went on, the price of wheat fell and wages rose, till now the working classes spend on the average less than a quarter of their incomes on bread; and in consequence the variations of commercial prosperity have got to exercise a preponderating influence on the marriage-rate.[3]

Since 1873 though the average real income of the population of England has indeed been increasing, its rate of increase has been less than in the preceding years, and meanwhile there has been a continuous fall of prices, and consequently a continuous fall in the money incomes of many classes of society. Now people are governed in their calculations as to whether they can afford to marry or not, more by the money income which they expect to be able to get, than by elaborate calculations of changes in its purchasing power. And therefore the standard of living among the working classes has been rising rapidly, perhaps more rapidly than at any other time in English history: their household expenditure measured in money has remained about stationary, and measured in goods has increased very fast. Meanwhile the price of wheat has also fallen very much, and a marked fall in the marriage-rate for the whole country has often accompanied a marked fall in the price of wheat. The marriage-rate is now reckoned on the basis that each marriage involves two persons and should therefore count for two. The

[1] See Farr's 17th Annual Report for 1854 as Registrar-General, or the abstract of it in *Vital Statistics* (pp. 72–5).

[2] For instance, representing the price of wheat in shillings and the number of marriages in England and Wales in thousands, we have for 1801 wheat at 119 and marriages at 67, for 1803 wheat at 59 and marriages at 94; for 1805 the numbers are 90 and 80, for 1807 they are 75 and 84, for 1812 they are 126 and 82, for 1815 they are 66 and 100, for 1817 they are 97 and 88, for 1822 they are 45 and 99.

[3] Since 1820 the average price of wheat has seldom exceeded 60s. and never 75s.: and the successive inflations of commerce which culminated and broke in 1826, 1836–9, 1848, 1856, 1866 and 1873 exercised an influence on the marriage-rate about equal with changes in the price of corn. When the two causes act together the effects are very striking: thus between 1829 and 1834, there was a recovery of prosperity accompanied by a steady fall in the price of wheat and marriages rose from a hundred and four to a hundred and twenty-one thousand. The marriage-rate rose again rapidly between 1842 and 1845 when the price of wheat was a little lower than in the preceding years, and the business of the country was reviving; and again under similar circumstances between 1847 and 1853 and between 1862 and 1865.

A comparison of the marriage-rate with the harvests in Sweden for the years 1749 to 1883 is given by Sir Rawson Rawson in the *Statistical Journal* for December 1885. The harvest does not declare itself till part of the year's tale of marriages is made up; and further the inequalities of harvests are to some extent compensated for by the storage of grain; and therefore the individual harvest figures do not correspond closely with the marriage-rate. But when several good or bad harvests come together, the effect in increasing or diminishing the marriage-rate is very clearly marked.

English rate fell from 17·6 per thousand in 1873 to 14·2 in IV, IV, 7.
1886. It rose to 16·5 in 1899; in 1907 it was 15·8, but in 1908 ——
only 14·9.[1]

There is much to be learnt from the history of population in Scotland.
Scotland and in Ireland. In the lowlands of Scotland a high standard of education, the development of mineral resources, and close
contact with their richer English neighbours have combined to afford
a great increase of average income to a rapidly increasing population.
On the other hand, the inordinate growth of population in Ireland Ireland.
before the potato-famine in 1847, and its steady diminution since
that time, will remain for ever landmarks in economic history.

Comparing the habits of different nations [2] we find that in the Inter-
Teutonic countries of Central and Northern Europe, the age of national
marriage is kept late, partly in consequence of the early years of statistics
manhood being spent in the army; but that it has been very early
in Russia; where, at all events under the old régime, the family
group insisted on the son's bringing a wife to help in the work of
the household as early as possible, even if he had to leave her for
a time and go to earn his living elsewhere. In the United Kingdom
and America there is no compulsory service, and men marry early.
In France, contrary to general opinion, early marriages on the part
of men are not rare; while on the part of women they are more
common than in any country for which we have statistics, except
the Slavonic countries, where they are much the highest.

The marriage-rate, the birth-rate and the death-rate are diminishing in almost every country. But the general mortality is high
where the birth-rate is high. For instance, both are high in Slavonic
countries, and both are low in the North of Europe. The death-
rates are low in Australasia, and the " natural " increase there is
fairly high, though the birth-rate is low and falling very fast. In

---

[1] Statistics of exports are among the most convenient indications of the fluctuations of commercial credit and industrial activity : and in the article already quoted,
Ogle has shown a correspondence between the marriage-rate and the exports per head.
Compare diagrams in Vol. II. p. 12 of Levasseur's *La Population Française*; and with
regard to Massachusetts by Willcox in the *Political Science Quarterly*, Vol. VIII. pp.
76–82. Ogle's inquiries have been extended and corrected in a paper read by R. H.
Hooker before the Manchester Statistical Society, in January 1898; who points out
that if the marriage-rate fluctuates, the birth-rate during an ascending phase of the
marriage-rate is apt to correspond to the marriage-rate not for that phase, but for
the preceding phase when the marriage-rate was declining : and *vice versa*. " Hence
the ratio of births to marriages declines when the marriage-rate is rising and rises
when the marriage-rate falls. A curve representing the ratio of births to marriages
will move inversely to the marriage-rate." He points out that the decline in the ratio of
births to marriages is not great, and is accounted for by the rapid decline of illegitimate
births. The ratio of legitimate births to marriages is not declining perceptibly.
[2] The following statements are based chiefly on statistics arranged by the late
Signor Bodio, by M. Levasseur, *La Population Française*, and by the English Registrar-
General in his Report for 1907.

IV, IV, 7. fact its fall in the various States ranged from 23 to 30 per cent. in the period 1881–1901.[1]

[1] Much instructive and suggestive matter connected with the subject of this chapter is contained in the *Statistical Memoranda and Charts relating to Public Health and Social Conditions* published by the Local Government Board in 1909 [Cd. 4671].

CHAPTER V

THE HEALTH AND STRENGTH OF THE POPULATION

§ 1. WE have next to consider the conditions on which depend
health and strength, physical, mental and moral. They are the
basis of industrial efficiency, on which the production of material
wealth depends; while conversely the chief importance of material
wealth lies in the fact that, when wisely used, it increases the health
and strength, physical, mental and moral of the human race.

In many occupations industrial efficiency requires little else
than physical vigour; that is, muscular strength, a good constitution and energetic habits. In estimating muscular, or indeed any
other kind of strength for industrial purposes, we must take account
of the number of hours in the day, of the number of days in the year,
and the number of years in the lifetime, during which it can be
exerted. But with this precaution we can measure a man's muscular
exertion by the number of feet through which his work would raise
a pound weight, if it were applied directly to this use; or in other
words by the number of " foot pounds " of work that he does.[1]

Although the power of sustaining great muscular exertion seems
to rest on constitutional strength and other physical conditions, yet
even it depends also on force of will, and strength of character.
Energy of this kind, which may perhaps be taken to be the strength

---

[1] This measure can be applied directly to most kinds of navvies' and porters'
work, and indirectly to many kinds of agricultural work. In a controversy that was
waged after the great agricultural lock-out as to the relative efficiency of unskilled
labour in the South and North of England, the most trustworthy measure was found
in the number of tons of material that a man would load into a cart in a day. Other
measures have been found in the number of acres reaped or mown, or the number of
bushels of corn reaped, etc. : but these are unsatisfactory, particularly for comparing
different conditions of agriculture : since the implements used, the nature of the crop
and the mode of doing the work all vary widely. Thus nearly all comparisons between
mediæval and modern work and wages based on the wages of reaping, mowing, etc.
are valueless until we have found means to allow for the effects of changes in the
methods of agriculture. It costs for instance less labour than it did to reap by hand
a crop that yields a hundred bushels of corn ; because the implements used are better
than they were : but it may not cost less labour to reap an acre of corn ; because
the crops are heavier than they were.

In backward countries, particularly where there is not much use of horses or other
draught animals, a great part of men's and women's work may be measured fairly
well by the muscular exertion involved in it. But in England less than one-sixth of
the industrial classes are now engaged on work of this kind ; while the force exerted
by steam-engines alone is more than twenty times as much as could be exerted by
the muscles of all Englishmen.

G

of the man, as distinguished from that of his body, is moral rather than physical; but yet it depends on the physical condition of nervous strength. This strength of the man himself, this resolution, energy and self-mastery, or in short this " vigour " is the source of all progress : it shows itself in great deeds, in great thoughts and in the capacity for true religious feeling.[1]

Vigour works itself out in so many forms, that no simple measure of it is possible. But we are all of us constantly estimating vigour, and thinking of one person as having more " backbone," more " stuff in him," or as being " a stronger man " than another. Business men even in different trades, and University men even when engaged in different studies, get to estimate one another's strength very closely. It soon becomes known if less strength is required to get a " first class " in one study than another.

The influence of climate and race.
§ 2. In discussing the growth of numbers a little has been said incidentally of the causes which determine length of life : but they are in the main the same as those which determine constitutional strength and vigour, and they will occupy our attention again in the present chapter.

The first of these causes is the climate. In warm countries we find early marriages and high birth-rates, and in consequence a low respect for human life : this has probably been the cause of a great part of the high mortality that is generally attributed to the insalubrity of the climate.[2]

---

[1] This must be distinguished from nervousness, which, as a rule, indicates a general deficiency of nervous strength ; though sometimes it proceeds from nervous irritability or want of balance. A man who has great nervous strength in some directions may have but little in others; the artistic temperament in particular often develops one set of nerves at the expense of others : but it is the weakness of some of the nerves, not the strength of the others, that leads to nervousness. The most perfect artistic natures seem not to have been nervous : Leonardo da Vinci and Shakespeare for example. The term " nervous strength " corresponds in some measure to *Heart* in Engel's great division of the elements of efficiency into (a) Body, (b) Reason, and (c) Heart (*Leib, Verstand und Herz*). He classifies activities according to the permutations a, ab, ac, abc, acb ; b, ba, bc, bca, bac ; c, ca, cb, cab, cba ; the order in each case being that of relative importance, and a letter being omitted where the corresponding element plays only a very small part.

In the war of 1870 Berlin University students, who seemed to be weaker than the average soldier, were found to be able to bear fatigue better.

[2] A warm climate impairs vigour. It is not altogether hostile to high intellectual and artistic work : but it prevents people from being able to endure very hard exertion of any kind for a long time. More sustained hard work can be done in the cooler half of the temperate zone than anywhere else ; and most of all in places such as England and her counterpart New Zealand, where sea-breezes keep the temperature nearly uniform. The summer heats and winter colds of many parts of Europe and America, where the mean temperature is moderate, have the effect of shortening the year for working purposes by about two months. Extreme and sustained cold is found to dull the energies, partly perhaps because it causes people to spend much of their time in close and confined quarters : inhabitants of the Arctic regions are generally incapable of long-continued severe exertion. In England popular opinion has insisted that a " warm Yule-tide makes a fat churchyard "; but statistics prove beyond question that it has the opposite effect : the average mortality is highest in the coldest quarter of the year, and higher in cold winters than in warm.

Vigour depends partly on race qualities : but these, so far as they can be explained at all, seem to be chiefly due to climate.[1]

§ 3. Climate has also a large share in determining the necessaries of life; the first of which is food. Much depends on the proper preparation of food; and a skilled housewife with ten shillings a week to spend on food will often do more for the health and strength of her family than an unskilled one with twenty. The great mortality of infants among the poor is largely due to the want of care and judgment in preparing their food; and those who do not entirely succumb to this want of motherly care often grow up with enfeebled constitutions.

In all ages of the world except the present, want of food has caused wholesale destruction of the people. Even in London in the seventeenth and eighteenth centuries the mortality was 8 per cent. greater in years of dear corn than in years of cheap corn.[2] But gradually the effects of increased wealth and improved means of communication are making themselves felt nearly all over the world; the severity of famines is mitigated even in such a country as India; and they are unknown in Europe and in the New World. In England now want of food is scarcely ever the direct cause of death : but it is a frequent cause of that general weakening of the system which renders it unable to resist disease; and it is a chief cause of industrial inefficiency.

We have already seen that the necessaries for efficiency vary with the nature of the work to be done, but we must now examine this subject a little more closely.

As regards muscular work in particular there is a close connection between the supply of food that a man has, and his available strength. If the work is intermittent, as that of some dock labourers, a cheap but nutritious grain diet is sufficient. But for very heavy continuous strain such as is involved in puddlers' and the hardest navvies' work, food is required which can be digested and assimilated even when the body is tired. This quality is still more essential in the food of the higher grades of labour, whose work involves great nervous strain; though the quantity required by them is generally small.

[1] Race history is a fascinating but disappointing study for the economist : for conquering races generally incorporated the women of the conquered; they often carried with them many slaves of both sexes during their migrations, and slaves were less likely than freemen to be killed in battle or to adopt a monastic life. In consequence nearly every race had much servile, that is mixed blood in it : and as the share of servile blood was largest in the industrial classes, a race history of industrial habits seems impossible.

[2] This was proved by Farr, who eliminated disturbing causes by an instructive statistical device (*Vital Statistics*, p. 139).

IV, v, 4.
———
Clothing,
houseroom
and firing.

After food, the next necessaries of life and labour are clothing, house-room and firing. When they are deficient, the mind becomes torpid, and ultimately the physical constitution is undermined. When clothing is very scanty, it is generally worn night and day; and the skin is allowed to be enclosed in a crust of dirt. A deficiency of house-room, or of fuel, causes people to live in a vitiated atmosphere which is injurious to health and vigour; and not the least of the benefits which English people derive from the cheapness of coal, is the habit, peculiar to them, of having well-ventilated rooms even in cold weather. Badly-built houses with imperfect drainage cause diseases which even in their slighter forms weaken vitality in a wonderful way; and overcrowding leads to moral evils which diminish the numbers and lower the character of the people.

Rest.

Rest is as essential for the growth of a vigorous population as the more material necessaries of food, clothing, etc. Overwork of every form lowers vitality; while anxiety, worry, and excessive mental strain have a fatal influence in undermining the constitution, in impairing fecundity and diminishing the vigour of the race.

Hope-
fulness,
freedom
and
change.

§ 4. Next comes three closely allied conditions of vigour, namely, hopefulness, freedom, and change. All history is full of the record of inefficiency caused in varying degrees by slavery, serfdom, and other forms of civil and political oppression and repression.[1]

In all ages colonies have been apt to outstrip their mother countries in vigour and energy. This has been due partly to the abundance of land and the cheapness of necessaries at their command; partly to that natural selection of the strongest characters for a life of adventure, and partly to physiological causes connected with the mixture of races: but perhaps the most important cause of all is to be found in the hope, the freedom and the changefulness of their lives.[2]

[1] Freedom and hope increase not only man's willingness but also his power for work; physiologists tell us that a given exertion consumes less of the store of nervous energy if done under the stimulus of pleasure than of pain: and without hope there is no enterprise. Security of person and property are two conditions of this hopefulness and freedom; but security always involves restraints on freedom, and it is one of the most difficult problems of civilization to discover how to obtain the security which is a condition of freedom without too great a sacrifice of freedom itself. Changes of work, of scene, and of personal associations bring new thoughts, call attention to the imperfections of old methods, stimulate a "divine discontent," and in every way develop creative energy.

[2] By converse with others who come from different places, and have different customs, travellers learn to put on its trial many a habit of thought or action which otherwise they would have always acquiesced in as though it were a law of nature. Moreover, a shifting of places enables the more powerful and original minds to find full scope for their energies and to rise to important positions: whereas those who stay at home are often over much kept in their places. Few men are prophets in their own land; neighbours and relations are generally the last to pardon the faults and to recognize the merits of those who are less docile and more enterprising than those around them. It is doubtless chiefly for this reason that in almost every part of

Freedom so far has been regarded as freedom from external bonds. But that higher freedom, which comes of self-mastery, is an even more important condition for the highest work. The elevation of the ideals of life on which this depends, is due on the one side to political and economic causes, and on the other to personal and religious influences; among which the influence of the mother in early childhood is supreme. IV, v, 5, 6.

§ 5. Bodily and mental health and strength are much influenced by occupation.[1] At the beginning of this century the conditions of factory work were needlessly unhealthy and oppressive for all, and especially for young children. But Factory and Education Acts have removed the worst of these evils from factories; though many of them still linger about domestic industries and the smaller workshops. *Influence of occupation.*

The higher wages, the greater intelligence, and the better medical facilities of townspeople should cause infant mortality to be much lower among them than in the country. But it is generally higher, especially where there are many mothers who neglect their family duties in order to earn money wages.

§ 6. In almost all countries there is a constant migration towards the towns.[2] The large towns and especially London absorb the *Influence of town life.*

England a disproportionately large share of the best energy and enterprise is to be found among those who were born elsewhere.

But change may be carried to excess; and when population shifts so rapidly, that a man is always shaking himself loose from his reputation, he loses some of the best external aids to the formation of a high moral character. The extreme hopefulness and restlessness of those who wander to new countries lead to much waste of effort in half acquiring technical skill, and half finishing tasks which are speedily abandoned in favour of some new occupation.

[1] The rate of mortality is low among ministers of religion and schoolmasters; among the agricultural classes, and in some other industries such as those of wheel-wrights, shipwrights and coal-miners. It is high in lead and tin mining, in file-making and earthenware manufacture. But neither these nor any other regular trade show as high a rate of mortality as is found among London general labourers and costermongers; while the highest of all is that of servants in inns. Such occupations are not directly injurious to health, but they attract those who are weak in physique and in character and they encourage irregular habits. A good account of the influence of occupation on death-rates is given in the supplement to the forty-fifth (1885) Annual Report of the Registrar-General, pp. xxv–lxiii. See also Farr's *Vital Statistics*, pp. 392–411, Humphreys' paper on *Class Mortality Statistics* in the *Statistical Journal* for June 1887, and the literature of the Factory Acts generally.

[2] Davenant (*Balance of Trade*, A.D. 1699, p. 20), following Gregory King, proves that according to official figures London has an excess of deaths over births of 2000 a year, but an immigration of 5000; which is more than half of what he calculates, by a rather risky method, to be the true net increase of the population of the country. He reckons that 530,000 people live in London, 870,000 in the other cities and market towns, and 4,100,000 in villages and hamlets. Compare these figures with the census of 1901 for England and Wales; where we find London with a population of over 4,500,000; five more towns with an average of over 500,000; and sixty-nine more exceeding 50,000 with an average of over 100,000. Nor is this all : for many suburbs whose population is not counted in, are often really parts of the big towns; and in some cases the suburbs of several adjacent towns run into one another, making them all into one gigantic, though rather scattered town. A suburb of Manchester is counted as a large town with 220,000 inhabitants; and the same is true of West

IV, v, 6.   very best blood from all the rest of England; the most enterprising, the most highly gifted, those with the highest *physique* and the strongest characters go there to find scope for their abilities. An increasing number of those who are most capable and have most strength of character, live in suburbs, where excellent systems of drainage, water supply and lighting, together with good schools and opportunities for open air play, give conditions at least as conducive to vigour as are to be found in the country; and though there are still many town districts only a little less injurious to vitality than were large towns generally some time ago, yet on the whole the increasing density of population seems to be for the present a diminishing source of danger. The recent rapid growth of facilities for living far from the chief centres of industry and trade must indeed slacken in time. But there seems no sign of any slackening in the movement of industries outwards to suburbs and even to new Garden Cities to seek and to bring with them vigorous workers.

Statistical averages are indeed unduly favourable to urban conditions, partly because many of the town influences which lower vigour do not much affect mortality; and partly because the majority of immigrants into the towns are in the full strength of youth, and of more than average energy and courage; while young people whose parents live in the country generally go home when they become seriously ill.[1]

Ham, a suburb of London with 275,000. The boundaries of some large towns are extended at irregular intervals to include such suburbs : and consequently the true population of a large town may be growing fast, while its nominal population grows slowly or even recedes, and then suddenly leaps forwards. Thus the nominal population of Liverpool was 552,000 in 1881; 518,000 in 1891; and 685,000 in 1901.

Similar changes are taking place elsewhere. Thus the population of Paris has grown twelve times as fast during the nineteenth century as that of France. The towns of Germany are increasing at the expense of the country by one half per cent. of the population yearly. In the United States there was in 1800 no town with more than 75,000 inhabitants; in 1905 there were three which together contained more than 7,000,000 and eleven more with above 300,000 each. More than a third of the population of Victoria are collected in Melbourne.

It must be recollected that the characteristics of town life increase in intensity for good and for evil with every increase in the size of a town, and its suburbs. Fresh country air has to pass over many more sources of noisome vapour before it reaches the average Londoner than before it reaches the average inhabitant of a small town. The Londoner has generally to go far before he can reach the freedom and the restful sounds and sights of the country. London therefore with 4,500,000 inhabitants adds to the urban character of England's life far more than a hundred times as much as a town of 45,000 inhabitants.

[1] For reasons of this kind Welton (*Statistical Journal*, 1897) makes the extreme proposal to omit all persons between 15 and 35 years of age in comparing the rates of mortality in different towns. The mortality of females in London between the ages of fifteen and thirty-five is, chiefly for this reason, abnormally low. If however a town has a stationary population its vital statistics are more easily interpreted; and selecting Coventry as a typical town, Galton has calculated that the adult children of artisan townsfolk are little more than half as numerous as those of labouring people who live in healthy country districts. When a place is decaying, the young and strong and hearty drift away from it; leaving the old and the infirm behind them, and consequently the birth-rate is generally low. On the other hand, a centre of industry

There is no better use for public and private money than in
providing public parks and playgrounds in large cities, in contracting
with railways to increase the number of the workmen's trains run
by them, and in helping those of the working classes who are willing
to leave the large towns to do so, and to take their industries with
them.[1]

§ 7. And there are yet other causes for anxiety. For there is
some partial arrest of that selective influence of struggle and competition which in the earlier stages of civilization caused those who
were strongest and most vigorous to leave the largest progeny behind them; and to which, more than any other single cause, the
progress of the human race is due. In the later stages of civilization
the rule has indeed long been that the upper classes marry late, and
in consequence have fewer children than the working classes : but
this has been compensated for by the fact that among the working
classes themselves the old rule was held ; and the vigour of the nation
that is tending to be damped out among the upper classes is thus
replenished by the fresh stream of strength that is constantly welling
up from below. But in France for a long time, and recently in
America, and England, some of the abler and more intelligent of the
working class population have shown signs of a disinclination to
have large families; and this is a source of danger.[2]

Thus there are increasing reasons for fearing, that while the
progress of medical science and sanitation is saving from death a
continually increasing number of the children of those who are feeble
physically and mentally; many of those who are most thoughtful

IV, v, 7.

Nature
left to
herself
tends to
weed out
the weak,
but man
has inter-
fered.

---

that is attracting population is likely to have a very high birth-rate, because it has
more than its share of people in the full vigour of life. This is especially the case in
the coal and iron towns, partly because they do not suffer, as the textile towns do,
from a deficiency of males; and partly because miners as a class marry early. In
some of them, though the death-rate is high, the excess of the birth-rate over it exceeds
20 per thousand of the population. The death-rate is generally highest in towns of
the second order, chiefly because their sanitary arrangements are not yet as good as
those of the very largest towns.

Prof. Haycraft (*Darwinism and Race Progress*) argues in the opposite direction.
He lays just stress on the dangers to the human race which would result from a
diminution of those diseases, such as phthisis and scrofula, which attack chiefly
people of weak constitution, and thus exercise a selective influence on the race, unless
it were accompanied by corresponding improvements in other directions. But
phthisis does not kill all its victims; there is some net gain in a diminution of its power
of weakening them.

[1] See an article entitled " Where to House the London Poor " by the present
writer in the *Contemporary Review*, Feb. 1884.

[2] In the Southern States of America, manual work became disgraceful to the white
man ; so that, if unable to have slaves himself, he led a paltry degenerate life, and
seldom married. Again, on the Pacific Slope, there were at one time just grounds for
fearing that all but highly skilled work would be left to the Chinese ; and that the
white men would live in an artificial way in which a family became a great expense.
In this case Chinese lives would have been substituted for American, and the average
quality of the human race would have been lowered.

IV, v, 8. and best endowed with energy, enterprise and self-control are tend-
———   ing to defer their marriages and in other ways to limit the number
of children whom they leave behind them.   The motive is sometimes
selfish, and perhaps it is best that hard and frivolous people should
leave but few descendants of their own type.   But more often it is
a desire to secure a good social position for their children.   This
desire contains many elements that fall short of the highest ideals of
human aims, and in some cases, a few that are distinctly base; but
after all it has been one of the chief factors of progress, and those
who are affected by it include many of those whose children would
probably be among the best and strongest of the race.

The State   It must be remembered that the members of a large family
gains   educate one another, they are usually more genial and bright, often
much
from large more vigorous in every way than the members of a small family.
families   Partly, no doubt, this is because their parents were of unusual
of healthy
children. vigour; and for a like reason they in their turn are likely to have
large and vigorous families.   The progress of the race is due to a
much greater extent than appears at first sight to the descendants
of a few exceptionally large and vigorous families.

The evils   But on the other hand there is no doubt that the parents can
of infant often do better in many ways for a small family than a large one.
mortality.
Other things being equal, an increase in the number of children who
are born causes an increase of infantile mortality; and that is an
unmixed evil.   The birth of children who die early from want of
care and adequate means is a useless strain to the mother and an
injury to the rest of the family.[1]

Practical   § 8. There are other considerations of which account ought to
conclusion. be taken; but so far as the points discussed in this chapter are concerned, it seems *primâ facie* advisable that people should not bring
children into the world till they can see their way to giving them at
least as good an education both physical and mental as they themselves had; and that it is best to marry moderately early provided
there is sufficient self-control to keep the family within the requisite
bounds without transgressing moral laws.   The general adoption of

---

[1] The extent of the infant mortality that arises from preventable causes may be
inferred from the facts that the percentage of deaths under one year of age to births
is generally about a third as much again in urban as in rural districts; and yet in
many urban districts which have a well-to-do population it is lower than the average
for the whole country (*Registrar-General's Report for* 1905, pp. xlii–xlv).   A few years
ago it was found that, while the annual death-rate of children under five years of
age was only about two per cent. in the families of peers and was less than three per
cent. for the whole of the upper classes, it was between six and seven per cent. for
the whole of England.   On the other hand Prof. Leroy Beaulieu says that in France
the parents of but one or two children are apt to indulge them, and be over-careful
about them to the detriment of their boldness, enterprise and endurance.   (See
Statistical Journal, Vol. 54, pp. 378, 9.)

these principles of action, combined with an adequate provision of I., v, 8.
fresh air and of healthy play for our town populations, could hardly
fail to cause the strength and vigour of the race to improve. And
we shall presently find reasons for believing that if the strength and
vigour of the race improves, the increase of numbers will not for a
long time to come cause a diminution of the average real income of
the people.

Thus then the progress of knowledge, and in particular of
medical science, the ever-growing activity and wisdom of Government in all matters relating to health, and the increase of material
wealth, all tend to lessen mortality and to increase health and
strength, and to lengthen life. On the other hand, vitality is
lowered and the death-rate raised by the rapid increase of town
life, and by the tendency of the higher strains of the population to
marry later and to have fewer children than the lower. If the
former set of causes were alone in action, but so regulated as to
avoid the danger of over-population, it is probable that man would
quickly rise to a physical and mental excellence superior to any that
the world has yet known; while if the latter set acted unchecked,
he would speedily degenerate.

The swaying to-and-fro forces of the good and evil.

As it is, the two sets hold one another very nearly in balance,
the former slightly preponderating. While the population of England is growing nearly as fast as ever, those who are out of health in
body or mind are certainly not an increasing part of the whole:
the rest are much better fed and clothed, and, except in overcrowded industrial districts, are generally growing in strength.
The average duration of life both for men and women has been
increasing steadily for many years.

The former slightly preponderate.

CHAPTER VI

INDUSTRIAL TRAINING

§ 1. HAVING discussed the causes which govern the growth of a numerous and vigorous population, we have next to consider the training that is required to develop its industrial efficiency.

The form which natural vigour takes depends largely on training.

The natural vigour that enables a man to attain great success in any one pursuit would generally have served him in good stead in almost any other. But there are exceptions. Some people, for instance, seem to be fitted from birth for an artistic career, and for no other; and occasionally a man of great practical genius is found to be almost devoid of artistic sensibility. But a race that has great nervous strength seems generally able, under favourable conditions, to develop in the course of a few generations ability of almost any kind that it holds in specially high esteem. A race that has acquired vigour in war or in the ruder forms of industry sometimes gains intellectual and artistic power of a high order very quickly; and nearly every literary and artistic epoch of classical and mediæval times has been due to a people of great nervous strength, who have been brought into contact with noble thoughts before they have acquired much taste for artificial comforts and luxuries.

The defects of our own age are apt to be over-estimated.

The growth of this taste in our own age has prevented us from taking full advantage of the opportunities our largely increased resources give us of consecrating the greater part of the highest abilities of the race to the highest aims. But perhaps the intellectual vigour of the age appears less than it really is, in consequence of the growth of scientific pursuits. For in art and literature success is often achieved while genius still wears the fascinating aspect of youth; but in modern science so much knowledge is required for originality, that before a student can make his mark in the world, his mind has often lost the first bloom of its freshness; and further the real value of his work is not often patent to the multitude as that of a picture or poem generally is.[1] In the same way the solid

---

[1] In this connection it is worth while to notice that the full importance of an epoch-making idea is often not perceived in the generation in which it is made : it starts the thoughts of the world on a new track, but the change of direction is not obvious until the turning-point has been left some way behind. In the same way the mechanical inventions of every age are apt to be underrated relatively to those of earlier times. For a new discovery is seldom fully effective for practical purposes

qualities of the modern machine-tending artisan are rated more IV, vi, 2.
cheaply than the lighter virtues of the mediæval handicraftsman. ———
This is partly because we are apt to regard as commonplace those
excellences which are common in our own time; and to overlook the
fact that the term " unskilled labourer " is constantly changing its
meaning.

§ 2. Very backward races are unable to keep on at any kind of Skilled and
work for a long time; and even the simplest form of what we regard unskilled labour.
as unskilled work is skilled work relatively to them; for they have
not the requisite assiduity, and they can acquire it only by a long
course of training. But where education is universal, an occupation
may fairly be classed as unskilled, though it requires a knowledge of
reading and writing. Again, in districts in which manufactures Skill with
have long been domiciled, a habit of responsibility, of carefulness which
and promptitude in handling expensive machinery and materials familiar
becomes the common property of all; and then much of the work of do not
tending machinery is said to be entirely mechanical and unskilled, recognize
and to call forth no human faculty that is worthy of esteem. But as skill.
in fact it is probable that not one-tenth of the present populations
of the world have the mental and moral faculties, the intelligence,
and the self-control that are required for it : perhaps not one-half
could be made to do the work well by steady training for two
generations. Even of a manufacturing population only a small part
are capable of doing many of the tasks that appear at first sight to
be entirely monotonous. Machine-weaving, for instance, simple as
it seems, is divided into higher and lower grades; and most of those
who work in the lower grades have not " the stuff in them " that is
required for weaving with several colours. And the differences are
even great in industries that deal with hard materials, wood, metals,
or ceramics.

Some kinds of manual work require long-continued practice in Mere
one set of operations, but these cases are not very common, and manual skill is
they are becoming rarer : for machinery is constantly taking over losing im-
work that requires manual skill of this kind. It is indeed true that portance relatively
a general command over the use of one's fingers is a very important to general
element of industrial efficiency; but this is the result chiefly of gence and
nervous strength, and self-mastery. It is of course developed by vigour of character.
training, but the greater part of this may be of a general character

---

till many minor improvements and subsidiary discoveries have gathered themselves
around it : an invention that makes an epoch is very often a generation older than
the epoch which it makes. Thus it is that each generation seems to be chiefly occupied
in working out the thoughts of the preceding one; while the full importance of its own
thoughts is as yet not clearly seen.

IV, VI, 3. and not special to the particular occupation; just as a good cricketer soon learns to play tennis well, so a skilled artisan can often move into other trades without any great and lasting loss of efficiency.

Manual skill that is so specialized that it is quite incapable of being transferred from one occupation to another is becoming steadily a less and less important factor in production. Putting aside for the present the faculties of artistic perception and artistic creation, we may say that what makes one occupation higher than another, what makes the workers of one town or country more efficient than those of another, is chiefly a superiority in general sagacity and energy which are not specialized to any one occupation.

To be able to bear in mind many things at a time, to have everything ready when wanted, to act promptly and show resource when anything goes wrong, to accommodate oneself quickly to changes in detail of the work done, to be steady and trustworthy, to have always a reserve of force which will come out in emergency, these are the qualities which make a great industrial people. They are not peculiar to any occupation, but are wanted in all; and if they cannot always be easily transferred from one trade to other kindred trades, the chief reason is that they require to be supplemented by some knowledge of materials and familiarity with special processes.

General and Specialised ability. We may then use the term *general ability* to denote those faculties and that general knowledge and intelligence which are in varying degrees the common property of all the higher grades of industry: while that manual dexterity and that acquaintance with particular materials and processes which are required for the special purposes of individual trades may be classed as *specialized ability*.

The causes that determine the supply of general ability. § 3. General ability depends largely on the surroundings of childhood and youth. In this the first and far the most powerful influence is that of the mother.[1] Next comes the influence of the father, of other children, and in some cases of servants.[2] As years

The home. pass on the child of the working man learns a great deal from what he sees and hears going on around him; and when we inquire into

---

[1] According to Galton the statement that all great men have had great mothers goes too far : but that shows only that the mother's influence does not outweigh all others; not that it is not greater than any one of them. He says that the mother's influence is most easily traceable among theologians and men of science, because an earnest mother leads her child to feel deeply about great things; and a thoughtful mother does not repress, but encourages that childish curiosity which is the raw material of scientific habits of thought.

[2] There are many fine natures among domestic servants. But those who live in very rich houses are apt to get self-indulgent habits, to overestimate the importance of wealth, and generally to put the lower aims of life above the higher, in a way that is not common with independent working people. The company in which the children of some of our best houses spend much of their time, is less ennobling than that of the average cottage. Yet in these very houses, no servant who is not specially qualified, is allowed to take charge of a young retriever or a young horse.

the advantages for starting in life which children of the well-to-do IV, VI, 4. classes have over those of artisans, and which these in their turn have over the children of unskilled labourers, we shall have to consider these influences of home more in detail. But at present we may pass to consider the more general influences of school education.

Little need be said of general education; though the influence School. even of that on industrial efficiency is greater than it appears. It is true that the children of the working classes must very often leave school, when they have but learnt the elements of reading, writing, arithmetic and drawing; and it is sometimes argued that part of the little time spent on these subjects would be better given to practical work. But the advance made at school is important not so much on its own account, as for the power of future advance which a school education gives. For a truly liberal general education adapts the mind to use its best faculties in business and to use business itself as a means of increasing culture; though it does not concern itself with the details of particular trades : that is left for technical education.[1]

§ 4. Technical education has in like manner raised its aims in Technical recent years. It used to mean little more than imparting that education. manual dexterity and that elementary knowledge of machinery and processes which an intelligent lad quickly picks up for himself when his work has begun; though if he has learnt it beforehand, he can perhaps earn a few shillings more at starting than if he had been quite ignorant. But such so-called education does not develop faculties; it rather hinders them from being developed. A lad, who has picked up the knowledge for himself, has educated himself by so doing; and he is likely to make better progress in the future than one who has been taught in a school of this old-fashioned kind. Technical education is however outgrowing its mistakes; and is aiming, firstly, at giving a general command over the use of eyes and fingers (though there are signs that this work is being taken

---

[1] The absence of a careful general education for the children of the working classes has been hardly less detrimental to industrial progress than the narrow range of the old grammar-school education of the middle classes. Till recently indeed it was the only one by which the average schoolmaster could induce his pupils to use their minds in anything higher than the absorption of knowledge. It was therefore rightly called liberal, because it was the best that was to be had. But it failed in its aim of familiarizing the citizen with the great thoughts of antiquity; it was generally forgotten as soon as school-time was over; and it raised an injurious antagonism between business and culture. Now however the advance of knowledge is enabling us to use science and art to supplement the curriculum of the grammar-school, and to give to those who can afford it an education that develops their best faculties, and starts them on the track of thoughts which will most stimulate the higher activities of their minds in after-life. The time spent on learning to spell is almost wasted : if spelling and pronunciation are brought into harmony in the English language as in most others, about a year will be added to the effective school education without any additional cost.

IV., VI, 4. over by general education, to which it properly belongs); and secondly at imparting artistic skill and knowledge, and methods of investigation, which are useful in particular occupations, but are seldom properly acquired in the course of practical work. It is however to be remembered that every advance in the accuracy and versatility of automatic machinery narrows the range of manual work in which command over hand and eye is at a high premium; and that those faculties which are trained by general education in its best forms are ever rising in importance.[1]

The aims of English education reform. According to the best English opinions, technical education for the higher ranks of industry should keep the aim of developing the faculties almost as constantly before it as general education does. It should rest on the same basis as a thorough general education, but should go on to work out in detail special branches of knowledge for the benefit of particular trades.[2] Our aim should be to add the scientific training in which the countries of Western Europe are ahead of us to that daring and restless energy and those practical instincts, which seldom flourish unless the best years of youth are spent in the workshop; recollecting always that whatever a youth learns for himself by direct experience in well-conducted works, teaches him more and stimulates his mental activity more than if it were taught him by a master in a technical school with model instruments.[3]

Apprenticeship. The old apprenticeship system is not exactly suited to modern conditions and it has fallen into disuse; but a substitute for it is wanted. Within the last few years many of the ablest manufacturers have begun to set the fashion of making their sons work through every stage in succession of the business they will ultimately

---

[1] As Nasmyth says; if a lad, having dropped two peas at random on a table, can readily put a third pea midway in a line between them, he is on the way to become a good mechanic. Command over eye and hand is gained in the ordinary English games, no less than in the playful work of the Kindergarten. Drawing has always been on the border line between work and play.

[2] One of the weakest points of technical education is that it does not educate the sense of proportion and the desire for simplicity of detail. The English, and to an even greater extent, the Americans, have acquired in actual business the faculty of rejecting intricacies in machinery and processes, which are not worth what they cost, and practical instinct of this kind often enables them to succeed in competition with Continental rivals who are much better educated.

[3] A good plan is that of spending the six winter months of several years after leaving school in learning science in College, and the six summer months as articled pupils in large workshops. The present writer introduced this plan about forty years ago at University College, Bristol (now the University of Bristol). But it has practical difficulties which can be overcome only by the cordial and generous co-operation of the heads of large firms with the College authorities. Another excellent plan is that adopted in the school attached to the works of Messrs. Mather and Platt at Manchester. "The drawings made in the school are of work actually in progress in the shops. One day the teacher gives the necessary explanations and calculations, and the next day the scholars see, as it were on the anvil, the very thing which has been the subject of his lecture."

have to control; but this splendid education can be had only by a IV, VI, 5.
few. So many and various are the branches of any great modern
industry that it would be impossible for the employers to undertake,
as they used to do, that every youth committed to their care should
learn all; and indeed a lad of ordinary ability would be bewildered
by the attempt. But it does not seem impracticable to revive the
apprenticeship system in a modified form.[1]

The great epoch-making inventions in industry came till recently Inventions in England and other countries.
almost exclusively from England. But now other nations are join-
ing in the race. The excellence of the common schools of the
Americans, the variety of their lives, the interchange of ideas
between different races among them, and the peculiar conditions
of their agriculture have developed a restless spirit of inquiry; while
technical education is now being pushed on with great vigour. On
the other hand, the diffusion of scientific knowledge among the
middle and even the working classes of Germany, combined with
their familiarity with modern languages and their habits of travelling
in pursuit of instruction, has enabled them to keep up with English
and American mechanics and to take the lead in many of the
applications of chemistry to business.[2]

§ 5. It is true that there are many kinds of work which can be A high education will in- crease the efficiency of the lower grades of industry
done as efficiently by an uneducated as by an educated workman :
and that the higher branches of education are of little direct use
except to employers and foremen and a comparatively small number
of artisans. But a good education confers great indirect benefits
even on the ordinary workman. It stimulates his mental activity;

[1] The employer binds himself to see that the apprentice is thoroughly taught in
the workshop all the subdivisions of one great division of his trade, instead of letting
him learn only one of these subdivisions, as too often happens now. The apprentice's
training would then often be as broad as if he had been taught the whole of the trade
as it existed a few generations ago; and it might be supplemented by a theoretical
knowledge of all branches of the trade, acquired in a technical school. Something
resembling the old apprenticeship system has recently come into vogue for young
Englishmen who desire to learn the business of farming under the peculiar conditions
of a new country : and there are some signs that the plan may be extended to the
business of farming in this country, for which it is in many respects admirably adapted.
But there remains a great deal of education suitable to the farmer and to the farm-
labourer which can best be given in agricultural colleges and dairy schools.

Meanwhile many great agencies for the technical education of adults are being
rapidly developed, such as public exhibitions, trade associations and congresses,
and trade journals. Each of them has its own work to do. In agriculture and
some other trades the greatest aid to progress is perhaps found in public shows. But
those industries, which are more advanced and in the hands of persons of studious
habits, owe more to the diffusion of practical and scientific knowledge by trade
journals; which, aided by changes in the methods of industry and also in its social
conditions, are breaking up trade secrets and helping men of small means in competition with their richer rivals.

[2] The heads of almost every progressive firm on the Continent have carefully
studied processes and machinery in foreign lands. The English are great travellers;
but partly perhaps on account of their ignorance of other languages they seem hardly
to set enough store on the technical education that can be gained by the wise use
of travel.

IV, VI, 5
—
indirectly
rather
than
directly.

it fosters in him a habit of wise inquisitiveness; it makes him more intelligent, more ready, more trustworthy in his ordinary work; it raises the tone of his life in working hours and out of working hours; it is thus an important means towards the production of material wealth; at the same time that, regarded as an end in itself, it is inferior to none of those which the production of material wealth can be made to subserve.

We must however look in another direction for a part, perhaps the greater part, of the immediate economic gain which the nation may derive from an improvement in the general and technical education of the mass of the people. We must look not so much at those who stay in the rank and file of the working classes, as at those who rise from a humble birth to join the higher ranks of skilled artisans, to become foremen or employers, to advance the boundaries of science, or possibly to add to the national wealth in art and literature.

Much of
the best
natural
ability in
the nation
is born
among the
working
classes,
and too
often runs
to waste
now.

The laws which govern the birth of genius are inscrutable. It is probable that the percentage of children of the working classes who are endowed with natural abilities of the highest order is not so great as that of the children of people who have attained or have inherited a higher position in society. But since the manual labour classes are four or five times as numerous as all other classes put together, it is not unlikely that more than half the best natural genius that is born into the country belongs to them; and of this a great part is fruitless for want of opportunity. There is no extravagance more prejudicial to the growth of national wealth than that wasteful negligence which allows genius that happens to be born of lowly parentage to expend itself in lowly work. No change would conduce so much to a rapid increase of material wealth as an improvement in our schools, and especially those of the middle grades, provided it be combined with an extensive system of scholarships, which will enable the clever son of a working man to rise gradually from school to school till he has the best theoretical and practical education which the age can give.

To the abilities of children of the working classes may be ascribed the greater part of the success of the free towns in the Middle Ages and of Scotland in recent times. Even within England itself there is a lesson of the same kind to be learnt : progress is most rapid in those parts of the country in which the greatest proportion of the leaders of industry are the sons of working men. For instance, the beginning of the manufacturing era found social distinctions more closely marked and more firmly established in the South than in the

North of England.   In the South something of a spirit of caste has IV, VI, 6.
held back the working men and the sons of working men from rising
to posts of command; and the old established families have been
wanting in that elasticity and freshness of mind which no social
advantages can supply, and which comes only from natural gifts.
This spirit of caste, and this deficiency of new blood among the
leaders of industry, have mutually sustained one another; and
there are not a few towns in the South of England whose decadence
within living memory can be traced in a great measure to this cause.

§ 6.   Education in art stands on a somewhat different footing Education
from education in hard thinking : for while the latter nearly always in art.
strengthens the character, the former not unfrequently fails to
do this.   Nevertheless the development of the artistic faculties of
the people is in itself an aim of the very highest importance, and is
becoming a chief factor of industrial efficiency.

We are here concerned almost exclusively with those branches of
art which appeal to the eye.   For though literature and music
contribute as much and more to the fulness of life, yet their development does not directly affect, and does not depend upon, the methods
of business, the processes of manufacture and the skill of artisans.

The artisan of Europe in the Middle Ages, and of eastern coun- Where
tries now, has perhaps obtained credit for more originality than he social and
industrial
has really possessed.   Eastern carpets, for instance, are full of grand change in
slow art is
conceptions : but if we examine a great many examples of the art guided by
of any one place, selected perhaps from the work of several centuries, matured
instincts,
we often find very little variety in their fundamental ideas.   But
in the modern era of rapid changes—some caused by fashion and
some by the beneficial movements of industrial and social progress—
everyone feels free to make a new departure, everyone has to rely
in the main on his own resources : there is no slowly matured public
criticism to guide him.[1]

This is however not the only, perhaps not the chief disadvantage and
under which artistic design labours in our own age.   There is no attracts
a large
good reason for believing that the children of ordinary workmen in share of
ability.

[1] In fact every designer in a primitive age is governed by precedent : only very
daring people depart from it; even they do not depart far, and their innovations are
subjected to the test of experience, which, in the long run, is infallible.   For though
the crudest and most ridiculous fashions in art and in literature will be accepted by
the people for a time at the bidding of their social superiors, nothing but true artistic
excellence has enabled a ballad or a melody, a style of dress or a pattern of furniture
to retain its popularity among a whole nation for many generations together.   These
innovations, then, which were inconsistent with the true spirit of art were suppressed,
and those that were on the right track were retained, and became the starting-point
for further progress; and thus traditional instincts played a great part in preserving
the purity of the industrial arts in Oriental countries, and to a less extent in mediæval
Europe.

IV, VI, 6. the middle Ages had more power of artistic origination than those of ordinary village carpenters or blacksmiths of to-day; but if one among ten thousand happened to have genius, it found vent in his work and was stimulated by the competition of the gilds and in other ways. But the modern artisan is apt to be occupied in the management of machinery; and though the faculties which he develops may be more solid and may help more in the long run towards the highest progress of the human race, than did the taste and fancy of his mediæval predecessor, yet they do not contribute directly towards the progress of art. And if he should find in himself a higher order of ability than among his fellows, he will probably endeavour to take a leading part in the management of a trades-union or some other society, or to collect together a little store of capital and to rise out of that trade in which he was educated. These are not ignoble aims; but his ambition would perhaps have been nobler and more fruitful of good to the world, if he had stayed in his old trade and striven to create works of beauty which should live after he had gone.

But in modern times design is almost limited to a narrow profession

It must however be admitted that he would have great difficulties in doing this. The shortness of the time which we allow ourselves for changes in the arts of decoration is scarcely a greater evil than the width of the area of the world over which they are spread; for that causes a further distraction of the hasty and hurried efforts of the designer, by compelling him to be always watching the world movements of the supply of and demand for art products. This is a task for which the artisan, who works with his own hands, is not well fitted; and in consequence now-a-days the ordinary artisan finds it best to follow and not to lead. Even the supreme skill of the Lyons weaver shows itself now almost exclusively in an inherited power of delicate manipulation, and fine perception of colour, that enable him to carry out perfectly the ideas of professional designers.

which is forced to pay court to fashion.

Increasing wealth is enabling people to buy things of all kinds to suit the fancy, with but a secondary regard to their powers of wearing; so that in all kinds of clothing and furniture it is every day more true that it is the pattern which sells the things. The influence of the late William Morris and others, combined with the lead which many English designers have derived from Oriental and especially Persian and Indian masters of colour is acknowledged by Frenchmen themselves to have attained the first rank for certain classes of English fabrics and decorative products. But in other directions France is supreme. Some English manufacturers who

hold their own against the world would, it is said, be driven out of IV, VI, 7.
the market if they had to depend on English patterns. This is
partly due to the fact that Paris having the lead in fashions, as the
result of an inherited quick and subtle taste in women's dress, a
Parisian design is likely to be in harmony with the coming fashions
and to sell better than a design of equal intrinsic worth from elsewhere.[1]

Technical education, then, though it cannot add much directly
to the supply of genius in art, any more than it can in science or
in business, can yet save much natural artistic genius from running
to waste; and it is called on to do this all the more because the training that was given by the older forms of handicraft can never be
revived on a large scale.[2]

§ 7. We may then conclude that the wisdom of expending Education
public and private funds on education is not to be measured by its a national
direct fruits alone. It will be profitable as a mere investment, to ment,
give the masses of the people much greater opportunities than they
can generally avail themselves of. For by this means many, who
would have died unknown, are enabled to get the start needed for
bringing out their latent abilities. And the economic value of one
great industrial genius is sufficient to cover the expenses of the
education of a whole town; for one new idea, such as Bessemer's
chief invention, adds as much to England's productive power as the
labour of a hundred thousand men. Less direct, but not less in
importance, is the aid given to production by medical discoveries
such as those of Jenner or Pasteur, which increase our health and
working power; and again by scientific work such as that of mathe-

---

[1] French designers find it best to live in Paris : if they stay for long out of contact
with the central movements of fashion they seem to fall behindhand. Most of them
have been educated as artists, but have failed of their highest ambition. It is only
in exceptional cases, as for instance for the Sèvres china, that those who have succeeded as artists find it worth their while to design. Englishmen can, however, hold
their own in designing for Oriental markets, and there is evidence that the English
are at least equal to the French in originality, though they are inferior in quickness
in seeing how to group forms and colours so as to obtain an effective result. (See the
Report on Technical Education, Vol. I. pp. 256, 261, 324, 325 and Vol. III. pp. 151,
152, 202, 203, 211 and passim.) It is probable that the profession of the modern
designer has not yet risen to the best position which it is capable of holding. For it
has been to a disproportionate extent under the influence of one nation; and that
nation is one whose works in the highest branches of art have seldom borne to be
transplanted. They have indeed often been applauded and imitated at the time by
other nations, but they have as yet seldom struck a key-note for the best work of
later generations.
[2] The painters themselves have put on record in the portrait-galleries the fact that
in mediæval times, and even later, their art attracted a larger share of the best intellect
than it does now ; when the ambition of youth is tempted by the excitement of modern
business, when its zeal for imperishable achievements finds a field in the discoveries
of modern science, and, lastly, when a great deal of excellent talent is insensibly
diverted from high aims by the ready pay to be got by hastily writing half-thoughts
for periodical literature.

IV, VI, 8. matics or biology, even though many generations may pass away before it bears visible fruit in greater material wellbeing. All that is spent during many years in opening the means of higher education to the masses would be well paid for if it called out one more Newton or Darwin, Shakespeare or Beethoven.

There are few practical problems in which the economist has a more direct interest than those relating to the principles on which the expense of the education of children should be divided between the State and the parents. But we must now consider the conditions that determine the power and the will of the parents to bear their share of the expense, whatever it may be.

and a duty of parents. Most parents are willing enough to do for their children what their own parents did for them; and perhaps even to go a little beyond it if they find themselves among neighbours who happen to have a rather higher standard. But to do more than this requires, in addition to the moral qualities of unselfishness and a warmth of affection that are perhaps not rare, a certain habit of mind which is as yet not very common. It requires the habit of distinctly realizing the future, of regarding a distant event as of nearly the same importance as if it were close at hand (discounting the future at a low rate of interest); this habit is at once a chief product and a chief cause of civilization, and is seldom fully developed except among the middle and upper classes of the more cultivated nations.

Mobility between grades and within grades. § 8. Parents generally bring up their children to occupations in their own grade, and therefore the total supply of labour in any grade in one generation is in a great measure determined by the numbers in that grade in the preceding generation, yet within the grade itself there is greater mobility. If the advantages of any one occupation in it rise above the average, there is a quick influx of youth from other occupations within the grade. The vertical movement from one grade to another is seldom very rapid or on a very large scale; but, when the advantages of a grade have risen relatively to the difficulty of the work required of it, many small streams of labour, both youthful and adult, will begin to flow towards it; and though none of them may be very large, they will together have a sufficient volume to satisfy before long the increased demand for labour in that grade.

Provisional conclusion. We must defer to a later stage a fuller discussion of the obstacles which the conditions of any place and time oppose to the free mobility of labour, and also of the inducements which they offer to anyone to change his occupation or to bring up his son to an occupation different from his own. But we have seen enough to conclude that, other things being equal, an increase in the earnings that are to be got by labour increases its rate of growth; or, in other words, a rise in its demand price increases the supply of it. If the state of knowledge, and of ethical, social and domestic habits be given; then the vigour of the people as a whole if not their numbers, and both the numbers and vigour of any trade in particular, may be said to have a supply price in this sense, that there is a certain level of the demand price which will keep them stationary; that a higher price would cause them to increase, and that a lower price would cause them to decrease. Thus economic causes play a part in governing the growth of population as a whole as well as the supply of labour in any particular grade. But their influence on the numbers of the population as a whole is largely indirect; and is exerted by way of the ethical, social and domestic habits of life. For these habits are themselves influenced by economic causes deeply, though slowly, and in ways some of which are difficult to trace, and impossible to predict.[1]

---

[1] Mill was so much impressed by the difficulties that beset a parent in the attempt to bring up his son to an occupation widely different in character from his own, that he said (*Principles*, II. xiv. 2):—" So complete, indeed, has hitherto been the separation, so strongly marked the line of demarcation, between the different grades of labourers, as to be almost equivalent to an hereditary distinction of caste; each employment being chiefly recruited from the children of those already employed in it, or in employments of the same rank with it in social estimation, or from the children of persons who, if originally of a lower rank, have succeeded in raising themselves by their exertions. The liberal professions are mostly supplied by the sons of either the professional or the idle classes: the more highly skilled manual employments are filled up from the sons of skilled artisans or the class of tradesmen who rank with them : the lower classes of skilled employments are in a similar case ; and unskilled labourers, with occasional exceptions, remain from father to son in their pristine condition. Consequently the wages of each class have hitherto been regulated by the increase of its own population, rather than that of the general population of the country." But he goes on, " The changes, however, now so rapidly taking place in usages and ideas are undermining all these distinctions."

His prescience has been vindicated by the progress of change since he wrote. The broad lines of division which he pointed out have been almost obliterated by the rapid action of those causes which, as we saw earlier in the chapter, are reducing the amount of skill and ability required in some occupations and increasing it in others. We cannot any longer regard different occupations as distributed among four great planes; but we may perhaps think of them as resembling a long flight of steps of unequal breadth, some of them being so broad as to act as landing stages. Or even better still we might picture to ourselves two flights of stairs, one representing the "hard-handed industries " and the other " the soft-handed industries " ; because the vertical division between these two is in fact as broad and as clearly marked as the horizontal division between any two grades.

Mill's classification had lost a great part of its value when Cairnes adopted it (*Leading Principles*, p. 72). A classification more suited to our existing conditions is offered by Giddings (*Political Science Quarterly*, Vol. II. pp. 69-71). It is open to the objection that it draws broad lines of division where nature has made no broad lines; but it is perhaps as good as any division of industry into four grades can be. His divisions are (i) *automatic manual labour*, including common labourers and machine tenders; (ii) *responsible manual labour*, including those who can be entrusted with some responsibility and labour of self-direction; (iii) *automatic brain workers*, such as book-keepers, and (iv) *responsible brain workers*, including the superintendents and directors.

The conditions and methods of the large and incessant movement of the population upwards and downwards from grade to grade are studied more fully below, VI. IV. v. and VII.

IV, vi, 8.   The growing demand for boys to run errands, and to do other work that has no educational value, has increased the danger that parents may send their sons into avenues that have no outlook for good employment in later years : and something is being done by public agency, and more by the devotion and energy of men and women in unofficial association, in giving out notes of warning against such " blind alley " occupations, and assisting lads to prepare themselves for skilled work.   These efforts may be of great national value.   But care must be taken that this guidance and help is as accessible to the higher strains of the working class population when in need of it as to the lower ; lest the race should degenerate.

CHAPTER VII

THE GROWTH OF WEALTH

§ 1. IN this chapter it is not necessary to distinguish the points of view in which wealth is regarded as the object of consumption and as an agent of production; we are concerned with the growth of wealth simply, and we have no need to emphasize its uses as capital.

The earliest forms of wealth were probably implements for hunting and fishing, and personal ornaments; and, in cold countries, clothing and huts.[1] During this stage the domestication of animals began; but at first they were probably cared for chiefly for their own sake, because they were beautiful, and it was pleasant to have them; they were, like articles of personal ornament, desired because of the immediate gratification to be derived from their possession rather than as a provision against future needs.[2] Gradually the herds of domesticated animals increased; and during the pastoral stage they were at once the pleasure and the pride of their possessors, the outward emblems of social rank, and by far the most important store of wealth accumulated as a provision against future needs.

Forms of wealth among barbarous peoples.

As numbers thickened and the people settled down to agriculture, cultivated land took the first place in the inventory of wealth; and that part of the value of the land which was due to improvements (among which wells held a conspicuous place) became the chief element of capital, in the narrower sense of the term. Next in importance came houses, domesticated animals, and in some places boats and ships; but the implements of production, whether for use in agriculture or in domestic manufactures, remained for a long time of little value. In some places, however, precious stones and the precious metals in various forms became early a leading object of

Forms of wealth in early stages of civilization.

---

[1] A short but suggestive study of the growth of wealth in its early forms, and of the arts of life, is given in Tylor's *Anthropology*.

[2] Bagehot (*Economic Studies*, pp. 163–5), after quoting the evidence which Galton has collected on the keeping of pet animals by savage tribes, points out that we find here a good illustration of the fact that however careless a savage race may be for the future, it cannot avoid making some provision for it. A bow, a fishing-net, which will do its work well in getting food for to-day, must be of service for many days to come : a horse or a canoe that will carry one well to-day, must be a stored-up source of many future enjoyments. The least provident of barbaric despots may raise a massive pile of buildings, because it is the most palpable proof of his present wealth and power.

IV, vii, 1. desire and a recognized means of hoarding wealth; while, to say nothing of the palaces of monarchs, a large part of social wealth in many comparatively rude civilizations took the form of edifices for public purposes, chiefly religious, and of roads and bridges, of canals and irrigation works.

Until recently there was little use of expensive forms of auxiliary capital. For some thousands of years these remained the chief forms of accumulated wealth. In towns indeed houses and household furniture took the first place, and stocks of the more expensive of raw materials counted for a good deal; but though the inhabitants of the towns had often more wealth per head than those of the country, their total numbers were small; and their aggregate wealth was very much less than that of the country. During all this time the only trade that used very expensive implements was the trade of carrying goods by water: the weaver's looms, the husbandman's ploughs and the blacksmith's anvils were of simple construction and were of little account beside the merchant's ships. But in the eighteenth century England inaugurated the era of expensive implements.

But in recent years they have increased very fast. The implements of the English farmer had been rising slowly in value for a long time; but the progress was quickened in the eighteenth century. After a while the use first of water power and then of steam power caused the rapid substitution of expensive machinery for inexpensive hand tools in one department of production after another. As in earlier times the most expensive implements were ships and in some cases canals for navigation and irrigation, so now they are the means of locomotion in general;— railways and tramways, canals, docks and ships, telegraph and telephone systems and water-works: even gas-works might almost come under this head, on the ground that a great part of their plant is devoted to distributing the gas. After these come mines and iron and chemical works, ship-building yards, printing-presses, and other large factories full of expensive machinery.

On whichever side we look we find that the progress and diffusion of knowledge are constantly leading to the adoption of new processes and new machinery which economize human effort on condition that some of the effort is spent a good while before the attainment of the ultimate ends to which it is directed. It is not easy to measure this progress exactly, because many modern industries had no counterpart in ancient times. But let us compare the past and present conditions of the four great industries the products of which have not changed their general character: viz. agriculture, the building, the cloth-making, and the carrying trades. In the first

two of these hand work still retains an important place : but even
in them there is a great development of expensive machinery.
Compare for instance the rude implements of an Indian Ryot even
of to-day with the equipment of a progressive Lowland farmer; [1]
and consider the brick-making, mortar-making, sawing, planing,
moulding and slotting machines of a modern builder, his steam
cranes and his electric light.   And if we turn to the textile trades,
or at least to those of them which make the simpler products, we find
each operative in early times content with implements the cost of
which was equivalent to but a few months of his labour; while in
modern times it is estimated that for each man, woman and child
employed there is a capital in plant alone of more than £200, or say
the equivalent of five years' labour.   Again the cost of a steam-ship
is perhaps equivalent to the labour for fifteen years or more of those
who work her; while a capital of about £1000,000,000 invested
in railways in England and Wales is equivalent to the work for
more than twenty years of the 300,000 wage-earners employed on
them.

§ 2. As civilization has progressed, man has always been developing new wants, and new and more expensive ways of gratifying them.
The rate of progress has sometimes been slow, and occasionally there
has even been a great retrograde movement; but now we are moving
on at a rapid pace that grows quicker every year; and we cannot
guess where it will stop.   On every side further openings are sure to
offer themselves, all of which will tend to change the character of
our social and industrial life, and to enable us to turn to account
vast stores of capital in providing new gratifications and new ways
of economizing effort by expending it in anticipation of distant
wants.   There seems to be no good reason for believing that we are
anywhere near a stationary state in which there will be no new
important wants to be satisfied; in which there will be no more
room for profitably investing present effort in providing for the
future, and in which the accumulation of wealth will cease to have

And they are likely to continue to increase.

---

[1] The farm implements for a first class Ryot family, including six or seven adult
males, are a few light ploughs and hoes chiefly of wood, of the total value of about
13 rupees (Sir G. Phear, *Aryan Village*, p. 233) or the equivalent of their work for
about a month; while the value of the machinery alone on a well equipped large
modern arable farm amounts to £3 an acre (*Equipment of the Farm*, edited by J. C.
Morton) or say a year's work for each person employed.   They include steam-engines,
trench, subsoil and ordinary ploughs, some to be worked by steam and some by horse
power; various grubbers, harrows, rollers, clod-crushers, seed and manure drills,
horse hoes, rakes, hay-making, mowing and reaping machines, steam or horse thresh-
ing, chaff cutting, turnip cutting, hay-pressing machines and a multitude of others.
Meanwhile there is an increasing use of silos and covered yards, and constant improvements in the fittings of the dairy and other farm buildings, all of which give great
economy of effort in the long run, but require a larger share of it to be spent in preparing the way for the direct work of the farmer in raising agricultural produce.

IV, VII, 3.   any reward. The whole history of man shows that his wants
———   expand with the growth of his wealth and knowledge.[1]

And   And with the growth of openings for the investment of capital
meanwhile   there is a constant increase in that surplus of production over the
there has   necessaries of life, which gives the power to save. When the arts
been and
probably   of production were rude, there was very little surplus, except where
will be   a strong ruling race kept the subject masses hard at work on the
a parallel bare necessaries of life, and where the climate was so mild that those
increase in
the power   necessaries were small and easily obtained. But every increase in
to accu-   the arts of production, and in the capital accumulated to assist and
mulate.   support labour in future production, increased the surplus out of
            which more wealth could be accumulated. After a time civilization
            became possible in temperate and even in cold climates; the
            increase of material wealth was possible under conditions which
            did not enervate the worker, and did not therefore destroy the
            foundations on which it rested.[2] Thus from step to step wealth
            and knowledge have grown, and with every step the power of saving
            wealth and extending knowledge has increased.

The slow   § 3. The habit of distinctly realizing the future and providing
and fitful for it has developed itself slowly and fitfully in the course of man's
develop-   history. Travellers tell us of tribes who might double their resources
ment of
the habit   and enjoyments without increasing their total labour, if they would
of pro-   only apply a little in advance the means that lie within their power
viding   and their knowledge; as, for instance, by fencing in their little plots
for the
future.   of vegetables against the intrusion of wild animals.

            But even this apathy is perhaps less strange than the wasteful-

---

[1] For instance, improvements which have recently been made in some American
cities indicate that by a sufficient outlay of capital each house could be supplied with
what it does require, and relieved of what it does not, much more effectively than
now, so as to enable a large part of the population to live in towns and yet be free
from many of the present evils of town life. The first step is to make under all the
streets large tunnels, in which many pipes and wires can be laid side by side, and
repaired when they get out of order, without any interruption of the general traffic
and without great expense. Motive power, and possibly even heat, might then be
generated at great distances from the towns (in some cases in coal-mines), and laid
on wherever wanted. Soft water and spring water, and perhaps even sea water and
ozonized air, might be laid on in separate pipes to nearly every house; while steam-
pipes might be used for giving warmth in winter, and compressed air for lowering the
heat of summer; or the heat might be supplied by gas of great heating power laid on
in special pipes, while light was derived from gas specially suited for the purpose or
from electricity; and every house might be in electric communication with the rest
of the town. All unwholesome vapours, including those given off by any domestic
fires which were still used, might be carried away by strong draughts through long
conduits, to be purified by passing through large furnaces and thence away through
huge chimneys into the higher air. To carry out such a scheme in the towns of England would require the outlay of a much larger capital than has been absorbed by
our railways. This conjecture as to the ultimate course of town improvement may
be wide of the truth; but it serves to indicate one of very many ways in which the
experience of the past foreshadows broad openings for investing present effort in
providing the means of satisfying our wants in the future.
[2] Comp. Appendix A.

ness that is found now among some classes in our own country.
Cases are not rare of men who alternate between earning two or
three pounds a week and being reduced to the verge of starvation :
the utility of a shilling to them when they are in employment is less
than that of a penny when they are out of it, and yet they never
attempt to make provision for the time of need.[1] At the opposite
extreme there are misers, in some of whom the passion for saving
borders on insanity; while, even among peasant proprietors and
some other classes, we meet not unfrequently with people who carry
thrift so far as to stint themselves of necessaries, and to impair their
power of future work. Thus they lose every way : they never
really enjoy life; while the income which their stored-up wealth
brings them is less than they would have got from the increase of
their earning power, if they had invested in themselves the wealth
that they have accumulated in a material form.

In India, and to a less extent in Ireland, we find people who do
indeed abstain from immediate enjoyment and save up considerable
sums with great self-sacrifice, but spend all their savings in lavish
festivities at funerals and marriages. They make intermittent
provision for the near future, but scarcely any permanent provision
for the distant future : the great engineering works by which their
productive resources have been so much increased, have been made
chiefly with the capital of the much less self-denying race of Englishmen.

Thus the causes which control the accumulation of wealth differ
widely in different countries and different ages. They are not quite
the same among any two races, and perhaps not even among any
two social classes in the same race. They depend much on social
and religious sanctions; and it is remarkable how, when the binding
force of custom has been in any degree loosened, differences of
personal character will cause neighbours brought up under like
conditions to differ from one another more widely and more frequently in their habits of extravagance or thrift than in almost any
other respect.

§ 4. The thriftlessness of early times was in a great measure due Security
to the want of security that those who made provision for the future as a con-
would enjoy it : only those who were already wealthy were strong dition of
enough to hold what they had saved; the laborious and self-denying saving.
peasant who had heaped up a little store of wealth only to see it
taken from him by a stronger hand, was a constant warning to his

---

[1] They " discount " future benefits (comp. Book III. ch. v. § 3) at the rate of
many thousands per cent. per annum.

IV, VII, 5. neighbours to enjoy their pleasure and their rest when they could. The border country between England and Scotland made little progress so long as it was liable to incessant forays; there was very little saving by the French peasants in the eighteenth century when they could escape the plunder of the tax-gatherer only by appearing to be poor, or by Irish cottiers, who, on many estates, even forty years ago, were compelled to follow the same course in order to avoid the landlords' claims of exorbitant rents.

Insecurity of this kind has nearly passed away from the civilized world. But we are still suffering in England from the effects of the Poor-law which ruled at the beginning of last century, and which introduced a new form of insecurity for the working classes. For it arranged that part of their wages should, in effect, be given in the form of poor relief; and that this should be distributed among them in inverse proportion to their industry and thrift and forethought, so that many thought it foolish to make provision for the future. The traditions and instincts which were fostered by that evil experience are even now a great hindrance to the progress of the working classes; and the principle which nominally at least underlies the present Poor-law, that the State should take account only of destitution and not at all of merit, acts in the same direction, though with less force.

Insecurity of this kind also is being diminished : the growth of enlightened views as to the duties of the State and of private persons towards the poor, is tending to make it every day more true that those who have helped themselves and endeavoured to provide for their own future will be cared for by society better than the idle and the thoughtless. But the progress in this direction is still slow, and there remains much to be done yet.

§ 5. The growth of a money-economy and of modern habits of business does indeed hinder the accumulation of wealth by putting new temptations in the way of those who are inclined to live extravagantly. In old times if a man wanted a good house to live in he must build it himself; now he finds plenty of good houses to be hired at a rent. Formerly, if he wanted good beer he must have a good brew-house, now he can buy it more cheaply and better than he could brew it. Now he can borrow books from a library instead of buying them; and he can even furnish his house before he is ready to pay for his furniture. Thus in many ways the modern systems of buying and selling, and lending and borrowing, together with the growth of new wants, lead to new extravagances, and to a subordination of the interests of the future to those of the present.

The growth of a money-economy gives new temptations to extravagance,

But on the other hand, a money-economy increases the variety
of the uses between which a person can distribute his future expendi- but also
ture. A person who in a primitive state of society stores up some a new
things against a future need, may find that after all he does not $\frac{\text{certainty}}{\text{that}}$
need those things as much as others which he has not stored up : savings
and there are many future wants against which it is impossible to provide
provide directly by storing up goods. But he who has stored up $\frac{\text{what is}}{\text{wanted in}}$
capital from which he derives a money income can buy what he will the future.
to meet his needs as they arise.[1]

Again, modern methods of business have brought with them And it has
opportunities for the safe investment of capital in such ways as to $\frac{\text{enabled}}{\text{people who}}$
yield a revenue to persons who have no good opportunity of engaging have no
in any business,—not even in that of agriculture, where the land $\frac{\text{faculty for}}{\text{business to}}$
will under some conditions act as a trustworthy savings-bank. $\frac{\text{reap the}}{\text{full fruits}}$
These new opportunities have induced some people who would not of saving.
otherwise have attempted it to put by something for their own old
age. And, what has had a far greater effect on the growth of
wealth, it has rendered it far easier for a man to provide a secure
income for his wife and children after his death : for, after all,
family affection is the main motive of saving.

§ 6. There are indeed some who find an intense pleasure in seeing A few
their hoards of wealth grow up under their hands, with scarcely any $\frac{\text{people}}{\text{save for}}$
thought for the happiness that may be got from its use by them- their own
selves or by others. They are prompted partly by the instincts of sakes :
the chase, by the desire to outstrip their rivals; by the ambition to
have shown ability in getting the wealth, and to acquire power and
social position by its possession. And sometimes the force of habit,
started when they were really in need of money, has given them, by
a sort of reflex action, an artificial and unreasoning pleasure in
amassing wealth for its own sake. But were it not for the family but the
affections, many who now work hard and save carefully would not $\frac{\text{chief}}{\text{motive of}}$
exert themselves to do more than secure a comfortable annuity for saving is
their own lives; either by purchase from an insurance company, or $\frac{\text{family}}{\text{affection.}}$
by arranging to spend every year, after they had retired from work,
part of their capital as well as all their income. In the one case
they would leave nothing behind them : in the other only provision
for that part of their hoped-for old age, from which they had been
cut off by death. That men labour and save chiefly for the sake of
their families, and not for themselves, is shown by the fact that they
seldom spend, after they have retired from work, more than the
income that comes in from their savings, preferring to leave their

[1] Comp. III. v. 2.

IV, vii, 7. stored-up wealth intact for their families; while in this country alone twenty millions a year are saved in the form of insurance policies and are available only after the death of those who save them.

A man can have no stronger stimulus to energy and enterprise than the hope of rising in life, and leaving his family to start from a higher round of the social ladder than that on which he began. It may even give him an over-mastering passion which reduces to insignificance the desire for ease, and for all ordinary pleasures, and sometimes even destroys in him the finer sensibilities and nobler aspirations. But, as is shown by the marvellous growth of wealth in America during the present generation, it makes him a mighty producer and accumulator of riches; unless indeed he is in too great a hurry to grasp the social position which his wealth will give him: for his ambition may then lead him into as great extravagance as could have been induced by an improvident and self-indulgent temperament.

The greatest savings are made by those who have been brought up on narrow means to stern hard work, who have retained their simple habits, in spite of success in business, and who nourish a contempt for showy expenditure and a desire to be found at their death richer than they had been thought to be. This type of character is frequent in the quieter parts of old but vigorous countries, and it was very common among the middle classes in the rural districts of England for more than a generation after the pressure of the great French war and the heavy taxes that lingered in its wake.

The source of accumulation is surplus income; whether that derived from capital,

§ 7. Next, as to the sources of accumulation. The power to save depends on an excess of income over necessary expenditure; and this is greatest among the wealthy. In this country most of the larger incomes, but only a few of the smaller, are chiefly derived from capital. And, early in the present century, the commercial classes in England had much more saving habits than either the country gentlemen or the working classes. These causes combined to make English economists of the last generation regard savings as made almost exclusively from the profits of capital.

or rent, the earnings of professional men, and of hired workers.

But even in modern England rent and the earnings of professional men and hired workers are an important source of accumulation: and they have been the chief source of it in all the earlier stages of civilization.[1] Moreover, the middle and especially the professional classes have always denied themselves much in order to invest capital in the education of their children; while a great part of the wages

---

[1] Comp. *Principles of Political Economy*, by Richard Jones.

of the working classes is invested in the physical health and strength IV, VII, 8. of their children. The older economists took too little account of the fact that human faculties are as important a means of production as any other kind of capital; and we may conclude, in opposition to them, that any change in the distribution of wealth which gives more to the wage receivers and less to the capitalists is likely, other things being equal, to hasten the increase of material production, and that it will not perceptibly retard the storing-up of material wealth. Of course other things would not be equal if the change were brought about by violent methods which gave a shock to public security. But a slight and temporary check to the accumulation of material wealth need not necessarily be an evil, even from a purely economic point of view, if, being made quietly and without disturbance, it provided better opportunities for the great mass of the people, increased their efficiency, and developed in them such habits of self-respect as to result in the growth of a much more efficient race of producers in the next generation. For then it might do more in the long-run to promote the growth of even material wealth than great additions to our stock of factories and steam-engines.

A people among whom wealth is well distributed, and who have The public high ambitions, are likely to accumulate a great deal of public accumulations of property; and the savings made in this form alone by some well-to-democracies. do democracies form no inconsiderable part of the best possessions cies. which our own age has inherited from its predecessors. The growth Co-operation. of the co-operative movement in all its many forms, of building societies, friendly societies, trades-unions, of working men's savings-banks etc., shows that, even so far as the immediate accumulation of material wealth goes, the resources of the country are not, as the older economists assumed, entirely lost when they are spent in paying wages.[1]

§ 8. Having looked at the development of the methods of saving We must and the accumulation of wealth, we may now return to that analysis revert to of the relations between present and deferred gratifications, which the distribution of a we began from another point of view in our study of Demand.[2] commodity between

We there saw that anyone, who has a stock of a commodity present which is applicable to several uses, endeavours to distribute it ferred and de-between them all in such a way as to give him the greatest satis- uses.

---

[1] It must however be admitted that what passes by the name of public property is often only private wealth borrowed on a mortgage of future public revenue. Municipal gas-works for instance are not generally the results of public accumulations. They were built with wealth saved by private persons, and borrowed on public account.

[2] Above, III. v.

IV, vii, 8. faction. If he thinks he could obtain more satisfaction by transferring some of it from one use to another he will do so. If, therefore, he makes his distribution rightly, he stops in applying it to
each several use at such a point that he gets an equal amount of
good out of the application that he is only just induced to make of
it to each separate use; (in other words, he distributes it between
the different uses in such a way that it has the same marginal utility
in each).

We saw, further, that the principle remains the same whether
all the uses are present, or some are present and others deferred :
but that in this latter case some new considerations enter, of which
the chief are, firstly, that the deferring of a gratification necessarily
introduces some uncertainty as to its ever being enjoyed; and
secondly, that, as human nature is constituted, a present gratification
is generally, though not always, preferred to a gratification that is
expected to be equal to it, and is as certain as anything can be in
human life.

A person may save, though he prefers present gratifications to future, and he does not increase his means by waiting. A prudent person who thought that he would derive equal gratifications from equal means at all stages of his life, would perhaps
endeavour to distribute his means equally over his whole life : and
if he thought that there was a danger that his power of earning
income at a future date would run short, he would certainly save
some of his means for a future date. He would do this not only if
he thought that his savings would increase in his hands, but even if
he thought they would diminish. He would put by a few fruit
and eggs for the winter, because they would then be scarce, though
they would not improve by keeping. If he did not see his way to
investing his earnings in trade or on loan, so as to derive interest or
profits from them, he would follow the example of some of our own
forefathers who accumulated small stores of guineas which they
carried into the country, when they retired from active life. They
reckoned that the extra gratification which they could get by spending a few more guineas while money was coming in fast, would be
of less service to them than the comfort which those guineas would
buy for them in their old age. The care of the guineas cost them a
great deal of trouble; and no doubt they would have been willing
to pay some small charge to any one who would have relieved them
from the trouble without occasioning them any sort of risk.

Some saving might therefore We can therefore imagine a state of things in which stored-up
wealth could be put to but little good use; in which many persons
wanted to make provision for their own future; while but few of
those who wanted to borrow goods, were able to offer good security

for returning them, or equivalent goods, at a future date. In such a state of things the postponement of, and waiting for enjoyments would be an action that incurred a penalty rather than reaped a reward : by handing over his means to another to be taken care of, a person could only expect to get a sure promise of something less, and not of something more than that which he lent : the rate of interest would be negative.[1]

Such a state of things is conceivable. But it is also conceivable, and almost equally probable, that people may be so anxious to work that they will undergo some penalty as a condition of obtaining leave to work. For, as deferring the consumption of some of his means is a thing which a prudent person would desire on its own account, so doing some work is a desirable object on its own account to a healthy person. Political prisoners, for instance, generally regard it as a favour to be allowed to do a little work. And human nature being what it is, we are justified in speaking of the interest on capital as the reward of the sacrifice involved in the waiting for the enjoyment of material resources, because few people would save much without reward ; just as we speak of wages as the reward of labour, because few people would work hard without reward.

The sacrifice of present pleasure for the sake of future, has been called *abstinence* by economists. But this term has been misunderstood : for the greatest accumulators of wealth are very rich persons, some of whom live in luxury, and certainly do not practise abstinence in that sense of the term in which it is convertible with abstemiousness. What economists meant was that, when a person abstained from consuming anything which he had the power of consuming, with the purpose of increasing his resources in the future, his abstinence from that particular act of consumption increased the accumulation of wealth. Since, however, the term is liable to be misunderstood, we may with advantage avoid its use, and say that the accumulation of wealth is generally the result of a postponement of enjoyment, or of a *waiting* for it.[2] Or, in other words again, it is dependent on man's *prospectiveness*; that is, his faculty of realizing the future.

IV, VII, 2.

conceivably be made even if interest were negative;

but it is equally true that some work would be done even if there were a penalty for it.

We may therefore call interest the reward of waiting : not of abstinence.

---

[1] The suggestion that the rate of interest may conceivably become a negative quantity was discussed by Foxwell in a paper on *Some Social Aspects of Banking*, read before the Bankers' Institute in January, 1886.

[2] Karl Marx and his followers have found much amusement in contemplating the accumulations of wealth which result from the abstinence of Baron Rothschild, which they contrast with the extravagance of a labourer who feeds a family of seven on seven shillings a week ; and who, living up to his full income, practises no economic abstinence at all. The argument that it is Waiting rather than Abstinence, which is rewarded by Interest and is a factor of production, was given by Macvane in the Harvard *Journal of Economics* for July, 1887.

IV, vii, 9.   The "demand price" of accumulation, that is, the future pleasure which his surroundings enable a person to obtain by working and waiting for the future, takes many forms : but the substance is always the same. The extra pleasure which a peasant who has built a weatherproof hut derives from its usance, while the snow is drifting into those of his neighbours who have spent less labour on building theirs, is the price earned by his working and waiting. It represents the extra *productiveness* of efforts wisely spent in providing against distant evils, or for the satisfaction of future wants, as compared with that which would have been derived from an impulsive grasping at immediate satisfactions. Thus it is similar in all fundamental respects to the interest which the retired physician derives from the capital he has lent to a factory or a mine to enable it to improve its machinery; and on account of the numerical definiteness of the form in which it is expressed, we may take that interest to be the type of and to represent the usance of wealth in other forms.

It matters not for our immediate purpose whether the power over the enjoyment for which the person waits, was earned by him directly by labour, which is the original source of nearly all enjoyment; or was acquired by him from others, by exchange or by inheritance, by legitimate trade or by unscrupulous forms of speculation, by spoliation or by fraud : the only points with which we are just now concerned are that the growth of wealth involves in general a deliberate waiting for a pleasure which a person has (rightly or wrongly) the power of commanding in the immediate present, and that his willingness so to wait depends on his habit of vividly realizing the future and providing for it.

The greater the rate of gain from present sacrifice the greater will often be the saving,   § 9. But let us look more closely at the statement that, as human nature is constituted, an increase in the future pleasure which can be secured by a present given sacrifice will in general increase the amount of present sacrifice that people will make. Suppose, for instance, that villagers have to get timber for building their cottages from the forests; the more distant these are, the smaller will be the return of future comfort got by each day's work in fetching the wood, the less will be their future gain from the wealth accumulated probably by each day's work : and this smallness of the return of future pleasure, to be got at a given present sacrifice, will tend to prevent them from increasing the size of their cottages; and will perhaps diminish on the whole the amount of labour they spend in getting timber. But this rule is not without exception. For, if

but not always.   custom has made them familiar with cottages of only one fashion, the

further they are from the woods, and the smaller the usance to be IV, VII, 9.
got from the produce of one day's work, the more days' work will
they give.

And similarly if a person expects, not to use his wealth himself, So the
but to let it out on interest, the higher the rate of interest the higher higher the
his reward for saving. If the rate of interest on sound investments interest
is 4 per cent., and he gives up £100 worth of enjoyment now, he may the greater
expect an annuity of £4 worth of enjoyment: but he can expect as a rule,
only £3 worth, if the rate is 3 per cent. And a fall in the rate of
interest will generally lower the margin at which a person finds it
just not worth while to give up present pleasures for the sake of
those future pleasures that are to be secured by saving some of his
means. It will therefore generally cause people to consume a little
more now, and to make less provision for future enjoyment. But
this rule is not without exception.

Sir Josiah Child remarked more than two centuries ago, that in but there
countries in which the rate of interest is high, merchants "when are excep-
they have gotten great wealth, leave trading" and lend out their the rule.
money at interest, "the gain thereof being so easy, certain and
great; whereas in other countries where interest is at a lower rate,
they continue merchants from generation to generation, and enrich
themselves and the state." And it is as true now, as it was then,
that many men retire from business when they are yet almost in the
prime of life, and when their knowledge of men and things might
enable them to conduct their business more efficiently than ever.
Again, as Sargant has pointed out, if a man has decided to go on
working and saving till he has provided a certain income for his old
age, or for his family after his death, he will find that he has to save
more if the rate of interest is low than if it is high. Suppose, for
instance, that he wishes to provide an income of £400 a year on
which he may retire from business, or to insure £400 a year for his
wife and children after his death: if then the current rate of interest
is 5 per cent., he need only put by £8,000, or insure his life for
£8,000; but if it is 4 per cent., he must save £10,000, or insure his
life for £10,000.

It is then possible that a continued fall in the rate of interest But in
may be accompanied by a continued increase in the yearly additions spite of
to the world's capital. But none the less is it true that a fall in the a fall in
distant benefits to be got by a given amount of working and waiting interest
for the future does tend on the whole to diminish the provision which tends to
people make for the future; or in more modern phrase, that a fall in saving less
the rate of interest tends to check the accumulation of wealth. For than it

IV, vii, 10.
———
otherwise
would be.

though with man's growing command over the resources of nature, he may continue to save much even with a low rate of interest; yet while human nature remains as it is every fall in that rate is likely to cause many more people to save less than to save more than they would otherwise have done.[1]

Provisional
conclusion.

§ 10. The causes which govern the accumulation of wealth and its relation to the rate of interest have so many points of contact with various parts of economic science, that the study of them cannot easily be brought together in one part of our inquiry. And although in the present Book we are concerned mainly with the side of supply; it has seemed necessary to indicate provisionally here something of the general relations between the demand for and the supply of capital. And we have seen that :—

The accumulation of wealth is governed by a great variety of causes : by custom, by habits of self-control and realizing the future, and above all by the power of family affection. Security is a necessary condition for it, and the progress of knowledge and intelligence furthers it in many ways.

A rise in the rate of interest offered for capital, *i.e.* in the demand price for saving, tends to increase the volume of saving. For in spite of the fact that a few people who have determined to secure an income of a certain fixed amount for themselves or their family will save less with a high rate of interest than with a low rate, it is a nearly universal rule that a rise in the rate increases the *desire* to save; and it often increases the *power* to save, or rather it is often an indication of an increased efficiency of our productive resources : but the older economists went too far in suggesting that a rise of interest (or of profits) at the expense of wages always increased the power of saving : they forgot that from the national point of view the investment of wealth in the child of the working man is as productive as its investment in horses or machinery.

It must however be recollected that the annual investment of wealth is a small part of the already existing stock, and that therefore the stock would not be increased perceptibly in any one year by even a considerable increase in the annual rate of saving.

[1] See also VI. vi. It may however be observed here that the dependence of the growth of capital on the high estimation of "future goods" appears to have been over-estimated by earlier writers; not under-estimated, as is argued by Prof. Böhm-Bawerk.

NOTE ON THE STATISTICS OF THE GROWTH OF WEALTH.

§ 11. The statistical history of the growth of wealth is singularly poor and misleading. This is partly due to difficulties inherent in any attempt to give a numerical measure of wealth which shall be applicable to different places and times, partly to the absence of systematic attempts to collect the necessary facts. The Government of the United States does indeed ask for returns of every person's property; and though the results thus obtained are not satisfactory, yet they are perhaps the best we have. IV, VII, 11.
——
Estimates of national wealth are seldom direct:

Estimates of the wealth of other countries have to be based almost exclusively on estimates of income, which are capitalized at various numbers of years' purchase; this number being chosen with reference (i) to the general rate of interest current at the time, (ii) to the extent to which the income derived from the use of wealth in any particular form is to be credited (a) to the permanent income-yielding power of the wealth itself; and (b) to either the labour spent in applying it, or the using up of the capital itself. This last head is specially important in the case of ironworks which depreciate rapidly, and still more in the case of such mines as are likely to be speedily exhausted; both must be capitalized at only a few years' purchase. On the other hand, the income-yielding power of land is likely to increase; and where that is the case, the income from land has to be capitalized at a great number of years' purchase (which may be regarded as making a negative provision under the head of ii. b). they are generally based on estimates of income.

Land, houses, and live stock are the three forms of wealth which have been in the first rank of importance always and everywhere. But land differs from other things in this, that an increase in its value is often chiefly due to an increase in its scarcity; and is therefore a measure rather of growing wants than of growing means of meeting wants. Thus the land of the United States in 1880 counted as of about equal value with the land of the United Kingdom, and about half that of France. Its money value was insignificant a hundred years ago; and if the density of population two or three hundred years hence is nearly the same in the United States as in the United Kingdom, the land of the former will then be worth at least twenty times as much as that of the latter. The money value of land is increased by its scarcity.

In the early middle ages the whole value of the land of England was much less than that of the few large-boned but small-sized animals that starved through the winter on it : now, though much of the best land is entered under the heads of houses, railways, etc.; though the live stock is now probably more than ten times as heavy in aggregate weight, and of better quality; and though there is now abundant farming capital of kinds which were then unknown; yet agricultural land is now worth more than three times as much as the farm stock. The few years of the pressure of the great French war nearly doubled the nominal value of the land of England. Since then free trade, improvements in transport, the opening of new countries, and other causes have lowered the nominal value of that part of the land which is devoted to agriculture. And they have made the general purchasing power of money in terms of commodities rise in England relatively to the Continent. Early in the last century 25 fr. would buy more, and especially more of the things needed by the working classes, in France and Germany than £1 would in England. But now the advantage is the other way : and this causes the recent growth of the wealth of France and Germany to appear to be greater relatively to that of England than it really is.

When account is taken of facts of this class, and also of the fact that a fall in the rate of interest increases the number of years' purchase at which any income has to be capitalized, and therefore increases the value of a property

IV, vii, 11. which yields a given income; we see that the estimates of national wealth would be very misleading, even if the statistics of income on which they were based were accurate. But still such estimates are not wholly without value.

Country and Author of Estimate.	Land, £ mill.	Houses, etc., £ mill.	Farm-capital, £ mill.	Other wealth, £ mill.	Total wealth, £ mill.	Wealth per cap. £
ENGLAND.						
1679 (Petty)	144	30	36	40	250	42
1690 (Gregory King).	180	45	25	70	320	58
1812 (Colquhoun)	750	300	143	653	1,846	180
1885 (Giffen)	1,333	1,700	382	3,012	6,427	315
UNITED KINGDOM.						
1812 (Colquhoun)	1,200	400	228	908	2,736	160
1855 (Edleston)	1,700	550	472	1,048	3,760	130
1865 (Giffen)	1,864	1,031	620	2,598	6,113	200
1875 —	2,007	1,420	668	4,453	8,548	260
1885 —	1,691	1,927	522	5,897	10,037	270
1905 (Money)	966	2,827	285	7,326	11,413	265
UNITED STATES.						
1880 (Census)	2,040	2,000	480	4,208	8,728	175
1890 —					13,200	208
1900 —					18,860	247
FRANCE.						
1892 (de Foville)	3,000	2,000	400	4,000	9,400	247
ITALY.						
1884 (Pantaleoni)	1,160	360			1,920	65

Sir R. Giffen's *Growth of Capital* and Mr. Chiozza Money's *Riches and Poverty* contain suggestive discussions on many of the figures in the above table. But their divergences show the great uncertainty of all such estimates. Mr. Money's estimate of the value of land, *i.e.* agricultural land with farm buildings, is probably too low. Sir R. Giffen estimates the value of public property at £m. 500 : and he omits public loans held at home, on the ground that the entries for them would cancel one another, as much being debited under the head of public property as is credited under that of private property. But Mr. Money reckons the gross value of public roads, parks, buildings, bridges, sewers, lighting and water works, tramways, etc. at £m. 1,650 : and, after deducting from this £m. 1,200 for public loans, he gets £m. 450 for the net value of public property; and he thus becomes free to count public loans held at home under private property. He estimates the value of foreign stock exchange securities and other foreign property held in the United Kingdom at £m. 1,821. These estimates of wealth are mainly based on estimates of income : and, as regards the statistics of income, attention may be directed to Mr. Bowley's instructive analysis in *National progress since* 1882; and in *The Economic Journal* for September 1904.

Sir R. Giffen estimates the wealth of the British Empire in 1903 (*Statistical Journal*, Vol. 66, p. 584) thus :

United Kingdom	£m.	15,000
Canada	„	1,350
Australasia	„	1,100
India	„	3,000
South Africa	„	600
Remainder of Empire	„	1,200

A tentative history of changes in the relative wealth of different parts of IV, vɪɪ, 11.
England has been deduced by Rogers from the assessment of the several ——
counties for the purpose of taxation. Le Vicomte d'Avenel's great work
L'Histoire Économique de la Propriété &c. 1200–1800 contains a rich store of
materials as to France; and comparative studies of the growth of wealth in
France and other nations have been made by Levasseur, Leroy Beaulieu,
Neymarck and de Foville.

Mr. Crammond, addressing the Institute of Bankers in March 1919,
estimated the national wealth of the United Kingdom to be £m. 24,000, and
the national income to be £m. 3,600. He reckoned the net value of the
country's foreign investments to have fallen to £m. 1,600, she having recently
sold securities amounting to £m. 1,600; and borrowed another £m. 1,400.
On the balance she appeared to be a creditor to the amount of £m. 2,600:
but a great part of this amount cannot be reckoned as adequately secured.

CHAPTER VIII

INDUSTRIAL ORGANIZATION

§ 1. WRITERS on social science from the time of Plato downwards have delighted to dwell on the increased efficiency which labour derives from organization. But in this, as in other cases, Adam Smith gave a new and larger significance to an old doctrine by the philosophic thoroughness with which he explained it, and the practical knowledge with which he illustrated it. After insisting on the advantages of the division of labour, and pointing out how they render it possible for increased numbers to live in comfort on a limited territory, he argued that the pressure of population on the means of subsistence tends to weed out those races who through want of organization or for any other cause are unable to turn to the best account the advantages of the place in which they live.

Before Adam Smith's book had yet found many readers, biologists were already beginning to make great advances towards understanding the real nature of the differences in organization which separate the higher from the lower animals; and before two more generations had elapsed, Malthus' historical account of man's struggle for existence started Darwin on that inquiry as to the effects of the struggle for existence in the animal and vegetable world, which issued in his discovery of the selective influence constantly played by it. Since that time biology has more than repaid her debt; and economists have in their turn owed much to the many profound analogies which have been discovered between social and especially industrial organization on the one side and the physical organization of the higher animals on the other. In a few cases indeed the apparent analogies disappeared on closer inquiry : but many of those which seemed at first sight most fanciful, have gradually been supplemented by others, and have at last established their claim to illustrate a fundamental unity of action between the laws of nature in the physical and in the moral world. This central unity is set forth in the general rule, to which there are not very many exceptions, that the development of the organism, whether social or physical, involves an increasing subdivision of functions between its separate parts on the one hand, and on the other a more

intimate connection between them.[1]   Each part gets to be less and IV, viii, 1.
less self-sufficient, to depend for its wellbeing more and more on —
other parts, so that any disorder in any part of a highly-developed
organism will affect other parts also.

This increased subdivision of functions, or " differentiation," as Differenti-
it is called, manifests itself with regard to industry in such forms as ation and
the division of labour, and the development of specialized skill, tion.
knowledge and machinery : while " integration," that is, a growing
intimacy and firmness of the connections between the separate parts
of the industrial organism, shows itself in such forms as the increase
of security of commercial credit, and of the means and habits of
communication by sea and road, by railway and telegraph, by post
and printing-press.

The doctrine that those organisms which are the most highly
developed, in the sense in which we have just used the phrase, are
those which are most likely to survive in the struggle for existence,
is itself in process of development.   It is not yet completely thought
out either in its biological or its economic relations.   But we may
pass to consider the main bearings in economics of the law that the
struggle for existence causes those organisms to multiply which are
best fitted to derive benefit from the environment.

The law requires to be interpreted carefully : for the fact that a The law of
thing is beneficial to its environment will not by itself secure its struggle
survival either in the physical or in the moral world.   The law of vival re-
" survival of the fittest " states that those organisms tend to be care-
survive which are best fitted to utilize the environment for their fully
own purposes.   Those that utilize the environment most, often turn preted.
out to be those that benefit those around them most ; but sometimes
they are injurious.

Conversely, the struggle for survival may fail to bring into
existence organisms that would be highly beneficial : and in the
economic world the demand for any industrial arrangement is not
certain to call forth a supply, unless it is something more than a
mere desire for the arrangement, or a need for it.   It must be an
efficient demand ; that is, it must take effect by offering adequate
payment or some other benefit to those who supply it.[2]   A mere
desire on the part of employees for a share in the management and

---

[1] See a brilliant paper by Häckel on *Arbeitstheilung in Menschen- und Thierleben*
and Schäffle's *Bau und Leben des socialen Körpers*.

[2] Like all other doctrines of the same class, this requires to be interpreted in the
light of the fact that the effective demand of a purchaser depends on his means, as
well as on his wants : a small want on the part of a rich man often has more effective
force in controlling the business arrangements of the world than a great want on the
part of a poor man.

IV, VIII, 2. the profits of the factory in which they work, or the need on the part of clever youths for a good technical education, is not a demand in the sense in which the term is used when it is said that supply naturally and surely follows demand. This seems a hard truth: but some of its harshest features are softened down by the fact that those races, whose members render services to one another without exacting direct recompense, are not only the most likely to flourish for the time, but most likely to rear a large number of descendants who inherit their beneficial habits.

Its harshest features softened by the principle of heredity.

§ 2. Even in the vegetable world a species of plants, however vigorous in its growth, which should be neglectful of the interests of its seeds, would soon perish from the earth. The standard of family and race duty is often high in the animal kingdom; and even those predatory animals which we are accustomed to regard as the types of cruelty, which fiercely utilize the environment and do nothing for it in return, must yet be willing as individuals to exert themselves for the benefit of their offspring. And going beyond the narrower interests of the family to those of the race, we find that among so-called social animals, such as bees and ants, those races survive in which the individual is most energetic in performing varied services for the society without the prompting of direct gain to himself.

Influence of parental care on survival of the species.

But when we come to human beings, endowed with reason and speech, the influence of a tribal sense of duty in strengthening the tribe takes a more varied form. It is true that in the ruder stages of human life many of the services rendered by the individual to others are nearly as much due to hereditary habit and unreasoning impulse, as are those of the bees and ants. But deliberate, and therefore moral, self-sacrifice soon makes its appearance; it is fostered by the far-seeing guidance of prophets and priests and legislators, and is inculcated by parable and legend. Gradually the unreasoning sympathy, of which there are germs in the lower animals, extends its area and gets to be deliberately adopted as a basis of action : tribal affection, starting from a level hardly higher than that which prevails in a pack of wolves or a horde of banditti, gradually grows into a noble patriotism; and religious ideals are raised and purified. The races in which these qualities are the most highly developed are sure, other things being equal, to be stronger than others in war and in contests with famine and disease; and ultimately to prevail. Thus the struggle for existence causes in the long run those races of men to survive in which the individual is most willing to sacrifice himself for the benefit of those around him; and

In man self-sacrifice becomes deliberate and is the basis of the strength of the race.

which are consequently the best adapted collectively to make use of IV, VIII, 3.
their environment.

Unfortunately however not all the qualities which enable one But evil
race to prevail over another benefit mankind as a whole. It would is mixed
with the
no doubt be wrong to lay very much stress on the fact that warlike good,
habits have often enabled half-savage races to reduce to submission
others who were their superiors in every peaceful virtue; for such
conquests have gradually increased the physical vigour of the world,
and its capacity for great things, and ultimately perhaps have done
more good than harm. But there is no such qualification to the
statement that a race does not establish its claim to deserve well of
the world by the mere fact that it flourishes in the midst or on the
surface of another race. For, though biology and social science alike
show that parasites sometimes benefit in unexpected ways the race
on which they thrive; yet in many cases they turn the peculiarities
of that race to good account for their own purposes without giving
any good return. The fact that there is an economic demand for especially
the services of Jewish and Armenian money-dealers in Eastern in the
case of a
Europe and Asia, or for Chinese labour in California, is not by itself parasitic
a proof, nor even a very strong ground for believing, that such race.
arrangements tend to raise the quality of human life as a whole.
For, though a race entirely dependent on its own resources can
scarcely prosper unless it is fairly endowed with the most important
social virtues; yet a race, which has not these virtues and which is
not capable of independent greatness, may be able to thrive on its
relations with another race. But on the whole, and subject to grave
exceptions, those races survive and predominate in which the best
qualities are most strongly developed.

§ 3. This influence of heredity shows itself nowhere more The caste
markedly than in social organization. For that must necessarily system
was use-
be a slow growth, the product of many generations : it must be ful at
the time,
based on those customs and aptitudes of the great mass of the people but not
which are incapable of quick change. In early times when religious, free from
draw-
ceremonial, political, military and industrial organization were backs.
intimately connected, and were indeed but different sides of the
same thing, nearly all those nations which were leading the van of
the world's progress were found to agree in having adopted a more
or less strict system of caste : and this fact by itself proved that the
distinction of castes was well suited to its environment, and that on
the whole it strengthened the races or nations which adopted it.
For since it was a controlling factor of life, the nations which adopted
it could not have generally prevailed over others, if the influence

IV, VIII, 3. exerted by it had not been in the main beneficial. Their pre-eminence proved not that it was free from defects, but that its excellences, relatively to that particular stage of progress, outweighed its defects.

Again we know that an animal or a vegetable species may differ from its competitors by having two qualities, one of which is of great advantage to it; while the other is unimportant, perhaps even slightly injurious, and that the former of these qualities will make the species succeed in spite of its having the latter : the survival of which will then be no proof that it is beneficial. Similarly the struggle for existence has kept alive many qualities and habits in the human race which were in themselves of no advantage, but which are associated by a more or less permanent bond with others that are great sources of strength. Such instances are found in the tendency to an overbearing demeanour and a scorn for patient industry among nations that owe their advance chiefly to military victories; and again in the tendency among commercial nations to think too much of wealth and to use it for the purposes of display. But the most striking instances are found in matters of organization; the excellent adaptation of the system of caste for the special work which it had to do, enabled it to flourish in spite of its great faults, the chief of which were its rigidity, and its sacrifice of the individual to the interests of society, or rather to certain special exigencies of society.

The same is true of the relations between different industrial classes in the modern Western world. Passing over intermediate stages and coming at once to the modern organization of the Western world, we find it offering a striking contrast, and a no less striking resemblance, to the system of caste. On the one hand, rigidity has been succeeded by plasticity : the methods of industry which were then stereotyped, now change with bewildering quickness; the social relations of classes, and the position of the individual in his class, which were then definitely fixed by traditional rules, are now perfectly variable and change their forms with the changing circumstances of the day. But on the other hand, the sacrifice of the individual to the exigencies of society as regards the production of material wealth seems in some respects to be a case of atavism, a reversion to conditions which prevailed in the far-away times of the rule of caste. For the division of labour between the different ranks of industry and between different individuals in the same rank is so thorough and uncompromising, that the real interests of the producer are sometimes in danger of being sacrificed for the sake of increasing the addition which his work makes to the aggregate production of material wealth.

§ 4. Adam Smith, while insisting on the general advantages of that minute division of labour and of that subtle industrial organization which were being developed with unexampled rapidity in his time, was yet careful to indicate many points in which the system failed, and many incidental evils which it involved.[1] But many of his followers with less philosophic insight, and in some cases with less real knowledge of the world, argued boldly that whatever is, is right. They argued for instance that, if a man had a talent for managing business, he would be surely led to use that talent for the benefit of mankind : that meanwhile a like pursuit of their own interests would lead others to provide for his use such capital as he could turn to best account; and that his own interest would lead him so to arrange those in his employment that everyone should do the highest work of which he was capable, and no other; and that it would lead him to purchase and use all machinery and other aids to production, which could in his hands contribute more than the equivalent of their own cost towards supplying the wants of the world.

This doctrine of natural organization contains more truth of the highest importance to humanity than almost any other which is equally likely to evade the comprehension of those who discuss grave social problems without adequate study : and it had a singular fascination for earnest and thoughtful minds.   But its exaggeration worked much harm, especially to those who delighted most in it. For it prevented them from seeing and removing the evil that was intertwined with the good in the changes that were going on around them.   It hindered them from inquiring whether many even of the broader features of modern industry might not be transitional, having indeed good work to do in their time, as the caste system had in its time; but being, like it, serviceable chiefly in leading the way towards better arrangements for a happier age.   And it did harm by preparing the way for exaggerated reaction against it.

§ 5. Moreover the doctrine took no account of the manner in which organs are strengthened by being used. Herbert Spencer has insisted with much force on the rule that, if any physical or mental exercise gives pleasure and is therefore frequent, those physical or mental organs which are used in it are likely to grow rapidly.   Among the lower animals indeed the action of this rule is so intimately interwoven with that of the survival of the fittest, that the distinction between the two need not often be emphasized. For as it might be guessed *a priori*, and as seems to be proved by observation, the struggle for survival tends to prevent animals from

Margin notes: IV, VIII, 4, 5. Adam Smith's moderation, the extravagance of some of his followers.

They paid too little attention to the conditions under which the faculties can best be developed.

---

[1] See above I. IV. 6 ; and below Appendix B, 3 and 6.

IV, vin, 5. taking much pleasure in the exercise of functions which do not contribute to their wellbeing.

But man, with his strong individuality, has greater freedom. He delights in the use of his faculties for their own sake; sometimes using them nobly, whether with the abandon of the great Greek burst of life, or under the control of a deliberate and steadfast striving towards important ends; sometimes ignobly, as in the case of a morbid development of the taste for drink. The religious, the moral, the intellectual and the artistic faculties on which the progress of industry depends, are not acquired solely for the sake of the things that may be got by them; but are developed by exercise for the sake of the pleasure and the happiness which they themselves bring : and, in the same way, that greater factor of economic prosperity, the organization of a well-ordered state, is the product of an infinite variety of motives; many of which have no direct connection with the pursuit of national wealth.[1]

No doubt it is true that physical peculiarities acquired by the parents during their life-time are seldom if ever transmitted to their offspring. But no conclusive case seems to have been made out for the assertion that the children of those who have led healthy lives, physically and morally, will not be born with a firmer fibre than they would have been had the same parents grown up under unwholesome influences which had enfeebled the fibre of their minds and their bodies. And it is certain that in the former case the children are likely after birth to be better nourished, and better trained; to acquire more wholesome instincts; and to have more of that regard for others and that self-respect, which are the mainsprings of human progress, than in the latter case.[2]

It is needful then diligently to inquire whether the present industrial organization might not with advantage be so modified as to increase the opportunities, which the lower grades of industry have for using latent mental faculties, for deriving pleasure from their use, and for strengthening them by use; since the argument that if such a change had been beneficial, it would have been already

---

[1] Man with his many motives, as he may set himself deliberately to encourage the growth of one peculiarity, may equally set himself to check the growth of another : the slowness of progress during the Middle Ages was partly due to a deliberate detestation of learning.

[2] See Note XI. in the Mathematical Appendix. Considerations of this class have little application to the development of mere animals, such as mice ; and none at all to that of peas and other vegetables. And therefore the marvellous arithmetical results which have been established, provisionally at all events, in regard to heredity in such cases, have very little bearing on the full problems of inheritance with which students of social science are concerned : and some negative utterances on this subject by eminent Mendelians seem to lack due reserve. Excellent remarks on the subject will be found in Prof. Pigou's *Wealth and Welfare*, Part I, ch. iv.

brought about by the struggle for survival, must be rejected as IV, VIII, 5. invalid.   Man's prerogative extends to a limited but effective control over natural development by forecasting the future and preparing the way for the next step.

Thus progress may be hastened by thought and work; by the application of the principles of Eugenics to the replenishment of the race from its higher rather than its lower strains, and by the appropriate education of the faculties of either sex : but however hastened it must be gradual and relatively slow.   It must be slow relatively to man's growing command over technique and the forces of nature; a command which is making ever growing calls for courage and caution, for resource and steadfastness, for penetrating insight and for breadth of view.   And it must be very much too slow to keep pace with the rapid inflow of proposals for the prompt reorganization of society on a new basis.   In fact our new command over nature, while opening the door to much larger schemes for industrial organization than were physically possible even a short time ago, places greater responsibilities on those who would advocate new developments of social and industrial structure.   For though, institutions may be changed rapidly; yet if they are to endure they must be appropriate to man : they cannot retain their stability if they change very much faster than he does.   Thus progress itself increases the urgency of the warning that in the economic world, *Natura non facit saltum*.[1]

Changes in industrial structure must wait on the development of man; and therefore must be either gradual or unstable.

Progress must be slow; but even from the merely material point of view it is to be remembered that changes, which add only a little to the immediate efficiency of production, may be worth having if they make mankind ready and fit for an organization, which will be more effective in the production of wealth and more equal in its distribution; and that every system, which allows the higher faculties of the lower grades of industry to go to waste, is open to grave suspicion.

[1] Compare Appendix A, 16.

CHAPTER IX

INDUSTRIAL ORGANIZATION, CONTINUED. DIVISION OF
LABOUR. THE INFLUENCE OF MACHINERY

IV, ɪx, 1.
———
The course
of inquiry
in this and
the three
following
chapters.

§ 1. The first condition of an efficient organization of industry
is that it should keep everyone employed at such work as his abilities
and training fit him to do well, and should equip him with the best
machinery and other appliances for his work. We shall leave on
one side for the present the distribution of work between those who
carry out the details of production on the one hand, and those who
manage its general arrangement and undertake its risk on the
other; and confine ourselves to the division of labour between
different classes of operatives, with special reference to the influence
of machinery. In the following chapter we shall consider the reciprocal effects of division of labour and localization of industry; in
a third chapter we shall inquire how far the advantages of division
of labour depend upon the aggregation of large capitals into the hands
of single individuals or firms, or, as is commonly said, on production
on a large scale; and lastly, we shall examine the growing specialization of the work of business management.

Practice
makes
perfect.

Everyone is familiar with the fact that " practice makes perfect," that it enables an operation, which at first seemed difficult,
to be done after a time with comparatively little exertion, and yet
much better than before; and physiology in some measure explains

Physio-
logical ex-
planation.

this fact. For it gives reasons for believing that the change is due
to the gradual growth of new habits of more or less " reflex " or
automatic action. Perfectly reflex actions, such as that of breathing
during sleep, are performed by the responsibility of the local nerve
centres without any reference to the supreme central authority of
the thinking power, which is supposed to reside in the cerebrum.
But all deliberate movements require the attention of the chief
central authority : it receives information from the nerve centres or
local authorities and perhaps in some cases direct from the sentient
nerves, and sends back detailed and complex instructions to the local
authorities, or in some cases direct to the muscular nerves, and so
co-ordinates their action as to bring about the required results.[1]

---

[1] For instance, the first time a man attempts to skate he must give his whole
attention to keeping his balance, his cerebrum has to exercise a direct control over
every movement, and he has not much mental energy left for other things. But

The physiological basis of purely mental work is not yet well understood; but what little we do know of the growth of brain structure seems to indicate that practice in any kind of thinking develops new connections between different parts of the brain. Anyhow we know for a fact that practice will enable a person to solve quickly, and without any considerable exertion, questions which he could have dealt with but very imperfectly a little while before, even by the greatest effort. The mind of the merchant, the lawyer, the physician, and the man of science, becomes gradually equipped with a store of knowledge and a faculty of intuition, which can be obtained in no other way than by the continual application of the best efforts of a powerful thinker for many years together to one more or less narrow class of questions. Of course the mind cannot work hard for many hours a day in one direction : and a hard-worked man will sometimes find recreation in work that does not belong to his business, but would be fatiguing enough to a person who had to do it all day long.

Some social reformers have indeed maintained that those who do the most important brain work might do a fair share of manual work also, without diminishing their power of acquiring knowledge or thinking out hard questions. But experience seems to show that the best relief from overstrain is in occupations taken up to suit the

Knowledge and intellectual ability.

Change of activity often a form of relaxation.

---

after a good deal of practice the action becomes semi-automatic, the local nerve centres undertake nearly all the work of regulating the muscles, the cerebrum is set free, and the man can carry on an independent train of thought; he can even alter his course to avoid an obstacle in his path, or to recover his balance after it has been disturbed by a slight unevenness, without in any way interrupting the course of his thoughts. It seems that the exercise of nerve force under the immediate direction of the thinking power residing in the cerebrum has gradually built up a set of connections, involving probably distinct physical change, between the nerves and nerve centres concerned; and these new connections may be regarded as a sort of capital of nerve force. There is probably something like an organized bureaucracy of the local nerve centres : the medulla, the spinal axis, and the larger ganglia generally acting the part of provincial authorities, and being able after a time to regulate the district and village authorities without troubling the supreme government. Very likely they send up messages as to what is going on : but if nothing much out of the way has happened, these are very little attended to. When however a new feat has to be accomplished, as for instance learning to skate backwards, the whole thinking force will be called into requisition for the time; and will now be able by aid of the special skating-organization of the nerves and nerve centres, which has been built up in ordinary skating, to do what would have been altogether impossible without such aid.

To take a higher instance : when an artist is painting at his best, his cerebrum is fully occupied with his work : his whole mental force is thrown into it, and the strain is too great to be kept up for a long time together. In a few hours of happy inspiration he may give utterance to thoughts that exert a perceptible influence on the character of coming generations. But his power of expression had been earned by numberless hours of plodding work in which he had gradually built up an intimate connection between eye and hand, sufficient to enable him to make good rough sketches of things with which he is tolerably familiar, even while he is engaged in an engrossing conversation and is scarcely conscious that he has a pencil in his hand.

IV, IX, 2. mood of the moment and stopped when the mood is passed, that is, in what popular instinct classes as " relaxation." Any occupation which is so far business-like that a person must sometimes force himself by an effort of the will to go on with it, draws on his nervous force and is not perfect relaxation : and therefore it is not economical from the point of view of the community unless its value is sufficient to outweigh a considerable injury to his main work.[1]

In the higher grades of work extreme specialization does not always increase efficiency.

§ 2. It is a difficult and unsettled question how far specialization should be carried in the highest branches of work. In science it seems to be a sound rule that the area of study should be broad during youth, and should gradually be narrowed as years go on. A medical man who has always given his attention exclusively to one class of diseases, may perhaps give less wise advice even in his special subject than another who, having learnt by wider experience to think of those diseases in relation to general health, gradually concentrates his study more and more on them, and accumulates a vast store of special experiences and subtle instincts. But there is no doubt that greatly increased efficiency can be attained through division of labour in those occupations in which there is much demand for mere manual skill.

But it is easy to acquire a high manual skill in a narrow range of work.

Adam Smith pointed out that a lad who had made nothing but nails all his life could make them twice as quickly as a first-rate smith who only took to nail-making occasionally. Anyone who has to perform exactly the same set of operations day after day on things of exactly the same shape, gradually learns to move his fingers exactly as they are wanted, by almost automatic action and with greater rapidity than would be possible if every movement had to wait for a deliberate instruction of the will. One familiar instance is seen in the tying of threads by children in a cotton-mill. Again, in a clothing or a boot factory, a person who sews, whether by hand or machinery, just the same seam on a piece of leather or cloth of just the same size, hour after hour, day after day, is able to do it with far less effort and far more quickly than a worker with much greater quickness of eye and hand, and of a much higher order of

---

[1] J. S. Mill went so far as to maintain that his occupations at the India Office did not interfere with his pursuit of philosophical inquiries. But it seems ⁿrobable that this diversion of his freshest powers lowered the quality of his best thought more than he was aware; and though it may have diminished but little his remarkable usefulness in his own generation, it probably affected very much his power of doing that kind of work which influences the course of thought in future generations. It was by husbanding every atom of his small physical strength that Darwin was enabled to do so much work of just that kind : and a social reformer who had succeeded in exploiting Darwin's leisure hours in useful work on behalf of the community, would have done a very bad piece of business for it.

general skill, who was accustomed to make the whole of a coat or IV, IX, 2
the whole of a boot.[1]

Again, in the wood and the metal industries, if a man has to The
perform exactly the same operations over and over again on the uniformity of many
same piece of material, he gets into the habit of holding it exactly in processes
the way in which it is wanted, and of arranging the tools and other in the
things which he has to handle in such positions that he is able to wood and metal
bring them to work on one another with the least possible loss of time trades.
and of force in the movements of his own body. Accustomed to find
them always in the same position and to take them in the same order,
his hands work in harmony with one another almost automatically :
and with increased practice his expenditure of nervous force
diminishes even more rapidly than his expenditure of muscular force.

But when the action has thus been reduced to routine it has The
nearly arrived at the stage at which it can be taken over by provinces of manual
machinery. The chief difficulty to be overcome is that of getting labour and
the machinery to hold the material firmly in exactly the position in machinery.
which the machine tool can be brought to bear on it in the right
way, and without wasting too much time in taking grip of it. But
this can generally be contrived when it is worth while to spend some
labour and expense on it; and then the whole operation can often
be controlled by a worker who, sitting before a machine, takes with
the left hand a piece of wood or metal from a heap and puts it in a
socket, while with the right he draws down a lever, or in some
other way sets the machine tool at work, and finally with his left
hand throws on to another heap the material which has been cut or
punched or drilled or planed exactly after a given pattern. It is in
these industries especially that we find the reports of modern trades-
unions to be full of complaints that unskilled labourers, and even
their wives and children, are put to do work which used to require
the skill and judgment of a trained mechanic, but which has been
reduced to mere routine by the improvement of machinery and the
ever-increasing minuteness of the subdivision of labour.

[1] The best and most expensive clothes are made by highly skilled and highly
paid tailors, each of whom works right through first one garment and then another :
while the cheapest and worst clothes are made for starvation wages by unskilled
women who take the cloth to their own homes and do every part of the sewing themselves. But clothes of intermediate qualities are made in workshops or factories, in
which the division and subdivision of labour are carried as far as the size of the staff
will permit; and this method is rapidly gaining ground at both ends at the expense
of the rival method. Lord Lauderdale (*Inquiry*, p. 282) quotes Xenophon's argument that the best work is done when each confines himself to one simple department,
as when one man makes shoes for men, and another for women; or better when one
man only sews shoes or garments, another cuts them out : the king's cooking is much
better than anybody's else's, because he has one cook who only boils, another who
only roasts meat; one who only boils fish, another who only fries it : there is not
one man to make all sorts of bread but a special man for special qualities.

IV, ix, 3.
___
The
division
of labour
in relation
to the
growth of
machinery.

§ 3. We are thus led to a general rule, the action of which is more prominent in some branches of manufacture than others, but which applies to all. It is, that any manufacturing operation that can be reduced to uniformity, so that exactly the same thing has to be done over and over again in the same way, is sure to be taken over sooner or later by machinery. There may be delays and difficulties; but if the work to be done by it is on a sufficient scale, money and inventive power will be spent without stint on the task till it is achieved.[1]

Thus the two movements of the improvement of machinery and the growing subdivision of labour have gone together and are in some measure connected. But the connection is not so close as is generally supposed. It is the largeness of markets, the increased demand for great numbers of things of the same kind, and in some cases of things made with great accuracy, that leads to subdivision of labour; the chief effect of the improvement of machinery is to cheapen and make more accurate the work which would anyhow

Machinery
displaces
purely
manual
skill;

have been subdivided. For instance, " in organizing the works at Soho, Boulton and Watt found it necessary to carry division of labour to the furthest practicable point. There were no slide-lathes, planing machines or boring tools, such as now render mechanical accuracy of construction almost a matter of certainty. Everything depended on the individual mechanic's accuracy of hand and eye; yet mechanics generally were much less skilled then than they are now. The way in which Boulton and Watt contrived partially to get over the difficulty was to confine their workmen to special classes of work, and make them as expert in them as possible. By continued practice in handling the same tools and fabricating the same articles, they thus acquired great individual proficiency." [2]

and thus
diminishes

Thus machinery constantly supplants and renders unnecessary that

[1] One great inventor is rumoured to have spent £300,000 on experiments relating to textile machinery, and his outlay is said to have been abundantly returned to him. Some of his inventions were of such a kind as can be made only by a man of genius; and however great the need, they must have waited till the right man was found for them. He charged not unreasonably £1000 as royalty for each of his combing machines; and a worsted manufacturer, being full of work, found it worth his while to buy an additional machine, and pay this extra charge for it, only six months before the expiry of the patent. But such cases are exceptional: as a rule, patented machines are not very dear. In some cases the economy of having them all produced at one place by special machinery has been so great that the patentee has found it to his advantage to sell them at a price lower than the old price of the inferior machines which they displaced: for that old price gave him so high a profit, that it was worth his while to lower the price still further in order to induce the use of the machines for new purposes and in new markets. In almost every trade many things are done by hand, though it is well known that they could easily be done by some adaptations of machines that are already in use in that or some other trade, and which are not made only because there would not as yet be enough employment for them to remunerate the trouble and expense of making them.

[2] Smiles' *Boulton and Watt*, pp. 170, 1.

purely manual skill, the attainment of which was, even up to Adam IV, IX, 4.
Smith's time, the chief advantage of division of labour. But this some of
influence is more than countervailed by its tendency to increase the the advan-
scale of manufactures and to make them more complex; and there- tages of division of
fore to increase the opportunities for division of labour of all kinds, labour: but
and especially in the matter of business management. increases the scope for it.

§ 4. The powers of machinery to do work that requires too much Machine-
accuracy to be done by hand are perhaps best seen in some branches made
of the metal industries in which the system of Interchangeable Parts machinery is intro-
is being rapidly developed. It is only after long training and with ducing the new era
much care and labour that the hand can make one piece of metal of Inter-
accurately to resemble or to fit into another: and after all the change-able
accuracy is not perfect. But this is just the work which a well made Parts.
machine can do most easily and most perfectly. For instance, if
sowing and reaping machines had to be made by hand, their first
cost would be very high; and when any part of them was broken,
it could be replaced only at great cost by sending the machine back
to the manufacturer or by bringing a highly skilled mechanic to the
machine. But as it is, the manufacturer keeps in store many fac-
similes of the broken part, which were made by the same machinery,
and are therefore interchangeable with it. A farmer in the North-
West of America, perhaps a hundred miles away from any good
mechanic's shop, can yet use complicated machinery with confidence;
since he knows that by telegraphing the number of the machine and
the number of any part of it which he has broken, he will get by
the next train a new piece which he can himself fit into its place.
The importance of this principle of interchangeable parts has been
but recently grasped; there are however many signs that it will do
more than any other to extend the use of machine-made machinery
to every branch of production, including even domestic and agricultural work.[1]

The influences which machinery exerts over the character of Illustra-
modern industry are well illustrated in the manufacture of watches. tion from the history
Some years ago the chief seat of this business was in French Switzer- of the
land; where the subdivision of labour was carried far, though a great watch-making
part of the work was done by a more or less scattered population. trade.
There were about fifty distinct branches of trade each of which did
one small part of the work. In almost all of them a highly specialized
manual skill was required, but very little judgment; the earnings

---

[1] The system owes its origin in great measure to Sir Joseph Whitworth's standard
gauges; but it has been worked out with most enterprise and thoroughness in America.
Standardization is most helpful in regard to things which are to be built up with others
into complex machines, buildings, bridges, etc.

IV, IX, 4. were generally low, because the trade had been established too long
for those in it to have anything like a monopoly, and there was no
difficulty in bringing up to it any child with ordinary intelligence.
But this industry is now yielding ground to the American system of
making watches by machinery, which requires very little specialized
manual skill.   In fact the machinery is becoming every year more
and more automatic, and is getting to require less and less assistance

Complex   from the human hand.   But the more delicate the machine's power,
machinery the greater is the judgment and carefulness which is called for from
increases
the   those who see after it.   Take for instance a beautiful machine
demand   which feeds itself with steel wire at one end, and delivers at the
for judg-
ment and   other tiny screws of exquisite form; it displaces a great many
general   operatives who had indeed acquired a very high and specialized
intelli-
gence;   manual skill, but who lived sedentary lives, straining their eyesight
through microscopes, and finding in their work very little scope for
any faculty except a mere command over the use of their fingers.
But the machine is intricate and costly, and the person who minds
it must have an intelligence, and an energetic sense of responsibility,
which go a long way towards making a fine character; and which,
though more common than they were, are yet sufficiently rare to
be able to earn a very high rate of pay.   No doubt this is an extreme
case; and the greater part of the work done in a watch factory is
much simpler.   But much of it requires higher faculties than the
old system did, and those engaged in it earn on the average higher
wages; at the same time it has already brought the price of a trustworthy watch within the range of the poorest classes of the community, and it is showing signs of being able soon to accomplish the
very highest class of work.[1]

and in   Those who finish and put together the different parts of a watch
some cases
weakens   must always have highly specialized skill : but most of the machines
the   which are in use in a watch factory are not different in general
barriers
that divide character from those which are used in any other of the lighter metal
different   trades : in fact many of them are mere modifications of the turning
trades.
lathes and of the slotting, punching, drilling, planing, shaping,
milling machines and a few others, which are familiar to all engineering trades.   This is a good illustration of the fact that while there is
a constantly increasing subdivision of labour, many of the lines of

---

[1] The perfection which the machinery has already attained is shown by the fact
that at the Inventions Exhibition held in London in 1885, the representative of an
American watch factory took to pieces fifty watches before some English representatives of the older system of manufacture, and after throwing the different parts into
different heaps, asked them to select for him one piece from each heap in succession;
he then set these pieces up in one of the watch-cases and handed them back a watch
in perfect order.

division between trades which are nominally distinct are becoming IV, IX, 5.
narrower and less difficult to be passed. In old times it would have
been very small comfort to watch-makers, who happened to be suffering from a diminished demand for their wares, to be told that the
gun-making trade was in want of extra hands; but most of the
operatives in a watch factory would find machines very similar to
those with which they were familiar, if they strayed into a gun-
making factory or sewing-machine factory, or a factory for making
textile machinery. A watch factory with those who worked in it
could be converted without any overwhelming loss into a sewing-
machine factory : almost the only condition would be that in the
new factory no one should be put to work which required a higher
order of general intelligence, than that to which he was already
accustomed.

§ 5. The printing trade affords another instance of the way in Illustra-
which an improvement of machinery and an increase in the volume tion from
of production causes an elaborate subdivision of labour. Everyone ing trade.
is familiar with the pioneer newspaper editor of newly settled districts
of America, who sets up the type of his articles as he composes them;
and with the aid of a boy prints off his sheets and distributes them
to his scattered neighbours. When however the mystery of printing
was new, the printer had to do all this for himself, and in addition
to make all his own appliances.[1] These are now provided for him
by separate " subsidiary " trades, from whom even the printer in
the backwoods can obtain everything that he wants to use. But
in spite of the assistance which it thus gets from outside, a large
printing establishment has to find room for many different classes
of workers within its walls. To say nothing of those who organize
and superintend the business, of those who do its office work and
keep its stores, of the skilled " readers " who correct any errors that
may have crept into the " proofs," of its engineers and repairers of
machinery, of those who cast, and who correct and prepare its stereotype plates; of the warehousemen and the boys and girls who assist
them, and several other minor classes; there are the two great
groups of the compositors who set up the type, and the machinists
and pressmen who print impressions from them. Each of these two Instance
groups is divided into many smaller groups, especially in the large of the
centres of the printing trade. In London, for instance, a minder cation in

---

[1] " The type-founder was probably the first to secede from the concern; then
printers delegated to others the making of presses; afterwards the ink and the rollers
found separate and distinct manufacturers; and there arose a class of persons who,
though belonging to other trades, made printing appliances a speciality, such as
printers' smiths, printers' joiners and printers' engineers " (Mr. Southward in the
Article on *Typography* in the *Encyclopædia Britannica*).

IV, IX, 5.
modern industry of thin lines of division,

who was accustomed to one class of machine, or a compositor who was accustomed to one class of work, if thrown out of employment would not willingly abandon the advantage of his specialized skill, and falling back on his general knowledge of the trade seek work at another kind of machine or in another class of work.[1] These barriers between minute subdivisions of a trade count for a great deal in many descriptions of the modern tendency towards specializa-

which can be passed without great difficulty.

tion of industry; and to some extent rightly, because though many of them are so slight that a man thrown out of work in one sub-division could pass into one of its neighbours without any great loss of efficiency, yet he does not do so until he has tried for a while to get employment in his old lines; and therefore the barriers are as effective as stronger ones would be so far as the minor fluctuations of trade from week to week are concerned. But they are of an altogether different kind from the deep and broad partitions which divided one group of mediæval handicraftsmen from another, and which caused the lifelong suffering of the handloom-weavers when their trade had left them.[2]

Instance of the increased

In the printing trades, as in the watch trade, we see mechanical and scientific appliances attaining results that would be impossible

---

[1] For instance, Mr. Southward tells us " a minder may understand only book machines or only news machines; he may know all about " machines that print from flat surfaces or those that print from cylinders; " or of cylinders he may know only one kind. Entirely novel machines create a new class of artisans. There are men perfectly competent to manage a Walter press who are ignorant how to work two-colour or fine book-work machines. In the compositor's department division of labour is carried out to a still minuter degree. An old-fashioned printer would set up indifferently a placard, a title-page, or a book. At the present day we have jobbing hands, book hands, and news hands, the word 'hand' suggesting the factory-like nature of the business. There are jobbing hands who confine themselves to posters. Book hands comprise those who set up the titles and those who set up the body of the work. Of these latter again, while one man composes, another, the 'maker-up,' arranges the pages."

[2] Let us follow still further the progress of machinery in supplanting manual labour in some directions and opening out new fields for its employment in others. Let us watch the process by which large editions of a great newspaper are set up and printed off in a few hours. To begin with, a good part of the type-setting is itself often done by a machine; but in any case the types are in the first instance on a plane surface, from which it is impossible to print very rapidly. The next step therefore is to make a papier-maché cast of them, which is bent on to a cylinder, and is then used as the mould from which a new metal plate is cast that fits the cylinders of the printing machine. Fixed on these it rotates alternately against the inking cylinders and the paper. The paper is arranged in a huge roll at the bottom of the machine and unrolls itself automatically, first against the damping cylinders and then against the printing cylinders, the first of which prints it on one side, and the second on the other : thence to the cutting cylinders, which cut it into equal lengths, and thence to the folding apparatus, which folds it ready for sale.

More recently the casting of the type has been brought under the new methods. The compositor plays on a keyboard like that of the type-writer, and the matrix of a corresponding letter goes into line : then after spacing out, molten lead is poured on the line of matrices, and a solid line of type is ready. And in a further develop-ment each letter is cast separately from its matrix; the machine reckons up the space taken by the letters, stops when there are enough for a line, divides out the free space equally into the requisite number of small spaces between the words; and finally casts the line. It is claimed that one compositor can work several such machines simultaneously in distant towns by electric currents.

without them; at the same time that they persistently take over
work that used to require manual skill and dexterity, but not much
judgment; while they leave for man's hand all those parts which
do require the use of judgment, and open up all sorts of new occupations in which there is a great demand for it.   Every improvement
and cheapening of the printer's appliances increases the demand for
the judgment and discretion and literary knowledge of the reader,
for the skill and taste of those who know how to set up a good title-
page, or how to make ready a sheet on which an engraving is to be
printed, so that light and shade will be distributed properly.   It
increases the demand for the gifted and highly-trained artists who
draw or engrave on wood and stone and metal, and for those who
know how to give an accurate report in ten lines of the substance
of a speech that occupied ten minutes—an intellectual feat the difficulty of which we underrate, because it is so frequently performed.
And again, it tends to increase the work of photographers and
electrotypers, and stereotypers, of the makers of printer's machinery,
and many others who get a higher training and a higher income from
their work than did those layers on and takers off, and those folders
of newspapers who have found their work taken over by iron fingers
and iron arms.

§ 6.   We may now pass to consider the effects which machinery
has in relieving that excessive muscular strain which a few generations ago was the common lot of more than half the working men
even in such a country as England.   The most marvellous instances
of the power of machinery are seen in large iron-works, and especially
in those for making armour plates, where the force to be exerted is
so great that man's muscles count for nothing, and where every
movement, whether horizontal or vertical, has to be effected by
hydraulic or steam force, and man stands by ready to govern the
machinery and clear away ashes or perform some such secondary
task.

Machinery of this class has increased our command over nature,
but it has not directly altered the character of man's work very
much; for that which it does he could not have done without it.
But in other trades machinery has lightened man's labours.   The
house carpenters, for instance, make things of the same kind as
those used by our forefathers, with much less toil for themselves.
They now give themselves chiefly to those parts of the task which
are most pleasant and most interesting; while in every country
town and almost every village there are found steam mills for
sawing, planing and moulding, which relieve them of that grievous

IV, ix, 6.
———
demand
for facul-
ties of a
high order
caused by
machinery.

Machinery
relieves
the strain
on human
muscles.

IV, IX, 6. fatigue which not very long ago used to make them prematurely old.[1]

Machinery takes over sooner or later all monotonous work in manufacture.

New machinery, when just invented, generally requires a great deal of care and attention. But the work of its attendant is always being sifted; that which is uniform and monotonous is gradually taken over by the machine, which thus becomes steadily more and more automatic and self-acting; till at last there is nothing for the hand to do, but to supply the material at certain intervals and to take away the work when finished. There still remains the responsibility for seeing that the machinery is in good order and working smoothly; but even this task is often made light by the introduction of an automatic movement, which brings the machine to a stop the instant anything goes wrong.

Illustration from the textile industries.

Nothing could be more narrow or monotonous than the occupation of a weaver of plain stuffs in the old time. But now one woman will manage four or more looms, each of which does many times as much work in the course of the day as the old hand-loom did; and her work is much less monotonous and calls for much more judgment than his did. So that for every hundred yards of cloth that are woven, the purely monotonous work done by human beings is probably not a twentieth part of what it was.[2]

It thus prevents monotony of work from involving monotony of life.

Facts of this kind are to be found in the recent history of many trades: and they are of great importance when we are considering the way in which the modern organization of industry is tending to narrow the scope of each person's work, and thereby to render it monotonous. For those trades in which the work is most subdivided are those in which the chief muscular strain is most certain to be taken off by machinery; and thus the chief evil of monotonous work is much diminished. As Roscher says, it is monotony of life much more than monotony of work that is to be dreaded: monotony of work is an evil of the first order only when it involves monotony of life. Now when a person's employment requires much physical exertion, he is fit for nothing after his work; and unless his mental faculties are called forth in his work, they have little chance of being

[1] The jack-plane, used for making smooth large boards for floors and other purposes, used to cause heart disease, making carpenters as a rule old men by the time they were forty. Adam Smith tells us that " workmen, when they are liberally paid, are very apt to overwork themselves and to ruin their health and constitution in a few years. A carpenter in London, and in some other places, is not supposed to last in his utmost vigour above eight years. . . . Almost every class of artificers is subject to some particular infirmity occasioned by excessive application to their peculiar species of work." *Wealth of Nations*, Book I. chapter VII.

[2] The efficiency of labour in weaving has been increased twelve-fold and that in spinning six-fold during the last seventy years. In the preceding seventy years the improvements in spinning had already increased the efficiency of labour two-hundred-fold (see Ellison's *Cotton Trade of Great Britain*, ch. IV. and V.).

developed at all.   But the nervous force is not very much exhausted IV, ix, 7.
in the ordinary work of a factory, at all events where there is not
excessive noise, and where the hours of labour are not too long.
The social surroundings of factory life stimulate mental activity in
and out of working hours; and many of those factory workers,
whose occupations are seemingly the most monotonous, have considerable intelligence and mental resource.[1]

It is true that the American agriculturist is an able man, and
that his children rise rapidly in the world.   But partly because land
is plentiful, and he generally owns the farm that he cultivates, he
has better social conditions than the English; he has always had to
think for himself, and has long had to use and to repair complex
machines.   The English agricultural labourer has had many great
disadvantages to contend with.   Till recently he had little education;
and he was in a great measure under a semi-feudal rule, which was
not without its advantages, but which repressed enterprise and even
in some degree self-respect.   These narrowing causes are removed.
He is now fairly well educated in youth.   He learns to handle various
machinery; he is less dependent on the good-will of any particular
squire or group of farmers; and, since his work is more various, and
educates intelligence more than the lowest grades of town work do,
he is tending to rise both absolutely and relatively.

§ 7. We must now proceed to consider what are the conditions The
under which the economies in production arising from division of economic
labour can best be secured.   It is obvious that the efficiency of specialized
specialized machinery or specialized skill is but one condition of its machinery

---

[1] Perhaps the textile industries afford the best instance of work that used to be
done by hand and is now done by machinery. They are especially prominent in
England, where they give employment to nearly half a million males and more than
half a million females, or more than one in ten of those persons who are earning
independent incomes. The strain that is taken off human muscles in dealing even
with those soft materials is shown by the fact that for every one of these million
operatives there is used about one horse-power of steam, that is, about ten times
as much as they would themselves exert if they were all strong men; and the history
of these industries will serve to remind us that many of those who perform the more
monotonous parts of manufacturing work are as a rule not skilled workers who have
come down to it from a higher class of work, but unskilled workers who have risen to
it.   A great number of those who work in the Lancashire cotton-mills have come there
from poverty-stricken districts of Ireland, while others are the descendants of paupers
and people of weak physique, who were sent there in large numbers early in the last
century from the most miserable conditions of life in the poorest agricultural districts,
where the labourers were fed and housed almost worse than the animals whom they
tended.   Again, when regret is expressed that the cotton factory hands of New
England have not the high standard of culture which prevailed among them a century
ago, we must remember that the descendants of those factory workers have moved
up to higher and more responsible posts, and include many of the ablest and wealthiest
of the citizens of America.   Those who have taken their places are in the process of
being raised; they are chiefly French Canadians and Irish, who though they may
learn in their new homes some of the vices of civilization, are yet much better off
and have on the whole better opportunities of developing the higher faculties of themselves and their children than they had in their old homes.

IV, IX, 7.

requires that they should be fully occupied.

economic use; the other is that sufficient work should be found to keep it well employed. As Babbage pointed out, in a large factory " the master manufacturer by dividing the work to be executed into different processes, each requiring different degrees of skill or force, can purchase exactly that precise quantity of both which is necessary for each process; whereas if the whole work were executed by one workman that person must possess skill to perform the most difficult and sufficient strength to execute the most laborious of the operations into which the work is divided." The economy of production requires not only that each person should be employed constantly in a narrow range of work, but also that, when it is necessary for him to undertake different tasks, each of these tasks should be such as to call forth as much as possible of his skill and ability. Just in the same way the economy of machinery requires that a powerful turning-lathe when specially arranged for one class of work should be kept employed as long as possible on that work; and if there is occasion to employ it on other work, that should be such as to be worthy of the lathe, and not such as could have been done equally well by a much smaller machine.

But the most economic use of man as an agent of production is wasteful if he is not himself developed by it.

Here then, so far as the economy of production goes, men and machines stand on much the same footing : but while machinery is a mere implement of production, man's welfare is also its ultimate aim. We have already been occupied with the question whether the human race as a whole gains by carrying to an extreme that specialization of function which causes all the most difficult work to be done by a few people : but we have now to consider it more nearly with special reference to the work of business management. The main drift of the next three chapters is to inquire what are the causes which make different forms of business management the fittest to profit by their environment, and the most likely to prevail over others; but it is well that meanwhile we should have in our minds the question, how far they are severally fitted to benefit their environment.

Many of those economies in the use of specialized skill and machinery which are commonly regarded as within the reach of very large establishments, do not depend on the size of individual factories. Some depend on the aggregate volume of production of the kind in the neighbourhood; while others again, especially those connected with the growth of knowledge and the progress of the arts, depend chiefly on the aggregate volume of production in the whole civilized world. And here we may introduce two technical terms.

We may divide the economies arising from an increase in the IV, ix, 7.
scale of production of any kind of goods, into two classes—firstly, *External*
those dependent on the general development of the industry; and, *and*
internal
secondly, those dependent on the resources of the individual houses *economies.*
of business engaged in it, on their organization and the efficiency of
their management.   We may call the former *external economies*, and
the latter *internal economies*.   In the present chapter we have been
chiefly discussing internal economies; but we now proceed to
examine those very important external economies which can often
be secured by the concentration of many small businesses of a similar
character in particular localities : or, as is commonly said, by the
localization of industry.

CHAPTER X

INDUSTRIAL ORGANIZATION, CONTINUED. THE CONCENTRA-
TION OF SPECIALIZED INDUSTRIES IN PARTICULAR
LOCALITIES

IV, x, 1.

Even
in early
stages of
civiliza-
tion the
production
of some
light and
valuable
wares
has been
localized.

§ 1. In an early stage of civilization every place had to depend
on its own resources for most of the heavy wares which it consumed;
unless indeed it happened to have special facilities for water carriage.
But wants and customs changed slowly : and this made it easy for
producers to meet the wants even of consumers with whom they had
little communication; and it enabled comparatively poor people to
buy a few expensive goods from a distance, in the security that they
would add to the pleasure of festivals and holidays during a life-
time, or perhaps even during two or three life-times. Consequently
the lighter and more expensive articles of dress and personal adorn-
ment, together with spices and some kinds of metal implements
used by all classes, and many other things for the special use of the
rich, often came from astonishing distances. Some of these were
produced only in a few places, or even only in one place; and they
were diffused all over Europe partly by the agency of fairs [1] and
professional pedlars, and partly by the producers themselves, who
would vary their work by travelling on foot for many thousand miles
to sell their goods, and see the world. These sturdy travellers took
on themselves the risks of their little businesses; they enabled the
production of certain classes of goods to be kept on the right track for
satisfying the needs of purchasers far away; and they created new
wants among consumers, by showing them at fairs or at their own
houses new goods from distant lands. An industry concentrated in
certain localities is commonly, though perhaps not quite accurately,
described as a localized industry.[2]

This elementary localization of industry gradually prepared the

[1] Thus in the records of the Stourbridge Fair held near Cambridge we find an
endless variety of light and precious goods from the older seats of civilization in
the East and on the Mediterranean; some having been brought in Italian ships, and
others having travelled by land as far as the shores of the North Sea.

[2] Not very long ago travellers in western Tyrol could find a strange and characteristic relic of this habit in a village called Imst. The villagers had somehow acquired
a special art in breeding canaries : and their young men started for a tour to distant
parts of Europe each with about fifty small cages hung from a pole over his shoulder,
and walked on till they had sold all.

way for many of the modern developments of division of labour in IV, x, 2.
the mechanical arts and in the task of business management. Even
now we find industries of a primitive fashion localized in retired
villages of central Europe, and sending their simple wares even to
the busiest haunts of modern industry. In Russia the expansion of a
family group into a village has often been the cause of a localized
industry; and there are an immense number of villages each of
which carries on only one branch of production, or even only a part
of one.[1]

§ 2. Many various causes have led to the localization of indus- The
tries; but the chief causes have been physical conditions; such as various
origins of
the character of the climate and the soil, the existence of mines and localized
industries;
quarries in the neighbourhood, or within easy access by land or physical
water. Thus metallic industries have generally been either near conditions;
mines or in places where fuel was cheap. The iron industries in
England first sought those districts in which charcoal was plentiful,
and afterwards they went to the neighbourhood of collieries.[2]
Staffordshire makes many kinds of pottery, all the materials of
which are imported from a long distance; but she has cheap coal
and excellent clay for making the heavy " seggars " or boxes in
which the pottery is placed while being fired. Straw plaiting has its
chief home in Bedfordshire, where straw has just the right proportion of silex to give strength without brittleness; and Buckingham-
shire beeches have afforded the material for the Wycombe chair-
making. The Sheffield cutlery trade is due chiefly to the excellent
grit of which its grindstones are made.

Another chief cause has been the patronage of a court. The the
rich fold there assembled made a demand for goods of specially high patronage
of courts;
quality, and this attracts skilled workmen from a distance, and
educates those on the spot. When an Eastern potentate changed
his residence—and, partly for sanitary reasons, this was constantly

---

[1] There are for instance over 500 villages devoted to various branches of woodwork; one village makes nothing but spokes for the wheels of vehicles, another
nothing but the bodies and so on; and indications of a like state of things are found
in the histories of oriental civilizations and in the chronicles of mediæval Europe.
Thus for instance we read (Rogers' *Six Centuries of Work and Wages*, ch. IV.) of a
lawyer's handy book written about 1250, which makes note of scarlet at Lincoln;
blanket at Bligh; burnet at Beverley; russet at Colchester; linen fabrics at Shaftesbury, Lewes, and Aylsham; cord at Warwick and Bridport; knives at Marstead;
needles at Wilton; razors at Leicester; soap at Coventry; horse girths at Doncaster;
skins and furs at Chester and Shrewsbury and so on.

The localization of trades in England at the beginning of the eighteenth century
is well described by Defoe, *Plan of English Commerce*, 85–7; *English Tradesmen*, II.
282–3.

[2] The later wanderings of the iron industry from Wales, Staffordshire and Shrop-
shire to Scotland and the North of England are well shown in the tables submitted
by Sir Lowthian Bell to the recent Commission on the Depression of Trade and Industry. See their Social Report, Part I. p. 320.

IV, x, 2. done—the deserted town was apt to take refuge in the development
of a specialized industry, which had owed its origin to the presence
the of the court. But very often the rulers deliberately invited artisans
deliberate from a distance and settled them in a group together. Thus the
invitation
of rulers. mechanical faculty of Lancashire is said to be due to the influence of
Norman smiths who were settled at Warrington by Hugo de Lupus
in William the Conqueror's time. And the greater part of England's
manufacturing industry before the era of cotton and steam had its
course directed by settlements of Flemish and other artisans;
many of which were made under the immediate direction of Plantagenet and Tudor kings. These immigrants taught us how to weave
woollen and worsted stuffs, though for a long time we sent our cloths
to the Netherlands to be fulled and dyed. They taught us how to
cure herrings, how to manufacture silk, how to make lace, glass, and
paper, and to provide for many of our other wants.[1]

The But how did these immigrants learn their skill? Their ancestors
industrial had no doubt profited by the traditional arts of earlier civilizations
develop-
ment of on the shores of the Mediterranean and in the far East : for nearly
nations all important knowledge has long deep roots stretching downwards
waits upon
opportuni- to distant times; and so widely spread have been these roots, so
ties and ready to send up shoots of vigorous life, that there is perhaps no
upon
character. part of the old world in which there might not long ago have flourished
many beautiful and highly skilled industries, if their growth had
been favoured by the character of the people, and by their social
and political institutions. This accident or that may have determined whether any particular industry flourished in any one town;
the industrial character of a whole country even may have been
largely influenced by the richness of her soil and her mines, and her
facilities for commerce. Such natural advantages may themselves
have stimulated free industry and enterprise : but it is the existence
of these last, by whatever means they may have been promoted,
which has been the supreme condition for the growth of noble forms
of the arts of life. In sketching the history of free industry and
enterprise we have already incidentally traced the outline of the
causes which have localized the industrial leadership of the world
now in this country and now in that. We have seen how physical
nature acts on man's energies, how he is stimulated by an invigorating climate, and how he is encouraged to bold ventures by the

_____
[1] Fuller says that Flemings started manufactures of cloths and fustians in Norwich,
of baizes in Sudbury, of serges in Colchester and Taunton, of cloths in Kent, Gloucester-
shire, Worcestershire, Westmorland, Yorkshire, Hants, Berks, and Sussex, of kerseys
in Devonshire, and of Levant cottons in Lancashire. Smiles' *Huguenots in England and
Ireland*, p. 109. See also Lecky's *History of England in the eighteenth century*, ch. II.

opening out of rich fields for his work : but we have also seen how IV, x, 3.
the use he makes of these advantages depends on his ideals of life,
and how inextricably therefore the religious, political and economic
threads of the world's history are interwoven; while together they
have been bent this way or that by great political events and the
influence of the strong personalities of individuals.

The causes which determine the economic progress of nations
belong to the study of international trade and therefore lie outside of
our present view.   But for the present we must turn aside from these
broader movements of the localization of industry, and follow the
fortunes of groups of skilled workers who are gathered within the
narrow boundaries of a manufacturing town or a thickly peopled
industrial district.

§ 3. When an industry has thus chosen a locality for itself, it is *The*
likely to stay there long : so great are the advantages which people *advan-*
following the same skilled trade get from near neighbourhood to one *tages of*
localized
another.   The mysteries of the trade become no mysteries; but are *industries;*
hereditary
as it were in the air, and children learn many of them unconsciously. *skill;*
Good work is rightly appreciated, inventions and improvements in
machinery, in processes and the general organization of the business
have their merits promptly discussed : if one man starts a new idea,
it is taken up by others and combined with suggestions of their
own; and thus it becomes the source of further new ideas.   And *the*
presently subsidiary trades grow up in the neighbourhood, supplying *growth of*
subsidiary
it with implements and materials, organizing its traffic, and in many *trades;*
ways conducing to the economy of its material.

Again, the economic use of expensive machinery can sometimes *the use*
be attained in a very high degree in a district in which there is a large *of highly*
specialized
aggregate production of the same kind, even though no individual *machin-*
capital employed in the trade be very large.   For subsidiary indus- *ery;*
tries devoting themselves each to one small branch of the process of
production, and working it for a great many of their neighbours, are
able to keep in constant use machinery of the most highly specialized
character, and to make it pay its expenses, though its original cost
may have been high, and its rate of depreciation very rapid.

Again, in all but the earliest stages of economic development a *a local*
localized industry gains a great advantage from the fact that it *market for*
special
offers a constant market for skill.   Employers are apt to resort to *skill.*
any place where they are likely to find a good choice of workers
with the special skill which they require; while men seeking employment naturally go to places where there are many employers who
need such skill as theirs and where therefore it is likely to find a good

I

IV, x, 3. market. The owner of an isolated factory, even if he has access to a plentiful supply of general labour, is often put to great shifts for want of some special skilled labour; and a skilled workman, when thrown out of employment in it, has no easy refuge. Social forces here co-operate with economic : there are often strong friendships between employers and employed : but neither side likes to feel that in case of any disagreeable incident happening between them, they must go on rubbing against one another : both sides like to be able easily to break off old associations should they become irksome. These difficulties are still a great obstacle to the success of any business in which special skill is needed, but which is not in the neighbourhood of others like it : they are however being diminished by the railway, the printing-press and the telegraph.

Sometimes however a localized industry makes too extensive demands for one kind of labour.   On the other hand a localized industry has some disadvantages as a market for labour if the work done in it is chiefly of one kind, such for instance as can be done only by strong men. In those iron districts in which there are no textile or other factories to give employment to women and children, wages are high and the cost of labour dear to the employer, while the average money earnings of each family are low. But the remedy for this evil is obvious, and is found in the growth in the same neighbourhood of industries of a supplementary character. Thus textile industries are constantly found congregated in the neighbourhood of mining and engineering industries, in some cases having been attracted by almost imperceptible steps; in others, as for instance at Barrow, having been started deliberately on a large scale in order to give variety of employment in a place where previously there had been but little demand for the work of women and children.

The advantages of variety of employment are combined with those of localized industries in some of our manufacturing towns, and this is a chief cause of their continued growth. But on the other hand the value which the central sites of a large town have for trading purposes, enables them to command much higher ground-rents than the situations are worth for factories, even when account is taken of this combination of advantages : and there is a similar competition for dwelling space between the employees of the trading houses and the factory workers. The result is that factories now congregate in the outskirts of large towns and in manufacturing districts in their neighbourhood rather in the towns themselves.[1]

---

[1] The movement has been specially conspicuous in the case of the textile manufacturers. Manchester, Leeds and Lyons are still chief centres of the trade in cotton, woollen and silk stuffs, but they do not now themselves produce any great part of the goods to which they owe their chief fame. On the other hand London and Paris

A district which is dependent chiefly on one industry is liable to extreme depression, in case of a falling-off in the demand for its produce, or of a failure in the supply of the raw material which it uses. This evil again is in a great measure avoided by those large towns or large industrial districts in which several distinct industries are strongly developed. If one of them fails for a time, the others are likely to support it indirectly; and they enable local shopkeepers to continue their assistance to workpeople in it. *IV, x, 4. Different industries in the same neighbourhood mitigate each other's depressions.*

So far we have discussed localization from the point of view of the economy of production. But there is also the convenience of the customer to be considered. He will go to the nearest shop for a trifling purchase; but for an important purchase he will take the trouble of visiting any part of the town where he knows that there are specially good shops for his purpose. Consequently shops which deal in expensive and choice objects tend to congregate together; and those which supply ordinary domestic needs do not.[1] *Localization of shops.*

§ 4. Every cheapening of the means of communication, every new facility for the free interchange of ideas between distant places alters the action of the forces which tend to localize industries. Speaking generally we must say that a lowering of tariffs, or of freights for the transport of goods, tends to make each locality buy more largely from a distance what it requires; and thus tends to concentrate particular industries in special localities : but on the other hand everything that increases people's readiness to migrate from one place to another tends to bring skilled artisans to ply their crafts near to the consumers who will purchase their wares. These two opposing tendencies are well illustrated by the recent history of the English people. *The influence of means of communication on the geographical distribution of industries.*

On the one hand the steady cheapening of freights, the opening of railways from the agricultural districts of America and India to the sea-board, and the adoption by England of a free-trade policy, have led to a great increase in her importation of raw produce. But on the other hand the growing cheapness, rapidity and comfort of foreign travel, are inducing her trained business men and her skilled artisans to pioneer the way for new industries in other lands, and to help them to manufacture for themselves goods which they have been wont to buy from England. English mechanics have taught people in almost every part of the world how to use English *Illustration from the recent history of England.*

---

retain their positions as the two largest manufacturing towns of the world, Philadelphia coming third. The mutual influences of the localization of industry, the growth of towns and habits of town life, and the development of machinery are well discussed in Hobson's *Evolution of Capitalism.*

[1] Comp. Hobson, *l. c.* p. 114.

IV, x, 4. machinery, and even how to make similar machinery; and English miners have opened out mines of ore which have diminished the foreign demand for many of England's products.

One of the most striking movements towards the specialization of a country's industries, which history records, is the rapid increase of the non-agricultural population of England in recent times. The exact nature of this change is however liable to be misunderstood; and its interest is so great, both for its own sake, and on account of the illustrations it affords of the general principles which we have been discussing in the preceding chapter and in this, that we may with advantage pause here to consider it a little.

The diminution of her agricultural population is less than at first sight appears. In the first place, the real diminution of England's agricultural industries is not so great as at first sight appears. It is true that in the Middle Ages three-fourths of the people were reckoned as agriculturists; that only one in nine was returned to the last census as engaged in agriculture, and that perhaps not more than one in twelve will be so returned at the next census. But it must be remembered that the so-called agricultural population of the Middle Ages were not exclusively occupied with agriculture; they did for themselves a great part of the work that is now done by brewers and bakers, by spinners and weavers, by bricklayers and carpenters, by dressmakers and tailors and by many other trades. These self-sufficing habits died slowly; but most of them had nearly disappeared by the beginning of the last century; and it is probable that the labour spent on the land at this time was not a much less part of the whole industry of the country than in the Middle Ages : for, in spite of her ceasing to export wool and wheat, there was so great an increase in the produce forced from her soil, that the rapid improvement in the arts of her agriculturists scarcely availed to hold in check the action of the law of diminishing return. But gradually a great deal of labour has been diverted from the fields to making expensive machinery for agricultural purposes. This change did not exert its full influence upon the numbers of those who were reckoned as agriculturists so long as the machinery was drawn by horses : for the work of tending them and supplying them with food was regarded as agricultural. But in recent years a rapid growth of the use of steam power in the fields has coincided with the increased importation of farm produce. The coal-miners who supply these steam-engines with fuel, and the mechanics who make them and manage them in the fields are not reckoned as occupied on the land, though the ultimate aim of their labour is to promote its cultivation.

The real diminution then of England's agriculture is not so great as at first sight appears; but there has been a change in its distribution. Many tasks which used once to be performed by agricultural labourers are now done by specialized workers who are classed as in the building, or road-making industries, as carriers and so on. And, partly for this reason the number of people who reside in purely agricultural districts has seldom diminished fast; and has often increased, even though the number of those engaged in agriculture has been diminishing rapidly. *IV, x, 4.*

Attention has already been called to the influence which the importation of agricultural produce exerts in altering the relative values of different soils : those falling most in value which depended chiefly on their wheat crops, and which were not naturally fertile, though they were capable of being made to yield fairly good crops by expensive methods of cultivation. Districts in which such soils predominate, have contributed more than their share to the crowds of agricultural labourers who have migrated to the large towns; and thus the geographical distribution of industries within the country has been still further altered. A striking instance of the influence of the new means of transport is seen in those pastoral districts in the remoter parts of the United Kindom, which send dairy products by special express trains to London and other large towns, meanwhile drawing their own supplies of wheat from the further shores of the Atlantic or even the Pacific Ocean. *Changes in the distribution of the agricultural population within the country.*

But next, the changes of recent years have not, as would at first sight appear probable, increased the proportion of the English people who are occupied in manufactures. The output of England's manufactures is certainly many times as great now as it was at the middle of the last century; but those occupied in manufacture of every kind were as large a percentage of the population in 1851 as in 1901; although those who make the machinery and implements which do a great part of the work of English agriculture, swell the numbers of the manufacturers. *Those set free from agriculture have gone not to manufactures*

The chief explanation of this result lies in the wonderful increase in recent years of the power of machinery. This has enabled us to produce ever increasing supplies of manufactures of almost every kind both for our own use and for exportation without requiring any considerable increase in the number of people who tend the machines. And therefore we have been able to devote the labour set free from agriculture chiefly to supplying those wants in regard to which the improvements of machinery help us but little : the efficiency of machinery has prevented the industries localized in England from *but chiefly to industries in which there has been no great increase in the efficiency of labour.*

IV, x, 4. becoming as exclusively mechanical as they otherwise would. Prominent among the occupations which have increased rapidly since 1851 in England at the expense of agriculture are the service of Government, central and local; education of all grades; medical service; musical, theatrical and other entertainments, besides mining, building, dealing and transport by road and railway. In none of these is very much direct help got from new inventions: man's labour is not much more efficient in them now than it was a century ago: and therefore if the wants for which they make provision increase in proportion to our general wealth, it is only to be expected that they should absorb a constantly growing proportion of the industrial population. Domestic servants increased rapidly for some years; and the total amount of work which used to fall to them is now increasing faster than ever. But much of it is now done, often with the aid of machinery, by persons in the employment of clothiers of all kinds, of hotel proprietors, confectioners, and even by various messengers from grocers, fishmongers and others who call for orders, unless they are sent by telephone. These changes have tended to increase the specialization and the localization of industries.

Transition to the subject of the next chapter.

Passing away from this illustration of the action of modern forces on the geographical distribution of industries, we will resume our inquiry as to how far the full economies of division of labour can be obtained by the concentration of large numbers of small businesses of a similar kind in the same locality; and how far they are attainable only by the aggregation of a large part of the business of the country into the hands of a comparatively small number of rich and powerful firms, or, as is commonly said, by production on a large scale; or, in other words, how far the economies of production on a large scale must needs be *internal*, and how far they can be *external*.[1]

---

[1] The percentage of the population occupied in the textile industries in the United Kingdom fell from 3·13 in 1881 to 2·43 in 1901; partly because much of the work done by them has been rendered so simple by semi-automatic machinery that it can be done fairly well by peoples that are in a relatively backward industrial condition; and partly because the chief textile goods retain nearly the same simple character as they had thirty or even three thousand years ago. On the other hand manufactures of iron and steel (including shipbuilding) have increased so greatly in complexity as well as in volume of output, that the percentage of the population occupied in them rose from 2·39 in 1881 to 3·01 in 1901; although much greater advance has been meanwhile made in the machinery and methods employed in them than in the textile group. The remaining manufacturing industries employed about the same percentage of the people in 1901 as in 1881. In the same time the tonnage of British shipping cleared from British ports increased by one half; and the number of dock labourers doubled, but that of seamen has slightly diminished. These facts are to be explained partly by vast improvements in the construction of ships and all appliances connected with them, and partly by the transference to dock labourers of nearly all tasks connected with handling the cargo some of which were even recently

performed by the crew.   Another marked change is the increased aggregate occupation of women in manufactures, though that of married women appears to have
diminished, and that of children has certainly diminished greatly.

The Summary Tables of the Census of 1911, published in 1915, show so many
changes in classification since 1901 that no general view of recent developments can
be safely made.   But Table 64 of that *Report* and Prof. D. Caradog Jones' paper read
before the Royal Statistical Society in December 1914 show that the developments
of 1901–1911 differ from their predecessors in detail rather than in general character.

CHAPTER XI

INDUSTRIAL ORGANIZATION, CONTINUED. PRODUCTION ON A LARGE SCALE

IV, xi, 1.

The typical industries for our .present purpose are those engaged in manufacture.

§ 1. THE advantages of production on a large scale are best shown in manufacture; under which head we may include all businesses engaged in working up material into forms in which it will be adapted for sale in distant markets. The characteristic of manufacturing industries which makes them offer generally the best illustrations of the advantages of production on a large scale, is their power of choosing freely the locality in which they will do their work. They are thus contrasted on the one hand with agriculture and other extractive industries (mining, quarrying, fishing, etc.), the geographical distribution of which is determined by nature; and on the other hand with industries that make or repair things to suit the special needs of individual consumers, from whom they cannot be far removed, at all events without great loss.[1]

The chief advantages of production on a large scale are economy of skill, economy of machinery and economy of materials : but the last of these is rapidly losing importance relatively to the other two. It is true that an isolated workman often throws away a number of small things which would have been collected and turned to good account in a factory ;[2] but waste of this kind can scarcely occur in a localized manufacture even if it is in the hands of small men; and there is not very much of it in any branch of industry in modern England, except agriculture and domestic cooking. No doubt many of the most important advances of recent years have been due to the utilizing of what had been a waste product; but this has been generally due to a distinct invention, either chemical or mechanical, the use of which has been indeed promoted by minute subdivision of labour, but has not been directly dependent on it.[3]

---

[1] "Manufacture" is a term which has long lost any connection with its original use : and is now applied to those branches of production where machine and not hand work is most prominent. Roscher made the attempt to bring it back nearer to its old use by applying it to domestic as opposed to factory industries : but it is too late to do this now.

[2] See Babbage's instance of the manufacture of horn. *Economy of Manufactures*, ch. XXII.

[3] Instances are the utilization of the waste from cotton, wool, silk and other textile materials; and of the by-products in the metallurgical industries, in the manufacture of soda and gas, and in the American mineral oil and meat packing industries.

Again, it is true that when a hundred sets of furniture, or of IV, xi, 2
clothing, have to be cut out on exactly the same pattern, it is worth ——
while to spend great care on so planning the cutting out of the boards
or the cloth, that only a few small pieces are wasted. But this is
properly an economy of skill; one planning is made to suffice for
many tasks, and therefore can be done well and carefully. We may
pass then to the economy of machinery.

§ 2. In spite of the aid which subsidiary industries can give to The
small manufacturers, where many in the same branch of trade are advantages
collected in one neighbourhood,[1] they are still placed under a great factory
disadvantage by the growing variety and expensiveness of machin- as regards
ery. For in a large establishment there are often many expensive specialized
machines each made specially for one small use. Each of them machinery.
requires space in a good light, and thus stands for something considerable in the rent and general expenses of the factory; and independently of interest and the expense of keeping it in repair, a heavy
allowance must be made for depreciation in consequence of its being
probably improved upon before long.[2] A small manufacturer
must therefore have many things done by hand or by imperfect
machinery, though he knows how to have them done better and
cheaper by special machinery, if only he could find constant employment for it.

But next, a small manufacturer may not always be acquainted Advan-
with the best machinery for his purpose. It is true that if the tages with
regard to
industry in which he is engaged has been long established on a large the inven-
scale, his machinery will be well up to the mark, provided he can improved
afford to buy the best in the market. In agriculture and the cotton machinery.
industries, for instance, improvements in machinery are devised
almost exclusively by machine makers; and they are accessible to
all, at any rate on the payment of a royalty for patent right. But
this is not the case in industries that are as yet in an early stage of
development or are rapidly changing their form; such as the chemical
industries, the watchmaking industry and some branches of the jute
and silk manufactures; and in a host of trades that are constantly
springing up to supply some new want or to work up some new
material.

---

[1] See the preceding chapter, § 3.
[2] The average time which a machine will last before being superseded is in many
trades not more than fifteen years, while in some it is ten years or even less.   There is
often a loss on the use of a machine unless it earns every year twenty per cent. on its
cost; and when the operation performed by such a machine costing £500 adds only a
hundredth part to the value of the material that passes through it—and this is not an
extreme case—there will be a loss on its use unless it can be applied in producing at
least £10,000 worth of goods annually.

IV, XI, 2.

The small
manufac-
turer
cannot
often
afford to
experi-
ment.

In all such trades new machinery and new processes are for the greater part devised by manufacturers for their own use. Each new departure is an experiment which may fail; those which succeed must pay for themselves and for the failure of others; and though a small manufacturer may think he sees his way to an improvement, he must reckon on having to work it out tentatively, at considerable risk and expense and with much interruption to his other work: and even if he should be able to perfect it, he is not likely to be able to make the most of it. For instance, he may have devised a new speciality, which would get a large sale if it could be brought under general notice: but to do this would perhaps cost many thousand pounds; and, if so, he will probably have to turn his back on it. For it is almost impossible for him to discharge, what Roscher calls a characteristic task of the modern manufacturer, that of creating new wants by showing people something which they had never thought of having before; but which they want to have as soon as the notion is suggested to them: in the pottery trade for example the small manufacturer cannot afford even to make experiments with new patterns and designs except in a very tentative way. His chance is better with regard to an improvement in making things for which there is already a good market. But even here he cannot get the full benefit of his invention unless he patents it; and sells the right to use it; or borrows some capital and extends his business; or lastly changes the character of his business and devotes his capital to that particular stage of the manufacture to which his improvement applies. But after all such cases are exceptional: the growth of machinery in variety and expensiveness presses hard on the small manufacturer everywhere. It has already driven him completely out of some trades and is fast driving him out of others.[1]

There are however some trades in which the advantages which a

---

[1] In many businesses only a small percentage of improvements are patented. They consist of many small steps, which it would not be worth while to patent one at a time. Or their chief point lies in noticing that a certain thing ought to be done; and to patent one way of doing it, is only to set other people to work to find out other ways of doing it against which the patent cannot guard. If one patent is taken out, it is often necessary to " block " it, by patenting other methods of arriving at the same result; the patentee does not expect to use them himself, but he wants to prevent others from using them. All this involves worry and loss of time and money: and the large manufacturer prefers to keep his improvement to himself and get what benefit he can by using it. While if the small manufacturer takes out a patent, he is likely to be harassed by infringements: and even though he may win " with costs " the actions in which he tries to defend himself, he is sure to be ruined by them if they are numerous. It is generally in the public interest that an improvement should be published, even though it is at the same time patented. But if it is patented in England and not in other countries, as is often the case, English manufacturers may not use it, even though they were just on the point of finding it out for themselves before it was patented; while foreign manufacturers learn all about it and can use it freely.

large factory derives from the economy of machinery almost vanish
as soon as a moderate size has been reached.   For instance in cotton
spinning, and calico weaving, a comparatively small factory will hold
its own and give constant employment to the best known machines
for every process : so that a large factory is only several parallel
smaller factories under one roof; and indeed some cotton-spinners,
when enlarging their works, think it best to add a weaving department.   In such cases the large business gains little or no economy in
machinery; and even then it generally saves something in building,
particularly as regards chimneys, and in the economy of steam
power, and in the management and repairs of engines and machinery.
Large soft-goods factories have carpenters' and mechanics' shops,
which diminish the cost of repairs, and prevent delays from accidents
to the plant.[1]

IV, xi, 2.

But in some trades a factory of moderate size can have the best machinery.

Akin to these last, there are a great many advantages which a
large factory, or indeed a large business of almost any kind, nearly
always has over a small one.   A large business buys in great quantities and therefore cheaply; it pays low freights and saves on carriage in many ways, particularly if it has a railway siding.   It often
sells in large quantities, and thus saves itself trouble; and yet at
the same time it gets a good price, because it offers conveniences to
the customer by having a large stock from which he can select and
at once fill up a varied order; while its reputation gives him confidence.   It can spend large sums on advertising by commercial
travellers and in other ways; its agents give it trustworthy information on trade and personal matters in distant places, and its own
goods advertise one another.

Advan-
tages of a large business, or of associated groups of businesses, in buying and selling.

The economies of highly organized buying and selling are among
the chief causes of the present tendency towards the fusion of many
businesses in the same industry or trade into single huge aggregates;
and also of trading federations of various kinds, including German
cartels and centralized co-operative associations.   They have also
always promoted the concentration of business risks in the hands

---

[1] It is a remarkable fact that cotton and some other textile factories form an
exception to the general rule that the capital required per head of the workers is
generally greater in a large factory than in a small one.   The reason is that in most
other businesses the large factory has many things done by expensive machines
which are done by hand in a small factory; so that while the wages bill is less in
proportion to the output in a large factory than in a small one, the value of the machinery
and the factory space occupied by the machinery is much greater.   But in the simpler
branches of the textile trades, small works have the same machinery as large works
have; and since small steam-engines, etc. are proportionately more expensive than
large ones, they require a greater fixed capital in proportion to their output than larger
factories do; and they are likely to require a floating capital also rather greater in
proportion.

IV, xi, 3, 4. of large capitalists who put out the work to be done by smaller
——   men.[1]

Advan-   § 3. Next, with regard to the economy of skill. Everything
tages of   that has been said with regard to the advantages which a large
a large
factory as   establishment has in being able to afford highly specialized machinery
regards   applies equally with regard to highly specialized skill. It can con-
specialized
skill,   trive to keep each of its employees constantly engaged in the most
             difficult work of which he is capable, and yet so to narrow the range
             of his work that he can attain that facility and excellence which
             come from long-continued practice. But enough has already been
             said on the advantage of division of labour : and we may pass to an
             important though indirect advantage which a manufacturer derives
             from having a great many men in his employment.

the   The large manufacturer has a much better chance than a small
selection   one has, of getting hold of men with exceptional natural abilities,
of leading
men, etc.   to do the most difficult part of his work—that on which the reputa-
             tion of his establishment chiefly depends. This is occasionally
             important as regards mere handiwork in trades which require much
             taste and originality, as for instance that of a house decorator, and
             in those which require exceptionally fine workmanship, as for
             instance that of a manufacturer of delicate mechanism.[2] But in
             most businesses its chief importance lies in the facilities which it
             gives to the employer for the selection of able and tried men, men
             whom he trusts and who trust him, to be his foremen and heads of
             departments. We are thus brought to the central problem of the
             modern organization of industry, viz. that which relates to the
             advantages and disadvantages of the subdivision of the work of
             business management.

The sub-   § 4. The head of a large business can reserve all his strength for
division of the broadest and most fundamental problems of his trade : he must
the work of
business   indeed assure himself that his managers, clerks and foremen are the
manage-   right men for their work, and are doing their work well; but beyond
ment :
advan-   this he need not trouble himself much about details. He can keep
tages of   his mind fresh and clear for thinking out the most difficult and vital
the large
manu-   problems of his business; for studying the broader movements of
facturer ;

---

[1] See below IV. xii. 3.

[2] Thus Boulton writing in 1770 when he had 700 or 800 persons employed as
metallic artists and workers in tortoiseshell, stones, glass, and enamel, says :—" I
have trained up many, and am training up more, plain country lads into good workmen ; and wherever I find indications of skill and ability, I encourage them. I
have likewise established correspondence with almost every mercantile town in Europe,
and am thus regularly supplied with orders for the grosser articles in common demand,
by which I am enabled to employ such a number of hands as to provide me with an
ample choice of artists for the finer branches of work : and I am thus encouraged to
erect and employ a more extensive apparatus than it would be prudent to employ for
the production of the finer articles only." Smiles' *Life of Boulton*, p. 128.

the markets, the yet undeveloped results of current events at home and abroad; and for contriving how to improve the organization of the internal and external relations of his business.

For much of this work the small employer has not the time if he has the ability; he cannot take so broad a survey of his trade, or look so far ahead; he must often be content to follow the lead of others. And he must spend much of his time on work that is below him; for if he is to succeed at all, his mind must be in some respects of a high quality, and must have a good deal of originating and organizing force; and yet he must do much routine work.

On the other hand the small employer has advantages of his own. *those of the small manufacturer.* The master's eye is everywhere; there is no shirking by his foremen or workmen, no divided responsibility, no sending half-understood messages backwards and forwards from one department to another. He saves much of the book-keeping, and nearly all of the cumbrous system of checks that are necessary in the business of a large firm; and the gain from this source is of very great importance in trades which use the more valuable metals and other expensive materials.

And though he must always remain at a great disadvantage in getting information and in making experiments, yet in this matter the general course of progress is on his side. For External economies are constantly growing in importance relatively to Internal in all matters of Trade-knowledge : newspapers, and trade and technical publications of all kinds are perpetually scouting for him and bringing him much of the knowledge he wants—knowledge which a little while ago would have been beyond the reach of anyone who could not afford to have well-paid agents in many distant places. Again, it is to his interest also that the secrecy of business is on the whole diminishing, and that the most important improvements in method seldom remain secret for long after they have passed from the experimental stage. It is to his advantage that changes in manufacture depend less on mere rules of thumb and more on broad developments of scientific principle; and that many of these are made by students in the pursuit of knowledge for its own sake, and are promptly published in the general interest. Although therefore the small manufacturer can seldom be in the front of the race of progress, he need not be far from it, if he has the time and the ability for availing himself of the modern facilities for obtaining knowledge. But it is true that he must be exceptionally strong if he can do this without neglecting the minor but necessary details of the business.

§ 5. In agriculture and other trades in which a man gains no very great new economies by increasing the scale of his production, it often happens that a business remains of about the same size for many years, if not for many generations. But it is otherwise in trades in which a large business can command very important advantages, which are beyond the reach of a small business. A new man, working his way up in such a trade, has to set his energy and flexibility, his industry and care for small details, against the broader economies of his rivals with their larger capital, their higher specialization of machinery and labour, and their larger trade connection. If then he can double his production, and sell at anything like his old rate, he will have more than doubled his profits. This will raise his credit with bankers and other shrewd lenders; and will enable him to increase his business further, and to attain yet further economies, and yet higher profits : and this again will increase his business and so on. It seems at first that no point is marked out at which he need stop. And it is true that, if, as his business increased, his faculties adapted themselves to his larger sphere, as they had done to his smaller; if he retained his originality, and versatility and power of initiation, his perseverance, his tact and his good luck for very many years together; he might then gather into his hands the whole volume of production in his branch of trade for his district. And if his goods were not very difficult of transport, nor of marketing, he might extend this district very wide, and attain something like a limited monopoly; that is, of a monopoly limited by the consideration that a very high price would bring rival producers into the field.

But long before this end is reached, his progress is likely to be arrested by the decay, if not of his faculties, yet of his liking for energetic work. The rise of his firm may be prolonged if he can hand down his business to a successor almost as energetic as himself.[1] But the continued very rapid growth of his firm requires the presence of two conditions which are seldom combined in the same industry. There are many trades in which an individual producer could secure much increased " internal " economies by a great increase of his output; and there are many in which he could market that output easily; yet there are few in which he could do both. And this is not an accidental, but almost a necessary result.

For in most of those trades in which the economies of production on a large scale are of first-rate importance, marketing is difficult.

---

[1] Means to this end and their practical limitations are discussed in the latter half of the following chapter.

IV, XI, 5.

Rapid growth of firms in some trades which offer great economies to production on a large scale.

Where marketing is easy, the

There are, no doubt, important exceptions. A producer may, for IV, XI, 6. instance, obtain access to the whole of a large market in the case of economies goods which are so simple and uniform that they can be sold whole- of produc- sale in vast quantities. But, most goods of this kind are raw pro- large scale duce; and nearly all the rest are plain and common, such as steel are mostly rails or calico; and their production can be reduced to routine, for firms of the very reason that they are plain and common. Therefore in the moderate industries which produce them, no firm can hold its own at all size. unless equipped with expensive appliances of nearly the latest type for its main work; while subordinate operations can be per- formed by subsidiary industries; and in short there remains no very great difference between the economies available by a large and by a very large firm; and the tendency of large firms to drive out small ones has already gone so far as to exhaust most of the strength of those forces by which it was originally promoted.

But many commodities with regard to which the tendency to But in increasing return acts strongly are, more or less, specialities : some specialities of them aim at creating a new want, or at meeting an old want in a is difficult. new way. Some of them are adapted to special tastes, and can never have a very large market; and some have merits that are not easily tested, and must win their way to general favour slowly. In all such cases the sales of each business are limited, more or less according to circumstances, to the particular market which it has slowly and expensively acquired; and though the production itself might be economically increased very fast, the sale could not.

Lastly, the very conditions of an industry which enable a new Causes firm to attain quickly command over new economies of production, which render that firm liable to be supplanted quickly by still younger firms firms with yet newer methods. Especially where the powerful quickly, economies of production on a large scale are associated with the use of often new appliances and new methods, a firm which has lost the excep- their fall. tional energy which enabled it to rise, is likely ere long quickly to decay; and the full life of a large firm seldom lasts very long.

§ 6. The advantages which a large business has over a small one Advan- are conspicuous in manufacture, because, as we have noticed, it large has special facilities for concentrating a great deal of work in a businesses small area. But there is a strong tendency for large establishments kinds. to drive out small ones in many other industries. In particular the retail trade is being transformed, the small shopkeeper is losing ground daily.

Let us look at the advantages which a large retail shop or store In retail has in competing with its smaller neighbours. To begin with, it trade they

IV, XI, 6.
are on the
increase
can obviously buy on better terms, it can get its goods carried more
cheaply, and can offer a larger variety to meet the taste of customers.
Next, it has a great economy of skill : the small shopkeeper, like the
small manufacturer, must spend much of his time in routine work
that requires no judgment : whereas the head of a large establishment, and even in some cases his chief assistants, spend their whole
time in using their judgment. Until lately these advantages have
been generally outweighed by the greater facilities which the small
shopkeeper has for bringing his goods to the door of his customers;
for humouring their several tastes; and for knowing enough of them
individually to be able safely to lend them capital, in the form of
selling them goods on credit.

owing to
the growth
of cash
payments
But within recent years there have been many changes all telling
on the side of large establishments. The habit of buying on credit
is passing away; and the personal relations between shopkeeper
and customer are becoming more distant. The first change is a
great step forwards : the second is on some accounts to be regretted,
but not on all; for it is partly due to the fact that the increase of
true self-respect among the wealthier classes is making them no
longer care for the subservient personal attentions they used to
require. Again, the growing value of time makes people less willing
than they were to spend several hours in shopping; they now often
prefer to spend a few minutes in writing out a long list of orders from
a varied and detailed price-list; and this they are enabled to do
easily by the growing facilities for ordering and receiving parcels by
post and in other ways. And when they do go shopping, tramcars
and local trains are often at hand to take them easily and cheaply to
the large central shops of a neighbouring town. All these changes
render it more difficult than it was for the small shopkeeper to hold
his own even in the provision trade, and others in which no great
variety of stock is required.

and the
increasing
variety of
the goods
in common
demand.
But in many trades the ever-growing variety of commodities,
and those rapid changes of fashion which now extend their baneful
influence through almost every rank of society, weight the balance
even more heavily against the small dealer, for he cannot keep a
sufficient stock to offer much variety of choice, and if he tries to follow
any movement of fashion closely, a larger proportion of his stock will
be left stranded by the receding tide than in the case of a large
shopkeeper. Again, in some branches of the clothing and furniture
and other trades the increasing cheapness of machine-made goods is
leading people to buy ready-made things from a large store instead
of having them made to order by some small maker and dealer in

their neighbourhood. Again, the large shopkeeper, not content
with receiving travellers from the manufacturers, makes tours either
himself or by his agent in the most important manufacturing districts at home and abroad; and he thus often dispenses with middlemen between him and the manufacturer. A tailor with moderate
capital shows his customers specimens of many hundreds of the
newest cloths, and perhaps orders by telegraph the selected cloth to
be sent by parcels' post. Again, ladies often buy their materials
direct from the manufacturer, and get them made up by dressmakers who have scarcely any capital. Small shopkeepers seem
likely always to retain some hold of the minor repairing trades :
and they keep their own fairly well in the sale of perishable food,
especially to the working classes, partly in consequence of their being
able to sell goods on credit and to collect small debts. In many
trades however a firm with a large capital prefers having many small
shops to one large one. Buying, and whatever production is desirable, is concentrated under a central management; and exceptional
demands are met from a central reserve, so that each branch has
large resources, without the expense of keeping a large stock. The
branch manager has nothing to divert his attention from his customers; and, if an active man, with direct interest in the success of
his branch, may prove himself a formidable rival to the small shopkeeper; as has been shown in many trades connected with clothing
and food.

§ 7. We may next consider those industries whose geographical The
position is determined by the nature of their work. carrying
trades.

Country carriers and a few cabmen are almost the only survivals
of small industry in the carrying trade. Railways and tramways are
constantly increasing in size, and the capital required to work them
is increasing at an even greater rate. The growing intricacy and
variety of commerce is adding to the advantages which a large fleet
of ships under one management derives from its power of delivering
goods promptly, and without breach of responsibility, in many
different ports; and as regards the vessels themselves time is on the
side of large ships, especially in the passenger trade.[1] As a consequence the arguments in favour of the State's undertaking

---

[1] A ship's carrying power varies as the cube of her dimensions, while the resistance
offered by the water increases only a little faster than the square of her dimensions;
so that a large ship requires less coal in proportion to its tonnage than a small one.
It also requires less labour, especially that of navigation : while to passengers it offers
greater safety and comfort, more choice of company and better professional attendance. In short, the small ship has no chance of competing with the large ship between
ports which large ships can easily enter, and between which the traffic is sufficient to
enable them to fill up quickly.

IV, xi, 7. business are stronger in some branches of the carrying trade than in any other, except the allied undertakings of carrying away refuse, and bringing in water, gas, etc.[1]

Mines and quarries.

The contest between large and small mines and quarries has not so clearly marked a tendency. The history of the State management of mines is full of very dark shadows; for the business of mining depends too much on the probity of its managers and their energy and judgment in matters of detail as well as of general principle, to be well managed by State officials : and for the same reason the small mine or quarry may fairly be expected, other things being equal, to hold its own against the large one. But in some cases the cost of deep shafts, of machinery and of establishing means of communication, are too great to be borne by any but a very large business.

The case of agriculture is deferred.

In agriculture there is not much division of labour, and there is no production on a very large scale; for a so-called " large farm " does not employ a tenth part of the labour which is collected in a factory of moderate dimensions. This is partly due to natural causes, to the changes of the seasons and to the difficulty of concentrating a great deal of labour in any one place; but it is partly also due to causes connected with varieties of land tenure. And it will be best to postpone discussion of all of them till we come to study demand and supply in relation to land in the sixth Book.

[1] It is characteristic of the great economic change of the last hundred years that when the first railway bills were passed, provision was made for allowing private individuals to run their own conveyances on them just as they do on a highway or a canal; and now we find it difficult to imagine how people could have expected, as they certainly did, that this plan would prove a practicable one.

CHAPTER XII

INDUSTRIAL ORGANIZATION, CONTINUED. BUSINESS MANAGEMENT

§ 1. HITHERTO we have been considering the work of management chiefly in regard to the operations of a manufacturing or other business employing a good deal of manual labour. But we now have to consider more carefully the variety of the functions which business men discharge; the manner in which they are distributed among the heads of a large business, and again between different classes of business which co-operate in allied branches of production and marketing. And incidentally we have to inquire how it occurs that, though in manufacturing at least nearly every individual business, so long as it is well managed, tends to become stronger the larger it has grown; and though *primâ facie* we might therefore expect to see large firms driving their smaller rivals completely out of many branches of industry, yet they do not in fact do so.

IV, XII, 1.

Problems to be solved.

" Business " is taken here broadly to include all provision for the wants of others which is made in the expectation of payment direct or indirect from those who are to be benefited. It is thus contrasted with the provision for his wants which each one makes for himself, and with those kindly services which are prompted by friendship and family affection.

The primitive handicraftsman managed his whole business for himself; but since his customers were with few exceptions his immediate neighbours, since he required very little capital, since the plan of production was arranged for him by custom, and since he had no labour to superintend outside of his own household, these tasks did not involve any very great mental strain. He was far from enjoying unbroken prosperity; war and scarcity were constantly pressing on him and his neighbours, hindering his work and stopping their demand for his wares. But he was inclined to take good and evil fortune, like sunshine and rain, as things beyond his control : his fingers worked on, but his brain was seldom weary.

The primitive handicraftsman dealt directly with the consumer

Even in modern England we find now and then a village artisan who adheres to primitive methods, and makes things on his own account for sale to his neighbours; managing his own business and

and so do as a rule the learned

undertaking all its risks. But such cases are rare: the most striking instances of an adherence to old-fashioned methods of business are supplied by the learned professions; for a physician or a solicitor manages as a rule his own business and does all its work. This plan is not without its disadvantages: much valuable activity is wasted or turned to but slight account by some professional men of first-rate ability, who have not the special aptitude required for obtaining a business connection; they would be better paid, would lead happier lives, and would do more good service for the world if their work could be arranged for them by some sort of a middleman. But yet on the whole things are probably best as they are: there are sound reasons behind the popular instinct which distrusts the intrusion of the middleman in the supply of those services which require the highest and most delicate mental qualities, and which can have their full value only where there is complete personal confidence.

English solicitors however act, if not as employers or undertakers, yet as agents for hiring that branch of the legal profession which ranks highest, and whose work involves the hardest mental strain. Again, many of the best instructors of youth sell their services, not directly to the consumer, but to the governing body of a college or school, or to a head master, who arranges for their purchase: the employer supplies to the teacher a market for his labour; and is supposed to give to the purchaser, who may not be a good judge himself, some sort of guarantee as to the quality of the teaching supplied.

Again, artists of every kind, however eminent, often find it to their advantage to employ someone else to arrange for them with customers; while those of less established repute are sometimes dependent for their living on capitalized traders, who are not themselves artists, but who understand how to sell artistic work to the best advantage.

§ 2. But in the greater part of the business of the modern world the task of so directing production that a given effort may be most effective in supplying human wants has to be broken up and given into the hands of a specialized body of employers, or to use a more general term, of business men. They "adventure" or "undertake" its risks; they bring together the capital and the labour required for the work; they arrange or "engineer" its general plan, and superintend its minor details. Looking at business men from one point of view we may regard them as a highly skilled industrial grade, from another as middlemen intervening between the manual worker and the consumer.

There are some kinds of business men who undertake great risks, IV, xii, 3. and exercise a large influence over the welfare both of the producers and of the consumers of the wares in which they deal, but who are not to any considerable extent direct employers of labour. The extreme type of these is the dealer on the stock exchange or the produce markets, whose daily purchases and sales are of vast dimensions, and who yet has neither factory nor warehouse, but at most an office with a few clerks in it. The good and the evil effects of the action of speculators such as these are however very complex; and we may give our attention at present to those forms of business in which administration counts for most and the subtler forms of speculation for least. Let us then take some illustrations of the more common types of business, and watch the relations in which the undertaking of risks stands to the rest of the work of the business man.

§ 3. The building trade will serve our purpose well, partly because Illustra- it adheres in some respects to primitive methods of business. Late tion from in the Middle Ages it was quite common for a private person to building. build a house for himself without the aid of a master builder; and the habit is not even now altogether extinct. A person who undertakes his own building must hire separately all his workmen, he must watch them and check their demands for payment; he must buy his materials from many quarters, and he must hire, or dispense with the use of, expensive machinery. He probably pays more than the current wages; but here others gain what he loses. There is however great waste in the time he spends in bargaining with the men and testing and directing their work by his imperfect knowledge; and again in the time that he spends in finding out what kinds and quantities he wants of different materials, and where to get them best, and so on. This waste is avoided by that division of labour which assigns to the professional builder the task of superintending details, and to the professional architect the task of drawing plans.

The division of labour is often carried still further when houses The chief are built not at the expense of those who are to live in them, but as risks of a building speculation. When this is done on a large scale, as for taking instance in opening out a new suburb, the stakes at issue are so sometimes large as to offer an attractive field to powerful capitalists with a very separated high order of general business ability, but perhaps with not much detailed technical knowledge of the building trade. They rely on their own manage judgment for the decision as to what are likely to be the coming building relations of demand and supply for different kinds of houses; but trades;

IV, XII, 4. they entrust to others the management of details. They employ
architects and surveyors to make plans in accordance with their
general directions; and then enter into contracts with professional
builders for carrying them out. But they themselves undertake
the chief risks of the business, and control its general direction.

in the textile trades; §4. It is well known that this division of responsibility prevailed
in the woollen trade just before the beginning of the era of large
factories : the more speculative work and the broader risks of buying and selling being taken over by the undertakers, who were not
themselves employers of labour; while the detailed work of superintendence and the narrower risks of carrying out definite contracts
were handed over to small masters.[1] This plan is still extensively
followed in some branches of the textile trades, especially those in
which the difficulty of forecasting the future is very great. Manchester warehousemen give themselves to studying the movements
of fashion, the markets for raw materials, the general state of trade,
of the money market and of politics, and all other causes that are
likely to influence the prices of different kinds of goods during the
coming season; and after employing, if necessary, skilled designers
to carry out their ideas (just as the building speculator in the previous case employed architects), they give out to manufacturers in
different parts of the world contracts for making the goods on which
they have determined to risk their capital.

in house industries; In the clothing trades especially we see a revival of what has
been called the "house industry," which prevailed long ago in the
textile industries; that is, the system in which large undertakers
give out work to be done in cottages and very small workshops to
persons who work alone or with the aid of some members of their
family, or who perhaps employ two or three hired assistants.[2]
In remote villages in almost every county of England agents of
large undertakers come round to give out to the cottagers partially
prepared materials for goods of all sorts, but especially clothes such
as shirts and collars and gloves; and take back with them the
finished goods. It is however in the great capital cities of the world,

---

[1] Compare Appendix A, 13.
[2] German economists call this "factory like" (fabrikmässig) house industry,
as distinguished from the "national" house industry, which uses the intervals
of other work (especially the winter interruptions of agriculture) for subsidiary
work in making textile and other goods. (See Schönberg on *Gewerbe* in his *Handbuch*)
Domestic workers of this last class were common all over Europe in the Middle Ages
but are now becoming rare except in the mountains and in eastern Europe. They
are not always well advised in their choice of work; and much of what they make could
be made better with far less labour in factories, so that it cannot be sold profitably in
the open market : but for the most part they make for their own or their neighbours'
use, and thus save the profits of a series of middlemen. Compare *Survival of domestic
industries* by Gonner in the *Economic Journal*, Vol. II.

and in other large towns, especially old towns, where there is a great   IV, xɪɪ, 4.
deal of unskilled and unorganized labour, with a somewhat low
physique and morale, that the system is most fully developed,
especially in the clothing trades, which employ two hundred thous-
and people in London alone, and in the cheap furniture trades.
There is a continual contest between the factory and the domestic
system, now one gaining ground and now the other : for instance
just at present the growing use of sewing machines worked by steam
power is strengthening the position of the factories in the boot trade;
while factories and workshops are getting an increased hold of the
tailoring trade.   On the other hand the hosiery trade is being
tempted back to the dwelling-house by recent improvements in hand
knitting machines; and it is possible that new methods of distributing power by gas and petroleum and electric engines may exercise a
like influence on many other industries.

Or there may be a movement towards intermediate plans, in Sheffield
similar to those which are largely followed in the Sheffield trades. trades;
Many cutlery firms for instance put out grinding and other parts of
their work, at piece-work prices, to working men who rent the steam
power which they require, either from the firm from whom they take
their contract or from someone else : these workmen sometimes
employing others to help them, sometimes working alone.

Again, the foreign merchant very often has no ships of his own, in the
but gives his mind to studying the course of trade, and undertakes shipping
himself its chief risks; while he gets his carrying done for him by trade;
men who require more administrative ability, but need not have the
same power of forecasting the subtler movements of trade; though it
is true that as puchasers of ships they have great and difficult
trade risks of their own.   Again, the broader risks of publishing a and in the
book are borne by the publisher, perhaps in company with the author; production
while the printer is the employer of labour and supplies the expensive etc.
types and machinery required for the business.   And a somewhat
similar plan is adopted in many branches of the metal trades, and of
those which supply furniture, clothing, etc.

Thus there are many ways in which those who undertake This plan
the chief risks of buying and selling may avoid the trouble of housing has ad-
and superintending those who work for them.   They all have their vantages;
advantages; and when the workers are men of strong character, as
at Sheffield, the results are on the whole not unsatisfactory.   But but is
unfortunately it is often the weakest class of workers, those with the liable to
abuse.
least resource and the least self-control who drift into work of this
kind.   The elasticity of the system which recommends it to the

IV, xii, 5. undertaker, is really the means of enabling him to exercise, if he chooses, an undesirable pressure on those who do his work.

For while the success of a factory depends in a great measure on its having a set of operatives who adhere steadily to it, the capitalist who gives out the work to be done at home has an interest in retaining a great many persons on his books; he is tempted to give each of them a little employment occasionally and play them off one against another; and this he can easily do because they do not know one another, and cannot arrange concerted action.

§ 5. When the profits of business are under discussion they are generally connected in people's minds with the employer of labour : " the employer " is often taken as a term practically coextensive with the receiver of business profits. But the instances which we have just considered are sufficient to illustrate the truth that the superintendence of labour is but one side, and often not the most important side of business work; and that the employer who undertakes the whole risks of his business really performs two entirely distinct services on behalf of the community, and requires a twofold ability.

Several distinct functions are combined in one hand by the ideal manufacturer :

the faculties required in him.

To return to a class of considerations already noticed (IV. xi. 4 and 5), the manufacturer who makes goods not to meet special orders but for the general market, must, in his first rôle as merchant and organizer of production, have a thorough knowledge of *things* in his own trade. He must have the power of forecasting the broad movements of production and consumption, of seeing where there is an opportunity for supplying a new commodity that will meet a real want or improving the plan of producing an old commodity. He must be able to judge cautiously and undertake risks boldly; and he must of course understand the materials and machinery used in his trade.

But secondly in this rôle of employer he must be a natural leader of *men*. He must have a power of first choosing his assistants rightly and then trusting them fully; of interesting them in the business and of getting them to trust him, so as to bring out whatever enterprise and power of origination there is in them; while he himself exercises a general control over everything, and preserves order and unity in the main plan of the business.

The abilities required to make an ideal employer are so great and so numerous that very few persons can exhibit them all in a very high degree. Their relative importance however varies with the nature of the industry and the size of the business; and while one employer excels in one set of qualities, another excels in another; scarcely

any two owe their success to exactly the same combination of advantages. Some men make their way by the use of none but noble
qualities, while others their prosperity to qualities in which there is
very little that is really admirable except sagacity and strength of
purpose.

Such then being the general nature of the work of business
management, we have next to inquire what opportunities different
classes of people have of developing business ability; and, when
they have obtained that, what opportunities they have of getting
command over the capital required to give it scope. We may thus
come a little closer to the problem stated at the beginning of the
chapter, and examine the course of development of a business firm
during several consecutive generations. And this inquiry may conveniently be combined with some examination of the different
forms of business management. Hitherto we have considered
almost exclusively that form in which the whole responsibility and
control rests in the hands of a single individual. But this form is
yielding ground to others in which the supreme authority is distributed among several partners or even a great number of shareholders. Private firms and joint-stock companies, co-operative
societies and public corporations are taking a constantly increasing
share in the management of business; and one chief reason of this is
that they offer an attractive field to people who have good business
abilities, but have not inherited any great business opportunities.

§ 6. It is obvious that the son of a man already established in
business starts with very great advantages over others. He has
from his youth up special facilities for obtaining the knowledge and
developing the faculties that are required in the management of
his father's business : he learns quietly and almost unconsciously
about men and manners in his father's trade and in those from which
that trade buys and to which it sells; he gets to know the relative
importance and the real significance of the various problems and
anxieties which occupy his father's mind : and he acquires a technical knowledge of the processes and the machinery of the trade.[1]
Some of what he learns will be applicable only to his father's trade;
but the greater part will be serviceable in any trade that is in any
way allied with that; while those general faculties of judgment and
resource, of enterprise and caution, of firmness and courtesy, which
are trained by association with those who control the larger issues of

IV, XII, 6.

*The supply
of business
ability
may
be dis-
cussed in
connection
with the
forms of
business
manage-
ment.*

*The son of
a business
man has a
good start.*

---

[1] We have already noticed how almost the only perfect apprenticeships of modern
times are those of the sons of manufacturers, who practise almost every important
operation that is carried on in the works sufficiently to be able in after years to enter
into the difficulties of all their employees and form a fair judgment on their work.

IV, xɪɪ, 6. any one trade, will go a long way towards fitting him for managing almost any other trade. Further, the sons of successful business men start with more material capital than almost anyone else except those who by nurture and education are likely to be disinclined for business and unfitted for it : and if they continue their fathers' work, they have also the vantage ground of established trade connections.

But business men do not form a caste, because their abilities and tastes are not always inherited; It would therefore at first sight seem likely that business men should constitute a sort of caste; dividing out among their sons the chief posts of command, and founding hereditary dynasties, which should rule certain branches of trade for many generations together. But the actual state of things is very different. For when a man has got together a great business, his descendants often fail, in spite of their great advantages, to develop the high abilities and the special turn of mind and temperament required for carrying it on with equal success. He himself was probably brought up by parents of strong earnest character; and was educated by their personal influence and by struggle with difficulties in early life. But his children, at all events if they were born after he became rich, and in any case his grandchildren, are perhaps left a good deal to the care of domestic servants who are not of the same strong fibre as the parents by whose influence he was educated. And while his highest ambition was probably success in business, they are likely to be at least equally anxious for social or academic distinction.[1]

For a time indeed all may go well. His sons find a firmly established trade connection, and what is perhaps even more important, a well-chosen staff of subordinates with a generous interest in the business. By mere assiduity and caution, availing themselves of the traditions of the firm, they may hold together for a long time. But when a full generation has passed, when the old traditions are no longer a safe guide, and when the bonds that held together the old staff have been dissolved, then the business almost invariably falls to pieces unless it is practically handed over to the management of new men who have meanwhile risen to partnership in the firm.

But in most cases his descendants arrive at this result by a

[1] Until lately there has ever been in England a kind of antagonism between academic studies and business. This is now being diminished by the broadening of the spirit of our great universities, and by the growth of colleges in our chief business centres. The sons of business men when sent to the universities do not learn to despise their fathers' trades as often as they used to do even a generation ago. Many of them indeed are drawn away from business by the desire to extend the boundaries of knowledge. But the higher forms of mental activity, those which are constructive and not merely critical, tend to promote a just appreciation of the nobility of business work rightly done.

shorter route. They prefer an abundant income coming to them IV, xii, 7.
without effort on their part, to one which though twice as large and after a
could be earned only by incessant toil and anxiety; and they sell time new
the business to private persons or a joint-stock company; or they blood must
be brought
become sleeping partners in it; that is sharing in its risks and in its in by some
method.
profits, but not taking part in its management : in either case the
active control over their capital falls chiefly into the hands of new
men.

§ 7. The oldest and simplest plan for renovating the energies of The
a business is that of taking into partnership some of its ablest method of
private
employees. The autocratic owner and manager of a large manu- partner-
facturing or trading concern finds that, as years go on, he has to ship.
delegate more and more responsibility to his chief subordinates;
partly because the work to be done is growing heavier, and partly
because his own strength is becoming less than it was. He still
exercises a supreme control, but much must depend on their energy
and probity : so, if his sons are not old enough, or for any other
reason are not ready to take part of the burden off his shoulders, he
decides to take one of his trusted assistants into partnership : he
thus lightens his own labours, at the same time that he secures that
the task of his life will be carried on by those whose habits he has
moulded, and for whom he has perhaps acquired something like a
fatherly affection.[1]

But there are now, and there always have been, private partnerships on more equal terms, two or more people of about equal
wealth and ability combining their resources for a large and difficult
undertaking. In such cases there is often a distinct partition of the
work of management : in manufactures for instance one partner
will sometimes give himself almost exclusively to the work of buying
raw material and selling the finished product, while the other is
responsible for the management of the factory : and in a trading
establishment one partner will control the wholesale and the other
the retail department. In these and other ways private partnership
is capable of adapting itself to a great variety of problems : it is
very strong and very elastic; it has played a great part in the past,
and it is full of vitality now.

---

[1] Much of the happiest romance of life, much that is most pleasant to dwell
upon in the social history of England from the Middle Ages up to our own day is
connected with the story of private partnerships of this class. Many a youth has
been stimulated to a brave career by the influence of ballads and tales which narrate
the difficulties and the ultimate triumph of the faithful apprentice, who has at length
been taken into partnership, perhaps on marrying his employer's daughter. There
are no influences on national character more far-reaching than those which thus give
shape to the aims of aspiring youth.

§ 8. But from the end of the Middle Ages to the present time there has been in some classes of trades a movement towards the substitution of public joint-stock companies, the shares of which can be sold to anybody in the open market, for private companies, the shares in which are not transferable without the leave of all concerned. The effect of this change has been to induce people, many of whom have no special knowledge of trade, to give their capital into the hands of others employed by them : and there has thus arisen a new distribution of the various parts of the work of business management.

The ultimate undertakers of the risks incurred by a joint-stock company are the shareholders; but as a rule they do not take much active part in engineering the business and controlling its general policy; and they take no part in superintending its details. After the business has once got out of the hands of its original promoters, the control of it is left chiefly in the hands of Directors; who, if the company is a very large one, probably own but a very small proportion of its shares, while the greater part of them have not much technical knowledge of the work to be done. They are not generally expected to give their whole time to it; but they are supposed to bring wide general knowledge and sound judgment to bear on the broader problems of its policy; and at the same time to make sure that the "Managers" of the company are doing their work thoroughly.[1] To the Managers and their assistants is left a great part of the work of engineering the business, and the whole of the work of superintending it: but they are not required to bring any capital into it; and they are supposed to be promoted from the lower ranks to the higher according to their zeal and ability. Since the joint-stock companies in the United Kingdom do a very great part of the business of all kinds that is done in the country, they offer very large opportunities to men with natural talents for business management, who have not inherited any material capital, or any business connection.

§ 9. Joint-stock companies have great elasticity and can expand themselves without limit when the work to which they have set themselves offers a wide scope; and they are gaining ground in

IV, xii, 8, 9.

The method of joint-stock companies

The shareholders undertake the risks;

the Directors control the Managers;

who superintend the details.

Those who undertake the risks cannot

[1] Bagehot delighted to argue (see for instance *English Constitution*, ch. vii.) that a Cabinet Minister often derives some advantage from his want of technical knowledge of the business of his Department. For he can get information on matters of detail from the Permanent Secretary and other officials who are under his authority; and, while he is not likely to set his judgment against theirs on matters where their knowledge gives them the advantage, his unprejudiced common sense may well overrule the traditions of officialism in broad questions of public policy : and in like manner the interests of a company may possibly sometimes be most advanced by those Directors who have the least technical knowledge of the details of its business.

nearly all directions. But they have one great source of weakness in IV, xii, 9.
the absence of any adequate knowledge of the business on the part always
of the shareholders who undertake its chief risks. It is true that judge
the head of a large private firm undertakes the chief risks of the the
business, while he entrusts many of its details to others; but his business
position is secured by his power of forming a direct judgment as managed.
to whether his subordinates serve his interests faithfully and
discreetly. If those to whom he has entrusted the buying or
selling of goods for him take commissions from those with whom
they deal, he is in a position to discover and punish the fraud. If
they show favouritism and promote incompetent relations or friends
of their own, or if they themselves become idle and shirk their work,
or even if they do not fulfil the promise of exceptional ability which
induced him to give them their first lift, he can discover what is
going wrong and set it right.

But in all these matters the great body of the shareholders of a The
joint-stock company are, save in a few exceptional instances, almost system is
powerless; though a few of the larger shareholders often exert workable
themselves to find out what is going on; and are thus able to exer- only by
cise an effective and wise control over the general management of modern
the business. It is a strong proof of the marvellous growth in recent business
times of a spirit of honesty and uprightness in commercial matters, morality.
that the leading officers of great public companies yield as little as
they do to the vast temptations to fraud which lie in their way.
If they showed an eagerness to avail themselves of opportunities
for wrong-doing at all approaching that of which we read in the
commercial history of earlier civilization, their wrong uses of the
trusts imposed in them would have been on so great a scale as to
prevent the development of this democratic form of business.
There is every reason to hope that the progress of trade morality
will continue, aided in the future as it has been in the past, by a
diminution of trade secrecy and by increased publicity in every
form; and thus collective and democratic forms of business management may be able to extend themselves safely in many directions in
which they have hitherto failed, and may far exceed the great services
they already render in opening a large career to those who have no
advantages of birth.

The same may be said of the undertakings of Governments Govern-
imperial and local : they also may have a great future before them, ment
but up to the present time the tax-payer who undertakes the ultimate takings.
risks has not generally succeeded in exercising an efficient control
over the businesses, and in securing officers who will do their work

IV, XII, 10. with as much energy and enterprise as is shown in private establishments.

The social perils of bureaucratic methods.

The problems of large joint-stock company administration, as well as of Governmental business, involve however many complex issues into which we cannot enter here. They are urgent, because very large businesses have recently increased fast, though perhaps not quite so fast as is commonly supposed. The change has been brought about chiefly by the development of processes and methods in manufacture and mining, in transport and banking, which are beyond the reach of any but very large capitals; and by the increase in the scope and functions of markets, and in the technical facilities for handling large masses of goods. The democratic element in Governmental enterprise was at first almost wholly vivifying: but experience shows creative ideas and experiments in business technique, and in business organization, to be very rare in Governmental undertakings, and not very common in private enterprises which have drifted towards bureaucratic methods as the result of their great age and large size. A new danger is thus threatened by the narrowing of the field of industry which is open to the vigorous initiative of smaller businesses.

Trusts and cartels.

Production on the largest scale of all is to be seen chiefly in the United States, where giant businesses, with some touch of monopoly, are commonly called "trusts." Some of these trusts have grown from a single root. But most of them have been developed by the amalgamation of many independent businesses; and a first step towards this combination was generally an association, or "cartel" to use a German term, of a rather loose kind.

Co-operative association in its ideal form

§ 10. The system of co-operation aims at avoiding the evils of these two methods of business management. In that ideal form of co-operative society, for which many still fondly hope, but which as yet has been scantily realized in practice, a part or the whole of those shareholders who undertake the risks of the business are themselves employed by it. The employees, whether they contribute towards the material capital of the business or not, have a share in its profits, and some power of voting at the general meetings at which the broad lines of its policy are laid down, and the officers appointed who are to carry that policy into effect. They are thus

might avoid the chief dangers of joint-stock companies.

the employers and masters of their own managers and foremen; they have fairly good means of judging whether the higher work of engineering the business is conducted honestly and efficiently, and they have the best possible opportunities for detecting any laxity or incompetence in its detailed administration. And lastly they render

unnecessary some of the minor work of superintendence that is IV, XII, 10.
required in other establishments; for their own pecuniary interests
and the pride they take in the success of their own business make
each of them averse to any shirking of work either by himself or by
his fellow-workmen.

But unfortunately the system has very great difficulties of its It has
own. For human nature being what it is, the employees themselves difficulties in the task
are not always the best possible masters of their own foremen and of business
managers; jealousies and frettings at reproof are apt to act like manage-ment,
sand, that has got mixed with the oil in the bearings of a great and
complex machinery. The hardest work of business management is
generally that which makes the least outward show; those who
work with their hands are apt to underrate the intensity of the strain
involved in the highest work of engineering the business, and to
grudge its being paid for at anything like as high a rate as it could
earn elsewhere. And in fact the managers of a co-operative society
seldom have the alertness, the inventiveness and the ready versatility of the ablest of those men who have been selected by the
struggle for survival, and who have been trained by the free and
unfettered responsibility of private business. Partly for these
reasons the co-operative system has seldom been carried out in its
entirety; and its partial application has not yet attained a conspicuous success except in retailing commodities consumed by working men. But within the last few years more hopeful signs have
appeared of the success of *bonâ fide* productive associations, or " co-
partnerships."

Those working men indeed whose tempers are strongly indivi- but it may
dualistic, and whose minds are concentrated almost wholly on their outgrow some of
own affairs, will perhaps always find their quickest and most con- these.
genial path to material success by commencing business as small
independent " undertakers," or by working their way upwards in a
private firm or a public company. But co-operation has a special
charm for those in whose tempers the social element is stronger, and
who desire not to separate themselves from their old comrades, but
to work among them as their leaders. Its aspirations may in some
respects be higher than its practice; but it undoubtedly does rest
in a great measure on ethical motives. The true co-operator combines a keen business intellect with a spirit full of an earnest faith;
and some co-operative societies have been served excellently by men
of great genius both mentally and morally—men who for the sake of
the co-operative faith that is in them, have worked with great ability
and energy, and with perfect uprightness, being all the time con-

IV, xii, 10. tent with lower pay than they could have got as business managers on their own account or for a private firm. Men of this stamp are more common among officers of co-operative societies than in other occupations; and though they are not very common even there, yet it may be hoped that the diffusion of a better knowledge of the true principles of co-operation, and the increase of general education, are every day fitting a larger number of co-operators for the complex problems of business management.

Profit-Sharing. Meanwhile many partial applications of the co-operative principle are being tried under various conditions, each of which presents some new aspect of business management. Thus under the scheme of Profit-Sharing, a private firm while retaining the un-fettered management of its business, pays its employees the full market rate of wages, whether by Time or Piece-work, and agrees in addition to divide among them a certain share of any profits that may be made above a fixed minimum; it being hoped that the firm will find a material as well as a moral reward in the diminution of friction, in the increased willingness of its employees to go out of their way to do little things that may be of great benefit compara-tively to the firm, and lastly in attracting to itself workers of more than average ability and industry.[1]

Partial Co-operation. Another partially co-operative scheme is that of some Oldham cotton-mills : they are really joint-stock companies; but among their shareholders are many working men who have a special knowledge of the trade, though they often prefer not to be employed in the mills of which they are part owners. And another is that of the Productive establishments, owned by the main body of co-operative stores, through their agents, the co-operative Wholesale Societies. In the Scotch Wholesale, but not in the English, the workers, as such, have some shares in the management and in the profits of the works.

At a later stage we shall have to study all those various co-operative and semi-co-operative forms of business more in detail, and to inquire into the cause of their success or failure in different classes of business, wholesale and retail, agricultural, manufacturing and trading. But we must not pursue this inquiry further now.

Hopes for the future. Enough has been said to show that the world is only just beginning to be ready for the higher work of the co-operative movement; and that its many different forms may therefore be reasonably expected to attain a larger success in the future than in the past; and to

[1] Compare Schloss, *Methods of Industrial Remuneration*; and Gilman, *A dividend to labour*.

offer excellent opportunities for working men to practise themselves IV, xII, 11. in the work of business management, to grow into the trust and confidence of others, and gradually rise to posts in which their business abilities will find scope.

§ 11. In speaking of the difficulty that a working man has in rising to a post in which he can turn his business ability to full account, the chief stress is commonly laid upon his want of capital: but this is not always his chief difficulty. For instance the co-operative distributive societies have accumulated a vast capital, on which they find it difficult to get a good rate of interest; and which they would be rejoiced to lend to any set of working men who could show that they had the capacity for dealing with difficult business problems. Co-operators who have firstly a high order of business ability and probity, and secondly the " personal capital " of a great reputation among their fellows for these qualities, will have no difficulty in getting command of enough material capital for a considerable undertaking : the real difficulty is to convince a sufficient number of those around them that they have these rare qualities. And the case is not very different when an individual endeavours to obtain from the ordinary sources the loan of the capital required to start him in business.

The rise of the working man is not hindered as much as at first sight appears, by his want of capital;

It is true that in almost every business there is a constant increase in the amount of capital required to make a fair start; but there is a much more rapid increase in the amount of capital which is owned by people who do not want to use it themselves, and are so eager to lend it out that they will accept a constantly lower and lower rate of interest for it. Much of this capital passes into the hands of bankers who promptly lend it to anyone of whose business ability and honesty they are convinced. To say nothing of the credit that can be got in many businesses from those who supply the requisite raw material or stock in trade, the opportunities for direct borrowing are now so great that a moderate increase in the amount of capital required for a start in business is no very serious obstacle in the way of a person who has once got over the initial difficulty of earning a reputation for being likely to use it well.

for the loan-fund is increasing in volume and in eagerness for employment.

But perhaps a greater though less conspicuous hindrance to the rise of the working man is the growing complexity of business. The head of a business has now to think of many things about which he never used to trouble himself in earlier days; and these are just the kind of difficulties for which the training of the workshop affords the least preparation. Against this must be set the rapid improvement of the education of the working man not only at school, but

He is hindered much by the growing complexity of business.

K

IV, xɪɪ, 11. what is more important, in after life by newspapers, and from the
—— work of co-operative societies and trades-unions, and in other ways.

But he   About three-fourths of the whole population of England belong
may   to the wage-earning classes; and at all events when they are well
overcome
these   fed, properly housed and educated, they have their fair share of
difficulties. that nervous strength which is the raw material of business ability.
Without going out of their way they are all consciously or unconsciously competitors for posts of business command.   The ordinary
workman if he shows ability generally becomes a foreman, from
that he may rise to be a manager, and to be taken into partnership
with his employer.   Or having saved a little of his own he may start
one of those small shops which can still hold their own in a working
man's quarter, stock it chiefly on credit, and let his wife attend to it
by day, while he gives his evenings to it.   In these or in other ways he
may increase his capital till he can start a small workshop, or factory.
Once having made a good beginning he will find the banks eager to
give him generous credit.   He must have time; and since he is not
likely to start in business till after middle age he must have a long
as well as a strong life; but if he has this and has also " patience,
genius and good fortune " he is pretty sure to command a goodly
capital before he dies.[1]   In a factory those who work with their
hands have better opportunities of rising to posts of command than
the book-keepers and many others to whom social tradition has
assigned a higher place.   But in trading concerns it is otherwise;
what manual work is done in them has as a rule no educating
character, while the experience of the office is better adapted for
preparing a man to manage a commercial than a manufacturing
business.

The rise   There is then on the whole a broad movement from below up-
may take   wards.   Perhaps not so many as formerly rise at once from the
two gener-
ations   position of working men to that of employers : but there are more
instead   who get on sufficiently far to give their sons a good chance of attain-
of one.

---

[1] The Germans say that success in business requires " Geld, Geduld, Genie and
Glück."   The chances that a working man has of rising vary somewhat with the
nature of the work, being greatest in those trades in which a careful attention to details
counts for most, and a wide knowledge, whether of science or of the world movements
of speculation, counts for least.   Thus for instance " thrift and the knowledge of practical details " are the most important elements of success in the ordinary work of the
pottery trade; and in consequence most of those who have done well in 't " have
risen from the bench like Josiah Wedgwood " (see G. Wedgwood's evidence before
the Commission on Technical Education); and a similar statement might be made
about many of the Sheffield trades.   But some of the working classes develop a great
faculty for taking speculative risks; and if the knowledge of facts by which successful
speculation must be guided, comes within their reach, they will often push their way
through competitors who have started above them.   Some of the most successful
wholesale dealers in perishable commodities such as fish and fruit have begun life as
market porters.

ing to the highest posts. The complete rise is not so very often IV, xii, 12.
accomplished in one generation; it is more often spread over two;
but the total volume of the movement upwards is probably greater
than it has ever been. And perhaps it is better for society as a
whole that the rise should be distributed over two generations. The
workmen who at the beginning of the last century rose in such large But that
numbers to become employers were seldom fit for posts of command : is not an
they were too often harsh and tyrannical; they lost their self- unmixed
control, and were neither truly noble nor truly happy; while their evil;
children were often haughty, extravagant, and self-indulgent,
squandering their wealth on low and vulgar amusements, having
the worst faults of the older aristocracy without their virtues.
The foreman or superintendent who has still to obey as well as to
command, but who is rising and sees his children likely to rise
further, is in some ways more to be envied than the small master.
His success is less conspicuous, but his work is often higher and more
important for the world, while his character is more gentle and
refined and not less strong. His children are well-trained; and if
they get wealth, they are likely to make a fairly good use of it.

It must however be admitted that the rapid extension of vast if the
businesses, and especially of joint-stock companies in many branches danger
of industry, is tending to make the able and thrifty workman, with of mere
high ambitions for his sons, seek to put them to office work. There office work
they are in danger of losing the physical vigour and the force of avoided.
character which attaches to constructive work with the hands, and
to become commonplace members of the lower middle classes.
But, if they can keep their force unimpaired, they are likely to become leaders in the world, though not generally in their father's
industry; and therefore without the benefit of specially appropriate
traditions and aptitude.

§ 12. When a man of great ability is once at the head of an An able
independent business, whatever be the route by which he has got business
there, he will with moderate good fortune soon be able to show such speedily
evidence of his power of turning capital to good account as to enable increases
him to borrow in one way or another almost any amount that he at his
may need. Making good profits he adds to his own capital, and this command.
extra capital of his own is a material security for further borrowings;
while the fact that he has made it himself tends to make lenders less
careful to insist on a full security for their loans. Of course fortune
tells for much in business : a very able man may find things going
against him; the fact that he is losing money may diminish his
power of borrowing. If he is working partly on borrowed capital,

IV, xii, 12. it may even make those who have lent it refuse to renew their loans, and may thus cause him to succumb to what would have been but a passing misfortune, if he had been using no capital but his own : [1] and in fighting his way upwards he may have a chequered life full of great anxieties, and even misfortunes. But he can show his ability in misfortune as well as in success : human nature is sanguine; and it is notorious that men are abundantly willing to lend to those who have passed through commercial disaster without loss to their business reputation. Thus, in spite of vicissitudes, the able business man generally finds that in the long run the capital at his command grows in proportion to his ability.

A man who has not great business ability loses his capital the more rapidly the larger his business is. Meanwhile, as we have seen, he, who with small ability is in command of a large capital, speedily loses it : he may perhaps be one who could and would have managed a small business with credit and left it stronger than he had found it : but if he has not the genius for dealing with great problems, the larger it is the more speedily will he break it up. For as a rule a large business can be kept going only by transactions which, after allowing for ordinary risks, leave but a very small percentage of gain. A small profit on a large turn-over quickly made, will yield a rich income to able men : and in those businesses which are of such a nature as to give scope to very large capitals, competition generally cuts the rate of profits on the turn-over very fine. A village trader may make five per cent. less profits on his turn-over than his abler rival, and yet be able to hold his head above water. But in those large manufacturing and trading businesses in which there is a quick return and a straight-forward routine, the whole profits on the turn-over are often so very small that a person who falls behind his rivals by even a small percentage loses a large sum at every turn-over; while in those large businesses which are difficult and do not rely on routine, and which afford high profits on the turn-over to really able management, there are no profits at all to be got by anyone who attempts the task with only ordinary ability.

These two forces tend to adjust the capital to the These two sets of forces, the one increasing the capital at the command of able men, and the other destroying the capital that is in the hands of weaker men, bring about the result that there is a far more close correspondence between the ability of business men and

---

[1] The danger of not being able to renew his borrowings just at the time when he wants them most, puts him at a disadvantage relatively to those who use only their own capital, much greater than is represented by the mere interest on his borrowings : and, when we come to that part of the doctrine of distribution which deals with earnings of management, we shall find that, for this among other reasons, profits are something more than interest in addition to net earnings of management, *i.e.* those earnings which are properly to be ascribed to the abilities of business men.

the size of the businesses which they own than at first sight would IV, xii, 12.
appear probable.   And when to this fact we add all the many routes, ability
which we have already discussed, by which a man of great natural required to use it well.
business ability can work his way up high in some private firm or
public company, we may conclude that wherever there is work on a
large scale to be done in such a country as England, the ability and
the capital required for it are pretty sure to be speedily forthcoming.

Further, just as industrial skill and ability are getting every day
to depend more and more on the broad faculties of judgment,
promptness, resource, carefulness and steadfastness of purpose—
faculties which are not specialized to any one trade, but which are
more or less useful in all—so it is with regard to business ability.   In
fact business ability consists more of these non-specialized faculties
than do industrial skill and ability in the lower grades : and the
higher the grade of business ability the more various are its applications.

Since then business ability in command of capital moves with Business
great ease horizontally from a trade which is over-crowded to one ability in command
which offers good openings for it : and since it moves with great ease of capital
vertically, the abler men rising to the higher posts in their own has a fairly defined
trade, we see, even at this early stage of our inquiry, some good supply price in
reasons for believing that in modern England the supply of business such a
ability in command of capital accommodates itself, as a general rule, country as England.
to the demand for it; and thus has a fairly defined supply price.

Finally, we may regard this supply price of business ability in
command of capital as composed of three elements.   The first is the
supply price of capital; the second is the supply price of business
ability and energy ; and the third is the supply price of that organization by which the appropriate business ability and the requisite
capital are brought together.   We have called the price of the first of Net and
these three elements *interest*; we may call the price of the second gross earnings
taken by itself *net earnings of management*, and that of the second of manage-
and third, taken together, *gross earnings of management*. ment.

CHAPTER XIII

CONCLUSION. CORRELATION OF THE TENDENCIES TO INCREASING AND TO DIMINISHING RETURN

The relation in which the later chapters of this Book stand to the earlier.

§ 1. At the beginning of the Book we saw how the extra return of raw produce which nature affords to an increased application of capital and labour, other things being equal, tends in the long run to diminish. In the remainder of the Book and especially in the last four chapters we have looked at the other side of the shield, and seen how man's power of productive work increases with the volume of the work that he does. Considering first the causes that govern the supply of labour, we saw how every increase in the physical, mental and moral vigour of a people makes them more likely, other things being equal, to rear to adult age a large number of vigorous children. Turning next to the growth of wealth, we observed how every increase of wealth tends in many ways to make a greater increase more easy than before. And lastly we saw how every increase of wealth and every increase in the numbers and intelligence of the people increased the facilities for a highly developed industrial organization, which in its turn adds much to the collective efficiency of capital and labour.

A summary of the later chapters of this Book.

Looking more closely at the economies arising from an increase in the scale of production of any kind of goods, we found that they fell into two classes—those dependent on the general development of the industry, and those dependent on the resources of the individual houses of business engaged in it and the efficiency of their management; that is, into *external* and *internal* economies.

Summary.

We saw how these latter economies are liable to constant fluctuations so far as any particular house is concerned. An able man, assisted perhaps by some strokes of good fortune, gets a firm footing in the trade, he works hard and lives sparely, his own capital grows fast, and the credit that enables him to borrow more capital grows still faster; he collects around him subordinates of more than ordinary zeal and ability; as his business increases they rise with him, they trust him and he trusts them, each of them devotes himself with energy to just that work for which he is specially fitted, so that no high ability is wasted on easy work, and no difficult

work is entrusted to unskilful hands. Corresponding to this steadily IV, XIII, 1.
increasing economy of skill, the growth of his business brings with it Summary.
similar economies of specialized machines and plant of all kinds;
every improved process is quickly adopted and made the basis of
further improvements; success brings credit and credit brings
success; credit and success help to retain old customers and to
bring new ones; the increase of his trade gives him great advantages
in buying; his goods advertise one another, and thus diminish
his difficulty in finding a vent for them. The increase in the scale
of his business increases rapidly the advantages which he has over
his competitors, and lowers the price at which he can afford to sell.
This process may go on as long as his energy and enterprise, his
inventive and organizing power retain their full strength and freshness, and so long as the risks which are inseparable from business
do not cause him exceptional losses; and if it could endure for a
hundred years, he and one or two others like him would divide
between them the whole of that branch of industry in which he is
engaged. The large scale of their production would put great
economies within their reach; and provided they competed to their
utmost with one another, the public would derive the chief benefit
of these economies, and the price of the commodity would fall very
low.

But here we may read a lesson from the young trees of the forest
as they struggle upwards through the benumbing shade of their older
rivals. Many succumb on the way, and a few only survive; those
few become stronger with every year, they get a larger share of
light and air with every increase of their height, and at last in their
turn they tower above their neighbours, and seem as though they
would grow on for ever, and for ever become stronger as they grow.
But they do not. One tree will last longer in full vigour and attain
a greater size than another; but sooner or later age tells on them all.
Though the taller ones have a better access to light and air than their
rivals, they gradually lose vitality; and one after another they give
place to others, which, though of less material strength, have on their
side the vigour of youth.

And as with the growth of trees, so was it with the growth of
businesses as a general rule before the great recent development of
vast joint-stock companies, which often stagnate, but do not readily
die. Now that rule is far from universal, but it still holds in many
industries and trades. Nature still presses on the private business
by limiting the length of the life of its original founders, and by
limiting even more narrowly that part of their lives in which their

IV, xiii, 2. faculties retain full vigour. And so, after a while, the guidance of
Summary. the business falls into the hands of people with less energy and less
creative genius, if not with less active interest in its prosperity. If
it is turned into a joint-stock company, it may retain the advantages
of division of labour, of specialized skill and machinery : it may even
increase them by a further increase of its capital; and under favourable conditions it may secure a permanent and prominent place
in the work of production. But it is likely to have lost so much of its
elasticity and progressive force, that the advantages are no longer
exclusively on its side in its competition with younger and smaller
rivals.

When therefore we are considering the broad results which the
growth of wealth and population exert on the economies of production, the general character of our conclusions is not very much
affected by the facts that many of these economies depend directly
on the size of the individual establishments engaged in the production, and that in almost every trade there is a constant rise and fall
of large businesses, at any one moment some firms being in the
ascending phase and others in the descending. For in times of
average prosperity decay in one direction is sure to be more than
balanced by growth in another.

Meanwhile an increase in the aggregate scale of production of
course increases those economies, which do not directly depend on
the size of individual houses of business. The most important of
these result from the growth of correlated branches of industry
which mutually assist one another, perhaps being concentrated in the
same localities, but anyhow availing themselves of the modern
facilities for communication offered by steam transport, by the
telegraph and by the printing-press. The economies arising from
such sources as this, which are accessible to any branch of production,
do not depend exclusively upon its own growth : but yet they are
sure to grow rapidly and steadily with that growth; and they are
sure to dwindle in some, though not in all respects, if it decays.

Forecast   § 2. These results will be of great importance when we come to
of our
study of   discuss the causes which govern the supply price of a commodity.
the cost of We shall have to analyse carefully the normal cost of producing a
production
in a repre- commodity, relatively to a given aggregate volume of production;
sentative   and for this purpose we shall have to study *the expenses of a repre-*
firm.
sentative producer for that aggregate volume. On the one hand we
shall not want to select some new producer just struggling into
business, who works under many disadvantages, and has to be content for a time with little or no profits, but who is satisfied with

the fact that he establishing a connection and taking the first IV, xm, 2.
steps towards building up a successful business; nor on the other
hand shall we want to take a firm which by exceptionally long-
sustained ability and good fortune has got together a vast business,
and huge well-ordered workshops that give it a superiority over
almost all its rivals.   But our representative firm must be one
which has had a fairly long life, and fair success, which is managed
with normal ability, and which has normal access to the economies,
external and internal, which belong to that aggregate volume of
production; account being taken of the class of goods produced, the
conditions of marketing them and the economic environment
generally.

Thus a representative firm is in a sense an average firm.   But
there are many ways in which the term " average " might be interpreted in connection with a business.   And a Representative firm
is that particular sort of average firm, at which we need to look in
order to see how far the economies, *internal and external,* of production on a large scale have extended generally in the industry and
country in question.   We cannot see this by looking at one or two
firms taken at random : but we can see it fairly well by selecting,
after a broad survey, a firm, whether in private or joint-stock management (or better still, more than one), that represents, to the best of
our judgment, this particular average.

The general argument of the present Book shows that an increase
in the aggregate volume of production of anything will generally
increase the size, and therefore the internal economies possessed by
such a representative firm; that it will always increase the external
economies to which the firm has access; and thus will enable it to
manufacture at a less proportionate cost of labour and sacrifice than
before.

In other words, we say broadly that while the part which nature *Laws of*
plays in production shows a tendency to diminishing return, the part *increasing*
which man plays shows a tendency to increasing return.   The *law of return,*
increasing return may be worded thus :—An increase of labour and
capital leads generally to improved organization, which increases the
efficiency of the work of labour and capital.

Therefore in those industries which are not engaged in raising
raw produce an increase of labour and capital generally gives a
return increased more than in proportion; and further this improved
organization tends to diminish or even override any increased
resistance which nature may offer to raising increased amounts of raw
produce.   If the actions of the laws of increasing and diminishing

IV, XIII, 2.
and of
constant
return.

The
straining
of the
tendencies
towards
increasing
and
diminish-
ing return
against
one
another.

return are balanced we have the *law of constant return*, and an increased produce is obtained by labour and sacrifice increased just in proportion.

For the two tendencies towards increasing and diminishing return press constantly against one another. In the production of wheat and wool, for instance, the latter tendency has almost exclusive sway in an old country, which cannot import freely. In turning the wheat into flour, or the wool into blankets, an increase in the aggregate volume of production brings some new economies, but not many; for the trades of grinding wheat and making blankets are already on so great a scale that any new economies that they may attain are more likely to be the result of new inventions than of improved organization. In a country however in which the blanket trade is but slightly developed, these latter may be important; and then it may happen that an increase in the aggregate production of blankets diminishes the proportionate difficulty of manufacturing by just as much as it increases that of raising the raw material. In that case the actions of the laws of diminishing and of increasing return would just neutralize one another; and blankets would conform to the law of constant return. But in most of the more delicate branches of manufacturing, where the cost of raw material counts for little, and in most of the modern transport industries the law of increasing return acts almost unopposed.[1]

Increasing
Return is a
relation of
quantities.

Increasing Return is a relation between a quantity of effort and sacrifice on the one hand, and a quantity of product on the other. The quantities cannot be taken out exactly, because changing methods of production call for machinery, and for unskilled and skilled labour of new kinds and in new proportions. But, taking a broad view, we may perhaps say vaguely that the output of a certain amount of labour and capital in an industry has increased by perhaps a quarter or a third in the last twenty years. To measure outlay and output in terms of money is a tempting, but a dangerous resource : for a comparison of money outlay with money returns is apt to slide into an estimate of the rate of profit on capital.[2]

[1] In an article on " The variation of productive forces " in the *Quarterly Journal of Economics*, 1902, Professor Bullock suggests that the term " Economy of Organization " should be substituted for Increasing Return. He shows clearly that the forces which make for Increasing Return are not of the same order as those that make for Diminishing Return : and there are undoubtedly cases in which it is better to emphasize this difference by describing causes rather than results, and contrasting Economy of Organization with the Inelasticity of Nature's response to intensive cultivation.

[2] There is no general rule that industries which yield increasing returns show also rising profits. No doubt a vigorous firm, which increases its scale of operations and obtains important (internal) economies which are peculiar to it, will show an increasing return and a rising rate of profit; because its increasing output will not materially affect the price of its produce. But profits tend to be low, as we shall see below

§ 3. We may now sum up provisionally the relations of industrial IV, xiii, 3.
expansion to social wellbeing. A rapid growth of population has A rapid
often been accompanied by unhealthy and enervating habits of life growth of
in overcrowded towns. And sometimes it has started badly, out- population
running the material resources of the people, causing them with under
imperfect appliances to make excessive demands on the soil; and conditions,
so to call forth the stern action of the law of diminishing return as some
regards raw produce, without having the power of minimizing its
effects. Having thus begun with poverty, an increase in numbers
may go on to its too frequent consequences in that weakness of
character which unfits a people for developing a highly organized
industry.

These are serious perils : but yet it remains true that the collec- but not
tive efficiency of a people with a given average of individual strength under
and energy may increase more than in proportion to their numbers. others.
If they can for a time escape from the pressure of the law of diminishing return by importing food and other raw produce on easy terms;
if their wealth is not consumed in great wars, and increases at least
as fast as their numbers; and if they avoid habits of life that would
enfeeble them; then every increase in their numbers is likely *for the
time* to be accompanied by a more than proportionate increase in
their power of obtaining material goods. For it enables them to
secure the many various economies of specialized skill and specialized
machinery, of localized industries and production on a large scale :
it enables them to have increased facilities of communication of all
kinds; while the very closeness of their neighbourhood diminishes
the expense of time and effort involved in every sort of traffic
between them, and gives them new opportunities of getting social
enjoyments and the comforts and luxuries of culture in every
form. No doubt deduction must be made for the growing difficulty
of finding solitude and quiet and even fresh air : but there is in
most cases some balance of good.[1]

Taking account of the fact that an increasing density of population generally brings with it access to new social enjoyments we may
give a rather broader scope to this statement and say :—An increase

---

(VI. viii. 1, 2), in such industries as plain weaving, because their vast scale has enabled
organization in production and marketing to be carried so far as to be almost dominated
by routine.

[1] The Englishman Mill bursts into unwonted enthusiasm when speaking (*Political
Economy*, Book iv. ch. vi. § 2) of the pleasures of wandering alone in beautiful scenery :
and many American writers give fervid descriptions of the growing richness of human
life as the backwoodsman finds neighbours settling around him, as the backwoods
settlement develops into a village, the village into a town, and the town into a vast
city. (See for instance Carey's *Principles of Social Science* and Henry George's
Progress and Poverty.)

IV, XIII, 3. of population accompanied by an equal increase in the material sources of enjoyment and aids to production is likely to lead to a more than proportionate increase in the aggregate income of enjoyment of all kinds; provided firstly, an adequate supply of raw produce can be obtained without great difficulty, and secondly there is no such overcrowding as causes physical and moral vigour to be impaired by the want of fresh air and light and of healthy and joyous recreation for the young.

The effects of a growth of numbers must be carefully distinguished from those of the growth of wealth by which it is generally accompanied.

The accumulated wealth of civilized countries is at present growing faster than the population : and though it may be true that the wealth per head would increase somewhat faster if the population did not increase quite so fast; yet as a matter of fact an increase of population is likely to continue to be accompanied by a more than proportionate increase of the material aids to production : and in England *at the present time*, with easy access to abundant foreign supplies of raw material, an increase of population is accompanied by a more than proportionate increase of the means of satisfying human wants other than the need for light, fresh air, etc. Much of this increase is however attributable not to the increase of industrial efficiency but to the increase of wealth by which it is accompanied : and therefore it does not necessarily benefit those who have no share in that wealth. And further, England's foreign supplies of raw produce may at any time be checked by changes in the trade regulations of other countries, and may be almost cut off by a great war, while the naval and military expenditure which would be necessary to make the country fairly secure against this last risk, would appreciably diminish the benefits that she derives from the action of the law of increasing return.

BOOK V

GENERAL RELATIONS OF DEMAND, SUPPLY AND VALUE

CHAPTER I

INTRODUCTORY. ON MARKETS

§ 1. A BUSINESS firm grows and attains great strength, and afterwards perhaps stagnates and decays; and at the turning point there is a balancing or equilibrium of the forces of life and decay: the latter part of Book IV has been chiefly occupied with such balancing of forces in the life and decay of a people, or of a method of industry or trading. And as we reach to the higher stages of our work, we shall need ever more and more to think of economic forces as resembling those which make a young man grow in strength, till he reaches his prime; after which he gradually becomes stiff and inactive, till at last he sinks to make room for other and more vigorous life. But to prepare the way for this advanced study we want first to look at a simpler balancing of forces which corresponds rather to the mechanical equilibrium of a stone hanging by an elastic string, or of a number of balls resting against one another in a basin.

margin: V, I, 1. Biological and mechanical notions of the balancing of opposed forces.

We have now to examine the general relations of demand and supply; especially those which are connected with that adjustment of price, by which they are maintained in " equilibrium." This term is in common use and may be used for the present without special explanation. But there are many difficulties connected with it, which can only be handled gradually : and indeed they will occupy our attention during a great part of this Book.

margin: Scope of this Book.

Illustrations will be taken now from one class of economic problems and now from another, but the main course of the reasoning will be kept free from assumptions which specially belong to any particular class.

Thus it is not descriptive, nor does it deal constructively with real problems. But it sets out the theoretical backbone of our

V, I, 2.   knowledge of the causes which govern value, and thus prepares the way for the construction which is to begin in the following Book. It aims not so much at the attainment of knowledge, as at the power to obtain and arrange knowledge with regard to two opposing sets of forces, those which impel man to economic efforts and sacrifices, and those which hold him back.

Markets described only provisionally here.   We must begin with a short and provisional account of markets : for that is needed to give precision to the ideas in this and the following Books. But the organization of markets is intimately connected both as cause and effect with money, credit, and foreign trade ; a full study of it must therefore be deferred to a later volume, where it will be taken in connection with commercial and industrial fluctuations, and with combinations of producers and of merchants, of employers and employed.

Definition of a market.   § 2. When demand and supply are spoken of in relation to one another, it is of course necessary that the markets to which they refer should be the same. As Cournot says, " Economists understand by the term *Market*, not any particular market place in which things are bought and sold, but the whole of any region in which buyers and sellers are in such free intercourse with one another that the prices of the same goods tend to equality easily and quickly." [1] Or again as Jevons says :—" Originally a market was a public place in a town where provisions and other objects were exposed for sale ; but the word has been generalized, so as to mean any body of persons who are in intimate business relations and carry on extensive transactions in any commodity. A great city may contain as many markets as there are important branches of trade, and these markets may or may not be localized. The central point of a market is the public exchange, mart or auction rooms, where the traders agree to meet and transact business. In London the Stock Market, the Corn Market, the Coal Market, the Sugar Market, and many others are distinctly localized ; in Manchester the Cotton Market, the Cotton Waste Market, and others. But this distinction of locality is not necessary. The traders may be spread over a whole town, or region of country, and yet make a market, if they are, by means of fairs, meetings, published price lists, the post-office or otherwise, in close communication with each other." [2]

Thus the more nearly perfect a market is, the stronger is the tendency for the same price to be paid for the same thing at the same

---

[1] *Recherches sur les Principes Mathématiques de la Théorie des Richesses*, ch. IV. See also above III. IV. 7.
[2] *Theory of Political Economy*, ch. IV.

time in all parts of the market : but of course if the market is large, allowance must be made for the expense of delivering the goods to different purchasers; each of whom must be supposed to pay in addition to the market price a special charge on account of delivery.[1]

§ 3. In applying economic reasonings in practice it is often difficult to ascertain how far the movements of supply and demand in any one place are influenced by those in another. It is clear that the general tendency of the telegraph, the printing-press and steam traffic is to extend the area over which such influences act and to increase their force. The whole Western World may, in a sense, be regarded as one market for many kinds of stock exchange securities, for the more valuable metals, and to a less extent for wool and cotton. and even wheat; proper allowance being made for expenses of transport, in which may be included taxes levied by any customs houses through which the goods have to pass. For in all these cases the expenses of transport, including customs duties, are not sufficient to prevent buyers from all parts of the Western World from competing with one another for the same supplies.

There are many special causes which may widen or narrow the market of any particular commodity : but nearly all those things for which there is a very wide market are in universal demand, and capable of being easily and exactly described. Thus for instance cotton, wheat, and iron satisfy wants that are urgent and nearly universal. They can be easily described, so that they can be bought and sold by persons at a distance from one another and at a distance also from the commodities. If necessary, samples can be taken of them which are truly representative : and they can even be "graded," as is the actual practice with regard to grain in America, by an independent authority; so that the purchaser may be secure that what he buys will come up to a given standard, though he has never seen a sample of the goods which he is buying and perhaps would not be able himself to form an opinion on it if he did.[2]

Commodities for which there a is a very wide market must also be such as will bear a long carriage : they must be somewhat durable, and their value must be considerable in proportion to their bulk.

Side notes: V, I, 3. Boundaries of a market. Instances of very wide markets. General conditions which affect the extent of the market for a thing. Suitability for grading and sampling. Portability.

---

[1] Thus it is common to see the prices of bulky goods quoted as delivered "free on board" (f. o. b.) any vessel in a certain port, each purchaser having to make his own reckoning for bringing the goods home.
[2] Thus the managers of a public or private "elevator," receive grain from a farmer, divide it into different grades, and return to him certificates for as many bushels of each grade as he has delivered. His grain is then mixed with those of other farmers; his certificates are likely to change hands several times before they reach a purchaser who demands that the grain shall be actually delivered to him; and little or none of what that purchaser receives may have come from the farm of the original recipient of the certificate.

A thing which is so bulky that its price is necessarily raised very much when it is sold far away from the place in which it is produced, must as a rule have a narrow market. The market for common bricks for instance is practically confined to the near neighbourhood of the kilns in which they are made : they can scarcely ever bear a long carriage by land to a district which has any kilns of its own. But bricks of certain exceptional kinds have markets extending over a great part of England.

The conditions of highly organized markets
§ 4. Let us then consider more closely the markets for things which satisfy in an exceptional way these conditions of being in general demand, cognizable and portable. They are, as we have said, stock exchange securities and the more valuable metals.

illustrated by reference to stock exchanges.
Any one share or bond of a public company, or any bond of a government is of exactly the same value as any other of the same issue : it can make no difference to any purchaser which of the two he buys. Some securities, principally those of comparatively small mining, shipping, and other companies, require local knowledge, and are not very easily dealt in except on the stock exchanges of provincial towns in their immediate neighbourhood. But the whole of England is one market for the shares and bonds of a large English railway. In ordinary times a dealer will sell, say, Midland Railway shares, even if he has not them himself; because he knows they are always coming into the market, and he is sure to be able to buy them.

But the strongest case of all is that of securities which are called " international," because they are in request in every part of the globe. They are the bonds of the chief governments, and of very large public companies such as those of the Suez Canal and the New York Central Railway. For bonds of this class the telegraph keeps prices at almost exactly the same level in all the stock exchanges of the world. If the price of one of them rises in New York or in Paris, in London or in Berlin, the mere news of the rise tends to cause a rise in other markets; and if for any reason the rise is delayed, that particular class of bonds is likely soon to be offered for sale in the high priced market under telegraphic orders from the other markets, while dealers in the first market will be making telegraphic purchases in other markets. These sales on the one hand, and purchases on the other, strengthen the tendency which the price has to seek the same level everywhere; and unless some of the markets are in an abnormal condition, the tendency soon becomes irresistible.

On the stock exchange also a dealer can generally make sure of selling at nearly the same price as that at which he buys; and he is often willing to buy first class stocks at a half, or a quarter, or an eighth, or in some cases even a sixteenth per cent. less than he offers in the same breath to sell them at. If there are two securities equally good, but one of them belongs to a large issue of bonds, and the other to a small issue by the same government, so that the first is constantly coming on the market, and the latter but seldom, then the dealers will on this account alone require a larger margin between their selling price and their buying price in the latter case than in the former.[1] This illustrates well the great law, that the larger the market for a commodity the smaller generally are the fluctuations in its price, and the lower is the percentage on the turnover which dealers charge for doing business in it.

Stock exchanges then are the pattern on which markets have been, and are being formed for dealing in many kinds of produce which can be easily and exactly described, are portable and in general demand. The material commodities however which possess these qualities in the highest degree are gold and silver. For that very reason they have been chosen by common consent for use as money, to represent the value of other things : the world market for them is most highly organized, and will be found to offer many subtle illustrations of the actions of the laws which are we now discussing.

The world market for the precious metals.

§ 5. At the opposite extremity to international stock exchange securities and the more valuable metals are, firstly, things which must be made to order to suit particular individuals, such as well-fitting clothes; and, secondly, perishable and bulky goods, such as fresh vegetables, which can seldom be profitably carried long distances. The first can scarcely be said to have a wholesale market at all; the conditions by which their price is determined are those of retail buying and selling, and the study of them may be postponed.[2] There are indeed wholesale markets for the second class, but they are confined within narrow boundaries; we may find our typical instance in the sale of the commoner kinds of vegetables in a country

Putting aside cases of retail dealing, we pass to a market which seems

---

[1] In the case of shares of very small and little known companies, the difference between the price at which a dealer is willing to buy and that at which he will sell may amount to from five per cent. or more of the selling value. If he buys, he may have to carry this security a long time before he meets with any one who comes to take it from him, and meanwhile it may fall in value : while if he undertakes to deliver a security which he has not himself got and which does not come on the market every day, he may be unable to complete his contract without much trouble and expense.

[2] A man may not trouble himself much about small retail purchases : he may give half-a-crown for a packet of paper in one shop which he could have got for two shillings in another. But it is otherwise with wholesale prices. A manufacturer cannot sell a ream of paper for six shillings while his neighbour is selling it at five. For those whose business it is to deal in paper know almost exactly the lowest price at which it can be bought, and will not pay more than this. The manufacturer has to sell at about the market price, that is at about the price at which other manufacturers are selling at the same time.

to be
narrowly
confined,

town. The market-gardeners in the neighbourhood have probably
to arrange for the sale of their vegetables to the townspeople with
but little external interference on either side. There may be some
check to extreme prices by the power on the one side of selling, and
on the other of buying elsewhere; but under ordinary circumstances
the check is inoperative, and it may happen that the dealers in such
a case are able to combine, and thus fix an artificial monopoly
price; that is, a price determined with little direct reference to cost
of production, but chiefly by a consideration of what the market
will bear.

though
even this
is subject
to indirect
influences
from great
distances.

On the other hand, it may happen that some of the market-
gardeners are almost equally near a second country town, and send
their vegetables now to one and now to the other; and some people
who occasionally buy in the first town may have equally good access
to the second. The least variation in price will lead them to prefer
the better market; and thus make the bargainings in the two
towns to some extent mutually dependent. It may happen that
this second town is in close communication with London or some
other central market, so that its prices are controlled by the prices
in the central market; and in that case prices in our first town also
must move to a considerable extent in harmony with them. As
news passes from mouth to mouth till a rumour spreads far away
from its forgotten sources, so even the most secluded market is
liable to be influenced by changes of which those in the market have
no direct cognizance, changes that have had their origin far away
and have spread gradually from market to market.

Thus at the one extreme are world markets in which competition acts directly from all parts of the globe; and at the other
those secluded markets in which all direct competition from afar is
shut out, though indirect and transmitted competition may make
itself felt even in these; and about midway between these extremes
lie the great majority of the markets which the economist and the
business man have to study.

Limita-
tions of
market
with
regard
to time
affect the
nature of
the causes
of which
we have
to take
account.

§ 6. Again, markets vary with regard to the period of time
which is allowed to the forces of demand and supply to bring themselves into equilibrium with one another, as well as with regard to
the area over which they extend. And this element of Time
requires more careful attention just now than does that of Space.
For the nature of the equilibrium itself, and that of the causes by
which it is determined, depend on the length of the period over
which the market is taken to extend. We shall find that if the
period is short, the supply is limited to the stores which happen to be

at hand: if the period is longer, the supply will be influenced,
more or less, by the cost of producing the commodity in question;
and if the period is very long, this cost will in its turn be influenced,
more or less, by the cost of producing the labour and the material
things required for producing the commodity. These three classes
of course merge into one another by imperceptible degrees. We
will begin with the first class; and consider in the next chapter
those temporary equilibria of demand and supply, in which " supply "
means in effect merely the stock available at the time for sale in the
market; so that it cannot be directly influenced by the cost of
production.

CHAPTER II

TEMPORARY EQUILIBRIUM OF DEMAND AND SUPPLY

§ 1. THE simplest case of balance or equilibrium between desire and effort is found when a person satisfies one of his wants by his own direct work. When a boy picks blackberries for his own eating, the action of picking is probably itself pleasurable for a while; and for some time longer the pleasure of eating is more than enough to repay the trouble of picking. But after he has eaten a good deal, the desire for more diminishes; while the task of picking begins to cause weariness, which may indeed be a feeling of monotony rather than of fatigue. Equilibrium is reached when at last his eagerness to play and his disinclination for the work of picking counterbalance the desire for eating. The satisfaction which he can get from picking fruit has arrived at its *maximum*: for up to that time every fresh picking has added more to his pleasure than it has taken away; and after that time any further picking would take away from his pleasure more than it would add.[1]

In a casual bargain that one person makes with another, as for instance when two backwoodsmen barter a rifle for a canoe, there is seldom anything that can properly be called an equilibrium of supply and demand : there is probably a margin of satisfaction on either side; for probably the one would be willing to give something besides the rifle for the canoe, if he could not get the canoe otherwise; while the other would in case of necessity give something besides the canoe for the rifle.

It is indeed possible that a true equilibrium may be arrived at under a system of barter; but barter, though earlier in history than buying and selling, is in some ways more intricate; and the simplest cases of a true equilibrium value are found in the markets of a more advanced state of civilization.

We may put aside as of little practical importance a class of dealings which has been much discussed. They relate to pictures by old masters, rare coins and other things, which cannot be "graded" at all. The price at which each is sold, will depend much on whether any rich persons with a fancy for it happen to be present

---

[1] See IV. i. 2, and Note XII. in the Mathematical Appendix.

at its sale. If not, it will probably be bought by dealers who
reckon on being able to sell it at a profit; and the variations in the
price for which the same picture sells at successive auctions, great
as they are, would be greater still if it were not for the steadying
influence of professional purchasers.

§ 2. Let us then turn to the ordinary dealings of modern life;
and take an illustration from a corn-market in a country town, and
let us assume for the sake of simplicity that all the corn in the market
is of the same quality. The amount which each farmer or other
seller offers for sale at any price is governed by his own need for
money in hand, and by his calculation of the present and future
conditions of the market with which he is connected. There are
some prices which no seller would accept, some which no one would
refuse. There are other intermediate prices which would be
accepted for larger or smaller amounts by many or all of the sellers.
Everyone will try to guess the state of the market and to govern his
actions accordingly. Let us suppose that in fact there are not
more than 600 quarters, the holders of which are willing to accept
as low a price as 35s.; but that holders of another hundred would be
tempted by 36s.; and holders of yet another three hundred by 37s.
Let us suppose also that a price of 37s. would tempt buyers for only
600 quarters; while another hundred could be sold at 36s., and
yet another two hundred at 35s. These facts may be put out in a
table thus :—

At the price.	Holders will be willing to sell.	Buyers will be willing to buy.
37s.	1000 quarters	600 quarters
36s.	700 ,,	700 ,,
35s.	600 ,,	900 ,,

Of course some of those who are really willing to take 36s.
rather than leave the market without selling, will not show at once
that they are ready to accept that price. And in like manner
buyers will fence, and pretend to be less eager than they really are.
So the price may be tossed hither and thither like a shuttlecock, as
one side or the other gets the better in the " higgling and bargaining " of the market. But unless they are unequally matched;
unless, for instance, one side is very simple or unfortunate in failing
to gauge the strength of the other side, the price is likely to be never
very far from 36s.; and it is nearly sure to be pretty close to 36s.
at the end of the market. For if a holder thinks that the buyers
will really be able to get at 36s. all that they care to take at that
price, he will be unwilling to let slip past him any offer that is well
above that price.

Illustra-
tion from
a local
corn-
market
of a true
though
temporary
equi-
librium.

V, ɪɪ, 3.   Buyers on their part will make similar calculations; and if at any time the price should rise considerably above 36s. they will argue that the supply will be much greater than the demand at that price : therefore even those of them who would rather pay that price than go unserved, wait; and by waiting they help to bring the price down.   On the other hand, when the price is much below 36s., even those sellers who would rather take the price than leave the market with their corn unsold, will argue that at that price the demand will be in excess of the supply : so they will wait, and by waiting help to bring the price up.

The price of 36s. has thus some claim to be called the true equilibrium price : because if it were fixed on at the beginning, and adhered to throughout, it would exactly equate demand and supply (*i.e.* the amount which buyers were willing to purchase at that price would be just equal to that for which sellers were willing to take that price); and because every dealer who has a perfect knowledge of the circumstances of the market expects that price to be established. If he sees the price differing much from 36s. he expects that a change will come before long, and by anticipating it he helps it to come quickly.

It is not indeed necessary for our argument that any dealers should have a thorough knowledge of the circumstances of the market.   Many of the buyers may perhaps underrate the willingness of the sellers to sell, with the effect that for some time the price rules at the highest level at which any buyers can be found; and thus 500 quarters may be sold before the price sinks below 37s. But afterwards the price must begin to fall and the result will still probably be that 200 more quarters will be sold, and the market will close on a price of about 36s.   For when 700 quarters have been sold, no seller will be anxious to dispose of any more except at a higher price than 36s., and no buyer will be anxious to purchase any more except at a lower price than 36s.   In the same way if the sellers had underrated the willingness of the buyers to pay a high price, some of them might begin to sell at the lowest price they would take, rather than have their corn left on their hands, and in this case much corn might be sold at a price of 35s.; but the market would probably close on a price of 36s. and a total sale of 700 quarters.[1]

§ 3. In this illustration there is a latent assumption which is in accordance with the actual conditions of most markets; but which

---

[1] A simple form of the influence which opinion exerts on the action of dealers, and therefore on market price, is indicated in this illustration : we shall be much occupied with more complex developments of it later on.

ought to be distinctly recognized in order to prevent its creeping V, II, 3. into those cases in which it is not justifiable. We tacitly assumed The that the sum which purchasers were willing to pay, and which sellers latent as- were willing to take, for the seven hundredth quarter would not be sumption, affected by the question whether the earlier bargains had been dealers' made at a high or a low rate. We allowed for the diminution in to spend the buyers' need of corn [its marginal utility to them] as the amount nearly bought increased. But we did not allow for any appreciable change constant in their unwillingness to part with money [its marginal utility]; through- we assumed that that would be practically the same whether the out, early payments had been at a high or a low rate.

This assumption is justifiable with regard to most of the market is gener- dealings with which we are practically concerned. When a person ally valid buys anything for his own consumption, he generally spends on it corn- a small part of his total resources; while when he buys it for the market; purposes of trade, he looks to re-selling it, and therefore his potential resources are not diminished. In either case there is no appreciable change in his willingness to part with money. There may indeed be individuals of whom this is not true; but there are sure to be present some dealers with large stocks of money at their command; and their influence steadies the market.[1]

The exceptions are rare and unimportant in markets for com- but in a modities; but in markets for labour they are frequent and important. labour When a workman is in fear of hunger, his need of money [its marginal exceptions utility to him] is very great; and, if at starting, he gets the worst of are often the bargaining, and is employed at low wages, it remains great, and important. he may go on selling his labour at a low rate. That is all the more probable because, while the advantage in bargaining is likely

---

[1] For instance a buyer is sometimes straitened for want of ready money, and has to let offers pass by him in no way inferior to others which he has gladly accepted : his own funds being exhausted, he could not perhaps borrow except on terms that would take away all the profit that the bargains had at first sight offered. But if the bargain is really a good one, some one else, who is not so straitened, is nearly sure to get hold of it.

Again, it is possible that several of those who had been counted as ready to sell corn at a price of 36s. were willing to sell only because they were in urgent need of a certain amount of ready money ; if they succeeded in selling some corn at a high price, there might be a perceptible diminution in the marginal utility of ready money to them ; and therefore they might refuse to sell for 36s. a quarter all the corn which they would have sold if the price had been 36s. throughout. In this case the sellers in consequence of getting an advantage in bargaining at the beginning of the market might retain to the end a price higher than *the* equilibrium price. The price at which the market closed would be *an* equilibrium price ; and though not properly described as *the* equilibrium price, it would be very unlikely to diverge widely from that price. Conversely, if the market had opened much to the disadvantage of the sellers and they had sold some corn very cheap, so that they remained in great want of ready money, the final utility of money to them might have remained so high that they would have gone on selling considerably below 36s. until the buyers had been supplied with all that they cared to take. The market would then close without the true equilibrium price having ever been reached, but a very near approach would have been made to it.

V, II, 3.   to be pretty well distributed between the two sides of a market for commodities, it is more often on the side of the buyers than on that of the sellers in a market for labour. Another difference between a labour market and a market for commodities arises from the fact that each seller of labour has only one unit of labour to dispose of. These are two among many facts, in which we shall find, as we go on, the explanation of much of that instinctive objection which the working classes have felt to the habit of some economists, particularly those of the employer class, of treating labour simply as a commodity and regarding the labour market as like every other market; whereas in fact the differences between the two cases, though not fundamental from the point of view of theory, are yet clearly marked, and in practice often very important.

This difference has important results in theory and in practice.

The theory of buying and selling becomes therefore much more complex when we take account of the dependence of marginal utility on amount in the case of money as well as of the commodity itself. The practical importance of this consideration is not very great. But a contrast is drawn in Appendix F between barter and dealings in which one side of each exchange is in the form of general purchasing power. In barter a person's stock of either commodity exchanged needs to be adjusted closely to his individual wants. If his stock is too large he may have no good use for it. If his stock is too small he may have some difficulty in finding any one who can conveniently give him what he wants and is also in need of the particular things of which he himself has a superfluity. But any one who has a stock of general purchasing power, can obtain any thing he wants as soon as he meets with any one who has a superfluity of that thing : he needs not to hunt about till he comes across " the double coincidence " of a person who can spare what he wants, and also wants what he can spare. Consequently every one, and especially a professional dealer, can afford to keep command over a large stock of money; and can therefore make considerable purchases without depleting his stock of money or greatly altering its marginal value.

Reference to an Appendix on Barter.

CHAPTER III

EQUILIBRIUM OF NORMAL DEMAND AND SUPPLY

§ 1. WE have next to inquire what causes govern supply prices, V, III, 1. that is prices which dealers are willing to accept for different amounts. Transition In the last chapter we looked at the affairs of only a single day; to normal and supposed the stocks offered for sale to be already in existence. values. But of course these stocks are dependent on the amount of wheat sown in the preceding year; and that, in its turn, was largely influenced by the farmers' guesses as to the price which they would get for it in this year. This is the point at which we have to work in the present chapter.

Even in the corn-exchange of a country town on a market-day Nearly all the equilibrium price is affected by calculations of the future dealings in relations of production and consumption; while in the leading corn- ties that markets of America and Europe dealings for future delivery already very predominate and are rapidly weaving into one web all the leading perishable, threads of trade in corn throughout the whole world. Some of affected these dealings in "futures" are but incidents in speculative lations of manœuvres; but in the main they are governed by calculations of the future; the world's consumption on the one hand, and of the existing stocks and coming harvests in the Northern and Southern hemispheres on the other. Dealers take account of the areas sown with each kind of grain, of the forwardness and weight of the crops, of the supply of things which can be used as substitutes for grain, and of the things for which grain can be used as a substitute. Thus, when buying or selling barley, they take account of the supplies of such things as sugar, which can be used as substitutes for it in brewing, and again of all the various feeding stuffs, a scarcity of which might raise the value of barley for consumption on the farm. If it is thought that the growers of any kind of grain in any part of the world have been losing money, and are likely to sow a less area for a future harvest; it is argued that prices are likely to rise as soon as that harvest comes into sight, and its shortness is manifest to all. Anticipations of that rise exercise an influence on present sales for future delivery, and that in its turn influences cash prices; so that these prices are indirectly affected by estimates of the expenses of producing further supplies.

V, III, 2.

and we are now to consider slow and gradual adjustments of supply and demand.

But in this and the following chapters we are specially concerned with movements of prices ranging over still longer periods than those for which the most far-sighted dealers in futures generally make their reckoning : we have to consider the volume of production adjusting itself to the conditions of the market, and the normal price being thus determined at the position of stable equilibrium of normal demand and normal supply.

The account of supply price carried a little further.

§ 2. In this discussion we shall have to make frequent use of the terms *cost* and *expenses* of production; and some provisional account of them must be given before proceeding further.

We may revert to the analogy between the supply price and the demand price of a commodity. Assuming for the moment that the efficiency of production depends solely upon the exertions of the workers, we saw that " the price required to call forth the exertion necessary for producing any given amount of a commodity may be called the supply price for that amount, with reference of course to a given unit of time." [1] But now we have to take account of the fact that the production of a commodity generally requires many different kinds of labour and the use of capital in many forms. The exertions of all the different kinds of labour that are directly or indirectly involved in making it; together with the abstinences or rather the waitings required for saving the capital used in making it : all these efforts and sacrifices together will be called the *real cost of production* of the commodity. The sums of money that have to be paid for these efforts and sacrifices will be called either its *money cost of production*, or, for shortness, its *expenses of production*; they are the prices which have to be paid in order to call forth an adequate supply of the efforts and waitings that are required for making it; or, in other words, they are its supply price. [2]

The analysis of the expenses of production of a commodity

Real and money cost of production.

Expenses of production.

---

[1] IV. I. 2.

[2] Mill and some other economists have followed the practice of ordinary life in using the term Cost of production in two senses, sometimes to signify the difficulty of producing a thing, and sometimes to express the outlay of money that has to be incurred in order to induce people to overcome this difficulty and produce it. But by passing from one use of the term to the other without giving explicit warning, they have led to many misunderstandings and much barren controversy. The attack on Mill's doctrine of Cost of Production in relation to Value, which is made in Cairnes' *Leading Principles*, was published just after Mill's death; and unfortunately his interpretation of Mill's words was generally accepted as authoritative, because he was regarded as a follower of Mill. But in an article by the present writer on " Mill's Theory of Value " (*Fortnightly Review*, April 1876) it is argued that Cairnes had mistaken Mill's meaning, and had really seen not more but less of the truth than Mill had done.

The expenses of production of any amount of a raw commodity may best be estimated with reference to the "margin of production" at which no rent is paid. But this method of speaking has great difficulties with regard to commodities that obey the law of increasing return. It seemed best to note this point in passing : it will be fully discussed later on, chiefly in ch. XII.

might be carried backward to any length; but it is seldom worth while to go back very far. It is for instance often sufficient to take the supply price of the different kinds of raw materials used in any manufacture as ultimate facts, without analysing these supply prices into the several elements of which they are composed; otherwise indeed the analysis would never end. We may then arrange the things that are required for making a commodity into whatever groups are convenient, and call them its *factors of production*. Its expenses of production when any given amount of it is produced are thus the supply prices of the corresponding quantities of its factors of production. And the sum of these is the supply price of that amount of the commodity.

Factors of production.

§ 3. The typical modern market is often regarded as that in which manufacturers sell goods to wholesale dealers at prices into which but few trading expenses enter. But taking a broader view, we may consider that the supply price of a commodity is the price at which it will be delivered for sale to that group of persons whose demand for it we are considering; or, in other words, in the market which we have in view. On the character of that market will depend how many trading expenses have to be reckoned to make up the supply price.[1] For instance, the supply price of wood in the neighbourhood of Canadian forests often consists almost exclusively of the price of the labour of lumber men : but the supply price of the same wood in the wholesale London market consists in a large measure of freights : while its supply price to a small retail buyer in an English country town is more than half made up of the charges of the railways and middlemen who have brought what he wants to his doors, and keep a stock of it ready for him. Again, the supply price of a certain kind of labour may for some purposes be divided up into the expenses of rearing, of general education and of special trade education. The possible combinations are numberless; and though each may have incidents of its own which will require separate treatment in the complete solution of any problem connected with it, yet all such incidents may be ignored, so far as the general reasonings of this Book are concerned.

There is great variety in the relative importance of different elements of cost of production.

In calculating the expenses of production of a commodity we must take account of the fact that changes in the amounts produced are likely, even when there is no new invention, to be accompanied by changes in the relative quantities of its several factors of pro-

[1] We have already (II. m.) noticed that the economic use of the term "production" includes the production of new utilities by moving a thing from a place in which it is less wanted to a place in which it is more wanted, or by helping consumers to satisfy their needs.

V, III, 4.

duction. For instance, when the scale of production increases, horse or steam power is likely to be substituted for manual labour; materials are likely to be brought from a greater distance and in greater quantities, thus increasing those expenses of production which correspond to the work of carriers, middlemen and traders of all kinds.

The principle of substitution.

As far as the knowledge and business enterprise of the producers reach, they in each case choose those factors of production which are best for their purpose; the sum of the supply prices of those factors which are used is, as a rule, less than the sum of the supply prices of any other set of factors which could be substituted for them; and whenever it appears to the producers that this is not the case, they will, as a rule, set to work to substitute the less expensive method. And further on we shall see how in a somewhat similar way society substitutes one undertaker for another who is less efficient in proportion to his charges. We may call this, for convenience of reference, *The principle of substitution.*

The applications of this principle extend over almost every field of economic inquiry.[1]

The position from which we start.

§ 4. The position then is this : we are investigating the equilibrium of normal demand and normal supply in their most general form; we are neglecting those features which are special to particular parts of economic science, and are confining our attention to those broad relations which are common to nearly the whole of it. Thus

We assume free play for demand and supply in the market.

we assume that the forces of demand and supply have free play; that there is no close combination among dealers on either side, but each acts for himself, and there is much free competition; that is, buyers generally compete freely with buyers, and sellers compete freely with sellers. But though everyone acts for himself, his knowledge of what others are doing is supposed to be generally sufficient to prevent him from taking a lower or paying a higher price than others are doing. This is assumed provisionally to be true both of finished goods and of their factors of production, of the hire of labour and of the borrowing of capital. We have already inquired to some extent, and we shall have to inquire further, how far these assumptions are in accordance with the actual facts of life. But meanwhile this is the supposition on which we proceed; we assume that there is only one price in the market at one and the same time; it being understood that separate allowance is made, when necessary, for differences in the expense of delivering goods to dealers in different parts of the market; including allowance for the special expenses of retailing, if it is a retail market.

[1] See III. v. and IV. vII. 8.

In such a market there is a demand price for each amount of the V, III, 4. commodity, that is, a price at which each particular amount of the General commodity can find purchasers in a day or week or year. The conditions of demand. circumstances which govern this price for any given amount of the commodity vary in character from one problem to another; but in every case the more of a thing is offered for sale in a market the lower is the price at which it will find purchasers; or in other words, the demand price for each bushel or yard diminishes with every increase in the amount offered.

The unit of time may be chosen according to the circumstances of each particular problem : it may be a day, a month, a year, or even a generation : but in every case it must be short relatively to the period of the market under discussion. It is to be assumed that the general circumstances of the market remain unchanged throughout this period; that there is, for instance, no change in fashion or taste, no new substitute which might affect the demand, no new invention to disturb the supply.

The conditions of normal supply are less definite; and a full study The of them must be reserved for later chapters. They will be found to vary conditions of supply in detail with the length of the period of time to which the investigation will vary refers; chiefly because both the material capital of machinery and with the length of other business plant, and the immaterial capital of business skill and time to which ability and organization, are of slow growth and slow decay. reference

Let us call to mind the " representative firm," whose economies is made. But we of production, internal and external, are dependent on the aggregate may provisionally volume of production of the commodity that it makes;[1] and, regard postponing all further study of the nature of this dependence, let us normal supply assume that the normal supply price of any amount of that com- price as modity may be taken to be its normal expenses of production the expenses of (including *gross* earnings of managements[2]) by that firm. That is, production, let us assume that this is the price the expectation of which will just including suffice to maintain the existing aggregate amount of production; gross earnings some firms meanwhile rising and increasing their output, and others of management, of falling and diminishing theirs; but the aggregate production a representative remaining unchanged. A price higher than this would increase the sentative firm. growth of the rising firms, and slacken, though it might not arrest, the decay of the falling firms; with the net result of an increase in the aggregate production. On the other hand, a price lower than this would hasten the decay of the falling firms, and slacken the growth of the rising firms; and on the whole diminish production : and a rise or fall of price would affect in like manner though perhaps

---

[1] See IV. XIII. 2.   [2] See last paragraph of IV. XII.

V, III, 5.

not in an equal degree those great joint-stock companies which often stagnate, but seldom die.

The construction of the list of prices at which a thing can be supplied; or its *supply schedule.*

§ 5. To give definiteness to our ideas let us take an illustration from the woollen trade. Let us suppose that a person well acquainted with the woollen trade sets himself to inquire what would be the normal supply price of a certain number of millions of yards annually of a particular kind of cloth. He would have to reckon (i) the price of the wool, coal, and other materials which would be used up in making it, (ii) wear-and-tear and depreciation of the buildings, machinery and other fixed capital, (iii) interest and insurance on all the capital, (iv) the wages of those who work in the factories, and (v) the gross earnings of management (including insurance against loss), of those who undertake the risks, who engineer and superintend the working. He would of course estimate the supply prices of all these different factors of production of the cloth with reference to the amounts of each of them that would be wanted, and on the supposition that the conditions of supply would be normal; and he would add them all together to find the supply price of the cloth.

Let us suppose a list of supply prices (or a supply schedule) made on a similar plan to that of our list of demand prices :[1] the supply price of each amount of the commodity in a year, or any other unit of time, being written against that amount.[2]   As the

[1] See III. III. 4.

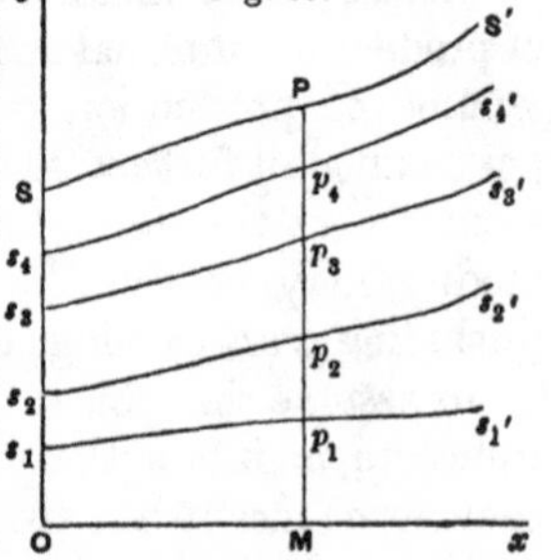

[2] Measuring, as in the case of the demand curve, amounts of the commodity along Ox and prices parallel to Oy, we get for each point M along Ox a line MP drawn at right angles to it measuring the supply price for the amount OM, the extremity of which, P, may be called a *supply point*; this price MP being made up of the supply prices of the several factors of production for the amount OM. The locus of P may be called the *supply curve.*

Fig. 18.

Suppose, for instance, that we classify the expenses of production of our representative firm, when an amount OM of cloth is being produced under the heads of (i) Mp_1, the supply price of the wool and other circulating capital which would be consumed in making it, (ii) p_1p_2 the corresponding wear-and-tear and depreciation on buildings, machinery and other fixed capital; (iii) p_2p_3 the interest and insurance on all the capital, (iv) p_3p_4 the wages of those who work in the lactory, and (v) p_4P the gross earnings of management, etc. of those who undertake the risks and direct the work.   Thus as M moves from O towards the right p_1, p_2, p_3, p_4 will each trace out a curve, and the ultimate supply curve traced out by P will be thus shown as obtained by superimposing the supply curves for the several factors of production of the cloth.

It must be remembered that these supply prices are the prices not of units of the several factors but of these amounts of the several factors which are required for producing a yard of cloth. Thus, for instance, p_3p_4 is the supply price not of any fixed amount of labour but of that amount of labour which is employed to making a yard where there is an aggregate production of OM yards.   (See above, § 3.)   We need not trouble ourselves to consider just here whether the ground-rent of the factory must be put into a class by itself : this belongs to a group of questions which will be discussed later. We are taking no notice of rates and taxes, for which he would of course have to make his account.

flow, or (annual) amount of the commodity increases, the supply price may either increase or diminish; or it may even alternately increase and diminish.[1] For if nature is offering a sturdy resistance to man's efforts to wring from her a larger supply of raw material, while at that particular stage there is no great room for introducing important new economies into the manufacture, the supply price will rise; but if the volume of production were greater, it would perhaps be profitable to substitute largely machine work for hand work and steam power for muscular force; and the increase in the volume of production would have diminished the expenses of production of the commodity of our representative firm. But those cases in which the supply price falls as the amount increases involve special difficulties of their own; and they are postponed to chapter XII of this Book.

§ 6. When therefore the amount produced (in a unit of time) is such that the demand price is greater than the supply price, then sellers receive more than is sufficient to make it worth their while to bring goods to market to that amount; and there is at work an active force tending to increase the amount brought forward for sale. On the other hand, when the amount produced is such that the demand price is less than the supply price, sellers receive less than is sufficient to make it worth their while to bring goods to market on that scale; so that those who were just on the margin of doubt as to whether to go on producing are decided not to do so, and there is an active force at work tending to diminish the amount brought forward for sale. When the demand price is equal to the supply price, the amount produced has no tendency either to be increased or to be diminished; it is in equilibrium.

What is meant by equilibrium.

When demand and supply are in equilibrium, the amount of the commodity which is being produced in a unit of time may be called the *equilibrium-amount*, and the price at which it is being sold may be called the *equilibrium-price*.

Equilibrium-amount and equilibrium-price.

Such an equilibrium is *stable*; that is, the price, if displaced a little from it, will tend to return, as a pendulum oscillates about its lowest point; and it will be found to be a characteristic of stable equilibria that in them the demand price is greater than the supply price for amounts just less than the equilibrium amount, and *vice versâ*. For when the demand price is greater than the supply price, the amount produced tends to increase. Therefore, if the demand

Stable equilibria, the conditions under which they occur.

---

[1] That is, a point moving along the supply curve towards the right may either rise or fall, or even it may alternately rise and fall; in other words, the supply curve may be inclined positively or negatively, or even at some parts of its course it may be inclined positively and at others negatively. (See p. 84, n.[1].)

V, III, 6. price is greater than the supply price for amounts just less than an equilibrium amount; then, if the scale of production is temporarily diminished somewhat below that equilibrium amount, it will tend to return; thus the equilibrium is stable for displacements in that direction. If the demand price is greater than the supply price for amounts just less than the equilibrium amount, it is sure to be less than the supply price for amounts just greater : and therefore, if the scale of production is somewhat increased beyond the equilibrium position, it will tend to return; and the equilibrium will be stable for displacements in that direction also.

Oscillations about a position of stable equilibrium

When demand and supply are in stable equilibrium, if any accident should move the scale of production from its equilibrium position, there will be instantly brought into play forces tending to push it back to that position; just as, if a stone hanging by a string is displaced from its equilibrium position, the force of gravity will at once tend to bring it back to its equilibrium position. The movements of the scale of production about its position of equilibrium will be of a somewhat similar kind.[1]

are seldom rhythmical.

But in real life such oscillations are seldom as rhythmical as those of a stone hanging freely from a string; the comparison would be more exact if the string were supposed to hang in the troubled waters of a mill-race, whose stream was at one time allowed to flow freely, and at another partially cut off. Nor are these complexities sufficient to illustrate all the disturbances with which the economist and the merchant alike are forced to concern themselves. If the person holding the string swings his hand with movements partly rhythmical and partly arbitrary, the illustration will not outrun the difficulties of some very real and practical problems of value. For indeed the demand and supply schedules do not

---

[1] Compare V. I. 1. To represent the equilibrium of demand and supply geometrically we may draw the demand and supply curves together as in Fig. 19. If then OR represents the rate at which production is being actually carried on, and Rd the demand price is greater than Rs the supply price, the production is exceptionally profitable, and will be increased. R, the *amount-index*, as we may call it, will move to the right. On the other hand, if Rd is less than Rs, R will move to the left. If Rd is equal to Rs, that is, if R is vertically under a point of intersection of the curves, demand and supply are in equilibrium.

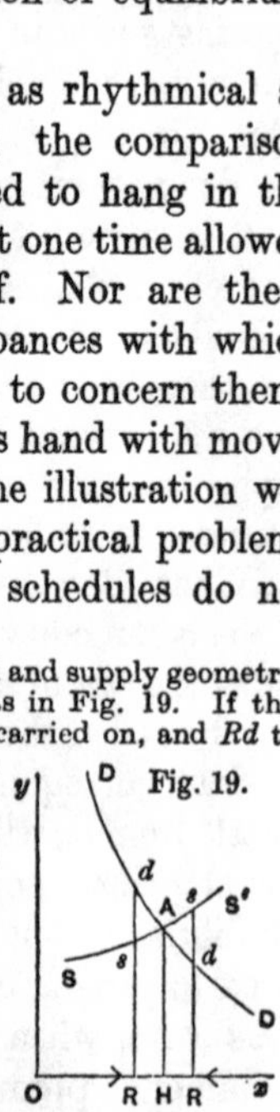

This may be taken as the typical diagram for stable equilibrium for a commodity that obeys the law of diminishing return. But if we had made SS' a horizontal straight line, we should have represented the case of "constant return," in which the supply price is the same for all amounts of the commodity. And if we made SS' inclined negatively, but less steeply than DD' (the necessity for this condition will appear more fully later on), we should have got a case of stable equilibrium for a commodity which obeys the law of increasing return. In either case the above reasoning remains unchanged without the alteration of a word or a letter; but the last case introduces difficulties which we have arranged to postpone.

Fig. 19.

in practice remain unchanged for a long time together, but are
constantly being changed; and every change in them alters the
equilibrium amount and the equilibrium price, and thus gives new
positions to the centres about which the amount and the price tend
to oscillate.

V, III, 7.

These considerations point to the great importance of the
element of time in relation to demand and supply, to the study of
which we now proceed. We shall gradually discover a great many
different limitations of the doctrine that the price at which a thing
can be produced represents its real cost of production, that is, the
efforts and sacrifices which have been directly devoted to its production. For, in an age of rapid change such as this, the equilibrium
of normal demand and supply does not thus correspond to any distinct relation of a certain aggregate of pleasures got from the consumption of the commodity and an aggregate of efforts and sacrifices
involved in producing it : the correspondence would not be exact,
even if normal earnings and interest were exact measures of the
efforts and sacrifices for which they are the money payments. This
is the real drift of that much quoted, and much-misunderstood
doctrine of Adam Smith and other economists that the normal, or
"natural," value of a commodity is that which economic forces
tend to bring about *in the long run*. It is the average value which
economic forces would bring about if the general conditions of life
were stationary for a run of time long enough to enable them all to
work out their full effect.[1]

Loose
connection
between
supply
price and
real cost
of pro-
duction;
signifi-
cance of
the
phrases
*Normal
equili-
brium* and
*In the
long run.*

But we cannot foresee the future perfectly. The unexpected
may happen; and the existing tendencies may be modified before
they have had time to accomplish what appears now to be their full
and complete work. The fact that the general conditions of life
are not stationary is the source of many of the difficulties that are
met with in applying economic doctrines to practical problems.

Of course Normal does not mean Competitive. Market prices
and Normal prices are alike brought about by a multitude of influences, of which some rest on a moral basis and some on a physical;
of which some are competitive and some are not. It is to the
persistence of the influences considered, and the time allowed for
them to work out their effects that we refer when contrasting Market
and Normal price, and again when contrasting the narrower and the
broader use of the term Normal price.[2]

§ 7. The remainder of the present volume will be chiefly occupied
with interpreting and limiting this doctrine that the value of a thing

Influences
of utility
and cost

---

[1] See below V. v. 2 and Appendix H. 4.   [2] See above pp. 28–30.

L

of production on value.

tends in the long run to correspond to its cost of production. In particular the notion of equilibrium, which has been treated rather slightly in this chapter, will be studied more carefully in chapters v. and XII. of this Book : and some account of the controversy whether " cost of production " or " utility " governs value will be given in Appendix I. But it may be well to say a word or two here on this last point.

We might as reasonably dispute whether it is the upper or the under blade of a pair of scissors that cuts a piece of paper, as whether value is governed by utility or cost of production. It is true that when one blade is held still, and the cutting is effected by moving the other, we may say with careless brevity that the cutting is done by the second ; but the statement is not strictly accurate, and is to be excused only so long as it claims to be merely a popular and not a strictly scientific account of what happens.

The former preponderates in market values :

In the same way, when a thing already made has to be sold, the price which people will be willing to pay for it will be governed by their desire to have it, together with the amount they can afford to spend on it. Their desire to have it depends partly on the chance that, if they do not buy it, they will be able to get another thing like it at as low a price : this depends on the causes that govern the supply of it, and this again upon cost of production. But it may so happen that the stock to be sold is practically fixed. This, for instance, is the case with a fish market, in which the value of fish for the day is governed almost exclusively by the stock on the slabs in relation to the demand : and if a person chooses to take the stock for granted, and say that the price is governed by demand, his brevity may perhaps be excused so long as he does not claim strict accuracy. So again it may be pardonable, but it is not strictly accurate to say that the varying prices which the same rare book fetches, when sold and resold at Christie's auction room, are governed exclusively by demand.

the latter in normal values.

Taking a case at the opposite extreme, we find some commodities which conform pretty closely to the law of constant return; that is to say, their average cost of production will be very nearly the same whether they are produced in small quantities or in large. In such a case the normal level about which the market price fluctuates will be this definite and fixed (money) cost of production. If the demand happens to be great, the market price will rise for a time above the level; but as a result production will increase and the market price will fall : and conversely, if the demand falls for a time below its ordinary level.

In such a case, if a person chooses to neglect market fluctuations, and to take it for granted that there will anyhow be enough demand for the commodity to insure that some of it, more or less, will find purchasers at a price equal to this cost of production, then he may be excused for ignoring the influence of demand, and speaking of (normal) price as governed by cost of production—provided only he does not claim scientific accuracy for the wording of his doctrine, and explains the influence of demand in its right place.

Thus we may conclude that, *as a general rule*, the shorter the period which we are considering, the greater must be the share of our attention which is given to the influence of demand on value; and the longer the period, the more important will be the influence of cost of production on value. For the influence of changes in cost of production takes as a rule a longer time to work itself out than does the influences of changes in demand. The actual value at any time, the market value as it is often called, is often more influenced by passing events and by causes whose action is fitful and short lived, than by those which work persistently. But in long periods these fitful and irregular causes in large measure efface one another's influence; so that in the long run persistent causes dominate value completely. Even the most persistent causes are however liable to change. For the whole structure of production is modified, and the relative costs of production of different things are permanently altered, from one generation to another.

When considering costs from the point of view of the capitalist employer, we of course measure them in money; because his direct concern with the efforts needed for the work of his employees lies in the money payments he must make. His concern with the real costs of their effort and of the training required for it is only indirect, though a monetary assessment of his own labour is necessary for some problems, as will be seen later on. But when considering costs from the social point of view, when inquiring whether the cost of attaining a given result is increasing or diminishing with changing economic conditions, then we are concerned with the real costs of efforts of various qualities, and with the real cost of waiting. If the purchasing power of money, in terms of effort has remained about constant, and if the rate of remuneration for waiting has remained about constant, then the money measure of costs corresponds to the real costs : but such a correspondence is never to be assumed lightly. These considerations will generally suffice for the interpretation of the term Cost in what follows, even where no distinct indication is given in the context.

The business man is concerned with money costs; but the evolution of normal value with real costs.

CHAPTER IV

THE INVESTMENT AND DISTRIBUTION OF RESOURCES

V, iv, 1.

The
policy
of invest-
ment
for a
distant
return
may be
clearly
seen in the
case of a
man who
makes a
thing for
his own
use.

§ 1. THE first difficulty to be cleared up in our study of normal values, is the nature of the motives which govern the investment of resources for a distant return. It will be well to begin by watching the action of a person who neither buys what he wants nor sells what he makes, but works on his own behalf; and who therefore balances the efforts and sacrifices which he makes on the one hand against the pleasures which he expects to derive from their fruit on the other, without the intervention of any money payments at all.

Let us then take the case of a man who builds a house for himself on land, and of materials, which nature supplies gratis; and who makes his implements as he goes, the labour of making them being counted as part of the labour of building the house. He would have to estimate the efforts required for building on any proposed plan; and to allow almost instinctively an amount increasing in geometrical proportion (a sort of compound interest) for the period that would elapse between each effort and the time when the house would be ready for his use. The utility of the house to him when finished would have to compensate him not only for the efforts, but for the waitings.[1]

If the two motives, one deterring, the other impelling, seemed equally balanced, he would be on the margin of doubt. Probably the gain would much more than outweigh the " real " cost with regard to some part of the house. But as he turned over more and more ambitious plans, he would at last find the advantages of any

---

[1] For he might have applied these efforts, or efforts equivalent to them, to producing immediate gratifications; and if he deliberately chose the deferred gratifications, it would be because, even after allowing for the disadvantages of waiting, he regarded them as outweighing the earlier gratifications which he could have substituted for them. The motive force then tending to deter him from building the house would be his estimate of the aggregate of these efforts, the evil or discommodity of each being increased in geometrical proportion (a sort of compound interest) according to the corresponding interval of waiting. The motive on the other hand impelling him to build it, would be expectation of the satisfaction which he would have from the house when completed; and that again might be resolved into the aggregate of many satisfactions more or less remote, and more or less certain, which he expected to derive from its use. If he thought that this aggregate of discounted values of satisfactions that it would afford him, would be more than a recompense to him for all the efforts and waitings which he had undergone, he would decide to build. (See III. v. 3, IV. vii. 8 and Note XIII in the Mathematical Appendix.)

further extension balanced by the efforts and waitings required for   V, IV, 2.
making it; and that extension of the building would be on the outer
limit, or margin of profitableness of the investment of his capital.

There would probably be several ways of building parts of the
house; some parts for instance might almost equally well be built
of wood or of rough stones : the investment of capital on each plan
for each part of the accommodation would be compared with the
advantages offered thereby, and each would be pushed forward till
the outer limit or margin of profitableness had been reached.
Thus there would be a great many margins of profitableness : one
corresponding to each kind of plan on which each kind of accommodation might be provided.

§ 2. This illustration may serve to keep before us the way in   *Transition
which the efforts and sacrifices which are the real cost of production   *to the in-
vestment
of a thing, underlie the expenses which are its money cost. But, as   *of capital
*by the
has just been remarked, the modern business man commonly   *modern
takes the payments which he has to make, whether for wages or raw   *under-
*taker of
material, as he finds them; without staying to inquire how far they   *business
are an accurate measure of the efforts and sacrifices to which they   *enter-
prises.
correspond. His expenditure is generally made piece-meal; and
the longer he expects to wait for the fruit of any outlay, the richer
must that fruit be in order to compensate him. The anticipated
fruit may not be certain; and in that case he will have to allow for
the risk of failure. After making that allowance, the fruit of the
outlay must be expected to exceed the outlay itself by an amount
which, independently of his own remuneration, increases at compound interest in proportion to the time of waiting.[1] Under this
head are to be entered the heavy expenses, direct and indirect,
which every business must incur in building up its connection.

For brevity we may speak of any element of outlay (allowance   *Accumula-
being made for the remuneration of the undertaker himself) when   *tion of
*past and
increased by compound interest in this way, as *accumulated*; just   *discount-
as we used the term *discounted* to represent the present value of a   *ing of
*future
future gratification. Each element of outlay has then to be accu-   *outlays
mulated for the time which will elapse between its being incurred   *and
receipts.
and its bearing fruit; and the aggregate of these accumulated
elements is the total outlay involved in the enterprise. The
balance between efforts and the satisfactions resulting from them

---

[1] We may, if we choose, regard the price of the business undertaker's own work as
part of the original outlay, and reckon compound interest on it together with the
rest. Or we may substitute for compound interest a sort of " compound profit."
The two courses are not strictly convertible : and at a later stage we shall find that
in certain cases the first is to be preferred, and in others the second.

may be made up to any day that is found convenient. But whatever day is chosen, one simple rule must be followed :—Every element whether an effort or a satisfaction, which dates from a time anterior to that day, must have compound interest for the interval accumulated upon it : and every element, which dates from a time posterior to that day, must have compound interest for the interval discounted from it. If the day be anterior to the beginning of the enterprise, then every element must be discounted. But if, as is usual in such cases, the day be that when the efforts are finished, and the house is ready for use; then the efforts must carry compound interest up to that day, and the satisfactions must all be discounted back to that day.

Waiting is an element of cost as truly as effort is, and it is entered in the cost when accumulated : it is therefore of course not counted separately. Similarly, on the converse side, whatever money or command over satisfaction " comes in " at any time is part of the income of that time : if the time is before the day for which accounts are balanced up, then it must be accumulated up to that day; if after, it must be discounted back. If, instead of being converted to immediate enjoyment, it is used as a stored up source of future income, that later income must not be counted as an *additional* return to the investment.[1]

If the enterprise were, say, to dig out a dock-basin on a contract, the payment for which would be made without fail when the work was finished; and if the plant used in the work might be taken to be worn out in the process, and valueless at the end of it; then the enterprise would be just remunerative if this aggregate of outlays, accumulated up to the period of payment, were just equal to that payment.

But, as a rule, the proceeds of the sales come in gradually; and we must suppose a balance-sheet struck, looking both backwards and forwards. Looking backwards we should sum up the net outlays, and add in accumulated compound interest on each element of outlay. Looking forwards we should sum up all net incomings, and from the value of each subtract compound interest

---

[1] In the aggregate the income from the saving will in the ordinary course be larger in amount than the saving by the amount of the interest that is the reward of saving. But, as it will be turned to account in enjoyment later than the original saving could have been, it will be discounted for a longer period (or accumulated for a shorter); and if entered in the balance sheet of the investment in place of the original saving, it would stand for exactly the same sum. (Both the original income which was saved and the subsequent income earned by it are assessed to income tax; on grounds similar to those which make it expedient to levy a larger income tax from the industrious than from the lazy man.) The main argument of this section is expressed mathematically in Note XIII.

for the period during which it would be deferred. The aggregate of V, IV, 3. the net incomings so discounted would be balanced against the aggregate of the accumulated outlays : and if the two were just equal, the business would be just remunerative. In calculating the outgoings the head of the business must reckon in the value of his own work.[1]

§ 3. At the beginning of his undertaking, and at every successive The stage, the alert business man strives so to modify his arrangements principle of substi- as to obtain better results with a given expenditure, or equal results tution. with a less expenditure. In other words, he ceaselessly applies the principle of substitution, with the purpose of increasing his profits; and, in so doing, he seldom fails to increase the total efficiency of work, the total power over nature which man derives from organization and knowledge.

Every locality has incidents of its own which affect in various ways the methods of arrangement of every class of business that is carried on in it : and even in the same place and the same trade no two persons pursuing the same aims will adopt exactly the same routes. The tendency to variation is a chief cause of progress; and the abler are the undertakers in any trade the greater will this tendency be. In some trades, as for instance cotton-spinning, the possible variations are confined within narrow limits; no one can hold his own at all who does not use machinery, and very nearly the latest machinery, for every part of the work. But in others, as for instance in some branches of the wood and metal trades, in farming, and in shopkeeping, there can be great variations. For instance, of two manufacturers in the same trade, one will perhaps

---

[1] Almost every trade has its own difficulties and its own customs connected with the task of valuing the capital that has been invested in a business, and of allowing for the depreciation which that capital has undergone from wear-and-tear, from the influence of the elements, from new inventions, and from changes in the course of trade. These two last causes may temporarily raise the value of some kinds of fixed capital, at the same time that they are lowering that of others. And people whose minds are cast in different moulds, or whose interests in the matter point in different directions, will often differ widely on the question what part of the expenditure required for adapting buildings and plant to changing conditions of trade, may be regarded as an investment of new capital; and what ought to be set down as charges incurred to balance depreciation, and treated as expenditure deducted from the current receipts, before determining the net profits or true income earned by the business. These difficulties, and the consequent difference of opinion, are greatest of all with regard to the investment of capital in building up a business connection, and the proper method of appraising the goodwill of a business, or its value " as a going concern."   On the whole of this subject see Matheson's *Depreciation of Factories and their Valuation.*

Another group of difficulties arises from changes in the general purchasing power of money. If that has fallen, or, in other words, if there has been a rise of general prices, the value of a factory may appear to have risen when it has really remained stationary. Confusions arising from this source introduce greater errors into estimates of the real profitableness of different classes of business than would at first sight appear probable. But all questions of this kind must be deferred till we have discussed the theory of money.

V, IV, 4. have a larger wages bill and the other heavier charges on account of machinery; of two retail dealers one will have a larger capital locked up in stock and the other will spend more on advertisements and other means of building up the immaterial capital of a profitable trade connection. And in minor details the variations are numberless.

Each man's actions are influenced by his special opportunities and resources, as well as by his temperament and his associations: but each, taking account of his own means, will push the investment of capital in his business in each several direction until what appears in his judgment to be the outer limit, or margin, of profitableness is reached; that is, until there seems to him no good reason for thinking that the gains resulting from any further investment in that particular direction would compensate him for his outlay. The margin of profitableness, even in regard to one and the same branch or sub-branch of industry, is not to be regarded as a mere point on any one fixed line of possible investment; but as a boundary line of irregular shape cutting one after another every possible line of investment.

The margin of profitableness is not a mere point on any one route, but a line intersecting all routes.

§ 4. This principle of substitution is closely connected with, and is indeed partly based on, that tendency to a diminishing rate of return from any excessive application of resources or of energies in any given direction, which is in accordance with general experience. It is thus linked up with the broad tendency of a diminishing return to increased applications of capital and labour to land in old countries which plays a prominent part in classical economics. And it is so closely akin to the principle of the diminution of marginal utility that results in general from increased expenditure, that some applications of the two principles are almost identical. It has already been observed that new methods of production bring into existence new commodities, or lower the price of old commodities so as to bring them within the reach of increased numbers of consumers: that on the other hand changes in the methods and volume of consumption cause new developments of production, and new distribution of the resources of production: and that though some methods of consumption which contribute most to man's higher life, do little if anything towards furthering the production of material wealth, yet production and consumption are intimately correlated.[1] But now we are to consider more in detail how the distribution of the resources of production between different industrial undertakings is the counterpart and reflex of the distribu-

Affinities between the principles of substitution, of diminishing utility and diminishing return. The correlation of consumption and production.

[1] See pp. 70–77, and 53–56.

tion of the consumers' purchases between different classes of com- V. iv, 4.
modities.[1]

Let us revert to the primitive housewife, who having " a limited The dis-
number of hanks of yarn from the year's shearing, considers all the tribution of re-
domestic wants for clothing and tries to distribute the yarn between sources in
them in such a way as to contribute as much as possible to the economy.
family wellbeing. She will think she has failed if, when it is done,
she has reason to regret that she did not apply more to making, say,
socks, and less to vests. But if, on the other hand, she hit on the
right points to stop at, then she made just so many socks and vests
that she got an equal amount of good out of the last bundle of yarn
that she applied to socks, and the last she applied to vests." [2] If
it happened that two ways of making a vest were open to her, which
were equally satisfactory as regards results, but of which one, while
using up a little more yarn, involved a little less trouble than the
other; then her problems would be typical of those of the larger
business world. They would include first decisions as to the relative
urgency of various ends; secondly, decisions as to the relative
advantages of various means of attaining each end; thirdly, decisions, based on these two sets of decisions, as to the margin up to
which she could most profitably carry the application of each means
towards each end.

These three classes of decisions have to be taken on a larger The dis-
scale by the business man, who has more complex balancings and tribution of readjustments to make before reaching each decision.[3] Let us take sources in
an illustration from the building trade. Let us watch the operations business economy.
of a "speculative builder" in the honourable sense of the term : Illustra-
that is, a man who sets out to erect honest buildings in anticipation of tion from the build-
general demand; who bears the penalty of any error in his judgment; ing trade.
and who, if his judgment is approved by events, benefits the community as well as himself. Let him be considering whether to erect
dwelling houses, or warehouses, or factories or shops. He is trained
to form at once a fairly good opinion as to the method of working
most suitable for each class of building, and to make a rough estimate
of its cost. He estimates the cost of various sites adapted for each
class of building : and he reckons in the price that he would have to

---

[1] The substance of part of this section was placed in VI. i. 7 in earlier editions.
But it seems to be needed here in preparation for the central chapters of Book V.
[2] See III. v. 1.
[3] The remainder of this section goes very much on the lines of the earlier half
of Note XIV. in the Mathematical Appendix; which may be read in connection
with it. The subject is one in which the language of the differential calculus—
not its reasonings—are specially helpful to clear thought : but the main outlines can
be presented in ordinary language.

V, IV, 4.   pay for any site as a part of his capital expenditure, just as he does the expense to which he would be put for laying foundations in it, and so on. He brings this estimate of cost into relation with his estimate of the price he is likely to get for any given building, together with its site. If he can find no case in which the demand price exceeds his outlays by enough to yield him a good profit, with some margin against risks, he may remain idle. Or he may possibly build at some risk in order to keep his most trusty workmen together, and to find some occupation for his plant and his salaried assistance : but more on this later on.

Suppose him now to have decided that (say) villa residences of a certain type, erected on a plot of ground which he can buy, are likely to yield him a good profit. The main end to be sought being thus settled, he sets himself to study more carefully the means by which it is to be obtained, and, in connection with that study, to consider possible modifications in the details of his plans.

Given the general character of the houses to be built, he will have to consider in what proportions to use various materials— brick, stone, steel, cement, plaster, wood, etc., with a view to obtaining the result which will contribute most, in proportion to its cost, to the efficiency of the house in gratifying the artistic taste of purchasers and in ministering to their comfort. In thus deciding what is the best distribution of his resources between various commodities, he is dealing with substantially the same problem as the primitive housewife, who has to consider the most economic distribution of her yarn between the various needs of her household.

Like her, he has to reflect that the yield of benefit which any particular use gave would be relatively large up to a certain point, and would then gradually diminish. Like her, he has so to distribute his resources that they have the same marginal utility in each use : he has to weigh the loss that would result from taking away a little expenditure here, with the gain that would result from adding a little there. In effect both of them work on lines similar to those which guide the farmer in so adjusting the application of his capital and labour to land, that no field is stinted of extra cultivation to which it would have given a generous return, and none receives so great an expenditure as to call into strong activity the tendency to diminishing return in agriculture.[1]

Thus it is that the alert business man, as has just been said, " pushes the investment of capital in his business in each several direction until what appears in his judgment to be the outer limit,

[1] See above III. III. 1; and the footnote on pp. 130.

or margin, of profitableness is reached; that is, until there seems to V, IV, 5. him no good reason for thinking that the gains resulting from any further investment in that particular direction would compensate him for his outlay." He never assumes that roundabout methods will be remunerative in the long run. But he is always on the look out for roundabout methods that promise to be more effective in proportion to their cost than direct methods : and he adopts the best of them, if it lies within his means.

*   *   *   *

§ 5. Some technical terms relating to costs may be considered *Prime cost.* here. When investing his capital in providing the means of carrying on an undertaking, the business man looks to being recouped by the price obtained for its various products; and he expects to be able under normal conditions to charge for each of them a sufficient price; that is, one which will not only cover the *special, direct,* or *Prime or* *prime cost,* but also bear its proper share of the general expenses of *special cost.* the business; and these we may call its general, or *supplementary cost.* These two elements together make its *total cost.*

There are great variations in the usage of the term Prime cost *Supple-* in business. But it is here taken in a narrow sense. Supplementary *mentary* *and total* costs are taken to include standing charges on account of the *cost.* durable plant in which much of the capital of the business has been invested, and also the salaries of the upper employees : for the charges to which the business is put on account of their salaries cannot generally be adapted quickly to changes in the amount of work there is for them to do. There remains nothing but the (money) cost of the raw material used in making the commodity and the wages of that part of the labour spent on it which is paid by the hour or the piece and the extra wear-and-tear of plant. This is the special cost which a manufacturer has in view, when his works are not fully employed, and he is calculating the lowest price at which it will be worth his while to accept an order, irrespectively of any effect that his action may have in spoiling the market for future orders, and trade being slack at the time. But in fact he must as a rule take account of this effect : the price at which it is just worth his while to produce, even when trade is slack, is in practice generally a good deal above this prime cost, as we shall see later on.[1]

---

[1] Especially in V. IX. " There are many systems of Prime Cost in vogue . . . we take Prime Cost to mean, as in fact the words imply, only the original or direct cost of production; and while in some trades it may be a matter of convenience to include in the cost of production a proportion of indirect expenses, and a charge for depreciation on plant and buildings, in no case should it comprise interest on capital or profit." (Garcke and Fells, *Factory Accounts,* ch. I.)

§ 6. Supplementary cost must generally be covered by the selling price to some considerable extent in the short run. And they must be completely covered by it in the long run; for, if they are not, production will be checked. Supplementary costs are of many different kinds; and some of them differ only in degree from prime costs. For instance, if an engineering firm is in doubt whether to accept an order at a rather low price for a certain locomotive, the absolute prime costs include the value of the raw material and the wages of the artisans and labourers employed on the locomotive. But there is no clear rule as to the salaried staff: for, if work is slack, they will probably have some time on their hands; and their salaries will therefore commonly be classed among general or supplementary costs. The line of division is however often blurred over. For instance, foremen and other trusted artisans are seldom dismissed merely because of a temporary scarcity of work ; and therefore an occasional order may be taken to fill up idle time, even though its price does not cover their salaries and wages. That is they may not be regarded as prime costs in such a case. But, of course the staff in the office can be in some measure adjusted to variations in the work of the firm by leaving vacancies unfilled and even by weeding out inefficient men during slack times; and by getting extra help or putting out some of the work in busy times.

If we pass from such tasks to larger and longer tasks, as for instance the working out a contract to deliver a great number of locomotives gradually over a period of several years, then most of the office work done in connection with that order must be regarded as special to it : for if it had been declined and nothing else taken in its place, the expenses under the head of salaries could have been reduced almost to a proportionate extent.

The case is much stronger when we consider a fairly steady market for any class of staple manufactures extending over a long time. For then the outlay incurred for installing specialized skill and organization, the permanent office staff, and the durable plant of the workshops can all be regarded as part of the costs necessary for the process of production. That outlay will be increased up to a margin at which the branch of manufacture seems in danger of growing too fast for its market.

In the next chapter the argument of Chapter III. and of this chapter is continued. It is shown in more detail how those costs which most powerfully act on supply and therefore on price, are limited to a narrow and arbitrary group in the case of a single contract for, say, a locomotive; but are much fuller, and correspond much more truly to the broad features of industrial economy in the case of a continuous supply to a fairly steady general market : the influence of cost of production on value does not show itself clearly except in relatively long periods; and it is to be estimated with regard to a whole process of production rather than a particular locomotive, or a particular parcel of goods. And a similar study is made in Chapters VIII.-X. of variations in the character of those prime and supplementary costs which consist of charges for interest (or profits) on investments in agents of production, according as the periods of the market under consideration are long or short.

V, IV, 6.

further developed in Chs. V. and VIII.—X.

Meanwhile it may be noticed that the distinction between prime and supplementary costs operates in every phase of civilization, though it is not likely to attract much attention except in a capitalistic phase. Robinson Crusoe had to do only with real costs and real satisfactions : and an old-fashioned peasant family, which bought little and sold little, arranged its investments of present " effort and waiting " for future benefits on nearly the same lines. But, if either were doubting whether it was worth while to take a light ladder on a trip to gather wild fruits, the prime costs alone would be weighed against the expected benefits : and yet the ladder would not have been made, unless it had been expected to render sufficient service in the aggregate of many little tasks, to remunerate the cost of making it. In the long run it had to repay its total costs, supplementary as well as prime.

The distinction between prime and supplementary costs operates even where neither are reckoned in money.

Even the modern employer has to look at his own labour as a real cost in the first instance. He may think that a certain enterprise is likely to yield a surplus of money incomings over money outgoings (after proper allowances for risks and for discountings of future happenings); but that the surplus will amount to less than the money equivalent of the trouble and worry that the enterprise will cause to himself : and, in that case, he will avoid it.[1]

---

[1] The Supplementary costs, which the owner of a factory expects to be able to add to the prime costs of its products, are the source of the quasi-rents which it will yield to him. If they come up to his expectation, then his business so far yields good profits : if they fall much short of it, his business tends to go to the bad. But his statement bears only on long-period problems of value : and in that connection the difference between Prime and Supplementary costs has no special significance. The importance of the distinction between them is confined to short-period problems.

CHAPTER V

EQUILIBRIUM OF NORMAL DEMAND AND SUPPLY, CONTINUED,
WITH REFERENCE TO LONG AND SHORT PERIODS

V, v, 1.

ficulties scussed this apter to the ement of ne are tent in dinary scourse,

§ 1. THE variations in the scope of the term *Normal*, according as the periods of time under discussion are long or short, were indicated in Chapter III. We are now ready to study them more closely.

In this case, as in others, the economist merely brings to light difficulties that are latent in the common discourse of life, so that by being frankly faced they may be thoroughly overcome. For in ordinary life it is customary to use the word Normal in different senses, with reference to different periods of time; and to leave the context to explain the transition from one to another. The economist follows this practice of every-day life: but, by taking pains to indicate the transition, he sometimes seems to have created a complication which in fact he has only revealed.

here the e of e term ormal is astic.

Thus, when it is said that the price of wool on a certain day was abnormally high though the average price for the year was abnormally low, that the wages of coal-miners were abnormally high in 1872 and abnormally low in 1879, that the (real) wages of labour were abnormally high at the end of the fourteenth century and abnormally low in the middle of the sixteenth; everyone understands that the scope of the term normal is not the same in these various cases.

The best illustrations of this come from manufactures where the plant is long-lived, and the product is short-lived. When a new textile fabric is first introduced into favour, and there is very little plant suitable for making it, its normal price for some months may be twice as high as those of other fabrics which are not less difficult to make, but for making which there is an abundant stock of suitable plant and skill. Looking at long periods we may say that its normal price is on a par with that of the others: but if during the first few months a good deal of it were offered for sale in a bankrupt's stock we might say that its price was abnormally low even when it was selling for half as much again as the others. Everyone takes the context as indicating the special use of the term in each several case; and a formal interpretation clause is seldom necessary, because in ordinary conversation misunderstandings can

be nipped in the bud by question and answer. But let us look at this
matter more closely.

We have noticed [1] how a cloth manufacturer would need to
calculate the expenses of producing all the different things required
for making cloth with reference to the amounts of each of them that
would be wanted; and on the supposition in the first instance that
the conditions of supply would be normal. But we have yet to
take account of the fact that he must give to this term a wider or
narrower range, according as he was looking more or less far ahead.

Thus in estimating the wages required to call forth an adequate
supply of labour to work a certain class of looms, he might take the
current wages of similar work in the neighbourhood : or he might
argue that there was a scarcity of that particular class of labour in
the neighbourhood, that its current wages there were higher than in
other parts of England, and that looking forward over several years
so as to allow for immigration, he might take the normal rate of
wages at a rather lower rate than that prevailing there at the time.
Or lastly, he might think that the wages of weavers all over the
country were abnormally low relatively to others of the same grade,
in consequence of a too sanguine view having been taken of the
prospects of the trade half a generation ago. He might argue that
this branch of work was overcrowded, that parents had already
begun to choose other trades for their children which offered greater
net advantages and yet were not more difficult; that in consequence
a few years would see a falling-off in the supply of labour suited for
his purpose; so that looking forward a long time he must take
normal wages at a rate higher than the present average.[2]

Again, in estimating the normal supply price of wool, he would
take the average of several past years. He would make allowance for
any change that would be likely to affect the supply in the immediate
future; and he would reckon for the effect of such droughts as from
time to time occur in Australia and elsewhere; since their occurrence
is too common to be regarded as abnormal. But he would not allow
here for the chance of our being involved in a great war, by which the
Australian supplies might be cut off; he would consider that any allowance for this should come under the head of extraordinary trade risks,
and not enter into his estimate of the normal supply price of wool.

V, v, 1.

Illustra-
tion from
the cloth
trade.

[1] V. III. 5.
[2] There are indeed not many occasions on which the calculations of a business
man for practical purposes need to look forward so far, and to extend the range
of the term Normal over a whole generation : but in the broader applications of
economic science it is sometimes necessary to extend the range even further, and
to take account of the slow changes that in the course of centuries affect the supply
price of the labour of each industrial grade.

V, v, 2

He would deal in the same way with the risk of civil tumult or any violent and long-continued disturbance of the labour market of an unusual character; but in his estimate of the amount of work that could be got out of the machinery, etc. under normal conditions, he would probably reckon for minor interruptions from trade disputes such as are continually occurring, and are therefore to be regarded as belonging to the regular course of events, that is as not abnormal.

In all these calculations he would not concern himself specially to inquire how far mankind are under the exclusive influence of selfish or self-regarding motives. He might be aware that anger and vanity, jealousy and offended dignity are still almost as common causes of strikes and lockouts, as the desire for pecuniary gain : but that would not enter into his calculations. All that he would want to know about them would be whether they acted with sufficient regularity for him to be able to make a reasonably good allowance for their influence in interrupting work and raising the normal supply price of the goods.[1]

The complex problem of value must be broken up.

§ 2. The element of time is a chief cause of those difficulties in economic investigations which make it necessary for man with his limited powers to go step by step; breaking up a complex question, studying one bit at a time, and at last combining his partial solutions into a more or less complete solution of the whole riddle. In breaking it up, he segregates those disturbing causes, whose wanderings happen to be inconvenient, for the time in a pound called *Cœteris Paribus*. The study of some group of tendencies is isolated by the assumption *other things being equal* : the existence of other tendencies is not denied, but their disturbing effect is neglected for a time. The more the issue is thus narrowed, the more exactly can it be handled : but also the less closely does it correspond to real life. Each exact and firm handling of a narrow issue, however, helps towards treating broader issues, in which that narrow issue is contained, more exactly than would otherwise have been possible. With each step more things can be let out of the pound; exact discussions can be made less abstract, realistic discussions can be made less inexact than was possible at an earlier stage.[2]

---

[1] Compare I. II. 7.

[2] As has been explained in the Preface, pp. vi–ix, this volume is concerned mainly with normal conditions; and these are sometimes described as Statical. But in the opinion of the present writer the problem of normal value belongs to economic Dynamics : partly because Statics is really but a branch of Dynamics, and partly because all suggestions as to economic rest, of which the hypothesis of a Stationary state is the chief, are merely provisional, used only to illustrate particular steps in the argument, and to be thrown aside when that is done.

Our first step towards studying the influences exerted by the element of time on the relations between cost of production and value may well be to consider the famous fiction of the "Stationary state" in which those influences would be but little felt; and to contrast the results which would be found there with those in the modern world.

This state obtains its name from the fact that in it the general conditions of production and consumption, of distribution and exchange remain motionless; but yet it is full of movement; for it is a mode of life. The average age of the population may be stationary; though each individual is growing up from youth towards his prime, or downwards to old age. And the same amount of things per head of the population will have been produced in the same ways by the same classes of people for many generations together; and therefore this supply of the appliances for production will have had full time to be adjusted to the steady demand.

Of course we might assume that in our stationary state every business remained always of the same size, and with the same trade connection. But we need not go so far as that; it will suffice to suppose that firms rise and fall, but that the "representative" firm remains always of about the same size, as does the representative tree of a virgin forest, and that therefore the economies resulting from its own resources are constant: and since the aggregate volume of production is constant, so also are those economies resulting from subsidiary industries in the neighbourhood, etc. [That is, its internal and external economies are both constant. The price, the expectation of which just induced persons to enter the trade, must be sufficient to cover in the long run the cost of building up a trade connection; and a proportionate share of it must be added in to make up the total cost of production.]

In a stationary state then the plain rule would be that cost of production governs value. Each effect would be attributable mainly to one cause; there would not be much complex action and reaction between cause and effect. Each element of cost would be governed by "natural" laws, subject to some control from fixed custom. There would be no reflex influence of demand; no fundamental difference between the immediate and the later effects of economic causes. There would be no distinction between long-period and short-period normal value, at all events if we supposed that in that monotonous world the harvests themselves were uniform: for the representative firm being always of the same size, and always doing the same class of business to the same extent and in the same

V, v, 3.

way, with no slack times, and no specially busy times, its normal expenses by which the normal supply price is governed would be always the same. The demand lists of prices would always be the same, and so would the supply lists; and normal price would never vary.

But in the real world a simple doctrine of value is worse than none.

But nothing of this is true in the world in which we live. Here every economic force is constantly changing its action, under the influence of other forces which are acting around it. Here changes in the volume of production, in its methods, and in its cost are ever mutually modifying one another; they are always affecting and being affected by the character and the extent of demand. Further all these mutual influences take time to work themselves out, and, as a rule, no two influences move at equal pace. In this world therefore every plain and simple doctrine as to the relations between cost of production, demand and value is necessarily false : and the greater the appearance of lucidity which is given to it by skilful exposition, the more mischievous it is. A man is likely to be a better economist if he trusts to his common sense, and practical instincts, than if he professes to study the theory of value and is resolved to find it easy.

Modifications of the fiction of a stationary state bring us nearer to real life and help to break up a complex problem.

§ 3. The Stationary state has just been taken to be one in which population is stationary. But nearly all its distinctive features may be exhibited in a place where population and wealth are both growing, provided they are growing at about the same rate, and there is no scarcity of land : and provided also the methods of production and the conditions of trade change but little; and above all, where the character of man himself is a constant quantity. For in such a state by far the most important conditions of production and consumption, of exchange and distribution will remain of the same quality, and in the same general relations to one another, though they are all increasing in volume.[1]

This relaxation of the rigid bonds of a purely stationary state brings us one step nearer to the actual conditions of life : and by relaxing them still further we get nearer still. We thus approach by gradual steps towards the difficult problem of the interaction of countless economic causes. In the stationary state all the conditions of production and consumption are reduced to rest : but less violent assumptions are made by what is, not quite accurately, called the *statical* method. By that method we fix our minds on some central point : we suppose it for the time to be reduced to a *stationary* state; and we then study in relation to it the forces

---

[1] See below, V. xi. 6; and compare Keynes, *Scope and Method of Political Economy*, vi. 2.

that affect the things by which it is surrounded, and any tendency there may be to equilibrium of these forces. A number of these partial studies may lead the way towards a solution of problems too difficult to be grasped at one effort.[1]

§ 4. We may roughly classify problems connected with fishing industries as those which are affected by very quick changes, such as uncertainties of the weather; or by changes of moderate length, such as the increased demand for fish caused by the scarcity of meat during the year or two following a cattle plague; or lastly, we may consider the great increase during a whole generation of the demand for fish which might result from the rapid growth of a high-strung artisan population making little use of their muscles.

The day to day oscillations of the price of fish resulting from uncertainties of the weather, etc., are governed by practically the same causes in modern England as in the supposed stationary state. The changes in the general economic conditions around us are quick; but they are not quick enough to affect perceptibly the short-period normal level about which the price fluctuates from day to day: and they may be neglected [impounded in *cæteris paribus*] during a study of such fluctuations.

Let us then pass on; and suppose a great increase in the general demand for fish, such for instance as might arise from a disease affecting farm stock, by which meat was made a dear and dangerous food for several years together. We now impound fluctuations due to the weather in *cæteris paribus*, and neglect them provisionally: they are so quick that they speedily obliterate one another, and are therefore not important for problems of this class. And for the opposite reason we neglect variations in the numbers of those who are brought up as seafaring men : for these variations are too slow to produce much effect in the year or two during which the scarcity of meat lasts. Having impounded these two sets for the time, we give our full attention to such influences as the inducements which good fishing wages will offer to sailors to stay in their fishing homes for a year or two, instead of applying for work on a ship. We consider what old fishing boats, and even vessels that were not specially made for fishing, can be adapted and sent to fish for a year or two. The normal price for any given daily supply of fish, which we are now seeking, is the price which will *quickly* call into the fishing trade capital and labour enough to obtain that supply in a day's fishing of average good fortune; the influence which the price of fish will have upon capital and labour available in the fishing trade

Marginal notes: V, v, 4. — Illustration from the fishing trade. — Day to day oscillations. — An increase in the amount demanded generally raises short-period supply price;

[1] Compare the Preface and Appendix H, 4.

V, v, 4.   being governed by rather narrow causes such as these. This new level about which the price oscillates during these years of exceptionally great demand, will obviously be higher than before. Here we see an illustration of the almost universal law that the term Normal being taken to refer to a short period of time *an increase in the amount demanded raises the normal supply* price. This law is almost universal even as regards industries which in long periods follow the tendency to increasing return.[1]

but not necessarily long-period supply price.   But if we turn to consider the normal supply price with reference to a *long period* of time, we shall find that it is governed by a different set of causes, and with different results. For suppose that the disuse of meat causes a permanent distaste for it, and that an increased demand for fish continues long enough to enable the forces by which its supply is governed to work out their action fully (of course oscillation from day to day and from year to year would continue : but we may leave them on one side). The source of supply in the sea might perhaps show signs of exhaustion, and the fishermen might have to resort to more distant coasts and to deeper waters, Nature giving a Diminishing Return to the increased application of capital and labour of a given order of efficiency. On the other hand, those might turn out to be right who think that man is responsible for but a very small part of the destruction of fish that is constantly going on; and in that case a boat starting with equally good appliances and an equally efficient crew would be likely to get nearly as good a haul after the increase in the total volume of the fishing trade as before. In any case the normal cost of equipping a good boat with an efficient crew would certainly not be higher, and probably be a little lower after the trade had settled down to its now increased dimensions than before. For since fishermen require only trained aptitudes, and not any exceptional natural qualities, their number could be increased in less than a generation to almost any extent that was necessary to meet the demand; while the industries connected with building boats, making nets, etc. being now on a larger scale would be organized more thoroughly and economically. If therefore the waters of the sea showed no signs of depletion of fish, an increased supply could be produced at a lower price after a time sufficiently long to enable the normal action of economic causes to work itself out : and, the term Normal being taken to refer to a long period of time, the normal price of fish would decrease with an increase in demand.[2]

---

[1] See V, xi, 1.

[2] Tooke (*History of Prices*, Vol. I. p. 104) tells us : "There are particular articles of which the demand for naval and military purposes forms so large a proportion to

Thus we may emphasize the distinction already made between average price and normal price.　An average may be taken of the prices of any set of sales extending over a day or a week or a year or any other time : or it may be the average of sales at any time in many markets; or it may be the average of many such averages. But the conditions which are normal to any one set of sales are not likely to be exactly those which are normal to the others : and therefore it is only by accident that an average price will be a normal price; that is, the price which any one set of conditions tends to produce.　In a stationary state alone, as we have just seen, the term normal always means the same thing : there, but only there, " average price " and " normal price " are convertible terms.[1]

§ 5.　To go over the ground in another way.　Market values are governed by the relation of demand to stocks actually in the market; with more or less reference to " future " supplies, and not without some influence of trade combinations.

But the current supply is in itself partly due to the action of producers in the past; and this action has been determined on as the result of a comparison of the prices which they expect to get for their goods with the expenses to which they will be put in producing them.　The range of expenses of which they take account depends on whether they are merely considering the extra expenses of certain extra production with their existing plant, or are considering whether to lay down new plant for the purpose.　In the case, for instance, of an order for a single locomotive, which was discussed a little while ago,[2] the question of readjusting the plant to demand would hardly arise : the main question would be whether more work could conveniently be got out of the existing plant.　But in view of an order for a large number of locomotives to be delivered gradually over a series of years, some extension of plant " specially " made for

Margin notes: V, v, 5. Average and normal prices. Restatement of the main result. Nature of marginal production.

---

he total supply, that no diminution of consumption by individuals can keep pace with the immediate increase of demand by government; and consequently, the breaking out of a war tends to raise the price of such articles to a great relative height. But even of such articles, if the consumption were not on a progressive scale of increase so rapid that the supply, with all the encouragement of a relatively high price, could not keep pace with the demand, the tendency is (supposing no impediment, natural or artificial, to production or importation) to occasion such an increase of quantity, as to reduce the price to nearly the same level as that from which it had advanced.　And accordingly it will be observed, by reference to the table of prices, that salt-petre, hemp, iron, etc., after advancing very considerably under the influence of a greatly extended demand for military and naval purposes, tended downwards again whenever that demand was not progressively and rapidly increasing."　Thus a continuously progressive increase in demand may raise the supply price of a thing even for several years together; though a steady increase of demand for that thing, at a rate not too great for supply to keep pace with it, would lower price.

[1] V. III. 6.　The distinction will be yet further discussed in V. XII. and Appendix H.　See also Keynes, *Scope and Method of Political Economy*, ch. VII.

[2] Pp. 300–1.

V, v, 5. the purpose, and therefore truly to be regarded as prime marginal costs would almost certainly be carefully considered.

Whether the new production for which there appears to be a market be large or small, the general rule will be that unless the price is expected to be very low that portion of the supply which can be most easily produced, with but small prime costs, will be produced : that portion is not likely to be on the margin of production. As the expectations of price improve, an increased part of the production will yield a considerable surplus above prime costs, and the margin of production will be pushed outwards. Every increase in the price expected will, as a rule, induce some people who would not otherwise have produced anything, to produce a little; and those, who have produced something for the lower price, will produce more for the higher price. That part of their production with regard to which such persons are on the margin of doubt as to whether it is worth while for them to produce it at the price, is to be included together with that of the persons who are in doubt whether to produce at all; the two together constitute the marginal production at that price. The producers, who are in doubt whether to produce anything at all, may be said to lie altogether on the margin of production (or, if they are agriculturists, on the margin of cultivation). But as a rule they are very few in number, and their action is less important than that of those who would in any case produce something.

The general drift of the term Normal supply price for short and long periods. The general drift of the term normal supply price is always the same whether the period to which it refers is short or long; but there are great differences in detail. In every case reference is made to a certain given rate of aggregate production; that is, to the production of a certain aggregate amount daily or annually. In every case the price is that the expectation of which is sufficient and only just sufficient to make it worth while for people to set themselves to produce that aggregate amount; in every case the cost of production is marginal; that is, it is the cost of production of those goods which are on the margin of not being produced at all, and which would not be produced if the price to be got for them were expected to be lower. But the causes which determine this margin vary with the length of the period under consideration. For short periods people take the stock of appliances for production as practically fixed; and they are governed by their expectations of demand in considering how actively they shall set themselves to work those appliances. In long periods they set themselves to adjust the flow of these appliances to their expectations of demand for the goods

which the appliances help to produce.   Let us examine this difference   V, v, 6.
closely.

§ 6. The immediate effect of the expectation of a high price is
to cause people to bring into active work all their appliances of
production, and to work them full time and perhaps overtime.
The supply price is then the money cost of production of that part of
the produce which forces the undertaker to hire such inefficient
labour (perhaps tired by working overtime) at so high a price, and to
put himself and others to so much strain and inconvenience that he is
on the margin of doubt whether it is worth his while to do it or not.
The immediate effect of the expectation of a low price is to throw
many appliances for production out of work, and slacken the work of
others; and if the producers had no fear of spoiling their markets,
it would be worth their while to produce for a time for any price
that covered the prime costs of production and rewarded them for
their own trouble.

But, as it is, they generally hold out for a higher price; each
man fears to spoil his chance of getting a better price later on from
his own customers; or, if he produces for a large and open market,
he is more or less in fear of incurring the resentment of other producers, should he sell needlessly at a price that spoils the common
market for all. The marginal production in this case is the production of those whom a little further fall of price would cause, either
from a regard to their own interest or by formal or informal agreement with other producers, to suspend production for fear of further
spoiling the market. The price which, for these reasons, producers
are just on the point of refusing, is the true marginal supply price
for short periods. It is nearly always above, and generally very
much above the special or prime cost for raw materials, labour and
wear-and-tear of plant, which is immediately and directly involved
by getting a little further use out of appliances which are not fully
employed. This point needs further study.

In a trade which uses very expensive plant, the prime cost of
goods is but a small part of their total cost; and an order at much
less than their normal price may leave a large surplus above their
prime cost. But if producers accept such orders in their anxiety to
prevent their plant from being idle, they glut the market and tend
to prevent prices from reviving. In fact however they seldom
pursue this policy constantly and without moderation. If they did,
they might ruin many of those in the trade, themselves perhaps
among the number; and in that case a revival of demand would
find little response in supply, and would raise violently the prices of

For short
periods the
stock of
appliances
of produc-
tion are
practically
fixed, but
their
employ-
ment
varies
with
demand.

Where
there is
much fixed
capital,
prices can
fall far
below their
normal
level
without
reaching
special or
prime
cost;

V, v, 6. the goods produced by the trade. Extreme variations of this kind are in the long run beneficial neither to producers nor to consumers; and general opinion is not altogether hostile to that code of trade morality which condemns the action of anyone who " spoils the market " by being too ready to accept a price that does little more than cover the prime cost of his goods, and allows but little on account of his general expenses.[1]

For example, if at any time the prime cost, in the narrowest sense of the word, of a bale of cloth is £100; and if another £100 are needed to make the cloth pay its due share of the general expenses of the establishment, including normal profits to its owners, then the practically effective supply price is perhaps not very likely to fall below £150 under ordinary conditions, even for short periods; though of course a few special bargains may be made at lower prices without much affecting the general market.

but such a fall is opposed by many causes, mostly indirect.

Thus, although nothing but prime cost enters *necessarily and directly* into the supply price for short periods, it is yet true that supplementary costs also exert some influence indirectly. A producer does not often isolate the cost of each separate small parcel of his output; he is apt to treat a considerable part of it, even in some cases the whole of it, more or less as a unit. He inquires whether it is worth his while to add a certain new line to his present undertakings, whether it is worth while to introduce a new machine and so on. He treats the extra output that would result from the change more or less as a unit beforehand; and afterwards he quotes the lowest prices, which he is willing to accept, with more or less reference to the whole cost of that extra output regarded as a unit.

The marginal unit is a whole process of production rather than a parcel of goods.

In other words he regards an increase in his processes of production, rather than an individual parcel of his products, as a unit in most of his transactions. And the analytical economist must follow suit, if he would keep in close touch with actual conditions. These considerations tend to blur the sharpness of outline of the theory of value : but they do not affect its substance.[2]

To sum up then as regards short periods. The supply of

---

[1] Where there is a strong combination, tacit or overt, producers may sometimes regulate the price for a considerable time together with very little reference to cost of production. And if the leaders in that combination were those who had the best facilities for production, it might be said, in apparent though not in real contradiction to Ricardo's doctrines, that the price was governed by that part of the supply which was most easily produced. But as a fact, those producers whose finances are weakest, and who are bound to go on producing to escape failure, often impose their policy on the rest of the combination : insomuch that it is a common saying, both in America and England, that the weakest members of a combination are frequently its rulers.

[2] This general description may suffice for most purposes : but in chapter XI. there will be found a more detailed study of that extremely complex notion, a marginal

specialized skill and ability, of suitable machinery and other material
capital, and of the appropriate industrial organization has not time
to be fully adapted to demand; but the producers have to adjust their
supply to the demand as best they can with the appliances already
at their disposal. On the one hand there is not time materially to
increase those appliances if the supply of them is deficient; and on
the other, if the supply is excessive, some of them must remain
imperfectly employed, since there is not time for the supply to be
much reduced by gradual decay, and by conversion to other uses.
Variations in the particular income derived from them do not *for
the time* affect perceptibly the supply; and do not directly affect the
price of the commodities produced by them. The income is a
surplus of total receipts over prime cost; [that is, it has something
of the nature of a rent as will be seen more clearly in chapter VIII.].
But unless it is sufficient to cover in the long run a fair share of the
general costs of the business, production will gradually fall off. In
this way a controlling influence over the relatively quick movements of supply price during short periods is exercised by causes in
the background which range over a long period; and the fear of
" spoiling the market " often makes those causes act more promptly
than they otherwise would.

§ 7. In long periods on the other hand all investments of capital
and effort in providing the material plant and the organization of a
business, and in acquiring trade knowledge and specialized ability,
have time to be adjusted to the incomes which are expected to be
earned by them : and the estimates of those incomes therefore
directly govern supply, and are the true long-period normal supply
price of the commodities produced.

A great part of the capital invested in a business is generally
spent on building up its internal organization and its external
trade connections. If the business does not prosper all that capital
is lost, even though its material plans may realize a considerable
part of its original cost. And anyone proposing to start a new
business in any trade must reckon for the chance of this loss. If
himself a man of normal capacity for that class of work, he may look
forward ere long to his business being a representative one, in the
sense in which we have used this term, with its fair share of the
economies of production on a large scale. If the net earnings of
such a representative business seem likely to be greater than he

increment in the processes of production by a representative firm; together with a
fuller explanation of the necessity of referring our reasonings to the circumstances of a
representative firm, especially when we are considering industries which show a tendency to increasing return.

V, v, 8.   could get by similar investments in other trades to which he has access, he will choose this trade. Thus that investment of capital in a trade, on which the price of the commodity produced by it depends in the long run, is governed by estimates on the one hand of the outgoings required to build up and to work a representative firm, and on the other of the incomings, spread over a long period of time, to be got by such a price.

At any particular moment some businesses will be rising and others falling : but when we are taking a broad view of the causes which govern normal supply price, we need not trouble ourselves with these eddies on the surface of the great tide. Any particular increase of production may be due to some new manufacturer who is struggling against difficulties, working with insufficient capital, and enduring great privations in the hope that he may gradually build up a good business. Or it may be due to some wealthy firm which by enlarging its premises is enabled to attain new economies, and thus obtain a larger output at a lower proportionate cost : and, as this additional output will be small relatively to the aggregate volume of production in the trade, it will not much lower the price; so that the firm will reap great gains from its successful adaptation to its surroundings. But while these variations are occurring in the fortunes of individual businesses, there may be a steady tendency of the long-period normal supply price to diminish, as a direct consequence of an increase in the aggregate volume of production.

There is no sharp division between long and short periods.

§ 8. Of course there is no hard and sharp line of division between " long " and " short " periods. Nature has drawn no such lines in the economic conditions of actual life; and in dealing with practical problems they are not wanted. Just as we contrast civilized with uncivilized races, and establish many general propositions about either group, though no hard and fast division can be drawn between the two; so we contrast long and short periods without attempting any rigid demarcation between them. If it is necessary for the purposes of any particular argument to divide one case sharply from the other, it can be done by a special interpretation clause : but the occasions on which this is necessary are neither frequent nor important.

Classification of problems of value by the periods to which they refer.

Four classes stand out. In each, price is governed by the relations between demand and supply. As regards *market* prices, Supply is taken to mean the stock of the commodity in question which is on hand, or at all events " in sight." As regards *normal* prices, when the term Normal is taken to relate to *short* periods of a few months or a year, Supply means broadly what can be produced for the price in question with the existing stock of plant, personal and

impersonal, in the given time.   As regards *normal* prices, when the
term Normal is to refer to *long* periods of several years, Supply
means what can be produced by plant, which itself can be remunera-
tively produced and applied within the given time;   while lastly,
there are very gradual or *Secular* movements of normal price,
caused by the gradual growth of knowledge, of population and of
capital, and the changing conditions of demand and supply from one
generation to another.[1]

The remainder of the present volume is chiefly concerned with
the third of the above classes :   that is, with the normal relations of
wages, profits, prices, etc., for rather long periods.   But occasionally
account has to be taken of changes that extend over very many
years;   and one chapter, Book VI. ch. XII., is given up to " The
Influence of Progress on Value," that is, to the study of *secular*
changes of value.

[1] Compare the first section of this chapter.   Of course the periods required to
adapt the several factors of production to the demand may be very different; the
number of skilled compositors, for instance, cannot be increased nearly as fast as
the supply of type and printing-presses.   And this cause alone would prevent any
rigid division being made between long and short periods.   But in fact a theoretically
perfect long period must give time enough to enable not only the factors of production of the commodity to be adjusted to the demand, but also the factors of
production of those factors of production to be adjusted and so on; and this, when
carried to its logical consequences, will be found to involve the supposition of a
stationary state of industry, in which the requirements of a future age can be anticipated an indefinite time beforehand.   Some such assumption is indeed unconsciously
implied in many popular renderings of Ricardo's theory of value, if not in his own
versions of it; and it is to this cause more than any other that we must attribute
that simplicity and sharpness of outline, from which the economic doctrines in fashion
in the first half of this century derived some of their seductive charm, as well as most
of whatever tendency they may have to lead to false practical conclusions.

Relatively short and long period problems go generally on similar lines.   In
both use is made of that paramount device, the partial or total isolation for special
study of some set of relations.   In both opportunity is gained for analysing and
comparing similar episodes, and making them throw light upon one another; and for
ordering and co-ordinating facts which are suggestive in their similarities, and are
still more suggestive in the differences that peer out through their similarities.   But
there is a broad distinction between the two cases.   In the relatively short-period
problem no great violence is needed for the assumption that the forces not specially
under consideration may be taken for the time to be inactive.   But violence is required for keeping broad forces in the pound of *Cæteris Paribus* during, say, a whole
generation, on the ground that they have only an indirect bearing on the question in
hand.   For even indirect influences may produce great effects in the course of a
generation, if they happen to act cumulatively; and it is not safe to ignore them
even provisionally in a practical problem without special study.   Thus the uses of the
statical method in problems relating to very long periods are dangerous; care and
forethought and self-restraint are needed at every step.   The difficulties and risks
of the task reach their highest point in connection with industries which conform to
the law of Increasing Return; and it is just in connection with those industries that
the most alluring applications of the method are to be found.   We must postpone
these questions to chapter XII. and Appendix H.

But an answer may be given here to the objection that since " the economic
world is subject to continual changes, and is becoming more complex, . . . the longer
the run the more hopeless the rectification " : so that to speak of that position which
value tends to reach in the long run is to treat " variables as constants." (Devas,
Political Economy, Book IV. ch. V.)   It is true that we do treat variables *provisionally*
as constants.   But it is also true that this is the only method by which science has
ever made any great progress in dealing with complex and changeful matter, whether
in the physical or moral world.   See above V. v. 2.

CHAPTER VI

JOINT AND COMPOSITE DEMAND. JOINT AND COMPOSITE SUPPLY

§ 1. BREAD satisfies man's wants directly : and the demand for it is said to be direct. But a flour mill and an oven satisfy wants only indirectly, by helping to make bread, etc., and the demand for them is said to be indirect. More generally :—

Indirect or derived demand.

The demand for raw materials and other means of production is *indirect* and is *derived* from the direct demand for those directly serviceable products which they help to produce.

The services of the flour mill and the oven are joined together in the ultimate product, bread : the demand for them is therefore called a joint demand. Again, hops and malt are complementary to one another; and are joined together in the common destination of ale : and so on. Thus the demand for each of several complementary things is derived from the services which they *jointly* render in the production of some ultimate product, as for instance a

Joint demand.

loaf of bread, a cask of ale. In other words there is a *joint demand* for the services which any of these things render in helping to produce a thing which satisfies wants directly and for which there is therefore a direct demand : the direct demand for the finished product is in effect split up into many derived demands for the things used in producing it.[1]

To take another illustration, the direct demand for houses gives rise to a joint demand for the labour of all the various building trades, and for bricks, stone, wood, etc. which are factors of production of building work of all kinds, or as we may say for shortness, of new houses. The demand for any one of these, as for instance the labour of plasterers, is only an indirect or derived demand.

Let us pursue this last illustration with reference to a class of

---

[1] Compare III. III. 6. It will be recollected that the things in a form ready for immediate use have been called *goods of the first order*, or *consumers' goods*; and that things used as factors of production of other goods have been called *producers' goods*, or *goods of the second and higher orders* or *intermediate* goods : also that it is difficult to say when goods are really finished; that many things are commonly treated as finished consumers' goods before they are really ready for consumption, *e.g.* flour. See II. III. 1. The vagueness of the notion of *instrumental goods*, regarded as things the value of which is derived from that of their products, is indicated in II. IV. 13.

events that are of frequent occurrence in the labour market; the V, VI, 1.
period over which the disturbance extends being short, and the causes
of which we have to take account as readjusting demand and supply
being only such as are able to operate within that short period.

Illustra-
tion taken
from a
labour

This case has important practical bearings, which give it a
special claim on our attention; but we should notice that, referring
as it does to short periods, it is an exception to our general rule of
selecting illustrations in this and the neighbouring chapters from
cases in which there is time enough for the full long-period action of
the forces of supply to be developed.

dispute
in the
building
trade.

Let us then suppose that the supply and demand for building being
in equilibrium, there is a strike on the part of one group of workers,
say the plasterers, or that there is some other disturbance to the
supply of plasterers' labour. In order to isolate and make a separate
study of the demand for that factor, we suppose firstly that the
general conditions of the demand for new houses remain unchanged
(that is, that the demand schedule for new houses remains valid);
and secondly we assume that there is no change in the general conditions of supply of the other factors, two of which are of course the
business faculties and the business organizations of the master
builders; (that is, we assume that their lists of supply prices also
remain valid). Then a temporary check to the supply of plasterers'
labour will cause a proportionate check to the amount of building :
the demand price for the diminished number of houses will be a little
higher than before; and the supply prices for the other factors of
production will not be greater than before.[1] Thus new houses
can now be sold at prices which exceed by a good margin the
sum of the prices at which these other requisites for the production
of houses can be bought; and that margin gives the limit to the
possible rise of the price that will be offered for plasterers' labour, on
the supposition that plasterers' labour is indispensable. The
different amounts of this margin, corresponding to different checks
to the supply of plasterers' labour, are governed by the general rule
that :—The price that will be offered for any thing used in producing Law of
a commodity is, for each separate amount for the commodity, derived
demand.
limited by the excess of the price at which that amount of the
commodity can find purchasers, over the sum of the prices at which
the corresponding supplies of the other things needed for making it
will be forthcoming.

---

[1] This is at any rate true under all ordinary conditions : there will be less extra
charges for overtime ; and the price of the labour of carpenters, bricklayers and others
is likely rather to go down than to go up, and the same is true of bricks and other
building materials.

V, VI, 1.

To use technical terms, the demand schedule for any factor of production of a commodity can be *derived* from that for the commodity by subtracting from the demand price of each separate amount of the commodity the sum of the supply prices for corresponding amounts of the other factors.[1]

[1] The broad account given in the text may suffice for most purposes; and the general reader should perhaps omit the remaining footnotes to this chapter.

It must be remembered that this Derived schedule has no validity except on the suppositions that we are isolating this one factor for separate study; that its own conditions of supply are disturbed; that there is at the time no independent disturbance affecting any other element in the problem; and that therefore in the case of each of the other factors of production the selling price may be taken to coincide always with the supply price.

In illustrating this by a diagram, it will be well, for the sake of shortness of wording, to divide the expenses of production of a commodity into the supply prices of two things of which it is made; let us then regard the supply price of a knife as the sum of the supply prices of its blade and handle, and neglect the expense of putting the two together. Let ss' be the supply curve for handles and SS' that for knives; so that M being any point on Ox, and MqQ being drawn vertically to cut ss' in q and SS' in Q, Mq is the supply price for OM handles, qQ the supply price for OM blades and MQ the supply price for OM knives. Let DD' the demand curve for knives cut SS' in A, and AaB be drawn vertically as in the figure. Then in equilibrium OB knives are sold at a price BA of which Ba goes for the handle and aA for the blade.

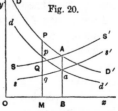

Fig. 20.

(In this illustration we may suppose that sufficient time is allowed to enable the forces which govern supply price to work themselves out fully; and we are at liberty therefore to make our supply curves inclined negatively. This change will not affect the argument; but on the whole it is best to take our typical instance with the supply curve inclined positively.)

Now let us suppose that we want to isolate for separate study the demand for knife handles. Accordingly we suppose that the demand for knives and the supply of blades conform to the laws indicated by their respective curves: also that the supply curve for handles still remains in force and represents the circumstances of normal supply of handles, although the supply of handles is temporarily disturbed. Let MQ cut DD' in P, then MP is the demand price for OM knives and Qq is the supply price for OM blades. Take a point p in MP such that Pp is equal to Qq, and therefore Mp is the excess of MP over Qq; then Mp is the demand price for OM handles. Let dd' be the locus of p obtained by giving M succesive positions along Ox and finding the corresponding positions of p; then dd' is the derived demand curve for handles. Of course it passes through a. We may now neglect all the rest of the figure except the curves dd', ss'; and regard them as representing the relations of demand for and supply of handles, other things being equal, that is to say, in the absence of any disturbing cause which affects the law of supply of blades and the law of demand for knives. Ba is then the equilibrium price of handles, about which the market price oscillates, in the manner investigated in the preceding chapter, under the influence of demand and supply, of which the schedules are represented by dd' and ss'. It has already been remarked that the ordinary demand and supply curves have no practical value except in the immediate neighbourhood of the point of equilibrium. And the same remark applies with even greater force to the equation of derived demand.

[Since $Mp - Mq = MP - MQ$; therefore A being a point of stable equilibrium, the equilibrium at a also is stable. But this statement needs to be somewhat qualified if the supply curves are negatively inclined: see Appendix H.]

In the illustration that has just been worked out the unit of each of the factors remains unchanged whatever be the amount of the commodity produced; for one blade and one handle are always required for each knife; but when a change in the amount of the commodity produced occasions a change in the amount of each factor that is required for the production of a unit of the commodity, the demand and supply curves for the factor got by the above process are not expressed in terms of fixed units of the factor. They must be translated back into fixed units before they are available for general use. (See Mathematical Note XIV *bis*.)

§ 2. When however we come to apply this theory to the actual
conditions of life, it will be important to remember that if the supply
of one factor is disturbed, the supply of others is likely to be disturbed also. In particular, when the factor of which the supply is
disturbed is one class of labour, as that of the plasterers, the employers' earnings generally act as a buffer. That is to say, the loss
falls in the first instance on them; but by discharging some of their
workmen and lowering the wages of others, they ultimately distribute a great part of it among the other factors of production.
The details of the process by which this is effected are various, and
depend on the action of trade combinations, on the higgling and
bargaining of the market, and on other causes with which we are
not just at present concerned.

Let us inquire what are the conditions, under which a check to the
supply of a thing that is wanted not for direct use, but as a factor
of production of some commodity, may cause a very great rise in its
price. The first condition is that the factor itself should be essential, or nearly essential to the production of the commodity, no good
substitute being available at a moderate price.

The second condition is that the commodity in the production
of which it is a necessary factor, should be one for which the demand
is stiff and inelastic; so that a check to its supply will cause consumers to offer a much increased price for it rather than go without
it; and this of course includes the condition that no good substitutes for the commodity are available at a price but little higher
than its equilibrium price. If the check to house building raises the
price of houses very much, builders, anxious to secure the exceptional profits, will bid against one another for such plasterers' labour
as there is in the market.[1]

The third condition is that only a small part of the expenses of
production of the commodity should consist of the price of this
factor. Since the plasterers' wages are but a small part of the total
expenses of building a house, a rise of even 50 per cent. in them
would add but a very small percentage to the expenses of production
of a house and would check demand but little.[2]

The fourth condition is that even a small check to the amount

---

[1] We have to inquire under what conditions the ratio pM to aB will be the greatest,
pM being the demand price for the factor in question corresponding to a supply
reduced from OB to OM, that is reduced by the given amount BM. The second
condition is that PM should be large; and since the elasticity of demand is measured
by the ratio which BM bears to the excess of PM over AB, the greater PM is, the
smaller, other things being equal, is the elasticity of demand.

[2] The third condition is that when PM exceeds AB in a given ratio, pM shall
be caused to exceed Ba in a large ratio : and other things being equal, that requires
Ba to be but a small part of BA.

demanded should cause a considerable fall in the supply prices of other factors of production; as that will increase the margin available for paying a high price for this one.[1] If, for instance, bricklayers and other classes of workmen, or the employers themselves cannot easily find other things to do, and cannot afford to remain idle, they may be willing to work for much lower earnings than before, and this will increase the margin available for paying higher wages to plasterers. These four conditions are independent, and the effects of the last three are cumulative.

Moderating influence of the principle of substitution.
The rise in plasterers' wages would be checked if it were possible either to avoid the use of plaster, or to get the work done tolerably well and at a moderate price by people outside the plasterers' trade : the tyranny, which one factor of production of a commodity might in some cases exercise over the other factors through the action of derived demand, is tempered by the principle of substitution.[2]

and of the power of modifying the proportions which the several factors of production of a commodity bear to one another.
Again, an increased difficulty in obtaining one of the factors of a finished commodity can often be met by modifying the character of the finished product. Some plasterers' labour may be indispensable; but people are often in doubt how much plaster work it is worth while to have in their houses, and if there is a rise in its price they will have less of it. The intensity of the satisfaction of which they would be deprived if they had a little less of it, is its marginal utility; the price which they are just willing to pay in order to have it, is the true demand price for plasterers' work up to the amount which is being used.

So again there is a joint demand for malt and hops in ale. But their proportions can be varied. A higher price can be got for an ale which differs from others only in containing more hops; and this excess price represents the demand for hops.[3]

The relations between plasterers, bricklayers, etc., are representative of much that is both instructive and romantic in the history of alliances and conflicts between trades-unions in allied trades. But the most numerous instances of joint demand are those of the demand for a raw material and the operatives who work it up; as

---

[1] That is, if Qq had been smaller than it is, Pp would have been smaller and Mp would have been larger. See also Mathematical Note XV.

[2] It is shown in Böhm-Bawerk's excellent *Grundzüge der Theorie des wirtschaftlichen Güterwerts* (*Jahrbuch für Nationalökonomie und Statistik*, vol. XIII. p. 59) that if all but one of the factors of production of a commodity have available substitutes in unlimited supply, by which their own price is rigidly fixed, the derived demand price for the remaining factor will be the excess of the demand price for the finished product over the sum of the supply prices thus fixed for the remaining factors. This is an interesting special case of the law given in the text.

[3] See Mathematical Note XVI.

for instance cotton or jute or iron or copper, and those who work up V, VI, 3, 4.
these several materials. Again, the relative prices of different
articles of food vary a good deal with the supply of skilled cooks'
labour : thus, for instance many kinds of meat and many parts of
vegetables which are almost valueless in America, where skilled
cooks are rare and expensive, have a good value in France, where the
art of cooking is widely diffused.

§ 3. We have already [1] discussed the way in which the aggregate *Composite*
demand for any commodity is compounded of the demands of the *or aggre-*
gate
different groups of people who may need it. But we now may *demand.*
extend this notion of *composite demand* to requisites of production
which are needed by several groups of producers.

Nearly every raw material and nearly every kind of labour is *Rival*
applied in many different branches of industry, and contributes to *demands.*
the production of a great variety of commodities. Each of these
commodities has its own direct demand; and from that the derived
demand for any of the things used in making it can be found, and
the thing is " distributed between its various uses " in the manner
which we have already discussed.[2] The various uses are rivals, or
competitors with one another; and the corresponding derived
demands are *rival* or *competitive demands* relatively to one another.
But in relation to the supply of the product, they co-operate with
one another; being " compounded " into the total demand that
carries off the supply : in just the same way as the partial demands
of several classes of society for a finished commodity are aggre-
gated, or compounded together into the total demand for it.[3]

§ 4. We may now pass to consider the case of *joint products* : *Joint*
i.e. of things which cannot easily be produced separately; but are *supply.*
joined in a common origin, and may therefore be said to have a

---

[1] See above, III. IV. 2, 4.   [2] See III. v.
[3] Thus, let a factor of production have three uses. Let d_1d_1' be the demand
curve for it in its first use.   From N any point on
Oy draw Np_1 horizontally to cut d_1d_1' in p_1; then
Np_1 is the amount that is demanded for the first
use at price ON. Produce Np_1 to p_2, and further
on to P making p_1p_2 and p_2P of such lengths as to
represent the amounts of the factor demanded at
price ON for the second and third uses respectively.
As N moves along Oy let p_2 trace out the curve d_2d_2'
and let P trace out the curve DD'. Thus d_2d_2'
would be the demand curve for the factor if it
had only its first and second uses. DD' is its
demand curve for all three uses.   It is immaterial
in what order we take the several uses. In the
case represented, the demand for the second use
begins at a lower price and that for the third use
begins at a higher price than does the demand for
the first use. (See Mathematical Note XVII.)

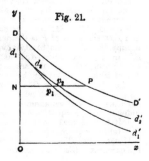

Fig. 21.

M

V, VI, 4. *joint supply*, such as beef and hides, or wheat and straw.[1] This case corresponds to that of things which have a joint demand, and it may be discussed almost in the same words, by merely substituting " demand " for " supply," and *vice versâ*. And there is a joint demand for things joined in a common destination : so there is a joint supply of things which have a common origin. The single supply of the common origin is split up into so many derived supplies of the things that proceed from it.[2]

For instance, since the repeal of the Corn Laws much of the wheat consumed in England has been imported, of course without any straw. This has caused a scarcity and a consequent rise in the price of straw, and the farmer who grows wheat looks to the straw for a great part of the value of the crop. The value of straw then is high in countries which import wheat, and low in those which export wheat. In the same way the price of mutton in the wool-producing districts of Australia was at one time very low. The wool was exported, the meat had to be consumed at home ; and as there was no great demand for it, the price of the wool had to defray almost the whole of the joint expenses of production of the wool and the meat. Afterwards the low price of meat gave a stimulus to the

----

[1] Professor Dewsnup (*American Economic Review, Supplement*, 1914, p. 89) suggests that things should be described as joint products, when their " total costs of production by a single plant are less than the sum of the costs of their production by separate plants." This definition is less general than that reached at the end of this section ; but it is convenient for some special uses.

[2] If it is desired to isolate the relations of demand and supply for a joint product, the derived supply price is found in just the same way as the derived demand price for a factor of production was found in the parallel case of demand. Other things must be assumed to be equal (that is, the supply schedule for the whole process of production must be assumed to remain in force and so must the demand schedule for each of the joint products except that to be isolated). The derived supply price is then found by the rule that it must equal the excess of the supply price for the whole process of production over the sum of the demand prices of all the other joint products ; the prices being taken throughout with reference to corresponding amounts.

We may again illustrate by a simple example in which it is assumed that the relative amounts of the two joint products are unalterable. Let SS' be the supply curve for bullocks which yield meat and leather in fixed quantities ; dd' the demand curve for their carcases, that is, for the meat derived from them. M being any point on Ox draw Mp vertically to cut dd' in p, and produce it to P so that pP represents the demand price for OM hides. Then MP is the demand price for OM bullocks, and DD' the locus of P is the demand curve for bullocks : it may be called the total demand curve. Let DD' cut SS' in A ; and draw AaB as in the figure. Then in equilibrium OB bullocks are produced and sold at price BA of which Ba goes for the carcase and aA for the hide.

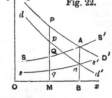

Fig. 22.

Let MP cut SS' in Q. From QM cut off Qq equal to Pp ; then q is a point on the derived supply curve for carcases. For if we assume that the selling price of OM hides is always equal to the corresponding demand price Pp, it follows that since it costs QM to produce each of OM bullocks there remains a price $QM - Pp$, that is qM, to be borne by each of the OM carcases. Then ss' the locus of q, and dd' are the supply and demand curves for carcases. (See Mathematical Note XVIII.)

industries preserving meat for exportation, and now its price in V, VI, 5.
Australia is higher.

There are very few cases of joint products the cost of production If the proof both of which together is exactly the same as that of one of them portions
of joint
alone. So long as any product of a business has a market value, products
can be
it is almost sure to have devoted to it some special care and expense, modified,
which would be diminished, or dispensed with if the demand for
that product were to fall very much. Thus, for instance, if straw
were valueless, farmers would exert themselves more than they do
to make the ear bear as large a proportion as possible to the stalk.
Again, the importation of foreign wool has caused English sheep to be
adapted by judicious crossing and selection so as to develop heavy
weights of good meat at an early age, even at the expense of some
deterioration of their wool. It is only when one of two things produced by the same process is valueless, unsaleable, and yet does not
involve any expense for its removal, that there is no inducement to
attempt to alter its amount; and, it is only in these exceptional their
cases that we have no means of assigning its separate supply price several
costs may
to each of the joint products. For when it is possible to modify the be dis-
proportions of these products, we can ascertain what part of the covered.
whole expense of the process of production would be saved, by so
modifying these proportions as slightly to diminish the amount of one
of the joint products without affecting the amounts of the others.
That part of the expense is the expense of production of the marginal
element of that product; it is the supply price of which we are in
search.[1]

But these are exceptional cases. It more frequently happens
that a business, or even an industry, finds its advantage in using a
good deal of the same plant, technical skill, and business organization for several classes of products. In such cases the cost of anything used for several purposes has to be defrayed by its fruits in
all of them : but there is seldom any rule of nature to determine
either the relative importance of these uses, or the proportions in
which the total cost should be distributed among them : much
depends on the changing features of markets.[2]

§ 5. We may pass to the problem of *composite supply* which is *Composite*
analogous to that of composite demand. A demand can often be *supply.*
satisfied by any one of several routes, according to the principle of
substitution. These various routes are rivals or competitiors with
one another; and the corresponding supplies of commodities are

---

[1] See Mathematical Note XIX.
[2] A little more is said on this subject in the next chapter : it is discussed fully
in the forthcoming work on *Industry and Trade.*

V, VI, 5.   *rival*, or *competitive* supplies relatively to one another. But in relation to the demand they co-operate with one another; being " compounded " into the total supply that meets the demand.[1]

If the causes which govern their production are nearly the same, they may for many purposes be treated as one commodity.[2] For instance, beef and mutton may be treated as varieties of one commodity for many purposes; but they must be treated as separate for others, as for instance for those in which the question of the supply of wool enters. Rival things are however often not finished commodities, but factors of production : for instance, there are many rival fibres which are used in making ordinary printing paper. We have just noticed how the fierce action of derived demand for one of several complementary supplies, as *e.g.* for the supply of plasterers' labour, was liable to be moderated, when the demand was met by competitive supply of a rival thing, which could be substituted for it.[3]

---

[1] The latter phrase " competing commodities " is used by Prof. Fisher in his brilliant *Mathematical Investigations in the theory of value and prices*, which throw much light on the subjects discussed in the present chapter.

[2] Comp. Jevons, *l. c.* pp. 145, 6. See also above, footnotes on pp. 84, 87.

[3] The want which all the rivals tend to satisfy is met by a composite supply, the total supply at any price being the sum of the partial supplies at that price.

Thus, for instance, N being any point on Oy draw Nq_1q_2Q parallel to Ox such that Nq_1, q_1q_2 and q_2Q are respectively the amounts of the first, second and third of those rivals which can be supplied at the price ON. Then NQ is the total composite supply at that price, and the locus of Q is the total supply curve of the means of satisfying the want in question. Of course the units of the several things which are rivals must be so taken that each of them satisfies the same amount of the want. In the case represented in the figure small quantities of the first rival can be put on the market at a price too low to call forth any supply of the other two, and small quantities of the second at a price too low to call forth any of the third. (See Mathematical Note XX.)

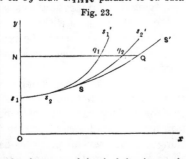

Fig. 23.

Continued rivalry is as a rule possible only when none of the rivals has its supply governed by the law of increasing return. The equilibrium is stable only when none of them is able to drive the others out; and this is the case when all of them conform to the law of diminishing return; because then if one did obtain a temporary advantage and its use increased, its supply price would rise, and then the others would begin to undersell it. But if one of them conformed to the law of increasing return, the rivalry would soon cease; for whenever it happened to gain a temporary advantage over its rivals its increased use would lower its supply price and therefore increase its sale—its supply price would then be further lowered, and so on : thus its advantage over its rivals would be continually increased until it had driven them out of the field. It is true that there are apparent exceptions to this rule; and things which conform to the law of increasing return do sometimes seem to remain for a long time in the field as rivals : such is the case perhaps with different kinds of sewing machines and of electric lights. But in these cases the things do not really satisfy the same wants, they appeal to slightly different needs or tastes; there is still some difference of opinion as to their relative merits; or else perhaps some of them are patented or in some other way have become the monopoly of particular firms. In

§ 6. All the four chief problems which have been discussed in this chapter have some bearing on the causes that govern the value of almost every commodity : and many of the most important cross connections between the values of different commodities are not obvious at first sight.

Thus when charcoal was generally used in making iron, the price of leather depended in some measure on that of iron; and the tanners petitioned for the exclusion of foreign iron in order that the demand on the part of English iron smelters for oak charcoal might cause the production of English oak to be kept up, and thus prevent oak bark from becoming dear.[1] This instance may serve to remind us of the way in which an excessive demand for a thing may cause its sources of supply to be destroyed, and thus render scarce any joint products that it may have : for the demand for wood on the part of the ironmakers led to a relentless destruction of many forests in England. Again, an excessive demand for lamb was assigned as a cause of the prevailing scarcity of sheep some years ago; while some argued on the contrary that the better the price to be got for spring lamb sold to the rich, the more profitable would be the production of sheep, and the cheaper would mutton be for the people. The fact is that an increase of demand may have opposite effects according as it does or does not act so suddenly as to prevent producers from adapting their action to it.

Again, the development of railways and other means of communication for the benefit of one trade, as for instance wheat growing in some parts of America and silver mining in others, greatly lowers some of the chief expenses of production of nearly every other product of those districts. Again, the prices of soda, and bleaching materials and other products of industries, the chief raw material of which is salt, move up and down relatively to one another with almost every improvement in the various processes which are used in those industries; and every change in those prices affects the prices of many other goods, for the various products of the salt industries are more or less important factors in many branches of manufacture.

Again, cotton and cotton-seed oil are joint products, and the recent fall in the price of cotton is largely due to the improved manufacture and uses of cotton-seed oil : and further, as the history

such cases custom and the force of advertising may keep many rivals in the field for a long time; particularly if the producers of those things which are really the best in proportion to their expenses of production are not able effectively to advertise and push their wares by travellers and other agencies.

[1] Toynbee (*Industrial Revolution*, p. 80).

V, VI, 6. of the cotton famine shows, the price of cotton largely affects that of wool, linen and other things of its own class; while cotton-seed oil is ever opening up new rivalries with things of its own class. Again, many new uses have been found for straw in manufacture; and these inventions are giving value to straw that used to be burnt in the West of America, and tend to hinder the rise in the marginal cost of producing wheat.[1]

[1] Again, since sheep and oxen compete for the use of land, leather and cloth compete in indirect demand for the use of a factor of production. But also in the upholsterer's shop they compete as supplying means for meeting the same want. There is thus a composite demand on the part of upholsterer and shoemaker for leather; and also for cloth when the upper part of a shoe is made of cloth : the shoe offers a joint demand for cloth and leather, they offering complementary supplies : and so on, in endless complications. See Mathematical Note XXI. The Austrian doctrine of " imputed value " has something in common with that of derived value given in this chapter. Whichever phrase be used, it is important that we should recognize the continuity between the old doctrine of value and the new; and that we should treat imputed or derived values merely as elements which take their place with many others in the broad problem of distribution and exchange. The new phrases merely give the means of applying to the ordinary affairs of life, some of that precision of expression which is the special property of mathematical language. Producers have always to consider how the demand for any raw material in which they are interested is dependent on the demand for the things in making which it is used, and how it is influenced by every change that affects them; and this is really a special case of the problem of ascertaining the efficient strength of any one of the forces, which contribute to a common result. In mathematical language this common result is called a *function* of the various forces : and the (marginal) contribution, which any of them is making to it, is represented by the (small) change in the result which would result from a (small) change in that force; that is by the *differential coefficient* of the result with regard to that force. In other words, the imputed value, or the derived value of a factor of production, if used for only one product, is the differential coefficient of that product with regard to that factor; and so on in successive complications, as indicated in Notes XIV.–XXI. of the Mathematical Appendix. (Some objections to parts of Prof. Wieser's doctrine of imputed values are well urged by Prof. Edgeworth, *Economic Journal*, Vol. v. pp. 279–85.)

CHAPTER VII

PRIME AND TOTAL COST IN RELATION TO JOINT PRODUCTS. COST OF MARKETING. INSURANCE AGAINST RISK. COST OF REPRODUCTION

§ 1. WE may now return to the consideration of prime and supplementary costs, with special reference to the proper distribution of the latter between the joint products of a business.

It often happens that a thing made in one branch of a business is used as a raw material in another, and then the question of the relative profitableness of the two branches can be accurately ascertained only by an elaborate system of book-keeping by double entry; though in practice it is more common to rely on rough estimates made by an almost instinctive guess. Some of the best illustrations of this difficulty are found in agriculture, especially when the same farm combines permanent pasture and arable land worked on long rotation.[1]

Another difficult case is that of the shipowner who has to apportion the expenses of his ship between heavy goods and goods that are bulky but not heavy. He tries, as far as may be, to get a mixed cargo of both kinds; and an important element in the struggle for existence of rival ports is the disadvantage under which those ports lie which are able to offer a cargo only of bulky or only of heavy goods : while a port whose chief exports are weighty but not bulky, attracts to its neighbourhood industries which make for export goods that can be shipped from it at low freights. The Staffordshire Potteries, for example, owe part of their success to the low freights at which their goods are carried by ships sailing from the Mersey with iron and other heavy cargoes.

But there is free competition in the shipowning trade, and it has great powers of variation as regards the size and shape of ships, the routes which they take, and the whole method of trading; and thus in many ways the general principle can be applied, that the relative proportions of the joint products of a business should be so modified that the marginal expenses of production of either product

V. VII, 1. Supplementary costs of joint products. Difficulty arising when one branch of a business supplies a raw material to another. Difficulties as to the joint products of the same business, are often overcome through the power of varying the details of the plan of production.

---

[1] There is scope for applications of mathematical or semi-mathematical analyses, such as are indicated in the last chapter, to some of the chief practical difficulties of book-keeping by double entry in different trades.

V, vii, 2. should be equal to its marginal demand price.[1]   Or, in other words, the amount of carrying power for each kind of cargo has a constant tendency to move towards equilibrium at a point at which the demand price for that amount in a normal state of trade is just sufficient to cover the expenses of providing it; these expenses being reckoned so as to include not only its (money) prime cost, but also all those general expenses of the business which are in the long run incurred on its account, whether directly or indirectly.[2]

A first approximation is sometimes got by treating supplementary as proportional to prime cost.

In some branches of manufacture it is customary to make a first approximation to the total cost of producing any class of goods, by assuming that their share of the general expenses of the business is proportionate either to their prime cost, or to the special labour bill that is incurred in making them.   Corrections can then be made to meet such cases as those of goods which require either more or less than an average share of space or light, or of the use of expensive machinery; and so on.

§ 2. There are two elements of the general expenses of a business, the sharing of which between the different branches requires some special attention.   They are the expense of marketing and that of insurance against risk.

The difficulty of assigning to each branch of a business its share of the expenses of marketing

Some kinds of goods are easily marketed; there is a steady demand for them, and it is always safe to make them for stock. But for that very reason competition cuts their price " very fine," and does not allow a large margin above the direct cost of making them.   Sometimes the tasks of making and selling them can be rendered almost automatic, so as to require very little to be charged on their account under the heads of the expenses of management and marketing.   But in practice it is not uncommon to charge such goods with even less than the small share that would properly fall to them, and to use them as a means of obtaining and maintaining a business connection, that will facilitate the marketing of other classes of goods, the production of which cannot so well be reduced to routine; for as to these there is not so close a competition.   Manufacturers, especially in trades connected with furniture and dress, and retailers in almost all trades, frequently find it best to use certain of their goods as a means of advertising others, and to

---

[1] Compare ch. vi. § 4.

[2] Of course this does not apply to railway rates.   For a railway company having little elasticity as to its methods of working, and often not much competition from outside, has no inducement to endeavour to adjust the charges which it makes for different kinds of traffic to their cost to itself.   In fact though it may ascertain the prime cost in each case easily enough, it cannot determine accurately what are the relative total costs of fast and slow traffic, of short and long distance traffic, of light and heavy traffic; nor again of extra traffic when its lines and its trains are crowded and when they are nearly empty.

charge the first with less and the second with more than their V, vii, 2.
proportionate share of Supplementary expenses. In the former
class they put those goods which are so uniform in character and so
largely consumed that nearly all purchasers know their value well,
in the second those with regard to which purchasers think more of
consulting their fancy than of buying at the lowest possible price.

All difficulties of this kind are much increased by that instability becomes
of supply price, which results whenever the tendency to increasing very great
return is acting strongly. We have seen that in seeking the normal law of
supply price in such cases we must select as representative a business return
which is managed with normal ability and so as to get its fair share acts
of the economies, both internal and external, resulting from indus- strongly;
trial organization : also that these economies, though they fluctuate
with the fortunes of particular businesses, yet increase generally
when the aggregate production increases. Now it is obvious that if a
manufacturer makes a commodity the increased production of which
would put largely increased internal economies within his reach, it is
worth his while to sacrifice a great deal in order to push its sales in a
new market. If he has a large capital, and the commodity is one
in much demand, his expenditure for this purpose may be very great,
even exceeding that which he devotes directly to the manufacture :
and if, as is likely, he is pushing at the same time several other
commodities, nothing more than a very rough guess can be made
as to what share of this expenditure should be charged to the sales of
each of them in the current year, and what share should be charged
to the connection which he is endeavouring to build up for them in
the future.

In fact when the production of a commodity conforms to the law especially
of increasing return in such a way as to give a very great advantage when the
to large producers, it is apt to fall almost entirely into the hands of a falls into
few large firms; and then the normal marginal supply price cannot of a few
be isolated on the plan just referred to, because that plan assumes large
the existence of a great many competitors with businesses of all firms.
sizes, some of them being young and some old, some in the ascending
and some in the descending phase. The production of such a commodity really partakes in a great measure of the nature of a monopoly; and its price is likely to be so much influenced by the incidents
of the campaign between rival producers, each struggling for an
extension of territory, as scarcely to have a true normal level.

Economic progress is constantly offering new facilities for Economies
marketing goods at a distance : it not only lowers cost of carriage, in produc-
but what is often more important, it enables producers and consumers tion are

V, VII, 3.

often balanced by local facilities for marketing.

in distant places to get in touch with one another. In spite of this, the advantages of the producer who lives on the spot are very great in many trades; they often enable him to hold his own against competitors at a distance whose methods of production are more economical. He can sell in his own neighbourhood as cheaply as they can, because though the cost of making is greater for his goods than for theirs, he escapes much of the cost which they incur for marketing. But time is on the side of the more economic methods of production; his distant competitors will gradually get a stronger footing in the place, unless he or some new man adopts their improved methods.

It remains to make a closer study of the relation in which insurance against the risks of a business stands to the supply price of any particular commodity produced in it.

An insurance cannot be effected at moderate rates against all business risks.

§ 3. The manufacturer and the trader commonly insure against injury by fire and loss at sea; and the premiums which they pay are among the general expenses, a share of which has to be added to the prime cost in order to determine the total cost of their goods. But no insurance can be effected against the great majority of business risks.

Even as regards losses by fire and sea, insurance companies have to allow for possible carelessness and fraud; and must therefore, independently of all allowances for their own expenses and profits, charge premiums considerably higher than the true equivalent of the risks run by the buildings or the ships of those who manage their affairs well. The injury done by fire or sea however is likely, if it occurs at all, to be so very great that it is generally worth while to pay this extra charge; partly for special trade reasons, but chiefly because the total utility of increasing wealth increases less than in proportion to its amount. But the greater part of business risks are so inseparably connected with the general management of the business that an insurance company which undertook them would really make itself responsible for the business : and in consequence every firm has to act as its own insurance office with regard to them. The charges to which it is put under this head are part of its general expenses, and a share of them has to be added to the prime cost of each of its products.

But here there are two difficulties. In some cases insurance against risk is apt to be left out of account altogether, in others it is apt to be counted twice over. Thus a large shipowner sometimes declines to insure his ships with the underwriters : and sets aside part at least of the premiums that he might have paid to them, to

build up an insurance fund of his own. But he must still, when V, VII, 4.
calculating the total cost of working a ship, add to its prime cost a *Caution*
charge on account of insurance. And he must do the same thing, *against*
in some form or other, with regard to those risks against which he *overlook-*
ing certain
could not buy an insurance policy on reasonable terms even if he *insurance*
expenses,
wanted to. At times, for instance, some of his ships will be idle in
port, or will earn only nominal freights : and to make his business
remunerative in the long run he must, in some form or other, charge
his successful voyages with an insurance premium to make up for his
losses on those which are unsuccessful.

In general, however, he does this, not by making a formal entry *and*
in his accounts under a separate head, but by the simple plan of *against*
counting
taking the average of successful and unsuccessful voyages together; *others*
and when that has once been done, insurance against these risks *twice over.*
cannot be entered as a separate item in cost of production, without
counting the same thing twice over. Having decided to run these
risks himself, he is likely to spend a little more than the average of his
competitors, in providing against their occurrence; and this extra
expense enters in the ordinary way into his balance-sheet. It is
really an insurance premium in another form; and therefore he must
not count insurance against this part of the risk separately, for then
he would be counting it twice over.[1]

When a manufacturer has taken the average of his sales of dress
materials over a long time, and bases his future action on the results
of his past experience, he has already allowed for the risk that the
machinery will be depreciated by new inventions rendering it nearly
obsolete, and for the risk that his goods will be depreciated by
changes in fashion. If he were to allow separately for insurance
against these risks, he would be counting the same thing twice
over.[2]

§ 4. Thus, though when we have counted up the average receipts *But un-*
of a risky trade, we must not make a separate full allowance for *'certainty*

---

[1] Again, certain insurance companies in America take risks against fire in factories
at very much less than the ordinary rates, on condition that some prescribed precautions are taken, such as providing automatic sprinklers and making the walls and
floor solid. The expense incurred in these arrangements is really an insurance
premium; and care must be taken not to count it twice over. A factory which
undertakes its own risks against fire will have to add to the prime cost of its goods an
allowance for insurance at a lower rate, if it is arranged on this plan, than if built in
the ordinary way.

[2] Again, when a farmer has calculated the expenses of raising any particular crop
with reference to an average year, he must not count in addition insurance against the
risk that the season may be bad, and the crop a failure : for in taking an average
year, he has already set off the chances of exceptionally good and bad seasons against
one another. When the earnings of a ferryman have been calculated on the average
of a year, allowance has already been made for the risk that he may sometimes have to
cross the stream with an empty boat.

V, vii, 5.
—
s an evil
n itself,
insurance against risk; though there may be something to be allowed as a charge on account of uncertainty. It is true that an adventurous occupation, such as gold mining, has special attractions for some people : the deterrent force of risks of loss in it is less than the attractive force of chances of great gain, even when the value of the latter estimated on the actuarial principle is much less than that of the former; and as Adam Smith pointed out, a risky trade, in which there is an element of romance, often becomes so overcrowded that the average earnings in it are lower than if there were no risks to be run.[1] But in the large majority of cases the influence of risk is in the opposite direction; a railway stock that is certain to pay four per cent. will sell for a higher price than one which is equally likely to pay one or seven per cent. or any intermediate amount.

ind an
iverage
;ain
;enerally
;ounts for
ess, the
nore un-
ertain the
lements
if which
t is
nade up.
Every trade then has its own peculiarities, but in most cases the evils of uncertainty count for something, though not very much : in some cases a slightly higher average price is required to induce a given outlay, if that average is the mean of widely divergent and uncertain results, than if the adventurer may reckon confidently on a return that differs but little from that average. To the average price therefore we must add a recompense for uncertainty, if that is unusually great; though if we added insurance against risk we should be counting the greater part of that twice over.[2]

To
ubstitute
ost of
eproduc-
ion for
ost of
roduction
n the
heory of
iormal
ralues is
o make
io real
hange;
§ 5. This discussion of the risks of trade has again brought before us the fact that the value of a thing, though it tends to equal its normal (money) cost of production, does not coincide with it at any particular time, save by accident. Carey, observing this, suggested that we should speak of value in relation to (money) cost of reproduction instead of in relation to cost of production.

The suggestion has, however, no significance so far as normal values are concerned. For normal cost of production and normal cost of reproduction are convertible terms; and no real change is made by saying that the normal value of a thing tends to equal its normal (money) cost of reproduction instead of its normal (money) cost of production. The former phrase is less simple than the latter, but means the same thing.

ind
hough
he market
ralue of
thing is
ometimes
iearer
ost of re-
And no valid argument for the change can be founded on the fact, which may be readily admitted, that there are some few cases in which the market value of a thing is nearer its cost of reproduction than the cost that was actually incurred in producing that particular thing. The present price of an iron ship for instance, made before

---

[1] *Wealth of Nations*, Book i. ch. x.

[2] The evils resulting from the uncertainty involved in great business risks are well shown by von Thünen (*Isolirter Staat*, II. i. p. 82).

the great recent improvements in the manufacture of iron, might
diverge less from the cost of reproducing it, that is of producing
another just like it by modern methods, than from that which was
actually incurred in producing it. But the price of the old ship
would be less than the cost of reproduction of the ship, because
the art of designing ships has improved as fast as that of manufacturing iron; and moreover steel has displaced iron as the material of
shipbuilding. It may still be urged that the price of the ship is
equal to that of producing a ship, which would be equally serviceable,
on a modern plan and by modern methods. But that would not be
the same thing as saying that the value of the ship is equal to its cost
of reproduction; and, as a matter of fact, when, as often happens,
an unexpected scarcity of ships causes freights to increase very
rapidly, those who are anxious to reap the harvest of profitable trade,
will pay for a ship in sailing order a price much above that for which
a shipbuilding firm would contract to produce another equally good
and deliver it some time hence. Cost of reproduction exerts little
direct influence on value, save when purchasers can conveniently
wait for the production of new supplies.

Marginal note: production than cost of production, it is not governed by cost of reproduction.

Again, there is no connection between cost of reproduction and
price in the case of food in a beleaguered city, of quinine the supply
of which has run short in a fever-stricken island, of a picture by
Raphael, of a book that nobody cares to read, of an armour-clad
ship of obsolete pattern, of fish when the market is glutted, of fish
when the market is nearly empty, of a cracked bell, of a dress
material that has gone out of fashion, or of a house in a deserted
mining village.

*   *   *

The reader, unless already experienced in economic analysis, is
recommended to omit the next seven chapters, and pass at once to
Chapter xv., which contains a brief summary of this Book. It is
true that the four chapters on marginal costs in relation to values,
and especially Chapters viii. and ix., bear upon some difficulties
which are latent in the phrase " the net product of labour "; and
that this phrase is used in Book VI. But the broad explanation of it
given there will suffice provisionally for most purposes; and the
intricacies connected with it may be best appreciated at a somewhat
advanced stage of economic studies.

CHAPTER VIII

MARGINAL COSTS IN RELATION TO VALUES. GENERAL PRINCIPLES

V, VIII, 1.

This and he next hree hapters ontinue he main rgument f chapters V.–VI.

§ 1. This Chapter and the three following are given to a study of the marginal costs of products in relation to the values of those products on the one hand, and on the other hand to the values of the land, machinery, and other appliances used in making them. *The study relates to normal conditions and long period results.* This fact must ever be borne in mind. The market value of anything may be much above or much below the normal cost of production : and the marginal costs of a particular producer at any time may stand in no close relation to marginal costs under normal conditions.[1]

It was indicated at the end of Chapter VI. that no one part of the problem can be isolated from the rest. There are comparatively few things the demand for which is not greatly affected by the demand for other things to the usefulness of which they contribute ; and it may even be said that the demand for the majority of articles of commerce is not direct but is derived from the demand for those commodities to the making of which they contribute, as materials or as implements. And again this demand, because it is so derived, is largely dependent on the supply of other things which will work with them in making those commodities. And again the supply of anything available for use in making any commodity is apt to be greatly influenced by the demand for that thing derived from its uses in making other commodities : and so on. These inter-relations can be and must be ignored in rapid and popular discussions on the business affairs of the world. But no study that makes any claim to thoroughness can escape from a close investigation of them. This requires many things to be borne in mind at the same time : and for that reason economics can never become a simple science.[2]

The contribution which this group of chapters aims at making

---

[1] Numerous objections have been urged against the important place assigned to marginal costs in modern analysis. But it will be found that most of them rely on arguments, in which statements referring to normal conditions and normal value are controverted by statements relating to abnormal or particular conditions.

[2] The reader is referred to the footnote on p. 326 with special reference to the compressed mathematical version of the central problem of value which begins in Note XIV. in the Mathematical Appendix and culminates in Note XXI.

covers little ground : but that ground is difficult : and we shall need
to work over it carefully, and from more than one point of view;
for it is thickly strewn with pitfalls and stumbling blocks. It deals
primarily with the earnings of land, machinery, and other material
agents of production. Its main argument applies to the earnings of
human beings; but they are influenced by some causes which do not
affect the earnings of material agents of production : and the matter
in hand is sufficiently difficult without further complicating it by side
issues.

§ 2. Let us begin by recalling the action of the principle of
substitution. In the modern world nearly all the means of production pass through the hands of employers and other business men,
who specialize themselves in organizing the economic forces of the
population. Each of them chooses in every case those factors of
production which seem best for his purpose. And the sum of the
prices which he pays for those factors which he uses is, as a rule, less
than the sum of the prices which he would have to pay for any other
set of factors which could be substituted for them : for, whenever
it appears that this is not the case, he will, as a rule, set to work to
substitute the less expensive arrangement or process.[1]

This statement is in close harmony with such common sayings
of every-day life, as that " everything tends to find its own level,"
that " most men earn just about what they are worth," that " if one
man can earn twice as much as another, that shows that his work is
worth twice as much," that " machinery will displace manual labour
whenever it can do the work cheaper." The principle does not
indeed act without hindrance. It may be restricted by custom or
law, by professional etiquette or trade-union regulation : it may be
weakened by want of enterprise, or it may be softened by a generous
unwillingness to part with old associates. But it never ceases to act,
and it permeates all the economic adjustments of the modern world.

Thus there are some kinds of field work for which horse-power is
clearly more suitable than steam-power, and *vice versâ*. If we may
now suppose that there have been no great recent improvements in
horse or steam machinery, and that therefore the experience of the
past has enabled farmers gradually to apply the law of substitution;
then, on this supposition the application of steam-power will have
been pushed just so far that any further use of it in the place of
horse-power would bring no net advantage. There will however
remain a margin on which they could be *indifferently* applied (as

---

[1] Compare V. III. 3; and V. IV. 3, 4; and Note XIV. in the Mathematical
Appendix.

v, viii, 3. Jevons would have said); and on that margin the net efficiency of either in adding to the money value of the total product will be proportionate to the cost of applying it.[1]

Similarly, if there are two methods of obtaining the same result, one by skilled and the other by unskilled labour, that one will be adopted which is the more efficient in proportion to its cost. There will be a margin on which either will be indifferently applied.[2] On that line the efficiency of each will be in proportion to the price paid for it, account being taken of the special circumstances of different districts and of different workshops in the same district. In other words, the wages of skilled and unskilled labour will bear to one another the same ratio that their efficiencies do at the margin of indifference.

Again, there will be a rivalry between hand-power and machine-power similar to that between two different kinds of hand-power or two different kinds of machine-power. Thus hand-power has the advantage for some operations, as, for instance, for weeding out valuable crops that have an irregular growth; horse-power in its turn has a clear advantage for weeding an ordinary turnip field; and the application of each of them will be pushed in each district till any further use of it would bring no net advantage there. On the margin of indifference between hand-power and horse-power their prices must be proportionate to their efficiency; and thus the influence of substitution will tend to establish a direct relation between the wages of labour and the price that has to be paid for horse-power.

The *net product* at the margin.

§ 3. As a rule many kinds of labour, of raw material, of machinery and other plant, and of business organization, both internal and external, go to the production of a commodity : and the advantages of economic freedom are never more strikingly manifest than when a business man endowed with genius is trying experiments, at his own risk, to see whether some new method, or combination of old methods, will be more efficient than the old. Every business man indeed, according to his energy and ability, is constantly endeavouring to obtain a notion of the relative efficiency of every agent of

[1] This margin will vary with local circumstances, as well as with the habits, inclinations, and resources of individual farmers. The difficulty of applying steam machinery in small fields and on rugged ground is overcome more generally in those districts in which labour is scarce than in those in which it is plentiful; especially if, as is probable, coal is cheaper, and the feed of horses dearer in the former than the latter.

[2] Skilled manual labour being generally used for special orders and for things of which not many are required of the same pattern; and unskilled labour aided by specialized machinery being used for others. The two methods are to be seen side by side on similar work in every large workshop : but the position of the line between them will vary a little from one workshop to another.

production that he employs; as well as of others that might possibly V, VIII, 4.
be substituted for some of them. He estimates as best he can how
much *net product* (*i.e.* net addition to the value of his total product)
will be caused by a certain extra use of any one agent; *net* that is
after deducting for any extra expenses that may be indirectly caused
by the change, and adding for any incidental savings. He endeavours to employ each agent up to that margin at which its net
product would no longer exceed the price he would have to pay for it.
He works generally by trained instinct rather than formal calculation; but his processes are substantially similar to those indicated
in our study of derived demand; and, from another point of view,
they may be described as those which might be reaped by a complex
and refined system of book-keeping by double entry.[1]

We have already followed some simple estimates of this sort. Illustra-
We have noticed, for instance, how the proportion of hops and malt tion of
in ale can be varied, how the extra price which can be got for ale by in which
increasing the quantity of hops in it is a representative of the causes product
which govern the demand price for hops. Assuming that no of an
further trouble or expense of any kind is involved by this additional production
use of hops, and that the expediency of using this extra amount is may be
doubtful, the extra value thus given to the ale is the marginal net estimated.
product of the hops of which we are in search. In this case, as in
most others, the net product is an improvement in quality or a
general contribution to the value of the product; it is not a definite
part of the produce which can be separated from the rest. But in
exceptional instances that can be done.[2]

§ 4. The notion of the marginal employment of any agent of The
production implies a possible tendency to diminishing return from diminish-
its increased employment. from dis-

Excessive applications of any means to the attainment of any tionate
end are indeed sure to yield diminishing returns in every branch of use of
business; and, one may say, in all the affairs of life. We may take of production, is

---

[1] The changes, which he desires, may be such as could only be made on a large
scale; as for instance the substitution of steam-power for hand-power in a certain
factory; and in that case there would be a certain element of uncertainty and risk
in the change. Such breaches of continuity are however inevitable both in production
and consumption if we regard the action of single individuals. But as there is a
continuous demand in a large market for hats and watches and wedding cakes, though
no individual buys many of them (see III. III. 5), so there will always be trades in
which small businesses are most economically conducted without steam-power, and
larger businesses with; while businesses of intermediate size are on the margin.
Again, even in large establishments in which steam is already in use, there will always
be some things done by hand-power which are done by steam-power elsewhere; and
so on.
[2] See p. 320, and Mathematical Note XVI. See also other illustrations in V. VI.,
VII. A further illustration of the relation between the wages of the marginal shepherd,
and the net product of his labour will be worked out in detail in VI. I. 7.

V, viii, 4.

akin to,
but dis-
tinct from,
Diminish-
ing Return
of land in
general to
more
intensive
cultiva-
tion, how-
ever ap-
propriate.

some additional examples of a principle that has already been illustrated.[1] In the manufacture of sewing machines some parts may well be made of cast iron; for others a common kind of steel will suffice; there are yet others for which a specially expensive steel-compound is needed; and all parts should be finished off more or less smoothly, so that the machine may work easily. Now if any one devoted a disproportionate care and expense to the selection of materials for the less important uses, it might truly be said that that expenditure was yielding a rapidly diminishing return; and that he would have done better to give some of it to making his machines work smoothly, or even to producing more machines : and the case might be even worse if he devoted an excessive expenditure to mere brilliancy of finish, and put low grade metal to work for which a higher grade was needed.

This consideration seems at first to simplify economic problems; but on the contrary it is a chief source of difficulty and confusion. For though there is some analogy between all these various tendencies to diminishing return, they yet are not identical. Thus the diminishing return which arises from an ill-proportioned application of the various agents of production into a particular task has little in common with that broad tendency to the pressure of a crowded and growing population on the means of subsistence. The great classical Law of Diminishing Return has its chief application, not to any one particular crop, but to all the chief food crops. It takes for granted that farmers raise, as a rule, those crops for which their land and other resources are best adapted, account being taken of the relative demands for the several crops; and that they distribute their resources appropriately between different routes. It does not attribute to them unlimited intelligence and wisdom, but it assumes that, taking one with another, they have shown a reasonable amount of care and discretion in the distribution of these resources. It refers to a country the whole land of which is already in the hands of active business men, who can supplement their own capital by loans from banks wherever they can show it is likely to be well applied; and asserts that an increase in the total amount of capital applied to agriculture in that country will yield diminishing returns of produce in general. This statement is akin to, but yet quite distinct from, the statement that if any farmer makes a bad distribution of his resources between different plans of cultivation, he will get a markedly diminishing return from those elements of expenditure which he has driven to excess.

[1] See V. iv. 4; see also the note on von Thünen, below, p. 433.

For instance, in any given case, there is a certain proportion between the amounts which may with best advantage be spent on ploughing and harrowing, or manuring. There might be some differences of opinion on the matter, but only within narrow limits. An inexperienced person who ploughed many times over land, which was already in fairly good mechanical condition, while he gave it little or none of the manure which it was craving, would be generally condemned as having so over applied ploughing as to make it yield a rapidly diminishing return. But this result of the mis-application of resources has no very close connection with the tendency of agriculture in an old country to yield a diminishing return to a general increase of resources well applied in cultivation : and indeed exactly parallel cases can be found of a diminishing return to particular resources when applied in undue proportion, even in industries which yield an increasing return to increased applications of capital and labour when appropriately distributed.[1]

§ 5. The part played by the net product at the margin of production in the modern doctrine of Distribution is apt to be misunderstood. In particular many able writers have supposed that it represents the marginal use of a thing as *governing* the value of the

V, VIII, 5.

Marginal uses and costs do not govern value, but are

---

[1] See above IV. III. 8; and Carver, *Distribution of Wealth*, ch. II., and above footnotes on pp. 266. Mr. J. A. Hobson is a vigorous and suggestive writer on the realistic and social sides of economics : but, as a critic of Ricardian doctrines, he is perhaps apt to underrate the difficulty of the problems which he discusses. He argues that if the marginal application of any agent of production be curtailed, that will so disorganize production that every other agent will be working to less effect than before; and that therefore the total resulting loss will include not only the true marginal product of that agent, but also a part of the products due to the other agents : but he appears to have overlooked the following points :—(1) There are forces constantly at work tending so to readjust the distribution of resources between their different uses, that any maladjustment will be arrested before it has gone far : and the argument does not profess to apply to exceptional cases of violent maladjustment. (2) When the adjustment is such as to give the best results, a slight change in the proportions in which they are applied diminishes the efficiency of that adjustment by a quantity which is very small relatively to that change—in technical language it is of " the second order of smalls "—; and it may therefore be neglected relatively to that change. (In pure mathematical phrase, efficiency being regarded as a function of the proportions of the agents; when the efficiency is at its maximum, its differential coefficient with regard to any one of these proportions is zero.) A grave error would therefore have been involved, if any allowance had been made for those elements which Mr. Hobson asserts to have been overlooked. (3) In economics, as in physics, changes are generally continuous. Convulsive changes may indeed occur, but they must be dealt with separately : and an illustration drawn from a convulsive change can throw no true light on the processes of normal steady evolution. In the particular problem before us, this precaution is of special importance : for a violent check to the supply of any one agent of production, may easily render the work of all other agents practically useless; and therefore it may inflict a loss out of all proportion to the harm done by a small check to the supply of that agent when applied up to that margin, at which there was doubt whether the extra net product due to a small additional application of it would be remunerative. The study of changes in complex quantitative relations is often vitiated by a neglect of this consideration, to which Mr. Hobson seems to be prone; as indeed is instanced by his remarks on a " marginal shepherd " in *The Industrial System*, p. 110. See Professor Edgeworth's masterly analyses of the two instances mentioned in this note, *Quarterly Journal of Economics*, 1904, p. 167; and *Scientia*, 1910, pp. 95—100.

V, VIII, 6.

governed
together
with value
by the
general
relations
of demand
and
supply.

whole. It is not so; the doctrine says we must *go to the margin to study the action of those forces which govern* the value of the whole: and that is a very different affair. Of course the withdrawal of (say) iron from any of its necessary uses would have just the same influence on its value as its withdrawal from its marginal uses; in the same way as the pressure in a boiler for cooking under high pressure would be affected by the escape of any other steam just as it would by the escape of the steam in one of the safety valves: but in fact the steam does not escape except through the safety valves. In like manner iron, or any other agent of production, is not (under ordinary circumstances) thrown out of use except at points at which its use yields no clear surplus of profit; that is, it is thrown out from its marginal uses only.

Again, the finger of an automatic weighing machine determines, in the sense of *indicating*, the weight sought for. So the escape of steam from a safety valve, governed by a spring representing a pressure of a hundred pounds to the square inch, determines the pressure of steam in the boiler, in the sense of indicating that it has reached a hundred pounds to the inch. The pressure is caused by the heat; the spring in the valve governs the pressure by yielding and letting out some of the steam when its amount is so great, at the existing heat, as to overbear the resistance of the spring.

Similarly, with regard to machinery and other appliances of production made by man, there is a margin through which additional supplies come in after overcoming the resistance of a spring, called " cost of production." For when the supply of those appliances is so small relatively to the demand that the earnings expected from new supplies are more than sufficient to yield normal interest (or profits, if earnings of management are reckoned in) on their cost of production, besides allowing for depreciation, etc., then the valve opens, and the new supplies come in. When the earnings are less than this, the valve remains shut : and as anyhow the existing supply is always in process of slow destruction by use and the lapse of time, the supply is always shrinking when the valve is closed. The valve is that part of the machinery by which the general relations of demand and supply govern value. But marginal uses do not govern value; because they, together with value, are themselves governed by those general relations.

The terms
Interest
and Profits
are
directly
applicable

§ 6. Thus, so long as the resources of an individual producer are in the form of general purchasing power, he will push every investment up to the margin at which he no longer expects from it a higher net return than he could get by investing in some other material, or machine, or advertisement, or in the hire of some additional labour : v, vɪɪɪ, 6. every investment will, as it were, be driven up to a valve which to fluid offers to it a resistance equal to its own expanding force. If he capital; invests in material or in labour, that is soon embodied in some saleable product : the sale replenishes his fluid capital, and that again is invested up to the margin at which any further investment would yield a return so diminished as not to be profitable.

But if he invests in land, or in a durable building or machine, but only the return which he gets from his investment may vary widely indirectly from his expectation. It will be governed by the market for his certain products, which may change its character largely through new assump- inventions, changes in fashion, etc., during the life of a machine, tions to to say nothing of the perpetual life of land. The incomes which he embodi- thus may derive from investments in land and in machinery differ capital. from his individual point of view mainly in the longer life of the land. But in regard to production in general, a dominant difference between the two lies in the fact that the supply of land is fixed (though in a new country, the supply of land utilized in man's service may be increased); while the supply of machines may be increased without limit. And this difference reacts on the individual producer. For if no great new invention renders his machines obsolete, while there is a steady demand for the things made by them, they will be constantly on sale at about their cost of production; and his machines will generally yield him normal profits on that cost of production, with deductions corresponding to their wear and tear.

Thus the rate of interest is a ratio : and the two things which it connects are both sums of money. So long as capital is " free," and the sum of money or general purchasing power over which it gives command is known, the net money income, expected to be derived from it, can be represented at once as bearing a given ratio (four or five or ten per cent.) to that sum. But when the free capital has been invested in a particular thing, its money value cannot as a rule be ascertained except by capitalizing the net income which it will yield : and therefore the causes which govern it are likely to be akin in a greater or less degree to those which govern rents.

We are thus brought to the central doctrine of this part of The economics, viz. :—" That which is rightly regarded as interest on doctrine ' free ' or ' floating ' capital, or on new investments of capital, is of this more properly treated as a sort of rent—a *Quasi-rent*—on old invest- chapters. ments of capital. And there is no sharp line of division between floating capital and that which has been ' sunk ' for a special branch of production, nor between new and old investments of capital;

V, VIII, 6. each group shades into the other gradually.   And thus even the rent
of land is seen, not as a thing by itself, but as the leading species of a
large genus; though indeed it has peculiarities of its own which are
of vital importance from the point of view of theory as well as of
practice." [1]

[1] This statement is reproduced from the Preface to the first edition of the present
volume.

CHAPTER IX

MARGINAL COSTS IN RELATION TO VALUES. GENERAL PRINCIPLES, CONTINUED

§ 1. THE incidents of the tenure of land are so complex : and so many practical issues connected with them have raised controversies on side issues of the problem of value, that it will be well to supplement our previous illustration from land. We may take another from an imaginary commodity so chosen that sharp outlines can be assigned to each stage of the problem, without inviting the objection that such sharp outlines are not found in the actual relations between landlord and tenant. V, IX, 1.

The essential features of rent proper are seen most clearly in an imaginary instance,

But before entering on this, we may prepare the way for using, as we go, illustrations drawn from the incidence of taxation to throw side-lights on the problem of value. For indeed a great part of economic science is occupied with the diffusion throughout the community of economic changes which primarily affect some particular branch of production or consumption; and there is scarcely any economic principle which cannot be aptly illustrated by a discussion of the shifting of the effects of some tax " forwards," *i.e.* towards the ultimate consumer, and away from the producer of raw material and implements of production; or else in the opposite direction, " backwards." But especially is this true of the class of problems now under discussion.[1]

aided by illustrations drawn from the incidence of taxes.

It is a general principle that if a tax impinges on anything used by one set of persons in the production of goods or services to be disposed of to other persons, the tax tends to check production. This tends to shift a large part of the burden of the tax forwards on to consumers, and a small part backwards on to those who supply the requirements of this set of producers. Similarly, a tax on the consumption of anything is shifted in a greater or less degree backwards on to its producer.

Shifting forwards and back-wards.

For instance, an unexpected and heavy tax upon printing would strike hard upon those engaged in the trade, for if they attempted to raise prices much, demand would fall off quickly : but the blow

Incidence of a tax on print-ing.

[1] The substance of this section is reproduced from answers to questions proposed by the Royal Commission on Local Taxation. See [C. 9528], 1899, pp. 112-126.

V, ix, 1.   would bear unevenly on various classes engaged in the trade. Since printing machines and compositors cannot easily find employment out of the trade, the prices of printing machines and wages of compositors would be kept low for some time. On the other hand, the buildings and steam engines, the porters, engineers, and clerks would not wait for their numbers to be adjusted by the slow process of natural decay to the diminished demand; some of them would be quickly at work in other trades, and very little of the burden would stay long on those of them who remained in the trade. A considerable part of the burden, again, would fall on subsidiary industries, such as those engaged in making paper and type; because the market for their products would be curtailed. Authors and publishers would also suffer a little; because they would be forced either to raise the price of books, with a consequent diminution of sales, or to see a greater proportion of their gross receipts swallowed up by costs. Finally, the total turnover of the booksellers would diminish, and they would suffer a little.

A local tax on printing.   So far it has been assumed that the tax spreads its net very wide, and covers every place to which the printing industry in question could be easily transferred. But, if the tax were only local, the compositors would migrate beyond its reach; and the owners of printing houses might bear a larger and not a smaller proportionate share of the burden than those whose resources were more specialized but more mobile. If the local tax were uncompensated by any effect which tended to attract population, part of the burden would be thrown on local bakers, grocers, etc., whose sales would be diminished.

A tax on printing presses.   Next suppose the tax to be levied on printing presses instead of on printed matter. In that case, if the printers had no semi-obsolete presses which they were inclined to destroy or to leave idle, the tax would not strike marginal production : it would not immediately affect the output of printing, nor therefore its price. It would merely intercept some of the earnings of the presses on the way to the owners, and lower the quasi-rents of the presses. But it would not affect the rate of net profits which was needed to induce people to invest fluid capital in presses : and therefore, as the old presses wore out, the tax would add to marginal expenses, that is to expenses which the producer was free to incur or not as he liked, and which he was in doubt whether to incur. Therefore the supply of printing would be curtailed; its price would rise : and new presses would be introduced only up to the margin at which they would be able, in the judgment of printers generally, to pay the tax and yet yield normal profits on the outlay. When this stage had been reached the distribution of the burden of a tax upon presses would henceforth be nearly the same as that of a tax upon printing : excepting only that there would be more inducement to get a great deal of work out of each press. For instance more of the presses might be made to work double shifts; in spite of the fact that night work involves special expenses.

We now pass to apply these principles of shifting of taxes to our main illustration.

§ 2. Let us suppose that a meteoric shower of a few thousand large stones harder than diamonds fell all in one place; so that they were all picked up at once, and no amount of search could find any more. These stones, able to cut every material, would revolutionize many branches of industry; and the owners of them would have a differential advantage in production, that would afford a large producer's surplus. This surplus would be governed wholly by the urgency and volume of the demand for their services on the one hand and the number of the stones on the other hand : it could not be affected by the cost of obtaining a further supply, because none could be had at any price. A cost of production might indeed influence their value indirectly : but it would be the cost of tools made of hard steel and other materials of which the supply can be increased to keep pace with demand. So long as any of the stones were habitually used by intelligent producers for work which could be done equally well by such tools, the value of a stone could not much exceed the cost of producing tools (allowance being made for wear and tear) equally efficient with it in these inferior uses.

A limited stock of large stones harder than diamonds.

The stones, being so hard as not to be affected by wear, would probably be kept in operation during all the working hours of the day. And if their services were very valuable, it might be worth while to keep people working overtime, or even in double or triple shifts, in order to extract the utmost service from them. But the more intensively they were applied, the less net return would be reaped from each additional service forced from them; thus illustrating the law that the intensive working not only of land, but of every other appliance of production is likely to yield a diminishing return if pressed far enough.

The total supply of stones is fixed. But of course any particular manufacturer might obtain almost as many as he liked to pay for : and in the long run he would expect his outlay on them to be returned with interest (or profits, if the remuneration for his own work were not reckoned separately), just in the same way as if he were

The purchaser would expect them to yield interest on their price.

V, IX, 2. buying machinery, the total stock of which could be increased indefinitely, so that its price conformed pretty closely to its cost of production.

But the net income which he actually reaped from them would be governed by the value of their services,

uncontrolled by fresh supplies dependent on cost.

But when he had once bought the stones, changes in the processes of production or of demand for the things made by their aid, might cause the income yielded by them to become twice as great or only half as great as he had expected. In the latter case it would resemble the income derived from a machine, which had not the latest improvements and could earn only half as much as a new machine of equal cost. The values of the stone and of the machine alike would be reached by capitalizing the income which they were capable of earning, and that income would be governed by the net value of the services rendered by them. The income earning power and therefore the value of each would be independent of its own costs of production, but would be governed by the general demand for its products in relation to the general supply of those products. But in the case of the machine that supply would be controlled by the cost of supply of new machines equally efficient with it; and in the case of the stone there would be no such limit, so long as all the stones in existence were employed on work that could not be done by anything else.

This argument may be put in another way. Since any one, who bought stones, would take them from other producers, his purchase would not materially affect the general relations of demand for the services of the stones to the supply of those services. It would not therefore affect the price of the stones; which would still be the capitalized value of the services which they rendered in those uses, in which the need for them was the least urgent: and to say that the purchaser expected normal interest on the price which represented the capitalized value of the services, would be a circular statement that the value of the services rendered by stones is governed by the value of those very services.[1]

---

[1] Such circular reasonings are sometimes nearly harmless : but they always tend to overlay and hide the real issues. And they are sometimes applied to illegitimate uses by company promoters; and by advocates of special interests, who desire to influence the course of legislation in their own favour. For instance a semi-monopolistic business aggregation or trust is often " over-capitalized." To effect this a time is chosen, at which the branch of production with which it is concerned is abnormally prosperous : when perhaps some solid firms are earning fifty per cent. net on their capital in a single year, and thus making up for lean years past and to come in which their receipts will do little more than cover prime costs. Financiers connected with the flotation sometimes even arrange that the businesses to be offered to the public shall have a good many orders to fill at specially favourable prices : the loss falling on themselves, or on other companies which they control. The gains to be secured by semi-monopolistic selling, and possibly by some further economies in production are emphasized : and the stock of the trust is absorbed by the public. If ultimately objection to the conduct of the trust is raised, and especially to the strengthening of its semi-monopolistic position by a high tariff or any other public favour, the answer is

Next let us suppose that the stones were not all found at once but were scattered over the surface of the earth on public ground, and that a laborious search might expect to be rewarded by finding one here and there. Then people would hunt for the stones only up to that point, or margin, at which the probable gain of so doing would in the long run just reward the outlay of labour and capital involved; and in the long run, the normal value of the stones would be such as to maintain equilibrium between demand and supply, the number of the stones gathered annually being in the long run just that for which the normal demand price was equal to the normal supply price. V, IX, 3.
Next sup-
pose that
the supply
of stones
can be
increased
slowly;

Finally, let us bring the case of the stones into accord with that of the lighter machinery and other plant ordinarily used in manufacture, by supposing that the stones were brittle, and were soon destroyed; and that an inexhaustible store existed from which additional supplies could be obtained quickly and certainly at a nearly uniform cost. In this case the value of the stones would always correspond closely to that cost: variations in demand would have but little influence on their price, because even a slight change in price would quickly effect a great change in the stock of them in the market. In this case the income derived from a stone (allowance being made for wear-and-tear) would always adhere closely to interest on its cost of production. and lastly
that it can
be in-
creased
quickly,
and that
the stones
are quickly
worn out.

§ 3. This series of hypotheses stretches continuously from the one extreme in which the income derived from the stones is a rent in the strictest sense of the term, to the other extreme in which it is to be classed rather with interest on free or floating capital. In the first extreme case the stones cannot be worn out or destroyed, and no more can be found. They of course tend to be distributed among the various uses to which they are applicable in such a way that there is no use to which an increased supply of them could be applied, without taking them away from some other use in which they were rendering net services at least as valuable. These margins of application of the several uses are thus *governed* by the relation in which the fixed stock of stones stands to the aggregate of demands for them in different uses. And the margins being thus governed, the prices that will be paid for their use are *indicated* by the value of the services which they render at any one of those margins. The above
string of
hypotheses
begins
with rents
proper,

---

given that the shareholders are receiving but a moderate return on their investments. Such cases are not uncommon in America. In this country a more moderate watering of the stock of some railways has been occasionally used indirectly as a defence of the shareholders against a lowering of rates, that threatens to reduce dividends on inflated capital below what would be a fair return on solid capital.

V, IX, 3.
and in this
case a tax
remains
on the
owners.
A uniform tax on them, collected from the user, will lower their net service in each use by the same amount : it will not affect their distribution between several uses; and it will fall wholly on the owner, after perhaps some little delay caused by a frictional resistance to readjustments.

At the
other ex-
treme are
incomes
kept close
to interest
(or profits)
on money
cost of
production
and here
a tax falls
upon
users.
At the opposite extreme of our chain of hypotheses, the stones perish so quickly, and are so quickly reproduced at about a uniform cost, that variations in the urgency and volume of the uses to which the stones can be put will be followed so promptly by changes in the stock of them available, that those services can never yield much more or much less than normal *interest* on the money cost of obtaining additional stones. In this case a business man, when making his estimates for the cost of any undertaking in which stones will be used, may enter *interest* (or if he is counting his own work in, *profits*), for the time during which those stones will be used (together with wear-and-tear), as part of the prime, special, or direct expenses of his undertaking. A tax on the stones under these conditions would fall entirely on any one who even a little while after the tax had come into force, gave out a contract for anything in making which the stones would be used.

Inter-
mediate
stages.
Taking an intermediate hypothesis as to the length of life of the stones and the rapidity with which new supplies could be obtained; we find that the charges which the borrower of stones must expect to pay, and the revenue which the owner of the stones could reckon on deriving from them at any time, might temporarily diverge some way from interest (or profits) on their cost. For changes in the urgency and volume of the uses to which they could be applied, might have caused the value of the services rendered by them in their marginal uses to rise or fall a great deal, even though there had been no considerable change in the difficulty of obtaining them. And if this rise or fall, arising from variations in demand, and not from variations in the cost of the stones, is likely to be great during the period of any particular enterprise, or any particular problem of value that is under discussion; then for that discussion the income yielded by the stones is to be regarded as more nearly akin to a rent than to interest on the cost of producing the stones. A tax upon the stones in such a case would tend to diminish the rental which people would pay for their use, and therefore to diminish the inducements towards investing capital and effort in obtaining additional supplies. It would therefore check the supply, and compel those who needed the stones to pay gradually increasing rentals for their use, up to the point at which the rentals fully covered the costs of

producing the stones. But the time needed for this re-adjustment v, ix, 3. might be long : and in the interval a great part of the tax would fall upon the owners of the stones.

If the life of the stones was long relatively to that process of *Prime* production in which the stones were used which was under discussion, *costs relatively* the stock of stones might be in excess of that needed to do all the *to long* work for which they were specially fitted. Some of them might be *periods become* lying almost idle, and the owner of these stones might make up his *supple-* estimate of the marginal price for which he was just willing to work *mentary relatively* without entering in that estimate interest on the value of the stones. *to short;* That is to say, some costs which would have been classed as prime costs in relation to contracts, or other affairs, which lasted over a long period, would be classed as supplementary costs in relation to a particular affair which would last but a short time, and which came under consideration when business was slack.

It is of course just as essential in the long run that the price obtained should cover general or supplementary costs as that it should cover prime costs. An industry will be driven out of existence in the long run as certainly by failing to return even a moderate interest on capital invested in steam engines, as by failing to replace the price of the coal or the raw material used up from day to day : just as a man's work will be stopped as certainly by depriving him of food as by putting him in chains. But the man can go on working fairly well for a day without food; while if he is put in chains the check to his work comes at once. So an industry may, and often does, keep tolerably active during a whole year or even more, in which very little is earned beyond prime costs, and the fixed plant has " to work for nothing." But when the price falls so low that it does not pay for the out of pocket expenses during the year for wages and raw material, for coal and for lighting, etc., then the production is likely to come to a sharp stop.

This is the fundamental difference between those incomes yielded *and there* by agents of production which are to be regarded as rents or quasi- *is a corre- sponding* rents and those which (after allowing for the replacement of wear- *transition* and-tear and other destruction) may be regarded as interest (or *from interest on* profits) on current investments. The difference is fundamental, but *free capital* it is only one of degree. Biology tends to show that the animal and *to quasi- rents of* vegetable kingdoms have a common origin. But yet there are *embodied capital.* fundamental differences between mammals and trees; while in a narrower sense the differences between an oak tree and an apple tree are fundamental; and so are in a still narrower sense those between an apple tree and a rose bush, though they are both classed as

V, ix, 4. *rosaceæ.* Thus our central doctrine is that interest on free capital and quasi-rent on an old investment of capital shade into one another gradually; even the rent of land being not a thing by itself, but the leading species of a large genus.[1]

Economics learns from physics to reason about pure elements, though they are rarely isolated by nature.

§ 4. Again, pure elements are seldom isolated from all others by nature either in the physical or moral world. Pure rent in the strict sense of the term is scarcely ever met with : nearly all income from land contains more or less important elements which are derived from efforts invested in building houses and sheds, in draining the land and so on. But economists have learnt to recognize diversity of nature in those composite things to which the names of rent, profits, wages etc. are given in popular language; they have learnt that there is an element of true rent in the composite product that is commonly called wages, an element of true earnings in what is commonly called rent and so on. They have learnt in short to follow the example of the chemist who seeks for the true properties of each element; and who is thus prepared to deal with the common oxygen or soda of commerce, though containing admixtures of other elements.[2]

They recognize that nearly all land in actual use contains an element of capital; that separate reasonings are required for those parts of its value which are, and those which are not, due to efforts of man invested in the land for the purposes of production; and that the results of these reasonings must be combined in dealing with any particular case of that income which commonly goes by the name " rent," but not all of which is rent in the narrower sense of the term. The manner in which the reasonings are to be combined depends on the nature of the problem. Sometimes the mere

[1] See above, p. 341–2.

[2] Professor Fetter seems to ignore this lesson in an article on " The passing of the concept of rent " in the *Quarterly Journal of Economics*, May 1901, p. 419; where he argues that " if only those things which owe nothing to labour are classed as land, and if it is then shown that there is no material thing in settled countries of which this can be said, it follows that everything must be classed as capital." Again he appears to have missed the true import of the doctrines which he assails, when he argues (*ib.* pp. 423–9) against " Extension as the fundamental attribute of land, and the basis of rent." The fact is that its extension (or rather the aggregate of " its space relations ") is the chief, though not the only property of land, which causes the income derived from it (in an old country) to contain a large element of true rent : and that the element of true rent, which exists in the income derived from land, or the " rent of land " in the popular use of the term, is in practice so much more important than any others that it has given a special character to the historical development of the Theory of Rent (see above, p. 123). If meteoric stones of absolute hardness, in high demand and incapable of increase, had played a more important part in the economic history of the world than land, then the elements of true rent which attracted the chief attention of students, would have been associated with the property of hardness; and this would have given a special tone and character to the development of the Theory of Rent. But neither extension nor hardness is a fundamental attribute of all things which yield a true rent. Professor Fetter seems also to have missed the point of the central doctrine as to rents, quasi-rents and interest, given above.

mechanical " composition of forces " suffices; more often allowance V, IX, 5.
must be made for a quasi-chemical interaction of the various forces;
while in nearly all problems of large scope and importance, regard
must be had to biological conceptions of growth.

§ 5. Finally a little may be said on a distinction that is sometimes The
made between " scarcity rents " and " differential rents." In a sense distinction between
all rents are scarcity rents, and all rents are differential rents. But differential
in some cases it is convenient to estimate the rent of a particular scarcity
agent by comparing its yield to that of an inferior (perhaps a mar- rents is
ginal) agent, when similarly worked with appropriate appliances. mental.
And in other cases it is best to go straight to the fundamental
relations of demand to the scarcity or abundance of the means for the
production of those commodities for making which the agent is
serviceable.

Suppose for instance that all the meteoric stones in existence
were equally hard and imperishable; and that they were in the
hands of a single authority : further that this authority decided,
not to make use of its monopolistic power to restrict production so
as to raise the price of its services artificially, but to work each of
the stones to the full extent it could be profitably worked (that is up
to the margin of pressure so intensive that the resulting product could
barely be marketed at a price which covered, with profits, its
expenses without allowing anything for the use of the stone). Then
the price of the services rendered by the stones would have been
governed by the natural scarcity of the aggregate output of their
services in relation to the demand for those services; and the
aggregate surplus or rent would most easily be reckoned as the
excess of this scarcity price over the aggregate expenses of working
the stones. It would therefore generally be regarded as a scarcity
rent. But on the other hand it could have been reckoned as the
differential excess of the aggregate value of the net services of the
stones over that which would have been reached if all their uses had
been as unproductive as their marginal uses. And exactly the
same would be true if the stones were in the hands of different
producers, impelled by competition with one another to work each
stone up to the margin at which its further use ceased to be profitable.

This last instance has been so chosen as to bring out the fact
that the " differential " as well as the " scarcity " routes for estimating rent are independent of the existence of inferior agents of
production : for the differential comparison in favour of the more
advantageous uses of the stones can be made by reference to the
marginal uses of good stones, as clearly as by reference to the use of

V, IX, 5. inferior stones which are on the margin of not being worth using at all.

The exist-
ence of
inferior
agents
does not
raise, but
lowers the
rents of
superior.

In this connection it may be noted that the opinion that the existence of inferior land, or other agents of production, tends to raise the rents of the better agents is not merely untrue. It is the reverse of the truth. For, if the bad land were to be flooded and rendered incapable of producing anything at all, the cultivation of other land would need to be more intensive; and therefore the price of the product would be higher, and rents generally would be higher, than if that land had been a poor contributor to the total stock of produce.[1]

---

[1] Compare Cassel, *Das Recht auf den vollen Arbeitsertrag*, p. 81.

The many misconceptions, that have appeared in the writings even of able economists, as to the nature of a quasi-rent, seem to arise from an inadequate attention to
the differences between short periods and long in regard to value and costs. Thus it
has been said that a quasi-rent is an " unnecessary profit," and that it is " no part of
cost." Quasi-rent is correctly described as an unnecessary profit in regard to short
periods, because no " special " or " prime " costs have to be incurred for the production
of a machine that, by hypothesis, is already made and waiting for its work. But it is a
necessary profit in regard to those other (supplementary) costs which must be incurred
in the long run in addition to prime costs; and which in some industries, as for
instance sub-marine telegraphy, are very much more important than prime costs.
It is no part of cost under any conditions : but the confident expectation of coming
quasi-rents is a necessary condition for the investment of capital in machinery, and for
the incurring of supplementary costs generally.

Again a quasi-rent has been described as a sort of " conjuncture " or " opportunity " profit; and, almost in the same breath, as no profit or interest at all, but
only a rent. For the time being, it is a conjuncture or opportunity income : while
in the long run it is expected to, and it generally does, yield a normal rate of interest
(or if earnings of management are counted in, of profit) on the free capital, represented by a definite sum of money that was invested in producing it. By definition
the rate of interest is a percentage; that is a relation between two numbers (see
above, p. 341). A machine is not a number : its value may be a certain number of
pounds or dollars : but that value is estimated, unless the machine be a new one,
as the aggregate of its (discounted) earnings, or quasi-rents. If the machine is
new, its makers have calculated that this aggregate will appear to probable purchasers
as the equivalent of a price which will repay the makers for it : in that case therefore
it is as a rule, *both* a cost price, *and* a price which represents an aggregate of (discounted)
future incomes. But when the machine is old and partially obsolete in pattern, there
is no close relation between its value and its cost of production : its value is then simply
the aggregate of the discounted values of the future quasi-rents, which it is expected
to earn.

CHAPTER X

MARGINAL COSTS IN RELATION TO AGRICULTURAL VALUES

§ 1. WE now pass from general considerations to those relating to land; and we begin with those specially applicable to agricultural land in an old country.

Suppose, that a war, which was not expected to last long, were to cut off part of the food supplies of England. Englishmen would set themselves to raise heavier crops by such extra application of capital or labour as was likely to yield a speedy return; they would consider the results of artificial manures, of the use of clod-crushing machines, and so on; and the more favourable these results were, the less would be the rise in the price of produce in the coming year which they regarded as necessary to make it worth their while to incur additional outlay in these directions. But the war would have very little effect on their action as to those improvements which would not bear fruit till it was over. In any inquiry then as to the causes that will determine the prices of corn during a short period, that fertility which the soil derives from slowly made improvements has to be taken for granted as it then is, almost in the same way as if it had been made by nature. Thus, the income derived from these permanent improvements gives a surplus above the *prime* or *special* costs needed for raising extra produce. But it is not a true surplus, in the same sense that rent proper is; *i.e.* it is not a surplus above the *total* costs of the produce : it is needed to cover the general expenses of the business.

To speak more exactly :—If the extra income derived from improvements that have been made in the land by its individual owner is so reckoned as not to include any benefit which would have been conferred on the land by the general progress of society independently of his efforts and sacrifices; then, as a rule, the whole of it is required to remunerate him for those efforts and sacrifices. He may have underestimated the gains which will result from them; but he is about equally likely to have made an overestimate. If he has estimated them rightly, his interest has urged him to make the investment as soon as it showed signs of being profitable : and in the absence of any special reason to the contrary we may suppose him

N

V, x, 1. to have done this. In the long run, then, the net returns to the investment of capital in the land, taking successful and unsuccessful returns together, do not afford more than an adequate motive to such investment. If poorer returns had been expected than those on which people actually based their calculations, fewer improvements would have been made.

That is to say :—for periods which are long in comparison with the time needed to make improvements of any kind, and bring them into full operation, the net incomes derived from them are but the price required to be paid for the efforts and sacrifices of those who make them : the expenses of making them thus directly enter into marginal expenses of production, and take a direct part in governing long-period supply price. But in short periods, that is, in periods short relatively to the time required to make and bring into full bearing improvements of the class in question, no such direct influence on supply price is exercised by the necessity that such improvements should in the long run yield net incomes sufficient to give normal profits on their cost. And therefore when we are dealing with such periods, these incomes may be regarded as quasi-rents which depend on the price of the produce.[1]

Summary of relations between marginal costs and value of agricultural produce in general in an old country. We may conclude then :—(1) The amount of produce raised, and therefore the position of the margin of cultivation (*i.e.* the margin of the profitable application of capital and labour to good and bad land alike) are both governed by the general conditions of demand and supply. They are governed on the one hand by demand; that is, by the numbers of the population who consume the produce, the intensity of their need for it, and their means of paying for it; and on the other hand by supply; that is, by the extent and fertility of the available land, and the numbers and resources of those ready to cultivate it. Thus cost of production, eagerness of demand, margin of production, and price of the produce mutually govern one another : and no circular reasoning is involved in speaking of any one as in part governed by the others. (2) That part of the produce which

---

[1] Of course the character and extent of the improvements depends partly on the conditions of land tenure, and the enterprise and ability and command over capital on the part of landlords and tenants which existed at the time and place in question. In this connection we shall find, when we come to study land tenure, that there are large allowances to be made for the special conditions of different places.

It may be noted, however, that rent proper is estimated on the understanding that the original properties of the soil are unimpaired. And when the income derived from improvements is regarded as a quasi-rent, it is to be understood that they are kept up in full efficiency : if they are being deteriorated, the equivalent of the injury done to them must be deducted from the income they are made to yield before we can arrive at that Net income which is to be regarded as their quasi-rent.

That part of the income which is required to cover wear-and-tear bears some resemblance to a royalty, which does no more than cover the injury done to a mine by taking ore out of it.

goes as rent is of course thrown on the market, and acts on prices, V, x, 2. in just the same way as any other part. But the general conditions of demand and supply, or their relations to one another, are not affected by the division of the produce into the share of rent and the share needed to render the farmer's expenditure profitable. The amount of that rent is not a governing cause; but is itself governed by the fertility of land, the price of the produce, and the position of the margin : it is the excess of the value of the total returns which capital and labour applied to land do obtain, over those which they would have obtained under circumstances as unfavourable as those on the margin of cultivation. (3) If the cost of production were estimated for parts of the produce which do not come from the margin, a charge on account of rent would of course need to be entered in this estimate; and if this estimate were used in an account of the causes which govern the price of the produce; then the reasoning would be circular. For that, which is wholly an effect, would be reckoned up as part of the cause of those things of which it is an effect. (4) The cost of production of the marginal produce can be ascertained without reasoning in a circle. The cost of production of other parts of the produce cannot. The cost of production on the margin of the profitable application of capital and labour is that to which the price of the whole produce tends, under the control of the general conditions of demand and supply : it does not govern price, but it focuses the causes which do govern price.

§ 2. It has sometimes been suggested that if all land were equally advantageous and all were occupied, the income derived from it would partake of the nature of a monopoly rent : but this seems to be an error. Of course the landowners might conceivably combine to stint production, whether their properties were of equal fertility or not; the raised prices which would thus be obtained for the produce would be monopoly prices; and the incomes of the owners would be monopoly revenues rather than rents. But, with a free market, the revenues from land would be rents, governed by the same causes and in the same way in a country where the land was all of equal advantage, as in those where good and bad land were intermingled.[1]

Scarcity
without in-
equalities
of fertility
gives rise
to rent.

It is, indeed, true that if there were more than enough land, all of about the same fertility, to enable everyone to have as much of it as was needed to give full scope to the capital he was prepared to apply to it, then it could yield no rent. But that merely illustrates the old paradox that water, when abundant, has no market value :

[1] Compare V. IX. 5.

V, x, 2.

for though the services of some part of it are essential to support life, yet everyone can get without effort to that margin of satiety at which any further supplies would be of no service to him. When every cottager has a well from which he can draw as much water as he needs, with no more labour than is required at his neighbour's well, the water in the well has no market value. But let a drought set in, so that the shallow wells are exhausted, and even the deeper wells are threatened, then the owners of those wells can exact a charge for every bucket which they allow anyone to draw for his own use. The denser population becomes, the more numerous will be the occasions on which such charges can be made (it being supposed that no new wells are developed) : and at last every owner of a well may find in it a permanent source of revenue.

When a new country is first settled, and land is free, immigration proceeds up to the margin at which the pioneer's endurance is just rewarded.

In the same way the scarcity value of land in a new country gradually emerges. The early settler exercises no exclusive privilege, for he only does what anyone else is at liberty to do. He undergoes many hardships, if not personal dangers; and perhaps he runs some risks that the land may turn out badly, and that he may have to abandon his improvements. On the other hand, his venture may turn out well; the flow of population may trend his way, and the value of his land may soon give as large a surplus over the normal remuneration of his outlay on it as the fishermen's haul does when they come home with their boat full. But in this there is no surplus above the rewards needed for his venture. He has engaged in a risky business which was open to all, and his energy and good fortune have given him an exceptionally high reward : anyone else might have taken the same chance as he did. Thus the income which he expects the land to afford in the future enters into the calculations of the settler, and adds to the motives which determine his action when in doubt as to how far to carry his enterprise. He regards its " discounted value " [1] as profits on his capital, and as earnings of his own labour, in so far as his improvements are made with his own hands.

Rent emerges as a surplus as demand for produce and the supply of labour increase.

A settler often takes up land with the expectation that the produce which it affords while in his possession, will fall short of an adequate reward for his hardships, his labour and his expenditure. He looks for part of his reward to the value of the land itself, which he may perhaps after a while sell to some new-comer who has no turn for the life of a pioneer. Sometimes even, as the British farmer learns to his cost, the new settler regards his wheat almost as a by-product; the main product for which he works is a farm, the

---

[1] Compare III. v. 3 and V. iv. 2.

title-deeds to which he will earn by improving the land : he reckons V, x, 3. that its value will steadily rise, not through his own efforts so much as through the growth of those comforts and resources, and of those markets in which to buy and in which to sell, that are the product of the growing *public* prosperity.

This may be put in another way. People are generally unwilling to face the hardships and isolation of pioneer agriculture, unless they can look forward with some confidence to much higher earnings, measured in terms of the necessaries of life, than they could get at home. Miners cannot be attracted to a rich mine, isolated from other conveniences and varied social opportunities of civilization, except by the promise of high wages : and those who superintend the investment of their own capital in such mines expect very high profits. For similar reasons pioneer farmers require high aggregate gains made up of receipts for the sale of their produce, together with the acquisition of valuable title-deeds, to remunerate them for their labour and endurance of hardships. And the land is peopled up to that margin at which it just yields gains adequate for this purpose, without leaving any surplus for rent, when no charge is made for the land. When a charge is made, immigration spreads only up to that margin, at which the gains will leave a surplus, of the nature of rent, to cover such charges, in addition to rewarding the pioneer's endurance.

§ 3. With all this it is to be remembered that land is but a particular form of capital from the point of view of the individual producer. The question whether a farmer has carried his cultivation of a particular piece of land as far as he profitably can; and whether he should try to force more from it, or to take in another piece of land; is of the same kind as the question whether he should buy a new plough, or try to get a little more work out of his present stock of ploughs, using them sometimes when the soil is not in a very favourable condition, and feeding his horses a little more lavishly. He weighs the net product of a little more land against the other uses to which he could put the capital sum that he would have to expend in order to obtain it : and in like manner he weighs the net product, to be got by working his ploughs under unfavourable circumstances, against that got by increasing his stock of ploughs, and thus working under more favourable conditions. That part of his produce which he is in doubt whether to raise by extra use of his existing ploughs, or by introducing a new plough, may be said to be derived from a marginal use of the plough. It pays nothing *net* (*i.e.* nothing beyond a charge for actual wear-and-tear) towards the net income earned by the plough.

Land is but one form of capital to the individual producer.

V, x, 3.

So again a manufacturer or trader, owning both land and buildings, regards the two as bearing similar relations to his business. Either will afford him aid and accommodation at first liberally; and afterwards with diminishing return, as he endeavours to force more and more from them : till at last he will doubt whether the overcrowding of his workshops or his storerooms is not so great a source of trouble, that it would answer his purpose to obtain more space. And when he comes to decide whether to obtain that space by taking in an extra piece of land or by building his factory a floor higher, he weighs the net income to be derived from further investments in the one against that to be derived from the other. That part of his production which he just forces out of his existing appliances (being in doubt whether it would not be better worth his while to increase those appliances than to work so intensively those which he has), does not contribute to the net income which those appliances yield him. This argument says nothing as to whether the appliances were made by man, or part of a stock given by nature; it applies to rents and quasi-rents alike.

Likeness amid unlikeness between true rent and quasi-rent.

But there is this difference from the point of view of society. If one person has possession of a farm, there is less land for others to have. His use of it is not in addition to, but in lieu of the use of a farm by other people : whereas if he invests in improvements of land or in buildings on it, he will not appreciably curtail the opportunities of others to invest capital in like improvements. Thus there is likeness amid unlikeness between land and appliances made by man. There is unlikeness because land in an old country is approximately (and in some senses absolutely) a *permanent and fixed stock* : while appliances made by man, whether improvements in land, or in buildings, or machinery, etc., are a flow capable of being increased or diminished according to variations in the effective demand for the products which they help in raising. So far there is unlikeness. But on the other hand there is likeness, in that, since some of them cannot be produced quickly, they are a practically *fixed stock for short periods* : and for those periods the incomes derived from them stand in the same relation to the value of the products raised by them, as do true rents.[1]

[1] The relations between rent and profits engaged the attention of the economists of the last generation; among whom may be specially mentioned Senior and Mill, Hermann and Mangoldt. Senior seemed almost on the point of perceiving that the key of the difficulty was held by the element of time: but here as elsewhere he contented himself with suggestions; he did not work them out. He says (*Political Economy*, p. 129), " for all useful purposes the distinction of profits from rent ceases as soon as the capital from which a given revenue arises has become, whether by gift or by inheritance, the property of a person to whose abstinence and exertions it did not owe its creation." Again, Mill says, *Political Economy*, Book III. ch. v. § 4, " Any

§ 4. Let us apply these considerations to the supposition that a permanent tax is to be levied on " corn," in the sense in which it was used by the classical economists as short for all agricultural produce. It is obvious that the farmer would try to make the consumer pay some part at least of the tax. But any rise in the price charged to the consumer would check demand, and thus react on the farmer. In order to decide how much of this tax would be shifted on to the consumer, we must study the *margin of profitable expenditure,* whether that be the margin of a little expenditure applied to poor land and land far removed from good markets, or the margin of a large expenditure applied to rich land, and land near to dense industrial districts.

V, x, 4.
———
Illustra-
tion
from the
ultimate
incidence
of a tax
on agri-
cultural
produce in
general.

If only a little corn had been raised near the margin, a moderate fall in the net price received by the farmer would not cause a great check to the supply of corn.   There would therefore be no great rise in the price paid for it by the consumer; and the consumer would bear very little of the tax.   But the surplus value of the corn over its expenses of production would fall considerably.   The farmer, if cultivating his own land, would bear the greater part of the tax. And, if he were renting the land, he could demand a great reduction of his rent.

If, on the other hand, a great deal of corn had been raised near the margin of cultivation, the tax would tend to cause a great shrinkage of production.   The consequent rise of price would arrest that shrinkage, leaving the farmer in a position to cultivate nearly as intensively as before : and the landlord's rent would suffer but little.[1]

Thus, on the one hand, a tax which is so levied as to discourage the cultivation of land or the erection of farm buildings on it, tends to be shifted forward on to the consumers of the produce of land. But, on the other hand, a tax on that part of the (annual) value of land, which arises from its position, its extension, its yearly income of sunlight and heat and rain and air, cannot settle anywhere except on

---

difference in favour of certain producers or in favour of production in certain circumstances is the source of a gain, which though not called rent unless paid periodically by
one person to another, is governed by laws entirely the same with it."

It has been well observed that a speculator, who, without manipulating prices
by false intelligence or otherwise, anticipates the future correctly ; and who makes his
gains by shrewd purchases and sales on the Stock Exchange or in Produce Markets,
generally renders a public service by pushing forward production where it is wanted,
and repressing it where it is not : but that a speculator in land in an old country can
render no such public service, because the stock of land is fixed.   At the best he can
prevent a site with great possibilities from being devoted to inferior uses in consequence
of the haste, ignorance, or impecuniosity of those in control of it.

[1] Of course the adjustments of rent to the true economic surplus from the land
are in practice slow and irregular.   These matters are discussed in VI. ix. and x.,
and the incidence of a tax on grain under certain rather arbitrary assumptions is
studied in some detail in Appendix K.

V, x, 5. the landlord; a lessee being, of course, landlord for the time. This (annual) value of the land is commonly called its " original value " or its " inherent value "; but much of that value is the result of the action of men, though not of its individual holders. For instance, barren heath land may suddenly acquire a high value from the growth of an industrial population near it; though its owners have

The *public* left it untouched as it was made by nature. It is, therefore, perhaps
value of more correct to call this part of the annual value of land its " *public*
land. *value* "; while that part which can be traced to the work and outlay of its individual holders may be called its " private value." The old terms " inherent value " and " original value " may however be retained for general use, with a note of caution as to their partial inaccuracy. And, using another term that has precedent in its favour, we may speak of this annual public value of the land as " true rent."

A tax on the public value of land does not greatly diminish the inducements to cultivate the land highly, nor to erect farm buildings on it. Such a tax therefore does not greatly diminish the supply of agricultural produce offered on the market, nor raise the price of produce; and it is not therefore shifted away from the owners of land.

Implicit   This assumes that the true rent of land on which the tax is levied
assump-   is assessed with reference to its general capabilities, and not to the
tion
that the   special use which the owner makes of it : its net product is supposed
land is   to be that which could be got by a cultivator of normal ability and
turned to
reasonably   enterprise, turning it to good account to the best of his judgment.
good   If an improved method of cultivation develops latent resources of
account.   the soil, so as to yield an increased return much in excess of what is required to remunerate the outlay with a good rate of profits; this excess of net return above normal profits belongs properly to true rent : and yet, if it is known, or even expected, that a very heavy special tax on true rent will be made to apply to this excess income, that expectation may deter the owner from making the improvement.[1]

Relations   § 5. A little has been said incidentally of the competition between
between   different branches of industry for the same raw material or appliances
marginal
costs and   for production. But now we have to consider the competition
value for   between various branches of agriculture for the same land. This
any one
kind of   case is simpler than that of urban land, because farming is a single
agri-   business so far as the main crops are concerned; though the rearing
cultural
produce.   of choice trees (including vines), flowers, vegetables, etc., affords scope for various kinds of specialized business ability. The classical economists were therefore justified in provisionally supposing that

---

[1] The exemption of vacant building land from taxes on its full value retards building. See Appendix G.

all kinds of agricultural produce can be regarded as equivalent to V, x, 5.
certain quantities of corn; and that all the land will be used for
agricultural purposes, with the exception of building sites which are a
small and nearly fixed part of the whole. But when we concentrate
our attention on any one product, as for instance, hops, it may seem
that a new principle is introduced. That is however not the case.
Let us look into this.

Hops are grown in varying rotations with other crops; and the The
farmer is often in doubt whether he shall grow hops or something marginal
else on one of his fields. Thus each crop strives against others for value of
the possession of the land; and if any one crop shows signs of being hops are
more remunerative than before relatively to others, the cultivators by Substi-
will devote more of their land and resources to it. The change combina-
may be retarded by habit, or diffidence, or obstinacy, or limitations of Diminish-
the cultivator's knowledge; or by the terms of his lease. But it ing Return
will still be true in the main that each cultivator—to recall once more tion in
the dominant principle of substitution—" taking account of his own general.
means, will push the investment of capital in his business in each
several direction until what appears in his judgment to be the
margin of profitableness is reached; that is, until there seems to
him no good reason for thinking that the gains resulting from any
further investment in that particular direction would compensate
him for his outlay."

Thus in equilibrium, oats and hops and every other crop will
yield the same net return to that outlay of capital and labour, which
the cultivator is only just induced to apply. For otherwise he would
have miscalculated; he would have failed to get the *maximum*
reward which his outlay can be made to yield : and it would still be
open to him to increase his gains by redistributing his crops, by
increasing or diminishing his cultivation of oats or some other crop.[1]

---

[1] In so far as the farmer is producing raw material, or even human food, for
market, his distribution of resources between different uses is a problem of business
economy : in so far as he is producing for his own domestic consumption, it is, in part at
least, a problem of domestic economy. Compare above V. IV. 4. It may be added
that Note XIV. in the Mathematical Appendix emphasizes the fact that that distribution of outlay between different enterprises, which will give a maximum aggregate
return, is fixed by the same set of equations as that for the similar problem in
domestic economy.

Mill (*Principles*, III. XVI. 2), when discussing " joint products," observed that all
questions relating to the competition of crops for the possession of particular soils are
complicated by the rotation of crops and similar causes; an intricate debit and credit
account by double entry needs to be kept between the various members of the rotation.
Practice and shrewd instinct enable the farmer to do this fairly well. The whole
problem might be expressed in simple mathematical phrases. But they would be
tedious, and perhaps unfruitful. They would therefore not be serviceable, so long
as they remained abstract; though they belong to a class which may ultimately be of
good use in the higher science of agriculture, when that has advanced far enough to
fill in realistic details.

V, x, 5.

Competi-
tion of
different
crops for
the same
land : the
incidence
of a special
tax on
hops.

This brings us to consider taxation in reference to the competition of different crops for the use of the same land. Let us suppose that a tax is imposed on hops, wherever grown; it is not to be a mere local rate or tax. The farmer can evade a part of the pressure of the tax by lessening the intensity of his cultivation of the land which he plants with hops; and a yet further part by substituting another crop on land which he had proposed to devote to hops. He will have recourse to this second plan in so far as he considers that he would get a better result by growing another crop, and selling it free from the tax, than by growing hops and selling them in spite of the tax. In this case the surplus which he could obtain from the land by growing, say, oats upon it would come into his mind when deciding where to set the limit to his production of hops. But even here there would be no simple numerical relation between the surplus, or rent, which the land would yield under oats, and the marginal costs which the price of hops must cover. And a farmer whose land produced hops of exceptionally high quality, and which happened to be in good condition at the time for hops, would have no doubt at all that it was best to grow hops on the land; though in consequence of the tax he might decide to curtail a little his expenditure on it.[1]

[1] If for instance he reckoned that he could get a surplus of £30 above his expenses (other than rent) in spite of the tax by growing hops, and a surplus of only £20 above similar expenses by growing any other crop, it could not be truly said that the rent which the field could be made to yield by growing other crops, " entered into " the marginal price of oats. But it is easier to interpret the classical doctrine that " Rent does not enter into cost of production " in a sense in which it is not true, and to scoff at it, than in the sense in which it was intended and is true. It seems best therefore to avoid the phrase.

The ordinary man is offended by the old phrase that rent does not enter into the price of oats; when he sees that an increase in the demand for land for other uses, manifests itself in a rise of the rental value of all land in the neighbourhood; leaves less land free for growing oats; consequently makes it worth while to force larger crops of oats out of the remaining oat-land, and thus raises the marginal expenses of oats and their price. A rise in rent does serve as a medium through which the growing scarcity of land available for hops and other produce obtrudes itself on his notice; and it is not worth while to try to force him to go behind these symptoms of the change in conditions to the truly operative causes. It is therefore inexpedient to say that the rent of land does not enter into their price. But it is worse than inexpedient to say that the rent of the land does enter into their price : that is false.

Jevons asks (Preface to *Theory of Political Economy*, p. liv) : " If land which has been yielding £2 per acre rent, as pasture, be ploughed up and used for raising wheat, must not the £2 per acre be debited against the expenses of production of wheat ? " The answer is in the negative. For there is no connection between this particular sum of £2 and the expenses of production of that wheat which only just pays its way. What should be said is :—" When land capable of being used for producing one commodity is used for producing another, the price of the first is raised by the consequent limitation of its field of production. The price of the second will be the expenses of production (wages and profits) of that part of it which only just pays its way, that which is produced on the margin of profitable expenditure. And if for the purposes of any particular argument we take together the whole expenses of the production on that land, and divide these among the whole of the commodity produced; then the rent which we ought to count in is not that which the land would pay if used for producing the first commodity, but that which it does pay when used for producing the second."

Meanwhile the tendency towards a general restriction in the
supply of hops would tend to raise their price. If the demand for
them were very rigid, and hops of adequate quality could not easily
be imported from beyond the range of this special tax, the price might
rise by nearly the full amount of the tax. In that case the tendency
would be checked, and very nearly as much hops would be grown as
before the tax had been levied. And here, as in the case of a tax
on printing, recently discussed, the effect of a local tax is in strong
contrast to that of a general tax. For unless the local tax covered
most of the ground in the country on which good hops could be
grown, its effect would be to drive them beyond its boundary :
very little revenue would be got from it, local farmers would suffer
a good deal, and the public would pay a rather higher price for their
hops.

§ 6. The argument of the last section applies, so far as short
periods are concerned, to the earning power of farm-buildings and to
other quasi-rents. When existing farm-buildings, or other appliances which could be used in producing one commodity, are diverted
to producing another because the demand for that is such as to
enable them to earn a higher income by producing it, then *for the
time* the supply of the first will be less, and its price higher than if the
appliances had not been able to earn a higher income by another use.
Thus, when appliances are capable of being used in more than one
branch of agriculture, the marginal cost in each branch will be
affected by the extent to which these appliances are called off for
work in other branches. Other agents of production will be pushed
to more intensive uses in the first branch, in spite of a diminishing
return; and the value of its product will rise, because only at a
higher value will the price be in equilibrium. The increased earning
power of the appliances due to the external demand will appear to
be the cause of this increase in value : for it will cause a relative
scarcity of the appliances in that branch of production, and therefore
raise marginal costs. And from this statement it appears super-
ficially to be a simple transition to the statement that the increased
earning power of the appliances enter into those costs which govern
value. But the transition is illegitimate. There will be no direct or
numerical relation between the increase in the price of the first
commodity and the income that the appliances can earn when they
have been transferred to the second industry and adapted for service
in it.

Similarly, if a tax be put on factories used in one industry,
some of them will be diverted to other industries; and consequently

V, x, 6.

arallel
use in
manu-
cture.

he
rinciples
f these
wo
hapters
re not
pplicable
o mines.

the marginal costs and therefore the values of the products in those industries will fall; simultaneously with a temporary fall in net rental values of factories in all uses. But these falls will vary in amount, and there will be no numerical relation between the fall in the prices of the product and in these rents, or rather quasi-rents.

These principles are not applicable to mines, whether for short periods or for long. A royalty is *not* a rent, though often so called. For, except when mines, quarries, etc., are practically inexhaustible, the excess of their income over their direct outgoings has to be regarded, in part at least, as the price got by the sale of stored-up goods—stored up by nature indeed, but now treated as private property; and therefore the marginal supply price of minerals includes a royalty in addition to the marginal expenses of working the mine. Of course the owner desires to receive the royalty without undue delay; and the contract between him and the lessee often provides, partly for this reason, for the payment of a rent as well as a royalty. But the royalty itself on a ton of coal, when accurately adjusted, represents that diminution in the value of the mine, regarded as a source of wealth in the future, which is caused by taking the ton out of nature's storehouse.[1]

---

[1] See above, p. 140–1. Adam Smith is attacked by Ricardo for putting rent on the same footing with wages and profits as parts of (money) cost of production; and no doubt he does this sometimes. But yet he says elsewhere, "Rent it is to be observed enters into the composition of the price of commodities in a different way from wages and profit. High or low wages and profit are the causes of high or low price : high or low rent is the effect of it. It is because high or low wages and profit must be paid in order to bring a particular commodity to market that its price is high or low. But it is because its price is high or low a great deal more, or very little more, or no more than what is sufficient to pay those wages and profits, that it affords a high rent, or a low rent, or no rent at all." (*Wealth of Nations*, I. xi.) In this, as in many other instances, he anticipated in one part of his writings truths which in other parts he has seemed to deny.

Adam Smith discusses the " price at which coals can be sold for any considerable time "; and contends that " the most fertile mine regulates the price of coals at all other mines in the neighbourhood." His meaning is not clear; but he does not appear to be referring to any temporary underselling; and he seems to imply that the mines are leased at so much a year. Ricardo, following on apparently the same lines, comes to the opposite conclusion that it " is the least fertile mine which regulates price "; which is perhaps nearer the truth than Adam Smith's doctrine. But in fact when the charge for the use of a mine is mainly in the form of a royalty, neither proposition seems to be applicable. Ricardo was technically right (or at all events not definitely wrong) when he said that rent does not enter into the marginal cost of production of mineral produce. But he ought to have added that if a mine is not practically inexhaustible, the income derived from it is partly rent and partly royalty ; and that though the rent does not, the minimum royalty does enter directly into the expenses incurred on behalf of every part of the produce, whether marginal or not.

The royalty is of course calculated in regard to those seams in the mine, which are neither exceptionally rich and easy of working, nor exceptionally poor and difficult. Some seams barely pay the expenses of working them; and some which run short, or have a bad fault, do not even nearly pay the wages of the labour spent on them. The whole argument however implicitly assumes the conditions of an old country. Professor Taussig is probably right when, having in view the circumstances of a new country (*Principles*, ii. p. 96), he " doubts whether any payment at all can be secured by the owner of the very poorest mine, assuming he has done nothing to develop it."

CHAPTER XI

MARGINAL COSTS IN RELATION TO URBAN VALUES

§ 1. THE last three chapters examined the relation in which cost of production stands to the income derived from the ownership of the " original powers " of land and other free gifts of nature, and also to that which is directly due to the investment of private capital. There is a third class, holding an intermediate position between these two, which consists of those incomes, or rather those parts of incomes which are the indirect result of the general progress of society, rather than the direct result of the investment of capital and labour by individuals for the sake of gain. This class has to be studied now, with special reference to the value of urban sites.

We have already noted that, though nature nearly always gives a less than proportionate return, when measured by *the amount* of the produce raised, to increasing applications of capital and labour in the cultivation of land; yet, on the other hand, if the more intensive cultivation is the result of the growth of a non-agricultural population in the neighbourhood, this very concourse of people is likely to raise *the value* of produce. We have seen how this influence opposes, and usually outweighs the action of the law of diminishing return when the produce is measured according to its value to the producer and not according to its amount; the cultivator gets good markets in which to supply his wants, as well as good markets in which to sell, he buys more cheaply while he sells more dearly, and the conveniences and enjoyments of social life are ever being brought more within his reach.[1]

Again, we have seen how the economies which result from a high industrial organization [2] often depend only to a small extent on the resources of individual firms. Those *internal* economies which each establishment has to arrange for itself are frequently very small as compared with those *external* economies which result from the general progress of the industrial environment; the situation of a business nearly always plays a great part in determining the extent to which it can avail itself of external economies; and the situation value which a site derives from the growth of a rich and active

[1] See IV. III. 6.   [2] See IV. X.–XIII.

V, xi, 2. population close to it, or from the opening up of railways and other good means of communication with existing markets, is the most striking of all the influences which changes in the industrial environment exert on cost of production.

Situation value. If in any industry, whether agricultural or not, two producers have equal facilities in all respects, except that one has a more convenient situation than the other, and can buy or sell in the same markets with less cost of carriage, the differential advantage which his situation gives him is the aggregate of the excess charges for cost of carriage to which his rival is put. And we may suppose that other advantages of situation, such for instance as the near access to a labour market specially adapted to his trade, can be translated in like manner into money values. When this is done, and all are added together we have the money value of the advantages of situation which the first business has over the second : and this becomes its special *situation value*, if the second has no situation value and its site is reckoned merely at agricultural value. The extra income which can be earned on the more favoured site gives rise to what

Site value may be called a special situation rent : and the aggregate *site value* of any piece of building land is that which it would have if cleared of buildings and sold in a free market. The " annual site value "—to use a convenient, though not strictly correct form of speaking—is the income which that price would yield at the current rate of interest. It obviously exceeds the special situation value, merely by agricultural value; which is often an almost negligible quantity in comparison.[1]

Exceptional cases in which the income derived from § 2. It is obvious that the greater part of situation value is " public value." (See above, p. 360.) There are however exceptional cases, which call for notice. Sometimes the settlement of a whole town, or even district, is planned on business principles, and

---

[1] If we suppose that two farms, which sell in the same market, return severally to equal applications of capital and labour amounts of produce, the first of which exceeds the second by the extra cost of carrying its produce to market, then the rent of the two farms will be the same. (The capital and labour applied to the two farms are here supposed to be reduced to the same money measure, or which comes to the same thing, the two farms are supposed to have equally good access to markets in which to buy.) Again, if we suppose that two mineral springs *A* and *B* supplying exactly the same water are capable of being worked each to an unlimited extent at a constant money cost of production; this cost being, say twopence a bottle at *A* whatever the amount produced by it, and twopence halfpenny at *B* ; then those places to which the cost of carriage per bottle from *B* is a halfpenny less than from *A*, will be the neutral zone for their competition. (If the cost of carriage be proportional to the distance, this neutral zone is a hyperbola of which *A* and *B* are foci.) *A* can undersell *B* for all places on *A*'s side of it, and *vice versâ* ; and each of them will be able to derive a monopoly rent from the sale of its produce within its own area. This is a type of a great many fanciful, but not uninstructive, problems which readily suggest themselves. Compare von Thünen's brilliant researches in *Der isolirte Staat.*

carried out as an investment at the expense and risk of a single person or company. The movement may be partly due to philanthropic or religious motives, but its financial basis will in any case be found in the fact that the concourse of numbers is itself a cause of increased economic efficiency. Under ordinary circumstances the chief gains arising from this efficiency would accrue to those who are already in possession of the place : but the chief hopes of commercial success, by those who undertake to colonize a new district or build a new town, are usually founded on securing these gains for themselves.

When, for instance, Mr. Salt and Mr. Pullman determined to take their factories into the country and to found Saltaire and Pullman City, they foresaw that the land, which they could purchase at its value for agricultural purposes, would obtain the special situation value which town property derives from the immediate neighbourhood of a dense population. And similar considerations have influenced those, who, having fixed upon a site adapted by nature to become a favourite watering-place, have bought the land and spent large sums in developing its resources : they have been willing to wait long for any net income from their investment in the hope that ultimately their land would derive a high situation value from the concourse of people attracted to it.[1]

In all such cases the yearly income derived from the land (or at all events that part of it which is in excess of the agricultural rent) is for many purposes to be regarded as profits rather than rent. And this is equally true, whether the land is that on which the factory itself at Saltaire or Pullman City is built, or that which affords a high " ground-rent " as the site of a shop or store, whose situation will enable it to do a brisk trade with those who work in the factory. For in such cases great risks have to be run ; and in all undertakings in which there are risks of great losses, there must also be hopes of great gains. The normal expenses of production of a commodity must include payment for the ventures required for producing it, sufficient to cause those who are on the margin of doubt whether to venture or not, to regard the probable net amount of their gains— net, that is, after deducting the probable amount of their losses— as compensating them for their trouble and their outlay. And that the gains resulting from such ventures are not much more than sufficient for this purpose is shown by the fact that they are not as yet very common. They are however likely to be more frequent in

V, xi, 2.
———
advantageous situation is earned by individual effort and outlay.

Illustrations from Saltaire and Pullman City.

[1] Cases of this kind are of course most frequent in new countries. But they are not very rare in old countries : Saltburn is a conspicuous instance ; while a more recent instance of exceptional interest is furnished by Letchworth Garden City.

V, xi, 2.   those industries which are in the hands of very powerful corporations.   A large railway company, for instance, can found a Crewe or a New Swindon for manufacturing railway plant without running any great risk.[1]

Improvements
effected at
the joint
expense of
the landowners
concerned.   Somewhat similar instances are those of a group of landowners who combine to make a railway, the net traffic receipts of which are not expected to pay any considerable interest on the capital invested in making it; but which will greatly raise the value of their land.   In such cases part of the increase of their incomes as landowners ought to be regarded as profits on capital which they have invested in the improvement of their land : though the capital has gone towards making a railway instead of being applied directly to their own property.

Other cases of like nature are main drainage schemes, and other plans for improving the general condition of agricultural or town property, in so far as they are carried out by the landowners at their own expense, whether by private agreement or by the levying of special rates on themselves.   Similar cases again are found in the investment of capital by a nation in building up its own social and political organization as well as in promoting the education of the people and in developing its sources of material wealth.

Thus that improvement of the environment, which adds to the value of land and of other free gifts of nature, is in a good many cases partly due to the deliberate investment of capital by the owners of the land for the purpose of raising its value; and therefore a portion of the consequent increase of income may be regarded as profits when we are considering long periods.   But in many cases it is not so; and any increase in the net income derived from the free gifts of nature which was not brought about by, and did not supply the direct motive to, any special outlay on the part of the landowners, is to be regarded as rent for all purposes.

Analogous
cases in   Cases somewhat analogous to these arise when the owner of a score or more of acres in the neighbourhood of a growing town

---

[1] Governments have great facilities for carrying out schemes of this kind, especially in the matter of choosing new sites for garrison towns, arsenals, and establishments for the manufacture of the materials of war.   In comparisons of the expenses of production by Government and by private firms, the sites of the Government works are often reckoned only at their agricultural value.   But such a plan is misleading.   A private firm has either to pay heavy annual charges on account of its site, or to run very heavy risks if it tries to make a town for itself.   And therefore in order to prove that Government management is for general purposes as efficient and economical as private management, a full charge ought to be made in the balance-sheets of Government factories for the town-value of their sites.   In those exceptional branches of production for which a Government can found a manufacturing town without incurring the risks that a private firm would incur in a similar case, that point of advantage may fairly be reckoned as an argument for Governments undertaking those particular businesses.

"develops" them for building. He probably lays out the roads, V, xi, 3. decides where houses are to be continuous, and where detached; the laying and prescribes the general style of architecture, and perhaps the out of minimum expenditure on each house; for the beauty of each adds suburban property. to the general value of all. This collective value, thus created by him, is of the nature of public value; and it is dependent, for the greater part, on that dormant public value, which the site as a whole derived from the growth of a prosperous town in its neighbourhood. But yet that share of it which results from his forethought, constructive faculty and outlay, is to be regarded as the reward of business enterprise, rather than as the appropriation of public value by a private person.

These exceptional cases must be reckoned with. But the But as a general rule holds that the amount and character of the building rule site put upon each plot of land is, in the main (subject to the local little to the building bylaws), that from which the most profitable results are owner of the site. anticipated, with little or no reference to its reaction on the situation value of the neighbourhood. In other words the site value of the plot is governed by causes which are mostly beyond the control of him who determines what buildings shall be put on it : and he adjusts his expenditure on it to his estimates of the income to be derived from various descriptions of buildings on it.

§ 3. The owner of building land sometimes builds on it himself : Causes sometimes he sells it outright : very often he lets it at a fixed ground- that rent for ninety-nine years, after which the land and the buildings on the capital it (which by covenant must be kept in good repair) revert to his value of successor in title. Let us consider what governs the value at which land. he can sell the land and the ground-rent at which he can let it.

The capitalized value of any plot of land is the actuarial " discounted " value of all the net incomes which it is likely to afford, allowance being made on the one hand for all incidental expenses, including those of collecting the rents, and on the other for its mineral wealth, its capabilities of development for any kind of business, and its advantages, material, social and æsthetic, for the purposes of residence. The money equivalent of that social status and those other personal gratifications which the ownership of land affords, does not appear in the returns of the money income derived from it, but does enter into its capital money value.[1]

---

[1] The value of agricultural land is commonly expressed as a certain number of times the current money rental, or in other words a certain "number of years' purchase " of that rental : and other things being equal it will be the higher, the more important these direct gratifications are, as well as the greater the chance that they and the money income afforded by the land will rise. The number of

V, xi, 4.

Ground-
rents for
long leases
are based
on esti-
mates of
future true
site values.

Next let us consider what governs the "ground-rent" which the owner can obtain for a plot which he lets on, say, a ninety-nine years' building lease. The present discounted value of all the fixed money payments under that lease tends to be equal to the present capital value of the land; after deducting, firstly, for the obligation to return the land with the buildings on it to the successor in title of the present owner at the end of the lease, and secondly for the possible inconvenience of any restrictions on the use of the land contained in the lease. In consequence of these deductions the ground-rent would be rather less than the "annual site value" of the land, if that site value were expected to remain fixed throughout. But in fact the site value is expected to rise in consequence of the growth of population, and other causes : and therefore the ground-rent is generally a little above the annual site value at the beginning of the lease, and much below it towards the end.[1]

Among the estimated outgoings on account of any building, which have to be deducted from its estimated gross yield before deciding what is the value of the privilege of erecting it on any given plot of land, are the taxes (central and local) which may be expected to be levied on the property, and to be paid by the owner of the property. But this raises difficult side-issues, which are postponed to Appendix G.

The
relations of
marginal
costs to
the value
of the

§ 4. Let us revert to the fact that the law of diminishing return applies to the use of land for the purposes of living and working on it in all trades.[2] Of course in the trade of building, as in agriculture, it is possible to apply capital too thinly. Just as a homesteader

---

years' purchase would be increased also by an expected fall either in the future normal rate of interest or in the purchasing power of money.

The discounted value of a very distant rise in the value of land is much less than is commonly supposed. For instance, if we take interest at five per cent. (and higher rates prevailed during the Middle Ages), £1 invested at compound interest would amount to about £17,000 in 200 years, and £40,000,000,000 in 500 years. Therefore an expenditure by the State of £1 in securing to itself the reversion of a rise in the value of land which came into operation now for the first time would have been a bad investment, unless the value of that rise now exceeded £17,000, if the payment was made 200 years ago; if 500 years ago to £40,000,000,000. This assumes that it would have been possible to invest a sum of this dimension at five per cent. : which of course it would not.

[1] A few site-values have fallen in districts which have been deserted by fashion or trade. But on the other hand annual site values have risen to be many times as great as the ground-rents in the case of land which was leased when it had no special situation value, but has since become a chief centre of fashion, or of trade : and all the more if the lease was granted in the first half of the eighteenth century, when gold was scarce and the incomes of all classes of the people, measured in money, were very low. The present discounted value of the return of property to the ground landlord a hundred years hence, which will then be worth £1000, is less perhaps than is commonly supposed; though the error is not so great as in the case of anticipations ranging over many hundred years, which were discussed in a recent note : if interest be taken at three per cent. it is about £50; if at five per cent., as was the rule three or four generations ago, it is but £8.

[2] See IV. iii. 7.

may find that he can raise more produce by cultivating only a half of the 160 acres allotted to him than by spreading his labour over the whole, so even when ground has scarcely any value, a very low house may be dear in proportion to its accommodation. But, as in agriculture, there is a certain application of capital and labour to the acre which gives the highest return, and further applications after this give a less return, so it is in building. The amount of capital per acre which gives the maximum return varies in agriculture with the nature of the crops, with the state of the arts of production, and with the character of the markets to be supplied; and similarly in building, the capital per square foot which would give the maximum return, if the site had no scarcity value, varies with the purpose for which the building is wanted. But when the site has a scarcity value, it is worth while to go on applying capital beyond this maximum rather than pay the extra cost of land required for extending the site. In places where the value of land is high, each square foot is made to yield perhaps twice the accommodation, at more than twice the cost, that it would be made to give, if used for similar purposes where the value of land is low.

v, xi, 4.

product and to the rent of the land used are similar in manufacture and agriculture.

We may apply the phrase *the margin of building* to that accommodation which it is only just worth while to get from a given site, and which would not be got from it if land were less scarce. To fix the ideas, we may suppose this accommodation to be given by the top floor of the building.[1]

The margin of building.

By erecting this floor, instead of spreading the building over more ground, a saving in the cost of land is effected, which just compensates for the extra expense and inconvenience of the plan. The accommodation given by this floor, when allowance has been made for its incidental disadvantages, is only just enough to be worth what it costs without allowing anything for the rent of land; and the expenses of production of the things raised on this floor, if it is part of a factory, are just covered by their price; there is no surplus

---

[1] Houses built in flats are often provided with a lift which is run at the expense of the owner of the house, and in such cases, at all events in America, the top floor sometimes lets for a higher rent than any other. If the site is very valuable and the law does not limit the height of his house in the interest of his neighbours, he may build very high : but at last he will reach the margin of building. At last he will find that the extra expenses for foundations and thick walls, and for his lift, together with some resulting depreciation of the lower floors, make him stand to lose more than he gains by adding one more floor; the extra accommodation which it only just answers his purpose to supply is then to be regarded as at the margin of building, even though the gross rent be greater for the higher floors than for the lower. Compare the footnote on p. 140.

But in England bylaws restrain an individual from building so high as to deprive his near neighbours of air and light. In the course of time those who build high will be forced to have a good deal of free space about their buildings; and this will render very high buildings unprofitable.

V, XI, 5.   for the rent of land. The expenses of production of manufactures may then be reckoned as those of the goods which are made on the margin of building, so as to pay no rent for land. That is to say the rent of the land does not enter into that set of expenses at the margin at which the action of the forces of demand and supply in governing value may be most clearly seen.

Suppose, for instance, that a person is planning a hotel or a factory; and considering how much land to take for the purpose. If land is cheap he will take much of it; if it is dear he will take less and build high. Suppose him to calculate the expenses of building and working his establishment with frontages of 100 and 110 feet respectively, in ways equally convenient on the whole to himself, his customers and employees, and therefore equally profitable to himself. Let him find that the difference between the two plans, after capitalizing future expenditure, shows an advantage of £500 in favour of the larger area; he will then be inclined to take the larger if the land is to be got at less than £50 per foot of frontage, but not otherwise; and £50 will be the marginal value of land to him. He might have reached this result by calculating the increased value of the business that could be done with the same outlay in other respects on the larger site as compared with the smaller, or again by building on less expensive ground instead of in a less favourable situation. But, by whatever route he makes his calculation, its character is similar to that by which he decides whether it is worth his while to buy business plant of any other kind : and he regards the net income (allowance being made for depreciation) which he expects to get from either investment as standing in the same general relation to his business; and if the advantages of the situation are such, that all the land available on it can find employments of different kinds in each of which its marginal use is represented by a capital value of £50 per foot of frontage, then that will be the current value of the land.

The competition of factories, warehouses, etc. for the same land.   § 5. This assumes that the competition for land for various uses will cause building in each locality and for each use to be carried up to that margin, at which it is no longer profitable to apply any more capital to the same site. As the demand for residential and business accommodation in a district increases, it becomes worth while to pay a higher and higher price for land, in order to avoid the expense and inconvenience of forcing more accommodation from the same ground area.

For instance, if the value of land in, say, Leeds rises because of the increased competition for it by shops, warehouses, iron works, etc.; then a woollen manufacturer finding his expenses of production increased, may move to another town or into the country; and thus leave the land on which he used to work to be built over with shops and warehouses, for which a town situation is more valuable than it is for factories.   For he may think that the saving in the cost of land that he will make by moving into the country, together with other advantages of the change, will more than counter-balance its disadvantages.   In a discussion as to whether it was worth while to do so, the rental value of the site of his factory would be reckoned among the expenses of production of his cloth; and rightly.

But we have to go behind that fact.   The general relations of demand and supply cause production to be carried up to a margin at which the expenses of production (nothing being entered for rent) are so high that people are willing to pay a high value for additional and in order to avoid the inconvenience and expense of crowding their work on to a narrow site.   These causes govern site value; and site value is therefore not properly regarded as governing marginal costs.

Thus the industrial demand for land is in all respects parallel to the agricultural.   The expenses of production of oats are increased by the fact that land, which could yield good crops of oats, is in great demand for growing other crops that enable it to yield a higher rent : and in the same way the printing-presses, which may be seen at work in London some sixty feet above the ground, could afford to do their work a little cheaper if the demand for ground for other uses did not push the margin of building up so high.   Again, a hop-grower may find that on account of the high rent which he pays for his land, the price of his hops will not cover their expenses of production where he is, and he may abandon hop-growing, or seek other land for it; while the land that he leaves may perhaps be let to a market-gardener.   After a while the demand for land in the neighbourhood may again become so great that the aggregate price which the market-gardener obtains for his produce will not pay its expenses of production, including rent; and so he in his turn makes room for, say, a building company.

In each case the rising demand for land alters the margin to which it is profitable to carry the intensive use of land : the costs at this margin indicate the action of those fundamental causes which govern the value of the land.   And at the same time they are themselves those costs to which the general conditions of demand and supply compel value to conform : and therefore it is right for our purpose to go straight to them; though any such inquiry would be irrelevant to the purposes of a private balance sheet.

V, xi, 6.

The
rents of
traders in
relation
to their
prices.

§ 6. The demand for exceptionally valuable urban land comes from traders of various kinds, wholesale and retail, more than from manufacturers; and it may be worth while to say something here as to the very interesting features of demand that are peculiar to their case.

If two factories in the same branch of trade have equal outputs they are sure to have nearly equal floor space. But there is no close relation between the size of trading establishments and their turn-overs. Plenty of space is for them a matter of convenience and a source of extra profit. It is not physically indispensable; but the larger their space, the greater the stock which they can keep on hand, and the greater the advantage to which they can display specimens of it; and especially is this the case in trades that are subject to changes of taste and fashion. In such trades the dealers exert themselves to collect within a comparatively small space representatives of all the best ideas that are in vogue, and still more of those that are likely soon to be so; and the higher the rental values of their sites the more prompt they must be in getting rid, even at a loss, of such things as are a little behind the time and do not improve the general character of their stocks. If the locality is one in which customers are more likely to be tempted by a well-chosen stock than by low prices, the traders will charge prices that give a high rate of profit on a comparatively small turn-over : but, if not, they will charge low prices and try to force a large business in proportion to their capital and the size of their premises; just as in some neighbourhoods the market-gardener finds it best to gather his peas young when they are full of flavour, and in others to let them grow till they weigh heavily in the scales. Whichever plan the traders follow, there will be some conveniences which they are in doubt whether it is worth while to offer to the public; since they calculate that the extra sales gained by such conveniences are only just remunerative, and do not contribute any surplus towards rent. The goods which they sell in consequence of these conveniences, are goods into whose expenses of marketing rent does not enter any more than it does into those of the peas which the market-gardener only just finds it worth his while to produce.

Prices are low in some very highly-rented shops, because their doors are passed by great numbers of people who cannot afford to pay high prices for the gratification of their fancy; and the shopkeeper knows that he must sell cheaply, or not sell at all. He has to be content with a low rate of profit each time he turns over his capital. But, as the wants of his customers are simple, he need not keep a large stock of goods; and he can turn over his capital many times a year. So his annual net profits are very great, and he is willing to pay a very high rent for the situation in which they can be earned. On the other hand, prices are very high in some of the quiet streets in the fashionable parts of London and in many villages; because in the one case customers must be attracted by a very choice stock, which can only be sold slowly; and in the other the aggregate turn-over is very small indeed. In neither place can the trader make profits that will enable him to pay as high a rent as those of some cheap but bustling shops in the East end of London.

It is however true that, if without any increase in traffic such as brings extra custom, a situation becomes more valuable for purposes other than shopkeeping; then only those shopkeepers will be able to pay their way who can manage to secure a large custom relatively to the prices which they charge and the class of business which they do. There will therefore be a smaller supply of shopkeepers in all trades for which the demand has not increased: and those who remain, will be able to charge a higher price than before, without offering any greater conveniences and attractions to their customers. The rise of ground values in the district will thus be an indication of a scarcity of space which, other things being equal, will raise the prices of retail goods; just in the same way as the rise of agricultural rents in any district will indicate a scarcity of land which will raise the marginal expenses of production, and therefore the price of any particular crop. A rise of ground values may be an indication of a scarcity of space that will tend to raise traders' prices.

§ 7. The rent of a house (or other building) is a composite rent, of which one part belongs to the site and the other to the buildings themselves. The relations between these two are rather intricate, and may be deferred to Appendix G. A few words may however be said here as to composite rents in general. At starting there may appear to be some contradiction in the statement that a thing is yielding at the same time two rents: for its rent is in some sense a residual income after deducting the expenses of working it; and there cannot be two residues in regard to the same process of working and the same resulting revenue. But when the thing is composite each of its parts may be capable of being so worked as to yield a surplus of revenue over the expenses of working it. The corresponding rents can always be distinguished analytically, and some-times they can be separated commercially.[1] The component elements of composite rent can be distinguished in some but not in all cases.

---

[1] It will be borne in mind that if a house is not appropriate to its site, its aggregate rent will not exceed its site rent by the full building rent which the house would command on an appropriate site. Similar limitations apply to most composite rents.

For instance, the rent of a flour-mill worked by water includes the rent of the site on which it is built, and the rent of the water power which it uses. Suppose that it is contemplated to build a mill in a place where there is a limited water power which could be applied equally well on any one of many sites; then the rent of the water power together with the site selected for it is the sum of two rents; which are respectively the equivalent of the differential advantages which possession of the site gives for production of any kind, and which the ownership of the water power gives for working a mill on any of the sites. And these two rents, whether they happen to be owned by the same person or not, can be clearly distinguished and separately estimated both in theory and in practice.

But this cannot be done if there are no other sites on which a mill can be built : and in that case, should the water power and the site belong to different persons, there is nothing but "higgling and bargaining" to settle how much of the excess of the value of the two together over that which the site has for other purposes shall go to the owner of the latter. And even if there were other sites at which the water power could be applied, but not with equal efficiency, there would still be no means of deciding how the owners of the site and the water power should share the excess of the producer's surplus which they got by acting together, over the sum of that which the site would yield for some other purpose, and of that which the water power would yield if applied elsewhere. The mill would probably not be put up till an agreement had been made for the supply of water power for a term of years : but at the end of that term similar difficulties would arise as to the division of the aggregate producer's surplus afforded by the water power and the site with the mill on it.

Difficulties of this kind are continually arising with regard to attempts by partial monopolists, such as railway, gas, water and electrical companies, to raise their charges on the consumer who has adapted his business arrangements to make use of their services, and perhaps laid down at his own expense a costly plant for the purpose. For instance, at Pittsburgh when manufacturers had just put up furnaces to be worked by natural gas instead of coal, the price of the gas was suddenly doubled. And the history of mines affords many instances of difficulties of this kind with neighbouring landowners as to rights of way, etc., and with the owners of neighbouring cottages, railways and docks.[1]

---

[1] The relations between the interests of different classes of workers in the same business and in the same trade, have some affinity to the subject of composite rents. See below VI. viii. 9, 10.

CHAPTER XII

EQUILIBRIUM OF NORMAL DEMAND AND SUPPLY, CONTINUED, WITH REFERENCE TO THE LAW OF INCREASING RETURN

§ 1. WE may now continue the study begun in chapters iii. and v.; and examine some difficulties connected with the relations of demand and supply as regards commodities the production of which tends to increasing return.

We have noted that this tendency seldom shows itself imme-diately on an increase of demand. To take an example, the first effect of a sudden fashion for watch-shaped aneroids would be a temporary rise of price, in spite of the fact that they contain no material of which there is but a scanty stock. For highly paid labour, that had no special training for the work, would have to be drawn in from other trades; a good deal of effort would be wasted, and for a time the real and the money cost of production would be increased.

The tendency to in-creasing return does not act quickly.

But yet, if the fashion lasted a considerable time, then even independently of any new invention, the cost of making aneroids would fall gradually. For specialized skill in abundance would be trained, and properly graduated to the various work to be done. With a large use of the method of interchangeable parts, specialized machinery would do better and more cheaply much of the work that is now done by hand; and thus a continued increase in the annual output of watch-shaped aneroids would lower their price very much.

Here there is to be noted an important difference between demand and supply. A fall in the price, at which a commodity is offered, acts on demand always in one direction. The amount of the commodity demanded may increase much or little according as the demand is elastic or inelastic : and a long or short time may be required for developing the new and extended uses of the commodity, which are rendered possible by the fall in price.[1] But—at all events if exceptional cases in which a thing is driven out of fashion by a fall in its price be neglected—the influence of price on demand is similar in character for all commodities : and, further, those demands which

Differences between demand and supply in regard to elas-ticity.

[1] See above III. iv. 5.

V, xii, 2. show high elasticity in the long run, show a high elasticity almost at once; so that, subject to a few exceptions, we may speak of the demand for a commodity as being of high or low elasticity without specifying how far we are looking ahead.

Elasticity of supply. But there are no such simple rules with regard to supply. An increase in the price offered by purchasers does indeed always increase supply : and thus it is true that, if we have regard to short periods only, and especially to the transactions of a dealer's market, there is an " elasticity of supply " which corresponds closely to elasticity of demand. That is to say, a given rise in price will cause a great or a small increase in the offers which sellers accept, according as they have large or small reserves in the background, and as they have formed low or high estimates of the level of prices at the next market : and this rule applies nearly in the same way to things which in the long run have a tendency to diminishing return as to those which have a tendency to increasing return. In fact if the large plant needed in a branch of manufacture is fully occupied, and cannot be rapidly increased, an increase in the price offered for its products may have no perceptible effect in increasing the output for some considerable time : while a similar increase in the demand for a handmade commodity might call forth quickly a great increase in supply, though in the long run its supply conformed to that of constant return or even of diminishing return.

In the more fundamental questions which relate to long periods, the matter is even more complex. For the ultimate output corresponding to an unconditional demand at even current prices would be theoretically infinite; and therefore the elasticity of supply of a commodity which conforms to the law of Increasing Return, or even to that of Constant Return, is theoretically infinite for long periods.[1]

We must distinguish the economies of a whole industry and of an individual firm. § 2. The next point to be observed is that this tendency to a fall in the price of a commodity as a result of a gradual development of the industry by which it is made, is quite a different thing from the tendency to the rapid introduction of new economies by an individual firm that is increasing its business.

We have seen how every step in the advance of an able and enterprising manufacturer makes the succeeding step easier and more

---

[1] Strictly speaking, the amount produced and the price at which it can be sold, are functions one of another, account being taken of the length of time allowed for the evolution of appropriate plant and organization for production on a large scale. But in real life, the cost of production per unit is deduced from the amount expected to be produced, and not *vice versâ*. Economists commonly follow this practice; and they follow also the practice of business life in inverting this order with regard to demand. That is, they consider the increase of sales that will follow from a given reduction of price, more frequently than the diminution of price which will be required to effect a given increase of sales.

rapid; so that his progress upwards is likely to continue so long as he V, xii, 2. has fairly good fortune, and retains his full energy and elasticity and his liking for hard work. But these cannot last for ever : and as soon as they decay, his business is likely to be destroyed through the action of some of those very causes which enabled it to rise; unless indeed he can pass it over into hands as strong as his used to be. Thus the rise and fall of individual firms may be frequent, while a great industry is going through one long oscillation, or even moving steadily forwards; as the leaves of a tree (to repeat an earlier illustration) grow to maturity, reach equilibrium, and decay many times, while the tree is steadily growing upwards year by year.[1]

The causes which govern the facilities for production at the command of a single firm, thus conform to quite different laws from those which control the whole output of an industry. And the contrast is perhaps heightened, when we take the difficulties of marketing into account. For instance, manufactures, which are adapted to special tastes, are likely to be on a small scale; and they are generally of such a character that the machinery and modes of organization already developed in other trades, could be easily adapted to them; so that a great increase in their scale of production would be sure to introduce vast economies at once. But these are the very industries in which each firm is likely to be confined more or less to its own particular market; and, if it is so confined, any hasty increase in its production is likely to lower the demand price in that market out of all proportion to the increased economies that it will gain; even though its production is but small relatively to the broad market for which in a more general sense it may be said to produce.

Facilities for increased production often opposed by difficulties of market-ing.

In fact, when trade is slack, a producer will often try to sell some of his surplus goods outside of his own particular market at prices that do little more than cover their prime costs : while within that market he still tries to sell at prices that nearly cover supplementary costs; and a great part of these are the returns expected on capital invested in building up the external organization of his business.[2]

Again supplementary costs are, as a rule, larger relatively to prime costs for things that obey the law of increasing return than for other things[3] ; because their production needs the investment of a

[1] See IV. ix.-xiii.; and especially xi. 5.

[2] This may be expressed by saying that when we are considering an individual producer, we must couple his supply curve—not with the general demand curve for his commodity in a wide market, but—with the particular demand curve of his own special market. And this particular demand curve will generally be very steep; perhaps as steep as his own supply curve is likely to be, even when an increased output will give him an important increase of internal economies.

[3] Of course this rule is not universal. It may be noted, for instance, that the net loss of an omnibus, that is short of passengers throughout its trip, and loses a

V, XII, 3. large capital in material appliances and in building up trade connections. This increases the intensity of those fears of spoiling his own peculiar market, or incurring odium from other producers for spoiling the common market; which we have already learnt to regard as controlling the short-period supply price of goods, when the appliances of production are not fully employed.

We cannot then regard the conditions of supply by an individual producer as typical of those which govern the general supply in a market. We must take account of the fact that very few firms have a long-continued life of active progress, and of the fact that the relations between the individual producer and his special market differ in important respects from those between the whole body of producers and the general market.[1]

The solution of the difficulty is in the action of a representative firm.

§ 3. Thus the history of the individual firm cannot be made into the history of an industry any more than the history of an individual man can be made into the history of mankind. And yet the history of mankind is the outcome of the history of individuals; and the aggregate production for a general market is the outcome of the motives which induce individual producers to expand or contract their production. It is just here that our device of a representative

---

fourpenny fare, is nearer fourpence than threepence, though the omnibus trade conforms perhaps to the law of constant return. Again, if it were not for the fear of spoiling his market, the Regent Street shoemaker, whose goods are made by hand, but whose expenses of marketing are very heavy, would be tempted to go further below his normal price in order to avoid losing a special order, than a shoe manufacturer who uses much expensive machinery and avails himself generally of the economies of production on a large scale. There are other difficulties connected with the supplementary costs of joint products, e.g. the practice of selling some goods at near prime cost, for the purpose of advertisement (see above V. VII. 2). But these need not be specially considered here.

[1] Abstract reasonings as to the effects of the economies in production, which an individual firm gets from an increase of its output are apt to be misleading, not only in detail, but even in their general effect. This is nearly the same as saying that in such case the conditions governing supply should be represented in their totality. They are often vitiated by difficulties which lie rather below the surface, and are especially troublesome in attempts to express the equilibrium conditions of trade by mathematical formulæ. Some, among whom Cournot himself is to be counted, have before them what is in effect the supply schedule of an individual firm; representing that an increase in its output gives it command over so great internal economies as much to diminish its expenses of production; and they follow their mathematics boldly, but apparently without noticing that their premises lead inevitably to the conclusion that, whatever firm first gets a good start will obtain a monopoly of the whole business of its trade in its district. While others avoiding this horn of the dilemma, maintain that there is no equilibrium at all for commodities which obey the law of increasing return; and some again have called in question the validity of any supply schedule which represents prices diminishing as the amount produced increases. See Mathematical Note XIV., where reference is made to this discussion.

The remedy for such difficulties as these is to be sought in treating each important concrete case very much as an independent problem, under the guidance of staple general reasonings. Attempts so to enlarge the *direct* applications of general propositions as to enable them to supply adequate solutions of all difficulties, would make them so cumbrous as to be of little service for their main work. The " principles " of economics must aim at affording guidance to an entry on problems of life, without making claim to be a substitute for independent study and thought.

firm comes to our aid.   We imagine to ourselves at any time a firm
that has its fair share of those internal and external economies, which
appertain to the aggregate scale of production in the industry to
which it belongs.   We recognize that the size of such a firm, while
partly dependent on changes in technique and in the costs of
transport, is governed, other things being equal, by the general
expansion of the industry.   We regard the manager of it as reckoning
up whether it would be worth his while to add a certain new line to
his undertakings;   whether he should introduce a certain new
machine and so on.   We regard him as treating the output which
would result from that change more or less as a unit, and weighing
in his mind the cost against the gain.[1]

This then is the marginal cost on which we fix our eyes.   We do
not expect it to fall immediately in consequence of a sudden increase
of demand.   On the contrary we expect the short-period supply
price to increase with increasing output.   But we also expect a
gradual increase in demand to increase gradually the size and the
efficiency of this representative firm;   and to increase the economies
both internal and external which are at its disposal.

We thus get at the true long-period marginal cost, falling with a gradual increase of demand.

That is to say, when making lists of supply prices (supply
schedules) for long periods in these industries, we set down a
diminished supply price against an increased amount of the flow of
the goods;   meaning thereby that a flow of that increased amount
will in the course of time be supplied profitably at that lower price,
to meet a fairly steady corresponding demand.   We exclude from
view any economies that may result from substantive new inventions;   but we include those which may be expected to arise naturally
out of adaptations of existing ideas;   and we look towards a position
of balance or equilibrium between the forces of progress and decay,
which would be attained if the conditions under view were supposed
to act uniformly for a long time.   But such notions must be taken
broadly.   The attempt to make them precise over-reaches our
strength.   If we include in our account nearly all the conditions of
real life, the problem is too heavy to be handled;   if we select a few,
then long-drawn-out and subtle reasonings with regard to them
become scientific toys rather than engines for practical work.

The theory of stable equilibrium of normal demand and supply
helps indeed to give definiteness to our ideas;   and in its elementary
stages it does not diverge from the actual facts of life, so far as to
prevent its giving a fairly trustworthy picture of the chief methods
of action of the strongest and most persistent group of economic

The pure theory in its earlier stages diverges but little from actual

[1] See above V. v. 6.

V, xii, 3.

facts; but if pushed far its practical value rapidly diminishes.

forces. But when pushed to its more remote and intricate logical consequences, it slips away from the conditions of real life. In fact we are here verging on the high theme of economic progress; and here therefore it is especially needful to remember that economic problems are imperfectly presented when they are treated as problems of statical equilibrium, and not of organic growth. For though the statical treatment alone can give us definiteness and precision of thought, and is therefore a necessary introduction to a more philosophic treatment of society as an organism, it is yet only an introduction.

The Statical theory of equilibrium is only an introduction to economic studies; and it is barely even an introduction to the study of the progress and development of industries which show a tendency to increasing return. Its limitations are so constantly overlooked, especially by those who approach it from an abstract point of view, that there is a danger in throwing it into definite form at all. But, with this caution, the risk may be taken; and a short study of the subject is given in Appendix H.

CHAPTER XIII

THEORY OF CHANGES OF NORMAL DEMAND AND SUPPLY IN RELATION TO THE DOCTRINE OF MAXIMUM SATISFACTION

§ 1. In earlier chapters of this Book, and especially in chapter V, xiii, 1. xii., we have considered gradual changes in the adjustment of demand and supply. But any great and lasting change in fashion; any substantive new invention; any diminution of population by war or pestilence; or the development or dwindling away of a source of supply of the commodity in question, or of a raw material used in it, or of another commodity which is a rival and possible substitute for it :—such a change as any of these may cause the prices set against any given annual (or daily) consumption and production of the commodity to cease to be its normal demand and supply prices for that volume of consumption and production; or, in other words, they may render it necessary to make out a new demand schedule or a new supply schedule, or both of them. We proceed to study the problems thus suggested.

Transition to substantive changes in the condition of demand and supply.

An increase of normal demand for a commodity involves an increase in the price at which each several amount can find purchasers; or, which is the same thing, an increase of the quantity which can find purchasers at any price. This increase of demand may be caused by the commodity's coming more into fashion, by the opening out of a new use for it or of new markets for it, by the permanent falling off in the supply of some commodity for which it can be used as a substitute, by a permanent increase in the wealth and general purchasing power of the community, and so on. Changes in the opposite direction will cause a falling off in demand and a sinking of the demand prices. Similarly an increase of normal supply means an increase of the amounts that can be supplied at each several price, and a diminution of the price at which each separate amount can be supplied.[1] This change may be caused

What is meant by an increase of normal demand,

or of normal supply.

---

[1] A rise or fall of the demand or supply prices involves of course a rise or fall of the demand or supply curve.

If the change is gradual, the supply curve will assume in succession a series of positions, each of which is a little below the preceding one; and in this way we might have represented the effects of that gradual improvement of industrial organization which arises from an increase in the scale of production, and which we have represented by assigning to it an influence upon the supply price for long-

V, XIII, 2.   by the opening up of a new source of supply, whether by improved
means of transport or in any other way, by an advance in the arts of
production, such as the invention of a new process or of new
machinery, or again, by the granting of a bounty on production.
Conversely, a diminution of normal supply (or a raising of the supply
schedule) may be caused by the closing up of a new source of supply
or by the imposition of a tax.

Effects of
an increase
of normal
demand.
§ 2. We have, then, to regard the effects of an increase of normal
demand from three points of view, according as the commodity in
question obeys the law of constant or of diminishing or of increasing
return : that is, its supply price is practically constant for all
amounts, or increases or diminishes with an increase in the amount
produced.

In the first case an increase of demand simply increases the
amount produced without altering its price; for the normal price
of a commodity which obeys the law of constant return is determined
absolutely by its expenses of production : demand has no influence
in the matter beyond this, that the thing will not be produced at all
unless there is some demand for it at this fixed price.

If the commodity obeys the law of diminishing return an increase
of demand for it raises its price and causes more of it to be produced;
but not so much more as if it obeyed the law of constant return.

On the other hand, if the commodity obeys the law of increasing
return, an increase of demand causes much more of it to be produced—more than if the commodity obeyed the law of constant
return—and at the same time lowers its price. If, for instance, a
thousand things of a certain kind have been produced and sold
weekly at a price of 10s., while the supply price for two thousand
weekly would be only 9s., a small rate of increase in normal
demand may gradually cause this to become the normal price;
since we are considering periods long enough for the full normal
action of the causes that determine supply to work itself out. The
converse holds in each case should normal demand fall off instead of
increasing.[1]

---

period curves. In an ingenious paper privately printed by Sir H. Cunynghame, a
suggestion is made, which seems to come in effect to proposing that a long-period
supply curve should be regarded as in some manner representing a series of short-
period curves; each of these curves would assume throughout its whole length that
development of industrial organization which properly belongs to the scale of production represented by the distance from Oy of the point in which that curve cuts
the long-period supply curve (compare Appendix H, 3) and similarly with regard to
demand.

[1] Diagrams are of especial aid in enabling us to comprehend clearly the problems
of this chapter.

The three figures 24, 25, 26 represent the three cases of constant, diminishing
and increasing return respectively. The return in the last case is a diminishing

The argument of this section has been thought by some writers to lend support to the claim that a Protective duty on manufactured imports in general increases the home market for those imports; and, by calling into play the Law of Increasing Return, *ultimately* lowers their price to the home consumer. Such a result may indeed ultimately be reached by a wisely chosen system of " Protection to nascent industries " in a new country; where manufactures, like young children, have a power of rapid growth. But even there the policy is apt to be wrenched from its proper uses, to the enrichment of particular interests : for those industries which can send the greatest number of votes to the poll, are those which are already on so large a scale, that a further increase would bring very few new economies. And of course the industries in a country so long familiar with machinery as England is, have generally passed the stage at which they can derive much real help from such Protection : while Protection to any one industry nearly always tends to narrow the markets, especially the foreign markets, for other industries. These few remarks show that the question is complex : they do not pretend to reach farther than that.

§ 3. We have seen that an increase in normal demand, while leading in every case to an increased production, will in some cases raise and in others lower prices. But now we are to see that increased facilities for supply (causing the supply schedule to be lowered) will always lower the normal price at the same time that it

V, xiii, 3.

Protection to nascent industries.

Effects of increased facilities of supply.

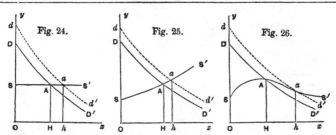

one in the earlier stages of the increase of production, but an increasing one in those subsequent to the attainment of the original position of equilibrium, *i.e.* for amounts of the commodity greater than *OH*. In each case *SS'* is the supply curve, *DD'* the old position of the demand curve, and *dd'* its position after there has been increase of normal demand. In each case *A* and *a* are the old and new positions of equilibrium respectively, *AH* and *ah* are the old and new normal or equilibrium prices, and *OH* and *Oh* the old and new equilibrium amounts. *Oh* is in every case greater than *OH*, but in fig. 25 it is only a little greater, while in fig. 26 it is much greater. (This analysis may be carried further on the plan adopted later on in discussing the similar but more important problem of the effects of changes in the conditions of normal supply.) In fig. 24 *ah* is equal to *AH*, in fig. 25 it is greater, in fig. 26 it is less.

The effect of a falling-off of normal demand can be traced with the same diagrams, *dd'* being now regarded as the old and *DD'* as the new position of this demand curve; *ah* being the old equilibrium price, and *AH* the new one.

O

v, xiii, 3. leads to an increase in the amount produced. For so long as the normal demand remains unchanged an increased supply can be sold only at a diminished price; but the fall of price consequent on a given increase of supply will be much greater in some cases than in others. It will be small if the commodity obeys the law of diminishing return; because then the difficulties attendant on an increased production will tend to counteract the new facilities of supply. On the other hand, if the commodity obeys the law of increasing return, the increased production will bring with it increased facilities, which will co-operate with those arising from the change in the general conditions of supply; and the two together will enable a great increase in production and consequent fall in price to be attained before the fall of the supply price is overtaken by the fall of the demand price. If it happens that the demand is very elastic, then a small increase in the facilities of normal supply, such as a new invention, a new application of machinery, the opening up of new and cheaper sources of supply, the taking off a tax or granting a bounty, may cause an enormous increase of production and fall of price.[1]

[1] All this can be most clearly seen by the aid of diagrams, and indeed there are some parts of the problem which cannot be satisfactorily treated without their aid. The three figures 27, 28, 29 represent the three cases of constant and diminishing and increasing returns, respectively. In each case DD' is the demand curve, SS' the old position, and ss' the new position of the supply curve. A is the old, and a the new position of stable equilibrium. Oh is greater than OH, and ah is less than AH in every case : but the changes are small in fig. 28 and great in fig. 29. Of course the demand curve must lie below the old supply curve to the right of A, otherwise A would be a point not of stable, but of unstable equilibrium. But subject to this

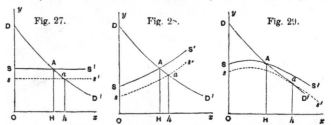

condition the more elastic the demand is, that is, the more nearly horizontal the demand curve is at A the further off will a be from A, and the greater therefore will be the increase of production and the fall of price.

The whole result is rather complex. But it may be stated thus. Firstly, given the elasticity of demand at A, the increase in the quantity produced and the fall in price will both be the greater, the greater be the return got from additional capital and labour applied to the production. That is, they will be the greater, the more nearly horizontal the supply curve is at A in fig. 28, and the more steeply inclined it is in fig. 29 (subject to the condition mentioned above, that it does not lie below the demand curve to the right of A, and thus turn A into a position of unstable equilibrium). Secondly, given the position of the supply curve at A, the greater the elasticity of demand the greater will be the increase of production in every case; but the smaller will be the fall of price in fig. 28, and the greater the fall of price in fig. 29. Fig. 27 may be regarded as a limiting case of either fig. 28 or 29.

If we take account of the circumstances of composite and joint supply and demand discussed in chapter VI., we have suggested to us an almost endless variety of problems which can be worked out by the methods adopted in these two chapters.

§ 4. We may now consider the effects which a change in the conditions of supply may exert on consumers' surplus or rent. For brevity of language a tax may be taken as representative of those changes which may cause a general increase, and a bounty as representative of those which may cause a general diminution in the normal supply price for each several amount of the commodity.

Changes that raise or lower the supply schedule may be represented by a tax or bounty.

Firstly, if the commodity is one, the production of which obeys the law of constant return, so that the supply price is the same for all amounts of the commodity, consumers' surplus will be diminished by more than the increased payments to the producer; and therefore, in the special case of a tax, by more than the gross receipts of the State. For on that part of the consumption of the commodity, which is maintained, the consumer loses what the State receives : and on that part of the consumption which is destroyed by the rise in price, the consumers' surplus is destroyed; and of course there is no payment for it to the producer or to the State.[1] Conversely, the gain of consumers' surplus caused by a bounty on a commodity that obeys the law of constant return, is less than the bounty itself. For on that part of the consumption which existed

The case of constant return.

All this reasoning assumes that the commodity either obeys the law of diminishing return or obeys the law of increasing return throughout. If it obeys first one, and then the other, so that the supply curve is at one part inclined positively and at another negatively, no general rule can be laid down as to the effect on price of increased facilities of supply, though in every case this must lead to an increased volume of production. A great variety of curious results may be got by giving the supply curve different shapes, and in particular such as cut the demand curve more than once.

This method of inquiry is not applicable to a tax on wheat in so far as it is consumed by a labouring class which spends a great part of its income on bread; and it is not applicable to a general tax on all commodities : for in neither of these cases can it be assumed that the marginal value of money to the individual remains approximately the same after the tax has been levied as it was before.

[1] This is most clearly seen by aid of a diagram. SS', the old constant return supply curve, cuts DD' the demand curve in A : DSA is the consumers' surplus. Afterwards a tax Ss being imposed the new equilibrium is found at a, and consumers' surplus is Dsa. The gross tax is only the rectangle $sSKa$, that is, a tax at the rate of Ss on an amount sa of the commodity. And this falls short of the loss of consumers' surplus by the area aKA. The net loss aKA is small or great, other things being equal, as aA is or is not inclined steeply. Thus it is smallest for those commodities the demand for which is most inelastic, that is, for necessaries. If therefore a given aggregate taxation has to be levied ruthlessly from any class it will cause less loss of consumers' surplus if levied on necessaries than if levied on comforts; though of course the consumption of luxuries and in a less degree of comforts indicates ability to bear taxation.

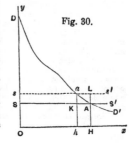

Fig. 30.

V, XIII, 4. before the bounty, consumers' surplus is increased by just the amount of the bounty; while on the new consumption that is caused by the bounty, the gain of the consumers' surplus is less than the bounty.[1]

The case of diminishing return. If however the commodity obeys the law of diminishing return, a tax by raising its price, and diminishing its consumption, will lower its expenses of production other than the tax : and the result will be to raise the supply price by something less than the full amount of the tax. In this case the gross receipts from the tax *may* be greater than the resulting loss of consumers' surplus, and they *will* be greater if the law of diminishing return acts so sharply that a small diminution of consumption causes a great falling-off in the expenses of production other than the tax.[2]

On the other hand, a bounty on a commodity which obeys the law of diminishing return will lead to increased production, and will extend the margin of cultivation to places and conditions in which the expenses of production, exclusive of the bounty, are greater than before. Thus it will lower the price to the consumer and increase consumers' surplus less than if it were given for the production of a commodity which obeyed the law of constant return. In that case the increase of consumers' surplus was seen to be less than the direct cost of the bounty to the State; and therefore in this case it is much less.[3]

[1] If we now regard ss' as the old supply curve which is lowered to the position SS' by the granting of a bounty, we find the gain of consumers' surplus to be $sSAa$. But the bounty paid is Ss on an amount SA, which is represented by the rectangle $sSAL$: and this exceeds the gain of consumers' surplus by the area aLA.

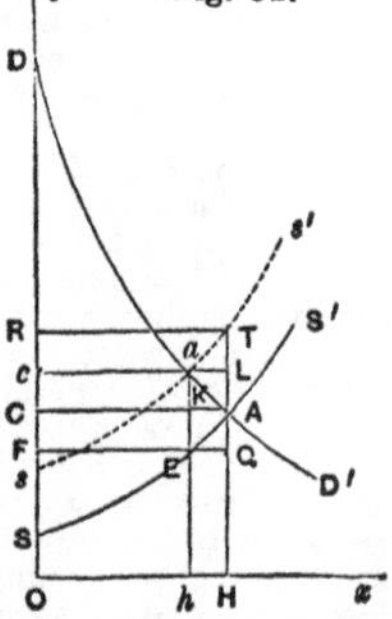

[2] Let the old supply curve be SS' fig. 31, and let the imposition of a tax raise it to ss'; let A and a be the old and new positions of equilibrium, and let straight lines be drawn through them parallel to Ox and Oy, as in the figure. Then the tax being levied, as shown by the figure, at the rate of aE on each unit; and Oh, that is, CK units, being produced in the new position of equilibrium, the gross receipts of the tax will be $cFEa$, and the loss of consumers' surplus will be $cCAa$; that is, the gross receipts from the tax will be greater or less than the loss of consumers' surplus as $CFEK$ is greater or less than aKA; and in the figure as it stands it is much greater. If SS' had been so drawn as to indicate only very slight action of the law of diminishing return, that is, if it had been nearly horizontal in the neighbourhood of A, then EK would have been very small; and $CFEK$ would have become less than aKA.

Fig. 31.

[3] To illustrate this case we may take ss' in fig. 31 to be the position of the supply curve before the granting of the bounty, and SS' to be its position afterwards. Thus a was the old equilibrium point, and A is the point to which the equilibrium moves when the bounty is awarded. The increase of consumers' surplus is only $cCAa$, while the payments made by the State under the bounty are, as shown by the figure, at the rate of AT on each unit of the commodity; and as in the new position of equilibrium there are produced OH, that is, CA units, they amount altogether to $RCAT$ which includes and is necessarily greater than the increase of consumers' surplus.

By similar reasoning it may be shown that a tax on a commodity which obeys the law of increasing return is more injurious to the consumer than if levied on one which obeys the law of constant return. For it lessens the demand and therefore the output. It thus probably increases the expenses of manufacture somewhat : sends up the price by more than the amount of the tax; and finally diminishes consumers' surplus by much more than the total payments which it brings in to the exchequer.[1] On the other hand, a bounty on such a commodity causes so great a fall in its price to the consumer, that the consequent increase of consumers' surplus may exceed the total payments made by the State to the producers; and certainly will do so in case the law of increasing return acts at all sharply.[2]

These results are suggestive of some principles of taxation which require careful attention in any study of financial policy; when it will be necessary to take account of the expenses of collecting a tax and of administering a bounty, and of the many indirect effects, some economic and some moral, which a tax or a bounty is likely to produce. But these partial results are well adapted for our immediate purpose of examining a little more closely than we have done hitherto the general doctrine that a position of (stable) equilibrium of demand and supply is a position also of *maximum satisfaction*: and there is one abstract and trenchant form of that doctrine which has had much vogue, especially since the time of

V, XIII, 4.

The case of increasing return.

These results throw light on the doctrine of *maximum satisfaction*.

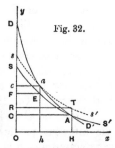

Fig. 32.

[1] Thus taking SS' in fig. 32 to be the old position of the supply curve, and ss' its position after the tax, A to be the old and a the new positions of equilibrium, we have, as in the case of fig. 31, the total tax represented by $cFEa$, and the loss of consumers' surplus by $cCAa$; the former being always less than the latter.

The statement in the text is put broadly and in simple outline. If it were applied to practical problems account would need to be taken of several considerations which have been ignored. An industry which yields an increasing return, is nearly sure to be growing, and therefore to be acquiring new economies of production on a large scale. If the tax is a small one, it may merely retard this growth and not cause a positive shrinking. Even if the tax is heavy and the industry shrinks, many of the economies gained will be in part at least preserved; as is explained above in Appendix H. In consequence ss' ought properly not to have the same shape as SS', and the distance aE ought to be less than AT.

[2] To illustrate this case we may take ss' in fig. 32 to be the position of the supply curve before the granting of the bounty, and SS' to be its position afterwards. Then, as in the case of fig. 31, the increase of consumers' surplus is represented by $cCAa$, while the direct payments made by the State under the bounty are represented by $RCAT$. As the figure is drawn, the former is much larger than the latter. But it is true that if we had drawn ss' so as to indicate a very slight action of the law of increasing return, that is, if it had been very nearly horizontal in the neighbourhood of a, the bounty would have increased relatively to the gain of consumers' surplus; and the case would have differed but little from that of a bounty on a commodity which obeys the law of constant return, represented in fig. 30.

V, xiii, 5.

Bastiat's *Economic Harmonics*, and which falls within the narrow range of the present discussion.

There is a limited sense in which the doctrine is generally true.

§ 5. There is indeed one interpretation of the doctrine according to which every position of equilibrium of demand and supply may fairly be regarded as a position of maximum satisfaction.[1] For it is true that so long as the demand price is in excess of the supply price, exchanges can be effected at prices which give a surplus of satisfaction to buyer or to seller or to both. The marginal utility of what he receives is greater than that of what he gives up, to at least one of the two parties; while the other, if he does not gain by the exchange, yet does not lose by it. So far then every step in the exchange increases the aggregate satisfaction of the two parties. But when equilibrium has been reached, demand price being now equal to supply price, there is no room for any such surplus : the marginal utility of what each receives no longer exceeds that of what he gives up in exchange : and when the production increases beyond the equilibrium amount, the demand price being now less than the supply price, no terms can be arranged which will be acceptable to the buyer, and will not involve a loss to the seller.

It is true then that a position of equilibrium of demand and supply is a position of maximum satisfaction in this limited sense, that the aggregate satisfaction of the two parties concerned increases until that position is reached; and that any production beyond the equilibrium amount could not be permanently maintained so long as buyers and sellers acted freely as individuals, each in his own interest.

But when not taken in this limited sense, the doctrine is open to great exceptions.

But occasionally it is stated, and very often it is implied, that a position of equilibrium of demand and supply is one of maximum aggregate satisfaction in the full sense of the term : that is, that an increase of production beyond the equilibrium level would directly (*i.e.* independently of the difficulties of arranging for it, and of any indirect evils it might cause) diminish the aggregate satisfaction of both parties. The doctrine so interpreted is not universally true.

It assumes that equal sums of money measure equal utilities to all concerned;

In the first place it assumes that all differences in wealth between the different parties concerned may be neglected, and that the satisfaction which is rated at a shilling by any one of them, may be taken as equal to one that is rated at a shilling by any other. Now it is obvious that, if the producers were as a class very much poorer than the consumers, the aggregate satisfaction might be increased by a stinting of supply when it would cause a great rise in demand price (*i.e.* when the demand is inelastic); and that if the consumers were

---

[1] Compare V. i. 1. Unstable equilibrium may now be left out of account.

as a class much poorer than the producers, the aggregate satisfaction might be increased by extending the production beyond the equilibrium amount and selling the commodity at a loss.[1]

This point however may well be left for future consideration. It is in fact only a special case of the broad proposition that the aggregate satisfaction can *primâ facie* be increased by the distribution, whether voluntarily or compulsorily, of some of the property of the rich among the poor; and it is reasonable that the bearings of this proposition should be set aside during the first stages of an inquiry into existing economic conditions. This assumption therefore may be properly made, provided only it is not allowed to slip out of sight.

But in the second place the doctrine of maximum satisfaction assumes that every fall in the price which producers receive for the commodity, involves a corresponding loss to them; and this is not true of a fall in price which results from improvements in industrial organization. When a commodity obeys the law of increasing return, an increase in its production beyond equilibrium point may cause the supply price to fall much; and though the demand price for the increased amount may be reduced even more, so that the production would result in some loss to the producers, yet this loss may be very much less than that money value of the gain to purchasers which is represented by the increase of consumers' surplus.

and it ignores the fact that a fall in price due to improvements benefits consumers without injuring producers.

In the case then of commodities with regard to which the law of increasing return acts at all sharply, or in other words, for which the normal supply price diminishes rapidly as the amount produced increases, the direct expense of a bounty sufficient to call forth a greatly increased supply at a much lower price, would be much less than the consequent increase of consumers' surplus. And if a general agreement could be obtained among consumers, terms might be arranged which would make such action amply remunerative to the producers, at the same time that they left a large balance of advantage to the consumers.[2]

Aggregate satisfaction can therefore primâ facie be increased beyond the level attained by the free play of demand and supply.

[1] In this illustration one of the two things exchanged is general purchasing power; but of course the argument would hold if a poor population of pearl divers were dependent for food on a rich population who took pearls in exchange.

[2] Though not of great practical importance, the case of multiple positions of (stable) equilibrium offers a good illustration of the error involved in the doctrine of maximum satisfaction when stated as a universal truth. For the position in which a small amount is produced and is sold at a high price would be the first to be reached, and when reached would be regarded according to that doctrine as that which gave the absolute maximum of aggregate satisfaction. But another position of equilibrium corresponding to a larger production and a lower price would be equally satisfactory to the producers, and would be much more satisfactory to the consumers; the excess of consumers' surplus in the second case over the first would represent the increase in aggregate satisfaction.

We are
not here
concerned
with the
indirect
evils of
artificial
arrange-
ments
for this
purpose.

§ 6. One simple plan would be the levying of a tax by the community on their own incomes, or on the production of goods which obey the law of diminishing return, and devoting the tax to a bounty on the production of those goods with regard to which the law of increasing return acts sharply.   But before deciding on such a course they would have to take account of considerations, which are not within the scope of the general theory now before us, but are yet of great practical importance.   They would have to reckon up the direct and indirect costs of collecting a tax and administering a bounty; the difficulty of securing that the burdens of the tax and the benefits of the bounty were equitably distributed; the openings for fraud and corruption; and the danger that in the trade which had got a bounty and in other trades which hoped to get one, people would divert their energies from managing their own businesses to managing those persons who control the bounties.

Besides these semi-ethical questions there will arise others of a strictly economic nature, relating to the effects which any particular tax or bounty may exert on the interests of landlords, urban or agricultural, who own land adapted for the production of the commodity in question.   These are questions which must not be overlooked; but they differ so much in their detail that they cannot fitly be discussed here.[1]

[1] The incidence of a tax on agricultural produce will be discussed later on by the aid of diagrams similar to those used to represent the fertility of land (see IV. III.). Landlords' rent absorbs a share of the aggregate selling price of almost all commodities : but it is most prominent in the case of those which obey the law of diminishing return ; and an assumption of no extreme violence will enable fig. 33 (a reproduction of 31) to represent roughly the leading features of the problem.

It will be argued in Appendix H, 1, that we are not properly at liberty to assume that the expenses of raising the produce from the richer lands and under the more favourable circumstances are independent of the extent to which the production is carried ; since an increased production is likely to lead to an improved organization, if not of farming industries themselves, yet of those subsidiary to them, and especially of the carrying trade. We may however permit ourselves to make this assumption provisionally, so as to get a clear view of the broad outlines of the problem ; though we must not forget that in any applications of the general reasonings based on it account must be taken of the facts which we here ignore. On this assumption then SS' being the supply curve before the imposition of a tax, landlords' rent is represented by CSA. After the tax has been imposed and the supply curve raised to ss' the landlords' rent becomes the amount by which cOha, the total price got for Oh produce sold at the rate ha, exceeds the total tax cFEa, together with OhES the total expenses of production, exclusive of rent, for Oh produce : that is, it becomes FSE. (In the figure the curve ss' has the same shape as SS', thereby implying that the tax is specific ; that is, is a uniform charge on each unit of the commodity whatever be its value. The argument so far does not depend on this assumption, but if it is made we can by a shorter route get the new landlords' rent at csa, which then is equal to FSE). Thus the loss of landlords' rent is CFEA ; and this added to cCAa the loss of consumers' surplus, makes up cFEAa, which exceeds the gross tax by aAE.

§ 7. Enough has been said to indicate the character of the second V, XIII, 7. great limitation which has to be introduced into the doctrine that Restate- the maximum satisfaction is *generally* to be attained by encouraging ment of each individual to spend his own resources in that way which suits exceptions him best. It is clear that if he spends his income in such a way as to the to increase the demand for the services of the poor and to increase that it is their incomes, he adds something more to the total happiness than best for all if he adds an equal amount to the incomes of the rich, because the should happiness which an additional shilling brings to a poor man is much income as greater than that which it brings to a rich one; and that he does good he pleases. by buying things the production of which raises, in preference to things the production of which lowers the character of those who make them.[1]   But further, even if we assume that a shilling's worth of happiness is of equal importance to whomsoever it comes, and that every shilling's worth of consumers' surplus is of equal importance from whatever commodity it is derived, we have to admit that the manner in which a person spends his income is a matter of direct economic concern to the community. For in so far as he spends it on things which obey the law of diminishing return, he makes those things more difficult to be obtained by his neighbours, and thus lowers the real purchasing power of their incomes; while in so far as he spends it on things which obey the law of increasing return, he makes those things more easy of attainment to others, and thus increases the real purchasing power of their incomes.

Again, it is commonly argued that an equal *ad valorem* tax levied on all economic commodities (material and immaterial), or which is the same thing a tax on expenditure, is *primâ facie* the best tax; because it does not divert the expenditure of individuals out of its natural channels : we have now seen that this argument is invalid. But ignoring for the time the fact that the direct economic effect of a tax or a bounty never constitutes the whole, and very often not even the chief part of the considerations which have to be weighed before deciding to adopt it, we have found :—firstly, that a tax on expenditure generally causes a greater destruction of consumers' surplus than one levied exclusively on commodities as to which there

---

On the other hand, the direct payments under a bounty would exceed the increase of consumers' surplus, and of landlords' surplus calculated on the above assumptions. For taking ss' to be the original position of the supply curve, and SS' to be its position after the bounty, the new landlords' surplus on these assumptions is CSA, or which is the same thing RsT; and this exceeds the old landlords' rent csa by $RcaT$. The increase of consumers' surplus is $cCAa$; and therefore the total bounty, which is $RCAT$, exceeds the gain of consumers' surplus and landlords' rent together by TaA.

For reasons stated in Appendix H, 3, the assumption on which this reasoning proceeds is inapplicable to cases in which the supply curve is inclined negatively.

[1] Compare III. VI.

v, xiii, 7. is but little room for the economies of production on a large scale, and which obey the law of diminishing return; and secondly, that it might even be for the advantage of the community that the government should levy taxes on commodities which obey the law of diminishing return, and devote part of the proceeds to bounties on commodities which obey the law of increasing return.

These conclusions, it will be observed, do not by themselves afford a valid ground for government interference. But they show that much remains to be done, by a careful collection of the statistics of demand and supply, and a scientific interpretation of their results, in order to discover what are the limits of the work that society can with advantage do towards turning the economic actions of individuals into those channels in which they will add the most to the sum total of happiness.[1]

[1] It is remarkable that Malthus, *Political Economy*, ch. iii. § 9, argued that, though the difficulties thrown in the way of importing foreign corn during the great war turned capital from the more profitable employment of manufacture to the less profitable employment of agriculture, yet if we take account of the consequent increase of agricultural rent, we may conclude that the new channel may have been one of "higher national, though not higher individual profits." In this no doubt he was right; but he overlooked the far more important injury inflicted on the public by the consequent rise in the price of corn, and the consequent destruction of consumers' surplus. Senior takes account of the interests of the consumer in his study of the different effects of increased demand on the one hand and of taxation on the other in the case of agricultural and manufactured produce (*Political Economy*, pp. 118-123). Advocates of Protection in countries which export raw produce have made use of arguments tending in the same direction as those given in this Chapter; and similar arguments are now used, especially in America (as for instance by Mr. H. C. Adams), in support of the active participation of the State in industries which conform to the law of increasing return. The graphic method has been applied, in a manner somewhat similar to that adopted in the present Chapter, by Dupuit in 1844; and, independently, by Fleeming Jenkin (*Edinburgh Philosophical Transactions*) in 1871.

CHAPTER XIV

THE THEORY OF MONOPOLIES

§ 1. It has never been supposed that the monopolist in seeking his own advantage is naturally guided in that course which is most conducive to the well-being of society regarded as a whole, he himself being reckoned as of no more importance than any other member of it. The doctrine of Maximum Satisfaction has never been applied to the demand for and supply of monopolized commodities. But there is much to be learnt from a study of the relations in which the interests of the monopolist stand to those of the rest of society, and of the general conditions under which it might be possible to make arrangements more beneficial to society as a whole than those which he would adopt if he consulted only his own interests : and with this end in view we are now to seek for a scheme for comparing the relative quantities of the benefits which may accrue to the public and to the monopolist from the adoption of different courses of action by him.

In a later volume a study will be made of the Protean shapes of modern trade combinations and monopolies, some of the most important of which, as for example " Trusts," are of very recent growth. At present we consider only those general causes determining monopoly values, that can be traced with more or less distinctness in every case in which a single person or association of persons has the power of fixing either the amount of a commodity that is offered for sale or the price at which it is offered.

§ 2. The *primâ facie* interest of the owner of a monopoly is clearly to adjust the supply to the demand, not in such a way that the price at which he can sell his commodity shall just cover its expenses of production, but in such a way as to afford him the greatest possible total net revenue.

But here we meet with a difficulty as to the meaning of the term Net revenue. For the supply price of a freely-produced commodity includes normal profits; the whole of which, or at all events what remains of them after deducting interest on the capital employed and insurance against loss, is often classed indiscriminately as net revenue. And when a man manages his own business, he often does not distinguish carefully that portion of his profits, which really is his own earnings of management, from any exceptional gains arising from the fact that the business is to some extent of the nature of a monopoly.

This difficulty however is in a great measure avoided in the case of a public company; where all, or nearly all, the expenses of management are entered in the ledger as definite sums, and are subtracted from the total receipts of the company before its net income is declared.

The net income divided among the shareholders includes interest on the capital invested and insurance against risk of failure, but little or no earnings of management; so that the amount by which the dividends are in excess of what may fairly be allowed as interest and insurance, is the *Monopoly Revenue* which we are seeking.

Since then it is much easier to specify exactly the amount of this net revenue when a monopoly is owned by a public company than when it is owned by an individual or private firm, let us take as a typical instance the case of a gas company that has the monopoly of the supply of gas to a town. For the sake of simplicity the company may be supposed to have already invested the whole of its own capital in fixed plant, and to borrow any more capital, that it may want to extend its business, on debentures at a fixed rate of interest.

'he
emand
shedule
as usual;
ut the
upply
shedule
ust be
rawn on
special
lan.

§ 3. The demand schedule for gas remains the same as it would be if gas were a freely-produced commodity; it specifies the price per thousand feet at which consumers in the town will among them use any given number of feet. But the supply schedule must represent the normal expenses of production of each several amount supplied; and these include interest on all its capital, whether belonging to its shareholders or borrowed on debentures, at a fixed normal rate; they include also the salaries of its directors, and permanent officials, adjusted (more or less accurately) to the work required of them, and therefore increasing with an increase in the output of gas. A

'he
Monopoly
evenue
shedule.

monopoly revenue schedule may then be constructed thus :—Having set against each several amount of the commodity its demand price, and its supply price estimated on the plan just described, subtract each supply price from the corresponding demand price and set the residue in the monopoly revenue column against the corresponding amount of the commodity.

Thus for instance if a thousand million feet could be sold annually at a price of 3s. per thousand feet, and the supply price for this amount were 2s. 9d. per thousand feet, the monopoly revenue schedule would show 3d. against this amount; indicating an aggre-

gate net revenue when this amount was sold, of three million pence, V, XIV, 4.
or £12,500.   The aim of the company, having regard only to their
own immediate dividends, will be to fix the price of their gas at such
a level as to make this aggregate net revenue the largest possible.[1]

§ 4. Now suppose that a change takes place in the conditions of
supply; some new expense has to be incurred, or some old expense
can be avoided; or perhaps a new tax is imposed on the undertaking
or a bounty is awarded to it.

First let this increase or diminution of the expenses be a fixed A tax,
sum, bearing on the undertaking as one undivided whole and not fixed in

---

[1] Thus DD' being the demand curve, and SS' the curve corresponding to the
supply schedule described in the text, let MP_2P_1 be drawn vertically from any
point M in Ox, cutting SS' in P_2 and DD' in P_1; and from it cut off $MP_3 = P_2P_1$,
then the locus of P_3 will be our third curve, QQ', which we may call the *monopoly
revenue curve*. The supply price for a small quantity of gas will of course be very
high; and in the neighbourhood of Oy the supply curve will be above the demand
curve, and therefore the net revenue curve will be below Ox. It will cut Ox in K
and again in H, points which are vertically under B and A, the two points of intersection of the demand and supply curves. The maximum monopoly revenue will
then be obtained by finding a point q_3 on QQ' such that Lq_3 being drawn perpendicular
to Ox, $OL \times Lq_3$ is a maximum. Lq_3 being produced to cut SS' in q_2 and DD^1 in q_1, the
company, if desiring to obtain the greatest immediate monopoly revenue, will fix the
price per thousand feet at Lq_1, and consequently will sell OL thousand feet; the expenses of production will be Lq_2 per thousand feet, and the aggregate net revenue
will be $OL \times q_2q_1$, or which is the same thing $OL \times Lq_3$.

The dotted lines in the diagram are known to mathematicians as rectangular
hyperbolas; but we may call them *constant revenue curves* : for they are such that if
from a point on any one of them
lines be drawn perpendicular to Ox
and Oy respectively (the one representing revenue per thousand
feet and the other representing the
number of thousand feet sold), then
the product of these will be a constant quantity for every point on one
and the same curve. This product
is of course a smaller quantity for
the inner curves, those nearer Ox
and Oy, than it is for the outer
curves. And consequently since P_3
is on a smaller constant revenue
curve than q_3 is, $OM \times MP_3$ is less
than $OL \times Lq_3$. It will be noticed
that q_3 is the point in which QQ'
touches one of these curves. That
is, q_3 is on a larger constant revenue
curve than is any other point on QQ';
and therefore $OL \times Lq_3$ is greater
than $OM \times MP_3$, not only in the
position given to M in the figure, but
also in any position that M can take
along Ox. That is to say, q_3 has
been correctly determined as the
point on QQ' corresponding to the
maximum total monopoly revenue.
And thus we get the rule :—If
through that point in which QQ'

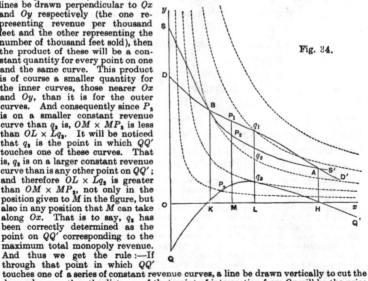

Fig. 34.

touches one of a series of constant revenue curves, a line be drawn vertically to cut the
demand curve, then the distance of that point of intersection from Ox will be the price
at which the commodity should be offered for sale in order that it may afford the
maximum monopoly revenue. See Note XXII. in the Mathematical Appendix.

V, xiv, 4

otal
mount,
n a
ionopoly
vill not
iminish
roduc-
ion;

varying with the amount of the commodity produced. Then, whatever be the price charged and the amount of the commodity sold, the monopoly revenue will be increased or diminished, as the case may be, by this sum; and therefore that selling price which afforded the maximum monopoly revenue before the change will afford it afterwards; the change therefore will not offer to the monopolist any inducement to alter his course of action. Suppose for instance that the maximum monopoly revenue is got when twelve hundred million cubic feet are sold annually; and that this is done when the price is fixed at 30d. per thousand feet: suppose that the expenses of production for this amount are at the rate of 26d., leaving a monopoly revenue at the rate of four pence per thousand feet, that is £20,000 in all. This is its maximum value: if the company fixed the price higher at, say, 31d. and sold only eleven hundred million feet, they would perhaps get a monopoly revenue at the rate of 4·2 pence per thousand feet, that is £19,250 in all; while in order to sell thirteen hundred millions they would have to lower their price to, say, 28d. and would get a monopoly revenue at the rate of perhaps 3·6d. per thousand feet, that is £19,500 in all. Thus by fixing the price at 30d. they get £750 more than by fixing it at 31d., and £500 more than by fixing it at 28d. Now let a tax of £10,000 a year be levied on the gas company as a fixed sum independent of the amount they sell. Their monopoly revenue will become £10,000 if they charge 30d., £9,250 if they charge 31d., and £9,500 if they charge 28d. They will therefore continue to charge 30d.

ior will
one pro-
portioned
to mono-
poly
evenue,

The same is true of a tax or a bounty proportioned not to the gross receipts of the undertaking, but to its monopoly revenue. For suppose next that a tax is levied, not of one fixed sum, but a certain percentage, say 50 per cent. of the monopoly revenue. The company will then retain a monopoly revenue of £10,000 if they charge 30d., of £9,625 if they charge 31d., and of £9,750 if they charge 28d. They will therefore still charge 30d.[1]

[1] If to the expenses of working a monopoly there be added (by a tax or otherwise) a lump sum independent of the amount produced, the result will be to cause every point on the monopoly revenue curve to move downwards to a point on a constant revenue curve representing a constant revenue smaller by a *fixed amount* than that on which it lies. Therefore the maximum revenue point on the new monopoly revenue curve lies vertically below that on the old : that is, the selling price and the amount produced remain unchanged, and conversely with regard to a fixed bounty or other fixed diminution of aggregate working expenses. As to the effects of a tax proportional to monopoly revenue, see Note XXIII. in the Mathematical Appendix.

　　It should however be noticed that if a tax or other new additional expense exceeds the maximum monopoly revenue, it will prevent the monopoly from being worked at all; it will convert the price which had afforded the maximum monopoly revenue into the price which would reduce to a minimum the loss that would result from continuing to work the monopoly.

On the other hand a tax proportional to the amount produced gives an inducement to the monopolist to lessen his output and raise his price. For by so doing he diminishes his expenses. And the excess of total receipts over total outlay may therefore be now increased by a diminution of output; though before the imposition of the tax it would have been lessened. Further, if before the imposition of the tax the net revenue was only a little greater than that which would have been afforded by much smaller sales, then the monopolist would gain by reducing his production very greatly; and hence in such cases as this, the change is likely to cause a very great diminution of production and rise of price. The opposite effects will be caused by a change which diminishes the expense of working the monopoly by a sum that varies directly with the amount produced under it.

V, XIV, 4.
———
but it will
have that
effect if it
is propor-
tional
to the
quantity
produced.

In the last example, for instance, a tax of 2d. on each thousand feet sold would have reduced the monopoly revenue to £10,083 if the company charged 31d. per thousand feet and therefore sold eleven hundred millions; to £10,000 if they charged 30d. and therefore sold twelve hundred millions, and to £8,666 if they charged 28d. and therefore sold thirteen hundred million feet. Therefore the tax would induce the company to raise the price to something higher than 30d.; they would perhaps go to 31d., perhaps somewhat higher; for the figures before us do not show exactly how far it would be their interest to go.

On the other hand, if there were a bounty of 2d. on the sale of each thousand feet, the monopoly revenue would rise to £28,416 if they charged 31d., to £30,000 if they charged 30d., and to £30,333 if they charged 28d.: it would therefore cause them to lower the price. And of course the same result would follow from an improvement in the method of making gas, which lowered its cost of production to the monopolist company by 2d. per 1000 feet.[1]

[1] In the text it is supposed that the tax or bounty is directly proportional to the sales: but the argument, when closely examined, will be found to involve no further assumption than that the aggregate tax or bounty increases with every increase in that amount: the argument does not really require that it should increase in exact proportion to that amount.

Much instruction is to be got by drawing diagrams to represent various conditions of demand and of (monopoly) supply, with the resultant shapes of the monopoly revenue curve. A careful study of the shapes thus obtained will give more assistance than any elaborate course of reasoning in the endeavour to realize the multiform action of economic forces in relation to monopolies. A tracing may be made on thin paper of the constant revenue curves in one of the diagrams; and this, when laid over a monopoly revenue curve, will indicate at once the point, or points, of maximum revenue. For it will be found, not only when the demand and supply curves cut one another more than once, but also when they do not, there will often be, as in fig. 35, several points on a monopoly revenue curve at which it touches a constant revenue curve. Each of these points will show a true maximum monopoly revenue; but one of them will generally stand out pre-eminently as being on a larger

§ 5. The monopolist would lose all his monopoly revenue if he produced for sale an amount so great that its supply price, as here defined, was equal to its demand price : the amount which gives the maximum monopoly revenue is always considerably less than that. It may therefore appear as though the amount produced under a monopoly is always less and its price to the consumer always higher than if there were no monopoly. But this is not the case.

---

constant revenue curve than any of the others and therefore indicating a larger monopoly revenue than they.

If it happens, as in fig. 35, that this chief maximum q'_3 lies a long way to the right of a smaller maximum q_3, then the imposition of a tax on the commodity, or any other change that raised its supply curve throughout, would lower by an equal

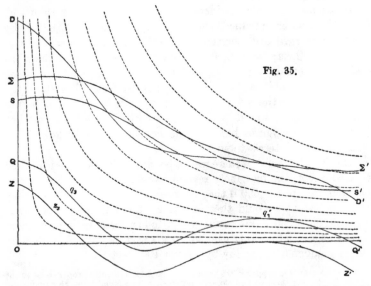

Fig. 35.

amount the monopoly revenue curve. Let the supply curve be raised from SS' to the position $\Sigma\Sigma'$; and in consequence let the monopoly revenue curve fall from its old position QQ' to ZZ'; then the chief point of maximum revenue will move from q'_3 to z_3, representing a great diminution of production, a great rise of price and a great injury to the consumers. The converse effects of any change, such as a bounty on the commodity, which lowers its supply price throughout and raises the monopoly revenue curve, may be seen by regarding ZZ' as the old and QQ' as the new position of that curve. It will be obvious on a little consideration (but the fact may with advantage be illustrated by drawing suitable diagrams), that the more nearly the monopoly revenue curve approximates to the shape of a constant revenue curve, the greater will be the change in the position of the maximum revenue point which results from any given alteration in the expenses of production of the commodity generally. This change is great in fig. 35 not because DD' and SS' intersect more than once, but because two parts of QQ', one a long way to the right of the other, lie in the neighbourhood of the same constant revenue curve.

For when the production is all in the hands of one person or company, the total expenses involved are generally less than would have to be incurred if the same aggregate production were distributed among a multitude of comparatively small rival producers. They would have to struggle with one another for the attention of consumers, and would necessarily spend in the aggregate a great deal more on advertising in all its various forms than a single firm would; and they would be less able to avail themselves of the many various economies which result from production on a large scale. In particular they could not afford to spend as much on improving methods of production and the machinery used in it, as a single large firm which knew that it was certain itself to reap the whole benefit of any advance it made.

V, XIV, 6

it must be remember-ed that a monopoly can generally be worked economi-cally.

This argument does indeed assume the single firm to be managed with ability and enterprise, and to have an unlimited command of capital—an assumption which cannot always be fairly made. But where it can be made, we may generally conclude that the supply schedule for the commodity, if not monopolized, would show higher supply prices than those of our monopoly supply schedule; and therefore the equilibrium amount of the commodity produced under free competition would be less than that for which the demand price is equal to the monopoly supply price.[1]

One of the most interesting and difficult applications of the theory of monopolies is to the question whether the public interest is best served by the allotment of a distinct basin to each great railway, and excluding competition there. For the proposal it is urged that a railway can afford to carry two million passengers, or tons of goods, cheaper than one million : and that a division of the public demand between two lines will prevent either of them from offering a cheap service. It must be admitted that, other things being equal, the " monopoly revenue price " fixed by a railway will be lowered by every increase in the demand for its services, and *vice versâ*. But, human nature being what it is, experience has shown that the breaking of a monopoly by the opening out of a competing line accelerates, rather than retards the discovery by the older line

But this raises questions which are incapable of general solution.

---

[1] In other words, though L lies necessarily a good deal to the left of H, according to the notation in fig. 34 ; yet the supply curve for the commodity, if there were no monopoly, might lie so much above the present position of SS' that its point of inter-section with DD' would lie much to the left of A in the figure, and might not improb-ably lie to the left of L.   Something has already been said (IV. XI., XII. ; and V. XI.), as to the advantages which a single powerful firm has over its smaller rivals in those industries in which the law of increasing return acts strongly ; and as to the chance which it might have of obtaining a practical monopoly of its own branch of produc-tion, if it were managed for many generations together by people whose genius, enterprise and energy equalled those of the original founders of the business.

V, xiv, 6. that it can afford to carry traffic at lower rates.   There still remains the suggestion that after a while the railways will combine and charge the public with the expense wasted on duplicating the services.   But this again only opens out new matters of controversy.   The theory of monopolies starts rather than solves practical issues such as these : and we must defer their study.[1]

The monopolist may lower his price with a view to the future development of his business,

§ 6. So far we have supposed the owner of a monopoly to fix the price of his commodity with exclusive reference to the immediate net revenue which he can derive from it.   But, in fact, even if he does not concern himself with the interests of the consumers, he is likely to reflect that the demand for a thing depends in a great measure on people's familiarity with it; and that if he can increase his sales by taking a price a little below that which would afford him the maximum net revenue, the increased use of his commodity will before long recoup him for his present loss.   The lower the price of gas, the more likely people are to have it laid on to their houses; and when once it is there, they are likely to go on making some use of it, even though a rival, such as electricity or mineral oil, may be competing closely with it.   The case is stronger when a railway company has a practical monopoly of the transport of persons and goods to a sea-port, or to a suburban district which is as yet but partly built over; the railway company may then find it worth while, as a matter of business, to levy charges much below those which would afford the maximum net revenue, in order to get merchants into the habit of using the port, to encourage the inhabitants of the port to develop their docks and warehouses; or to assist speculative builders in the new suburb to build houses cheaply and to fill them quickly with tenants, thus giving to the suburb an air of early prosperity which goes far towards insuring its permanent success.   This sacrifice by a monopolist of part of his present gains in order to develop future business differs in extent rather than kind from the sacrifices which a young firm commonly makes in order to establish a connection.

In such cases as these a railway company though not pretending to any philanthropic motives, yet finds its own interests so closely

---

[1] The full theoretical treatment of questions relating to the influence exerted on monopoly price by an increase of demand requires the use of mathematics for which the reader is referred to an article on monopolies by Professor Edgeworth in the *Giornale degli Economisti* for Oct. 1897.   But an inspection of fig. 34 will show that a uniform raising of DD' will push L much to the right; and that the resulting position of q_1 will probably be lower than before.   If, however, a new class of residents come into the district, who are so well to do, that their willingness to travel is very little affected by the railway charges, then the shape of DD' will be altered; its left side will be raised more in proportion than its right : and the new position of q_1 may be higher than the old.

connected with those of the purchasers of its services, that it gains by making some temporary sacrifice of net revenue with the purpose of increasing consumers' surplus. And an even closer connection between the interests of the producers and the consumers is found when the landowners of any district combine to make a branch railway through it, without much hope that the traffic will afford the current rate of interest on the capital which they invest—that is, without much hope that the monopoly revenue of the railway, as we have defined it, will be other than a negative quantity—but expecting that the railway will add so much to the value of their property as to make their venture on the whole a profitable one. And when a municipality undertakes the supply of gas or water, or facilities for transport by improved roads, by new bridges, or by tramways, the question always arises whether the scale of charges should be high, so as to afford a good net revenue and relieve the pressure on the rates; or should be low, so as to increase consumers' surplus.

§ 7. It is clear then that some study is wanted of calculations by which a monopolist should govern his actions, on the supposition that he regards an increase of consumers' surplus as equally desirable to him, if not with an equal increase of his own monopoly revenue, yet with an increase, say, one-half or one-quarter as great.

If the consumers' surplus which arises from the sale of the commodity at any price, is added to the monopoly revenue derived from it, the sum of the two is the money measure of the net benefits accruing from the sale of the commodity to producers and consumers together, or as we may say the *total benefit* of its sale. And if the monopolist regards a gain to the consumers as of equal importance with an equal gain to himself, his aim will be to produce just that amount of the commodity which will make this total benefit a maximum.[1]

---

[1] In fig. 36 DD', SS', and QQ' represent the demand, supply, and monopoly revenue curves drawn on the same plan as in fig. 34. From P_1 draw P_1F perpendicular to Oy; then DFP_1 is the consumers' surplus derived from the sale of OM thousand feet of gas at the price MP_1. In MP_1 take a point P_4 such that $OM \times MP_4 =$ the area DFP_1 : then as M moves from O along Ox, P_4 will trace out our fourth curve, OR, which we may call the *consumers' surplus curve*. (Of course it passes through O, because when the sale of the commodity is reduced to nothing, the consumers' surplus also vanishes.)

Next from P_3P_1 cut off P_3P_5 equal to MP_4, so that $MP_5 = MP_3 + MP_2$. Then $OM \times MP_5 = OM \times MP_3 + OM \times MP_4$; but $OM \times MP_3$ is the total monopoly revenue when an amount OM is being sold at a price MP_1, and $OM \times MP_4$ is the corresponding consumers' surplus. Therefore $OM \times MP_5$ is the sum of the monopoly revenue and the consumers' surplus, that is the (money measure of the) total benefit which the community will derive from the commodity when an amount OM is produced. The locus of P_5 is our fifth curve, QT, which we may call the *total*

V, xiv, 7.

But if the consumers' surplus be counted at only a fraction of its actual value, the sum of the two may be called *compromise benefit.*

But it will seldom happen that the monopolist can and will treat £1 of consumers' surplus as equally desirable with £1 of monopoly revenue. Even a government which considers its own interests coincident with those of the people has to take account of the fact that, if it abandons one source of revenue, it must in general fall back on others which have their own disadvantages. For they will necessarily involve friction and expense in collection, together with some injury to the public, of the kind which we have described as a loss of consumers' surplus : and they can never be adjusted with perfect fairness, especially when account is taken of the unequal shares that different members of the community will get of the benefits for the sake of which it is proposed that the government should forego some of its revenue.

Suppose then that the monopolist makes a compromise, and reckons £1 of consumers' surplus as equivalent to say 10*s.* of monopoly revenue. Let him calculate the monopoly revenue to be got from selling his commodity at any given price, and to it let him add

benefit curve. It touches one of the constant revenue curves at t_5, and this shows that the (money measure of the) total benefit is a maximum when the amount offered

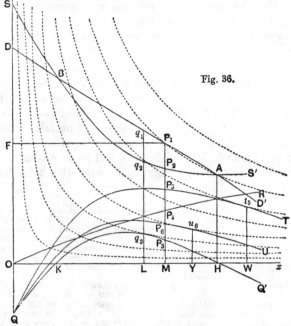

Fig. 36.

for sale is OW ; or, which is the same thing, when the price of sale is fixed at the demand price for OW.

one half the corresponding consumers' surplus : the sum of the two
may be called the *compromise benefit*; and his aim will be to fix on
that price which will make the compromise benefit as large as
possible.[1]

The following general results are capable of exact proof; but on
a little consideration they will appear so manifestly true as hardly to
require proof. Firstly, the amount which the monopolist will offer
for sale will be greater (and the price at which he will sell it will be
less) if he is to any extent desirous to promote the interests of
consumers than if his sole aim is to obtain the greatest possible monopoly revenue; and secondly, the amount produced will be greater
(and the selling price will be less) the greater be the desire of the
monopolist to promote the interests of consumers; *i.e.* the larger be
the percentage of its actual value at which he counts in consumers'
surplus with his own revenue.[2]

§ 8. Not many years ago it was commonly argued that : " An
English ruler, who looks upon himself as the minister of the race he
rules, is bound to take care that he impresses their energies in no
work that is not worth the labour that is spent upon it, or—to
translate the sentiment into plainer language—that he engages in
nothing that will not produce an income sufficient to defray the
interest on its cost." [3] Such phrases as this may sometimes have
meant little more than that a benefit which consumers were not
willing to purchase at a high price and on a large scale, was likely to
exist for the greater part only in the specious counsels of those who
had some personal interest in the proposed undertakings; but
probably they more often indicated a tendency to under-estimate
the magnitude of that interest which consumers have in a low price,
and which we call consumers' surplus.[4]

General results.

The importance of the interests of consumers has been under-estimated,

---

[1] If he compromises on the basis that £1 of consumers' surplus is equally desirable
with £n of monopoly revenue, n being a proper fraction, let us take a point P_6 in
P_3P_5 such that $P_3P_6 = n.P_3P_5$, or, which is the same thing, nMP_4. Then $OM \times MP_6 = OM \times MP_3, + nOM \times MP_4$; that is, it is equal to the monopoly revenue
derived from selling an amount OM of the commodity at the price MP_1, + n times
the consumers' surplus derived from this sale : and is therefore the compromise benefit
derived from that sale. The locus of P_6 is our sixth curve, QU, which we may call
the *compromise benefit curve*. It touches one of the constant revenue curves in u_6; which
shows that the compromise benefit attains its maximum when amount OY is sold;
or which is the same thing, when the selling price is fixed at the demand price for the
amount OY.
[2] That is to say, firstly, OY fig. 36 is always greater than OL; and secondly, the
greater n is, the greater OY is. (See Note XXIII. *bis* in the Mathematical Appendix.)
[3] The words are quoted from a leading article in *The Times* for July 30, 1874 :
they fairly represent a great body of public opinion.
[4] Fig. 37 may be taken to represent the case of a proposed Government undertaking in India. The supply curve is above the demand curve during its whole
length, showing that the enterprise to which it refers is unremunerative, in the sense
that whatever price the producers fix, they will lose money ; their monopoly revenue
will be a negative quantity. But QT the total benefit curve rises above Ox; and

V, xiv, 8.
——
because
direct
personal
experience
seldom
helps
much
towards
forming
correct
estimates
of them,

One of the chief elements of success in private business is the faculty of weighing the advantages and disadvantages of any proposed course, and of assigning to them their true relative importance. He who by practice and genius has acquired the power of attributing to each factor its right quantity, is already well on the way to fortune; and the increase in the efficiency of our productive forces is in a great measure due to the large number of able minds who are devoting themselves ceaselessly to acquiring these business instincts. But unfortunately the advantages thus weighed against one another are nearly all regarded from one point of view, that of the producer; and there are not many who concern themselves to weigh against

---

touches a constant revenue curve in t_5. If then they offer for sale an amount OW (or, which is the same thing, fix the price at the demand price for OW), the resultant consumers' surplus, if taken at its full value, will outweigh the loss on working by an

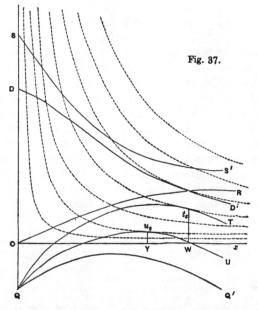

Fig. 37.

amount represented by $OW \times Wt_5$. But suppose that, in order to make up the deficiency, Government must levy taxes, and that taking account of all indirect expenses and other evils, these cost the public twice what they bring in to the Government, it will then be necessary to count two rupees of the consumers' surplus as compensating for a Government outlay of only one rupee; and in order to represent the net gain of the undertaking on this supposition, we must draw the compromise benefit curve QU as in fig. 36, but putting $n = \frac{1}{2}$. Thus $MP_5 = MP_3 \times \frac{1}{2}MP_4$. (Another way of putting the same thing is to say that QU is drawn midway between the monopoly revenue (negative) curve QQ' and the total benefit curve QT.) QU so drawn in fig. 37 touches a constant revenue curve in u_6, showing that if the amount OY is offered for sale, or, which is the same thing, if the price is fixed at the demand price for OY, there will result a net gain to India represented by $OY \times Yu_6$.

one another the relative quantities of the interests which the con- V, xiv, 8.
sumers and the producers have in different courses of action. For
indeed the requisite facts come within the direct experience of only a
very few persons, and even in the case of those few, only to a very
limited extent and in a very imperfect way. Moreover when a great
administrator has acquired those instincts with regard to public
interests which able business men have with regard to their own
affairs, he is not very likely to be able to carry his plans with a free
hand. At all events in a democratic country no great public undertaking is secure of being sustained on consistent lines of policy,
unless its advantages can be made clear, not only to the few who
have direct experience of high public affairs, but also to the many
who have no such experience and have to form their judgment on
the materials set before them by others.

Judgments of this kind must always be inferior to those which an and our
able business man forms, by the aid of instincts based on long public statistics
experience with regard to his own business. But they may be made are not yet
much more trustworthy than they are at present, if they can be properly organized.
based on statistical measures of the relative quantities of the
benefits and the injuries which different courses of public action
are likely to cause to the several classes of the community. Much of
the failure and much of the injustice, in which the economic policies
of governments have resulted, have been due to the want of statistical
measurement. A few people who have been strongly interested on
one side have raised their voices loudly, persistently and all together;
while little has been heard from the great mass of people whose
interests have lain in the opposite direction; for, even if their attention has been fairly called to the matter, few have cared to exert
themselves much for a cause in which no one of them has more than
a small stake. The few therefore get their way, although if statistical measures of the interests involved were available, it might
prove that the aggregate of the interests of the few was only a
tenth or a hundredth part of the aggregate of the interests of the
silent many.

No doubt statistics can be easily misinterpreted; and are often Statistical arguments
very misleading when first applied to new problems. But many are often
of the worst fallacies involved in the misapplications of statistics misleading at first;
are definite and can be definitely exposed, till at last no one ventures but free
to repeat them even when addressing an uninstructed audience: discussion clears
and on the whole arguments which can be reduced to statistical away
forms, though still in a backward condition, are making more sure statistical fallacies.
and more rapid advances than any others towards obtaining the

V, xiv, 9. general acceptance of all who have studied the subjects to which they refer. The rapid growth of collective interests, and the increasing tendency towards collective action in economic affairs, make it every day more important that we should know what quantitative measures of public interests are most needed and what statistics are required for them, and that we should set ourselves to obtain these statistics.

Hopes for the future from the statistical study of demand and consumers' surplus.

It is perhaps not unreasonable to hope that as time goes on, the statistics of consumption will be so organized as to afford demand schedules sufficiently trustworthy, to show in diagrams that will appeal to the eye, the quantities of consumers' surplus that will result from different courses of public and private action. By the study of these pictures the mind may be gradually trained to get juster notions of the relative magnitudes of the interests which the community has in various schemes of public and private enterprise; and sounder doctrines may replace those traditions of an earlier generation, which had perhaps a wholesome influence in their time, but which damped social enthusiasm by throwing suspicion on all projects for undertakings by the public on its own behalf which would not show a balance of direct pecuniary profit.

The practical bearings of many of the abstract reasonings in which we have recently been engaged will not be fully apparent till we approach the end of this treatise. But there seemed to be advantages in introducing them thus early, partly because of their close connection with the main theory of equilibrium of demand and supply, and partly because they throw side lights on the character and the purposes of that investigation of the causes which determine distribution on which we are about to enter.

The problem of two monopolies dependent on each other's aid is incapable of a universal solution.

§ 9. So far it has been assumed that the monopolist can buy and sell freely. But in fact monopolistic combinations in one branch of industry foster the growth of monopolistic combinations in those which have occasion to buy from or sell to it : and the conflicts and alliances between such associations play a rôle of ever increasing importance in modern economics. Abstract reasoning of a general character has little to say on the subject. If two absolute monopolies are complementary, so that neither can turn its products to any good account, without the other's aid, there is no means of determining where the price of the ultimate product will be fixed. Thus if we supposed, following Cournot's lead, that copper and zinc were each of them useless except when combined to make brass : and if we supposed that one man, A, owned all the available sources of supply of copper; while another, B, owned all those of zinc; there would then be no means of determining beforehand what amount of brass would be produced, nor therefore the price at which it could be sold. Each would try to get the better of the other in bargaining; and though the issue of the contest would greatly affect the purchasers, they would not be able to influence it.[1]

Under the conditions supposed, A could not count on reaping the whole, nor even any share at all of the benefit, from increased sales, that would be got by lowering the price of copper in a market in which the price of zinc was fixed by natural causes rather than strategical higgling and bargaining. For, if he reduced his price, B might take the action as a sign of commercial weakness, and raise the price of zinc; thus causing A to lose both on price and on amount sold. Each would therefore be tempted to bluff the other; and consumers might find that less brass was put on the market, and that therefore a higher price could be exacted for it, than if a single monopolist owned the whole supplies both of copper and of zinc : for he might see his way to gaining in the long run by a low price which stimulated consumption. But neither A nor B could reckon on the effects of his own action, unless the two came together and agreed on a common policy : that is unless they made a partial, and perhaps temporary fusion of their monopolies. On this ground, and because monopolies are likely to disturb allied industries it may reasonably be urged that the public interest generally requires that complementary monopolies should be held in a single hand.

But there are other considerations of perhaps greater importance on the other side. For in real life there are scarcely any monopolies as absolute and permanent as that just discussed. On the contrary there is in the modern world an ever increasing tendency towards the substitution of new things and new methods for old, which are not being developed progressively in the interests of consumers; and the direct or indirect competition thus brought to bear is likely to weaken the position of one of the complementary monopolies more than the other. For instance if there be only one factory for spinning and only one for weaving in a small isolated country, it may be for the time to the public interest that the two should be in

(margin notes:) V, xiv, 9. — There are *primâ facie* reasons for thinking that the public interest calls for their fusion, but such a fusion would in many cases introduce greater and more lasting discords than it removed.

---

[1] Thus there is a slight analogy between this case and that of composite rent of water power, and the only site on which it could be turned to account (see above V. xi. 7), so far as the indeterminateness of the division of the producer's surplus is concerned. But in this case there is no means of knowing what the producer's surplus will be. Cournot's fundamental equations appear to be based on inconsistent assumptions, see *Recherches sur les principes mathématiques des Richesses*, Ch. ix. p. 113. Here, as elsewhere, he opened up new ground, but overlooked some of its most obvious features. Prof. H. L. Moore (*Quarterly Journal of Economics*, Feb. 1906), basing himself partly on the work of Bertrand and Prof. Edgeworth, lays down clearly the assumptions which are appropriate to monopoly problems.

V, xiv, 9. the same hands. But the monopoly so established will be much harder to shake than would either half of it separately. For a new venturer might push his way into the spinning business and compete with the old spinning mill for the custom of the old weaving sheds.

Consider again a through route, partly by rail and partly by sea, between two great centres of industry. If competition on either half of the route were permanently impossible, it would probably be to the public interest that the ships and the railway line should be in the same hands. But as things are, no such general statement can be made. Under some conditions it is more to the public interest that they should be in one hand; under others, and those perhaps the conditions that occur the more frequently, it is in the long run to the public interest that they should remain in different hands.

Similarly the *primâ facie* arguments in favour of the fusion of monopolistic cartels, or other associations, in complementary branches of industry, though often plausible and even strong, will generally be found on closer examination to be treacherous. They point to the removal of prominent social and industrial discords; but at the probable expense of larger and more enduring discords in the future.[1]

---

[1] Book III. of *Industry and Trade* is occupied with a study of problems akin to those which have been sketched in this chapter.

CHAPTER XV

SUMMARY OF THE GENERAL THEORY OF EQUILIBRIUM OF DEMAND AND SUPPLY

§ 1. THE present chapter contains no new matter : it is a mere V, xv, 1. summary of the results of Book V. The second half of it may be of service to anyone who has omitted the later chapters : for it may indicate, though it cannot explain, their general drift.

In Book V we have studied the theory of the mutual relations of demand and supply in their most general form; taking as little account as possible of the special incidents of particular applications of the theory, and leaving over for the following Book the study of the bearings of the general theory on the special features of the several agents of production, Labour, Capital, and Land.

The difficulties of the problem depend chiefly on variations in the Ch. I. On markets. area of space, and the period of time over which the market in question extends; the influence of time being more fundamental than that of space.

Even in a market of very short period, such as that of a provincial Ch. II. Temporary equilibrium of demand and supply corn-exchange on market-day, the "higgling and bargaining" might probably oscillate about a mean position, which would have some sort of a right to be called the equilibrium price : but the action of dealers in offering one price or refusing another would depend little, if at all, on calculations with regard to cost of production. They would look chiefly at present demand on the one hand, and on the other at the stocks of the commodity already available. It is true that they would pay some attention to such movements of production in the near future as might throw their shadow before; but in the case of perishable goods they would look only a very little way beyond the immediate present. Cost of production has for instance no perceptible influence on the day's bargaining in a fish-market.

In a rigidly stationary state in which supply could be perfectly Chs. III. IV. V. Equilibrium of normal demand and supply. adjusted to demand in every particular, the normal expenses of production, the marginal expenses, and the average expenses (rent being counted in) would be one and the same thing, for long periods and for short. But, as it is, the language both of professed writers on

V, xv, 1.

The
element
of time.

Long
period
or true
normal
price.

economics and of men of business shows much elasticity in the use of the term Normal when applied to the causes that determine value. And one fairly well marked division needs study.

On the one side of this division are long periods, in which the normal action of economic forces has time to work itself out more fully; in which therefore a temporary scarcity of skilled labour, or of any other of the agents of production, can be remedied; and in which those economies that normally result from an increase in the scale of production—normally, that is without the aid of any substantive new invention—have time to develop themselves. The expenses of a representative firm, managed with normal ability and having normal access to the internal and external economies of production on a large scale, may be taken as a standard for estimating normal expenses of production : and when the period under survey is long enough to enable the investment of capital in building up a new business to complete itself and to bear full fruits; then the marginal supply price is that, the expectation of which in the long run just suffices to induce capitalists to invest their material capital, and workers of all grades to invest their personal capital in the trade.

Short-
period
normal
price or
sub-normal
price.

On the other side of the line of division are periods of time long enough to enable producers to adapt their production to changes in demand, in so far as that can be done with the existing provision of specialized skill, specialized capital, and industrial organization; but not long enough to enable them to make any important changes in the supplies of these factors of production. For such periods the stock of material and personal appliances of production has to be taken in a great measure for granted; and the marginal increment of supply is determined by estimates of producers as to the amount of production it is worth their while to get out of those appliances. If trade is brisk all energies are strained to their utmost, overtime is worked, and then the limit to production is given by want of power rather than by want of will to go farther or faster. But if trade is slack every producer has to make up his mind how near to prime cost it is worth his while to take fresh orders. And here there is no definite law, the chief operative force is the fear of spoiling the market; and that acts in different ways and with different strengths on different individuals and different industrial groups. For the chief motive of all open combinations and of all informal silent and "customary" understandings whether among employers or employed is the need for preventing individuals from spoiling the common market by action that may bring them immediate gains, but at the cost of a greater aggregate loss to the trade.

§ 2. We next turned aside to consider the relations of demand and V, xv, 2, 3.
supply with reference to things that need to be combined together Ch. VI.
for the purposes of satisfying a joint demand; of which the most Joint and
important instance is that of the specialized material capital, and the composite
specialized personal skill that must work together in any trade. and
For there is no direct demand on the part of consumers for either supply.
alone, but only for the two conjointly; the demand for either
separately is a derived demand, which rises, other things being equal,
with every increase in the demand for the common products, and
with every diminution in the supply price of the joint factors
of production.   In like manner commodities of which there is a joint
supply, such as gas and coke, or beef and hides, can each of them
have only a derived supply price, governed by the expenses of the
whole process of production on the one hand, and on the other by
the demand for the remaining joint products.

The composite demand for a thing, resulting from its being used
for several different purposes, and the composite supply of a thing,
that has several sources of production, present no great difficulty;
for the several amounts demanded for the different purposes, or
supplied from different sources, can be added together, on the same
plan as was adopted in Book III., for combining the demands of the
rich, the middle classes and the poor for the same commodity.

Next we made some study of the division of the supplementary Ch. VII.
costs of a business—and especially those connected with building Distribu-
up a trade connection, with marketing, and with insurance—among tion of
the various products of that business. supple-
mentary
costs.

§ 3. Returning to those central difficulties of the equilibrium of Chs. VIII.
normal demand and supply which are connected with the element of —XI.
time, we investigated more fully the relation between the value of an The value
appliance for production and that of the things produced by it. of an
appliance
for pro-
When different producers have different advantages for pro- duction in
ducing a thing, its price must be sufficient to cover the expenses of relation to
production of those producers who have no special and exceptional that of the
things
facilities; for if not they will withhold or diminish their production, produced
and the scarcity of the amount supplied, relatively to the demand, by it.
will raise the price.   When the market is in equilibrium, and the
thing is being sold at a price which covers these expenses, there
remains a surplus beyond their expenses for those who have the
assistance of any exceptional advantages.   If these advantages arise
from the command over free gifts of nature, the surplus is called a
producer's surplus or producer's rent : there is a surplus in any case,
and if the owner of a free gift of nature lends it out to another, he can

V, xv, 4. generally get for its use a money income equivalent to this surplus.

The price of the produce is equal to the cost of production of that part of it, which is raised on the margin, that is under such unfavourable conditions as to yield no rent. The cost of this part can be reckoned up without reasoning in a circle; and the cost of other parts cannot.

If land which had been used for growing hops, is found capable of yielding a higher rent as market-garden land, the area under hops will undoubtedly be diminished; and this will raise their marginal cost of production and therefore their price. The rent which land will yield for one kind of produce, calls attention to the fact that a demand for the land for that kind of produce increases the difficulties of supply of other kinds; though it does not directly enter into those expenses. And similar arguments apply to the relation between the site values of urban land and the costs of things made on it.

Thus when we are taking a broad view of normal value, when we are investigating the causes which determine normal value " in the long run," when we are tracing the " ultimate " effects of economic causes; then the income that is derived from capital in these forms enters into the payments by which the expenses of production of the commodity in question have to be covered; and estimates as to the probable amount of that income directly control the action of the producers, who are on the margin of doubt as to whether to increase the means of production or not. But, on the other hand, when we are considering the causes which determine normal prices for a period which is short relatively to that required for largely increasing the supply of those appliances for production; then their influence on value is chiefly indirect and more or less similar to that exerted by the free gifts of nature. The shorter the period which we are considering, and the slower the process of production of those appliances, the less part will variations in the income derived from them play in checking or increasing the supply of the commodity produced by them, and in raising or lowering its supply price.

Ch. XII.
The influence of the law of increasing return on supply price does not show its true character in short periods.

§ 4. This leads to the consideration of some difficulties of a technical character connected with the marginal expenses of production of a commodity that obeys the law of increasing return. The difficulties arise from the temptation to represent supply price as dependent on the amount produced, without allowing for the length of time that is necessarily occupied by each individual business in extending its internal, and still more its external organization; and in consequence they have been most conspicuous in mathematical and semi-mathematical discussions of the theory of

value. For when changes of supply price and amount produced are V, xv, 5.
regarded as dependent exclusively on one another without any
reference to gradual growth, it appears reasonable to argue that
the marginal supply price for each individual producer is the addition
to his aggregate expenses of production made by producing his last
element; that this marginal price is likely in many cases to be
diminished by an increase in his output much more than the demand
price in the general market would be by the same cause.

The statical theory of equilibrium is therefore not wholly applic- Short-
able to commodities which obey the law of increasing return. It comings
should however be noted that in many industries each producer of the
has a special market in which he is well known, and which he cannot Statical
extend quickly; and that therefore, though it might be physically Method.
possible for him to increase his output rapidly, he would run the
risk of forcing down very much the demand price in his special
market, or else of being driven to sell his surplus production outside
on less favourable terms. And though there are industries in which
each producer has access to the whole of a large market, yet in these
there remain but few internal economies to be got by an increase of
output, when the existing plant is already well occupied. No
doubt there are industries as to which neither of these statements is
true : they are in a transitional state, and it must be conceded that
the statical theory of equilibrium of normal demand and supply
cannot be profitably applied to them. But such cases are not
numerous; and with regard to the great bulk of manufacturing
industries, the connection between supply price and amount shows a
fundamentally different character for short periods and for long.

For short periods, the difficulties of adjusting the internal and
external organization of a business to rapid changes in output are so
great that the supply price must generally be taken to rise with an
increase, and to fall with a diminution in the amount produced.

But in long periods both the internal and the external economies Its
of production on a large scale have time to develop themselves. operation
The marginal supply price is not the expenses of production of any periods.
particular bale of goods : but it is the whole expenses (including
insurance, and gross earnings of management) of a marginal increment in the aggregate process of production and marketing.

§ 5. Some study of the effects of a tax, regarded as a special Ch. XIII.
case of a change in the general conditions of demand and supply Changes
suggests that, when proper allowance is made for the interests of demand
consumers, there is on abstract grounds rather less *primâ facie* cause and
than the earlier economists supposed, for the general doctrine of so-

V, xv, 5.
—
with some
reference
to the
doctrine of
Maximum
Satisfac-
tion.
called " Maximum Satisfaction " ; *i.e.* for the doctrine that the free
pursuit by each individual of his own immediate interest, will lead
producers to turn their capital and labour, and consumers to turn
their expenditure into such courses as are most conducive to the
general interests. We have nothing to do at this stage of our inquiry,
limited as it is to analysis of the most general character, with the
important question how far, human nature being constituted as
it is at present, collective action is likely to be inferior to individualistic action in energy and elasticity, in inventiveness and directness of purpose; and whether it is not therefore likely to waste
through practical inefficiency more than it could save by taking
account of all the interests affected by any course of action. But
even without taking account of the evils arising from the unequal
distribution of wealth, there is *primâ facie* reason for believing that
the aggregate satisfaction, so far from being already a maximum,
could be much increased by collective action in promoting the production and consumption of things in regard to which the law of
increasing return acts with especial force.

Ch. XIV.
Theory
of mono-
polies.
This position is confirmed by the study of the theory of monopolies. It is the immediate interest of the monopolist so to adjust
the production and sale of his wares as to obtain for himself the
maximum net revenue, and the course which he thus adopts is
unlikely to be that which affords the aggregate maximum satisfaction. The divergence between individual and collective interests
is *primâ facie* less important with regard to those things which obey
the law of diminishing return, than with regard to those which obey
the law of increasing return : but, in the case of the latter, there
is strong *primâ facie* reason for believing that it might often be to
the interest of the community directly or indirectly to intervene,
because a largely increased production would add much more to
consumers' surplus than to the aggregate expenses of production
of the goods. More exact notions on the relations of demand and
supply, particularly when expressed in the form of diagrams, may
help us to see what statistics should be collected, and how they
should be applied in the attempt to estimate the relative magnitudes
of various conflicting economic interests, public and private.

Ricardo's
theory of
value.
Ricardo's theory of cost of production in relation to value occupies
so important a place in the history of economics that any misunderstanding as to its real character must necessarily be very
mischievous; and unfortunately it is so expressed as almost to invite
misunderstanding. In consequence there is a widely spread belief
that it has needed to be reconstructed by the present generation of

economists.   Cause is shown in Appendix I for not accepting this
opinion; and for holding on the contrary that the foundations of the
theory as they were left by Ricardo remain intact; that much has
been added to them, and that very much has been built upon them,
but that little has been taken from them.   It is there argued that he
knew that demand played an essential part in governing value,
but that he regarded its action as less obscure than that of cost of
production, and therefore passed it lightly over in the notes which
he made for the use of his friends, and himself; for he never essayed
to write a formal treatise : also that he regarded cost of production
as dependent—not as Marx asserted him to have done on the mere
quantity of labour used up in production, but—on the quality as
well as quantity of that labour; together with the amount of stored
up capital needed to aid labour, and the length of time during which
such aid was invoked.

BOOK VI

THE DISTRIBUTION OF THE NATIONAL INCOME

CHAPTER I

PRELIMINARY SURVEY OF DISTRIBUTION

§ 1. THE keynote of this Book is in the fact that free human beings are not brought up to their work on the same principles as a machine, a horse, or a slave. If they were, there would be very little difference between the distribution and the exchange side of value; for every agent of production would reap a return adequate to cover its own expenses of production with wear-and-tear, etc.; at all events after allowance had been made for casual failures to adjust supply to demand. But as it is, our growing power over nature makes her yield an ever larger surplus above necessaries; and this is not absorbed by an unlimited increase of the population. There remain therefore the questions :—What are the general causes which govern the distribution of this surplus among the people? What part is played by conventional necessaries, *i.e.* the Standard of Comfort? What by the influence which methods of consumption and of living generally exert on efficiency; by wants and activities, *i.e.* by the Standard of Life? What by the many-sided action of the principle of substitution, and by the struggle for survival between hand-workers and brain-workers of different classes and grades? What by the power which the use of capital gives to those in whose hands it is? What share of the general flow is turned to remunerate those who work (including here the undertaking of ventures) and " wait," as contrasted with those who work and consume at once the fruits of their endeavours? An attempt is made to give a broad answer to those and some similar questions.

We shall begin a preliminary survey of the subject by noting how French and English writers a century ago represented value as governed almost wholly by cost of production, demand taking a subordinate place. Next we shall observe how near to the truth these results would be in a stationary state; and what corrections

need to be introduced in order to bring these results into harmony VI, I, 2.
with the actual conditions of life and work : and thus the remainder
of Chapter I will be given mainly to the demand for labour.

In Chapter II we shall first consider its supply under modern Drift of Chapter II.
conditions; and thence we shall turn to a general view of the causes
which fix the broad lines of distribution of the national income
between labour, and the owners of capital and land. In this rapid
survey we shall pass by unnoticed many details : to fill in some
of these is the task of the remainder of the Book; but others must
stand over for a later Volume.

§ 2. The simplest account of the causes which determine the The Physiocrats assumed, in
distribution of the national income is that given by the French
economists who just preceded Adam Smith; and it is based upon the accordance with facts
peculiar circumstances of France in the latter half of last century. near at
The taxes, and other exactions levied from the French peasant, hand, that wages were
were then limited only by his ability to pay; and few of the labouring at their lowest
classes were far from starvation. So the Economists or Physiocrats, possible
as they were called, assumed for the sake of simplicity, that there level,
was a natural law of population according to which the wages of
labour were kept at starvation limit.[1] They did not suppose
that this was true of the whole working population, but the exceptions were so few, that they thought that the general impression
given by their assumption was true : somewhat in the same way as
it is well to begin an account of the shape of the earth, by saying
that it is an oblate spheroid, although a few mountains do project
as much as a thousandth part of its radius beyond the general level.

Again, they knew that the rate of interest in Europe had fallen and that
during the five preceding centuries, in consequence of the fact that much the same was
" economy had in general prevailed over luxury." But they were true of the
impressed very much by the sensitiveness of capital, and the quick- interest on Capital.
ness with which it evaded the oppressions of the tax-gatherer by
retiring from his grasp; and they therefore concluded that there
was no great violence in the supposition that if its profits were
reduced below what they then were, capital would speedily be
consumed or migrate. Accordingly they assumed, again for the

---

[1] Thus Turgot, who for this purpose may be reckoned with the Physiocrats,
says (*Sur la Formation et Distribution des Richesses*, § VI.), " In every sort of occupation
it must come to pass, and in fact it does come to pass, that the wages of the artisan
are limited to that which is necessary to procure him a subsistence . . . He earns no
more than his living (Il ne gagne que sa vie.)" When however Hume wrote, pointing
out that this statement led to the conclusion that a tax on wages must raise wages;
and that it was therefore inconsistent with the observed fact that wages are often
low where taxes are high, and *vice versâ*; Turgot replied (March, 1767) to the effect
that his iron law was not supposed to be fully operative in short periods, but only in
long. See Say's *Turgot*, English Ed. pp. 53, etc.

sake of simplicity, that there was something like a natural, or necessary rate of profit, corresponding in some measure to the natural rate of wages; that if the current rate exceeded this necessary level, capital would grow rapidly, till it forced down the rate of profit to that level; and that, if the current rate went below that level, capital would shrink quickly, and the rate would be forced upwards again. They thought that, wages and profits being thus fixed by natural laws, the natural value of everything was governed simply as the sum of wages and profits required to remunerate the producers.[1]

These rigid assumptions were partially relaxed by Adam Smith, Adam Smith worked out this conclusion more fully than the Physiocrats did; though it was left for Ricardo to make clear that the labour and capital needed for production must be estimated at the margin of cultivation, so as to avoid the element of rent. But Adam Smith saw also that labour and capital were not at the verge of starvation in England, as they were in France. In England the wages of a great part of the working classes were sufficient to allow much more than the mere necessaries of existence; and capital had too rich and safe a field of employment there to be likely to go out of existence, or to emigrate. So when he is carefully weighing his words, his use of the terms " the natural rate of wages," and " the natural rate of profit," has not that sharp definition and fixedness which it had in the mouths of the Physiocrats; and he goes a good way towards explaining how they are determined by the ever-fluctuating conditions of demand and supply. He even insists that the liberal reward of labour " increases the industry of the common people "; that " a plentiful subsistence increases the bodily strength of the labourer; and the comfortable hope of bettering his condition, and of ending his days perhaps in ease and plenty, animates him to exert that strength to the utmost. Where wages are high, accordingly, we shall always find the workman more active, diligent and expeditious, than where they are low; in England, for example, than in Scotland; in the neighbourhood of great towns than in remote country places." [1] And yet he some-

---

[1] From these premises the Physiocrats logically deduced the conclusion that the only net produce of the country disposable for the purposes of taxation is the rent of land ; that when taxes are placed on capital or labour, they make it shrink till its net price rises to the natural level. The landowners have, they argued, to pay a gross price which exceeds this net price by the taxes together with all the expenses of collecting them in detail, and an equivalent for all the impediments which the tax-gatherer puts in the way of the free course of industry; and therefore the land-owners would lose less in the long run if, being the owners of the only true surplus that exists, they would undertake to pay direct whatever taxes the King required; especially if the King would consent " laisser faire, laisser passer," that is, to let every one make whatever he chose, and take his labour and send his goods to whatever market he liked.

[1] *Wealth of Nations*, Bk. I. ch. VIII.

times falls back into the old way of speaking, and thus makes
careless readers suppose that he believes the mean level of the
wages of labour to be fixed by an iron law at the bare necessaries of
life.

Malthus again, in his admirable survey of the course of wages in
England from the thirteenth to the eighteenth centuries, shows how
their mean level oscillated from century to century, falling sometimes down to about half a peck of corn a day, and rising sometimes
up to a peck and a half or even, in the fifteenth century, to about two
pecks. But although he observes that " an inferior mode of living
may be a cause as well as a consequence of poverty," he traces
this effect almost exclusively to the consequent increase of numbers;
he does not anticipate the stress which economists of our own
generation lay on the influence which habits of living exercise on the
efficiency, and therefore on the earning power of the labourer.[1]

Ricardo's language is even more unguarded than that of Adam
Smith and Malthus. It is true, indeed, that he says distinctly [2] :—
" It is not to be understood that the natural price of labour estimated
in food and necessaries is absolutely fixed and constant . . . It essentially depends on the habits and customs of the people." But,
having said this once, he does not take the trouble to repeat it
constantly; and most of his readers forget that he says it. In the
course of his argument he frequently adopts a mode of speaking
similar to that of Turgot and the Physiocrats [3]; and seems to
imply that the tendency of population to increase rapidly as soon as
wages rise above the bare necessaries of life, causes wages to be
fixed by " a natural law " to the level of these bare necessaries.
This law has been called, especially in Germany, Ricardo's " iron "
or " brazen " law : many German socialists believe that this law is in
operation now even in the western world; and that it will continue
to be so, as long as the plan on which production is organized remains
" capitalistic " or " individualistic "; and they claim Ricardo as an
authority on their side.[4]

In fact, however, Ricardo was not only aware that the necessary
or natural limit of wages was fixed by no iron law, but is determined
by the local conditions and habits of each place and time : he was

---

[1] *Political Economy,* IV. 2. There is some doubt as to the extent of the rise of
real wages in the fifteenth century. It is only in the last two generations that the real
wages of common labour in England have exceeded two pecks.
[2] *Principles,* v.   [3] Compare above, IV. III. 8.
[4] Some German economists, who are not socialists, and who believe that no
such law exists, yet maintain that the doctrines of Ricardo and his followers stand or
fall with the truth of this law; while others (*e.g.* Roscher, *Gesch. der Nat. Oek. in
Deutschland,* p. 1022) protest against the socialist misunderstandings of Ricardo.

VI, I, 2. further keenly sensitive to the importance of a higher " standard of living," and called on the friends of humanity to exert themselves to encourage the growth of a resolve among the working classes not to allow their wages to fall anywhere near the bare necessaries of life.[1]

The persistency with which many writers continue to attribute to him a belief in the " iron law " can be accounted for only by his delight " in imagining strong cases," and his habit of not repeating a hint, which he had once given, that he was omitting for the sake of simplicity the conditions and limitations that were needed to make his results applicable to real life.[2]

Mill also insisted on the progressive deterioration caused by unduly low wages.
Mill did not make any great advance in the theory of wages beyond his predecessors, in spite of the care with which he set himself to emphasize the distinctly human element in economics. He, however, followed Malthus in dwelling on those lessons of history which show that, if a fall of wages caused the labouring classes to lower their standard of comfort " the injury done to them will be permanent, and their deteriorated condition will become a new minimum tending to perpetuate itself as the more ample minimum did before." [3]

But it was only in the last generation that a careful study was

[1] It may be well to quote his words. " The friends of humanity cannot but wish that in all countries the labouring classes should have a taste for comforts and enjoyments, and that they should be stimulated by all legal means in their exertions to procure them. There cannot be a better security against a super-abundant population. In those countries, where the labouring classes have the fewest wants, and are contented with the cheapest food, the people are exposed to the greatest vicissitudes and miseries. They have no place of refuge from calamity; they cannot seek safety in a lower station; they are already so low, that they can fall no lower. On any deficiency of the chief article of their subsistence, there are few substitutes of which they can avail themselves, and dearth to them is attended with almost all the evils of famine." (*Principles*, ch. v.) It is noteworthy that McCulloch, who has been charged, not altogether unjustly, with having adopted the extremest tenets of Ricardo, and applied them harshly and rigidly, yet chooses for the heading of the fourth Chapter of his Treatise *On Wages* :—" Disadvantage of Low Wages, and of having the Labourers habitually fed on the cheapest species of food. Advantage of High Wages."

[2] This habit of Ricardo's is discussed in Appendix I. (See also V. xiv. 5.) The English classical economists frequently spoke of the minimum of wages as depending on the price of corn. But the term " corn " was used by them as short for agricultural produce in general, somewhat as Petty (*Taxes and Contributions*, ch. xiv.) speaks of " the Husbandry of Corn, which we will suppose to contain all necessaries of life, as in the Lord's Prayer we suppose the word Bread doth." Of course Ricardo took a less hopeful view of the prospects of the working classes than we do now. Even the agricultural labourer can now feed his family well and have something to spare : while even the artisan would then have required the whole of his wages, at all events after a poor harvest, to buy abundant and good food for his family. Sir W. Ashley insists on the narrowness of Ricardo's hopes as compared with those of our own age; he describes instructively the history of the passage quoted in the last note; and shows that even Lassalle did not attribute absolute rigidity to his brazen law. See Appendix I, 2.

[3] Book II. ch. XI. § 2. He had just complained that Ricardo supposed the standard of comfort to be invariable, having apparently overlooked passages such as that quoted in the last note but one. He was however well aware that Ricardo's " minimum rate of wages " depended on the prevalent standard of comfort, and had no connection with the bare necessaries of life.

begun to be made of the effects that high wages have in increasing the efficiency not only of those who receive them, but also of their children and grandchildren. In this matter the lead has been taken by Walker and other American economists; and the application of the comparative method of study to the industrial problems of different countries of the old and new worlds is forcing constantly more and more attention to the fact that highly paid labour is generally efficient and therefore not dear labour; a fact which, though it is more full of hope for the future of the human race than any other that is known to us, will be found to exercise a very complicating influence on the theory of distribution.

VI, i, 3.

But the last generation was the first to study carefully the influence of wages on efficiency.

It has now become certain that the problem of distribution is much more difficult than it was thought to be by earlier economists, and that no solution of it which claims to be simple can be true. Most of the old attempts to give an easy answer to it, were really answers to imaginary questions that might have arisen in other worlds than ours, in which the conditions of life were very simple. The work done in answering these questions was not wasted. For a very difficult problem can best be solved by being broken up into pieces : and each of these simple questions contained a part of the great and difficult problem which we have to solve. Let us profit by this experience and work our way by successive steps in the remainder of this chapter towards understanding the general causes which govern the demand for labour and capital in real life.[1]

The problem is difficult : simple illustrations are needed.

§ 3. Let us begin by studying the influence of demand on the earnings of labour, drawn from an imaginary world in which every-one owns the capital that aids him in his labour; so that the problem of the relations of capital and labour do not arise in it. That is, let us suppose but little capital to be used; while everyone owns what-ever capital he does use, and the gifts of nature are so abundant that they are free and unappropriated. Let us suppose, further, that everyone is not only of equal capacity, but of equal willingness to work, and does in fact work equally hard : also that all work is unskilled—or rather unspecialized in this sense, that if any two people were to change occupations, each would do as much and as good work as the other had done. Lastly, let us suppose that every-one produces things ready for sale without the aid of others, and that he himself disposes of them to their ultimate consumers : so that the demand for everything is direct.

First, all supposed industri-ally equal and inter-change-able, population stationary;

In this case the problem of value is very simple. Things exchange for one another in proportion to the labour spent in

demand is then

<hr />

[1] Compare V. v., especially §§ 2, 3.

the main
regulator
of distri-
bution;

producing them.   If the supply of any one thing runs short, it may for a little time sell for more than its normal price : it may exchange for things the production of which had required more labour than it had : but, if so, people will at once leave other work to produce it, and in a very short time its value will fall to the normal level. There may be slight temporary disturbances, but as a rule anyone's earnings will be equal to those of anyone else.   In other words, each will have an equal share in the net sum total of things and services produced; or, as we may say, the *national income* or *dividend*; which will constitute the demand for labour.[1]

If now a new invention doubles the efficiency of work in any trade, so that a man can make twice as many things of a certain kind in a year without requiring additional appliances, then those things will fall to half their old exchange value.   The effective demand for everyone's labour will be a little increased, and the share which each can draw from the common earnings-stream will be a little larger than before.   He may if he chooses take twice as many things of this particular kind, together with his old allowance of other things : or he may take somewhat more than before of everything. If there be an increase in the efficiency of production in many trades the common earnings-stream or dividend will be considerably larger; the commodities produced by those trades will constitute a considerably larger demand for those produced by others, and increase the purchasing power of everyone's earnings.

as also in
the next
case, in
which pop-
ulation is
stationary,
and all
are in-
dustrially
equal but
each has
his own
trade;

§ 4.   Nor will the position be greatly changed if we suppose that some specialized skill is required in each trade, provided other things remain as before : that is, provided the workers are still supposed to be all of equal capacity and industry; and all trades to be equally agreeable and equally easy to be learnt.   The normal rate of earnings will still be the same in all trades; for if a day's labour in one trade produces things that sell for more than a day's labour in others, and this inequality shows any signs of lasting, people will bring up their children by preference to the favoured trade.   It is true that there may be some slight irregularities.   The drifting from one trade to another must occupy time; and some trades may for a while get more than their normal share of the earnings-stream, while others get less, or even lack work.   But in spite of these disturbances, the current value of everything will fluctuate about its normal value; which will in this case, as in the preceding, depend simply on the amount of labour spent on the thing : for the normal value of all kinds of labour will still be equal.   The productive power

[1] See below, § 10.

of the community will have been increased by the division of labour; VI, I, 5.
the common national dividend or earnings-stream will be larger;
and as all will, putting aside passing disturbances, share alike in it,
each will be able to buy with the fruits of his own labour things more
serviceable to him than he could have produced for himself.

In this stage, as in those considered before, it is still true that the
value of each thing corresponds closely to the amount of labour spent
upon it; and that the earnings of everyone are governed simply by
the bounty of nature and by the progress of the arts of production.

§ 5. Next, let us still neglect the influence which the liberality and
of the expenditure on rearing and training workers exerts on their again if population
efficiency, leaving that matter to be discussed with other aspects of increases,
the supply side of distribution in the next chapter : and let us look but not under the
at the influence that changes in the numbers of the population influence of econo-
exert on the incomes which nature will yield. We suppose then mic causes,
that the growth of population proceeds at a rate, which is either all workers still
fixed; or, at all events, not affected by the rate of wages : it may be belonging to one
influenced by changes in custom, in moral opinion and in medical grade;
knowledge. And we still suppose all labour to be of the same
grade, and the national dividend to be divided out equally to each
family, save for some slight passing inequalities. In this case every
improvement in the arts of production or transport, every new
discovery, every new victory over nature will increase equally the
comforts and luxuries at the command of each family.

But this case differs from the last; because in this case, the even
increase of population, if maintained long enough, must ultimately though the tendency
outgrow the improvements in the arts of production, and cause the to dimin-
law of diminishing return to assert itself in agriculture. That is to ishing return
say, those who work on the land will get less wheat and other produce asserts itself.
in return for their labour and capital. An hour's labour will
represent a less quantity of wheat than before throughout the
agricultural trades, and therefore throughout all other trades;
since all labour is supposed to be of the same grade, and earnings are
therefore as a rule equal in all trades.

Further we must note that the surplus or rental value of land
will tend to rise. For the value of any kind of produce must
equal that of the labour, aided on our supposition by a uniform
quantity of capital throughout, which is required to produce it,
whether on good land or bad, under barely remunerative, or marginal
conditions. More labour and capital than before will be needed to
raise a quarter of wheat, etc., on the margin; and therefore the
wheat, etc., which is returned by nature to the labour applied under

VI, I, 6, 7. advantageous circumstances, will have a higher value relatively to that labour and capital than before : or, in other words, it will yield a larger surplus value over that of the labour and capital used in raising it.

If there are many grades, but the numbers in each grade are not governed by economic causes, demand is still the main regulator of value.

§ 6. Let us now drop the supposition that labour is so mobile as to ensure equal remuneration for equal efforts, throughout the whole of society, and let us approach much nearer to the actual condition of life by supposing that labour is not all of one industrial grade, but of several. Let us suppose that parents always bring up their children to an occupation in their own grade; that they have a free choice within that grade, but not outside it. Lastly, let us suppose that the increase of numbers in each grade is governed by other than economic causes : as before it may be fixed, or it may be influenced by changes in custom, in moral opinion, etc. In this case also the aggregate national dividend will be governed by the abundance of nature's return to man's work in the existing state of the arts of production; but the distribution of that dividend between the different grades will be unequal. It will be governed by the demand of the people themselves. The share of those in any industrial compartment will be the higher, the more extensive and urgent the needs which they are able to satisfy on the part of those who are themselves drawing large shares of the national income.

Suppose, for instance, artists to form a grade or caste or industrial compartment by themselves; then, their number being fixed, or at least controlled by causes independent of their earnings, their earnings will be governed by the resources and the eagerness of those classes of the population who care for such gratifications as artists can furnish.

Return to the real conditions of life, which are however considered only on the side of demand.

§ 7. We may now leave the imaginary world, in which everyone owns the capital that aids him in his work; and return to our own, where the relations of labour and capital play a great part in the problem of distribution. But let us still confine our attention to the distribution of the national dividend among the various agents of production, in accordance with the quantity of each agent, and the services which it renders; and leave the reflex influence which the remuneration of each agent exerts on the supply of that agent, to be considered in the next chapter.

Margin at which the further application of an agent of production ceases to be profitable,

We have seen how the alert business man is ever seeking for the most profitable application of his resources, and endeavouring to make use of each several agent of production up to that margin, or limit, at which he would gain by transferring a small part of his expenditure to some other agent; and how he is thus, so far as his influence goes, the medium through which the principle of substitution so adjusts the employment of each agent that, in its marginal VI, I, 7. application, its cost is proportionate to the additional net product resulting from its use. We have to apply this general reasoning to the case of the hire of labour.[1]

A question constantly in the mind of the careful business man illustrated by the case of labour. is whether he has the right number of men for his work. In some cases that is settled for him by his plant : there must be one and only one engine-driver on each express locomotive. But some express trains have only one guard; and when the traffic is heavy they may lose a few minutes which could be saved by a second guard : therefore an alert manager is constantly weighing the net product in saving of time and of annoyance to passengers, that will accrue from the aid of a second guard on an important train, and considering whether it will be worth its cost. This question is similar in kind to, but simpler in form than, the question whether " it would pay " to put an additional train on the time-table, which would call for more expenditure on plant as well as on labour.

Again one sometimes hears it said that a certain farmer starves A marginal employee. his land for labour. Perhaps he has enough horses and plant; but " if he took on another man, he would get his money back, and a good deal more " : that is, the net product of an additional man would more than cover his wages. Let us suppose that a farmer is raising such a question as to the number of his shepherds. For simplicity, we may suppose that an additional man would not require any further expenditure on plant or stock : that he would save the farmer himself just as much trouble in some ways as he gives in others; so that nothing has to be allowed for earnings of manage-ment (even when these are interpreted broadly so as to include insurance against risk, etc.) : and lastly that the farmer reckons that he would do just so much in preventing the wastage of lambs, and in others ways as will increase by twenty his annual output of sheep in good condition. That is to say, he reckons that the net product of an additional man will be twenty sheep. If he can be got for much less than the equivalent of their price, the alert farmer will certainly hire him; but, if only for about that price, the farmer will be on the margin of doubt; and the man may then be called a *marginal* shepherd, because his employment is marginal.

---

[1] See above V. IV. 1–4. A little later we shall have to consider in what respects the hire of human labour differs from the hire of a house or a machine : but, for the present, we may neglect this difference, and look at the problem only in its broad outlines. Even so, some technical difficulties will be passed on the way : and those readers, who, in accordance with the suggestion made at the end of V. VII., have omitted the later chapters of that Book, must be asked, if dissatisfied with the general treatment offered here, to turn back and read V. VIII. and IX.

VI, I, 7.

e is to be
pposed
normal
ficiency,
id
orking
ider
rmal
nditions.

It is best to assume throughout that the man is of normal efficiency. He would indeed be the marginal shepherd even if he were of exceptional efficiency, provided only that his net produce were equal to his wages : the farmer might have reckoned that a shepherd of normal efficiency would have added only sixteen sheep to output; and therefore have been willing to hire this man at a quarter more than the ordinary wages. But to assume him to be thus exceptional would be most inexpedient. He should be representative : that is, of normal efficiency.[1]

[1] See the remarks on labour standardization below, VI. XIII. 8, 9.

An arithmetical illustration is given in the following table. Column (2) represents the number of sheep that might probably be marketed annually, together with a due complement of wool, from a large British sheep run if worked by 8, 9, 10, 11 and 12 shepherds respectively. (In Australasia, where men are scarce, land is abundant, and a sheep of relatively small value, there are often less than ten men, except at shearing time, to each 2,000 sheep; Sir Albert Spicer in Ashley's *British Dominions*, p. 61.) We are assuming that an increase in the number of shepherds from 8 to 12 does not increase the general expenses of working the farm; and that it takes off the shoulders of the farmer as much trouble in some directions, as it imposes in others : so that there is nothing to be reckoned either way on these accounts. Accordingly the product due to each successive additional man, set out in column (3), is the excess of the corresponding number in column (2) over the preceding number in that same column (2). Column (4) is got by dividing the numbers in column (2) by those in column (1). Column (5) shows the cost for shepherds' labour at the rate of 20 sheep per man. Column (6) shows the surplus remaining for general expenses, including farmer's profit and rent.

(1) Number of shepherds.	(2) Number of sheep.	(3) Product due to last man.	(4) Average product per man.	(5) Wages bill.	(6) Excess of (2) over (5).
8	580	—	72½	160	420
9	615	35	68⅓	180	435
10	640	25	64	200	440
11	660	20	60	220	440
12	676	16	56⅓	240	436

As we move downwards the figures in (3) constantly diminish ; but those in (6) increase, then remain without change, and at last diminish. This indicates that the farmer's interests are equally served by hiring 10 or 11 men; but that they are less well served by hiring 8, or 9, or 12. The eleventh man (supposed to be of *normal* efficiency) is the marginal man, when the markets for labour and sheep are such that one man can be hired for a year for the price of 20 sheep. If the markets had put that hire at 25 sheep, the numbers in (6) would have been 380, 390, 390, 385 and 376 respectively. Therefore that particular farmer would *probably* have employed one less shepherd, and sent less sheep to market; and among many sheep farmers there would *certainly* have been a large proportion who would have done so.

It has been argued at length in regard to similar cases (see V. VIII. 4, 5) that the price which it is just worth while for the farmer to pay for this labour, merely gauges the outcome of multitudinous causes which between them govern the wages of shepherds; as the movements of a safety-valve may gauge the outcome of the multitudinous causes that govern the pressure in a boiler. Theoretically a deduction from this has to be made for the fact that, by throwing twenty extra sheep on the market, the farmer will lower the price of sheep generally, and therefore lose a little on his other sheep. This correction may be of appreciable importance in special cases. But in general discussions such as this, in which we are dealing with a very small addition to the supply thrown by one of many producers on a large market, it becomes very small (mathematically a small quantity of the second order), and may be neglected. (See above, footnote on p. 339.)

Of course the net product of the shepherd in this exceptional case plays no greater part in governing the wages of shepherds, than does that of any of the marginal shepherds on farms where they cannot be profitably employed without considerable extra outlay in other directions; as for land, buildings, implements, labour of management, etc.

If he is representative, and his employer is representative, the VI, I, 7.
twenty sheep will represent the net product and therefore the
earning power of a shepherd.   But if the employer is a bad manager,
if for instance he lets his men run short of necessaries for the sheep,
the man may save only fifteen sheep instead of twenty.   Net product
tends to represent normal wages only if the worker and his conditions
of employment are both normal.

The additional product to be got by this shepherd's labour is
largely influenced by the number of shepherds whom the farmer
already employs.   And this again is governed by general conditions
of demand and supply, and especially by the number of those from
whom the ranks of shepherds could have been recruited during the
current generation; by the demand for mutton and wool and by the
area from which supplies of them can be obtained; by the effectiveness of the shepherds on all other farms; and so on.   And the
amount of the marginal product is further largely influenced by the
competition of other uses for land : the space available for sheep-
farming is curtailed by the demand for land for growing timber or
oats, preserving deer, etc.[1]

This illustration has been chosen from a simple industry; but,
though the form may be different, the substance of the problem is
the same in every industry.   Subject to conditions which are indicated in the footnote, but are not important for our main purpose,
the wages of every class of labour tend to be equal to the net
product due to the additional labour of the marginal labourer of
that class.[2]

This doctrine has sometimes been put forward as a theory of This
wages. But there is no valid ground for any such pretension. doctrine
is not a
The doctrine that the earnings of a worker tend to be equal to the

---

Column (4) in the above table is deduced from (1) and (2), just as (3) is. But
the table shows how many men the farmer can afford to hire, when they are to be
had at wages equivalent to the value of the number of sheep in (3), and therefore
goes to the heart of the problem of wages : while (4) has no direct bearing on the
problem.   When therefore Mr. J. A. Hobson, remarking on a similar table of his own
(in which however the numbers chosen are inappropriate to the hypothesis which he
criticises), says :—"In other words the so-called final or marginal productivity turns
out to be nothing other than an average productivity. . . . The whole notion that there
is a marginal productivity . . . is entirely fallacious" (*The Industrial System*, p. 110),
he appears to be mistaken.

[1] Compare p. 362.

[2] Such a method of illustrating the net product of a man's labour is not easily
applicable to industries in which a great deal of capital and effort has to be invested
in gradually building up a trade connection, and especially if they are such as obey
the law of increasing return.   This is a practical difficulty of the same order as those
discussed in V. XII. and Appendix H. See also IV. XII.; V. VII. 1, 2; and XI.   The
influence of an additional man employed in any considerable business on its general
economies might also be considered from a purely abstract point of view; but it is
too small to be taken seriously. (See the footnote on p. 339.)

VI, I, 8.
ieory of
ages;
net product of his work, has by itself no real meaning; since in order to estimate net product, we have to take for granted all the expenses of production of the commodity on which he works, other than his own wages.

it is a
ieful
irt of a
ieory.
But though this objection is valid against a claim that it contains a theory of wages; it is not valid against a claim that the doctrine throws into clear light the action of one of the causes that govern wages.

emarks
inerally
iply
the
imand
r capital.
§ 8. In later chapters we shall need to take other illustrations for special purposes of the principle illustrated in the last section from the case of manual labour; and in particular to show how the value of some parts of the work of business management can be measured, when it is found that the effective output of a business is increased as much by some additional superintendence, as it would be by the hire of an additional ordinary worker. Again, the earnings of a machine can sometimes be estimated by the addition to the output of a factory which it might effect in certain cases without involving any incidental extra expense.

Generalizing from the work of a particular machine to that of machinery of a given aggregate value, we may suppose that in a certain factory an extra £100 worth of machinery can be applied so as not to involve any other extra expense, and so as to add annually £4 worth to the net output of the factory, after allowing for its own wear-and-tear. If the investors of capital push it into every occupation in which it seems likely to gain a high reward; and if, after this has been done and equilibrium has been found, it still pays and only just pays to employ this machinery, we can infer from this fact that the yearly rate of interest is 4 per cent. But illustrations of this kind merely indicate part of the action of the great causes which govern value. They cannot be made into a theory of interest, any more than into a theory of wages, without reasoning in a circle.

It may however be well to carry a little further our illustration of the nature of the demand for capital for any use; and to observe the way in which the aggregate demand for it is made up of the demands for many different uses.

lustra-
in of the
imand
r capital
a
irticular
ade.
To fix the ideas, let us take some particular trade, say that of hat-making, and inquire what determines the amount of capital which it absorbs. Suppose that the rate of interest is 4 per cent. per annum on perfectly good security; and that the hat-making trade absorbs a capital of one million pounds. This implies that the hat-making trade can turn the whole million pounds' worth of capital to so good

account that they would pay 4 per cent. per annum *net* for the use of VI, I, 8.
it rather than go without any of it.[1]

Some things are necessary to them; they must have not only
some food, clothing, and house room, but also some circulating
capital, such as raw material, and some fixed capital, such as tools
and perhaps a little machinery. And though competition prevents
anything more than the ordinary trade profit being got by the use
of this necessary capital; yet the loss of it would be so injurious that
those in the trade would have been willing to pay 50 per cent. on it,
if they could not have got the use of it on easier terms. There
may be other machinery which the trade would have refused to
dispense with if the rate of interest had been 20 per cent. per annum,
but not if it had been higher. If the rate had been 10 per cent.,
still more would have been used; if it had been 6 per cent., still more;
if 5 per cent., still more; and finally the rate being 4 per cent. they
use more still. When they have this amount, the marginal utility
of the machinery, *i.e.* the utility of that machinery which it is only
just worth their while to employ, is measured by 4 per cent.

A rise in the rate of interest would diminish their use of
machinery; for they would avoid the use of all that did not give a
net annual surplus of more than 4 per cent. on its value. And a fall
in the rate of interest would lead them to demand the aid of more
capital, and to introduce machinery which gave a net annual surplus
of something less than 4 per cent. on its value. Again, the lower the
rate of interest, the more substantial will be the style of building
used for the hat-making factories and the homes of the hat-makers;
and a fall in the rate of interest will lead to the employment of more
capital in the hat-making trade in the form of larger stocks of raw
material, and of the finished commodity in the hands of retail
dealers.[2]

The methods in which capital will be applied may vary much The
even within the same trade. Each undertaker having regard to his aggregate
 demand
own means, will push the investment of capital in his business in for
each several direction until what appears in his judgment to be the capital.
margin of profitableness is reached; and that margin is, as we have
said, a boundary line cutting one after another every possible line of
investment, and moving irregularly outwards in all directions

---

[1] The charge made to traders for loans is generally much more than 4 per cent.
per annum; but as we shall see in chapter VI. it includes other things besides true
net interest. Before the recent great destruction of capital by war, it seemed
reasonable to speak of 3 per cent. : but even 4 per cent. may scarcely avail for some
years after its close.

[2] Compare V. IV. : also Appendix I, 3; where some remarks are made on Jevons'
doctrine of interest.

whenever there is a fall in the rate of interest at which extra capital can be obtained. Thus the demand for the loan of capital is the aggregate of the demands of all individuals in all trades; and it obeys a law similar to that which holds for the sale of commodities : just as there is a certain amount of a commodity which can find purchasers at any given price. When the price rises the amount that can be sold diminishes, and so it is with regard to the use of capital.

And as with borrowings for productive purposes, so with those of spendthrifts or governments who mortgage their future resources in order to obtain the means of immediate expenditure. It is true that their actions are often but little governed by cool calculation, and that they frequently decide how much they want to borrow with but little reference to the price they will have to pay for the loan; but still the rate of interest exercises a perceptible influence on borrowings even of this kind.

§ 9. To sum up the whole in a comprehensive, if difficult, statement :—Every agent of production, land, machinery, skilled labour, unskilled labour, etc., tends to be applied in production as far as it profitably can be. If employers, and other business men, think that they can get a better result by using a little more of any one agent they will do so. They estimate the net product (that is the net increase of the money value of their total output after allowing for incidental expenses) that will be got by a little more outlay in this direction, or a little more outlay in that; and if they can gain by shifting a little of their outlay from one direction to another, they will do so.[1]

Thus then the uses of each agent of production are governed by the general conditions of demand in relation to supply : that is, on the one hand, by the urgency of all the uses to which the agent can be put, taken together with the means at the command of those who need it; and, on the other hand, by the available stocks of it. And equality is maintained between its values for each use by the constant tendency to shift it from uses, in which its services are of less value to others in which they are of greater value, in accordance with the principle of substitution.

If less use is made of unskilled labour or any agent, the reason will be that at some point at which people were on the margin of doubt whether it was worth while to use that agent, they have decided that it is not worth their while. That is what is meant by saying that we must watch the *marginal* uses, and the *marginal* efficiency

Provisional conclusion as to the influence of demand, guided by the principle of substitution, on the earnings of each agent.

---

[1] This statement follows closely the lines of V. IV. and VIII.

of each agent. We must do so, simply because it is only at the VI, I, 10.
margin that any of those shiftings can occur by which changed
relations of supply and demand manifest themselves.

If we neglected differences between the grades of labour, and Explicit
regarded all labour as of one kind, or at least as all expressed in applica-tions of
terms of a certain kind of labour of standard efficiency, we might this law
look for the margin of indifference between the direct application to distri-bution
of labour and that of material capital; and we might say shortly, were
to quote von Thünen's words, that " the efficiency of capital must first made by von
be the measure of its earnings, since if the labour of capital were Thünen.
cheaper than that of men, the undertaker would dismiss some of
his workmen, and in the opposite case he would increase their
number." [1]

But, of course, the increased competition of capital in general
for employment is of a different character from the competition of
machinery for employment in any single trade. The latter may
push a particular kind of labour out of employment altogether;
the former cannot displace labour in general, for it must cause an
increased employment of the makers of those things which are used
as capital. And in fact, the substitution of capital for labour is
really the substitution of labour, combined with much waiting, in
the place of other forms of labour combined with little waiting.[2]

§ 10. When we speak of the national dividend, or distributable Common
net income of the whole nation, as divided into the shares of land, usage is followed in
labour and capital, we must be clear as to what things we are delimiting
including, and what things we are excluding. It will seldom make income, whether
very much difference to our argument whether we use all the terms that which
broadly, or all the terms narrowly. But it is essential that our goes into or that

---

[1] *Der Isolirte Staat*, II. I. p. 123. He argues (*ib.* p. 124) that therefore " the
rate of interest is the element by which the relation of the efficiency of capital to that
of human labour is expressed "; and finally, in words, very similar to those, which
Jevons, working independently a generation later, adopted for the same purpose,
he says (p. 162): " The utility of the last applied little bit of capital defines (bestimmt)
the height of the rate of interest." With characteristic breadth of view, von Thünen
enunciated a general law of diminishing return for successive doses of capital in any
branch of production; and what he said on this subject has even now much interest,
though it does not show how to reconcile the fact that an increase in the capital
employed in an industry may increase the output more than in proportion, with the
fact that a continued influx of capital into an industry must ultimately lower the rate
of profits earned in it. His treatment of these and other great economic principles,
though primitive in many respects, yet stands on a different footing from his fanciful
and unreal assumptions as to the causes that determine the accumulation of capital,
and as to the relations in which wages stand to the stock of capital. From these he
deduces the quaint result that the natural rate of wages of labour is the geometric
mean between the labourer's necessaries, and that share of the product which is due
to his labour when aided by capital. By the natural rate he means the highest
that can be sustained; if the labourer were to get more than this for a time, the supply
of capital would, von Thünen argues, be so checked as to cause him in the long run to
lose more than he gained.

[2] As von Thünen was well aware. *Ib.* p. 127. See also below, VI. II. 9, 10.

VI, i, 10.

which comes out from the national dividend.

usage should be consistent throughout any one argument; and that, whatever is included on one side of the account of the demand for, and supply of, land, labour, and capital, should be included also on the other.

The labour and capital of the country, acting on its natural resources, produce annually a certain *net* aggregate of commodities, material and immaterial, including services of all kinds. The limiting word " net " is needed to provide for the using up of raw and half-finished commodities, and for the wearing out and depreciation of plant which is involved in production : all such waste must of course be deducted from the gross produce before the true or net income can be found. And net income due on account of foreign investments must be added in. (See above II. iv. 6.) This is the true net annual income, or revenue, of the country; or, the national dividend : we may, of course, estimate it for a year or for any other period. The terms National Income and National Dividend are convertible; only the latter is the more significant when we are looking at the national income in the character of the sum of the new sources of enjoyments that are available for distribution. But it is best here to follow the common practice, and not count as part of the national income or dividend anything that is not commonly counted as part of the income of the individual. Thus, unless anything is said to the contrary, the services which a person renders to himself, and those which he renders gratuitously to members of his family or friends; the benefits which he derives from using his own personal goods, or public property such as toll-free bridges, are not reckoned as parts of the national dividend, but are left to be accounted for separately.

The correlation of production and consumption.

Some part of production goes to increase the stock of raw material, machinery, etc., and does not merely replace material that has been used up, or machinery that has been worn out : and this part of the national income or dividend does not pass direct into personal consumption. But it does pass into consumption in the broad sense of the term which is commonly used by, say, a manufacturer of printing machines, when some of his stock is sold to printers. And in this broad sense it is true that all production is for consumption; that the national dividend is convertible with the aggregate of net production, and also with the aggregate of consumption. Under ordinary conditions of industry, production and consumption move together : there is no consumption except that for which the way has been prepared by appropriate production : and all production is followed by the consumption for which it was

designed. There may indeed be some miscalculation in particular VI, I, 10.
branches of production ; and a collapse of commercial credit may fill
nearly all warehouses for a time with unsold goods. But such
conditions are exceptional and are not within our present view.
(See below V. XIII. 10 ; and Appendix J, 3.)

CHAPTER II

PRELIMINARY SURVEY OF DISTRIBUTION, CONTINUED

Purpose of this chapter.

§ 1. As was indicated at the beginning of last chapter, we are now to supplement the study of the influence of demand on distribution, by a study of the reflex influence of remuneration on the supply of different agents of production. We have to combine the two in a preliminary general view of the parts played by cost of production and by utility or desirability in governing the distribution of the national dividend between different kinds of labour and the owners of capital and land.

Ricardo and his followers laid insufficient stress on demand; but were right in laying the greater stress on cost of production.

Ricardo and the able business men who followed in his wake took the operation of demand too much for granted as a thing which did not need to be explained : they did not emphasize it, nor study it with sufficient care; and this neglect has caused much confusion, and has obscured important truths. In the reaction, too much insistence has been laid on the fact that the earnings of every agent of production come from, and are for the time mainly governed by the value of the product which it takes part in producing; its earnings being so far governed on the same principle as the rent of land; and some have even thought it possible to constitute a complete theory of Distribution out of multifold applications of the law of rent. But they will not reach to that end. Ricardo and his followers seem to have been rightly guided by their intuitions, when they silently determined that the forces of supply were those, the study of which is the more urgent and involves the greater difficulty.

When we inquire what it is that governs the [marginal] efficiency of a factor of production, whether it be any kind of labour or material capital, we find that the immediate solution requires a knowledge of the available supply of that factor; for if the supply is increased, the thing will be applied to uses for which it is less needed, and in which it is less efficient. And the ultimate solution requires a knowledge also of the causes that determine that supply. The nominal value of everything, whether it be a particular kind of labour or capital or anything else, rests, like the keystone of an arch, balanced in equilibrium between the contending pressures of

ts two opposing sides; the forces of demand press on the one side,
ınd those of supply on the other.

The production of everything, whether an agent of production *The amounts and prices of the several agents of production mutually govern one another.*
)r a commodity ready for immediate consumption, is carried forward
ıp to that limit or margin at which there is equilibrium between the
'orces of demand and supply. The amount of the thing and its
)rice, the amounts of the several factors or agents of production
ısed in making it, and their prices—all these elements mutually
;overn one another, and if an external cause should alter any one of
:hem the effect of the disturbance extends to all the others.

In the same way, when several balls are lying in a bowl, they *Parallel instances from physics.*
nutually govern one another's positions; and again when a heavy
veight is suspended by several elastic strings of different strengths
ınd lengths (all of them being stretched) attached to different
)oints in the ceiling, the equilibrium positions of all the strings and
)f the weight mutually govern one another. If any one of the
:trings is shortened, everything else will change its position, and the
ength and the tension of every other string will be altered also.

§ 2. We have seen that the effective supply of any agent of *Influence of his remuneration on the individual's willingness to work.*
)roduction at any time depends firstly on the stock of it in existence,
ınd secondly on the willingness of those, in whose charge it is, to
ıpply it in production. This willingness is not decided simply by
:he immediate return which is expected; though there may be a
ower limit, which in some cases may be described as a prime cost,
)elow which no work will be done at all. A manufacturer for
nstance has no hesitation in declining to put his machinery in motion
'or an order that will not cover the extra direct money outlay caused
)y the work, together with the actual wear-and-tear of the
nachinery; while there are somewhat similar considerations with
·egard to the wear-and-tear of the worker's own strength and to the
'atigue and other discommodities of his work. And, though for
:he present we are concerned with cost and remuneration under
iormal conditions rather than with the direct cost to the individual
)f any particular piece of work that he does; yet it may be well to
nake a short statement on the subject here in order to avoid
misconceptions.

It has already been noticed [1] that when a man is fresh and eager, *Some work is pleasurable;*
ınd doing work of his own choice, it really costs him nothing. For
ıs some socialists have urged with pardonable exaggeration, few
people know how much they enjoy moderate work, till something
)ccurs to prevent them from working altogether. But rightly or

[1] See II. III. 2; IV. I. 2; IV. IX. 1.

VI, II, 2.

wrongly, most persons believe that the greater part of the work which they do, when earning their living, yields them no surplus of pleasure; but on the contrary costs them something. They are glad when the hour for stopping arrives : perhaps they forget that the earlier hours of their work have not cost them as much as the last : they are rather apt to think of nine hours' work as costing them nine times as much as the last hour; and it seldom occurs to them to think of themselves as reaping a producer's surplus or rent, through being paid for every hour at a rate sufficient to compensate them for the last, and most distressing hour.[1]

but generally, though not always, increased remuneration stimulates to increased exertions.

The longer a man works, or even is on duty, the greater is his desire for a respite, unless indeed he has become numbed by his work; while every hour's additional work gives him more pay, and brings him nearer to the stage at which his most urgent wants are satisfied; and the higher the pay, the sooner this stage is reached. It depends then on the individual, whether with growing pay new wants arise, and new desires to provide comforts for others or for himself in after years; or he is soon satiated with those enjoyments that can be gained only by work, and then craves more rest, and more opportunities for activities that are themselves pleasurable. No universal rule can be laid down; but experience seems to show that

---

[1] Recent discussions on the eight hours day have often turned very little on the fatigue of labour; for indeed there is much work in which there is so little exertion, either physical or mental, that what exertion there is counts rather as a relief from ennui than as fatigue. A man is on duty, bound to be ready when wanted, but perhaps not doing an hour's actual work in the day; and yet he will object to very long hours of duty because they deprive his life of variety, of opportunities for domestic and social pleasures, and perhaps of comfortable meals and rest.

If a man is free to cease his work when he likes, he does so when the advantages to be reaped by continuing seem no longer to over-balance the disadvantages. If he has to work with others, the length of his day's work is often fixed for him; and in some trades the number of days' work which he does in the year is practically fixed for him. But there are scarcely any trades, in which the amount of exertion which he puts into his work is rigidly fixed. If he be not able or willing to work up to the minimum standard that prevails where he is, he can generally find employment in another locality where the standard is lower; while the standard in each place is set by the general balancing of the advantages and disadvantages of various intensities of work by the industrial populations settled there. The cases therefore in which a man's individual volition has no part in determining the amount of work he does in a year, are as exceptional as the cases in which a man has to live in a house of a size widely different from that which he prefers, because there is none other available. It is true that a man who would rather work eight hours a day than nine at the same rate of tenpence an hour, but is compelled to work nine hours or none, suffers a loss from the ninth hour : but such cases are rare; and, when they occur, one must take the day as the unit. But the general law of costs is not disturbed by this fact, any more than the general law of utility is disturbed by the fact that a concert or a cup of tea has to be taken as a unit : and that a person who would rather pay five shillings for half a concert than ten for a whole, or twopence for half a cup of tea than fourpence for a whole cup, may incur a loss on the second half. There seems therefore to be no good foundation for the suggestion made by v. Böhm-Bawerk (*The Ultimate Standard of Value*, § IV. published in the *Zeitschrift für Volkswirtschaft*, vol. II.) that value must be determined generally by demand, without direct reference to cost, because the effective supply of labour is a fixed quantity : for even if the number of hours of work in the year were rigidly fixed, which it is not, the intensity of work would remain elastic.

the more ignorant and phlegmatic of races and of individuals, VI, II, 3.
especially if they live in a southern clime, will stay at their work a
shorter time, and will exert themselves less while at it, if the rate of
pay rises so as to give them their accustomed enjoyments in return
for less work than before. But those whose mental horizon is
wider, and who have more firmness and elasticity of character, will
work the harder and the longer the higher the rate of pay which is
open to them; unless indeed they prefer to divert their activities
to higher aims than work for material gain. But this point will
need to be discussed more fully under the head of the influence of
progress on value. Meanwhile we may conclude that increased
remuneration causes an immediate increase in the supply of efficient
work, as a rule; and that the exceptions to this rule, just noticed,
are seldom on a large scale, though they are not devoid of
significance.[1]

§ 3. When however we turn from the immediate influence
exerted by a rise in wages on the work done by an individual to its
ultimate effect after a generation or two, the result is less uncertain.
It is indeed true that, though a temporary improvement will give a
good many young people the opportunity to marry and set up
house, for which they have been waiting; yet a permanent increase
of prosperity is quite as likely to lower as to raise the birth-rate.
But on the other hand, an increase of wages is almost certain to
diminish the death-rate, unless it has been obtained at the price of
the neglect by mothers of their duties to their children. And the
case is much stronger when we look at the influence of high wages
on the physical and mental vigour of the coming generation.

For there is a certain consumption which is strictly necessary for
each grade of work in this sense, that if any of it is curtailed the
work cannot be done efficiently : the adults might indeed take good
care of themselves at the expense of their children, but that would
only defer the decay of efficiency for one generation. Further there
are conventional necessaries, which are so strictly demanded by

The dependence in the long run of the supply of efficient labour on the rate of earnings and on the manner in which they are spent.

---

[1] See ch. XII. Bad harvests, war prices, and convulsions of credit have at
various times compelled some workers, men, women and children, to over-work
themselves. And cases of ever-increasing exertion in return for a constantly sinking
wage, though not as numerous now as is often alleged, have not been very rare in
past times. They may be compared with the exertions of a failing firm to secure
some return for their outlay by taking contracts at little more than enough to recompense them for their prime, or special and direct cost. And on the other hand almost
every age, our own perhaps less than most others, has stories of people who in a
sudden burst of prosperity, have contented themselves with the wages to be earned
by very little work, and have thus contributed to bring the prosperity to a close. But
such matters must be deferred till after a study of commercial fluctuations. In
ordinary times the artisan, the professional man or the capitalist undertaker decides,
as an individual or as a member of a trade association, what is the lowest price against
which he will not strike.

VI, II, 3.   custom and habit, that in fact people generally would give up much of their necessaries, strictly so called, rather than go without the greater part of these. Thirdly there are habitual comforts, which some, though not all, would not entirely relinquish even when hardly pressed. Many of these conventional necessaries and customary comforts are the embodiment of material and moral progress, and their extent varies from age to age and from place to place. The greater they are, the less economical is man as an agent of production. But if they are wisely chosen they attain in the highest degree the end of all production : for they then raise the tone of human life.

The supply of labour corresponds quickly to the demand for it, when the workers' income is spent mainly on necessaries for efficiency.   Any increase in consumption that is strictly necessary to efficiency pays its own way and adds to, as much as it draws from, the national dividend. But an increase of consumption, that is not thus necessary, can be afforded only through an increase in man's command over nature : and that can come about through advance in knowledge and the arts of production, through improved organization and access to larger and richer sources of raw material, and lastly through the growth of capital and the material means of attaining desired ends in any form.

Thus the question how closely the supply of labour responds to the demand for it, is in a great measure resolved into the question how great a part of the present consumption of the people at large consists of necessaries, strictly so called, for the life and efficiency of young and old; how much consists of conventional necessaries which theoretically could be dispensed with, but practically would be preferred by the majority of the people to some of those things that were really necessary for efficiency; and how much is really superfluous regarded as a means towards production, though of course part of it may be of supreme importance regarded as an end in itself.

Most expenditure of the working classes conduces to efficiency in backward countries.   The earlier French and English economists, as we noted at the beginning of the preceding chapter, classed nearly all the consumption of the working classes under the first head. They did so, partly for simplicity, and partly because those classes were then poor in England and very poor in France; and they inferred that the supply of labour would correspond to changes in the effective demand for it in the same way, though of course not quite as fast as that of machinery would. And an answer not very different from theirs must be given to the question with regard to the less advanced countries even now. For throughout the greater part of the world the working classes can afford but few luxuries and not even many

conventional necessaries; and any increase in their earnings would
result in so great an increase of their numbers as to bring down
their earnings quickly to nearly the old level at their mere expenses
of rearing. Over a great part of the world wages are governed,
nearly after the so-called iron or brazen law, which ties them close
to the cost of rearing and sustaining a rather inefficient class of
labourers.

As regards the modern western world the answer is materially *The same*
different; so great has been the recent advance in knowledge and *is true*
freedom, in vigour and wealth, and in the easy access to rich distant *to some extent*
fields for the supply of food and raw material. But it is still true *even in the rich*
even in England to-day that much the greater part of the con- *western*
sumption of the main body of the population conduces to sustain *world.*
life and vigour; not perhaps in the most economical manner, but
yet without any great waste. Doubtless some indulgences are
positively harmful; but these are diminishing relatively to the rest,
the chief exception perhaps being that of gambling. Most of that
expenditure which is not strictly economical as a means towards
efficiency, yet helps to form habits of ready resourceful enterprise,
and gives that variety to life without which men become dull and
stagnant, and achieve little though they may plod much; and it is
well recognized that even in western countries skilled labour is
generally the cheapest where wages are the highest. It may be
admitted that the industrial development of Japan is tending to show
that some of the more expensive conventional necessaries might
conceivably be given up without a corresponding diminution of
efficiency : but, though this experience may be fruitful of far-
reaching results in the future, yet it has little bearing on the past and
the present. It remains true that, taking man as he is, and has been
hitherto, in the western world the earnings that are got by efficient
labour are not much above the lowest that are needed to cover the
expenses of rearing and training efficient workers, and of sustaining
and bringing into activity their full energies.[1]

We conclude then that an increase of wages, unless earned under

[1] On all locomotives there is some brass or copper work designed partly for
ornament, and which could be omitted or displaced without any loss to the efficiency
of the steam-engine. Its amount does in fact vary with the taste of the officials
who select the patterns for the engines of different railways. But it might happen
that custom required such expenditure; that the custom would not yield to argument,
and that the railway companies could not venture to offend against it. In that case,
when dealing with periods during which the custom ruled, we should have to include
the cost of that ornamental metal work in the cost of producing a certain amount of
locomotive horse-power, on the same level with the cost of the piston itself. And
there are many practical problems, especially such as relate to periods of but moderate
length, in which conventional and real necessaries may be placed on nearly the same
footing.

VI, II, 3.

General conclusion.

unwholesome conditions, almost always increases the strength, physical, mental and even moral of the coming generation; and that, other things being equal, an increase in the earnings that are to be got by labour increases its rate of growth; or, in other words, a rise in its demand-price increases the supply of it.   If the state of knowledge, and of social and domestic habits be given; then the vigour of the people as a whole if not their numbers, and both the numbers and vigour of any trade in particular, may be said to have a supply-price in this sense, that there is a certain level of the demand-price which will keep them stationary; that a higher price would cause them to increase, and that a lower price would cause them to decrease.

The influences of demand and supply on wages are co-ordinate.

Thus again we see that demand and supply exert co-ordinate influences on wages; neither has a claim to predominance; any more than has either blade of a pair of scissors, or either pier of an arch.   Wages tend to equal the net product of labour; its marginal productivity rules the demand-price for it; and, on the other side, wages tend to retain a close though indirect and intricate relation with the cost of rearing, training and sustaining the energy of efficient labour.   The various elements of the problem mutually determine (in the sense of governing) one another; and incidentally this secures that supply-price and demand-price tend to equality: wages are not governed by demand-price nor by supply-price, but by the whole set of causes which govern demand and supply.[1]

The phrase "general rate of wages" presents difficulties.

A word should be said as to the common phrase " the general rate of wages," or " the wages of labour in general."   Such phrases are convenient in a broad view of distribution, and especially when we are considering the general relations of capital and labour.   But in fact there is no such thing in modern civilization as a general rate of wages.   Each of a hundred or more groups of workers has its own wage problem, its own set of special causes, natural and artificial, controlling the supply-price, and limiting the number of its members; each has its own demand-price governed by the need that other agents of production have of its services.

---

[1] The reiteration in this section has seemed to be unavoidable in consequence of the misunderstandings of the main argument of the present Book by various critics; among whom must be included even the acute Prof. v. Böhm-Bawerk.   For in the article recently quoted (see especially Section 5), he seems to hold that a self-contradiction is necessarily involved in the belief that wages correspond both to the net product of labour and also to the cost of rearing and training labour and sustaining its efficiency (or, more shortly, though less appropriately, the cost of production of labour).   On the other hand the mutual interactions of the chief economic forces are set forth in an able article by Prof. Carver in the *Quarterly Journal of Economics* for July 1894; see also his *Distribution of Wealth*, ch. IV.

§ 4. Somewhat similar difficulties arise with regard to the phrase "the general rate of interest." But here the chief trouble comes from the fact that the income derived from capital already invested in particular things, such as factories or ships, is properly a quasi-rent and can be regarded as interest only on the assumption that the capital value of the investment has remained unaltered. Leaving this difficulty on one side for the present [1]; and recollecting that the phrase "the general rate of interest" applies in strictness only to the anticipated net earnings from new investments of free capital, we may resume briefly the results of our earlier studies of the growth of capital.

We have seen [2] that the accumulation of wealth is governed by a great variety of causes : by custom, by habits of self-control and of realizing the future, and above all by the power of family affection : security is a necessary condition for it, and the progress of knowledge and intelligence furthers it in many ways. But though saving in general is affected by many causes other than the rate of interest : and though the saving of many people is but little affected by the rate of interest; while a few, who have determined to secure an income of a certain fixed amount for themselves or their family, will save less with a high rate than with a low rate of interest : yet a strong balance of evidence seems to rest with the opinion that a rise in the rate of interest, or demand-price for saving, tends to increase the volume of saving.

Thus then interest, being the price paid for the use of capital in any market, tends towards an equilibrium level such that the aggregate demand for capital in that market, at that rate of interest, is equal to the aggregate stock forthcoming there at that rate. If the market, which we are considering, is a small one—say a single town, or a single trade in a progressive country—an increased demand for capital in it will be promptly met by an increased supply drawn from surrounding districts or trades. But if we are con-sidering the whole world, or even the whole of a large country as one market for capital, we cannot regard the aggregate supply of it as altered quickly and to a considerable extent by a change in the rate of interest. For the general fund of capital is the product of labour and waiting; and the extra work, and the extra waiting, to which a rise in the rate of interest would act as an incentive, would not quickly amount to much as compared with the work and waiting, of which the total existing stock of capital is the result. An extensive increase in the demand for capital in general will therefore be met

---

[1] See below, VI. VI. 6.　　　　[2] See IV. VII., summarized in § 10.

VI, ii, 5. for a time not so much by an increase of supply, as by a rise in the rate of interest; which will cause capital to withdraw itself partially from those uses in which its marginal utility is lowest. It is only slowly and gradually that the rise in the rate of interest will increase the total stock of capital.

Land is on a different footing from other agents of production.

§ 5. Land is on a different footing from man himself and those agents of production which are made by man; among which are included improvements made by him on the land itself.[1] For while the supplies of all other agents of production respond in various degrees and various ways to the demand for their services, land makes no such response. Thus an exceptional rise in the earnings of any class of labour, tends to increase its numbers, or efficiency, or both; and the increase in the supply of efficient work of that class tends to cheapen the services which it renders to the community. If the increase is in their numbers then the rate of earnings of each will tend downwards towards the old level. But if the increase is in their efficiency; then, though they will probably earn more per head than before, the gain to them will come from an increased national dividend, and will not be at the expense of other agents of production. And the same is true as regards capital : but it is not true as regards land. While therefore the value of land, in common with the values of other agents of production, is subject to those influences which were discussed towards the end of the preceding chapter; it is not subject to those which have been brought into the reckoning in the present discussion.

It is true that land is but a particular form of capital from the point of view of the individual manufacturer or cultivator. And land shares the influences of the laws of demand and of substitution which were discussed in the last chapter, because the existing stock of it, like the existing stock of capital or of labour of any kind, tends to be shifted from one use to another till nothing could be gained for production by any further shifting. And, so far as the discussions of the last chapter are concerned, the income that is derived from a factory, a warehouse, or a plough (allowance being made for wear-and-tear, etc.) is governed in the same way as is the income from land. In each case the income tends to equal the value of the marginal net product of the agent : in each case this is governed for the time by the total stock of the agent and the need that other agents have of its aid.

That is one side of the question. The other is that land (in an

---

[1] The argument of this section is put broadly. For a technical and more thorough treatment the reader is referred to V. x.

old country) does not share the reflex influences, discussed in this chapter, which a high rate of earnings exerts on the supply of other agents of production, and consequently on their contributions to the national dividend, and consequently on the real cost at which their services are purchased by other agents of production. The building an additional floor on one factory or putting an extra plough on one farm, does not generally take a floor from another factory or a plough from another farm; the nation adds a factory floor or a plough to its business as the individual does to his. There is thus a larger national dividend which is to be shared out; and in the long run the increased earnings of the manufacturer or farmer are not as a rule at the cost of other producers. In contrast to this the stock of land (in an old country) at any time is the stock for *all* time; and when a manufacturer or cultivator decides to take in a little more land to his business, he decides in effect to take it away from someone else's business. He adds a little more land to his business; but the nation adds no land to its business, the change does not in itself increase the national income.

§ 6. To conclude this stage of our argument :—The net aggregate of all the commodities produced is itself the true source from which flow the demand prices for all these commodities, and therefore for the agents of production used in making them. Or, to put the same thing in another way, this national dividend is at once the aggregate net product of, and the sole source of payment for, all the agents of production within the country : it is divided up into earnings of labour; interest of capital; and lastly the producer's surplus, or rent, of land and of other differential advantages for production. It constitutes the whole of them, and the whole of it is distributed among them; and the larger it is, the larger, other things being equal, will be the share of each of them.

It is distributed among them, speaking generally, in proportion to the need which people have for their several services—*i.e.* not the *total* need, but the *marginal* need. By this is meant the need at that point, at which people are indifferent whether they purchase a little more of the services (or the fruits of the services) of one agent, or devote their further resources to purchasing the services (or the fruits of the services) of other agents. Other things being equal, each agent is likely to increase the faster, the larger the share which it gets, unless indeed it is not capable of being increased at all. But every such increase will do something towards filling up the more urgent needs for that agent; and will thus lessen the marginal need for it, and lower the price at which it can find a market. That is to

The earnings of the several agents of production according to their marginal services, exhaust the national dividend.

VI, II, 7. say, an increase in the proportionate share, or rate of remuneration, of any agent is likely to bring into play forces, that will reduce that share, and leave a larger proportionate share of the dividend to be shared among others. This reflex action may be slow. But, if there is no violent change in the arts of production or in the general economic condition of society, the supply of each agent will be closely governed by its cost of production : account being taken of those conventional necessaries, which constantly expand as the growing richness of the national income yields to one class after another an increasing surplus above the mere necessaries for efficiency.

An increase in the supply of any agent will benefit most other agents, but not necessarily all. § 7. In studying the influence which increased efficiency and increased earnings in one trade exert on the condition of others we may start from the general fact that, other things being equal, the larger the supply of any agent of production, the farther will it have to push its way into uses for which it is not specially fitted; the lower will be the demand price with which it will have to be contented in those uses in which its employment is on the verge or margin of not being found profitable; and, in so far as competition equalizes the price which it gets in all uses, this price will be its price for all uses. The extra production resulting from the increase in that agent of production will go to swell the national dividend, and other agents of production will benefit thereby : but that agent itself will have to submit to a lower rate of pay.

For instance, if without any other change, capital increases fast, the rate of interest must fall; if without any other change, the number of those ready to do any particular kind of labour increases, their wages must fall. In either case there will result an increased production, and an increased national dividend : in either case the loss of one agent of production must result in a gain to others; but not necessarily to all others. Thus the opening up of rich quarries of slate or the increase in numbers or efficiency of quarrymen, would tend to improve the houses of all classes; and it would tend to increase the demand for bricklayers' and carpenters' labour, and raise their wages. But it would injure the makers of roofing tiles as producers of building materials, more than it benefited them as consumers. The increase in the supply of this one agent increases the demand for many others by a little, and for some others by much; but for some it lessens the demand.

Wages of a worker expressed provision- We know that the wages of any worker, say an operative in a boot and shoe factory, tend to equal the net product of his labour. They are not governed by that net product; for net products, like

all other incidents of marginal uses, are governed together with VI, II, 7.
value by the general relations of demand and supply.[1] But when, ally in
(1) the aggregate application of capital and labour to the boot and terms of
shoe industry up to that limit, at which the additional products ducts of
resulting from any further application could barely be made at workers of
profitable rates; (2) the distribution of resources between plant, grades.
labour, and other agents of production has been appropriately made;
(3) we have in view a factory, working with normally good fortune,
conducted with normal ability, and where the conditions are such
that there is a doubt whether to take on an additional operative of
normal ability and energy, who offers himself at the normal wage :—
when all these things are done, then we may fairly conclude that
the loss of that man's work would be likely to cause a diminution in
the net output of that factory, the value of which was about equal
to his wages.   The inversion of this statement runs that his wages
are about equal to that net product : (of course the net product of
an individual cannot be separated mechanically from that of others
who are working together with him).[2]

The work done by the various classes of operatives in a boot and
shoe factory is not all of the same difficulty : but we may ignore
differences in industrial rank between the classes, and suppose them
to be all of the same rank.   (This supposition greatly simplifies the
wording of the argument, without affecting its general character.)

Now under the rapidly changing conditions of modern work,
one industry or another is apt to be from time to time rather over
supplied or rather under supplied with labour : and these inevitable
inequalities are apt to be increased by restrictive combinations and
other influences.   But yet the fluidity of labour is sufficient to make
it true that the wages of labour of the same industrial grade or rank
tend to equality in different occupations throughout the same western
country.   Accordingly no considerable inaccuracy is involved in the
statement that in general, every worker of the same industrial rank
with a normal boot-operative will be able to buy a pair of boots of
any kind (after providing the cost of their material), with the
wages earned by him, in about the same time as is required by such
an operative to contribute a pair of boots of that kind to the net
product of his factory.   Putting this statement into a more general
form we may say that every worker will in general be able with the

---

[1] See V. VIII. 5; and VI. I. 7.
[2] See above pp. 428–9.   The net product of a factory is now commonly taken,
as it is in the official Census of Production, to be the work which it puts into its
material : thus the value of its net product is the excess of the gross value of its
output over the value of the material used by it.

earnings of a hundred days' labour to buy the net products of a hundred days' labour of other workers in the same grade with himself : he may select them in whatever way he chooses, so as to make up that aggregate sum.

If the normal earnings of workers in another grade are half as high again as his own, the boot-operative must spend three days' wages in order to get the net product of two days' labour of a worker in that grade ; and so in proportion.

Increased efficiency in any trade tends to raise real wages in others.

Thus, other things being equal, every increase in the net efficiency of labour in any trade, including his own, will raise in the same proportion the real value of that part of his wages which the boot-operative spends on the products of that trade ; and other things being equal, the equilibrium level of the real wages of the boot-operative depends directly on, and varies directly with, the average efficiency of the trades, including his own, which produce those things on which he spends his wages. Conversely, the rejection by the workers in any industry of an improvement, by which its efficiency could be increased ten per cent., inflicts on the boot-operative an injury measured by ten per cent. of that part of his wages which he spends on the products of that industry. But an increased efficiency on the part of workers, whose products compete with his own, may injure him temporarily at least, especially if he is not himself a consumer of those products.

The relations between grades. An increased supply of business ability raises the wages of manual labour.

Again, the boot-operative will gain by anything that changes the relative positions of different grades in such a way as to raise his grade relatively to others. He will gain by an increase of medical men whose aid he occasionally needs. And he will gain more if those grades which are occupied chiefly with the tasks of managing business, whether manufacturing, trading, or any other, receive a great influx from other grades : for then the earnings of management will be lowered permanently relatively to the earnings of manual work, there will be a rise in the net product of every kind of manual labour ; and, other things being equal, the boot-operative will get more of every commodity on which he spends those wages that represent his own net product.

We do not assume perfect knowledge and freedom of competition,

§ 8. The process of substitution, of which we have been discussing the tendencies, is one form of competition ; and it may be well to insist again that we do not assume that competition is perfect. Perfect competition requires a perfect knowledge of the state of the market ; and though no great departure from the actual facts of life is involved in assuming this knowledge on the part of dealers when we are considering the course of business in Lombard Street, the Stock Exchange, or in a wholesale Produce Market; it would VI, n. 9. be an altogether unreasonable assumption to make when we are examining the causes that govern the supply of labour in any of the lower grades of industry. For if a man had sufficient ability to know everything about the market for his labour, he would have too much to remain long in a low grade. The older economists, in constant contact as they were with the actual facts of business life, must have known this well enough; but partly for brevity and simplicity, partly because the term " free competition " had become almost a catchword, partly because they had not sufficiently classified and conditioned their doctrines, they often seemed to imply that they did assume this perfect knowledge.

It is therefore specially important to insist that we do not assume *but only* the members of any industrial group to be endowed with more *the enter-prise and* ability and forethought, or to be governed by motives other than *business habits* those which are in fact normal to, and would be attributed by every *which are* well-informed person to, the members of that group; account being *in fact normal* taken of the general conditions of time and place. There may be a *to each several* good deal of wayward and impulsive action, sordid and noble motives *rank of* may mingle their threads together; but there is a constant tendency *industry.* for each man to select such occupations for himself and his children as seem to him on the whole the most advantageous of those which are within the range of his resources, and of the efforts which he is able and willing to make in order to reach them.[1]

§ 9. The last group of questions, which still remain to be dis- *We pass* cussed, is concerned with the relation of capital in general to wages *to the relations* in general. It is obvious that though capital in general is constantly *of capital* competing with labour for the field of employment in particular *and labour in general.* trades; yet since capital itself is the embodiment of labour as well as *There is* of waiting, the competition is really between some kinds of labour *a real if* aided by a good deal of waiting, and other kinds of labour aided by *restricted competi-* less waiting. When for instance it is said that " capitalistic *tion for the field* machinery has displaced much labour that was employed in making *of employ-* boots," what is meant is, that formerly there were many who made *ment between* boots by hand, and a very few who made awls and other simple *capital and* implements, aided by a little waiting; while now there are rather *labour.* fewer persons occupied in boot making; and they make a much larger number of boots than before by aid of powerful machines, made by engineers aided by a good deal of waiting. There is a real and effective competition between labour in general and waiting in

---

[1] Differences between the adjustments of demand and supply in the case of commodities and in the case of labour are discussed in the following chapters.

Q

VI, II, 10. general.   But it covers a small part of the whole field, and is of small importance relatively to the benefits which labour derives from obtaining cheaply the aid of capital, and therefore of efficient methods in the production of things that it needs.[1]

For speaking generally, an increase in the power and the willingness to save will cause the services of waiting to be pushed constantly farther; and will prevent it from obtaining employment at as high a rate of interest as before.   That is, the rate of interest will constantly fall, unless indeed invention opens new advantageous uses of roundabout methods of production.   But this growth of capital will increase the national dividend; open out new and rich fields for the employment of labour in other directions; and will thus more than compensate for the partial displacement of the services of labour by those of waiting.[2]

An increase of capital lowers the marginal charge for its use and raises real wages.   The increase of the national dividend owing to the growth of capital and invention is certain to affect all classes of commodities; and to enable the shoemaker, for instance, to purchase with his earnings more food and clothes, more and better supplies of water, artificial light and heat, travel, and so on.   It may be admitted that a few improvements affect only commodities consumed by the rich, in the first instance at least; that no part of the corresponding increase of the national dividend goes directly to the labouring classes; and that they do not at once gain anything to compensate for the probable disturbance of some of their members in particular trades.   But such cases are rare, and generally on a small scale : and even in them there is nearly always some indirect compensation. For improvements, designed for the luxuries of the rich, soon spread themselves to the comforts of other classes.   And, though it is not a necessary consequence, yet in fact a cheapening of luxuries does generally lead in various ways to increased desires on the part of the rich for things made by hand and for personal services, and increases also the means at their disposal for gratifying those desires.   This points to another aspect of the relation between capital in general and wages in general.

Further explanations.   § 10.   It is to be understood that the share of the national dividend, which any particular industrial class receives during the year, consists either of things that were made during the year, or of

---

[1] We are leaving on one side here the competition for employment between labour in the narrower sense of the term, and the work of the undertaker himself and his assistant managers and foremen.   A great part of chs. VII. and VIII. is given to this difficult and important problem.

[2] Capital is here reckoned broadly : it is not confined to trade capital.   This point is of secondary interest and is relegated to Appendix J, 4.

the equivalents of those things. For many of the things made, or VI, n, 10.
partly made, during the year are likely to remain in the possession
of capitalists and undertakers of industry and to be added to the
stock of capital; while in return they, directly or indirectly, hand
over to the working classes some things that had been made in
previous years.

The ordinary bargain between labour and capital is that the The sense
wage-receiver gets command over commodities in a form ready for in which it is true
immediate consumption, and in exchange carries his employer's that the
goods a stage further towards being ready for immediate consump- earnings of labour
tion. But while this is true of most employees, it is not true of those depend on advances
who finish the processes of production. For instance, those who made by
put together and finish watches, give to their employers far more capital.
commodities in a form ready for immediate consumption, than they
obtain as wages. And if we take one season of the year with
another, so as to allow for seed and harvest time, we find that workmen as a whole hand over to their employers more finished commodities than they receive as wages. There is, however, a rather
forced sense in which we may perhaps be justified in saying that the
earnings of labour depend upon advances made to labour by capital.
For—not to take account of machinery and factories, of ships and
railroads—the houses loaned to workmen, and even the raw
materials in various stages which will be worked up into commodities consumed by them, represent a far greater provision of capital
for their use than the equivalent of the advances which they make
to the capitalist, even when they work for a month for him before
getting any wages.

In all this then there is nothing to make the relations between The older
capital in general and labour in general differ widely from those theories of wages
between any other two agents of production, in the general scheme of were
distribution already explained. The modern doctrine of the rela- working their way
tions between labour and capital is the outcome to which all the towards
earlier doctrines on the subject were working their way; and differs modern doctrine.
only in its greater exactness, completeness and homogeneity, from
that given by Mill in the third chapter of his fourth book; the only
place in which he collects together all the various elements of the
problem.

To conclude another stage of the argument :—Capital in general The broad
and labour in general co-operate in the production of the national theory of distri-
dividend, and draw from it their earnings in the measure of their bution
respective (marginal) efficiencies. Their mutual dependence is of already given
the closest; capital without labour is dead; the labourer without covers the

VI, II. 10. the aid of his own or someone else's capital would not long be alive.

general relations of capital and labour

Where labour is energetic, capital reaps a high reward and grows apace; and, thanks to capital and knowledge, the ordinary labourer in the western world is in many respects better fed, clothed and even housed than were princes in earlier times. The co-operation of capital and labour is as essential as that of the spinner of yarn and the weaver of cloth : there is a little priority on the part of the spinner; but that gives him no pre-eminence. The prosperity of each is bound up with the strength and activity of the other; though each may gain temporarily, if not permanently, a somewhat larger share of the national dividend at the expense of the other.

In the modern world, private employers and officials of joint-stock companies, many of whom have but little capital of their own, act as the centre of the great industrial wheel. The interests of owners of capital and of workers radiate towards them and from

though the rôle of the undertaker is of growing importance.

them : and they hold the whole together in a firm grip. They will therefore take a predominant place in those discussions of fluctuations of employment and of wages, which are deferred to the second volume of this treatise; and a prominent, though not predominant, place in those discussions of the secondary features in the mode of action of demand and supply peculiar to labour, capital and land respectively, which will occupy the next eight chapters.

Appendices J and K.

In Appendix J some account will be given of the " Wages-fund " doctrine. Reason will be shown for thinking that it laid excessive stress on the side of demand for labour, to the neglect of the causes which govern its supply; and that it suggested a correlation between the *stock* of capital and the *flow* of wages, instead of the true correlation between the *flow* of the products of labour aided by capital and the flow of wages. But reason will also be given for the opinion that the classical economists themselves—though perhaps not nearly all their followers—if cross examined, would have explained away the misleading suggestions of the doctrine; and thus have brought it into close accord, so far as it went, with modern doctrines. In Appendix K some study will be made of the various kinds of producers' and consumers' surpluses; raising questions of some abstract interest, but of little practical importance.

Our problem is too complex to be focused in a single view

As has already been intimated, the efficiencies (total and marginal) of the several factors of production, their contributions direct and indirect to the aggregate net product, or national dividend; and the shares of that dividend which accrue to them severally are correlated by a number of mutual interactions so complicated, that it is impossible to comprehend the whole in a single statement.

But yet by aid of the terse, compact, precise language of Mathematics it is possible to lead up to a fairly unified general view;
though of course it can take no account of differences of quality,
except in so far as they can be interpreted more or less crudely into
differences of quantity.[1]

VI, II, 10.

——

without
technical
language.

[1] Such a survey is focused in Notes XIV.–XXI. of the Mathematical Appendix :
the last of them is easy of comprehension, and shows the complexity of the problems.
Most of the rest are developments of details arising out of Note XIV., the substance
of part of which is translated into English in V. IV.

CHAPTER III

EARNINGS OF LABOUR

VI, III, 1, 2.

The scope of the present and the following seven Chapters.

§ 1. WHEN discussing the general theory of equilibrium of demand and supply in the last Book, and the main outlines of the central problem of distribution and exchange in the first two chapters of this Book, we left on one side, as far as might be, all considerations turning on the special qualities and incidents of the agents of production. We did not inquire in detail how far the general theories of the relations between the value of an appliance for production and that of the product, which it helps to make, are applicable to the incomes earned by natural abilities, or by skill and knowledge acquired long ago, whether in the ranks of the employers, the employed, or the professional classes. We avoided difficulties connected with the analysis of Profits, paying no attention to the many different scopes which the usage of the market-place assigns to this term, and even the more elementary term Interest; and we took no account of the influence of varieties of tenure on the form of demand for land. These and some other deficiencies will be made good by more detailed analysis in the following three groups of chapters on demand and supply in relation to labour, to capital and business power, and to land, respectively.

Problems relating to methods of estimating and reckoning earnings, to which the present chapter is devoted, belong mainly to the province of arithmetic or book-keeping: but much error has arisen from treating them carelessly.

Competition tends to make weekly wages in similar employments not equal, but proportionate to the efficiency of the workers.

§ 2. When watching the action of demand and supply with regard to a material commodity, we are constantly met by the difficulty that two things which are being sold under the same name in the same market, are really not of the same quality and not of the same value to the purchasers. Or, if the things are really alike, they may be sold even in the face of the keenest competition at prices which are nominally different, because the conditions of sale are not the same: for instance, a part of the expense or risk of delivery which is borne in the one case by the seller may in the other be transferred to the buyer. But difficulties of this kind are much greater in the case of labour than of material commodities:

the true price that is paid for labour often differs widely, and in ways that are not easily traced, from that which is nominally paid.

There is a preliminary difficulty as to the term " efficiency." When it is said that about equal earnings (or rather equal "net advantages," see above II. IV. 2) are obtained in the long run in different occupations by persons of about equal *efficiency*, the term " efficiency " must be interpreted broadly.   It must refer to *general* industrial efficiency, as defined above (IV. v. 1).   But when reference is made to differences of earning power of different people in the same occupation, then efficiency is to be estimated with special reference to those particular elements of efficiency which are needed for that occupation.

It is commonly said that the tendency of competition is to equalize the earnings of people engaged in the same trade or in trades of equal difficulty; but this statement requires to be interpreted carefully.   For competition tends to make the earnings got by two individuals of unequal efficiency in any given time, say, a day or a year, not equal, but unequal; and, in like manner, it tends not to equalize, but to render unequal the average weekly wages in two districts in which the average standards of efficiency are unequal. Given that the average strength and energy of the working-classes are higher in the North of England than in the South, it then follows that the more completely " competition makes things find their own level," the more certain is it that average weekly wages will be higher in the North than in the South [1]

Cliffe Leslie and some other writers have naïvely laid stress on local variations of wages as tending to prove that there is very little mobility among the working-classes, and that the competition among them for employment is ineffective.   But most of the facts which they quote relate only to wages reckoned by the day or week : they are only half-facts, and when the missing halves are supplied, they generally support the opposite inference to that on behalf of which they are quoted.   For it is found that local variations of weekly wages and of efficiency generally correspond : and thus the facts tend to prove the effectiveness of competition, so far as they bear on the question at all.   We shall however presently find that

[1] About fifty years ago correspondence between farmers in the North and the South of England led to an agreement that putting roots into a cart was an excellent measure of physical efficiency : and careful comparison showed that wages bore about the same proportion to the weights which the labourers commonly loaded in a day's work in the two districts.   The standards of wages and of efficiency in the South are perhaps now more nearly on a level with those in the North than they were then. But the standard trade union wages are generally higher in the North than in the South : and many men, who go North to reach the higher rate, find that they cannot do what is required, and return.

VI, III, 2. the full interpretation of such facts as these is a task of great difficulty and complexity.

Time-earnings.

The earnings, or wages, which a person gets in any given time, such as a day, a week, or a year, may be called his *time-earnings*, or *time-wages* : and we may then say that Cliffe Leslie's instances of unequal time-wages tend on the whole to support, and not to weaken, the presumption that competition adjusts earnings in occupations of equal difficulty and in neighbouring places to the efficiency of the workers.

Payment by piece-work.

But the ambiguity of the phrase, " the efficiency of the workers," has not yet been completely cleared away. When the payment for work of any kind is apportioned to the quantity and quality of the work turned out, it is said that uniform rates of *piece-work* wages are being paid; and if two persons work under the same conditions and with equally good appliances, they are paid in proportion to their efficiencies when they receive piece-work wages calculated by the same lists of prices for each several kind of work. If however the appliances are not equally good, a uniform rate of piece-work wages gives results disproportionate to the efficiency of the workers. If, for instance, the same lists of piece-work wages were used in cotton mills supplied with old-fashioned machinery, as in those which have the latest improvements, the apparent equality would represent a real inequality. The more effective competition is, and the more perfectly economic freedom and enterprise are developed, the more surely will the lists be higher in the mills that have old-fashioned machinery than in the others.

In order therefore to give its right meaning to the statement that economic freedom and enterprise tend to equalize wages in occupations of the same difficulty and in the same neighbourhood,

Efficiency earnings.

we require the use of a new term. We may find it in *efficiency-wages*, or more broadly *efficiency-earnings*; that is, earnings measured, not as time-earnings are with reference to the time spent in earning them; and not as piece-work earnings are with reference to the amount of output resulting from the work by which they are earned; but with reference to the exertion of ability and *efficiency* required of the worker.

The tendency towards equality of efficiency-earnings.

The tendency then of economic freedom and enterprise (or, in more common phrase, of competition), to cause every one's earnings to find their own level, is a tendency to equality of efficiency-earnings in the same district. This tendency will be the stronger, the greater is the mobility of labour, the less strictly specialized it is, the more keenly parents are on the look-out for the most advantageous

occupations for their children, the more rapidly they are able to
adapt themselves to changes in economic conditions, and lastly the
slower and the less violent these changes are.

This statement of the tendency is, however, still subject to a
slight correction. For we have hitherto supposed that it is a matter
of indifference to the employer whether he employs few or many
people to do a piece of work, provided his total wages-bill for the
work is the same. But that is not the case. Those workers who
earn most in a week when paid at a given rate for their work, are
those who are cheapest to their employers; and they are the cheapest
also to the community, unless indeed they overstrain themselves,
and work themselves out prematurely. For they use only the same
amount of fixed capital as their slower fellow-workers; and, since
they turn out more work, each part of it has to bear a less charge
on this account. The prime costs are equal in the two cases; but
the total cost of that done by those who are more efficient, and get
the higher time-wages, is lower than the total cost of that done by
those who get the lower time-wages at the same rate of piece-work
payment.[1]

This point is seldom of much importance in out-of-door work,
where there is abundance of room, and comparatively little use of
expensive machinery; for then, except in the matter of superintendence, it makes very little difference to the employer, whose
wages-bill for a certain piece of work is £100, whether that sum is
divided between twenty efficient or thirty inefficient workers. But
when expensive machinery is used which has to be proportioned to
the number of workers, the employer would often find the total cost
of his goods lowered if he could get twenty men to turn out for a
wages-bill of £50 as much work as he had previously got done by
thirty men for a wages-bill of £40. In all matters of this kind the
leadership of the world lies with America, and it is not an uncommon
saying there, that he is the best business man who contrives to pay
the highest wages.

The corrected law then stands that the tendency of economic
freedom and enterprise is generally to equalize efficiency-earnings in
the same district : but where much expensive fixed capital is used,
it would be to the advantage of the employer to raise the time-
earnings of the more efficient workers more than in proportion to

---

[1] This argument would be subject to corrections in cases in which the trade
admitted of the employment of more than one shift of workpeople. It would often
be worth an employer's while to pay to each of two shifts as much for an eight hours'
day as he now pays to one shift for a ten hours' day. For though each worker would
produce less, each machine would produce more on the former than on the latter
plan. But to this point we shall return.

VI, III 3. their efficiency.   Of course this tendency is liable to be opposed by
———   special customs and institutions; and, in some cases, by trades-
union regulations.[1]

§ 3.   Thus much with regard to estimates of the work for which
the earnings are given : but next we have to consider most carefully
the facts, that in estimating the real earnings of an occupation
account must be taken of many things besides its money receipts,
and that on the other side of the account we must reckon for many
incidental disadvantages besides those directly involved in the
strain and stress of the work.

Real wages   As Adam Smith says, " the *real wages* of labour may be said to
and nomi-   consist in the quantity of the necessaries and conveniences of life
nal wages.   that are given for it; its *nominal wages* in the quantity of money.....
The labourer is rich or poor, is well or ill rewarded, in proportion to
the real, not to the nominal, price of his labour." [2]   But the words
" that are given for it " must not be taken to apply only to the
necessaries and conveniences that are directly provided by the
purchaser of the labour or its products; for account must be taken
also of the advantages which are attached to the occupation, and
require no special outlay on his part.

Allowance   In endeavouring to ascertain the real wages of an occupation at
must be   any place or time, the first step is to allow for variations in the
made for   purchasing power of the money in which nominal wages are returned.
variations   This point cannot be thoroughly dealt with till we come to treat of
in the   the theory of money as a whole.   But it may be remarked in passing
purchasing   that this allowance would not be a simple arithmetical reckoning,
power of   even if we had perfectly accurate statistics of the history of the
money,   price of all commodities.   For if we compare distant places or
with   distant times, we find people with different wants, and different
special
reference
to the con-
sumption
of the

[1] Ricardo did not overlook the importance of the distinction between variations
in the amount of commodities paid to the labourer as wages, and variations in the
profitableness of the labourer to his employer.   He saw that the real interest of the
employer lay not in the amount of wages that he paid to the labourer, but in the ratio
which those wages bore to the value of the produce resulting from the labourer's
work : and he decided to regard the rate of wages as measured by this ratio : and to
say that wages rose when this ratio increased, and that they fell when it diminished.
It is to be regretted that he did not invent some new term for this purpose; for his
artificial use of a familiar term has seldom been understood by others, and was in
some cases even forgotten by himself.   (Compare Senior's *Political Economy*, pp. 142–
8.)   The variations in the productiveness of labour which he had chiefly in view were
those which result from improvements in the arts of production on the one hand, and
on the other from the action of the law of diminishing return, when an increase of
population required larger crops to be forced from a limited soil.   Had he paid
careful attention to the increase in the productiveness of labour that results directly
from an improvement in the labourer's condition, the position of economic science,
and the real wellbeing of the country, would in all probability be now much further
advanced than they are.   As it is, his treatment of wages seems less instructive than
that in Malthus' *Political Economy*.
[2] *Wealth of Nations*, I. v.

means of supplying those wants : and even when we confine our VI, III, 4, 5
attention to the same time and place we find people of different grade of
classes spending their incomes in very differ ent ways. For instance, labour concerned
the prices of velvet, of operatic entertainments and scientific books
are not very important to the lower ranks of industry; but a fall in
the price of bread or of shoe leather affects them much more than it
does the higher ranks. Differences of this kind must always be
borne in mind, and it is generally possible to make some sort of
rough allowance for them.[1]

§ 4. We have already noticed that a person's total real income is
found by deducting from his gross income the outgoings that belong
to its production; and that this gross income includes many things
which do not appear in the form of money payments and are in
danger of being overlooked.[2]

Firstly, then, with regard to the outgoings. We do not here Allowance
reckon the expenses of education, general and special, involved in must be made for
the preparation for any trade : nor do we take account of the ex- trade expenses.
haustion of a person's health and strength in his work. Allowance
for them may be best made in other ways. But we must deduct all
trade expenses, whether they are incurred by professional men or
artisans. Thus from the barrister's gross income we must deduct
the rent of his office and the salary of his clerk; from the carpenter's
gross income we must deduct the expenses which he incurs for tools;
and when estimating the earnings of quarrymen in any district we
must find out whether local custom assigns the expenses of tools
and blasting powder to them or their employers. Such cases are
comparatively simple; but it is more difficult to decide how large a
part of the expenses, which a medical man incurs for house and
carriage and social entertainments, should be regarded as trade
expenses.[3]

§ 5. Again, when servants or shop assistants have to supply Where
themselves at their own cost with expensive clothes, which they wages are partly paid
would not buy if free to do as they liked, the value of their wages in kind,
to them is somewhat lowered by this compulsion. And when the the allow- ances

---

[1] *The Report of the Poor Law Commissioners on the Employment of Women and Children in Agriculture*, 1843, p. 297, contains some interesting specimens of yearly wages paid in Northumberland, in which very little money appeared. Here is one :—
10 bushels of wheat, 30 of oats, 10 of barley, 10 of rye, 10 of peas; a cow's keep for a year; 800 yards of potatoes; cottage and garden; coal-shed; £3 10s. in cash; and 2 bushels of barley in lieu of hens.

[2] See II. IV. 7.

[3] This class of questions is closely allied to those raised when discussing the defini- tions of Income and Capital in Book II.; where a caution has already been entered against overlooking elements of income that do not take the form of money. Earnings of many even of the professional and wage-receiving classes are in a considerable measure dependent on their being in command of some material capital.

I, III, 6.
—
ust be
ken at
eir value
those
ho re-
ive them,
ot at
eir cost
those
ho give
iem.
employer provides expensive liveries, houseroom and food for his servants, these are generally worth less to them than they cost to him : it is therefore an error to reckon the real wages of domestic servants, as some statisticians have done, by adding to their money wages the equivalent of the cost to their employer of everything that he provides for them.

On the other hand, when a farmer hauls coals free for his men, he chooses, of course, times when his horses have little to do, and the real addition to their earnings is much greater than the cost to him. The same applies to many perquisites and allowances, as, for instance, when the employer allows his men to have without payment commodities which though useful to them, are almost valueless to him on account of the great expenses involved in marketing them; or, again, when he allows them to buy for their own use at the wholesale price commodities which they have helped to produce. When, however, this permission to purchase is changed into an obligation to purchase, the door is open to grave abuses. The farmer who in old times used to compel his men to take from him spoilt grain at the wholesale price of good grain, was really paying them lower wages than he appeared to be. And on the whole when this so-called *truck-system* prevails in any trade in an old country, we may fairly assume that the real rate of wages is lower than the nominal.[1]

Incer-
ainty of
access
iay be
llowed for
y striking
§ 6. Next we have to take account of the influences exerted on the real rate of earnings in an occupation by the uncertainty of success and the inconstancy of employment in it.

We should obviously start by taking the earnings of an occupa-

---

[1] Employers, whose main business is in a healthy condition, are generally too busy to be willing to manage such shops unless there is some strong reason for doing so; and consequently in old countries those who have adopted the Truck system, have more often than not done so with the object of getting back by underhand ways part of the wages which they have nominally paid. They have compelled those who work at home to hire machinery and implements at exorbitant rents; they have compelled all their workpeople to buy adulterated goods at short weights and high prices; and in some cases even to spend a very large part of their wages on goods on which it was easiest to make the highest rate of profits, and especially on spirituous liquors. Mr. Lecky, for instance, records an amusing case of employers who could not resist the temptation to buy theatre tickets cheap, and compel their workpeople to buy them at full price (*History of the Eighteenth Century*, VI. p. 158). The evil is however at its worst when the shop is kept not by the employer, but by the foreman or by persons acting in concert with him; and when he, without openly saying so, gives it to be understood that those, who do not deal largely at the shop, will find it difficult to get his good word. For an employer suffers more or less from anything that injures his workpeople, while the exactions of an unjust foreman are but little held in check by regard for his own ultimate interest.

On the whole evils of this kind are now relatively small. And it must be remembered that in a new country large businesses often spring up in remote places, in which there is no access to even moderately good retail stores or shops; and then it may be necessary that the employers should supply their workpeople with nearly everything they want, either by paying part of their wages in the form of allowances of food, clothing, etc., or by opening stores for them.

tion as the average between those of the successful and unsuccessful members of it; but care is required to get the true average. For if the average earnings of those who are successful are £2000 a year, and of those who are unsuccessful are £400 a year, the average of the whole will be £1200 a year if the former group is as large as the latter; but if, as is perhaps the case with barristers, the unsuccessful are ten times as numerous as the successful, the true average is but £550. And further, many of those who have failed most completely, are likely to have left the occupation altogether, and thus to escape being counted.

And again, though, by taking this average, we obviate the necessity of making any separate allowance for insurance against risk, account generally remains to be taken of the evil of uncertainty. For there are many people of a sober steady-going temper, who like to know what is before them, and who would far rather have an appointment which offered a certain income of say £400 a year than one which was not unlikely to yield £600, but had an equal chance of affording only £200. Uncertainty, therefore, which does not appeal to great ambitions and lofty aspirations, has special attractions for very few; while it acts as a deterrent to many of those who are making their choice of a career. And as a rule the certainty of moderate success attracts more than an expectation of an uncertain success that has an equal actuarial value.

But on the other hand, if an occupation offers a few extremely high prizes, its attractiveness is increased out of all proportion to their aggregate value. For this there are two reasons. The first is that young men of an adventurous disposition are more attracted by the prospects of a great success than they are deterred by the fear of failure; and the second is that the social rank of an occupation depends more on the highest dignity and the best position which can be attained through it than on the average good fortune of those engaged in it. It is an old maxim of statecraft that a Government should offer a few good prizes in every department of its service : and in aristocratic countries the chief officials receive very high salaries, while those of the lower grades are comforted in the receipt of salaries below the market level for similar services by their hopes of ultimately rising to a coveted post, and by the social consideration which in such countries always attends on public officers. This arrangement has the incidental effect of favouring those who are already rich and powerful; and partly for that reason it is not adopted in democratic countries. They often go to the opposite extreme, and pay more than the market rates for their

VI, III, 6.
———
an aver-
age, as
a first
approxi-
mation;

but
separate
allowance
must be
made for
the evils of
uncer-
tainty and
anxiety.

Though
a few
extremely
high prizes
have a dis-
propor-
tionately
great
attractive
force.

VI, III, 7. services to the lower ranks, and less to the upper ranks. But that plan, whatever be its merits on other grounds, is certainly an expensive one.

Similarly with regard to irregularity of employment.

We may next consider the influence which inconstancy of employment exerts on wages. It is obvious that in those occupations in which employment is irregular, the pay must be high in proportion to the work done : the medical man and the shoeblack must each receive when at work a pay which covers a sort of retaining fee for the time when he has nothing to do. If the advantages of their occupations are in other respects equal, and their work equally difficult, the bricklayer when at work must be paid a higher rate than the joiner, and the joiner than the railway guard. For work on the railways is nearly constant all the year round; while the joiner and the bricklayer are always in danger of being made idle by slackness of trade, and the bricklayer's work is further interrupted by frost and rain. The ordinary method of allowing for such interruptions is to add up the earnings for a long period of time and to take the average of them; but this is not quite satisfactory unless we assume that the rest and leisure, which a man gets when out of employment, are of no service to him directly or indirectly.[1]

This assumption may be fairly made in some cases; for waiting for work often involves so much anxiety and worry that it causes more strain than the work itself would do.[2] But that is not always so. Interruptions of work that occur in the regular course of business, and therefore raise no fears about the future, give opportunity for the system to recruit itself and lay in stores of energy for future exertions. The successful barrister, for instance, is subject to a severe strain during some parts of the year; and that is itself an evil. But when allowance has been made for it, he may be regarded as losing very little by being prevented from earning any fees during the legal vacations.[3]

Supplementary earnings.

§ 7. Next we must take account of the opportunities which a man's surroundings may afford of supplementing the earnings which he gets in his chief occupation, by doing work of other kinds. And account may need to be taken also of the opportunities which these surroundings offer for the work of other members of his family.

---

[1] These considerations are specially important with regard to piece-work; the rates of earnings being in some cases much reduced by short supplies of material to work on, or by other interruptions, avoidable or unavoidable.

[2] The evils of irregularity of employment are trenchantly stated in a lecture on that subject given by Prof. Foxwell in 1886.

[3] Workers in the higher grades are generally allowed holidays with pay; but those in the lower grades generally forfeit their pay when they take holidays. The causes of this distinction are obvious; but it naturally raises a feeling of grievance of a kind, to which the inquiries by the Labour Commission gave vent. See e.g. Group B. 24, 431-6.

Many economists have even proposed to take as their unit the earnings of a family : and there is much to be said for this plan with reference to agriculture and those old-fashioned domestic trades in which the whole family works together, provided that allowance is made for the loss resulting from any consequent neglect by the wife of her household duties.   But in modern England trades of this kind are exceptional; the occupation of the head of a family seldom exerts much direct influence on those of its other members, except those of his sons whom he introduces into his own trade; though of course when the place in which he works is fixed, the employments, to which his family can get easy access, are limited by the resources of the neighbourhood.

§ 8. Thus then the attractiveness of a trade depends on many other causes besides the difficulty and strain of the work to be done in it on the one hand, and the money-earnings to be got in it on the other.   And when the earnings in any occupation are regarded as acting on the supply of labour in it, or when they are spoken of as being its supply price, we must always understand that the term earnings is only used as a short expression for its " net advantages." [1] We must take account of the facts that one trade is healthier or cleanlier than another, that it is carried on in a more wholesome or pleasant locality, or that it involves a better social position; as is instanced by Adam Smith's well-known remark that the aversion which many people have for the work of a butcher, and to some extent for the butcher himself, raises earnings in the butchers' trade above those in other trades of equal difficulty.

Of course individual character will always assert itself in estimat- ing particular advantages at a high or a low rate.   Some persons, for instance, are so fond of having a cottage to themselves that they prefer living on low wages in the country to getting much higher wages in the town; while others are indifferent as to the amount of houseroom they get, and are willing to go without the comforts of life provided they can procure what they regard as its luxuries. This was the case, for example, with a family of whom the Royal Commission on the Housing of the Working Classes in 1884 were told : their joint earnings were £7 a week, but they chose to live in one room, so as to be able to spend money freely on excursions and amusements.

Personal peculiarities, such as these, prevent us from predicting with certainty the conduct of particular individuals.   But if each advantage and disadvantage is reckoned at the average of the money values it has for the class of people who would be likely to enter an

[1] See II. IV. 2.

VI, III, 8. occupation, or to bring up their children to it, we shall have the
means of estimating roughly the relative strengths of the forces that
tend to increase or diminish the supply of labour in that occupation
at the time and place which we are considering. For it cannot be
too often repeated that grave errors are likely to result from taking
over an estimate of this kind based on the circumstances of one
time and place, and applying it without proper precaution to those
of another time or another place.

Between races, In this connection it is interesting to observe the influence of
differences of national temperament in our own time. Thus in
America we see Swedes and Norwegians drift to agriculture in the
North-west, while the Irish, if they go on the land at all, choose
farms in the older Eastern States. The preponderance of Germans
in the furniture and the brewing industries; of Italians in railway
building; of Slavs in meat packing and in some groups of mines,
and of Irish and French Canadians in some of the textile industries
of the United States; and the preference of the Jewish immigrants
in London for the clothing industries and for retail trade—all these
are due partly to differences in national aptitudes, but partly also
to differences in the estimates that people of different races form of
the incidental advantages and disadvantages of different trades.

and between industrial trades. Lastly, the disagreeableness of work seems to have very little
effect in raising wages, if it is of such a kind that it can be done by
those whose industrial abilities are of a very low order. For the
progress of science has kept alive many people who are unfit for any
but the lowest grade of work. They compete eagerly for the comparatively small quantity of work for which they are fitted, and in
their urgent need they think almost exclusively of the wages they
can earn : they cannot afford to pay much attention to incidental
discomforts, and indeed the influence of their surroundings has
prepared many of them to regard the dirtiness of an occupation as
an evil of but minor importance.

An evil paradox. Hence arises the paradoxical result that the dirtiness of some
occupations is a cause of the lowness of the wages earned in them.
For employers find that this dirtiness adds much to the wages they
would have to pay to get the work done by skilled men of high
character working with improved appliances; and so they often
adhere to old methods which require only unskilled workers of but
indifferent character, and who can be hired for low (Time-) wages,
because they are not worth much to any employer. There is no
more urgent social need than that labour of this kind should be made
scarce and therefore dear.

CHAPTER IV

EARNINGS OF LABOUR, CONTINUED

§ 1. THE action of demand and supply with regard to labour was discussed in the last chapter with reference to the difficulties of ascertaining the real as opposed to the nominal price of labour. But some peculiarities in this action remain to be studied, which are of a more vital character. For they affect not merely the form, but also the substance of the action of the forces of demand and supply; and to some extent they limit and hamper the free action of those forces. We shall find that the influence of many of them is not at all to be measured by their first and most obvious effects : and that those effects which are cumulative are generally far more important in the long run than those which are not, however prominent the latter may appear.

The problem has thus much in common with that of tracing the economic influence of custom. For it has already been noticed, and it will become more clear as we go on, that the direct effects of custom in causing a thing to be sold for a price sometimes a little higher and sometimes a little lower than it would otherwise fetch, are not really of very great importance, because any such divergence does not, as a rule, tend to perpetuate and increase itself; but on the contrary, if it becomes considerable, it tends itself to call into action forces that counteract it. Sometimes these forces break down the custom altogether; but more often they evade it by gradual and imperceptible changes in the character of the thing sold, so that the purchaser really gets a new thing at the old price under the old name. These direct effects then are obvious, but they are not cumulative. On the other hand, the indirect effects of custom in hindering the methods of production and the character of producers from developing themselves freely are not obvious; but they generally are cumulative, and therefore exert a deep and controlling influence over the history of the world. If custom checks the progress of one generation, then the next generation starts from a lower level than it otherwise would have done; and any retardation which it suffers itself is accumulated

VI, IV, 2. and added to that of its predecessor, and so on from generation to generation.[1]

And so it is with regard to the action of demand and supply on the earnings of labour. If at any time it presses hardly on any individuals or class, the direct effects of the evils are obvious. But the sufferings that result are of different kinds : those, the effects of which end with the evil by which they were caused, are not generally to be compared in importance with those that have the indirect effect of lowering the character of the workers or of hindering it from becoming stronger. For these last cause further weakness and further suffering, which again in their turn cause yet further weakness and further suffering, and so on cumulatively. On the other hand, high earnings, and a strong character, lead to greater strength and higher earnings, which again lead to still greater strength and still higher earnings, and so on cumulatively.

First peculiarity : the worker sells his work, but retains property in himself.

§ 2. The first point to which we have to direct our attention is the fact that human agents of production are not bought and sold as machinery and other material agents of production are. The worker sells his work, but he himself remains his own property : those who bear the expenses of rearing and educating him receive but very little of the price that is paid for his services in later years.[2]

Consequently the investment of capital in him is limited by the means, the forethought, and the unselfishness of his parents.

Whatever deficiencies the modern methods of business may have, they have at least this virtue, that he who bears the expenses of production of material goods, receives the price that is paid for them. He who builds factories or steam-engines or houses, or rears slaves, reaps the benefit of all net services which they render so long as he keeps them for himself; and when he sells them he gets a price which is the estimated net value of their future services; and therefore he extends his outlay until there seems to him no good reason for thinking that the gains resulting from any further investment would compensate him. He must do this prudently and boldly, under the penalty of finding himself worsted in competition with others who follow a broader and more far-sighted policy, and

[1] It ought, however, to be remarked that some of the beneficial effects of custom are cumulative. For among the many different things that are included under the wide term " custom " are crystallized forms of high ethical principles, rules of honourable and courteous behaviour, and of the avoidance of troublesome strife about paltry gains; and much of the good influence which these exert on race character is cumulative. Compare I. II. 1, 2.

[2] This is consistent with the well-known fact that slave labour is not economical, as Adam Smith remarked long ago that " The fund destined for replacing or repairing, if I may say so, the wear-and-tear of the slave is commonly managed by a negligent master or careless overseer. That destined for performing the same office for the free man is managed by the free man himself . . . with strict frugality and parsimonious attention."

of ultimately disappearing from the ranks of those who direct the VI, IV, 2.
course of the world's business.   The action of competition, and the
survival in the struggle for existence of those who know best how to
extract the greatest benefits for themselves from the environment,
tend in the long run to put the building of factories and steam-
engines into the hands of those who will be ready and able to incur
every expense which will add more than it costs to their value as
productive agents.   But the investment of capital in the rearing
and early training of the workers of England is limited by the
resources of parents in the various grades of society, by their power
of forecasting the future, and by their willingness to sacrifice themselves for the sake of their children.

This evil is indeed of comparatively small importance with *This evil is com-paratively small in the higher ranks of society;* regard to the higher industrial grades.   For in those grades most
people distinctly realize the future, and " discount it at a low rate
of interest."   They exert themselves much to select the best careers
for their sons, and the best trainings for those careers; and they are
generally willing and able to incur a considerable expense for the
purpose.   The professional classes especially, while generally eager
to save some capital *for* their children, are even more on the alert
for opportunities of investing it *in* them.   And whenever there
occurs in the upper grades of industry a new opening for which an
extra and special education is required, the future gains need not
be very high relatively to the present outlay, in order to secure a
keen competition for the post.

But in the lower ranks of society the evil is great.   For the slender *but very great in the lower ranks,* means and education of the parents, and the comparative weakness
of their power of distinctly realizing the future, prevent them from
investing capital in the education and training of their children with
the same free and bold enterprise with which capital is applied to
improving the machinery of any well-managed factory.   Many of
the children of the working-classes are imperfectly fed and clothed;
they are housed in a way that promotes neither physical nor moral
health;   they receive a school education which, though in modern
England it may not be very bad so far as it goes, yet goes only a
little way;   they have few opportunities of getting a broader view
of life or an insight into the nature of the higher work of business,
of science or of art;   they meet hard and exhausting toil early on the
way, and for the greater part keep to it all their lives.   At least they
go to the grave carrying with them undeveloped abilities and faculties;   which, if they could have borne full fruit, would have added
to the material wealth of the country—to say nothing of higher

VI, IV, 3.

considerations—many times as much as would have covered the expense of providing adequate opportunities for their development.

and the evil is cumulative.

But the point on which we have specially to insist now is that this evil is cumulative. The worse fed are the children of one generation, the less will they earn when they grow up, and the less will be their power of providing adequately for the material wants of their children; and so on to following generations. And again, the less fully their own faculties are developed, the less will they realize the importance of developing the best faculties of their children, and the less will be their power of doing so. And conversely any change that awards to the workers of one generation better earnings, together with better opportunities of developing their best qualities, will increase the material and moral advantages which they have the power to offer to their children : while by increasing their own intelligence, wisdom and forethought, such a change will also to some extent increase their willingness to sacrifice their own pleasures for the wellbeing of their children; though there is much of that willingness now even among the poorest classes, so far as their means and the limits of their knowledge will allow.

The son of the artisan has a better start in life than the son of the unskilled labourer;

§ 3. The advantages which those born in one of the higher grades of society have over those born in a lower, consist in a great measure of the better introductions and the better start in life which they receive from their parents; and the importance of this good start in life is nowhere seen more clearly than in a comparison of the fortunes of the sons of artisans and of unskilled labourers. There are not many skilled trades to which the son of an unskilled labourer can get easy access; and in the large majority of cases the son follows the father's calling. In the old-fashioned domestic industries this was almost a universal rule; and, even under modern conditions, the father has often great facilities for introducing his son to his own trade. Employers and their foremen generally give to a lad whose father they already know and trust, a preference over one for whom they would have to incur the entire responsibility. And in many trades a lad, even after he has got entrance to the works, is not very likely to make good progress and obtain a secure footing, unless he is able to work by the side of his father, or some friend of his father's, who will take the trouble to teach him and to let him do work that requires careful supervision, but has an educational value.

he is brought up in a more refined home and with more

And the son of the artisan has further advantages. He generally lives in a better and cleaner house, and under material surroundings that are more consistent with refinement than those with which the ordinary labourer is familiar. His parents are likely to be better educated, and to have a higher notion of their duties to their children; and, last but not least, his mother is likely to be able to give more of her time to the care of her family.

If we compare one country of the civilized world with another, or one part of England with another, or one trade in England with another, we find that the degradation of the working-classes varies almost uniformly with the amount of rough work done by women. The most valuable of all capital is that invested in human beings; and of that capital the most precious part is the result of the care and influence of the mother, so long as she retains her tender and unselfish instincts, and has not been hardened by the strain and stress of unfeminine work.

This draws our attention to another aspect of the principle already noticed, that in estimating the cost of production of efficient labour, we must often take as our unit the family. At all events we cannot treat the cost of production of efficient men as an isolated problem; it must be taken as part of the broader problem of the cost of production of efficient men together with the women who are fitted to make their homes happy, and to bring up their children vigorous in body and mind, truthful and cleanly, gentle and brave.[1]

VI, IV, 3.

of a mother's care. The great importance of this last element.

---

[1] Sir William Petty discussed " The Value of the People " with much ingenuity; and the relation in which the cost of rearing an adult male stands to the cost of rearing a family unit was examined in a thoroughly scientific manner by Cantillon, *Essai*, Part I. chap. XI., and again by Adam Smith, *Wealth of Nations*, Book I. ch. VIII.: and in more recent times by Dr. Engel, in his brilliant Essay *Der Preis der Arbeit*, and by Dr. Farr and others.   Many estimates have been made of the addition to the wealth of a country caused by the arrival of an immigrant whose cost of rearing in his early years was defrayed elsewhere, and who is likely to produce more than he consumes in the country of his adoption.   The estimates have been made on many plans, all of them rough, and some apparently faulty in principle : but most of them find the average value of an immigrant to be about £200.   It would seem that, if we might neglect provisionally the difference between the sexes, we should calculate the value of the immigrant on the lines of the argument of V. IV. 2.   That is, we should " discount " the probable value of all the future services that he would render; add them together, and deduct from them the sum of the " discounted " values of all the wealth and direct services of other persons that he would consume : and it may be noted that in thus calculating each element of production and consumption at its probable value, we have incidentally allowed for the chances of his premature death and sickness, as well as of his failure or success in life.   Or again we might estimate his value at the money cost of production which his native country had incurred for him; which would in like manner be found by adding together the " accumulated " values of all the several elements of his past consumption and deducting from them the sum of the " accumulated " values of all the several elements of his past production.

So far we have taken no account of the difference between the sexes.   But it is clear that the above plans put the value of the male immigrants too high and that of the female too low : unless allowance is made for the service which women render as mothers, as wives and as sisters, and the male immigrants are charged with having consumed these services, while the female immigrants are credited with having supplied them.   (See Mathematical Note XXIV.)

Many writers assume, implicitly at least, that the net production of an average individual and the consumption during the whole of his life are equal; or, in other words, that he would neither add to nor take from the material wellbeing of a country, in which he stayed all his life.   On this assumption the above two plans of estimating his value would be convertible; and then of course we should make our calculations

VI, IV, 4.   § 4. As the youth grows up, the influence of his parents and his
schoolmaster declines; and thenceforward to the end of his life his
character is moulded chiefly by the nature of his work and the
influence of those with whom he associates for business, for pleasure
and for religious worship.

The
technical
training
of the
workshop
depends in
a great
measure
on the un-
selfishness
of the
employer.

A good deal has already been said of the technical training of
adults, of the decadence of the old apprenticeship system, and of the
difficulty of finding anything to take its place.   Here again we meet
the difficulty that whoever may incur the expense of investing capital
in developing the abilities of the workman, those abilities will be the
property of the workman himself : and thus the virtue of those who
have aided him must remain for the greater part its own reward.

It is true that high-paid labour is really cheap to those employers
who are aiming at leading the race, and whose ambition it is to turn
out the best work by the most advanced methods.   They are likely
to give their men high wages and to train them carefully; partly
because it pays them to do so, and partly because the character
that fits them to take the lead in the arts of production is likely also
to make them take a generous interest in the wellbeing of those who
work for them.   But though the number of such employers is
increasing, they are still comparatively few.   And even they cannot
always afford to carry the investment of capital in the training of
their men as far as they would have done, if the results of the investment accrued to them in the same way as the results of any improvements they might make in their machinery.   Even they are sometimes checked by the reflection that they are in a similar position
to that of a farmer who, with an uncertain tenure and no security
of compensation for his improvements, is sinking capital in raising
the value of his landlord's property.

Its benefits
are cumu-
lative, but
accrue
only in
part to
him or
his heirs.

Again, in paying his workpeople high wages and in caring for
their happiness and culture, the liberal employer confers benefits
which do not end with his own generation.   For the children of his
workpeople share in them, and grow up stronger in body and in
character than otherwise they would have done.   The price which
he has paid for labour will have borne the expenses of production
of an increased supply of high industrial faculties in the next genera-

---

by the latter and easier method.   We may, for instance, guess that the total amount
spent on bringing up an average child of the lower half of the labouring classes, say
two-fifths of the population, is £100; for the next fifth we may put the sum at £175;
for the next fifth at £300; for the next tenth at £500, and the remaining tenth at
£1200 : or an average of £300.   But of course some of the population are very young
and have had but little spent on them; others have got nearly to their life's end;
and therefore, on these assumptions, the average value of an individual is perhaps £200.

tion : but these faculties will be the property of others, who will
have the right to hire them out for the best price they will fetch :
neither he nor even his heirs can reckon on reaping much material
reward for this part of the good that he has done.

§ 5. The next of those characteristics of the action of demand Second peculiarity.
and supply peculiar to labour, which we have to study, lies in the
fact that when a person sells his services, he has to present himself
where they are delivered. It matters nothing to the seller of bricks
whether they are to be used in building a palace or a sewer : but it
matters a great deal to the seller of labour, who undertakes to per- The seller of labour must deliver it himself.
form a task of given difficulty, whether or not the place in which it
is to be done is a wholesome and a pleasant one, and whether or
not his associates will be such as he cares to have. In those yearly
hirings which still remain in some parts of England, the labourer
inquires what sort of a temper his new employer has, quite as
carefully as what rate of wages he pays.

This peculiarity of labour is of great importance in many indi- The effects of this are not generally cumulative, and their real importance is seldom very great.
vidual cases, but it does not often exert a broad and deep influence
of the same nature as that last discussed. The more disagreeable
the incidents of an occupation, the higher of course are the wages
required to attract people into it : but whether these incidents do
lasting and widespreading harm depends on whether they are such
as to undermine men's physical health and strength or to lower their
character. When they are not of this sort, they are indeed evils in
themselves, but they do not generally cause other evils beyond themselves; their effects are seldom cumulative.

Since however no one can deliver his labour in a market in which
he is not himself present, it follows that the mobility of labour and
the mobility of the labourer are convertible terms : and the unwillingness to quit home, and to leave old associations, including
perhaps some loved cottage and burial-ground, will often turn the
scale against a proposal to seek better wages in a new place. And
when the different members of a family are engaged in different
trades, and a migration, which would be advantageous to one
member would be injurious to others, the inseparability of the
worker from his work considerably hinders the adjustment of the
supply of labour to the demand for it. But of this more hereafter.

§ 6. Again, labour is often sold under special disadvantages, Third and fourth peculiarities. Labour is perishable,
arising from the closely connected group of facts that labour power
is " perishable," that the sellers of it are commonly poor and have
no reserve fund, and that they cannot easily withhold it from the
market.

VI, IV, 6.

and the sellers of it are often at a disadvantage in bargaining. But many material commodities are perishable.

Perishable is an attribute common to the labour of all grades : the time lost when a worker is thrown out of employment cannot be recovered, though in some cases his energies may be refreshed by rest.[1] It must however be remembered that much of the working power of material agents of production is perishable in the same sense; for a great part of the income, which they also are prevented from earning by being thrown out of work, is completely lost. There is indeed some saving of wear-and-tear on a factory, or a steam-ship, when it is lying idle : but this is often small compared with the income which its owners have to forego: they get no compensation for their loss of interest on the capital invested, or for the depreciation which it undergoes from the action of the elements or from its tendency to be rendered obsolete by new inventions.

Again, many vendible commodities are perishable. In the strike of dock labourers in London in 1889, the perishableness of the fruit, meat, etc. on many of the ships told strongly on the side of the strikers.

Disadvantages in bargaining are greatest generally among the lowest grades of labour.

The want of reserve funds and of the power of long withholding their labour from the market is common to nearly all grades of those whose work is chiefly with their hands. But it is especially true of unskilled labourers, partly because their wages leave very little margin for saving, partly because when any group of them suspends work, there are large numbers who are capable of filling their places. And, as we shall see presently when we come to discuss trade combinations, it is more difficult for them than for skilled artisans to form themselves into strong and lasting combinations; and so to put themselves on something like terms of equality in bargaining with their employers. For it must be remembered that a man who employs a thousand others, is in himself an absolutely rigid combination to the extent of one thousand units among buyers in the labour market.

They do not attach to domestic servants,

But these statements do not apply to all kinds of labour. Domestic servants though they have not large reserve funds, and seldom any formal trades-union, are sometimes better able than their employers to act in concert. The total real wages of domestic servants of fashionable London are very high in comparison with other skilled trades in which equal skill and ability are required. But on the other hand those domestic servants who have no specialized skill, and who hire themselves to persons with very narrow means, have not been able to make even tolerably good terms for themselves : they work very hard for very low wages.

[1] See above, VI. III.

Turning next to the highest grades of industry, we find that as
a rule they have the advantage in bargaining over the purchaser of
their labour.   Many of the professional classes are richer, have
larger reserve funds, more knowledge and resolution, and much
greater power of concerted action with regard to the terms on which
they sell their services, than the greater number of their clients and
customers.

If further evidence were wanted that the disadvantages of
bargaining under which the vendor of labour commonly suffers,
depend on his own circumstances and qualities, and not on the fact
that the particular thing which he has to sell is labour; such evidence could be found by comparing the successful barrister or
solicitor or physician, or opera singer or jockey with the poorer
independent producers of vendible goods.   Those, for instance, who
in remote places collect shell-fish to be sold in the large central
markets, have little reserve funds and little knowledge of the world,
and of what other producers are doing in other parts of the country :
while those to whom they sell, are a small and compact body of
wholesale dealers with wide knowledge and large reserve funds;
and in consequence the sellers are at a great disadvantage in bargaining.   And much the same is true of the women and children
who sell hand-made lace, and of the garret masters of East London
who sell furniture to large and powerful dealers.

It is however certain that manual labourers as a class are at a
disadvantage in bargaining; and that the disadvantage wherever
it exists is likely to be cumulative in its effects.   For though, so long
as there is any competition among employers at all, they are likely
to bid for labour something not very much less than its real value
to them, that is, something not very much less than the highest
price they would pay rather than go on without it; yet anything
that lowers wages tends to lower the efficiency of the labourer's
work, and therefore to lower the price which the employer would
rather pay than go without that work.   The effects of the labourer's
disadvantage in bargaining are therefore cumulative in two ways.
It lowers his wages; and as we have seen, this lowers his efficiency
as a worker, and thereby lowers the normal value of his labour.   And
in addition it diminishes his efficiency as a bargainer, and thus
increases the chance that he will sell his labour for less than its
normal value.[1]

---

[1] On the subject of this Section compare Book V. II. 3, and Appendix F on Barter.
Prof. Brentano was the first to call attention to several of the points discussed in this
chapter.   See also Howell's *Conflicts of Capital and Labour.*

CHAPTER V

EARNINGS OF LABOUR, CONTINUED

§ 1. THE next peculiarity in the action of demand and supply with regard to labour, which we have to consider, is closely connected with some of those we have already discussed. It consists in the length of time that is required to prepare and train labour for its work, and in the slowness of the returns which result from this training.

This discounting of the future, this deliberate adjustment of supply of expensively trained labour to the demand for it, is most clearly seen in the choice made by parents of occupations for their children, and in their efforts to raise their children into a higher grade than their own.

It was these chiefly that Adam Smith had in view when he said :—" When any expensive machine is erected, the extraordinary work to be performed by it before it is worn out, it must be expected, will replace the capital laid out upon it, with at least the ordinary profits. A man educated at the expense of much labour and time to any of those employments which require extraordinary dexterity and skill, may be compared to one of those expensive machines. The work which he learns to perform, it must be expected, over and above the usual wages of common labour, will replace to him the whole expense of his education, with at least the ordinary profits of an equally valuable capital. It must do this too in a reasonable time, regard being had to the very uncertain duration of human life, in the same manner as to the more certain duration of the machine."

But this statement is to be received only as a broad indication of general tendencies. For independently of the fact that in rearing and educating their children, parents are governed by motives different from those which induce a capitalist undertaker to erect a new machine, the period over which the earning power extends is generally greater in the case of a man than of a machine; and therefore the circumstances by which the earnings are determined are less capable of being foreseen, and the adjustment of supply to demand is both slower and more imperfect. For though factories

---

Margin notes:

VI, v, 1.

The fifth peculiarity consists in the great length of time required for providing additional supplies of specialized ability.

Adam Smith's comparison of the incomes earned by machinery and by a skilled worker.

must be modified on account of the shortness of the lives of most machines;

though there are

and houses, the main shafts of a mine and the embankments of a railway, may have much longer lives than those of the men who made them; yet these are exceptions to the general rule.

§ 2. Not much less than a generation elapses between the choice by parents of a skilled trade for one of their children, and his reaping the full results of their choice. And meanwhile the character of the trade may have been almost revolutionized by changes, of which some probably threw long shadows before them, but others were such as could not have been foreseen even by the shrewdest persons and those best acquainted with the circumstances of the trade.

VI, v, 2.
important exceptions.
Parents in choosing trades for their children must look forward a whole generation, and their forecasts are very liable to error.

The working classes in nearly all parts of England are constantly on the look-out for advantageous openings for the labour of themselves and their children; and they question friends and relations, who have settled in other districts, as to the wages that are to be got in various trades, and as to their incidental advantages and disadvantages. But it is very difficult to ascertain the causes that are likely to determine the distant future of the trades which they are selecting for their children; and there are not many who enter on this abstruse inquiry. The majority assume without a further thought that the condition of each trade in their own time sufficiently indicates what it will be in the future; and, so far as the influence of this habit extends, the supply of labour in a trade in any one generation tends to conform to its earnings not in that but in the preceding generation.

Again, some parents, observing that the earnings in one trade have been for some years rising relatively to others in the same grade, assume that the course of change is likely to continue in the same direction. But it often happens that the previous rise was due to temporary causes, and that, even if there had been no exceptional influx of labour into the trade, the rise would have been followed by a fall instead of a further rise : and, if there is such an exceptional influx, the consequence may be a supply of labour so excessive, that its earnings remain below their normal level for many years.

Next we have to recall the fact that, although there are some trades which are difficult of access except to the sons of those already in them, yet the majority draw recruits from the sons of those in other trades in the same grade : and therefore when we consider the dependence of the supply of labour on the resources of those who bear the expenses of its education and training, we must often regard the whole grade, rather than any one trade, as our

In this connection we must often take as our unit not a particular trade, but a whole grade of labour,

VI, v, 3, 4. unit; and say that, in so far as the supply of labour is limited by the funds available for defraying its cost of production, the supply of labour in any grade is determined by the earnings of that grade in the last rather than in the present generation.

It must, however, be remembered that the birth-rate in every grade of society is determined by many causes, among which deliberate calculations of the future hold but a secondary place: though, even in a country in which tradition counts for as little as it does in modern England, a great influence is exerted by custom and public opinion which are themselves the outcome of the experience of past generations.

Allowance must however be made for the movements of adult labour,

§ 3. But we must not omit to notice those adjustments of the supply of labour to the demand for it, which are effected by movements of adults from one trade to another, one grade to another, and one place to another. The movements from one grade to another can seldom be on a very large scale; although it is true that exceptional opportunities may sometimes develop rapidly a great deal of latent ability among the lower grades. Thus, for instance, the sudden opening out of a new country, or such an event as the American war, will raise from the lower ranks of labour many men who bear themselves well in difficult and responsible posts

which are of growing importance in consequence of the increasing demand for general ability.

But the movements of adult labour from trade to trade and from place to place can in some cases be so large and so rapid as to reduce within a very short compass the period which is required to enable the supply of labour to adjust itself to the demand. That general ability which is easily transferable from one trade to another, is every year rising in importance relatively to that manual skill and technical knowledge which are specialized to one branch of industry. And thus economic progress brings with it on the one hand a constantly increasing changefulness in the methods of industry, and therefore a constantly increasing difficulty in predicting the demand for labour of any kind a generation ahead; but on the other hand it brings also an increasing power of remedying such errors of adjustment as have been made.[1]

We pass to differences between causes that are most powerful in long and

§ 4. Let us now revert to the principle that the income derived from the appliances for the production of a commodity exerts a controlling influence in the long run over their own supply and price, and therefore over the supply and the price of the commodity itself; but that within short periods there is not time for the exercise of

---

[1] On the subject of this section compare Bk. IV. VI. 8; Mr. Charles Booth's *Life and Labour in London*; and Sir H. Ll. Smith's *Modern Changes in the Mobility of Labour*.

any considerable influence of this kind. And let us inquire how *VI, v, 5.* this principle needs to be modified when it is applied not to the *in short* material agents of production, which are only a means towards an *periods.* end, and which may be the private property of the capitalist, but to human beings who are ends as well as means of production and who remain their own property.

To begin with we must notice that, since labour is slowly pro- *A "long* duced and slowly worn out, we must take the term " long period " *period"* more strictly, and regard it as generally implying a greater duration, *gard to the* when we are considering the relations of normal demand and supply *supply of* for labour, than when we are considering them for ordinary com- *must gene-* modities. There are many problems, the period of which is long *very long.* enough to enable the supply of ordinary commodities, and even of most of the material appliances required for making them, to be adjusted to the demand; and long enough therefore to justify us in regarding the average prices of those commodities during the period as " normal," and as equal to their normal expenses of production in a fairly broad use of the term; while yet the period would not be long enough to allow the supply of labour to be adjusted at all well to the demand for it. The average earnings of labour during this period therefore would not be at all certain to give about a normal return to those who provided the labour; but they would rather have to be regarded as determined by the available stock of labour on the one hand, and the demand for it on the other. Let us consider this point more closely.

§ 5. Market variations in the price of a commodity are governed *The inde-* by the temporary relations between demand and the stock that is *pendent* in the market or within easy access of it. When the market price *craftsman.* so determined is above its normal level, those who are able to bring new supplies into the market in time to take advantage of the high price receive an abnormally high reward; and if they are small handicraftsmen working on their own account, the whole of this rise in price goes to increase their earnings.

In the modern industrial world, however, those who undertake *Fluctua-* the risks of production and to whom the benefits of any rise in *tions of* price, and the evils of any fall, come in the first instance, are capitalist *under the* undertakers of industry. Their net receipts in excess of the im- *modern* mediate outlay involved for making the commodity, that is, its *industry.* prime (money) cost, are a return derived for the time being from the capital invested in their business in various forms, including their own faculties and abilities. But, when trade is good, the force of competition among the employers themselves, each desiring to

VI, v, 6. extend his business, and to get for himself as much as possible of
this high return, makes them consent to pay higher wages to their
employees in order to obtain their services; and even if they act
in concert, and refuse for a time any concession, a combination
among their employees may force it from them under penalty of
foregoing the harvest, which the favourable turn of the market is
offering. The result generally is that before long a great part of
the gains are being distributed among the employees; and that
their earnings remain above the normal level so long as the prosperity
lasts.

Illustration from the coal trade. Thus the high wages of miners during the inflation which culminated in 1873, were governed for the time by the relation in
which the demand for their services stood to the amount of skilled
mining labour available, the unskilled labour imported into the
trade being counted as equivalent to an amount of skilled labour of
equal efficiency. Had it been impossible to import any such labour
at all, the earnings of miners would have been limited only by the
elasticity of the demand for coal on the one hand, and the gradual
coming to age of the rising generation of miners on the other. As
it was, men were drawn from other occupations which they were
not eager to leave; for they could have got high wages by staying
where they were, since the prosperity of the coal and iron trades was
but the highest crest of a swelling tide of credit. These new men
were unaccustomed to underground work; its discomforts told
heavily on them, while its dangers were increased by their want of
technical knowledge, and their want of skill caused them to waste
much of their strength. The limits therefore which their competition imposed on the rise of the special earnings of miners' skill were
not narrow.

When the tide turned those of the new-comers who were least
adapted for the work left the mines; but even then the miners who
remained were too many for the work to be done, and their wage
fell; till it reached that limit, at which those who were least adapted
for the work and life of a miner, could get more by selling their
labour in other trades. And that limit was a low one; for the
swollen tide of credit, which culminated in 1873, had undermined
solid business, impaired the true foundations of prosperity, and left
nearly every industry in a more or less unhealthy and depressed
condition.

In estimating the return for the § 6. We have already remarked that only part of the return
derived from an improvement which is being exhausted can be
regarded as being its net earnings; for a sum equivalent to the

exhaustion of the capital value of the improvement must be de- VI, v, 6.
ducted from these returns, before they can be counted as net income labourer's
of any kind. Similarly allowance must be made for the wear-and- skill,
tear of a machine, as well as for the cost of working it, before we account
can arrive at its net earnings. Now the miner is as liable to wear- taken not
and-tear as machinery is; and a deduction must be made from his his wear-
earnings also on account of wear-and-tear, when the special return and-tear,
of his skill is being estimated.[1]

But in his case there is a further difficulty. For while the owner but also
of machinery does not suffer from its being kept long at work when fatigue,
the expenses of working it, including wear-and-tear, have once been and other
allowed for; the owner of skilled faculties does suffer when they are veniences
kept long at work, and he suffers incidental inconveniences, such as of his
loss of recreation and of freedom of movement, etc. If the miner work.
has only four days' work in one week and earns £1, and in the next
week he has six days' work and earns £1 10s.; only part of this
extra 10s. can be regarded as return for his skill, for the remainder
must be reckoned as the recompense of his additional fatigue as
well as wear-and-tear.[2]

To conclude this part of our argument. The market price of Conclu-
everything, i.e. its price for short periods, is determined mainly by sion, and
the relations in which the demand for it stands to the available mentof the
stocks of it; and in the case of any agent of production, whether it argument
be a human or a material agent, this demand is " derived " from gard to the
the demand for those things which it is used in making. In these ence of
relatively short periods fluctuations in wages follow, and do not tions of
precede, fluctuations in the selling prices of the goods produced. earnings
on the
But the incomes which are being earned by all agents of pro- state of the
duction, human as well as material, and those which appear likely market.
to be earned by them in the future, exercise a ceaseless influence on
those persons by whose action the future supplies of these agents are
determined. There is a constant tendency towards a position of
normal equilibrium, in which the supply of each of these agents shall
stand in such a relation to the demand for its services, as to give to
those who have provided the supply a sufficient reward for their
efforts and sacrifices. If the economic conditions of the country
remained stationary sufficiently long, this tendency would realize
itself in such an adjustment of supply to demand, that both machines

---

[1] There is some ground for regarding this special return as a quasi-rent. See
VI. v. 7 and VIII. 8.
[2] Compare above, VI. II. 2. If they have any considerable stock of trade implements, they are to that extent capitalists; and part of their income is quasi-rent on
this capital.

and human beings would earn generally an amount that corresponded fairly with their cost of rearing and training, conventional necessaries as well as those things which are strictly necessary being reckoned for. But conventional necessaries might change under the influence of non-economic causes, even while economic conditions themselves were stationary : and this change would affect the supply of labour, and would lessen the national dividend and slightly alter its distribution. As it is, the economic conditions of the country are constantly changing, and the point of adjustment of normal demand and supply in relation to labour is constantly being shifted.

The extra income earned by rare natural abilities may be regarded as a surplus when analysing the incomes of individuals;

§ 7. We may now discuss the question under what head to class those extra incomes which are earned by extraordinary natural abilities. Since they are not the result of the investment of human effort in an agent of production for the purpose of increasing its efficiency, there is a strong *primâ facie* cause for regarding them as a producer's surplus, resulting from the possession of a differential advantage for production, freely given by nature. This analogy is valid and useful so long as we are merely analysing the component parts of the income earned by an individual. And there is some interest in the inquiry how much of the income of successful men is due to chance, to opportunity, to the conjuncture, how much to the good start that they have had in life; . how much is profits on the capital invested in their special training, how much is the reward of exceptionally hard work; and how much remains as a producer's surplus or rent resulting from the possession of rare natural gifts.

but not when we are considering the normal earnings of a trade;

But when we are considering the whole body of those engaged in any occupation, we are not at liberty to treat the exceptionally high earnings of successful men as rent, without making allowance for the low earnings of those who fail. For the supply of labour in any occupation is governed, other things being equal, by the earnings of which it holds out the prospect. The future of those who enter the occupation cannot be predicted with certainty : some, who start with the least promise, turn out to have great latent ability, and, aided perhaps by good luck, they earn large fortunes; while others, who made a brilliant promise at starting, come to nothing. For the chances of success and failure are to be taken together, much as are the chances of good and bad hauls by a fisherman or of good and bad harvests by a farmer; and a youth when selecting an occupation, or his parents when selecting one for him, are very far from leaving out of account the fortunes of successful men. These fortunes are therefore part of the price that is paid in the long run

for the supply of labour and ability that seeks the occupation : VI, v, 7.
they enter into the true or "long period" normal supply price of
labour in it.

It may be conceded, however, that, if a certain class of people save in the
were marked out from their birth as having special gifts for some extreme
case of a
particular occupation, and for no other, so that they would be sure class of
persons
to seek that occupation in any case, then the earnings which such born with
men would get might be left out of account as exceptional, when we rare
abilities
were considering the chances of success or failure for ordinary specialized
to parti-
persons. But as a matter of fact that is not the case; for a great cular
part of a person's success in any occupation depends on the develop- branches
of pro-
ment of talents and tastes, the strength of which cannot be clearly duction.
predicted until he has already committed himself to a choice of
occupation. Such predictions are at least as fallible as those which
a new settler can make as to the future fertility and advantages of
situation of the various plots of land that are offered for his selection.[1]
And partly for this reason the extra income derived from rare natural
qualities bears a closer analogy to the surplus produce from the
holding of a settler who has made an exceptionally lucky selection,
than to the rent of land in an old country. But land and human
beings differ in so many respects, that even that analogy, if pursued
very far, is apt to mislead : and the greatest caution is required in
the application of the term producer's surplus to the earnings of
extraordinary ability.

Finally, it may be observed that the argument of V. VIII.—XI.,
with regard to the special earnings (whether of the nature of rents
or quasi-rents) of appliances capable of being used in several branches
of production, is applicable to the special earnings of natural abilities,
and of skill. When land or machinery capable of being used for
producing one commodity is used for another, the supply price of
the first is raised, though not by an amount dependent on the
incomes which those appliances for production would yield in the
second use. So when trained skill or natural abilities which could
have been applied to produce one commodity, are applied for
another, the supply price of the first is raised through the narrowing
of its sources of supply.

[1] Comp. V. x. 2.

R

CHAPTER VI

INTEREST OF CAPITAL

VI, vi, 1.

Chapters I.
and II.
discussed
the main
principles
of the
action of
demand
and supply
in relation
to capital;
we go now
to details.

§ 1. The relations between demand and supply cannot be studied by themselves in the case of capital any more than they could in the case of labour. All the elements of the great central problem of distribution and exchange mutually govern one another: and the first two chapters of this Book, and more especially the parts that relate directly to capital, may be taken as an introduction to this and the next two chapters. But before entering on the detailed analysis with which they will be mainly occupied, something may be said as to the position which the modern study of capital and interest holds in relation to earlier work.

The funda-
mental
doctrines
of eco-
nomics as
to capital
are not
new, but
are the
basis of
action in
ordinary
life.

The aid which economic science has given towards understanding the part played by capital in our industrial system is solid and substantial; but it has made no startling discoveries. Everything of importance which is now known to economists has long been acted upon by able business men, though they may not have been able to express their knowledge clearly, or even accurately.

Everyone is aware that no payment would be offered for the use of capital unless some gain were expected from that use; and further that these gains are of many kinds. Some borrow to meet a pressing need, real or imaginary, and pay others to sacrifice the present to the future in order that they themselves may sacrifice the future to the present. Some borrow to obtain machinery, and other " intermediate " goods, with which they may make things to be sold at a profit; some to obtain hotels, theatres and other things which yield their services directly, but are yet a source of profit to those who control them. Some borrow houses for themselves to live in, or else the means wherewith to buy or build their own houses; and the absorption of the resources of the country in such things as houses increases, other things being equal, with every increase in those resources and every consequent fall in the rate of interest, just as does the absorption of those resources in machinery, docks, etc. The demand for durable stone houses in place of wood houses which give nearly equal accommodation for the time indicates that a country is growing in wealth, and that capital is to be had at a lower rate of interest; and it acts on the market for capital and on the rate of interest in the same way as would a demand for new factories or railways.

Everyone knows that people will not lend gratis as a rule; because, even if they have not themselves some good to which to turn the capital or its equivalent, they are sure to be able to find others to whom its use would be of benefit, and who would pay for the loan of it : and they stand out for the best market.[1]

Everyone knows that few, even among the Anglo-Saxon and other steadfast and self-disciplined races, care to save a large part of their incomes; and that many openings have been made for the use of capital in recent times by the progress of discovery and the opening up of new countries : and thus everyone understands generally the causes which have kept the supply of accumulated wealth so small relatively to the demand for its use, that that use is on the balance a source of gain, and can therefore require a payment when loaned. Everyone is aware that the accumulation of wealth is held in check, and the rate of interest so far sustained, by the preference which the great mass of humanity have for present over deferred gratifications, or, in other words, by their unwillingness to "wait." And indeed the true work of economic analysis in this respect is, not to emphasize this familiar truth, but to point out how much more numerous are the exceptions to this general preference than would appear at first sight.[2]

These truths are familiar; and they are the basis of the theory of capital and interest. But in the affairs of ordinary life truths are apt to present themselves in fragments. Particular relations are seen clearly one at a time; but the interactions of mutually self-determining causes are seldom grouped as a whole. The chief task of economics then as regards capital is to set out in order and in their mutual relations, all the forces which operate in the production and accumulation of wealth and the distribution of income; so that as regards both capital and other agents of production they may be seen *mutually governing* one another.

---

[1] That the supply of capital is held back by the *prospectiveness* of its uses, and men's unreadiness to look forward, while the demand for it comes from its *productiveness*, in the broadest sense of the term, is indicated in II. iv.

[2] See Book III. v. 3, 4; and IV. vii. 8. It is a good corrective of this error to note how small a modification of the conditions of our own world would be required to bring us to another in which the mass of the people would be so anxious to provide for old age and for their families after them, and in which the new openings for the advantageous use of accumulated wealth in any form were so small, that the amount of wealth for the safe custody of which people were willing to pay would exceed that which others desired to borrow; and where in consequence even those who saw their way to make a gain out of the use of capital, would be able to exact a payment for taking charge of it; and interest would be negative all along the line.

VI, VI, 1.
and in
analysis,

Next it has to analyse the influences which sway men in their choice between present and deferred gratifications, including leisure and opportunities for forms of activity that are their own reward. But here the post of honour lies with mental science; the received doctrines of which economics applies, in combination with other material, to its special problems.[1]

especially
of the con-
stituents
of profits
and their
mutual
relations.

Its work is therefore heavier in that analysis, on which we are to be engaged in this and the next two chapters, of the gains that are derived from the aid of accumulated wealth in the attainment of desirable ends, especially when that wealth takes the form of trade capital. For these gains or profits contain many elements, some of which belong to interest for the use of capital in a broad sense of the term; while others constitute *net* interest, or interest properly so called. Some constitute the reward of managing ability and of enterprise, including the bearing of risks; and others again belong not so much to any one of these agents of production as to their combination.

The eco-
nomic
doctrine of
capital has
progressed
continu-
ously and
without
abrupt
change.

The scientific doctrine of capital has had a long history of continuous growth and improvement in these three directions during the last three centuries. Adam Smith appears to have seen indistinctly, and Ricardo to have seen distinctly, almost everything of primary importance in the theory, very much as it is known now : and though one writer has preferred to emphasize one of its many sides, and another another, there seems no good reason for believing that any great economist since the time of Adam Smith has ever completely overlooked any side; and especially is it certain that nothing which would be familiar to men of business was overlooked by the practical financial genius of Ricardo. But there has been progress; almost everyone has improved some part, and given it a sharper and clearer outline; or else has helped to explain the complex relations of its different parts. Scarcely anything done by any great thinker has had to be undone, but something new has constantly been added.[2]

---

[1] Compare III. v. and IV. vii.

[2] Prof. v. Böhm-Bawerk appears to have underrated the acumen of his predecessors in their writings on capital and interest. What he regards as mere naïve fragments of theories appear rather to be the utterances of men well acquainted with the practical workings of business; and who, partly for some special purpose, and partly through want of system in exposition, gave such disproportionate stress to some elements of the problem as to throw others into the background. Perhaps part of the air of paradox with which he invests his own theory of capital may be the result of a similar disproportionate emphasis, and an unwillingness to recognize that the various elements of the problem *mutually* govern one another. Attention has already been called to the fact that, though he excludes houses and hotels, and indeed everything that is not strictly speaking an intermediate good, from his definition of capital, yet the demand for the use of goods, that are not intermediate, acts as directly on the rate of interest, as does that for capital as defined by him. Connected with this use

§ 2. But if we go back to mediæval and ancient history we certainly do seem to find an absence of clear ideas as to the nature of the services which capital renders in production, and for which interest is the payment; and since this early history is exercising an indirect influence on the problems of our own age, something should be said of it here.

In primitive communities there were but few openings for the employment of fresh capital in enterprise, and anyone who had property that he did not need for his own immediate use, would seldom forego much by lending it on good security to others without charging any interest for the loan. Those who borrowed were generally the poor and the weak, people whose needs were urgent and whose powers of bargaining were very small. Those who lent were as a rule either people who spared freely of their superfluity to help their distressed neighbours, or else professional money-lenders. To these last the poor man had resort in his need; and they frequently made a cruel use of their power, entangling him in meshes from which he could not escape without great suffering, and perhaps the loss of the personal freedom of himself or his children. Not only uneducated people, but the sages of early times, the fathers of the mediæval church, and the English rulers of India in our own time, have been inclined to say, that money-lenders " traffic in other people's misfortunes, seeking gain through their adversity : under the pretence of compassion they dig a pit for the oppressed." [1] In such a state of society it may be a question for discussion, whether it is to the public advantage that people should be encouraged to borrow wealth under a contract to return it with increase after a time : whether such contracts, taken one with another, do not on

---

of the term capital is a doctrine on which he lays great stress, viz. that " methods of production which take time are more productive " (*Positive Capital*, Book V. ch. IV. p. 261), or again that " every lengthening of a roundabout process is accompanied by a further increase in the technical result " (*Ib.* Book II. ch. II. p. 84). There are however innumerable processes which take a long time and are roundabout; but are not productive and therefore are not used; and in fact he seems to have inverted cause and effect. The true doctrine appears to be that, because interest has to be paid for, and can be gained by the use of capital; therefore those long and roundabout methods, which involve much locking up of capital, are avoided unless they are more productive than others. The fact that many roundabout methods are in various degrees productive is one of the causes that affect the rate of interest; and the rate of interest and the extent to which roundabout methods are employed are two of the elements of the central problem of distribution and exchange that mutually determine one another. See Appendix I, 3.

[1] From St. Chrysostom's Fifth Homily, see above I. II. 8. Compare also Ashley's *Economic History*, VI. vi.; and Bentham *On Usury*. The sentiment against usury had its origin in tribal relationships, in many other cases besides that of the Israelites, perhaps in all cases; and, as Cliffe Leslie remarks (*Essays*, 2nd Edition, p. 244):— It was " inherited from prehistoric times, when the members of each community still regarded themselves as kinsmen; when communism in property existed at least in practice, and no one who had more than he needed could refuse to share his superfluous wealth with a fellow-tribesman in want."

VI, VI, 3. the whole diminish rather than increase the sum total of human
happiness.

and this But unfortunately attempts were made to solve this difficult and
fact retard- important practical question by a philosophical distinction between
ed the
growth of the interest for the loan of money and the rental of material wealth.
clear Aristotle had said that money was barren, and that to derive interest
notions
as to the from lending it out was to put it to an unnatural use. And following
nature
of the his lead Scholastic writers argued with much labour and ingenuity
services that he who lent out a house or a horse might charge for its use,
rendered
by capital. because he gave up the enjoyment of a thing that was directly productive of benefit. But they found no similar excuse for the interest
on money : that, they said, was wrong, because it was a charge for
a service which did not cost the lender anything.[1]

Mediæval If the loan really cost him nothing, if he could have made no
confusion
of thought use of the money himself, if he was rich and the borrower poor and
on this needy, then it might no doubt be argued that he was morally bound
subject. to lend his money gratis : but on the same grounds he would have
been bound to lend without charge to a poor neighbour a house
which he would not himself inhabit, or a horse for a day's work of
which he had himself no need. The doctrine of these writers therefore
really implied, and in fact it did convey to people's minds the mischievous fallacy that—independently of the special circumstances
of the borrower and the lender—the loan of money, *i.e.* of command
over things in general, is not a sacrifice on the part of the lender
and a benefit to the borrower, of the same kind as the loan of a particular commodity : they obscured the fact that he who borrows
money can buy, for instance, a young horse, whose services he can
use, and which he can sell, when the loan has to be returned, at as
good a price as he paid for him. The lender gives up the power of
doing this, the borrower acquires it : there is no substantial difference
between the loan of the purchase price of a horse and the loan of
a horse.[2]

In the § 3. History has in part repeated itself : and in the modern
modern
world Western World a new reforming impulse has derived strength from,
similar and given strength to, another erroneous analysis of the nature of

---

[1] They also make a distinction between *hiring* things which were themselves to be
returned, and *borrowing* things the equivalent of which only had to be returned. This
distinction, however, though interesting from an analytical point of view, has very
little practical importance.

[2] Archdeacon Cunningham has described well the subtleties by which the mediæval church explained away her prohibition of loans at interest, in most of those cases
in which the prohibition would have been seriously injurious to the body politic.
These subtleties resemble the legal fictions by which the judges have gradually explained away the wording of laws, the natural interpretation of which seemed likely
to be mischievous. In both cases some practical evil has been avoided at the expense
of fostering habits of confused and insincere thought.

interest. As civilization has progressed, the loans of wealth to *VI, vi, 3.*
needy people have become steadily more rare, and a less important *causes*
part of the whole; while the loans of capital for productive use in *have pro-*
business have grown at an ever-increasing rate. An in consequence, *moted the spread of*
though the borrowers are not now regarded as the subjects of oppres- *erroneous analysis.*
sion, a grievance has been found in the fact that all producers,
whether working with borrowed capital or not, reckon interest on
the capital used by them as among the expenses which they require
to have returned to them in the long run in the price of their wares
as a condition of their continuing business. On this account, and
on account of the openings which the present industrial system offers
of amassing great wealth by sustained good fortune in speculation,
it has been argued that the payment of interest in modern times
oppresses the working classes indirectly, though not directly; and
that it deprives them of their fair share of the benefits resulting from
the growth of knowledge. And hence is derived the practical conclusion that it would be for the general happiness and therefore right,
that no private person should be allowed to own any of the means
of production, nor any direct means of enjoyment, save such as he
needs for his own use.

This practical conclusion has been supported by other arguments *Connection*
which will claim our attention; but at present we are only concerned *between the prac-*
with the doctrine that has been used by William Thompson, Rod- *tical pro-*
bertus, Karl Marx, and others in support of it. They argued that *posals of Rodbertus*
labour always produces a " Surplus " [1] above its wages and the *and Karl Marx and*
wear-and-tear of capital used in aiding it : and that the wrong done *their*
to labour lies in the exploitation of this surplus by others. But this *doctrine of value.*
assumption that the whole of this Surplus is the produce of labour, *Their main*
already takes for granted what they ultimately profess to prove by *conclusion*
it; they make no attempt to prove it; and it is not true. It is *was assumed*
not true that the spinning of yarn in a factory, after allowance has *in an*
been made for the wear-and-tear of the machinery, is the product *untrue premiss.*
of the labour of the operatives. It is the product of their labour,
together with that of the employer and subordinate managers, and
of the capital employed; and that capital itself is the product of
labour and waiting : and therefore the spinning is the product of
labour of many kinds, and of waiting. If we admit that it is the
product of labour alone, and not of labour and waiting, we can no
doubt be compelled by inexorable logic to admit that there is no
justification for Interest, the reward of waiting; for the conclusion
is implied in the premiss. Rodbertus and Marx do indeed boldly

---

[1] This is Marx's phrase. Rodbertus had called it a " Plus."

VI, vi, 4.   claim the authority of Ricardo for their premiss; but it is really as
———   opposed to his explicit statement and the general tenor of his theory
of value, as it is to common sense.[1]

To put the same thing in other words; if it be true that the postponement of gratifications involves *in general* a sacrifice on the part
of him who postpones, just as additional effort does on the part of
him who labours; and if it be true that this postponement enables
man to use methods of production of which the first cost is great;
but by which the aggregate of enjoyment is increased, as certainly
as it would be by an increase of labour; then it cannot be true that
the value of a thing depends simply on the amount of labour spent
on it. Every attempt to establish this premiss has necessarily
assumed implicitly that the service performed by capital is a " free "
good, rendered without sacrifice, and therefore needing no interest
as a reward to induce its continuance; and this is the very conclusion which the premiss is wanted to prove. The strength of
Rodbertus' and Marx's sympathies with suffering must always
claim our respect : but what they regarded as the scientific foundation of their practical proposals appears to be little more than a
series of arguments in a circle to the effect that there is no economic
justification for interest, while that result has been all along latent
in their premisses; though, in the case of Marx, it was shrouded by
mysterious Hegelian phrases, with which he " coquetted," as he tells
us in his Preface.

Net and   § 4. We may now proceed with our analysis. The interest of
Gross   which we speak when we say that interest is the earnings of capital
interest.   simply, or the reward of waiting simply, is *Net* interest; but what
commonly passes by the name of Interest, includes other elements
besides this, and may be called *Gross* interest.

Gross   These additional elements are the more important, the lower and
interest   more rudimentary the state of commercial security and of the
includes   organization of credit. Thus, for instance, in mediæval times, when
some   a prince wanted to forestall some of his future revenues, he borrowed
Insurance
against   perhaps a thousand ounces of silver, and undertook to pay back
risk,   fifteen hundred at the end of a year. There was however no perfect
security that he would fulfil the promise; and perhaps the lender
would have been willing to exchange that promise for an absolute
certainty of receiving thirteen hundred at the end of the year. In
that case, while the nominal rate at which the loan was made was
fifty per cent., the real rate was thirty.

The necessity for making this allowance for insurance against

———
[1] See Appendix I, 2.

risk is so obvious, that it is not often overlooked. But it is less obvious that every loan causes some trouble to the lender; that when, from the nature of the case, the loan involves considerable risk, a great deal of trouble has often to be taken to keep these risks as small as possible; and that then a great part of what appears to the borrower as interest, is, from the point of view of the lender, earnings of management of a troublesome business.

At the present time the net interest on capital in England is a little under three per cent. per annum; for no more than that can be obtained by investing in such first-rate stock-exchange securities as yield to the owner a secure income without appreciable trouble or expense on his part. And when we find capable business men borrowing on perfectly secure mortgages, at (say) four per cent., we may regard that gross interest of four per cent. as consisting of net interest, or interest proper, to the extent of a little under three per cent., and of earnings of management by the lenders to the extent of rather more than one per cent.[1]

Again, a pawnbroker's business involves next to no risk; but his loans are generally made at the rate of 25 per cent. per annum, or more; the greater part of which is really earnings of management of a troublesome business. Or to take a more extreme case, there are men in London, and Paris, and probably elsewhere, who make a living by lending money to costermongers. The money is often lent at the beginning of the day for the purchase of fruit, etc., and returned at the end of the day, when the sales are over, at a profit of ten per cent. : there is a little risk in the trade, and the money is seldom lost.[2] Now a farthing invested at ten per cent. a day would amount to a billion pounds at the end of a year. But no one can become rich by lending to costermongers; because no one can lend much in this way. The so-called interest on the loans really consists almost entirely of earnings of a kind of work for which few capitalists have a taste.

[1] Mortgages for long periods are sometimes more sought after by lenders than those for short periods, and sometimes less. The former save the trouble of frequent renewal, but they deprive the lender of command over his money for a long time, and thus limit his freedom. First-class stock-exchange securities combine the advantages of very long and very short mortgages. For their holder can hold them as long as he likes, and can convert them into money when he will; though, if at the time credit is shaken and other people want ready money, he will have to sell at a loss. If they could always be realized without a loss, and if there were no broker's commissions to be paid on buying and selling, they would not yield a higher income than money lent " on call " at the lender's choice of time; and that will always be less than the interest on loans for any fixed period, short or long.

[2] Again, Dr. Jessop (*Arcady*, p. 114) tells us " there are hosts of small money-lenders in the purlieus of the cattle markets who make advances to speculators *with an eye*," lending sums, amounting in exceptional cases up to £200, at a gross interest of ten per cent. for the twenty-four hours.

VI, vi, 5.

Further analysis of gross interest.

§ 5. It is then necessary to analyse a little more carefully the extra risks which are introduced into business when much of the capital used in it has been borrowed. Let us suppose that two men are carrying on similar businesses, the one working with his own, the other chiefly with borrowed capital.

Trade risks.

There is one set of risks which is common to both; which may be described as the *trade risks* of the particular business in which they are engaged. They arise from fluctuations in the markets for their raw materials and finished goods, from unforeseen changes of fashion, from new inventions, from the incursion of new and powerful rivals into their respective neighbourhoods, and so on. But there is another set of risks, the burden of which has to be borne by the man working with borrowed capital, and not by the other; and we

Personal risks.

may call them *personal risks*. For he who lends capital to be used by another for trade purposes, has to charge a high interest as insurance against the chances of some flaw or deficiency in the borrower's personal character or ability.[1]

Analysis of personal risks.

The borrower may be less able than he appears, less energetic, or less honest. He has not the same inducements, as a man working with his own capital has, to look failure straight in the face, and withdraw from a speculative enterprise as soon as it shows signs of going against him. On the contrary, should his standard of honour not be high, he may be not very keen of sight as to his losses. For if he withdraws at once, he will have lost all he has of his own; and if he allows the speculation to run on, any additional loss will fall on his creditors; and any gain will come to himself. Many creditors lose through semi-fraudulent inertness of this kind on the part of their debtors, and a few lose through deliberate fraud : the debtor for instance may conceal in subtle ways the property that is really his creditors', until his bankruptcy is over, and he has entered on a new business career; he can bring gradually into play his secret reserve funds without exciting over-much suspicion.

Gross interest does not tend to equality

The price then that the borrower has to pay for the loan of capital, and which he regards as interest, is from the point of view of the lender more properly to be regarded as profits : for it includes insurance against risks which are often very heavy, and earnings of management for the task, which is often very arduous, of keeping those risks as small as possible. Variations in the nature of these risks and of the task of management will of course occasion corresponding variations in the gross interest, so called, that is paid for the use of money. The tendency of competition is therefore not

[1] See also below, ch. viii. § 2.

towards equalizing this gross interest : on the contrary, the more VI, vi, 5.
thoroughly lenders and borrowers understand their business, the
more certainly will some classes of borrowers obtain loans at a lower
rate than others.

We must defer to a later stage our study of the marvellously but net
efficient organization of the modern money market by which capital interest does.
is transferred from one place where it is superabundant to another
where it is wanted; or from one trade that is in the process of
contraction to another which is being expanded : and at present we
must be contented to take it for granted that a very small difference
between the rates of net interest to be got on the loan of capital in
two different modes of investment in the same Western country
will cause capital to flow, though perhaps by indirect channels,
from the one to the other.

It is true that if either of the investments is on a small scale, and
few people know much about it, the flow of capital may be slow.
One person, for instance, may be paying five per cent. on a small
mortgage, while his neighbour is paying four per cent. on a mortgage
which offers no better security. But in large affairs the rate of net
interest (so far as it can be disentangled from the other elements of
profits) is nearly the same all over England. And further the diver-
gencies between the average rates of net interest in different countries of the Western World are rapidly diminishing, as a result of
the general growth of intercourse, and especially of the fact that
the leading capitalists of all these countries hold large quantities of
stock-exchange securities, which yield the same revenue and are
sold practically at the same price on the same day all over the
world.

When we come to discuss the Money Market we shall have to
study the causes which render the supply of capital for immediate
use much larger at some times than at others; and which at certain
times make bankers and others contented with an extremely low
rate of interest, provided the security be good and they can get
their money back into their own hands quickly in case of need. At
such times they are willing to lend for short periods even to borrowers, whose security is not of the first order, at a rate of interest
that is not very high. For their risks of loss are much reduced by
their power of refusing to renew the loan, if they notice any indication of weakness on the part of the borrower; and since short loans
on good security are fetching only a nominal price, nearly the whole
of what interest they get from him is insurance against risk, and
remuneration of their own trouble. But on the other hand such

loans are not really very cheap to the borrower : they surround him by risks, to avoid which he would often be willing to pay a much higher rate of interest. For if any misfortune should injure his credit, or if a disturbance of the money market should cause a temporary scarcity of loanable capital, he may be quickly brought into great straits. Loans to traders at nominally low rates of interest, if for short periods only, do not therefore really form exceptions to the general rule just discussed.

The rate of interest applies strictly to new investments only : the value of old investments is governed by their earnings.

§ 6. The flow of investment of resources from their common source in production consists of two streams. The smaller consists of new additions to the accumulated stock. The larger merely replaces that which is destroyed; whether by immediate consumption, as in the case of food, fuel, etc.; by wear-and-tear, as in that of railway irons; by the lapse of time, as in that of a thatched roof or a trade directory; or by all these combined. The annual flow of this second stream is probably not less than a quarter of the total stock of capital, even in a country in which the prevailing forms of capital are as durable as in England. It is therefore not unreasonable to assume for the present that the owners of capital in general have been able in the main to adapt its forms to the normal conditions of the time, so as to derive as good a *net* income from their investments in one way as another.

It is only on this supposition that we are at liberty to speak of capital in general as being accumulated under the expectation of a certain net interest which is the same for all its forms. For it cannot be repeated too often that the phrase " the rate of interest " is applicable to old investments of capital only in a very limited sense. For instance, we may perhaps estimate that a trade capital of some seven thousand millions is invested in the different trades of this country at about three per cent. net interest. But such a method of speaking, though convenient and justifiable for many purposes, is not accurate. What ought to be said is that, taking the rate of net interest on the investments of new capital in each of those trades [*i.e.* on marginal investments] to be about three per cent.; then the aggregate net income rendered by the whole of the trade-capital invested in the various trades is such that, if capitalized at 33 years' purchase (that is on the basis of interest at three per cent.), it would amount to some seven thousand million pounds. For the value of the capital already invested in improving land or erecting a building; in making a railway or a machine is the aggregate discounted value of its estimated future net incomes [or quasi-rents]; and if its prospective income-yielding power should diminish, its value would fall accordingly and would be the capitalized value of that smaller income after allowing for depreciation.

§ 7. Throughout the present volume we are supposing, in the absence of any special statement to the contrary, that all values are expressed in terms of money of fixed purchasing power, just as astronomers have taught us to determine the beginning or the ending of the day with reference not to the actual sun but to a *mean sun* which is supposed to move uniformly through the heavens. Further, the influences which changes in the purchasing power of money do exert on the terms on which loans are arranged, are most conspicuous in the market for short loans—a market which differs in many of its incidents from any other, and a full discussion of their influences must be deferred. But they should be noticed here in passing, at all events as a point of abstract theory. For the rate of interest which the borrower is willing to pay measures the benefits that he expects to derive from the use of the capital only on the assumption that the money has the same purchasing power when it is borrowed and when it is returned.

Let us suppose, for instance, that a man borrows £100 under contract to pay back £105 at the end of the year. If meanwhile the purchasing power of money has risen 10 per cent. (or which is the same thing, general prices have fallen in the ratio of 10 to 11), he cannot get the £105 which he has to pay back without selling one-tenth more commodities than would have been sufficient for the purpose at the beginning of the year. Assuming, that is, that the things which he handles have not changed in value relatively to things in general, he must sell at the end of the year commodities which would have cost him £115 10s. at the beginning, in order to pay back with interest his loan of £100; and therefore he has lost ground unless the commodities have increased under his hands 15½ per cent. While nominally paying 5 per cent. for the use of his money, he has really been paying 15½ per cent.

On the other hand, if prices had risen so much that the purchasing power of money had fallen 10 per cent. during the year, and he could get £100 for things which cost him £90 at the beginning of the year; then, instead of paying 5 per cent. for the loan, he would really be paid 5½ per cent. for taking charge of the money.[1]

When we come to discuss the causes of alternating periods of inflation and depression of commercial activity, we shall find that they are intimately connected with those variations in the real rate

Margin notes:

VI, VI, .7

Estimates of true, as contrasted with nominal, interest rest on assumptions as to the future purchasing power of money.

For short periods this may be best measured in commodities. A rise in the value of money makes the true rate of interest higher than the nominal.

---

[1] Compare Fisher's *Appreciation and Interest* 1896 : and *The rate of interest* 1907, especially Chapters V, XIV and their respective Appendices.

of interest which are caused by changes in the purchasing power of money. For when prices are likely to rise, people rush to borrow money and buy goods, and thus help prices to rise; business is inflated, and is managed recklessly and wastefully; those working on borrowed capital pay back less real value than they borrowed, and enrich themselves at the expense of the community. When afterwards credit is shaken and prices begin to fall, everyone wants to get rid of commodities and get hold of money which is rapidly rising in value; this makes prices fall all the faster, and the further fall makes credit shrink even more, and thus for a long time prices fall because prices have fallen.

We shall find that fluctuations in prices are caused only to a very slight extent by fluctuations in the supply of the precious metals; and that they would not be much diminished by the adoption of gold and silver instead of gold as the basis of our currency. But the evils which they cause are so great, that it is worth while to do much in order to diminish them a little. These evils however are not necessarily inherent in those slow changes in the purchasing power of money, which follow the course of man's changing command over nature : and in such changes there is generally both loss and gain. In the fifty years preceding the great war, improvements in the arts of production and in the access to rich sources of supply of raw material doubled the efficiency of man's labour in procuring many of the things which he wants. An injury would have been done to those members of the working classes (now indeed rapidly diminishing in number) whose money wages are much influenced by custom; if the purchasing power of a sovereign in terms of commodities had remained stationary, instead of following, as it has, the increasing command by man over nature. But this matter will require full discussion in another place.

CHAPTER VII

PROFITS OF CAPITAL AND BUSINESS POWER

§ 1. In the concluding chapters of Book IV we made some study of the various forms of business management, and the faculties
required for them; and we saw how the supply of business power
in command of capital may be regarded as consisting of three elements, the supply of capital, the supply of the business power to
manage it, and the supply of the organization by which the two are
brought together and made effective for production. In the last
chapter we were concerned mainly with interest, the earnings of the
first of these elements. In the earlier part of this chapter we shall
be occupied with the earnings of the second and third taken together,
which we have called *gross* earnings of management; and afterwards we shall pass to the relation in which this stands to the earnings
of the second taken by itself which we have called *net* earnings of
management.[1] We have to inquire more closely into the nature
of the services which are rendered to society by those who undertake
and manage business enterprises, and the rewards of their work;
and we shall find that the causes by which these are governed are
less arbitrary, and present closer analogies to those which govern
other kinds of earnings, than is commonly supposed.

This chapter and the following continue the analyses of IV. XII., XIII.

We must however make a distinction at starting. We must call
to mind [2] the fact that the struggle for survival tends to make those
methods of organization prevail, which are best fitted to *thrive in*
their environment; but not necessarily those best fitted to *benefit*
their environment, unless it happens that they are duly rewarded
for all the benefits which they confer, whether direct or indirect.
And in fact this is not so. For as a general rule the law of substitution—which is nothing more than a special and limited application of the law of survival of the fittest—tends to make one method
of industrial organization supplant another when it offers a direct
and immediate service at a lower price. The indirect and ultimate
services which either will render have, as a general rule, little or
no weight in the balance; and as a result many businesses languish
and die, which might in the long run have done good work for society

The success of any form of business manage-
ment depends on its immediate rather than its ultimate efficiency.

[1] See p. 261.   [2] See IV. VIII.

VI, VII, 1. if only they could have obtained a fair start.   This is especially true of some forms of co-operative associations.

In this connection we may divide employers and other undertakers into two classes, those who open out new and improved methods of business, and those who follow beaten tracks.   The services which the latter perform for society are chiefly direct and seldom miss their full reward : but it is otherwise with the former class.

For instance, economies have lately been introduced into some branches of iron manufacture by diminishing the number of times which the metal is heated in passing from iron ore to its final form; and some of these new inventions have been of such a nature that they could neither be patented nor kept secret.   Let us suppose then that a manufacturer with a capital of £50,000 is getting in normal times a net profit of £4,000 a year, £1,500 of which we may regard as his earnings of management, leaving £2,500 for the other two elements of profits.   We assume that he has been working so far in the same way as his neighbours, and showing an amount of ability which, though great, is no more than the normal or average ability of the people who fill such exceptionally difficult posts; that is, we assume that £1,500 a year is the normal earnings for the kind of work he has been doing.   But as time goes on, he thinks out a way of dispensing with one of the heatings that have hitherto been customary; and in consequence, without increasing his expenses, he is able to increase his annual output by things which can be sold for £2,000 net.   So long, therefore, as he can sell his wares at the old price, his earnings of management will be £2,000 a year above the average; and he will earn the full reward of his services to society.   His neighbours however will copy his plan, and probably make more than average profits for a time.   But soon competition will increase the supply, and lower the price of their wares, until their profits fall to about their old level; for no one could get extra high wages for making eggs stand on their ends after Columbus's plan had become public property.

Many business men whose inventions have in the long run been of almost priceless value to the world, have earned even less by their discoveries than Milton by his *Paradise Lost* or Millet by his *Angelus*; and while many men have amassed great wealth by good fortune, rather than by exceptional ability in the performance of public services of high importance, it is probable that those business men who have pioneered new paths have often conferred on society benefits out of all proportion to their own gains, even though they have died millionaires. Although then we shall find that the rewards VI, vii, 2. of every business undertaker tend to be proportionate to the *direct* services he renders to the community, this will by itself go but a small way towards proving that the existing industrial organization of society is the best conceivable, or even the best attainable; and it must not be forgotten that the scope of our present inquiry is limited to a study of the action of causes that determine the earnings of business undertaking and management *under existing social institutions.*

We will begin by tracing the adjustment of the rewards of the services rendered to society by ordinary workmen, by foremen, and by employers of different grades : we shall find the principle of substitution everywhere at work.

§ 2. We have already noticed that a great part of the work done by the head of a small business himself, is relegated in a large business to salaried heads of departments, managers, foremen and others. And this thread will guide us to much that is useful for our present inquiry. The simplest case is that of the earnings of the ordinary foreman; with which we may begin.

Adjustment of demand for the services of foremen as compared with those of ordinary workmen.

Let us suppose, for instance, that a railway contractor or a dockyard manager finds that it answers best to have one foreman to every twenty labourers, the wages of a foreman being twice those of a labourer. This means that, if he found himself with 500 labourers and 24 foremen, he would expect to get just a little more work done at the same expense by adding one more foreman, than by adding two more ordinary labourers : while if he had had 490 labourers and 25 foremen, he would have found it better to add two more labourers. If he could have got his foreman for one and a half times the wages of a labourer, perhaps he would have employed one foreman to every fifteen labourers. But, as it is, the number of foremen employed is determined at one-twentieth of that of the labourers, and their demand price at twice the labourers' wages.[1]

In exceptional cases the foremen may earn their wages by overdriving those whose work they superintend. But we may now suppose them to contribute to the success of the undertaking in a legitimate way, by securing a better organization of its details; so that fewer things are done amiss and need to be undone; so that everyone finds the help that he wants in moving heavy weights, etc., ready for him just when he wants it; so that all machinery and implements are kept in good working order, and no one has to waste his time and strength by working with inadequate appliances, and

---

[1] With this argument may be compared that of VI. i. 7.

VI, VII, 3. so on. The wages of foremen who do work of this kind may be taken as typical of a great part of the earnings of management : society, acting through the individual employer, offers an effective demand for their services until that margin is reached at which the aggregate efficiency of industry would be increased by adding workers of some other trade more than by adding the foremen whose wages would add an equal amount to the expenses of production.

So far the employer has been regarded as the agent through whom competition acts in contriving and arranging the factors of production so that the maximum of direct services (estimated by their money measure) should be performed at a minimum money cost. But now we have to look at the work of the employers themselves being contrived and arranged for them, though of course in a more haphazard fashion, by the immediate action of their own competition.

Adjustment of demand for organizing ability. Illustration from the gradual rise of a working carpenter.
§ 3. Let us then look next at the way in which the work of foremen and salaried managers is constantly being weighed against that of the heads of businesses. It will be interesting to watch the course of a small business as it gradually expands. A house carpenter, for instance, steadily increases his stock of tools, till he can hire a small workshop, and undertake odd jobs for private persons, who have to agree with him as to what is to be done. The work of management and of undertaking what little risks there are, is shared between them and him; and, as this gives them a great deal of trouble, they are not willing to pay him at a high rate for what work of management he does.[1]

His work as a small master-builder.
So his next step is to undertake all the different sides of small repairs. He has now entered on the career of a master-builder; and if his business grows, he gradually withdraws himself from manual labour, and to some extent even from the superintendence of its details. Substituting for his own work that of hired men, he has now to deduct their wages from his receipts, before he can begin to reckon his profits : and unless he proves himself to have a business ability up to the normal level of that grade of industry which he has now entered, he will probably soon lose all the little capital which he has gained, and after a short struggle return to that humbler rank of life in which he has prospered. Should his ability be just about that level, he will, with average good fortune, retain his position and perhaps gain a little ground : and the excess of his receipts over his outgoings will be representative of the normal earnings of management in his grade.

[1] Comp. IV. XII. 3.

If his ability be greater than that which is normal in his grade, VI, VII, 4.
he will be able to obtain as good a result with a given outlay for Changes
wages and other expenses, as most of his rivals can with a larger in the
outlay : he will have substituted his extra ability in organization character of his
for some of their outlay; and his earnings of management will include work as
the value of that outlay with which he has dispensed. He will thus the scale of his
increase his capital and his credit : and be able to borrow more, and business
at a lower rate of interest. He will obtain a wider business acquain- increases.
tanceship and connection; and he will get an increased knowledge
of materials and processes, and opportunities for bold but wise and
profitable adventure; until at last he has delegated to others nearly
all those duties which occupied his whole time even after he had
ceased to do manual work himself.[1]

§ 4. Having watched the adjustment of the earnings of foremen The ad-
and of ordinary workmen, and again of employers and foremen, we justment between
may now look at the earnings of employers on a small and a large the earn-
scale. ings of business

Our carpenter having become a master-builder on a very large men on a
scale, his undertakings will be so many and so great as to have large and on a small
occupied the time and energies of some scores of employers who scale.
superintended all the details of their several businesses. Throughout this struggle between large businesses and small, we see the
principle of substitution constantly in operation; the large employer substituting a little of his own work and a good deal of that
of salaried managers and foremen for that of a small employer.
When, for instance, tenders are invited for erecting a building, a
builder with a large capital often finds it worth his while to enter
the lists, even though he lives at a distance. The local builders
secure great economies in having workshops and men whom they
can trust already near the spot; while he gains something through
buying his materials on a large scale, through his command of

---

[1] The employer of a large number of workmen has to economize his energies on
the same plan that is followed by the leading officers of a modern army. For as
Mr. Wilkinson says (*The Brain of an Army*, pp. 42–6) :—" Organization implies that
every man's work is defined, that he knows exactly what he must answer for, and
that his authority is coextensive with his responsibility. . . . [In the German army]
every commander above the rank of captain deals with a body composed of units,
with the interior affairs of none of which he meddles, except in the case of failure on
the part of the officer directly responsible. . . . The general commanding an army corps
has to deal directly with only a few subordinates. . . . He inspects and tests the condition of all the various units, but . . . he is as far as possible unhampered by the worry
of detail. He can make up his mind coolly.". Bagehot in characteristic fashion had
remarked (*Lombard Street*, ch. VIII.) that if the head of a large business " is very busy,
it is a sign of something wrong "; and had compared (Essay on the *Transferability of
Capital*) the primitive employer with a Hector or Achilles mingling in the fray, and
the typical modern employer with " a man at the far end of a telegraph wire—a Count
Moltke with his head over some papers—who sees that the proper persons are slain,
and who secures the victory."

VI. VII. 5. machinery, especially for woodwork, and perhaps through being able to borrow what capital he wants on easier terms. These two sets of advantages frequently about balance one another; and the contest for the field of employment often turns on the relative efficiencies of the undivided energies of the small builder, and of that slight supervision which is all that the abler but busier large builder can afford to give himself, though he supplements it by the work of his local manager and of the clerks in his central office.[1]

A business man working with borrowed capital is at a disadvantage in some trades.
§ 5. So far we have been considering the gross earnings of management of a man who applies his own capital in business, and therefore can himself reap the equivalent of the costs direct and indirect, which are entailed when command over capital has to be collected from owners, who do not care to apply it to business uses themselves, and to be transferred to those whose own capital is insufficient for their enterprises.

We are next to consider the struggle for survival in pushing forward in some trades business men working chiefly with their own capital and in others those who work chiefly with borrowed capital. The personal risks, against which the lender of capital to be used in business requires to be indemnified, vary to some extent with the nature of that business, as well as with the circumstances of the individual borrower. They are very high in some cases, as for instance when a man is starting in a new branch of the electrical trades, in which there is very little past experience to go by, and the lender cannot easily form any independent judgment as to the progress which is being made by the borrower; and in all such cases the man working with borrowed capital is at a great disadvantage; the rate of profit is determined chiefly by the competition of those who apply their own capital. It may happen that not many such men have access to the trade; and in that case the competition may not be keen, and the rate of profit may be high; that is, it may exceed considerably net interest on the capital together with earnings of management on a scale commensurate with the difficulty of the business done, though that difficulty will probably be above the average.

And again, the new man with but little capital of his own is at a disadvantage in trades which move slowly and in which it is necessary to sow a long time before one reaps.

But in others he plays a leading part;
But in all those industries in which bold and tireless enterprise can reap a quick harvest; and in particular wherever high profits are to be made for a time by cheaper reproductions of costly wares,

[1] Comp. IV. XI. 4.

there the new man is in his element : it is he who by his quick resolu- VI, vii, 6.
tions and dexterous contrivances, and perhaps also a little by his
natural recklessness, " forces the pace."

And he often holds his own with great tenacity even under for he will
considerable disadvantages; for the freedom and dignity of his work hard
position are very attractive to him. Thus the peasant proprietor reward.
whose little plot is heavily mortgaged, the small so-called " sweater "
or " garret master " who takes out a sub-contract at a low price,
will often work harder than the ordinary workman, and for a lower
net income. And the manufacturer who is doing a large business
with comparatively little capital of his own will reckon his labour
and anxiety almost as nothing, for he knows that he must anyhow
work for his living, and he is unwilling to go into service to another :
he will therefore work feverishly for a gain that would not count
much in the balance with a wealthier rival, who, being able to retire
and live in comfort on the interest of his capital, may be doubting
whether it is worth while to endure any longer the wear-and-tear
of business life.

The inflation of prices which culminated in 1873, enriched borrowers in general, and in particular business undertakers, at the
expense of other members of society. New men therefore found
their way into business made very smooth; and those who had
already made or inherited business fortunes, found their way made
smooth for retiring from active work. Thus Bagehot, writing about
that time,[1] argued that the growth of new men was making English
business increasingly democratic : and, though admitting that " the
propensity to variation in the social as in the animal kingdom is the
principle of progress," he pointed out regretfully how much the
country might have gained by the long duration of families of
merchant princes. But in recent years there has been some reaction, due partly to social causes, and partly to the influence of a
continued fall in prices. The sons of business men are rather more
inclined than they were a generation ago to take pride in their
fathers' callings; and they find it harder to satisfy the demands of
an ever-increasing luxury on the income which would be theirs if
they withdrew from business.

§ 6. But the weighing in the balance of the services and therefore Joint-
the earnings of employees against the earnings of management of stock
business men is in some ways best illustrated by reference to Joint- companies.
stock companies. For in them most of the work of management is
divided between salaried directors (who indeed hold a few shares

[1] *Lombard Street*, Introductory chapter.

VI, VII, 7. themselves) and salaried managers and other subordinate officials, most of whom have little or no capital of any kind; and their earnings, being almost the pure earnings of labour, are governed in the long run by those general causes which rule the earnings of labour of equal difficulty and disagreeableness in ordinary occupations.

As has already been observed,[1] joint-stock companies are hampered by internal frictions, and conflicts of interest between shareholders and debenture holders, between ordinary and preferred shareholders, and between all these and the directors; and by the need for an elaborate system of checks and counterchecks. They seldom have the enterprise, the energy, the unity of purpose and the quickness of action of a private business. But these disadvantages are of relatively small importance in some trades. That publicity, which is one of the chief drawbacks of public companies in many branches of manufacture and of speculative commerce, is a positive advantage in ordinary banking and insurance and kindred businesses; while in these, as well as in most of the transport industries (railways, tramways, canals, and the supply of gas, water, and electricity), their unbounded command over capital gives them almost undisputed sway.

When powerful joint-stock companies are working in harmony, and are not directly or indirectly involved in speculative ventures on the stock exchange, or in campaigns for the crushing or for the compulsory fusion of rivals, they generally look forward to a distant future, and pursue a far-seeing if a sluggish policy. They are seldom willing to sacrifice their reputation for the sake of a temporary gain; they are not inclined to drive such extremely hard bargains with their employees as will make their service unpopular.

Modern methods of business exercise in the aggregate a powerful tendency to adjust earnings of management to the difficulty of the work done.

§ 7. Thus then each of the many modern methods of business has its own advantages and disadvantages: and its application is extended in every direction until that limit or margin is reached, at which its special advantages for that use no longer exceed its disadvantages. Or, to put the same thing in another way, the margin of profitableness of different methods of business organization for any particular purpose, is to be regarded not as a point on any one line, but a boundary line of irregular shape cutting one after another every possible line of business organization; and these modern methods, partly on account of their great variety, but partly also on account of the scope which many of them offer to men of business ability who have no capital, render possible a much closer correspondence between the earnings of undertaking and manage-

[1] See IV. XII. 9, 10.

ment and the services by which those earnings are got than could be VI, VII, 7. generally attained under the primitive system in which capital was scarcely ever applied to production by any save its owners. For then it could only be by a fortunate accident that those who had the capital and the opportunity for carrying on any trade or performing any service, of which the public was in need, had the aptitudes and the abilities required for the task. But, as it is, that share of the normal expenses of production of any commodity which is commonly classed as profits, is so controlled on every side by the action of the principle of substitution, that it cannot long diverge from the normal supply price of the capital needed, added to the normal supply price of the ability and energy required for managing the business, and lastly the normal supply price of that organization by which the appropriate business ability and the requisite capital are brought together.

The supply of business power is large and elastic, since the area The supply of business ability is drawn from a wide area, and is non-specialized. from which it is drawn is wide. Everyone has the business of his own life to conduct; and in this he can gain some training for business management, if he has the natural aptitudes for it. There is therefore no other kind of useful rare and therefore highly-paid ability which depends so little on labour and expense applied specially to obtaining it, and so much on " natural qualities." And, further, business power is highly non-specialized; because in the large majority of trades, technical knowledge and skill become every day less important relatively to the broad and non-specialized faculties of judgment, promptness, resource, carefulness and steadfastness of purpose.[1]

It is true that in small businesses, in which the master is little more than the head workman, specialized skill is very important. And it is true that " each sort of trade has a tradition of its own, which is never written, probably could not be written, which can only be learnt in fragments, and which is best taken in early life, before the mind is shaped and the ideas fixed. But each trade in modern commerce is surrounded by subsidiary and kindred trades, which familiarize the imagination with it, and make its state known." [2] Moreover those general faculties, which are characteristic of the modern business man, increase in importance as the scale of business increases. It is they which make him out as a

---

[1] IV. XII. 12. When the forms of productions cease to be few and simple, it becomes " no longer true that a man becomes an employer because he is a capitalist. Men command capital because they have the qualifications to profitably employ labour. To these captains of industry . . . capital and labour resort for opportunity to perform their several functions." (Walker, *Wages Question*, ch. XIV.)

[2] Bagehot, *Postulates*, p. 75.

VI, VII, 7. leader of men; and which enable him to go straight to the kernel of the practical problems with which he has to deal, to see almost instinctively the relative proportions of things, to conceive wise and far-reaching policies, and to carry them out calmly and resolutely.[1]

Difficulties of obtaining accurate knowledge as to the true earnings of management in different trades.

It must be admitted indeed that the adjustment of supply to demand in the case of business ability is somewhat hindered by the difficulty of ascertaining exactly what is the price that is being paid for it in any trade. It is comparatively easy to find out the wages of bricklayers or puddlers by striking an average between the wages that are earned by men of various degrees of efficiency, and allowing for the inconstancy of their employment. But the gross earnings of management which a man is getting can only be found after making up a careful account of the true profits of his business, and deducting interest on his capital. The exact state of his affairs is often not known by himself; and it can seldom be guessed at all accurately even by those who are in the same trade with himself. It is not true even in a little village at the present day that everyone knows all his neighbour's affairs. As Cliffe Leslie said, " The village innkeeper, publican or shopkeeper, who is making a small fortune does not invite competition by telling his neighbours of his profits, and the man who is not doing well does not alarm his creditors by exposing the state of his affairs." [2]

They do not reach far;

But though it may be difficult to read the lessons of an individual trader's experience, those of a whole trade can never be completely hidden, and cannot be hidden at all for long. Although one cannot tell whether the tide is rising or falling by merely watching half-a-dozen waves breaking on the seashore, yet a very little patience settles the question; and there is a general agreement among business men that the average rate of profits in a trade cannot rise or fall much without general attention being attracted to the change before long. And though it may sometimes be a more difficult task for a business man than for a skilled labourer, to find out whether

---

[1] Bagehot (l. c. pp. 94–5) says that the great modern commerce has " certain general principles which are common to all kinds of it, and a person can be of considerable use in more than one kind if he understands these principles and has the proper sort of mind. But the appearance of this common element is in commerce, as in politics, a sign of magnitude, and primitive commerce is all petty. In early tribes there is nothing but the special man—the clothier, the mason, the weapon-maker. Each craft tried to be, and very much was, a mystery except to those who carried it on. The knowledge required for each was possessed by few, kept secret by these few, and nothing else was of use but this monopolised and often inherited acquirement; there was no ' general ' business knowledge. The idea of a general art of money making is very modern: almost everything ancient about it is individual and particular."

[2] *Fortnightly Review*, June 1879, reprinted in his *Essays*.

he could improve his prospects by changing his trade, yet the busi- VI, vii, 7.
ness man has great opportunities for discovering whatever can be
found out about the present and future of other trades; and if he
should wish to change his trade, he will generally be able to do so
more easily than the skilled workman could.

On the whole then we may conclude that the rarity of the natural *and on the whole the adjust-ment of those earnings to the difficulty and im-portance of the work done is fairly accurate.*
abilities and the expensiveness of the special training required for
the work affect normal earnings of management in much the same
way as they do the normal wages of skilled labour. In either case,
a rise in the income to be earned sets in operation forces tending to
increase the supply of those capable of earning it; and in either
case, the extent to which the supply will be increased by a given rise
of income, depends upon the social and economic condition of those
from whom the supply is drawn. For though it is true that an able
business man who starts in life with a great deal of capital and a
good business connection is likely to obtain higher earnings of
management than an equally able man who starts without these
advantages; yet there are similar, though smaller, inequalities
between the earnings of professional men of equal abilities who start
with unequal social advantages; and the wages even of a working
man depend on the start he has had in life almost as much as on
the expense which his father has been able to afford for his
education.[1]

[1] See VI. iv. 3. On the general functions of those who undertake the chief
responsibilities of business, see Brentano, *Der Unternehmer*, 1907.

CHAPTER VIII

PROFITS OF CAPITAL AND BUSINESS POWER, CONTINUED

VI, VIII, 1.

On the supposed general tendency of the rate of profits to equality.

§ 1. THE causes that govern Earnings of Management have not been studied with any great care till within the last fifty years. The earlier economists did not do much good work in this direction because they did not adequately distinguish the component elements of profits, but searched for a simple general law governing the average rate of profits—a law which, from the nature of the case, cannot exist.

In analysing the causes that govern profits the first difficulty which we meet is in some measure verbal. It arises from the fact that the head of a small business does himself much of the work which in a large business is done by salaried managers and foremen, whose earnings are deducted from the net receipts of the large business before its profits are reckoned, while the earnings of the whole of his labour are reckoned among his profits. This difficulty has long been recognized. Adam Smith himself pointed out that :— " The whole drugs which the best employed apothecary in a large market-town will sell in a year may not perhaps cost him above thirty or forty pounds. Though he should sell them, therefore, for three or four hundred, or at a thousand per cent. profit this may frequently be no more than the reasonable wages of his labour charged in the only way in which he can charge them, upon the price of the drugs. The greater part of the apparent profit is real wages disguised in the garb of profit. In a small seaport town a little grocer will make forty or fifty per cent. upon a stock of a single hundred pounds, while a considerable wholesale merchant in the same place will scarce make eight or ten per cent. upon a stock of ten thousand." [1]

It is here important to distinguish between the *annual* rate of profits on the capital invested in a business, and the rate of profits

---

[1] *Wealth of Nations*, Book I. ch. x. Senior, *Outlines*, p. 203, puts the normal rate of profits on a capital of £100,000 at less than 10 per cent., on one of £10,000 or £20,000 at about 15 per cent., on one of £5,000 or £6,000 at 20 per cent., and " a much larger per-centage " on smaller capitals. Compare also § 4 of the preceding Chapter of the present Book. It should be noted that the nominal rate of profits of a private firm is increased when a manager, who brings no capital with him, is taken into partnership and rewarded by a share of the profits instead of a salary.

that are made every time the capital of the business is turned over; VI, VIII, 1.
that is, every time sales are made equal to that capital, or the rate and *on the*
turnover.
of profits *on the turnover*.   At present we are concerned with profits
per annum.

The greater part of the nominal inequality between the normal A correc-
rates of profit per annum in small businesses and in large would tion of this
anomaly of
disappear, if the scope of the term profits were narrowed in the language
former case or widened in the latter, so that it included in both removes
the chief
cases the remuneration of the same classes of services.   There are source of
the opinion
indeed some trades in which the rate of profit, rightly estimated, on that profits
large capitals tends to be higher than on small, though if reckoned are high in
a small
in the ordinary way it would appear lower.   For of two businesses business.
competing in the same trade, that with the larger capital can nearly
always buy at the cheaper rate, and can avail itself of many economies in the specialization of skill and machinery and in other ways,
which are out of the reach of the smaller business : while the only
important special advantage, which the latter is likely to have,
consists of its greater facilities for getting near its customers and
consulting their individual wants.   In trades in which this last
advantage is not important, and especially in some manufacturing
trades in which the large firm can sell at a better price than the small
one, the outgoings of the former are proportionately less and the
incomings larger; and therefore, if profits are so reckoned as to
include the same elements in both cases, the rate of profit in the
former case must be higher than in the latter.

But these are the very businesses in which it most frequently Small
happens that large firms after first crushing out small ones, either businesses
in trades
combine with one another and thus secure for themselves the gains which offer
of a limited monopoly, or by keen competition among themselves great
technical
reduce the rate of profit very low.   There are many branches of advantages
to large
the textile, the metal, and the transport trades in which no business capitals
can be started at all except with a large capital; while those that make very
low profits.
are begun on a moderate scale struggle through great difficulties, in
the hope that, after a time, it may be possible to find employment
for a large capital, which will yield earnings of management high in
the aggregate though low in proportion to the capital.

There are some trades which require a very high order of ability,
but in which it is nearly as easy to manage a very large business as
one of moderate size.   In rolling mills, for instance, there is little
detail which cannot be reduced to routine, and a capital of £1,000,000
invested in them can be easily controlled by one able man.   A rate
of profits of 20 per cent. is not a very high average rate for some

VI, VIII, 2. branches of the iron trade, which demand incessant thought and contrivance in matters of detail : but it would yield £150,000 a year as earnings of management to the owner of such works.   And even stronger cases are offered by recent fusions of giant firms in successive branches of the heavy iron industry.   Their profits fluctuate much with the state of trade : but, though enormous in the aggregate, they are said to be on the average at a low rate.

The rate of profits is low in nearly all those trades which require very little ability of the highest order, and in which a public or private firm with a good connection and a large capital can hold its own against new-comers, so long as it is managed by men of industrious habits with sound common sense and a moderate share of enterprise.   And men of this kind are seldom wanting either to a well-established public company or to a private firm which is ready to take the ablest of its servants into partnership.

On the whole, then, we may conclude firstly that the true rate of profits in large businesses is higher than at first sight appears, because much that is commonly counted as profits in the small business ought to be classed under another head, before the rate of profits in it is compared with that in a large business : and secondly that, even when this correction has been made, the rate of profit reckoned in the ordinary way declines generally as the size of the business increases.

Profits per annum are generally high in trades in which the work of management is difficult and risky;

§ 2. The normal earnings of management are of course high in proportion to the capital, and therefore the rate of profits per annum on the capital is high, when the work of management is heavy in proportion to the capital.   The work of management may be heavy because it involves great mental strain in organizing and devising new methods; or because it involves great anxiety and risk : and these two things frequently go together.   Individual trades have indeed peculiarities of their own, and all rules on the subject are liable to great exceptions.   But the following general propositions will be found to be valid, other things being equal, and to explain many inequalities in the normal rates of profit in different trades.

where capital is relatively small and the wages-bill is relatively large.

First, the extent of the work of management needed in a business depends more on the amount of the circulating capital used than on that of the fixed.   The rate of profit tends therefore to be low in trades in which there is a disproportionately large amount of durable plant, that requires but little trouble and attention when once it has been laid down.   As we have seen, these trades are likely to get into the hands of joint-stock companies : and the

aggregate salaries of the directors and higher officials bear a very VI, vɪɪɪ, 2.
small proportion to the capital employed in the case of railway and
water companies, and, even in a more marked degree, of companies
that own canals and docks and bridges.

Further, given the proportion between the fixed and circulating
capital of a business; the work of management will generally be
the heavier, and the rate of profits the higher, the more important
the wages-bill is relatively to the cost of material and the value of
the stock-in-trade.

In trades that handle costly materials, success depends very Risk as an
much upon good fortune and ability in buying and selling; and the element of
profits and
order of mind required for interpreting rightly and reducing to their of cost.
proper proportions the causes that are likely to affect price is rare,
and can command high earnings. The allowance to be made for
this is so important in certain trades as to have induced some
American writers to regard profits as remuneration of risk simply;
and as consisting of what remains after deducting interest and
earnings of management from gross profits. But this use of the
term seems on the whole not advantageous, because it tends to
class the work of management with mere routine superintendence.
It is of course true that as a rule a person will not enter on a risky
business, unless, other things being equal, he expects to gain from
it more than he would in other trades open to him, after his probable
losses had been deducted from his probable gains on a fair actuarial
estimate. If there were not a positive evil in such risk, people
would not pay premia to insurance companies; which they know
are calculated on a scale sufficiently above the true actuarial value
of the risk to pay the companies' great expenses of advertising and
working, and yet to yield a surplus of net profits. And where the
risks are not insured for, they must be compensated in the long run
on a scale about as high as would be required for the premia of an
insurance company, if the practical difficulties of insurance against
business risks could be overcome. But further many of those who
would be most competent to manage difficult businesses with wisdom and enterprise, are repelled from great risks, because their own
capital is not large enough to bear great losses. Thus a risky trade
is apt to get into the hands of rather reckless people; or perhaps
into the hands of a few powerful capitalists, who work it ably, but
arrange among themselves that the market shall not be forced so
as to prevent them from having a high rate of profit on the average.[1]

[1] On risk as an element of cost see V. vɪɪ. 4. There would be an advantage in a
careful analytical and inductive study of the attractive or repellent force which various

VI, VIII, 2.

In ordinary trades, profits often vary nearly with the wages-bill.

In trades in which the speculative element is not very important, so that the work of management consists chiefly of superintendence, the earnings of management will follow pretty closely on the amount of work done in the business; and a very rough but convenient measure of this is found in the wages-bill. And perhaps the least inaccurate of all the broad statements that can be made with regard to a general tendency of profits to equality in different trades, is that where equal capitals are employed, profits tend to be a certain percentage per annum on the total capital, together with a certain percentage on the wages-bill.[1]

The normal rate of profits in an industry may be lowered by a great gradual increase in production.

A manufacturer of exceptional ability and energy will apply better methods, and perhaps better machinery than his rivals : he will organize better the manufacturing and the marketing sides of his business; and he will bring them into better relation to one another. By these means he will extend his business; and therefore he will be able to take greater advantage from the specialization both of labour and of plant.[2] Thus he will obtain increasing return and also increasing profit : for if he is only one among many producers his increased output will not materially lower the prices of his goods, and nearly all the benefit of his economies will accrue to himself. If he happens to have a partial monopoly of his branch

---

kinds of risks exert on persons of various temperaments, and as a consequence on earnings and profits in risky occupations ; it might start from Adam Smith's remarks on the subject.

[1] There is a great difficulty in ascertaining even approximately the amounts of capital of different kinds invested in different classes of business. But guided mainly by the valuable statistics of American Bureaux, inexact as they avowedly are in this particular matter, we may conclude that the annual output is less than the capital in industries where the plant is very expensive, and the processes through which the raw material has to go are very long, as watch and cotton factories : but that it is more than four times the capital in businesses in which the raw material is expensive and the process of production rapid, e.g. boot factories ; as well as in some industries, which make only a slight change in the form of their material, such as sugar-refining, and slaughtering and meat-packing.

Next, analysing the turnover of circulating capital and comparing the cost of raw material to the wages-bill, we find that the former is much less than the latter in watch-factories, where the bulk of the material is small, and in stone, brick and tile works, where it is of a common sort : but in the large majority of industries the cost of material is much greater than the wages-bill ; and on the average of all the industries it is three and a half times as great. And in the Slight-change industries it is generally from twenty-five to fifty times as great.

Many of these inequalities disappear if the value of the raw material, coal, etc. used in a business is deducted before reckoning its output. This plan is commonly followed by careful statisticians in estimating the manufacturing output of a country, so as to avoid counting say yarn and cloth twice over ; and similar reasons should make us avoid counting both cattle and fodder crops in the agricultural product of a country. This plan is however not quite satisfactory. For logically one ought to deduct the looms which a weaving factory buys as well as its yarn. Again, if the factory itself was reckoned as a product of the building trades, its value should be deducted from the output (over a term of years) of the weaving trade. Similarly with regard to farm buildings. Farm horses ought certainly not to be counted, nor for some purposes any horses used in trade. However the plan of deducting nothing but raw material has its uses, if its inaccuracy is clearly recognized.

[2] See above IV. XI. 2–4.

of industry, he will so regulate his increased output, that his VI, vIII, 3.
monopoly profits increase.[1]

But when such improvements are not confined to one or two
producers : when they arise from a general increase in demand and
the output which corresponds to it; or from improved methods or
machinery, that are accessible to the whole industry; or from
advances made by subsidiary industries, and increased " external "
economies generally; then the prices of the products will keep close
to a level which yields only a normal rate of profits to that class of
industry. And in the process, the industry is likely to have passed
over to a class in which the normal rate of profits is lower than in its
old class; because there is in it more uniformity and monotony, and
less mental strain than before; and, though this is nearly the same
thing in other words, because it is more suited to joint-stock management. Thus a general increase in the proportion which the *quantity*
of product bears to the *quantity* of labour and capital in an industry
is likely to be accompanied by a fall in the rate of profits; which
may, from some points of view, be regarded as a diminishing return
measured in *values*.[2]

§ 3. We may now pass from profit per annum and examine the The rate of
causes that govern profit on the turnover. It is obvious that while profits on
the normal rate of profit per annum varies within narrow limits, the over varies
profit on the turnover may vary very widely from one branch of much more
widely
trade to another, because it depends on the length of time and the than the
annual
amount of work required for the turnover. Thus wholesale dealers, rate of
who buy and sell large quantities of produce in single transactions, profits
on capital.
and who are able to turn over their capital very rapidly, may make
large fortunes though their average profit on the turnover is less
than one per cent.; and, in the extreme case of large stock-exchange
dealings, even when it is only a small fraction of one per cent. But
a shipbuilder who has to put labour and material into the ship, and
to provide a berth for it, a long while before it is ready for sale,
and who has to take care for every detail connected with it, must
add a very high percentage to his direct and indirect outlay in order
to remunerate him for his labour, and the locking up of his capital.[3]

---

[1] See above p. 399–400.   [2] Compare pp. 266–7.

[3] He would however not need to charge a high rate of profits per annum on that
part of his capital which he had sunk in the earlier stages of building the ship; for that
capital, when once invested, would no longer require any special exercise of his ability
and industry, and it would be sufficient for him to reckon his outlay " accumulated "
at a high rate of compound interest; but in that case he must count the value of his
own labour as part of his early outlay. On the other hand, if there be any trade in
which a continuous and nearly uniform expenditure of trouble is called for on all the
capital invested, then it would be reasonable in that trade to find the " accumulated "
value of the earlier investments by the addition of a " compound " rate of profit

VI, VIII, 4.   Again, in the textile industries some firms buy raw material and turn out finished goods, while others confine themselves to spinning, to weaving or to finishing; and it is obvious that the rate of profit on the turnover of one of the first class must be equal to the sum of the rates of profit of one of each of the three other classes.[1] Again, the retail dealer's profit on the turnover is often only five or ten per cent. for commodities which are in general demand, and which are not subject to changes of fashion; so that while the sales are large, the necessary stocks are small, and the capital invested in them can be turned over very rapidly, with very little trouble and no risk. But a profit on the turnover of nearly a hundred per cent. is required to remunerate the retailer of some kinds of fancy goods which can be sold but slowly, of which varied stocks must be kept, which require a large place for their display, and which a change of fashion may render unsaleable except at a loss; and even this high rate is often exceeded in the case of fish, fruit, flowers and vegetables.[2]

But each branch of trade has its customary or fair rate of profit on the turnover.   § 4. We see then that there is no general tendency of profits on the turnover to equality; but there may be, and as a matter of fact there is in each trade and in every branch of each trade, a more or less definite rate of profits on the turnover which is regarded as a " fair " or normal rate. Of course these rates are always changing in consequence of changes in the methods of trade; which are generally begun by individuals who desire to do a larger trade at a lower rate of profit on the turnover than has been customary, but at a larger rate of profit per annum on their capital. If however there happens to be no great change of this kind going on, the traditions of the trade that a certain rate of profit on the turnover should be charged for a particular class of work are of great practical service to those in the trade. Such traditions are the outcome of much experience tending to show that, if that rate is charged, a proper allowance will be made for all the costs (supplementary as well as prime) incurred for that particular purpose, and in addition

---

(*i.e.* a rate of profit increasing geometrically as compound interest does). And this plan is frequently adopted in practice for the sake of simplicity even where it is not theoretically quite correct.

[1] Strictly speaking it will be a little greater than the sum of these three, because it will include compound interest over a longer period.

[2] The fishmongers and greengrocers in working-class quarters especially lay themselves out to do a small business at a high rate of profits; because each individual purchase is so small that the customer would rather buy from a dear shop near at hand than go some way to a cheaper one. The retailer therefore may not be getting a very good living though he charges a penny for what he bought for less than a halfpenny. The same thing was however perhaps sold by the fisherman or the farmer for a farthing or even less : and the direct cost of carriage and insurance against loss will not account for any great part of this last difference. Thus there seems to be some justification for the popular opinion that the middlemen in these trades have special facilities for obtaining abnormally high profits by combination among themselves.

the normal rate of profits per annum in that class of business will
be afforded. If they charge a price which gives much less than this
rate of profit on the turnover they can hardly prosper; and if they
charge much more they are in danger of losing their custom, since
others can afford to undersell them. This is the " fair " rate of
profit on the turnover which an honest man is expected to charge
for making goods to order, when no price has been agreed on beforehand; and it is the rate which a court of law will allow, in case a
dispute should arise between buyer and seller.[1]

§ 5. During all this inquiry we have had in view chiefly the
ultimate, or long-period or true normal results of economic forces;
we have considered the way in which the supply of business ability
in command of capital tends in the long run to adjust itself to the
demand; we have seen how it seeks constantly every business and
every method of conducting every business in which it can render
services that are so highly valued by persons who are able to pay
good prices for the satisfaction of their wants, that those services
will in the long run earn a high reward. The motive force is the
competition of undertakers : each one tries every opening, forecasting probable future events, reducing them to their true relative
proportions, and considering what surplus is likely to be afforded
by the receipts of any undertaking over the outlay required for it.
All his prospective gains enter into the profits which draw him
towards the undertaking; all the investments of his capital and

VI, VIII, 5.

Profits are a constituent element of normal supply price.

---

[1] The expert evidence that is given in such cases is full of instruction to the
economist in many ways, and in particular because of the use of mediæval phrases as
to the customs of the trade, with a more or less conscious recognition of the causes
which have produced those customs, and to which appeal must be made in support
of their continued maintenance. And it is almost always comes out finally that if the
" customary " rate of profit on the turnover is higher for one class of job than another,
the reason is that the former does (or did a little while ago) require a longer locking-up
of capital; or a greater use of expensive appliances (especially such as are liable to
rapid depreciation, or cannot be kept always employed, and therefore must pay their
way on a comparatively small number of jobs); or that it requires more difficult or
disagreeable work, or a greater amount of attention on the part of the undertaker;
or that it has some special element of risk for which insurance has to be made. And
the unreadiness of experts to bring to light these justifications of custom, which are
lying almost hidden from themselves in the recesses of their own minds, gives ground
for the belief that if we could call to life and cross-examine mediæval business men,
we should find much more half-conscious adjustment of the rate of profit to the exigencies of particular cases than has been suggested by historians. Many of them
fail sometimes to make it clear whether the customary rate of profits of which they
are speaking is a certain rate on the turnover, or such a rate on the turnover as will
afford in the long run a certain rate of profits per annum on the capital. Of course
the greater uniformity of the methods of business in mediæval times, would enable a
tolerably uniform rate of profits on the capital per annum to exist without causing so
great variations in the rate on the turnover as are inevitable in modern business. But
still it is clear that if one kind of rate of profits were nearly uniform, the other would
not be; and the value of much that has been written on mediæval economic history
seems to be somewhat impaired by the absence of a distinct recognition of the differences between the two kinds, and between the ultimate sanctions on which customs
relating severally to them must depend.

S

VI, VIII, 5. energies in making the appliances for future production, and in building up the "immaterial" capital of a business connection, have to show themselves to him as likely to be profitable, before he will enter on them : the whole of the profits which he expects from them enter into the reward, which he expects in the long run for his venture. And if he is a man of normal ability (normal that is for that class of work), and is on the margin of doubt whether to make the venture or not, they may be taken as true representatives of the (marginal) normal expenses of production of the services in question. Thus the whole of the normal profits enter into true or long-period supply price.

The causes which govern the normal levels of wages and the various elements of profits, resemble one another   The motives which induce a man and his father to invest capital and labour in preparing him for his work as an artisan, as a professional man, or as a business man, are similar to those which lead to the investment of capital and labour in building up the material plant and the organization of a business. In each case the investment (so far as man's action is governed by deliberate motive at all) is carried up to that margin at which any further investment appears to offer no balance of gain, no excess or surplus of utility over " disutility "; and the price, that is expected as a reward for all this investment, is therefore a part of the normal expenses of production of the services rendered by it.

A long period of time is however needed in order to get the full operation of all these causes, so that exceptional success may be balanced against exceptional failure. On the one hand are those who succeed abundantly because they turn out to have rare ability or rare good fortune either in the particular incidents of their speculative enterprises, or in meeting with a favourable opportunity for the general development of their business. And on the other are those who are mentally or morally incapable of making good use of their training and their favourable start in life, who have no special aptitude for their calling, whose speculations are unfortunate, or whose businesses are cramped by the encroachment of rivals, or left stranded by the tide of demand receding from them and flowing in some other direction.

more nearly than those which govern fluctuations in their values.   But though these disturbing causes may thus be neglected in problems relating to normal earnings and normal value; they assume the first rank, and exert a predominating influence, with regard to the incomes earned by particular individuals at particular times. And, since these disturbing causes affect profits and the earnings of management in very different ways from those in which they affect ordinary earnings, there is a scientific necessity for treating differently profits and ordinary earnings when we are discussing temporary fluctuations and individual incidents. Questions relating to market fluctuations cannot indeed be properly handled till the theories of money, credit and foreign trade have been discussed : but even at this stage we may note the following contrast between the ways in which disturbing causes such as we have just described affect profits and ordinary earnings. VI, VIII, 6, 7.

§ 6. In the first place the undertaker's profits bear the first brunt of any change in the price of those things which are the product of his capital (including his business organization), of his labour and of the labour of his employees; and as a result fluctuations of his profits generally precede fluctuations of their wages, and are much more extensive. For, other things being equal, a comparatively small rise in the price for which he can sell his product is not unlikely to increase his profit manyfold, or perhaps to substitute a profit for a loss. That rise will make him eager to reap the harvest of good prices while he can; and he will be in fear that his employees will leave him or refuse to work. He will therefore be more able and more willing to pay the high wages; and wages will tend upwards. But experience shows that (whether they are governed by sliding scales or not) they seldom rise as much in proportion as prices; and therefore they do not rise nearly as much in proportion as profits. First difference. Profits fluctuate with prices and in even greater ratio :
but the wages of employees lag behind, and their fluctuations are less.

Another aspect of the same fact is that when trade is bad, the employee at worst is earning nothing towards the support of himself and his family; but the employer's outgoings are likely to exceed his incomings, particularly if he is using much borrowed capital. In that case even his gross earnings of management are a negative quantity : that is, he is losing his capital. In very bad times this happens to a great number, perhaps the majority of undertakers; and it happens almost constantly to those who are less fortunate, or less able, or less well fitted for their special trade than others.

§ 7. To pass to another point, the number of those who succeed in business is but a small percentage of the whole; and in their hands are concentrated the fortunes of others several times as numerous as themselves, who have made savings of their own, or who have inherited the savings of others and lost them all, together with the fruits of their own efforts, in unsuccessful business. In order therefore to find the average profits of a trade we must not divide the aggregate profits made in it by the number of those who are reaping them, nor even by that number added to the number who have failed : but from the aggregate profits of the successful Second difference. The profits of individuals differ more widely than ordinary earnings do, and their average value is over.

VI, VIII, 8.

estimated,
because
those who
lose all
their
capital
disappear
from sight.
we must subtract the aggregate losses of those who have failed, and perhaps disappeared from the trade; and we must then divide the remainder by the sum of the numbers of those who have succeeded and those who have failed. It is probable that the true gross earnings of management, that is, the excess of profits over interest, is not on the average more than a half, and in some risky trades not more than a tenth part, of what it appears to be to persons who form their estimate of the profitableness of a trade by observation only of those who have secured its prizes. There are, however, as we shall presently see, reasons for thinking that the risks of trade are on the whole diminishing rather than increasing.[1]

Third
difference.
The true
earnings
of effort
are nearly
always a
consider-
able part
of the
income of
the artisan
and pro-
fessional
man; but
not of the
business
man.
§ 8. We may pass to another difference between the fluctuations of profits and ordinary earnings. We have seen that before free capital and labour have been invested in securing the skill required for the work of the artisan or professional man, the income expected to be derived from them is of the nature of profits : though the rate of such profits which is required, is often high for two reasons :— the people who make the outlay do not themselves reap the greater part of the reward arising from it; and they are frequently in straitened circumstances, and not able to invest for a distant return without great self-denial. And we have seen that, when the artisan or professional man has once obtained the skill required for his work, a part of his earnings are for the future really a quasi-rent of the capital and labour invested in fitting him for his work, in obtaining

[1] A century ago many Englishmen returned from the Indies with large fortunes, and the belief spread that the average rate of profits to be made there was enormous. But, as Sir W. Hunter points out (*Annals of Rural Bengal*, ch. VI.), the failures were numerous, but only "those who drew prizes in the great lottery returned to tell the tale." And at the very time when this was happening, it used commonly to be said in England that the families of a rich man and his coachman would probably change places within three generations. It is true that this was partly due to the wild extra-vagance common among young heirs at that time, and partly to the difficulty of finding secure investments for their capital. The stability of the wealthy classes of England has been promoted almost as much by the spread of sobriety and education as by the growth of methods of investment, which enable the heirs of a rich man to draw a secure and lasting income from his wealth though they do not inherit the busi-ness ability by which he acquired it. There are however even now districts in Eng-land, in whch the majority of manufacturers are workmen or the sons of workmen. And in America, though foolish prodigality is perhaps less common than in England, yet the greater changefulness of conditions, and the greater difficulty of keeping a business abreast of the age, have caused it commonly to be said that a family passes "from shirt sleeves to shirt sleeves" in three generations. Wells says (*Recent Economic Changes*, p. 351), "There has long been a substantial agreement among those competent to form an opinion, that ninety per cent. of all the men who try to do business on their own account fail of success." And Mr. J. H. Walker gives (*Quarterly Journal of Economics*, Vol. II. p. 448) some detailed statistics with regard to the origin and careers of the manufacturers in the leading industries of Worcester in Massachusetts between 1840 and 1888. More than nine-tenths of them began life as journeymen; and less than ten per cent. of the sons of those who were on the list of manufacturers in 1840, 1850 and 1860, had any property in 1888, or had died leaving any. And as to France, M. Leroy Beaulieu says (*Répartition des Richesses*, ch. XI.) that out of every hundred new businesses that are started twenty disappear almost at once, fifty or sixty vegetate, neither rising nor falling, and only ten or fifteen are successful.

his start in life, his business connections, and generally his oppor- VI, VIII, 8.
tunity for turning his faculties to good account; and only the
remainder of his income is true earnings of effort. But this remainder
is generally a large part of the whole. And here lies the contrast.
For when a similar analysis is made of the profits of the business
man, the proportions are found to be different: in his case the
greater part is quasi-rent.

The income which the undertaker of business on a large scale
gets from the capital, material and immaterial, invested in his
business is so great, and liable to such violent fluctuations from a
considerable negative to a large positive quantity, that he often
thinks very little of his own labour in the matter. If profitable
business opens out to him, he regards the harvest accruing from it as
almost pure gain; there is so little difference between the trouble
of having his business on his hands only partially active, and that
of working it to its full capacity, that as a rule it scarcely occurs to
him to set off his own extra labour as a deduction from those gains :
they do not present themselves to his mind as to any considerable
extent earnings purchased by extra fatigue, in the same way as the
extra earnings got by working overtime do to the artisan. This
fact is the chief cause, and to some extent the justification, of the
imperfect recognition by the general public, and even by some
economists, of the fundamental unity underlying the causes that
determine normal profits and normal wages.

Closely allied to the preceding difference is another. When an Fourth
artisan or a professional man has exceptional natural abilities, which difference.
are not made by human effort, and are not the result of sacrifices A large
share of the
undergone for a future gain, they enable him to obtain a surplus income of
income over what ordinary persons could expect from similar successful
business
exertions following on similar investments of capital and labour in men is a
their education and start in life; a surplus which is of the nature of surplus
due to rare
rent.   natural
faculties.

But, to revert to a point mentioned at the end of last chapter,
the class of business undertakers contains a disproportionately large
number of persons with high natural ability; since, in addition to
the able men born within its ranks it includes also a large share of
the best natural abilities born in the lower ranks of industry. And
thus while profits on capital invested in education is a specially
important element in the incomes of professional men taken as a
class, the rent of rare natural abilities may be regarded as a specially
important element in the incomes of business men, so long as we
consider them as individuals. (In relation to normal value the

VI, VIII, 8. earnings even of rare abilities are, as we have seen, to be regarded rather as a quasi-rent than as a rent proper.)

But there are exceptions to this rule. The humdrum business man, who has inherited a good business and has just sufficient force to keep it together, may reap an income of many thousands a year, which contains very little rent of rare natural qualities. And, on the other hand, the greater part of incomes earned by exceptionally successful barristers, and writers, and painters, and singers, and jockeys may be classed as the rent of rare natural abilities—so long at least as we regard them as individuals, and are not considering the dependence of the normal supply of labour in their several occupations on the prospects of brilliant success which they hold out to aspiring youth.

Changes in the industrial environment affect the profits of individual businesses more than they do ordinary earnings.

The income of a particular business is often very much affected by changes in its industrial environment and opportunity or conjuncture. But similar influences affect the special income derived from the skill of many classes of workers. The discovery of rich copper-mines in America and Australia lowered the earning power of the skill of Cornish miners, so long as they stayed at home : and every new discovery of rich mines in the new districts raised the earning power of the skill of those miners who had already gone there. And again, the growth of a taste for theatrical amusements, while raising the normal earnings of actors, and inducing an increased supply of their skill, raises the earning power of the skill of those already in the profession, a great part of which is, from the point of view of the individual, a producer's surplus due to rare natural qualities.[1]

[1] The late General Walker rendered excellent service in explaining the causes that govern wages on the one hand and earnings of management on the other. But he maintained (*Political Economy*, § 311) that profits do not form a part of the price of manufactured products; and he does not limit that doctrine to short periods, for which, as we have seen, the income derived from all skill, whether exceptional or not, whether that of an employer or a workman, may be regarded as a quasi-rent. He uses the word " profits " in an artificial sense; for, having excluded interest altogether from profits, he assumes that the " No-profits employer " earns " on the whole or in the long run the amount which he could have expected to receive as wages if employed by others " (*First Lessons*, 1889, § 190): that is to say, the " No-profits employer " obtains, in addition to interest on his capital, normal net earnings of management of men of his ability whatever that may be. Thus profits in Walker's sense exclude four-fifths of what are ordinarily classed as profits in England (the proportion would be rather less in America, and rather more on the Continent than in England). So that his doctrine would appear to mean only that that part of the employer's income, which is due to exceptional abilities or good fortune, does not enter into price. But the prizes as well as the blanks of every occupation, whether it be that of an employer or not, take their part in determining the number of persons who seek that occupation and the energy with which they give themselves to their work : and therefore do enter into *normal* supply price. Walker appears to rest his argument mainly on the important fact, which he has done much to make prominent, that the ablest employers, who in the long run get the highest profits, are as a rule those who pay the highest wages to the workman and sell at the lowest price to the consumer. But it is an

§ 9. Next let us consider in relation to one another the interests of different industrial classes engaged in the same trade.

VI, VIII, 9, 10.

This solidarity is a special case of the general fact that the demand for the several factors of production of any commodity is a joint demand, and we may refer back to the illustration of this general fact which is given in Book V. chapter VI. We there saw how a change in the supply of (say) plasterers' labour would affect the interests of all other branches of the building trades in the same way, but much more intensely than it would the general public. The fact is that the incomes derived from the specialized capital and the specialized skill belonging to all the various industrial classes engaged in producing houses, or calico, or anything else, depend very much on the general prosperity of the trade. And in so far as this is the case they may be regarded for short periods as shares of a composite or joint income of the whole trade. The share of each class tends to rise when this aggregate income is increased by an increase in their own efficiency or by any external cause. But when the aggregate income is stationary, and any one class gets a better share than before, it must be at the expense of the others. This is true of the whole body of those engaged in any trade; and it is true in a special sense of those who have spent a great part of their lives in working together in the same business establishment.

Relations between the interests of different classes of workers in the same trade.

§ 10. The earnings of a successful business, looked at from the point of view of the business man himself, are the aggregate of the earnings, firstly, of his own ability, secondly, of his plant and other material capital, and thirdly, of his good-will, or business organization and connection. But really it is more than the sum of these: for his efficiency depends partly on his being in that particular business; and if he were to sell it at a fair price, and then engage himself in another business, his income would probably be much diminished. The whole value of his business connection to him when working it is a notable instance of Conjuncture or Opportunity *value*. It is mainly a product of ability and labour, though good fortune may have contributed to it. That part which is transferable, and may be bought by a private individual, or by a large amalgamation of firms, must be entered among their costs; and is in a sense a Conjuncture or Opportunity *cost*.

A part of the gains of a business is derived from its connections and organization, and would often be lost if the employees deserted it.

The point of view of the employer however does not include the whole gains of the business: for there is another part which attaches

---

equally true and an even more important fact that those workmen who get the highest wages are as a rule those who turn their employers' plant and material to best account (see VI. III. 2), and thus enable him both to get high profits for himself and to charge low prices to the consumer.

VI, VIII,
10.

to his employees. Indeed, in some cases and for some purposes, nearly the whole income of a business may be regarded as a quasi-rent, that is an income determined for the time by the state of the market for its wares, with but little reference to the cost of preparing for their work the various things and persons engaged in it. In other words it is a *composite quasi-rent* [1] divisible among the different persons in the business by bargaining, supplemented by custom and by notions of fairness—results which are brought about by causes, that bear some analogy to those that, in early forms of civilization, have put the producer's surplus from the land almost permanently into the hands not of single individuals, but of cultivating firms. Thus the head clerk in a business has an acquaintance with men and things, the use of which he could in some cases sell at a high price to rival firms. But in other cases it is of a kind to be of no value save to the business in which he already is; and then his departure would perhaps injure it by several times the value of his salary, while probably he could not get half that salary elsewhere. [2]

When there would be no such loss, the quasi-rent of the employees' skill depends on the prosperity of the trade in general.

It is important to see how the position of such employees differs from that of others, whose services would be of almost equal value to any business in a large trade. The income of one of these in any week consists, as we have seen, partly of a recompense for the fatigue incurred by the work of that week, and partly of a quasi-rent of his specialized skill and ability : and, assuming competition to be perfectly efficient, this quasi-rent is determined by the price which either his present employers, or any other, would be willing to pay for his services in the state in which the market for their wares is during that week. The prices, that have to be paid for given work of a given kind, being thus determined by the general conditions of the trade, these prices enter into the direct outgoings which have to be deducted from its gross earnings in order to ascertain the quasi-rent of this particular firm at the time : but in the rise or fall of that quasi-rent the employees would have no share. In fact however competition is not thus perfectly efficient. Even

---

[1] Compare V. x. 8.

[2] When a firm has a speciality of its own, many even of its ordinary workmen would lose a great part of their wages by going away, and at the same time injure the firm seriously. The chief clerk may be taken into partnership, and the whole of the employees may be paid partly by a share in the profits of the concern; but whether this is done or not, their earnings are determined, not so much by competition and the direct action of the law of substitution, as by a bargain between them and their employers, the terms of which are theoretically arbitrary. In practice however they will probably be governed by a desire to " do what is right," that is, to agree on payments that represent the normal earnings of such ability, industry and special training as the employees severally possess, with something added if the fortunes of the firm are good, and something subtracted if they are bad.

where the same price is paid all over the market for the same work
with the same machinery, the prosperity of a firm increases the
chance of advancement for each of its employees, and also his chance
of continuous employment when trade is slack, and much-coveted
overtime when trade is good.

Thus there is *de facto* some sort of profit-and-loss sharing between
almost every business and its employees; and perhaps this is in its
very highest form when, without being embodied in a definite contract, the solidarity of interests between those who work together
in the same business is recognized with cordial generosity as the
result of true brotherly feeling. But such cases are not very common;
and as a rule the relations between employers and employed are
raised to a higher plane both economically and morally by the adoption of the system of profit-sharing; especially when it is regarded
as but a step towards the still higher but much more difficult level
of true co-operation.

If the employers in any trade act together and so do the employed, the solution of the problem of wages becomes indeterminate;
and there is nothing but bargaining to decide the exact shares in
which the excess of its incomings over its outgoings for the time
should be divided between employers and employed. Leaving out
of account industries which are being superseded, no lowering of
wages will be permanently in the interest of employers, which drives
many skilled workers to other markets, or even to other industries
in which they abandon the special earnings of skill; and wages
must be high enough in an average year to attract young people to
the trade. This sets lower limits to wages, and upper limits are set
by corresponding necessities as to the supply of capital and business
power. But what point between these limits should be taken at
any time can be decided only by higgling and bargaining; which are
however likely to be tempered somewhat by ethico-prudential considerations, especially if there be a good court of conciliation in the
trade.

The problem is in practice even more complex. For each group
of employees is likely to have its own union, and to fight for its own
hand. The employers act as buffers : but a strike for higher wages
on the part of one group may, in effect, deplete the wages of some
other group almost as much as the employers' profits.

This is not a fitting place for a study of the causes and effects
of trade combinations and of alliances and counter-alliances among
employers and employed, as well as among traders and manufacturers. They present a succession of picturesque incidents and

VI, VIII, 10.

romantic transformations, which arrest public attention and seem to indicate a coming change of our social arrangements now in one direction and now in another; and their importance is certainly great and grows rapidly. But it is apt to be exaggerated; for indeed many of them are little more than eddies, such as have always fluttered over the surface of progress. And though they are on a larger and more imposing scale in this modern age than before; yet now, as ever, the main body of movement depends on the deep silent strong stream of the tendencies of normal distribution and exchange; which " are not seen," but which control the course of those episodes which " are seen." For even in conciliation and arbitration, the central difficulty is to discover what is that normal level from which the decisions of the court must not depart far under penalty of destroying their own authority.

CHAPTER IX

RENT OF LAND

§ 1. IT has been argued in Book V. that the rent of land is no unique fact, but simply the chief species of a large genus of economic phenomena; and that the theory of the rent of land is no isolated economic doctrine, but merely one of the chief applications of a particular corollary from the general theory of demand and supply; that there is a continuous gradation from the true rent of those free gifts which have been appropriated by man, through the income derived from permanent improvements of the soil, to those yielded by farm and factory buildings, steam-engines and less durable goods. In this and the following chapter we are to make a special study of the net income of land. That study has two parts. One part relates to the total quantity of the net income, or producer's surplus from land : the other to the way in which this income is distributed between those who have an interest in the land. The first is general, whatever be the form of land tenure. We will begin with it, and *suppose that the cultivation of the land is undertaken by its owner.*

We begin by supposing land to be cultivated by its owners, to avoid questions affecting its tenure.

We may call to mind that the land has an " inherent " income of heat and light and air and rain, which man cannot greatly affect; and advantages of situation, many of which are wholly beyond his control, while but few of the remainder are the direct result of the investment of capital and effort in the land by its individual owners. These are the chief of its properties, the supply of which is not dependent on human effort, and which would therefore not be increased by extra rewards to that effort : and a tax on which would always fall exclusively on the owners.[1]

The income attributed to the inherent properties of land.

On the other hand those chemical or mechanical properties of the soil, on which its fertility largely depends, can be modified, and in extreme cases entirely changed by man's action. But a tax on the income derived from improvements which, though capable of general application are yet slowly made and slowly exhausted, would not appreciably affect the supply of them during a short period, nor therefore the supply of produce due to them. It would consequently fall in the main on the owner; a leaseholder being regarded for the

The income derived from permanent improvements.

---

[1] But compare V. XI. 2 for exceptions to the rule as to situation rent.

time as owner, subject to a mortgage. In a long period, however, it would diminish the supply of them, would raise the normal supply price of produce and fall on the consumer.

Résumé and application of the discussion in Book IV. as to the tendency to diminishing return.

§ 2. Now let us revert to our study of the tendency to diminishing return in agriculture in the fourth Book; still supposing that the owner of the land undertakes its cultivation, so that our reasoning may be general, and independent of the incidents of particular forms of land tenure.

We saw how the return to successive doses of capital and labour, though it may increase for the first few doses, will begin to diminish, when the land is already well cultivated. The cultivator continues to apply additional capital and labour, till he reaches a point at which the return is only just sufficient to repay his outlay and reward him for his own work. That will be the dose on the margin of cultivation, whether it happens to be applied to rich or to poor land; an amount equal to the return to it will be required, and will be sufficient to repay him for each of his previous doses. The excess of the gross produce over this amount is his producer's surplus.

He looks forward as far as he can : but it is seldom possible to look forward very far. And at any given time he takes for granted all that richness of the soil which results from permanent improvements and the income (or quasi-rent) derived from those improvements, together with that due to the original qualities of the soil, constitutes his producer's surplus or rent. Henceforth it is only the income derived from new investments that appears as earnings and profits : he carries these new investments up to the margin of profitableness; and his producer's surplus or rent is the excess of the gross income from the improved land over what is required to remunerate him for the fresh doses of capital and labour he annually applies.

This surplus depends on, firstly, the richness of the land, and secondly, the relative values of those things which he has to sell and of those things which he needs to buy. The richness or fertility of the land, we have seen, cannot be measured absolutely, for it varies with the nature of the crops raised, and with the methods and intensity of cultivation. Two pieces of land cultivated even by the same man with equal expenditures of capital and labour, are likely, if they yield equal crops of barley, to give unequal crops of wheat; if they return equal crops of wheat when cultivated slightly or in a primitive fashion, they are likely to yield unequal crops when cultivated intensively, or on modern methods. Further, the prices at which the various requisites of the farm can be bought, and its various products sold, depend on the industrial environment; and changes in that are continually changing the relative values of different crops and therefore the relative values of land in different situations.

Lastly, we suppose the cultivator to be of normal ability relatively to the task he has undertaken, and the circumstances of time and place. If he is of less ability his actual gross produce will be less than that which normally should come from the land: it will be yielding to him less than its true producer's surplus. If, on the contrary, he is of more than normal ability, he will be getting in addition to the producer's surplus due to the land, some producer's surplus due to rare ability.

The cultivators must be supposed to be of normal ability and enterprise.

§ 3. We have already traced in some detail the way in which a rise in the value of agricultural produce increases the producer's surplus, measured in terms of produce, from all lands, but especially from those where the tendency to diminishing return acts but feebly.[1] We have seen that generally speaking it raises the value of poor lands relatively to rich: or in other words, that if a person anticipates a rise in the value of produce, he may expect a larger future income from investing a given sum of money in poor land at present prices than from investing it in rich land.[2]

A rise in the real value of produce generally raises the produce value of the surplus,

Next, the real value of the producer's surplus, *i.e.* its value measured in terms of general purchasing power, will rise relatively to its produce value, in the same ratio as the value of produce measured in the same way has risen: that is to say, a rise in the value of produce causes a double rise in the value of producer's surplus.

and its real value even more.

The term the "real value" of produce is indeed ambiguous. Historically it has most often been used to mean the real value from the point of view of the consumer. This use is rather dangerous: for there are some purposes for which it is better to consider real value from the point of view of the producer. But with this caution we may use the term "labour-value" to express the amount of labour of a given kind that the produce will purchase; and "real value" to mean the amount of necessaries, comforts, and luxuries

Necessity for distinguishing between changes in the labour value of produce, and in its general purchasing power.

---

[1] IV. III. 3. Thus we see that if the value of produce rises from OH' to OH (figs. 12, 13, 14), so that while an amount of produce OH was required to remunerate a dose of capital and labour before the rise, an amount OH' would suffice after the rise, then the producer's surplus will be increased a little in the case of lands of the class represented in fig. 12, with regard to which the tendency to diminishing return acts quickly; much more with regard to the second class of lands (fig. 13), and most of all with regard to the third class (fig. 14).

[2] *Ib.* § 4. Comparing two pieces of land (figs. 16 and 17) with regard to which the tendency to diminishing return acts in a similar way, but of which the first is rich and the second poor, we found that the rise of producer's surplus from AHC to $AH'C'$, caused by a rise in the price of produce in the ratio OH to OH', was much larger in proportion in the second case.

of life that a given amount of produce will purchase. A rise in the labour-value of raw produce may imply an increasing pressure of population on the means of subsistence; and a rise of the producer's surplus from land due to that cause goes together with, and is a sort of measure of, the degradation of the people. But if, on the other hand, the rise in the real value of raw produce has been caused by an improvement of the arts of production, other than agricultural, it will probably be accompanied by a rise in the purchasing power of wages.

§ 4. In all this it has been clear that the producer's surplus from land is not evidence of the greatness of the bounty of nature, as was held by the Physiocrats and in a more modified form by Adam Smith : it is evidence of the limitations of that bounty. But it must be remembered that inequalities of situation relatively to the best markets are just as powerful causes of inequalities of producer's surplus, as are inequalities of absolute productiveness.[1]

This truth and its chief consequences, many of which seem now so obvious, were first made manifest by Ricardo. He delighted to argue that no surplus can be reaped from the ownership of those of nature's gifts the supply of which is everywhere practically unlimited : and in particular that there would be no surplus from land if there were an unlimited supply of it all equally fertile and all equally accessible. He carried this argument further, and showed that an improvement in the arts of cultivation, equally applicable to all soils (which is equivalent to a general increase in the natural fertility of land), will be nearly sure to lower the aggregate corn-surplus and quite sure to lower the aggregate real surplus derived

---

[1] England is so small and so thickly peopled, that even milk and vegetables which require to be marketed quickly, and even hay in spite of its bulk, can be sent across the country at no inordinate expense : while for the staple products, corn and live stock, the cultivator can get nearly the same net price in whatever part of England he is. For this reason English economists have ascribed to fertility the first rank among the causes which determine the value of agricultural land; and have treated situation as of secondary importance. They have therefore often regarded the producer's surplus, or rental value, of land as the excess of the produce which it yields, over what is returned to equal capital and labour (applied with equal skill) to land that is so barren as to be on the margin of cultivation; without taking the trouble to state explicitly either that the two pieces of land must be in the same neighbourhood, or that separate allowance must be made for differences in the expense of marketing. But this method of speaking did not come naturally to economists in new countries, where the richest land might lie uncultivated, because it had not good access to markets. To them situation appeared at least equally important with fertility in determining the value of land. In their view land on the margin of cultivation, was land far from markets; and, especially, land far from railways that lead to good markets : and the producer's surplus presented itself to them as the excess value of the produce from well-situated land over that which equal labour, capital (and skill), would get on the worst-situated land; allowance being of course made for differences of fertility, if necessary. In this sense the United States cannot any longer be regarded as a new country : for all the best land is taken up, and nearly all of it has obtained access by cheap railways to food markets.

from the land that supplies a given population with raw produce. VI, IX, 4.
He also pointed out that, if the improvements affected chiefly those
lands that were already the richest, it might raise the aggregate
surplus; but that, if it affected chiefly the poorer class of lands, it
would lower that aggregate very much.

It is quite consistent with this proposition to admit that an
improvement in the arts of cultivation of the land of England now
would raise the aggregate surplus from her land, because it would
increase the produce without materially lowering its price, unless it
were accompanied by a similar improvement in those countries from
which she imports raw produce; or, which comes to the same thing
for this purpose, by an improvement in the means of communication
with them. And as Ricardo himself says, improvements that apply
equally to all the land supplying the same market, " as they give a
great stimulus to population, and at the same time enable us to
cultivate poorer lands with less labour, are ultimately of immense
advantage to the landlords." [1]

There is some interest in the attempt to distinguish that part of Original
the value of land which is the result of man's labour, from that which and
acquired
is due to the original bounty of nature. Part of its value is caused properties
by highways and other improvements that were made for the general of land.
purposes of the country, and are not a special charge on its agriculture. Counting these in, List, Carey, Bastiat and others contend
that the expense of bringing land from its original to its present
condition would exceed the whole value it has now; and hence
they argue that all of its value is due to man's labour. Their facts
may be disputed; but they are really not relevant to their conclusions. What is wanted for their argument is that the present
value of land should not exceed the expense, in so far as it can
properly be charged to agricultural account, of bringing the land
from its original condition to one in which it would be as fertile and
generally useful for agricultural purposes as it now is. Many of the
changes wrought in it were made to suit agricultural methods that
are long since obsolete; and some of them even deduct from, rather
than add to, the value of the land. And further, the expenses of
making the change must be the net expenses after adding indeed
interest on the gradual outlay, but also after deducting the aggregate
value of the extra produce which has, from first to last, been attributable to the improvement. The value of land in a well-peopled district
is generally much greater than these expenses, and often many times
as great.

[1] Footnote to his third Chapter.

VI, ix, 5.

The argument so far applicable to all systems of land tenure.

§ 5. The argument of this chapter so far is applicable to all systems of land tenure, which recognize private ownership of land in any form; for it is concerned with that producer's surplus, which accrues to the owner if he cultivates his land himself; or, if he does not, then accrues to him and his tenants, regarded as a firm engaged in the business of cultivation. Thus it holds true, whatever be the division which custom or law or contract may have arranged between them with regard to their several shares of the cost of cultivation on the one hand, and the fruits of the cultivation on the other. The greater part of it is also independent of the stage of economic development which has been reached; and it is valid even if little or no produce is sent to market, and dues are levied in kind and so on.[1]

The division between the landlord's and the farmer's share in the English system is the most important for science.

At the present day, in those parts of England where custom and sentiment count for least, and free competition and enterprise for most in the bargaining for the use of land, it is commonly understood that the landlord supplies, and in some measure maintains, those improvements which are slowly made and slowly worn out. That being done, he requires of his tenant the whole producer's surplus which the land thus equipped is estimated to afford in a year of normal harvests and normal prices, after deducting enough to replace the farmer's capital with normal profits, the farmer standing to lose in bad years and gain in good years. In this estimate it is implicitly assumed that the farmer is a man of normal ability and enterprise for that class of holding; and therefore, if he rises above that standard, he will himself reap the benefit; and if he falls below it will himself bear the loss, and perhaps ultimately leave the farm. In other words, that part of the income derived from the land which the landlord obtains, is governed, for all periods of moderate length, mainly by the market for the produce, with but little reference to the cost of providing the various agents employed in raising it; and it therefore is of the nature of a rent. And that part which the tenant retains, is to be regarded, even for short periods, as profits entering directly into the normal price of the produce; because the produce would not be raised unless it were expected to yield those profits.

[1] Petty's memorable statement of the law of rent (*Taxes and Contributions*, IV. 13) is so worded as to apply to all forms of tenure and to all stages of civilization :—
" Suppose a man could with his own hands plant a certain scope of Land with Corn, that is, could Digg, or Plough; Harrow, Weed, Reap, Carry home, Thresh, and Winnow, so much as the Husbandry of this Land requires; and had withal Seed wherewith to sow the same. I say, that when this man hath subducted his seed out of the proceed of his Harvest, and also what himself hath both eaten and given to others in exchange for Clothes, and other Natural necessaries; that the Remainder of Corn, is the natural and true Rent of the Land for that year; and the *medium* of seven years, or rather of so many years as make up the Cycle, within which Dearths and Plenties make their revolution, doth give the ordinary Rent of the Land in Corn."

The more fully therefore the distinctively English features of VI, IX, 5. land tenure are developed, the more nearly is it true that the line of division between the tenant's and the landlord's share coincides with the deepest and most important line of cleavage in economic theory.[1] This fact perhaps more than any other was the cause of the ascendancy of English economic theory early in this century; it helped English economists to pioneer the way so far ahead, that even in our own generation, when as much intellectual activity has been devoted to economic studies in other countries as in England, nearly all the new constructive ideas are found to be but developments of others which were latent in the older English work.

The fact itself appears accidental : but perhaps it was not. For this particular line of cleavage involves less friction, less waste of time and trouble in checks and counter checks than any other. It may be doubted whether the so-called English system will endure. It has great disadvantages, and it may not be found the best in a future stage of civilization. But when we come to compare it with other systems, we shall see that it afforded great advantages to a country, which pioneered the way for the world in the development of free enterprise; and which therefore was impelled early to adopt all such changes as give freedom and vigour, elasticity and strength.

---

[1] In technical language it is the distinction between the quasi-rents which do not, and the profits which do, directly enter into the normal supply prices of produce for periods of moderate length.

LAND TENURE

VI, x, 1.

'arly
orms of
and
enure
ave
enerally
een based
n partner-
hips, con-
:olled by
radition
ather
han by
onscious
ontract.
'he
o-called
andlord is
enerally
he
leeping
artner,

§ 1. IN early times, and in some backward countries even in our own age, all rights to property depend on general understandings rather than on precise laws and documents. In so far as these understandings can be reduced to definite terms and expressed in the language of modern business, they are generally to the following effect :—The ownership of land is vested, not in an individual, but in a firm of which one member or group of members is the sleeping partner, while another member or group of members (it may be a whole family) is the working partner.[1]

The sleeping partner is sometimes the ruler of the State, sometimes he is an individual who inherits what was once the duty of collecting the payments due to this ruler from the cultivators of a certain part of the soil; but what, in the course of silent time, has become a right of ownership, more or less definite, more or less absolute. If, as is generally the case, he retains the duty to make certain payments to the ruler of the State, the partnership may be regarded as containing three members, of whom two are sleeping partners.[2]

nd his
hare
f the
roduce
i not a
rue rent.

The sleeping partner, or one of them, is generally called the proprietor, or landholder or landlord, or even the landowner. But this is an incorrect way of speaking, when he is restrained by law, or by custom which has nearly the force of law, from turning the culti-

---

[1] The sleeping partner may be a village community; but recent investigations, especially those of Mr. Seebohm, have given cause for believing that the communities were not often " free " and ultimate owners of the land. For a summary of the controversy as to the part which the village community has played in the history of England the reader is referred to the first chapter of Ashley's *Economic History*. Mention has already been made of the ways in which primitive forms of divided ownership of the land hindered progress, I. II. 2.

[2] The firm may be further enlarged by the introduction of an intermediary who collects payments from a number of cultivators, and after deducting a certain share, hands them over to the head of the firm. He is not a middleman in the sense in which the word is used ordinarily in England; that is, he is not a sub-contractor, liable to be dismissed at the end of a definite period for which he has contracted to collect the payments. He is a partner in the firm, having rights in the land as real as those of the head partner, though, it may be, of inferior value. The case may be even more complex than this. There may be many intermediate holders between the actual cultivators and the person who holds direct from the State. The actual cultivators also vary greatly in the character of their interests; some having a right to sit at fixed rents and to be altogether exempt from enhancement, some to sit at rents which are enhanceable only under certain prescribed conditions, some being mere tenants from year to year.

vator out of the holding by an arbitrary increase of the payments VI, x, 2.
exacted from him or by any other means.   In that case the property
in the land vests not in him alone, but in the whole of the firm of
which he is only the sleeping partner, the payment made by the
working partner is not a rent at all, but is that fixed sum, or that
part of the gross proceeds, as the case may be, which the constitution
of the firm binds him to pay; and, in so far as the custom or law
which regulates these payments is fixed and unalterable, the theory
of rent has but little direct application.

§ 2. But in fact the payments and dues, which custom is supposed *But custom is much more plastic than at first appears,* to stereotype, nearly always contain elements which are incapable
of precise definition; while the accounts of them handed down by
tradition are embodied in loose and vague impressions, or at best are
expressed in words that make no attempt at scientific exactness.[1]

We can watch the influence of this vagueness in the agreements *as is shown even by recent English history.* between landlord and tenant even in modern England; for they
have always been interpreted by the aid of customs, which have
ever been imperceptibly growing and dwindling again, to meet the
changing exigencies of successive generations. We change our
customs more quickly than our forefathers did, and we are more
conscious of our changes and more willing to convert our customs
into legal enactments, and to make them uniform.[2]

At the present day, in spite of minute legislation and carefully *Even now the adjustment of rents to the changes in the letting value of the land is partly tacit and almost unconscious.* drawn agreements, there remains a wide margin of uncertainty as to
the amount of capital which the landlord will from time to time
invest in maintaining and extending the farm buildings and other
improvements. It is in these matters, quite as much as in his direct
money relations with the tenant, that the generous and liberal
landlord shows himself; and, what is specially important for the
general argument of this chapter, alterations in the real net rent
required of the tenant are as often made by a quiet readjustment of
the shares of the expenses of working the farm that are borne by

---

[1] Prof. Maitland in the article on *Court Rolls* in the *Dictionary of Political Economy* observes that " we shall never know how far the tenure of the mediæval tenant was precarious until these documents have been examined."

[2] Thus Mr. Pusey's Committee of the House of Commons in 1848 reported, " That different usages have long prevailed in different counties and districts of the country, conferring a claim on an outgoing tenant for various operations of husbandry. . . . That these local usages are imported into leases or agreements, . . . unless the terms of the agreement expressly, or by implication, negative such a presumption.   That in certain parts of the country a modern usage has sprung up, which confers a right on the outgoing tenant to be reimbursed certain expenses . . . other than those above referred to. . . . That this usage appears to have grown out of improved and spirited systems of farming, involving a large outlay of capital. . . . That these [new] usages have gradually grown into general acceptance in certain districts, until they have ultimately become recognized there as the custom of the country."   Many of them are now enforced by law.   See below, § 10.

VI, x, 3. the landlord and the tenant as by a change in the money rent. Thus corporate bodies and many large private landowners often let their tenants go on from year to year, without any attempt to make the money rents follow the changes in the real letting value of the land; and there are many farms which are not let on lease and yet the rent of which has nominally remained unchanged during the agricultural inflation which culminated in 1874, and during the depression which followed. But in the earlier period the farmer, who knew he was under-rented, could not put pressure on his landlord to lay out capital in drainage or new buildings or even in repairs, and had to humour him as regards the game and in other matters; while just now the landlord, who has a steady tenant, will do many things, that are not stipulated for in the agreement, in order to retain him. Thus, while the money rent has remained stationary, the real rent has changed.

Thus caution is needed when applying the Ricardian analysis to modern English land problems;

This fact is an important illustration of the general proposition, that the economic theory of rent, the Ricardian theory as it is sometimes called, does not apply to modern English land tenure without many corrections and limitations both as regards substance and form; and that a further extension of these corrections and limitations will make the theory applicable to all forms of Mediæval and Oriental land tenure, in which any sort of private ownership is recognized. The difference is only one of degree.

as well as to earlier systems.

§ 3. But the difference of degree is very great. This is partly because in primitive times and backward countries the sway of custom is more undisputed; partly because, in the absence of scientific history, shortlived man has little better means of ascertaining whether custom is quietly changing, than the fly, born to-day and dead to-morrow, has of watching the growth of the plant on which it rests. But the chief reason is that the conditions of partnership were expressed in terms which were seldom capable of exact definition and measurement.

For the terms of partnership in them were vague, elastic, and capable of unconscious modification in many ways.

For the share of the senior partner in the firm, or the landlord as we may for shortness call him, generally included (either with or without a right to a certain share of the produce) the right to claim certain labour services and dues, tolls and presents; and the amount which he obtained under each of those heads varied from time to time, from place to place, and from one landlord to another. Whenever payments of all kinds made by the cultivator left him a margin beyond the necessaries of life for him and his family, together with those comforts and luxuries which were established by custom, the landlord was likely to use his superior strength to raise the payments in some form or other. If the chief payments were a certain share of the produce, he might increase that share : but, as that could seldom be done without an appearance of violence, he would be more likely to increase the number and weight of his minor imposts, or to insist that the land be more intensively cultivated, and a larger part of it be given to crops that cost much labour and are of great value. Thus changes went on, smoothly for the most part, silently and almost imperceptibly, like the hour-hand of a clock; but in the long run they were very thorough.[1]

The protection which custom afforded to the tenant was not indeed unimportant even as regards these dues. For he always knew pretty well what demands he would have to meet at any particular time. The moral sense of all around him, high and low, protested against any attempt on the part of his landlord to make a sudden and violent increase in the payments and dues, the tolls and fines which were recognized as usual; and thus custom rounded off the edges of change.

It is moreover true that these vague and variable elements of rent were generally but a small part of the whole; and that in those not very rare cases in which the money rent remained fixed for very long periods together, the tenant had a kind of partnership in the soil, which he owed partly to the forbearance of his landlord if it happened that the true net value of the land had risen, but partly also to the constraining force of custom and public opinion. This force in some measure resembled the force which holds raindrops on the lower edge of a window frame : the repose is complete till the window is violently shaken, and then they fall together; and in like way the legal rights of the landlord which had long lain latent were sometimes brought suddenly into action in a period of great economic change.[2]

---

[1] Thus the value of a service of a certain number of days' work would depend partly on the promptness with which the labourer left his own hayfield when called to that of his landlord, and on the energy he put into his work. His own rights, such as that of cutting wood or turf, were elastic ; and so were those of his landlord which bound him to allow flocks of pigeons to devour his crops unmolested, to grind his corn in the lord's mill, and to pay tolls levied on the lord's bridges and in his markets. Next, the fines or presents, or " abwabs " as they are called in India, which the tenant might be called on to pay, were more or less elastic, not only in their amounts but in the occasions on which they were levied. Under the Moguls the tenants in chief had often to pay a vast number of such imposts in addition to their nominally fixed share of the produce : and they passed these on, increased in weight and with additions of their own, to the inferior tenants. The British Government has not levied them itself; but it has not been able, in spite of many efforts, to protect the inferior tenants from them. For instance, in some parts of Orissa, Sir W. W. Hunter found that the tenants had to pay, besides their customary rent, 33 different cesses. They paid whenever one of their children married, they paid for leave to erect embankments, to grow sugar-cane, to attend the festival of Juggernaut, etc. (*Orissa*, I. 55-9.)

[2] In India at the present time we see very various forms of tenure existing side by side, sometimes under the same name and sometimes under different names. There

§ 4. The question whether the payments made by the cultivator for the use of his land should be reckoned in money or in produce

are places in which the raiyats and the superior holders own between them the property in the land subject to definite dues to Government, and where the raiyat is safe not only from being ejected, but also from being compelled by fear of violence to pay over to his superior holder more than that share of the producer's surplus, which custom strictly prescribes. In that case the payment which he makes is, as has already been said, simply the handing over to the other partner in the firm of that share of the receipts of the firm which under the unwritten deed of partnership belongs to him. It is not a rent at all. This form of tenure, however, exists only in those parts of Bengal in which there have been no great recent dislocations of the people, and in which the police are sufficiently active and upright to prevent the superior holders from tyrannizing over the inferior.

In the greater part of India the cultivator holds directly from the Government under a lease the terms of which can be revised at intervals. And the principle on which those leases are arranged, especially in the North-West and North-East, where new land is being settled, is to adjust the annual payments due for it to the probable Surplus Produce of the land, after deducting the cultivator's necessaries and his little luxuries, according to the customary standard of the place, and on the supposition that he cultivates with the energy and skill that are normal in that place. Thus as between man and man in the same place the charge is of the nature of economic rent. But, since unequal charges will be levied in two districts of equal fertility, of which one is cultivated by a vigorous and the other by a feeble population, its method of adjustment as between different districts is rather that of a tax, than a rent. For taxes are supposed to be apportioned to the net income which actually is earned, and rents to that which would be earned by an individual of normal ability : a successful trader will pay on ten times as large an actual income ten times as large a tax as his neighbour who lives in equally advantageous premises and pays equal rents.

The whole history of India records little of that quiet stability which has come over the rural parts of England since war, famine, and plague have ceased to visit us. Extensive movements seem to have been nearly always in progress, partly in consequence of the recurrence of famines (for, as the Statistical Atlas of India shows, there are very few districts which have not been visited at least once by a severe famine during this century); partly of the devastating wars which one set of conquerors after another has inflicted on the patient people; and partly of the rapidity with which the richest land reverts to a thick jungle. The land which has supported the largest population is that which, when deprived of its human inhabitants, most quickly provides shady harbours for wild beasts, for venomous snakes, and for malaria; these prevent the return of the refugees to their old homes, and cause them often to wander far before they settle. When land has been depopulated, those who have the control over it, whether the Government or private persons, offer very favourable terms in order to attract cultivators from elsewhere; this competition for tenants very much influences the relations of cultivators and superior holders for a long distance around them; and therefore, in addition to the changes of customary tenure, which, though impalpable at any time, have been always going on, there have been in almost every place many epochs in which the continuity even of the former custom has been broken and keen competition has reigned supreme.

These disturbing forces of war, famine, and plague were frequent in mediæval England, but their violence was less. And further, the rate of movement of nearly all changes in India has been greater than it would have been if the average period of a generation were as long as in the colder climate of England. Peace and prosperity therefore enable Indian populations to recover from their calamities more quickly; and the traditions which each generation holds of the doings of its fathers and grandfathers run back for a shorter time, so that usages of comparatively recent growth are more easily believed to have the sanction of antiquity. Change can move faster without being recognized as change.

Modern analysis may be applied to the contemporary conditions of land tenure in India and other Oriental countries, the evidence as to which we can examine and cross-examine, in such a way as to throw light on the obscure and fragmentary records of mediæval land tenures, which may indeed be examined, but cannot be cross-examined. There is of course great danger in applying modern methods to primitive conditions : it is easier to misapply them than to apply them rightly. But the assertion, which has been sometimes made, that they cannot be usefully applied at all appears to be based on a conception of the aims, methods and results of analysis, which has little in common with that presented in this, and other modern treatises. See *A Reply* in the *Economic Journal,* Sept. 1892.

is of growing interest with reference to both India and England. VI, x, 4.

But we may pass it by for the present and consider the more funda- *Metayage* mental distinction between the " English " system of rental and *or rental* that of holding land on " shares," as it is called in the New World, *by shares* or the " Metayer " [1] system as it is called in the Old.

In a great part of Latin Europe the land is divided into holdings, *has many* which the tenant cultivates by the labour of himself and his family, *forms in* and sometimes, though rarely, that of a few hired labourers, and *and* for which the landlord supplies buildings, cattle and, sometimes *America.* even, farm implements. In America there are few agricultural tenancies of any kind, but two-thirds of those few are small holdings, let out to white men of the poorer class, or to freed negroes, on some plan by which labour and capital share in the produce.[2]

This plan enables a man who has next to no capital of his own *It offers to* to obtain the use of it at a lower charge than he could in any other *the man* way, and to have more freedom and responsibility than he would *capital* as a hired labourer; and thus the plan has many of the advantages *some of* of the three modern systems of co-operation, profit sharing, and *the ad-* payment by piece-work.[3] But though the metayer has more free- *operative* dom than the hired labourer he has less than the English farmer. *produc-* His landlord has to spend much time and trouble, either of his own *it involves* or of a paid agent, in keeping the tenant to his work; and he must *friction.* charge for these a large sum, which, though going by another name, is really earnings of management. For, when the cultivator has to *If the* give to his landlord half of the returns to each dose of capital and *control* labour that he applies to the land, it will not be to his interest to *of the* apply any doses the total return to which is less than twice enough *slight the*
cultivation
is poor;

[1] The term Metayer applies properly only to cases in which the landlord's share of the produce is one-half; but it is usually applied to all arrangements of this kind whatever the landlord's share be. It must be distinguished from the Stock lease system in which the landlord provided part at least of the stock, but the tenant managed the farm entirely, at his own risk subject to a fixed annual payment to the landlord for land and stock. In mediæval England this system was much used, and the Metayer system appears not to have been unknown. (See Rogers, *Six Centuries of Work and Wages*, ch. x.)

[2] In 1880 74 per cent. of the farms of the United States were cultivated by their owners, 18 per cent., or more than two-thirds of the remainder, were rented for a share of the produce, and only 8 per cent. were held on the English system. The largest proportion of farms that were cultivated by persons other than their owners were in the Southern States. In some cases the landowner—the farmer as he is called there—supplies not only horses and mules, but their feed; and in that case the cultivator—who in France would be called not a Metayer but a Maître Valet—is almost in the position of a hired labourer paid by a share of what he gets; as is for instance a hired fisherman whose pay is the value of a part of the catch. The tenant's share varies from one-third, where the land is rich and the crops such as to require little labour, to four-fifths, where there is much labour and the landlord supplies little capital. There is much to be gained from a study of the many various plans on which the share contract is based.

[3] The relations between publisher and author on the " half-profits " system resemble in many ways those between landlord and metayer.

VI, x, 4. to reward him. If, then, he is free to cultivate as he chooses, he will cultivate far less intensively than on the English plan; he will apply only so much capital and labour as will give him returns more than twice enough to repay himself : so that his landlord will get a smaller share even of those returns than he would have on the plan of a fixed payment.[1]

This is the case in many parts of Europe, in which the tenant has practical fixity of tenure; and then it is only by constant interference that the landlord can keep up the amount of labour he puts on his farm, and keep down the use he makes of the farm cattle for outside work, the fruits of which he does not share with his landlord.

ut if it is ffective he results aay not e very ifferent rom those n the Cnglish lan.

But even in the most stationary districts the amount and quality of the stock which custom requires the landlord to provide are being constantly, though imperceptibly, modified to suit the changing relations of demand and supply. And if the tenant has no fixity of tenure, the landlord can deliberately and freely arrange the amount of capital and labour supplied by the tenant and the amount of capital supplied by himself to suit the exigencies of each special case.[2]

[1] This can be most clearly seen by aid of diagrams of the same kind as those used in IV. III. A *tenant's-share curve* would be drawn standing one-half (or one-third or two-thirds) as high above OD as AC does; the area below that curve would represent the tenant's share, that above the landlord's. OH being, as before, the return required to remunerate the tenant for one dose; he will, if left to his own devices, not carry cultivation beyond the point at which the tenant's-share curve cuts HC : and the landlord's will therefore be a less proportion of the returns to a slighter cultivation than under the English plan. Diagrams of this kind may be used to illustrate the way in which Ricardo's analysis of the causes that govern the Producer's Surplus from land, apply to systems of tenure other than the English. A little further change will adapt them to such customs as those found in Persia, where land itself is of small value; and " the harvest is divided into five parts, which are apportioned as follows, one part to each : 1, land; 2, water for irrigation, etc.; 3, seed; 4, labour; 5, bullocks. The landlord generally owns two, so he gets two-fifths of the harvest."

[2] This is already done in America, and in many parts of France; and some good judges think that the practice may be extended largely, and infuse new life into what a little while ago was regarded as the decaying system of Metayage. If worked out thoroughly, it will result in the cultivation being carried just about as far and affording the landlord the same income as he would have on the English plan for equally fertile and well-situated land equipped with the same capital, and in a place in which the normal ability and enterprise of candidates for farms is the same.

On the elasticity of Metayage in France see an article by Higgs and Lambelin in the *Economic Journal*, March 1894; and Leroy-Beaulieu, *Répartition des Richesses*, ch. IV.

Starting as in the last note, let the Circulating capital supplied by the landlord be represented by the distance OK marked off along OD. Then, if the landlord controls the amount OK freely and in his own interest, and can bargain with his tenant as to the amount of labour he applies, it can be proved geometrically that he will so adjust it as to force the tenant to cultivate the land just as intensively as he would under the English tenure; and his share will then be the same as under it. If he cannot modify the amount OK, but can still control the amount of the tenant's labour, then with certain shapes of the produce curve, the cultivation will be more intensive than it would be on the English plan; but the landlord's share will be somewhat less. This paradoxical result has some scientific interest, but little practical importance.

It is obvious then that the advantages of the metayer system are considerable when the holdings are very small, the tenants poor, and the landlords not averse to taking much trouble about small things : but that it is not suitable for holdings large enough to give scope to the enterprise of an able and responsible tenant. It is commonly associated with the system of peasant proprietorship; and we may consider that next. VI, x, 5.

§ 5. The position of a peasant proprietor has great attractions. He is free to do what he likes, he is not worried by the interference of a landlord, and the anxiety lest another should reap the fruits of his work and self-denial. His feeling of ownership gives him self-respect, and stability of character, and makes him provident and temperate in his habits. He is scarcely ever idle, and seldom regards his work as mere drudgery; it is all for the land that he loves so well. *The peasant proprietor has many virtues and many sources of happiness;*

"The magic of property turns sand into gold," said Arthur Young. It undoubtedly has done so in many cases in which the proprietors have been men of exceptional energy. But such men might perhaps have done as well or better if their horizon had not been limited to the narrow hopes of a peasant proprietor. For indeed there is another side to the picture. "Land," we are told, "is the best savings-bank for the working man." Sometimes it is the second best. But the very best is the energy of himself and his children; and the peasant proprietors are so intent on their land that they often care for little else. Many even of the richest of them stint the food of themselves and their families : they pride themselves on the respectability of their houses and furniture; but they live in their kitchens for economy, and are practically worse housed and far worse fed than the better class of English cottagers. And the poorest of them work hard during very long hours; but they do not get through much work, because they feed themselves worse than the poorest English labourers. They do not understand that wealth is useful only as the means towards a real income of happiness; they sacrifice the end to the means.[1] *but he is wastefully penurious, and is an industrious but inefficient worker.*

And it must be recollected that the English labourers represent the failure rather than the success of the English system. They are the descendants of those who for many successive generations *There are some well-to-do French and*

---

[1] The term "peasant proprietor" is a very vague one : it includes many who by thrifty marriages have collected into one hand the results of several generations of hard work and patient saving; and in France some of these were able to lend freely to the Government after the great war with Germany. But the savings of the ordinary peasant are on a very small scale; and in three cases out of four his land is starved for want of capital : he may have a little money hoarded or invested, but no good grounds have been shown for believing that he often has much.

VI, x, 6.

German peasants, but against them must be set the many rich men in the Old World and the New who are descended from English labourers.

have not availed themselves of the opportunities by which their abler and more adventurous neighbours were rising to leading posts at home, and, what is far more important, were acquiring the fee simple of a great part of the surface of the globe. Of the causes which have contributed to make the English race the chief owners of the New World, the most important is that bold enterprise which has made a man, who is rich enough to be a peasant proprietor, generally refuse to be content with the humdrum life and the narrow income of a peasant. And among the causes which have fostered this enterprise, none is more important than the absence of temptations to wait for a petty inheritance, and to marry for the sake of property rather than in the free exercise of individual choice—temptations which have often dulled the energy of youth in places in which peasant properties have predominated.

The American farmer.

It is partly in consequence of the absence of these temptations that the " farmers " of America, though they are men of the working class cultivating their own land with their own hands, do not resemble "peasant proprietors." They invest their income freely and wisely in developing the energies of themselves and their children; and these energies constitute the chief part of their capital, for their land generally is as yet of but little value. Their minds are always active, and though many of them have little technical knowledge of agriculture, their acuteness and versatility enable them to find out almost unerringly the best solution of the problem immediately before them.

American methods of cultivation.

That problem is generally to obtain a produce large in proportion to the labour spent on it, though small in proportion to the abundant land at their disposal. In some parts of America, however, in which land is beginning to get a scarcity value, and in which the immediate neighbourhood of good markets is making an intensive cultivation profitable, the methods of farming and of tenure are rearranging themselves on the English model. And within the last few years there have been signs of a tendency on the part of native Americans to hand over to persons of recent European origin the farms of the West, as they have already done the farms of the East, and as they did long ago the textile industries.

The English system though somewhat harsh gives great power.

§ 6. Let us then turn to that English system of tenure. It is faulty and harsh in many respects; but it stimulated and economized the enterprise and energy, which, aided by England's geographical advantages and freedom from devastating wars, gave her the leadership of the world in the arts of manufacture and colonization and, though in a less marked degree, in agriculture. England has learnt

lessons in agriculture from many countries and especially the Netherlands; but on the whole she has taught far more than she has learnt.
And there is now no country except the Netherlands which can
compare with her in the amount of produce per acre of fertile land;
and no country in Europe which obtains nearly so high returns in
proportion to the labour expended in getting them.[1]

The chief merit of the system is that it enables the landlord to
keep in his own hands the responsibility for that part and only that
part of the property which he can look after with but little trouble
to himself, and little vexation to his tenant; and the investment of
which, though requiring both enterprise and judgment, does not
demand constant supervision of minor details. His part consists
of land, buildings and permanent improvements, and averages in
England five times that which the farmer has to supply himself;
and he is willing to supply his part in the enterprise with this great
capital at a net rent which seldom gives interest at as much as
three per cent. on its cost. There is no other business in which a
man can borrow what capital he wants at so low a rate, or can often
borrow so large a part of his capital at any rate at all. The metayer
indeed may be said to borrow an even larger share, but at a much
higher rate.[2]

For it enables the landlord to supply that part of the capital for which he can be easily and effectively responsible;

The second merit of the English system, which partly follows
from the first, is that it gives the landlord considerable freedom in
the selection of an able and responsible tenant. So far as the
management of land, as opposed to its ownership, goes, the accident
of birth counts for less in England than in any other country of
Europe. But we have already seen that even in modern England
the accident of birth counts for a good deal in the access to posts of
command in all kinds of business, to the learned professions and
even to skilled manual trades. And it counts for somewhat more
in English agriculture: for the good and bad qualities of landlords

and it gives considerable freedom to the forces of selection.

---

[1] It would seem that England gets more produce per acre of fertile land than even
the Netherlands, though there is some doubt about it. The Netherlands have led
the way for England in more paths of industrial enterprise than any other country
has; and this enterprise has diffused itself from their thickly scattered towns over
the whole land. But there is error in the common opinion that they support as dense
a population as England does, and yet export on the balance a great deal of agricultural
produce. For Belgium imports a great part of her food; and even Holland imports
as much food as she exports, though her non-agricultural population is small. In
France, farm crops and even potatoes are on the average only about half as heavy as
in England proper; and France has only about half the weight of cattle and sheep in
proportion to her area. On the other hand, the small cultivators of France excel in
poultry and fruit and other light branches of production for which her superb climate
is well suited.

[2] For long periods the landlord may be regarded as an active partner and the
predominant partner in the business: for short periods his place is rather that of the
sleeping partner. On the part played by his enterprise compare the Duke of Argyll's
Unseen Foundations of Society, especially p. 374.

VI, x, 7. combine to prevent their selecting tenants on strictly commercial principles, and they do not very often go far afield for a new tenant.[1]

Improvements in agriculture come slowly.

§ 7. The number of people who have the opportunity of making a step forward in the arts of agriculture is very great. And since the different branches of agriculture differ from one another in general character less than do those of manufacture, it might have been expected that new ideas in it would have followed one another quickly and have been speedily diffused. But on the contrary progress has been slow. For the most enterprising agriculturists drift towards the town; those who stay behind live more or less isolated lives; and, as a result of natural selection and education, their minds have always been more staid than those of townsmen, and less ready to suggest or even to follow new paths. And further, though a manufacturer is nearly always safe in copying a plan that has worked well with his neighbour in the same trade, a farmer is not: for every farm has slight peculiarities of its own, so that the blind adoption of a plan, that has worked well close by, is likely to fail; and its failure encourages others in the belief that old and tried ways are the best.

The difficulty of keeping exact farming accounts.

Again, the variety in agricultural detail makes the proper keeping of farming accounts very difficult. There are so many joint products and so many by-products, so many complex and shifting relations of debtor and creditor between the several crops and methods of feeding, that an ordinary farmer, even if he were as fond of accounts as he is in fact averse to them, would have great difficulty in ascertaining, otherwise than by a semi-instinctive guess, what is the price that will just pay him to raise a certain amount of extra produce. He may know its prime cost with fair certainty, but he seldom knows its true total cost; and this increases the difficulty of reading quickly the teachings of experience and making progress by their aid.[2]

---

[1] There is still (1907) considerable difference of opinion as to the extent to which the habits of the landlords combined with the existing system of tenure hinder the formation of new small holdings, which might provide an intelligent labourer with an opportunity for starting an independent business of his own, as easily as the artisan can start a retail shop and repairing business in metal or other goods.

[2] The difficulty is even greater in small holdings. For the capitalist farmer does at all events measure the prime cost in terms of money. But the cultivator working with his own hands often puts into his land as much work as he feels able to do, without estimating carefully its money value in relation to its product.

Although peasant proprietors resemble the heads of other small businesses in their willingness to work harder than those whom they hire and for less reward; yet they differ from the small masters in manufacture in this, that they often do not hire extra labour even when it would pay them well to do so. If all that they and their family can do for their land is less than enough for it, it is generally under-cultivated: if more, it is often cultivated beyond the remunerative limit. It is a common rule that those who give the time which is free from their main occupation to some other industry, often regard their earnings in this last, however low, as an extra gain;

And there is another difference between the mode of action of VI, x, 8.
competition in agriculture and in manufacture. If one manu- Want of
facturer is unenterprising, others may be able to step into the opening ability on
which he leaves vacant : but when one landowner does not develop the part of one
the resources of his land in the best way, others cannot make up undertaker
for the deficiency without calling into play the tendency to diminish- is not com-
pensated
ing return; so that his want of wisdom and enterprise makes the by great
ability on
(marginal) supply price a little higher than it otherwise would be.[1] the part
of others,
It is however true that the difference between the two cases is only as it is
one of degree; since the growth of any branch of manufacture may in manu-
factures.
be retarded perceptibly by any falling-off in the ability and enterprise
of the leading firms engaged in it. The chief agricultural improvements have been made by landlords who have themselves been
townsmen or at least have associated a good deal with townsmen,
and by manufacturers in trades subsidiary to agriculture.[2]

§ 8. Though nature yields generally a less than proportionate Man's
return to an increased amount of labour of a given efficiency; man's part in
agriculture
part conforms generally to the law of increasing return (*i.e.* it in- conforms
creases in aggregate efficiency more than in proportion to the number to the
law of
of workers), in agriculture as well as in manufacture.[3] But yet the increasing
return.
economies of production on a large scale are not quite similar in the
two cases.

Firstly, agriculture must be spread over the broad land : raw Agricul-
material can be brought to the manufacturer for him to work on; ture can-
not be
but the agriculturist must seek his work. Again, the workers on a localized
the land must adapt their work to the seasons, and can seldom nor a
highly
confine themselves entirely to one class of work; and in consequence specialized
agriculture, even under the English system, cannot move fast in industry;
the direction of the methods of manufacture.

But yet there are considerable forces tending to push it in that but there
direction. The progress of invention is constantly increasing the are forces
tending to
number of serviceable, but expensive machines, for most of which a move it to-
small farmer can find employment during only a very short time. wards the
methods
He may hire some of them; but there are many the use of which he of manu-
can get only by co-operation with his neighbours; and the uncer- facture.

---

and they sometimes even work below what would be a starvation wage to those who
depend on that industry for support. This is especially true when the side-industry
is that of cultivating, partly for the pleasure of doing it, a small plot of land with
imperfect appliances.

[1] See VI. ii. 5, and the references given there.

[2] Prothero's *English Farming*, ch. vi. gives some instances of prolonged resistance
to changes, and adds that an Act had to be passed in England as late as 1634 " agaynst
plowynge by the taile."

[3] See IV. iii. 5, 6.

VI, x, 8. tainties of the weather prevent this plan from working very smoothly in practice.[1]

It requires a constantly increasing knowledge.

Again, the farmer must go beyond the results of his own and his father's experience in order to keep abreast of the changes of the day. He should be able to follow the movements of agricultural science and practice closely enough to see their chief practical applications to his own farm. To do all this properly requires a trained and versatile mind; and a farmer who has these qualities could find time to direct the general course of the management of several hundred, or even of several thousand acres; and the mere superintendence of his men's work in matters of detail is not a task fitting for him. The work which he ought to do is as difficult as that of a large manufacturer, who would not spend his own strength on minute supervision which he can easily hire subordinates to do. A farmer, who can do this higher work, must be wasting his strength on work that is beneath him, unless he employs many gangs of workmen each of them under a responsible foreman. But there are not many farms which give scope for this, and there is therefore very little inducement for really able men to enter the business of farming; the best enterprise and ability of the country generally avoid agriculture and go to trades in which there is room for a man of first-rate ability to do nothing but high class work, to do a great deal of it, and therefore to get high earnings of management.[2]

The economies of rather small farms in the work of which the

If it be assumed, as is the modern fashion, that the farmer is not to work habitually with his men and to encourage them by his presence, it seems best for the economy of production that farms should be as large as is practicable under the existing conditions of land tenure; so as to give room for the use of highly specialized

[1] Horse-power is dearer relatively to both steam-power and hand-power in England than in most other countries. England has taken the lead in the improvement of field steam machinery. The cheapness of horse-power tells generally on the side of moderate sized farms *versus* very small ones; but the cheapness of steam-power and "motor" power obtained from petrol, etc., tells on the side of very large farms, except in so far as the use of field steam machinery can be hired economically and at convenient times.

[2] The experiment of working farms on a very large scale is difficult and expensive, because it requires farm buildings and means of communication specially adapted to it; and it may have to overcome a good deal of resistance from custom and sentiment not altogether of an unhealthy kind. The risk also would be great; for in such cases those who pioneer often fail, though their route when well trodden may be found to be the easiest and best.

Our knowledge on many disputed points would be much increased and valuable guidance gained for the future if some private persons, or joint-stock companies, or co-operative associations, would make a few careful experiments of what have been called "Factory farms." On this plan there would be a central set of buildings (there might be more than one) from which roads and even light tramways extended in all directions. In these buildings the recognized principles of factory management would be applied, machinery would be specialized and economized, waste of material would be avoided, by-products would be utilized, and above all the best skill and managing power would be employed, but only for its proper work.

machines and for the exercise of great ability on the part of the farmer. But if a farm is not very large, and if, as is often the case, the farmer has no greater ability and activity of mind than is commonly to be found among the better class of working foremen in manufactures; then it would be best for others, and in the long run for himself, that he should return to the old plan of working among his men. Perhaps also his wife might return to some of those lighter tasks in and near the farmhouse which tradition ascribes to her. They require discretion and judgment, they are not inconsistent with education and culture; and combined with it they would raise and not lower the tone of her life, and her real claims to a good social position. There is some reason for thinking that the stern action of the principle of natural selection is now displacing those farmers, who have not the faculty to do difficult head-work, and yet decline to do hand-work. Their places are being taken by men of more than average natural ability who, with the help of modern education, are rising from the ranks of labourers; who are quite able to manage the ordinary routine work of a model farm; and who are giving to it a new life and spirit by calling their men to come and work, instead of telling them to go and work. Very large farms being left out of view, it is with rather small farms worked on these principles that the immediate future of English agriculture seems to lie. Small holdings have great advantages wherever so much care has to be given to individual plants, that machinery is out of place. But modern applications of scientific methods are giving an increasing importance to that economy of technical skill which can be attained in a large nursery for choice flowers and fruits, with several highly paid assistants.

§ 9. We may next consider how far landlords will in their own interest adjust the size of holdings to the real needs of the people. Small holdings often require more expensive buildings, roads and fences, and involve greater trouble and incidental expenses of management to the landlord in proportion to their acreage than do large holdings; and while a large farmer who has some rich land can turn poor soils to good account, small holdings will not flourish generally except on good soil.[1] Their gross rental per acre must therefore always be at a higher rate than that of large farms. But

Marginal notes: VI, x, 9. farmer and his wife take some share. / The gross rent of small holdings must be high relatively to their acreage.

---

[1] The interpretation of this term varies with local conditions and individual wants. On permanent pasture near a town or an industrial district the advantages of small holdings are perhaps at their maximum, and the disadvantages at their minimum. For small arable holdings the land should not be light, but strong, and the richer the better; and this is especially the case with holdings so small as to make much use of the spade. The small cultivator can often pay his rent most easily where the land is hilly and broken, because there he loses but little from his want of command of machinery.

VI, x, 9. it is contended that, especially when land is heavily burdened by
settlements, landlords are unwilling to incur the expense of sub-
dividing farms, unless they see their way to rents for small holdings

But it is
sometimes
at a
scarcity
value;
that will give them, in addition to high profits on their outlay, a
heavy insurance fund against the chance of having to throw the
holdings together again; and that the rental for small holdings, and
especially for those of only a few acres, is extravagantly high in
many parts of the country. Sometimes the prejudices of the landlord and his desire for undisputed authority make him positively
refuse to sell or let land to persons who are not in harmony with
him on social, political or religious questions. It seems certain that
evils of this kind have always been confined to a few districts, and

and that is
contrary
to the
public
interest.
that they are rapidly diminishing, but they rightly attract much
attention; for there is a public need in every district for small
holdings, as well as large; for allotments and large gardens; and
generally for holdings so small that they can be worked by people
who have some other occupation.[1]

There
should be
no artificial
hindrances
to peas-
ants' pro-
perties.
And lastly though peasant proprietorship, as a system, is unsuited to the economic conditions of England, to her soil, her climate,
and the temper of her people, yet there are a few peasant proprietors
in England who are perfectly happy in this condition; and there
are a few others who would buy small plots of land and would live
happily on them, if they could get just what they wanted where
they wanted it. Their temper is such that they do not mind
working hard and living sparely, provided they need call no one
master; they love quiet and dislike excitement; and they have a
great capacity for growing fond of land. Reasonable opportunity
should be given to such people to invest their savings in small plots
of land, on which they may raise suitable crops with their own hands;
and at the very least the present grievous legal charges on the transfer
of small plots should be diminished.

[1] They increase the number of people who are working in the open air with their
heads and their hands : they give to the agricultural labourer a stepping-stone upwards, prevent him from being compelled to leave agriculture to find some scope for
his ambition, and thus check the great evil of the continued flow of the ablest and
bravest farm lads to the towns. They break the monotony of existence, they give a
healthy change from indoor life, they offer scope for variety of character and for the
play of fancy and imagination in the arrangement of individual life; they afford a
counter attraction to the grosser and baser pleasures; they often enable a family to
hold together that would otherwise have to separate; under favourable conditions
they improve considerably the material condition of the worker; and they diminish
the fretting as well as the positive loss caused by the inevitable interruptions of their
ordinary work.

The evidence before the Committee on small holdings, 1906 [Cd. 3278] discusses very
fully the advantages and disadvantages of ownership for small holders; with apparently a balance of opinion against ownership.

In 1904 there were in Great Britain 111,000 holdings between 1 and 5 acres;
232,000 between 5 and 50 acres; 150,000 between 50 and 300; and 18,000 above
300 acres. See Ib. Appendix II.

Co-operation might seem likely to flourish in agriculture and to combine the economies of production on a large scale with many of the joys and the social gains of small properties. It requires habits of mutual trust and confidence; and unfortunately the bravest and the boldest, and therefore the most trustful, of the countrymen have always moved to the towns, and agriculturists are a suspicious race. But Denmark, Italy, Germany, and lastly Ireland have led the way in a movement which seems full of promise for organized co-operation in the handling of dairy produce, in the making of butter and cheese; in buying farmers' requisites and in selling farmers' produce: and Britain is following in their wake. The movement is however of limited scope: it scarcely touches work in the field itself.

As co-operation might combine more of the advantages of all systems of tenure, so the cottier system of Ireland often combined the disadvantages of all; but its worst evils and their causes have almost disappeared and the economic elements of the problem are just now overshadowed by the political. We must therefore pass it by.[1]

§ 10. The failures of the English system of land tenure in Ireland have brought into clear relief difficulties which are inherent in it, but which have been kept in the background in England by the conformity of the system to the business habits and the character of the people. The chief of these difficulties arise from the fact that while the system is competitive in its essence, the conditions of agriculture even in England offer a strong resistance to the full action of free competition. To begin with, there are special difficulties in ascertaining the facts on which that action must be based. We have just noticed the difficulty of keeping exact farming accounts: to this must be added that a farmer's calculations as to the rent which it is worth his while to undertake to pay, are further hampered by the difficulty of deciding what is a normal harvest and a normal level of prices. For good and bad seasons come so much

Marginal notes:
VI, x, 10.

Co-operation has great opportunities and increasing prospects in agriculture.

The English system of tenure is competitive, but competition does not act easily in agriculture.

Difficulty of deciding what are normal prices and harvests.

---

[1] The Ricardian theory of rent ought to not bear the greater part of the blame that has been commonly thrown on it, for those mistakes which English legislators made during the first half of this century in trying to force the English system of land tenure on India and Ireland. The theory concerns itself with the causes that determine the amount of the Producer's surplus from land at any time; and no great harm was done when this surplus was regarded as the landlord's share, in a treatise written for the use of Englishmen in England. It was an error in jurisprudence and not in economics that caused our legislators to offer to the Bengal tax-collector and Irish landlord facilities for taking to themselves the whole property of a cultivating firm, which consisted of tenant and landlord in the case of Ireland, and in the case of Bengal, of the Government and tenants of various grades; for the tax-collector was in most cases not a true member of the firm, but only one of its servants. But wiser and juster notions are prevailing now in the Government of India as well as of Ireland.

T

VI, x, 10.   in cycles that many years are required to afford a trustworthy average of them : [1] and in those many years the industrial environment is likely to have changed much; the local demand, the facilities for selling his own produce in distant markets and those which assist competitors from a distance to sell their produce in his local markets may all have changed.

Difficulty arising from local variations in the standard of normal farming skill and enterprise.

The landlord in determining what rent to accept is met by this difficulty and also by another, arising out of variations in the standards of ability among farmers in different parts of the country. The producer's surplus, or English rent, of a farm is that excess which its produce yields over its expenses of cultivation, including normal profits to the farmer: it being assumed that that farmer's ability and enterprise are such as are normal for farms of that class *in that place*. The difficulty in view is to decide whether these last words are to be interpreted broadly or narrowly.

Ethical and economic elements are here closely intermingled.

It is clear that if a farmer falls below the standard of ability of his own district, if his only forte is in driving hard bargains, if his gross produce is small and his net produce even smaller in proportion; in such a case the landlord acts in the interest of all when he hands over the farm to a more competent tenant, who will pay better wages, obtain a much higher net produce and pay a somewhat higher rent. On the other hand, when the local standard of normal ability and enterprise is low, it is not clearly right from an ethical point of view, nor is it clearly in the business interests of the landlord in the long run, that he should endeavour to take to himself a greater rent than can be paid by a farmer who reaches that standard; even though it could be obtained by importing a farmer from another district in which the standard is higher.[2]

The tenant's freedom to make and reap the fruits of improvements;

Closely related to this question is one as to the freedom the tenant should have to develop the natural capabilities of his land at his own risk, with the understanding that if he is successful he is to retain something more than mere normal profits on his enterprise. So far as minor improvements go, this difficulty is in a great measure met by long leases. These have done much for Scotland:

---

[1] Compare Tooke and Newmarch, *History of Prices*, Vol. VI. App. III.

[2] Difficulties of this kind are practically solved by compromises which experience has justified, and which are in accordance with the scientific interpretation of the term "normal." If a local tenant showed extraordinary ability, the landlord would be thought grasping who, by threatening to import a stranger, tried to extort a higher rent than the normal local farmer could make the land pay. On the other hand, a farm being once vacant, the landlord would be thought to act reasonably if he imported a stranger who would set a good model to the district, and who shared about equally with the landlord the extra net surplus due to his ability and skill, which, though not strictly speaking exceptional, were yet above the local standard. Compare the action of Settlement Officers in India with regard to equally good land cultivated by energetic and unenergetic races, noticed in the footnote on p. 533–4.

but they have disadvantages of their own. And as has been often VI, x, 10.
observed, " the English tenant has always something of a lease latent
even when he has no lease " : and again, " there are traces of partner-
métayage even in tenures which are thoroughly English." When ship between
seasons and markets are favourable to the farmer, he pays his full tenant and landlord.
rent and avoids making demands on the landlord that might set
him thinking whether the rent ought not to be raised. When
things go badly, the landlord, partly from sympathy and partly as
a matter of business, makes temporary remissions of rent, and bears
the expense of repairs, etc., which he would otherwise have left for
the farmer. There may thus be much give and take between landlord and tenant without any change of nominal rent.[1]

Custom has always given to the English tenant some partial
security for compensation for improvements made by him; and
legislation has recently caught up custom, and even passed it. The
tenant is not practically secure against the raising of his rent on
account of increased yield of the soil due to improvements of a
reasonable nature made by himself : and on leaving he can claim
compensation for the unexhausted value of them, to be fixed by
arbitration.[2]

Finally a word may be said as to private and public interests Conflict
with regard to open spaces in towns. Wakefield and the American between public and
economists have taught us how a sparsely inhabited new district is private in-
enriched by the advent of every new settler. The converse truth is terests in the matter
that a closely peopled district is impoverished by every one who of building
adds a new building or raises an old one higher. The want of air on open spaces.
and light, of peaceful repose out-of-doors for all ages and of healthy
play for children, exhausts the energies of the best blood of England

---

[1] Compare Nicholson, *Tenants' Gain not Landlords' Loss*, ch. x.

[2] The Agricultural Holdings Act of 1883 enforced customs which Mr. Pusey's
committee eulogized, but did not propose to enforce. Many improvements are made
partly at the expense of the landlord and partly at that of the tenant, the former
supplying the materials, and the latter the labour. In other cases it is best that the
landlord should be the real undertaker of the improvements, bearing the whole
expense and risk, and realizing the whole gain. The Act of 1900 recognized this;
and, partly for the sake of simplicity in working, it provided that compensation for
some improvements can be claimed only if they have been made with the consent
of the landlord. In the case of drainage notice of the tenant's wishes must be served
on the landlord; so that he may have the opportunity of himself undertaking the
risks and reaping a share of the accruing benefits. In reference to manuring, and
some kinds of repairs, etc., the tenant may act without consulting the landlord,
merely taking the risk that his outlay will not be regarded by the arbitrator as calling
for compensation.

Under the Act of 1900 the arbitrator was to assign such compensation as would
" represent fairly the value of the improvement to an incoming tenant," after deduction
for any part of that value which might be due to evoking dormant " inherent capabilities of the soil." But this deduction was struck out by the Act of 1906; the
interests of the landlord being regarded as sufficiently secured by the provisions
requiring his consent in some of those cases, in which such dormant capabilities might
be evoked; and by giving him an opportunity of taking the risks himself in the rest.

VI, x, 10. which is constantly flowing towards our large towns. By allowing
vacant spaces to be built on recklessly we are committing a great
blunder from a business point of view. For the sake of a little
material wealth we are wasting those energies which are the factors
of production of all wealth : we are sacrificing those ends towards
which material wealth is only a means.[1]

[1] This matter is further discussed in Appendix G.

CHAPTER XI

GENERAL VIEW OF DISTRIBUTION

§ 1. THE argument of the preceding ten chapters may now be summarized. It falls far short of a complete solution of the problem before us : for that involves questions relating to foreign trade, to fluctuations of credit and employment, and to the influences of associated and collective action in its many forms. But yet it extends to the broad action of the most fundamental and permanent influences which govern distribution and exchange. In the summary at the end of Book V we traced a continuous thread running through and connecting the applications of the general theory of equilibrium of demand and supply to different periods of time; from those so short that cost of production could exercise no direct influence on value, to those so long that the supply of the appliances of production could be fairly well adjusted to the indirect demand for them, which is derived from the direct demand for the commodities which they produce. In the present Book we have been concerned with another thread of continuity, which lies transversely to the thread connecting different periods of time. It connects the various agents and appliances for production, material and human; and establishes a fundamental unity between them, in spite of their important differences of outward feature.

Firstly, wages and other earnings of effort have much in common with interest on capital. For there is a general correspondence between the causes that govern the supply prices of material and of personal capital : the motives which induce a man to accumulate personal capital *in* his son's education, are similar to those which control his accumulation of material capital *for* his son. There is a continuous transition from the father who works and waits in order that he may bequeath to his son a rich and firmly-established manufacturing or trading business, to one who works and waits in order to support his son while he is slowly acquiring a thorough medical education, and ultimately to buy for him a lucrative practice. Again, there is the same continuous transition from him to one who works and waits in order that his son may stay long at school; and may afterwards work for some time almost without pay while learning a skilled trade, instead of being forced to support himself early in an occupation, such as that of an errand-boy, which offers comparatively high wages to young lads, because it does not lead the way to a future advance.

in spite of important differences. It is indeed true that the only persons, who, as society is now constituted, are very likely to invest much in developing the personal capital of a youth's abilities are his parents : and that many first-rate abilities go for ever uncultivated because no one, who can develop them, has had any special interest in doing so. This fact is very important practically, for its effects are cumulative. But it does not give rise to a fundamental difference between material and human agents of production : for it is analogous to the fact that much good land is poorly cultivated because those who would cultivate it well have not access to it.

Again, since human beings grow up slowly and are slowly worn out, and parents in choosing an occupation for their children must as a rule look forward a whole generation, changes in demand take a longer time to work out their full effects on supply in the case of human agents than of most kinds of material appliances for production; and a specially long period is required in the case of labour to give full play to the economic forces which tend to bring about a normal adjustment between demand and supply. Thus on the whole the *money* cost of any kind of labour to the employer corresponds in the long run fairly well to the *real* cost of producing that labour.[1]

Business men weigh the services of the different industrial classes; and thus give effect to the principle of substitution; § 2. The efficiency of human agents of production on the one hand, and that of material agents on the other, are weighed against one another and compared with their *money* costs; and each tends to be applied as far as it is more efficient than the other in proportion to its money cost. A chief function of business enterprise is to facilitate the free action of this great principle of substitution. Generally to the public benefit, but sometimes in opposition to it, business men are constantly comparing the services of machinery, and of labour, and again of unskilled and skilled labour, and of extra foremen and managers; they are constantly devising and experimenting with new arrangements which involve the use of different factors of production, and selecting those most profitable for themselves.[2]

The efficiency as compared with the cost of almost every class of labour, is thus continually being weighed in the balance in one

[1] Compare IV. v. VI. VII. and XII.; and VI. IV. v. and VII.
[2] Compare V. III. 3; and VI. VII. 2.

or more branches of production against some other classes of labour :
and each of these in its turn against others. This competition is
primarily " vertical " : it is a struggle for the field of employment
between groups of labour belonging to different grades, but engaged
in the same branch of production, and inclosed, as it were, between
the same vertical walls. But meanwhile " horizontal " competition
is always at work, and by simpler methods : for, firstly, there is
great freedom of movement of adults from one business to another
within each trade; and secondly, parents can generally introduce
their children into almost any other trade of the same grade with
their own in their neighbourhood. By means of this combined
vertical and horizontal competition there is an effective and closely
adjusted balance of payments to services as between labour in
different grades; in spite of the fact that the labour in any one
grade is mostly recruited even now from the children of those in the
same grade.[1]

The working of the principle of substitution is thus chiefly which is
indirect. When two tanks containing fluid are joined by a pipe, in the
the fluid, which is near the pipe in the tank with the higher level, long run.
will flow into the other, even though it be rather viscous; and thus
the general levels of the tanks will tend to be brought together,
though no fluid may flow from the further end of the one to the
further end of the other; and if several tanks are connected by
pipes, the fluid in all will tend to the same level, though some tanks
have no direct connection with others. And similarly the principle
of substitution is constantly tending by indirect routes to apportion
earnings to efficiency between trades, and even between grades,
which are not directly in contact with one another, and which
appear at first sight to have no way of competing with one another.

§ 3. There is no breach of continuity as we ascend from the But as
unskilled labourer to the skilled, thence to the foreman, to the head the work
of a department, to the general manager of a large business paid of business
partly by a share of the profits, to the junior partner, and lastly to selves
the head partner of a large private business : and in a joint-stock substitu-
company there is even somewhat of an anti-climax when we pass highly
from the directors to the ordinary shareholders, who undertake the organized.
chief ultimate risks of the business. Nevertheless business undertakers are to a certain extent a class apart.

For while it is through their conscious agency that the principle
of substitution chiefly works in balancing one factor of production
against another; with regard to them it has no other agency than

[1] Compare IV. VI. 7; and VI. v. 2.

VI, xi, 3. the indirect influence of their own competition. So it works blindly, or rather wastefully; it forces many to succumb who might have done excellent work if they had been favoured at first : and, in conjunction with the tendency to increasing return, it strengthens those who are strong, and hands over the businesses of the weak to those who have already obtained a partial monopoly.

But on the other hand there is also a constant increase in the forces which tend to break up old monopolies, and to offer to men, who have but little capital of their own, openings both for starting new businesses and for rising into posts of command in large public and private concerns; and these forces tend to put business ability in command of the capital required to give it scope.

Their work may be done more cheaply hereafter, but it is worth to society even now more than it costs.
On the whole the work of business management is done cheaply —not indeed as cheaply as it may be in the future when men's collective instincts, their sense of duty and their public spirit are more fully developed; when society exerts itself more to develop the latent faculties of those who are born in a humble station of life, and to diminish the secrecy of business; and when the more wasteful forms of speculation and of competition are held in check. But yet it is done so cheaply as to contribute to production more than the equivalent of its pay. For the business undertaker, like the skilled artisan, renders services which society needs, and which it would probably have to get done at a higher cost if he were not there to do them.

Contrasts between fluctuations of current profits and wages.
The similarity between the causes that determine the normal rewards of ordinary ability on the one hand, and of business power in command of capital on the other, does not extend to the fluctuations of their current earnings. For the employer stands as a buffer between the buyer of goods and all the various classes of labour by which they are made. He receives the whole price of the one and pays the whole price of the others. The fluctuations of his profits go with fluctuations of the prices of the things he sells, and are more extensive : while those of the wages of his employees come later and are less extensive. The earnings at any particular time of his capital and ability are sometimes large, but sometimes also a negative quantity : whereas those of the ability of his employees are never very large, and are never a negative quantity. The wage-receiver is likely to suffer much when out of work; but that is because he has no reserve, not because he is a wage-receiver.[1]

The income
That part of a man's income which he owes to the possession of extraordinary natural abilities is a free boon to him; and from an

[1] Compare V. ii. 3, and VI. iv. 6, and viii. 7-9.

abstract point of view bears some resemblance to the rent of other free gifts of nature, such as the inherent properties of land. But in reference to normal prices, it is to be classed rather with the profits derived by free settlers from the cultivation of new land, or again with the find of the pearl-fisher. The plot of one settler turns out better and that of another worse than was expected; the good find of one dive of the pearl-fisher compensates for many others that are fruitless : and the high income which one barrister, or engineer, or trader earns by his natural genius has to be counted with the comparative failures of many others; who perhaps appeared of no less promise when young and received as costly an education and start in life, but whose services to production were less than his in proportion to their cost. The ablest business men are generally those who get the highest profits, and at the same time do their work most cheaply; and it would be as wasteful if society were to give their work to inferior people who would undertake to do it more cheaply, as it would be to give a valuable diamond to be cut by a low waged but unskilled cutter.

§ 4. Returning to the point of view of the second Chapter of this Book, we may call to mind the double relation in which the various agents of production stand to one another. On the one hand they are often rivals for employment; any one that is more efficient than another in proportion to its cost tending to be substituted for it, and thus limiting the demand price for the other. And on the other hand they all constitute the field of employment for each other : there is no field of employment for any one, except in so far as it is provided by the others : the national dividend which is the joint product of all, and which increases with the supply of each of them, is also the sole source of demand for each of them.

Thus an increase of material capital causes it to push its way into new uses; and though in so doing it may occasionally diminish the field of employment for manual labour in a few trades, yet on the whole it will very much increase the demand for manual labour and all other agents of production. For it will much increase the national dividend, which is the common source of the demand for all; and since by its increased competition for employment it will have forced down the rate of interest, therefore the joint product of a dose of capital and labour will now be divided more in favour of labour than before.

This new demand for labour will partly take the form of the opening-out of new undertakings which hitherto could not have paid their way; while a new demand will come from the makers of

Margin notes:

VI, XI, 4.

derived from rare natural abilities.

The various agents of production are the sole source of employment for one another.

How an increase of capital enriches the field for the employment of labour.

VI, xi, 5.   new and more expensive machinery. For when it is said that machinery is substituted for labour, this means that one class of labour combined with much waiting is substituted for another combined with less waiting : and for this reason alone, it would be impossible to substitute capital for labour in general, except indeed locally by the importation of capital from other places.

It remains true, however, that the chief benefit which an increase of capital confers upon labour is not by opening out to it new employments, but by increasing the joint product of land, labour and capital (or of land, labour and waiting), and by reducing the share of that product which any given amount of capital (or of waiting) can claim as its reward.

If any group of workers becomes more efficient its wages rise and other wages rise also : if it becomes more numerous its wages fall while other wages rise. § 5. In discussing the influence which a change in the supply of work of any one industrial group exerts on the field of employment for other kinds of labour, there was no need to raise the question whether the increase of work came from an increase in the numbers or in the efficiency of those in the group : for that question is of no direct concern to the others. In either case there is the same addition to the national dividend : in either case competition will compel them to force themselves to the same extent into uses in which their marginal utility is lower; and will thus lessen to the same extent the share of the joint product which they are able to claim in return for a given amount of work of a given kind.

But the question is of vital importance to the members of that group. For, if the change is an increase of one-tenth in their average efficiency, then each ten of them will have as high an aggregate income as each eleven of them would have if their numbers had increased by one-tenth, their efficiency remaining unchanged.[1]

This and other influences of the environment on wages take part in governing the net product of the worker of normal efficiency to which normal wages approximate. This dependence of the wages of each group of workers on the numbers and efficiency of others is a special case of the general rule that the environment (or *Conjuncture*) plays a part at least co-ordinate with a man's energy and ability in governing that net product to which his wages ever approximate under the influence of competition.

The net product to which the normal wages of any group of workers approximate, must be estimated on the assumption that production has been pushed to that limit at which the output can be just marketed with normal profits, but not more : and it must

[1] Suppose, for instance, that an increase in the supply of work of the group by one-tenth forced them into work in which their marginal uses were lower, and thus lowered by a thirtieth their wages for any given amount of work; then, if the change came from an increase in their numbers, their average wages would fall by a thirtieth. But if it came from an increase in their efficiency, their wages would rise by about a sixteenth. (More exactly they would be $\frac{11}{10} \times \frac{29}{30} = 1\frac{19}{300}$ of what they were before.)

be estimated with reference to a worker of normal efficiency; whose VI, XI, 5. additional output repays an employer of normal ability and normal good fortune and normal resources with normal profits, but not more. (Something must be added to or subtracted from this net product to find the normal wages of a worker whose efficiency is more or less than normal.) The time chosen must be one of normal prosperity; and when the supplies of different kinds of labour are relatively appropriate. For instance if the building trade is exceptionally depressed, or exceptionally prosperous : or if its development is checked by an inadequate supply of bricklayers or carpenters, while the supply of other classes of building operatives is superabundant, then the occasion is one which does not afford a convenient opportunity for estimating the relations of net product to normal wages of either bricklayers or carpenters.[1]

---

[1] As regards the relation between wages and the marginal net product of labour see VI. I. and II. and especially pp. 427–9 and 446–8 : the matter is further discussed in VI. XIII. especially p. 588 n. As regards the need to seek a truly representative margin see V. VIII. 4, 5 : where it is argued (p. 339 n.) that when that has been reached, the influence of the supply of any group of workers on the wages of others has already been reckoned : and that the influence which any one individual worker exerts on the general economic environment of the industries of a country is infinitesimal, and is not relevant to an estimate of his net product in relation to his wages. In V. XII. and Appendix H something is said of the hindrances to a rapid increase of output even where such an increase would theoretically yield great economies; and of the special care needed in the use of the term " margin " in regard to them.

CHAPTER XII

GENERAL INFLUENCES OF ECONOMIC PROGRESS

VI, xii, 1.

The field of employment for capital and labour

§ 1. The field of employment which any place offers for labour and capital depends, firstly, on its natural resources; secondly, on the power of turning them to good account, derived from its progress of knowledge and of social and industrial organization; and thirdly, on the access that it has to markets in which it can sell those things of which it has a superfluity. The importance of this last condition is often underrated; but it stands out prominently when we look at the history of new countries.

is not always rich in new countries which have no good access to the markets of the old world.

It is commonly said that wherever there is abundance of good land to be had free of rent, and the climate is not unhealthy, the real earnings of labour and the interest on capital must both be high. But this is only partially true. The early colonists of America lived very hardly. Nature gave them wood and meat almost free: but they had very few of the comforts and luxuries of life. And even now there are, especially in South America and Africa, many places to which nature has been abundantly generous, which are nevertheless shunned by labour and capital, because they have no ready communications with the rest of the world. On the other hand high rewards may be offered to capital and labour by a mining district in the midst of an alkaline desert, when once communications have been opened up with the outer world, or again by a trading centre on a barren sea-coast; though, if limited to their own resources, they could support but a scanty population, and that in abject poverty. And the splendid markets which the old world has offered to the products of the new, since the growth of steam communication have rendered North America, Australia and parts of Africa and South America, the richest large fields for the employment of capital and labour that there have ever been.

Old countries offer a market for mortgages of the future incomes of a new country,

But after all the chief cause of the modern prosperity of new countries lies in the markets that the old world offers, not for goods delivered on the spot, but for promises to deliver goods at a distant date. A handful of colonists having assumed rights of perpetual property in vast tracts of rich land, are anxious to reap in their own generation its future fruits; and as they cannot do this directly, they do it indirectly, by selling in return for the ready goods of the old world promises to pay much larger quantities of the goods that their own soil will produce in a future generation. In one form or another they mortgage their new property to the old world at a very high rate of interest. Englishmen and others, who have accumulated the means of present enjoyment, hasten to barter them for larger promises in the future than they can get at home : a vast stream of capital flows to the new country, and its arrival there raises the rate of wages very high. The new capital filters but slowly towards the outlying districts : it is so scarce there, and there are so many persons eager to have it, that it often commands for a long time two per cent. a month, from which it falls by gradual stages down to six, or perhaps even five per cent., a year. For the settlers being full of enterprise, and seeing their way to acquiring private title-deeds to property that will shortly be of great value, are eager to become independent undertakers, and if possible employers of others; so wage-earners have to be attracted by high wages, which are paid in a great measure out of the commodities borrowed from the old world on mortgages, or in other ways.

VI, xii, 1.

and the consequent influx of capital into the latter

raises daily wages very high;

It is, however, difficult to estimate exactly the real rate of wages in outlying parts of new countries. The workers are picked men with a natural bias towards adventure; hardy, resolute, and enterprising; men in the prime of life, who do not know what illness is; and the strain of one kind and another which they go through, is more than the average English, and much more than the average European labourer could sustain. There are no poor among them, because there are none who are weak : if anyone becomes ailing, he is forced to retire to some more thickly-peopled place where there is less to be earned, but where also a quieter and less straining life is possible. Their earnings are very high if reckoned in money; but they have to buy at very high prices, or altogether dispense with, many of the comforts and luxuries which they would have obtained freely, or at low prices, if they had lived in more settled places. Many of these things however meet only artificial wants; and they can be easily foregone, where no one has them and no one expects them.

but labour is efficient, and therefore not dear.

As population increases, the best situations being already occupied, nature gives generally less return of raw produce to the marginal effort of the cultivators; and this tends a little to lower wages. But even in agriculture the law of increasing return is constantly contending with that of diminishing return, and many of the lands

As time goes on, though the tendency to diminishing return

VI, xii, 1.
may not be
acting very
strongly,

which were neglected at first give a generous response to careful cultivation; and meanwhile the development of roads and railroads, and the growth of varied markets and varied industries, render possible innumerable economies in production. Thus the tendencies to increasing and diminishing return appear pretty well balanced, sometimes the one, sometimes the other being the stronger.

If labour and capital increase at equal rates; and if, taking one thing with another, the law of production is that of constant return, there will be no change in the reward to be divided between a dose of capital and labour; that is, between capital and labour working together in the same proportions as before; there need not therefore be any change in wages or interest.

If however capital increases much faster than labour, the rate of interest is likely to fall; and then the rate of wages will probably rise at the expense of the share of a given quantum of capital. But yet the aggregate share of capital may increase faster than the aggregate share of labour.[1]

the influx
of capital
becomes
relatively
slower and
wages tend
to fall.

But whether the law of production of commodities be one of constant return or not, that of the production of new title-deeds to land is one of rapidly diminishing return. The influx of foreign capital, though perhaps as great as ever, becomes less in proportion to the population; wages are no longer paid largely with commodities borrowed from the old world: and this is the chief reason of the subsequent fall in the necessaries, comforts and luxuries of life which can be earned by work of a given efficiency. But two other causes tend to lower average daily wages measured in money. For, as the comforts and luxuries of civilization increase, the average efficiency of labour is generally lowered by the influx of immigrants of a less sturdy character than the earlier settlers : and

---

[1] Suppose for instance that an amount of capital, c, co-operating with an amount of labour, l, had raised a product $4p$; of which p goes as interest to capital, and the remaining $3p$ to labour. (The labour is of many grades, including management, but it is all referred to a common standard in a day's unskilled labour of given efficiency : see above IV. iii. 8.) Suppose that the quantity of labour has doubled, and that of capital has quadrupled : while the absolute efficiency in production of any given amount of each of the agents has not changed. Then we may expect $4c$ in co-operation with $2l$ to produce $2 \times 3p + 4p = 10p$. Now suppose the rate of interest, i.e. the reward for any quantum of capital (exclusive that is of the work of management etc.) to have fallen to two-thirds of its original amount; so that $4c$ receives only $\frac{8}{3}p$ instead of $4p$ as interest; then there will be left for labour of all kinds $7\frac{1}{3}p$ instead of $6p$. The amount, that goes to each quantum of capital, will have decreased; and that which goes to each quantum of labour, will have increased. But the aggregate amount that goes to capital will have increased in the ratio of $8 : 3$; while that which goes to labour will have increased in the lower ratio of $22 : 9$.

It is best in such matters to isolate *interest*, but, of course, we might have spoken of profits instead of interest, and contrasted the share of capitalists (rather than capital) with that of hired labour.

many of these new comforts and luxuries do not enter directly into money wages, but are an addition to it.[1]

§ 2. England's present economic condition is the direct result of tendencies to production on a large scale, and to wholesale dealings in labour as well as in goods which had long been slowly growing; but which in the eighteenth century received a twofold impetus from mechanical inventions, and the growth of consumers beyond the seas, who imported large quantities of goods of the same pattern. Then were the first beginnings of machine made interchangeable parts, and the application of special machinery to make special machinery for use in every branch of industry. Then first was seen the full force which the law of increasing return gives in a manufacturing country with localized industries and large capitals; particularly when many of the large stocks of capital are combined together either into Joint-stock or Regulated companies, or into modern Trusts. And then began that careful " grading " of goods for sale in distant markets, which has already led to national and even international speculative combinations in produce markets and stock-exchanges; and the future of which, no less than that of more lasting combinations among producers, whether undertakers of industry or working men, is the source of some of the gravest practical problems with which the coming generation will have to deal.

They key-notes of the modern movement are the reduction of a great number of tasks to one pattern; the diminution of friction of every kind which might hinder powerful agencies from combining their action and spreading their influence over vast areas; and the development of transport by new methods and new forces. The macadamized roads and the improved shipping of the eighteenth century broke up local combinations and monopolies, and offered facilities for the growth of others extending over a wider area : and in our own age the same double tendency is resulting from every new extension and cheapening of communication by land and sea, by printing-press and telegraph and telephone.

§ 3. But though in the eighteenth century, as now, the real national dividend of England depended much on the action of the

VI, XII, 2, 3.

England's present industrial problems are a development of those of the eighteenth century.

The key-notes of the modern movement.

In the eighteenth

---

[1] We took account of them when arriving at the conclusion that the tendency to increasing return would on the whole countervail that to diminishing return : and we ought to count them in at their full value when tracing the changes in real wages. Many historians have compared wages at different epochs with exclusive reference to those things which have always been in common consumption. But from the nature of the case, these are just the things to which the law of diminishing return applies, and which tend to become scarce as population increases, and the view thus got is therefore one-sided and misleading in its general effect.

VI, xii, 3.
century foreign trade affected chiefly that part of the national dividend which consisted of comforts and luxuries.

law of increasing return with regard to her exports, the mode of dependence has very much changed. Then England had something approaching to a monopoly of the new methods of manufacture; and each bale of her goods would be sold—at all events when their supply was artificially limited—in return for a vast amount of the produce of foreign countries. But, partly because the time was not yet ripe for carrying bulky goods great distances, her imports from the far-east and the far-west consisted chiefly of comforts and luxuries for the well-to-do; they had but little direct effect in lowering the labour-cost of necessaries to the English workman. Indirectly indeed her new trade lowered the cost of hardware, clothing and such other English manufactures as he consumed; because the production on a large scale of these things for consumers beyond the sea cheapened them for him. But it had very little effect on the cost of his food; and that was left to rise under the tendency to diminishing return, which was called into action by the rapid increase of population in new manufacturing districts where the old customary restraints of a narrow village life did not exist. A little later the great French war, and a series of bad harvests, raised that cost to much the highest point it has ever reached in Europe.

But now it gives England an immense command over necessaries.

But gradually the influence of foreign trade began to tell on the cost of production of our staple food. As the population of America spread westward from the Atlantic, richer and still richer wheat soils have come under cultivation; and the economies of transport have increased so much, especially in recent years, that the total cost of importing a quarter of wheat from the farms on the outskirts of cultivation has diminished rapidly, though the distance of that margin has been increasing. And thus England has been saved from the need of more and more intensive cultivation. The bleak hill-sides, up which the wheat-fields were laboriously climbing in Ricardo's time, have returned to pasture; and the ploughman works now only where land will yield plentiful returns to his labour: whereas if England had been limited to her own resources, he must have plodded over ever poorer and poorer soils, and must have gone on continually reploughing land that had already been well ploughed, in the hope of adding by this heavy toil an extra bushel or two to the produce of each acre. Perhaps in an average year now, the ploughing which only just pays its expenses, the ploughing " on the margin of cultivation," gives twice as much produce as it gave in Ricardo's time, and fully five times as much as it would have given now if with her present population England had been compelled to raise all her own food.

§ 4. Every improvement in the manufacturing arts increased England's power of meeting the various wants of backward countries; so that it answered their purpose to divert their energies from making things by hand for their own use, to growing raw material with which to buy manufactures from her. In this way the progress of invention opened a wider field for the sale of her special products, and enabled her more and more to confine her own production of food to conditions under which the law of diminishing return did not make itself much felt. But this good fortune has been short-lived. Her improvements have been followed, and latterly often anticipated, by America and Germany and other countries: and her special products have lost nearly all their monopoly value. Thus the amount of food and other raw material which can be bought in America with a ton of steel cannot be more than the produce of as much capital and labour as would make a ton of steel there by the new processes; and therefore it has fallen as the efficiency of English and American labour in making steel has increased. It is for this reason, as well as because of the heavy tariffs levied on her goods by many countries, that in spite of England's large trade, the progress of invention in the manufacturing arts has added less than might have been otherwise expected to her real national dividend.

VI, XII, 4, 5.

England has gained less than at first appears from the recent improvements in manufactures.

It is no slight gain that she can make cheaply clothes and furniture and other commodities for her own use: but those improvements in the arts of manufacture which she has shared with other nations, have not directly increased the amount of raw produce which she can obtain from other countries with the product of a given quantity of her own capital and labour. Probably more than three-fourths of the whole benefit she has derived from the progress of manufactures during the nineteenth century has been through its indirect influences in lowering the cost of transport of men and goods, of water and light, of electricity and news: for the dominant economic fact of our own age is the development not of the manufacturing, but of the transport industries. It is these that are growing most rapidly in aggregate volume and in individual power, and which are giving rise to the most anxious questions as to the tendencies of large capitals to turn the forces of economic freedom to the destruction of that freedom: but, on the other hand, it is they also which have done by far the most towards increasing England's wealth.

Her highest gains have come from the cheapening of transport of various kinds.

§ 5. Thus the new economic age has brought with it great changes in the relative values of labour and the chief requisites of life; and

Some of the influences

VI, xii, 5.
of progress
on the
normal
labour-
values:
firstly, of
the chief
requisites
of a
civilized
life, viz.
corn,

many of these changes are of a character which could not have been anticipated at the beginning of last century. The America then known was ill-suited for growing wheat; and the cost of carrying it great distances by land was prohibitive. The labour value of wheat —that is the amount of labour which will purchase a peck of wheat —was then at its highest point, and now is at its lowest. It would appear that agricultural wages have been generally below a peck of wheat a day; but that in the first half of the eighteenth century they were about a peck, in the fifteenth a peck and a half or perhaps a little more, while now they are two or three pecks. Prof. Rogers's estimates for the middle ages are higher : but he seems to have taken the wages of the more favoured part of the population as representative of the whole. In the middle ages, even after a fairly good harvest, the wheat was of a lower quality than the ordinary wheat of to-day; while after a bad harvest much of it was so musty that now-a-days it would not be eaten at all; and the wheat seldom became bread without paying a high monopoly charge to the mill belonging to the lord of the manor.

It is true that, where population is very sparse, nature supplies grass and therefore animal food almost *gratis*; and in South America beggars pursue their calling on horseback. During the middle ages however the population of England was always dense enough to give a considerable labour value to meat, though it was of poor quality. For cattle, though only about a fifth as heavy as now, had very large frames : their flesh was chiefly in those parts from which the coarsest joints come; and since they were nearly starved in the winter and fed up quickly on the summer grass, the meat contained a large percentage of water, and lost a great part of its weight in cooking. At the end of the summer they were slaughtered and salted : and salt was dear. Even the well-to-do scarcely tasted fresh meat during the winter. A century ago very little meat was eaten by the working classes; while now, though its price is a little higher than it was then, they probably consume more of it, on the average, than at any other time in English history.

Turning next to the rent of house-room, we find that ground-rents in town have risen, both extensively and intensively. For an increasing part of the population is living in houses on which ground-rents at an urban scale have to be paid, and that scale is rising. But house rent proper, that is what remains of the total rent after deducting the full rental value of the ground, is probably little, if at all, higher than at any previous time for similar accommodation; for the rate of profits on the turnover which is earned by capital engaged in building is now low, and the labour cost of building vi, xii, 5. materials has not much altered. And it must be remembered that those who pay the high town rents get in return the amusements and other advantages of modern town life, which many of them would not be willing to forego for the sake of a much greater gain than their total rent.

The labour value of wood, though lower than at the beginning of the century, is higher than in the middle ages : but that of mud, brick or stone walls has not much changed; while that of iron—to say nothing of glass—has fallen much.

And indeed the popular belief that house rent proper has risen, appears to be due to an imperfect acquaintance with the way in which our forefathers were really housed. The modern suburban artisan's cottage contains sleeping accommodation far superior to that of the gentry in the middle ages; and the working classes had then no other beds than loose straw, reeking with vermin, and resting on damp mud floors. Even these were probably less unwholesome, when bare and shared between human beings and live stock, than when an attempt at respectability covered them with rushes, which were nearly always vile with long accumulated refuse : but it is undeniable that the housing of the very poorest classes in our towns now is destructive both of body and soul; and that with our present knowledge and resources we have neither cause nor excuse for allowing it to continue.[1]

Fuel, like grass, is often a free gift of nature to a sparse popula- fuel, tion; and during the middle ages the cottagers could generally, though not always, get the little brushwood fire needed to keep them warm as they huddled together round it in huts which had no chimney through which the heat could go to waste. But as population increased the scarcity of fuel pressed heavily on the working classes, and would have arrested England's progress altogether, had not coal been ready to take the place of wood as fuel for domestic purposes, as well as for smelting iron. It is now so cheap that even the comparatively poor can keep themselves warm indoors without living in an unwholesome and stupefying atmosphere.

This is one of the great services that coal has wrought for modern clothing, civilization. Another is to provide cheap underclothing, without which cleanliness is impossible for the masses of the people in a cold

---

[1] The evils of the past were however greater than is commonly supposed. See e.g. the striking evidence of the late Lord Shaftesbury and of Miss Octavia Hill upon the Commission on Housing of 1885. London air is full of smoke; but it is probably less unwholesome than it was before the days of scientific sanitation, even though the population was then relatively small.

VI, XII, 6.   climate : and that is perhaps the chief of the benefits that England has gained from the direct application of machinery to making commodities for her own use.   Another, and not less important service, is to provide abundant water, even in large towns; [1] and another to supply, with the aid of mineral oil, that cheap and artificial light which is needed not only for some of man's work, but, what is of higher moment, for the good use of his evening leisure.   To this group of requisites for a civilized life, derived from coal on the one hand, and modern means of transport on the other, we must add, as has just been noticed, the cheap and thorough means of communication of news and thought by steam-presses, by steam-carried letters and steam-made facilities for travel.   These agencies, aided by electricity, are rendering possible the civilization of the masses in countries the climate of which is not so warm as to be enervating; and are preparing the way for true self-government and united action by the whole people, not merely of a town such as Athens, Florence or Bruges, but a broad country, and even in some respects of the whole civilized world.[2]

water, light,

news and travel.

The influence of progress on the values of the chief agents of production :

§ 6. We have seen that the national dividend is at once the aggregate net product of, and the sole source of payment for, all the agents of production within the country; that the larger it is, the larger, other things being equal, will be the share of each agent of production, and that an increase in the supply of any agent will generally lower its price, to the benefit of other agents.

it has sometimes lowered the value of English agricultural land,

This general principle is specially applicable to the case of land. An increase in the amount of productiveness of the land that supplies any market redounds in the first instance to the benefit of those capitalists and workers who are in possession of other agents of production for the same market.   And the influence on values which has been exerted in the modern age by the new means of transport is nowhere so conspicuous as in the history of land; its value rises with every improvement in its communications with markets in which its produce can be sold, and its value falls with every new access to its own markets of produce from more distant places.   It is not very long ago that the home counties were full of fears that the making of good roads would enable the more distant parts of England to compete with them in supplying London with food; and now the differential advantages of English farms are in some

---

[1] Primitive appliances will bring water from high ground to a few public fountains : but the omnipresent water supply which both in its coming and its going performs essential services for cleanliness and sanitation, would be impossible without coal-driven steam-pumps and coal-made iron pipes.

[2] See Appendix A, especially § 6.

respects being lowered by the importation of food that has travelled VI, XII, 7.
on Indian and American railroads, and been carried in ships made
of steel and driven by steam turbines.

But as Malthus contended, and Ricardo admitted, anything that but not of
promotes the prosperity of the people promotes also in the long run agricul-
that of the landlords of the soil. It is true that English rents rose urban land
very fast when, at the beginning of last century, a series of bad together.
harvests struck down a people that could not import their food;
but a rise so caused could not from the nature of the case have gone
very much further.   And the adoption of free trade in corn in the
middle of the century, followed by the expansion of American wheat-
fields, is rapidly raising the real value of the land urban and rural
taken together; that is, it is raising the amount of the necessaries,
comforts and luxuries of life which can be purchased by the aggregate
rental of all the landowners urban and rural taken together.[1]

§ 7. But though the development of the industrial environment Progress
tends on the whole to raise the value of land, it more often than not the value
lessens the value of machinery and other kinds of fixed capital, in so of the
far as their value can be separated from that of the sites on which of produc-
they rest. A sudden burst of prosperity may indeed enable the tion where
existing stock of appliances in any trade to earn for a time a very separated
high income. But things which can be multiplied without limit of their
cannot retain for long a scarcity value; and if they are fairly durable, sites;
as for instance ships and blast furnaces and textile machinery, they
are likely to suffer great depreciation from the rapid progress of
improvement.

The value of such things as railways and docks however depends but not if
in the long run chiefly on their situation. If that is good, the of their
progress of their industrial environment will raise their net value sites is
even after allowance has been made for the charges to which they in.
may be put in keeping their appliances abreast of the age.[2]

---

[1] Mr. W. Sturge (in an instructive paper read before the Institute of Surveyors,
Dec. 1872) estimates that the agricultural (money) rent of England doubled between
1795 and 1815, and then fell by a third till 1822; after that time it has been alternately
rising and falling; and it is now about 45 or 50 millions as against 50 or 55 millions
about the year 1873, when it was at its highest. It was about 30 millions in 1810,
16 millions in 1770, and 6 millions in 1600. (Compare Giffen's *Growth of Capital*,
ch. v., and Porter's *Progress of the Nation*, Sect. II. ch. I.) But the rental of urban
land in England is now much greater than the rent of agricultural land : and in order
to estimate the full gain of the landlords from the expansion of population and general
progress, we must reckon in the values of the land on which there are now railroads,
mines, docks, etc. Taken all together, the money rental of England's soil is more
than twice as high, and its real rental is perhaps four times as high, as it was when the
corn laws were repealed.

[2] Of course there are exceptions. Economic progress may take the form of
building new railways that will draw off much of the traffic of some of those already
existing, or of increasing the size of ships till they can no longer enter docks the
entrance to which is through shallow waters.

VI, xii, 8.

It has greatly increased the supply of capital. The growth of wealth is promoted by man's increased willingness to sacrifice the present for the future,

§ 8. Political Arithmetic may be said to have begun in England in the seventeenth century; and from that time onwards we find a constant and nearly steady increase in the amount of accumulated wealth per head of the population.[1]

Man, though still somewhat impatient of delay, has gradually become more willing to sacrifice ease or other enjoyment in order to obtain them in the future. He has acquired a greater " telescopic " faculty; that is, he has acquired an increased power of realizing the future and bringing it clearly before his mind's eye : he is more prudent, and has more self-control, and is therefore more inclined to estimate at a high rate future ills and benefits—these terms being used broadly to include the highest and lowest affections of the human mind. He is more unselfish, and therefore more inclined to work and save in order to secure a future provision for his family; and there are already faint signs of a brighter time to come, in which there will be a general willingness to work and save in order to increase the stores of public wealth and of public opportunities for leading a higher life.

in spite of a slackening in his willingness to work very long hours.

But though he is more willing than in earlier ages to incur present ills for the sake of future benefits, it is doubtful whether we can now trace a continued increase in the amount of exertion which he is willing to undergo for the sake of obtaining positive pleasures, whether present or future. During many generations the industry of the western world has steadily become more sedulous : holidays have diminished, the hours of work have increased, and people have from choice or necessity contented themselves with less and less search for pleasure outside their work. But it would seem that this movement has reached its maximum, and is now declining. In all grades of work except the very highest, people are getting to prize relaxation more highly than before, and are becoming more impatient of the fatigue that results from excessive strain; and they are perhaps on the whole less willing than they used to be to undergo the constantly increasing " discommodity " of very long hours of work, for the sake of obtaining present luxuries. These causes would make them less willing than before to work hard in order to provide against distant needs, were it not that there is an even more rapid increase in their power of realizing the future, and perhaps— though this is more doubtful—in their desire for that social distinction which comes from the possession of some small store of accumulated wealth.

This increase of capital per head tended to diminish its marginal

[1] See IV. vii.

utility; and therefore the rate of interest on new investments fell, VI, xii, 9.
though not uniformly. It was reported to be 10 per cent. during a
great part of the middle ages; but it fell to 3 per cent. in the earlier Recent
half of the eighteenth century. The subsequent vast industrial fluctuations in
and political demand for capital raised it again, and it was relatively the rate
high during the great war. It fell when the political drain had of interest.
ceased, the gold supply at the time being very small; but it rose in
the third quarter of last century, when new gold abounded, and
capital was much needed for railways and the development of new
countries. After 1873 an era of peace, combined with a slackening
of the gold supply, lowered interest; but now it is rising again,
partly in consequence of an increased gold supply.[1]

§ 9. The growth of general enlightenment and of a sense of There is a
responsibility towards the young has turned a great deal of the relative
increasing wealth of the nation from investment as material capital fall in the
to investment as personal capital. There has resulted a largely ability.
increased supply of trained abilities, which has much increased the
national dividend, and raised the average income of the whole people:
but it has taken away from these trained abilities much of that
scarcity value which they used to possess, and has lowered their
earnings not indeed absolutely, but relatively to the general advance;
and it has caused many occupations, which not long ago were
accounted skilled and which are still spoken of as skilled, to rank
with unskilled labour as regards wages.

A striking instance is that of writing. It is true that many
kinds of office work require a rare combination of high mental and
moral qualities; but almost any one can be easily taught to do the
work of a copying clerk, and probably there will soon be few men or
women in England who cannot write fairly well. When all can
write, the work of copying, which used to earn higher wages than
almost any kind of manual labour, will rank among unskilled trades.
In fact the better kinds of artisan work educate a man more, and
will be better paid than those kinds of clerk's work which call for
neither judgment nor responsibility. And, as a rule, the best thing
that an artisan can do for his son is to bring him up to do thoroughly
the work that lies at his hand, so that he may understand the
mechanical, chemical or other scientific principles that bear upon
it; and may enter into the spirit of any new improvement that may
be made in it. If his son should prove to have good natural abilities,
he is far more likely to rise to a high position in the world from the
bench of an artisan than from the desk of a clerk.

[1] See above VI. vi. 7.

VI, XII, 9.

Earnings
in old and
familiar
skilled
occupa-
tions tend
to fall
relatively
to those in
new.
Again a new branch of industry is often difficult simply because it is unfamiliar; and men of great force and skill are required to do work, which can be done by men of ordinary capacity or even by women and children, when the track has once been well beaten : its wages are high at first, but they fall as it becomes familiar. And this has caused the rise of average wages to be underrated, because it so happens that many of the statistics, which seem typical of general movements of wages, are taken from trades which were comparatively new a generation or two ago, and are now within the grasp of men of much less real ability than those who pioneered the way for them.[1]

The consequence of such changes as these is to increase the number of those employed in occupations which are called skilled, whether the term is now properly applied or not : and this constant increase in the numbers of workers in the higher classes of trades has caused the average of all labour to rise much faster than the average of representative wages in each trade.[2]

In the middle ages, though some men of great ability remained artisans all their lives, and became artists; yet as a class the artisans ranked more nearly with the unskilled labourers than they do now. At the beginning of the new industrial era in the middle of the eighteenth century the artisans had lost much of their old artistic traditions and had not yet acquired that technical command over their instruments, that certainty and facility in the exact performance of difficult tasks which belong to the modern skilled artisan. A change set in early in last century, and observers were struck by the social gulf that was opening out between skilled and unskilled labour; and the rise of the wages of the artisan, to about double

---

[1] Comp. IV. VI. 1, 2; and IX. 6. As the trade progresses, improvements in machinery are sure to lighten the strain of accomplishing any given task; and therefore to lower task wages rapidly. But meanwhile the pace of the machinery, and the quantity of it put under the charge of each worker, may be increased so much that the total strain involved in the day's work is greater than before. On this subject employers and employed frequently differ. It is for instance certain that time wages have risen in the textile trades; but the employees aver, in contradiction to the employers, that the strain imposed on them has increased more than in proportion. In this controversy wages have been estimated in money; but when account is taken of the increase in the purchasing power of money, there is no doubt that real efficiency wages have risen; that is, the exertion of a given amount of strength, skill and energy is rewarded by a greater command over commodities than formerly.

[2] This may be made clearer by an example. If there are 500 men in grade A earning 12s. a week, 400 in grade B earning 25s. and 100 in grade C earning 40s., the average wages of the 1000 men are 20s. If after a time 300 from grade A have passed on to grade B, and 300 from grade B to grade C, the wages in each grade remaining stationary, then the average wages of the whole thousand men will be about 28s. 6d. And even if the rate of wages in each grade had meanwhile fallen 10 per cent., the average wages of all would still be about 25s. 6d., that is, would have risen more than 25 per cent. Neglect of such facts as these, as Sir R. Giffen has pointed out, is apt to cause great errors.

those of ordinary labour. For indeed the great increase in the VI, XII, 10.
demand for highly skilled labour, especially in the metal trades, unskilled
stimulated a rapid absorption of the strongest characters among labour at the begin-
the labourers and their children into the ranks of the artisans. The ning of
breaking down just at that time of the old exclusiveness of the century: but now
artisans, was making them less than before an aristocracy by birth that ten-
and more than before an aristocracy by worth; and this rise in the dency is reversed.
quality of artisans enabled them to maintain a rate of wages much
above that of ordinary labour for a long while. But gradually some
of the simpler forms of skilled trades began to lose their scarcity
value, as their novelty wore off; and at the same time continually
increasing demands began to be made on the ability of those in some
trades, that were traditionally ranked as unskilled. The navvy for
instance, and the agricultural labourer, have been increasingly
trusted with expensive and complicated machinery, which had been
thought to belong only to the skilled trades, and the real wages of
these two representative occupations have risen fast. The rise of
wages of agricultural labourers would be more striking than it is,
did not the spread of modern notions to agricultural districts cause
many of the ablest children born there to leave the fields for the
railway or the workshop, to become policemen, or to act as carters
or porters in towns. Those who are left behind in the fields
have received a better education than was to be had in earlier
times; and, though having perhaps less than an average share
of natural ability, they earn much higher real wages than their
fathers.

There are some skilled and responsible occupations, such as those
of the head heaters and rollers in iron works, which require great
physical strength, and involve much discomfort : and in them wages
are very high. For the temper of the age makes those who can do
high-class work and can earn good wages easily, refuse to undergo
hardship, except for a very high reward.[1]

§ 10. We may next consider the changes in the relative wages of There is a
old and young men, of women and children. relative fall in the

The conditions of industry change so fast that long experience wages of
is in some trades almost a disadvantage, and in many it is of far elderly men;
less value than a quickness in taking hold of new ideas and adapting
one's habits to new conditions. A man is likely to earn less after

---

[1] The above brief remarks on the evolution of wages may well be supplemented
by Prof. Schmoller's survey in his *Volkswirtschaftslehre*, III. 7 (Vol. II. pp. 259–316).
It is specially notable for its breadth of view, and its careful coordination of the
material and psychical elements of progress. See also the latter half of his second
Book.

VI, xii, 11. he is fifty years old than before he is thirty; and the knowledge of this is tempting artisans to follow the example of unskilled labourers, whose natural inclination to marry early has always been encouraged by the desire that their family expenses may begin to fall off before their own wages begin to shrink.

and a rise in the wages of boys and girls,   A second and even more injurious tendency of the same kind is that of the wages of children to rise relatively to those of their parents. Machinery has displaced many men, but not many boys; the customary restrictions which excluded them from some trades are giving way; and these changes, together with the spread of education, while doing good in almost every other direction, are doing harm in this that they are enabling boys, and even girls, to set their parents at defiance and start in life on their own account.

and of women.   The wages of women are for similar reasons rising fast relatively to those of men. And this is a great gain in so far as it tends to develop their faculties; but an injury in so far as it tempts them to neglect their duty of building up a true home, and of investing their efforts in the personal capital of their children's character and abilities.

The earnings of exceptional genius are rising,   § 11. The relative fall in the incomes to be earned by moderate ability, however carefully trained, is accentuated by the rise in those that are obtained by many men of extraordinary ability. There never was a time at which moderately good oil paintings sold more cheaply than now, and there never was a time at which first-rate paintings sold so dearly. A business man of average ability and average good fortune gets now a lower rate of profits on his capital than at any previous time; while yet the operations, in which a man exceptionally favoured by genius and good luck can take part, are so extensive as to enable him to amass a huge fortune with a rapidity hitherto unknown.

as a result of two causes   The causes of this change are chiefly two; firstly, the general growth of wealth; and secondly, the development of new facilities for communication, by which men, who have once attained a commanding position, are enabled to apply their constructive or speculative genius to undertakings vaster, and extending over a wider area, than ever before.

of which one acts almost alone on professional incomes,   It is the first cause, almost alone, that enables some barristers to command very high fees; for a rich client whose reputation, or fortune, or both, are at stake will scarcely count any price too high to secure the services of the best man he can get : and it is this again that enables jockeys and painters and musicians of exceptional ability to get very high prices. In all these occupations the highest incomes earned in our own generation are the highest that the world VI, xii, 12. has yet seen.   But so long as the number of persons who can be reached by a human voice is strictly limited, it is not very likely that any singer will make an advance on the £10,000, said to have been earned in a season by Mrs. Billington at the beginning of last century, nearly as great as that which the business leaders of the present generation have made on those of the last.

For the two causes have co-operated to put enormous power and wealth in the hands of those business men of our own generation in America and elsewhere, who have had first-rate genius and have been favoured by fortune.   It is true that a great part of these gains have come, in some cases, from the wrecks of the rival speculators who had been worsted in the race.   But in others they were earned mainly by the supreme economizing force of a great constructive genius working at a new and large problem with a free hand : for instance the founder of the Vanderbilt family, who evolved the New York Central Railroad system out of chaos, probably saved to the people of the United States more than he accumulated himself.[1]

while both act fully with regard to business incomes.

§ 12. But these fortunes are exceptional.   The diffusion of education, and prudent habits among the masses of the people, and the opportunities which the new methods of business offer for the safe investment of small capitals, are telling on the side of moderate incomes.   The returns of the income tax and the house tax, the statistics of consumption of commodities, the records of salaries paid to the higher and the lower ranks of employees of Government and public companies, all indicate that middle class incomes are increasing faster than those of the rich ; that the earnings of artisans are increasing faster than those of the professional classes, and that the wages of healthy and vigorous unskilled labourers are increasing faster even than those of the average artisan.   The aggregate

Progress is fast improving the condition of the great body of the working classes.

[1] It should be noticed however that some of these gains may be traced to those opportunities for the formation of trade combinations engineered by a few able, wealthy and daring men to exploit for their own benefit a great body of manufactures, or the trade and traffic of a large district.   That part of this power, which depends on political conditions, and especially on the Protective tariff, may pass away.   But the area of America is so large, and its condition so changeful, that the slow and steady-going management of a great joint-stock company on the English plan is at a disadvantage in competition with the vigorous and original scheming, the rapid and resolute force of a small group of wealthy capitalists, who are willing and able to apply their own resources in great undertakings to a much greater extent than is the case in England.   The ever-shifting conditions of business life in America enable natural selection to bring to the front the best minds for the purpose from their vast population, almost every one of whom, as he enters on life, resolves to be rich before he dies.   The modern developments of business and of business fortunes are of exceptional interest and instruction to Englishmen : but their lessons will be misread unless the essentially different conditions of business life in the old world and the new are constantly borne in mind.

VI, xii, 12. income of the very rich is perhaps not a larger part of the whole in England now than in earlier times. But in America the aggregate value of land is rising fast; the higher strains of the working population are yielding ground to lower strains of immigrants; and great financiers are acquiring vast power : and it may possibly be true that the aggregate income from property is rising relatively to that from labour, and that the aggregate income of the very rich is rising fastest of all.

The inconstancy of employment in modern industry is apt to be exaggerated. It must be admitted that a rise in wages would lose part of its benefit, if it were accompanied by an increase in the time spent in enforced idleness. Inconstancy of employment is a great evil, and rightly attracts public attention. But several causes combine to make it appear to be greater than it really is.

When a large factory goes on half time, rumour bruits the news over the whole neighbourhood, and perhaps the newspapers spread it all over the country. But few people know when an independent workman, or even a small employer, gets only a few days' work in a month; and in consequence, whatever suspensions of industry there are in modern times, are apt to seem more important than they are relatively to those of earlier times. In earlier times some labourers were hired by the year : but they were not free, and were kept to their work by personal chastisement. There is no good cause for thinking that the mediæval artisan had constant employment. And the most persistently inconstant employment now to be found in Europe is in those non-agricultural industries of the West which are most nearly mediæval in their methods, and in those industries of Eastern and Southern Europe in which mediæval traditions are strongest.[1]

In many directions there is a steady increase in the proportion of employees who are practically hired by the year. This is for instance the general rule in many of those trades connected with transport which are growing fastest; and which are, in some respects, the representative industries of the second half of the nineteenth century, as the manufacturing trades were of the first half. And though the rapidity of invention, the fickleness of fashion, and above

[1] An instance, which came under the present writer's observation, may be mentioned here. In Palermo there is a semi-feudal connection between the artisans and their patrons. Each carpenter or tailor has one or more large houses to which he looks for employment; and so long as he behaves himself fairly well, he is practically secure from competition. There are no great waves of depression of trade; the newspapers are never filled with accounts of the sufferings of those out of work, because their condition changes very little from time to time. But a larger percentage of artisans are out of employment at the best of times in Palermo, than in England in the centre of the worst depression of recent years. Something further is said as to inconstancy of employment below, VI. xiii. 10.

all the instability of credit, do certainly introduce disturbing VI, XII. 12 elements into modern industry; yet, as we shall see presently, other influences are working strongly in the opposite direction, and there seems to be no good reason for thinking that inconstancy of employment is increasing on the whole.

CHAPTER XIII

PROGRESS IN RELATION TO STANDARDS OF LIFE

Activities and wants.

§ 1. LET us begin by pursuing a little further the line of thought on which we started in Book III, when considering wants in relation to activities. We there saw reasons for thinking that the true key-note of economic progress is the development of new activities rather than of new wants; and we may now make some study of a question that is of special urgency in our own generation; viz.—what is the connection between changes in the manner of living and the rate of earnings; how far is either to be regarded as the cause of the other, and how far as the effect?

By the standard of life we mean the standard of activities adjusted to wants.

The term the *standard of life* is here taken to mean the standard of activities adjusted to wants. Thus a rise in the standard of life implies an increase of intelligence and energy and self-respect; leading to more care and judgment in expenditure, and to an avoidance of food and drink that gratify the appetite but afford no strength, and of ways of living that are unwholesome physically and morally. A rise in the standard of life for the whole population will much increase the national dividend, and the share of it which accrues to each grade and to each trade. A rise in the standard of life for any one trade or grade will raise their efficiency and therefore their own real wages : it will increase the national dividend a little; and it will enable others to obtain their assistance at a cost somewhat less in proportion to its efficiency.

When a rise in the standard of comfort raises wages, it is chiefly by raising the standard of activities.

But many writers have spoken of the influence exerted on wages by a rise, not in the standard of *life*, but in that of *comfort*;—a term that may suggest a mere increase of artificial wants, among which perhaps the grosser wants may predominate. It is true that every broad improvement in the standard of comfort is likely to bring with it a better manner of living, and to open the way to new and higher activities; while people who have hitherto had neither the necessities nor the decencies of life, can hardly fail to get some increase of vitality and energy from an increase of comfort, however gross and material the view which they may take of it. Thus a rise in the standard of comfort will probably involve some rise in the standard of life; and, in so far as this is the case, it tends to increase the national dividend and to improve the condition of the VI, XIII, 2 people.

Some writers however of our own and of earlier times have gone further than this, and have implied that a mere increase of wants tends to raise wages. But the only direct effect of an increase of wants is to make people more miserable than before. And if we put aside its possible indirect effect in increasing activities, and otherwise raising the standard of life, it can raise wages only by diminishing the supply of labour. It will be well to go into this matter more closely.

§ 2. It has already been noted that if population increased in Assumptions which underlie the iron law of wages in its extreme form. high geometrical progession uninterruptedly for many generations together in a country which could not import food easily, then the total produce of labour and capital, working on the resources provided by nature, would barely cover the cost of rearing and training each generation as it came : this would be true even if we supposed that nearly the whole of the national dividend went to labour, scarcely any share being allotted to capitalist or landowner.[1] If the allowance fell below that level, the rate of increase of the population must necessarily shrink; unless indeed the expenses of their nurture and rearing were curtailed, with a resulting lowering of efficiency, and therefore of the national dividend, and therefore of earnings.

But in fact the check to the rapid growth of population would Conditions under which a rise in the standard of comfort would raise wages a little, have not been very rare in the history of the world. probably come earlier, because the population at large would not be likely to limit its consumption to bare necessaries : some part of the family income would almost certainly be spent on gratifications which contributed but little to the maintenance of life and efficiency. That is to say, the maintenance of a standard of comfort, raised more or less above that which was necessary for life and efficiency, would necessarily involve a check to the growth of population at a rather earlier stage than would have been reached if family expenditure had been directed on the same principles as is the expenditure on the nurture and training of horses or slaves. This analogy reaches further.

Three necessaries for full efficiency—hope, freedom and change [2] —cannot easily be brought within the slave's reach. But as a rule the shrewd slave-owner goes to some trouble and expense to promote rough musical and other entertainments, on the same principle that he provides medicines : for experience shows that melancholy in a

[1] See VI. II. 2, 3; also IV. IV. and V. : and VI. IV.
[2] See IV. V. 4.

VI, xiii, 2. slave is as wasteful as disease, or as cinders that clog the furnace of a boiler. Now if the standard of comfort of the slaves were to rise in such a way that neither punishment nor the fear of death would make them work unless provided with expensive comforts and even luxuries, they would get those comforts and luxuries; or else they would disappear, in the same way as would a breed of horses that did not earn their keep. And if it were true that the real wages of labour were forced down chiefly by the difficulty of obtaining food, as was in fact the case in England a hundred years ago; then indeed the working classes might relieve themselves from the pressure of Diminishing Return by reducing their numbers.

But in England now wages are not kept down by extreme pressure of numbers on the resources of agriculture, and can be raised only by increased efficiency.   But they cannot do so now, because there is no such pressure. The opening of England's ports, in 1846, was one among many causes of the development of railways connecting the vast agricultural lands of North and South America and Australia with the sea. Wheat grown under the most advantageous circumstances is brought to the English working man in sufficient quantities for his family at a total cost equal to but a small part of his wages. An increase in numbers gives many new opportunities for increased efficiency of labour and capital working together to meet men's wants; and thus may raise wages in one direction as much as it lowers them in another; provided only the stock of capital required for the new developments increases fast enough. Of course the Englishman is not unaffected by the law of diminishing return : he cannot earn his food with as little labour as if he were near spacious virgin prairies. But its cost to him, being now governed mainly by the supplies which come from new countries, would not be greatly affected either by an increase or by a diminution in the population of this country. If he can make his labour more efficient in producing things which can be exchanged for imported food, then he will get his food at less real cost to himself, whether the population of England grows fast or not.

When the wheat-fields of the world are worked at their full power (or even earlier, if the free entry of food unto England's ports should ever be obstructed), then indeed an increase of her population may lower wages, or at all events check the rise that would otherwise have come from the continued improvement in the arts of production : and, in such a case a rise in the standard of comfort may raise wages merely by stinting the growth of numbers.

Contrast between changes in numbers and in   But, while the present good fortune of abundant imported food attends on the English people, a rise in their standard of comfort could not increase their wages, merely by its action on their numbers. And further if it were obtained by measures which forced

down the rate of profits on capital even further below the level, VI, xiii, 3.
which can be got in countries which have a greater power of absorb- average
ing capital than England has, it might both check accumulation in activities.
England, and hasten the exportation of capital : and in that case
wages in England would fall both absolutely, and relatively to the
rest of the world. If on the other hand a rise in the standard of
comfort went together with a great increase in efficiency; then—
whether it were accompanied by an increase in numbers or not—it
would enlarge the national dividend relatively to population, and
establish a rise of real wages on an enduring basis. Thus a diminution by one-tenth of the number of workers, each doing as much
work as before, would not materially raise wages; and therefore a
diminution by one-tenth in the amount of work done by each, the
number remaining unchanged, would lower wages in general by one-
tenth.

This argument is of course consistent with the belief that a com- Even
pact group of workers can for a time raise their wages at the expense a single
of the rest of the community by making their labour scarce. But workers
such strategy seldom succeeds for more than a short time. However maintain
strong the anti-social obstacles which they erect against those who ally high
would like a share of their gains, interlopers find their way in; some wages
over the obstacles, some under them, and some through them. increasing
Meanwhile invention is set on foot to obtain in some other way, or efficiency.
from some other place, things of the production of which the compact
group thought to have a partial monopoly : and, what is even more
dangerous to them, new things are invented and brought into general
use, which satisfy nearly the same wants, and yet make no use of
their labour. Thus after a while those, who have striven to make a
shrewd use of monopoly, are apt to find their numbers swollen rather
than reduced, while the total demand for their labour has shrunk :
in that case their wages fall heavily.

§ 3. The relations between industrial efficiency and the hours of Standards
labour are complex. If the strain is very great, a man is apt to be in relation
so tired by long work that he is seldom at his best, and is often much to hours
below it or even idling. As a general, though not universal rule, his of work.
work is more intense when paid by piece, than when paid by time;
and, in so far as this is the case, short hours are specially suitable to
industries in which piece-work prevails.[1]

---

[1] The facts are much in question, partly because they vary much from one industry
to another; and those who have the most intimate knowledge of them, are apt to be
biassed. When piece-work can be brought under collective bargaining by trade unions,
the first effect of an improvement in plant is to raise real wages : and the onus of
claiming a readjustment of piece rates in order to keep wages in just proportion to
those which are being earned by equally difficult and responsible work in other occu-

U

VI, xiii, 3.

Leisure and rest, when turned to good account, make for economy.

When the hours, the nature of the work done, the physical conditions under which it is done, and the method by which it is remunerated, are such as to cause great wear-and-tear of body or mind or both, and to lead to a low standard of living; when there has been a want of that leisure, rest and repose, which are among the necessaries for efficiency; then the labour has been extravagant from the point of view of society at large, just as it would be extravagant on the part of the individual capitalist to keep his horses or slaves overworked or underfed. In such a case a moderate diminution of the hours of labour would diminish the national dividend only temporarily : for as soon as the improved standard of life had had time to exert its full effect on the efficiency of the workers, their increased energy, intelligence and force of character would enable them to do as much as before in less time; and thus, even from the point of view of material production, there would be no ultimate loss, any more than there would be in sending a sick worker into hospital to get his strength renovated. The coming generation is interested in the rescue of men, and still more in that of women, from excessive work; at least as much as it is in the handing down to it of a good stock of material wealth.

Exceptional case of the lowest grade of workers.

This argument assumes that the new rest and leisure raise the standard of life. And such a result is almost certain to follow in the extreme cases of overwork which we have been now considering; for in them a mere lessening of tension is a necessary condition for taking the first step upwards. The lowest grade of honest workers seldom work very hard. But they have little stamina; and many of them are so over-strained that they might probably, after a time, do as much in a shorter day as they now do in a long one.[1]

In some trades shorter hours combined with double shifts

Again there are some branches of industry which at present turn to account expensive plant during nine or ten hours a day; and in which the gradual introduction of two shifts of eight hours, or even less, would be a gain. The change would need to be introduced gradually; for there is not enough skilled labour in existence to

---

pations, is thus thrown upon the employers. In such cases, piece-work is generally in favour with employees. And where their organization is good, as in some classes of mining work, they approve it even in regard to work that is not uniform. But in many other cases it arouses their suspicion of unfair advantage. See below, § 8. According to Professor Schmoller, it is estimated that piece-work increases output by 20 to 100 per cent. according to the race of the workers and the character and technique of the industry, *Volkswirtschaftslehre*, § 208. An instructive detailed statement of the causes which lead workers generally to oppose payment by results in certain industries, while welcoming it in others, is given by Cole, *The payment of wages*, ch. ii.

[1] The history of British industries offers the most various, the most clearly defined, and the most generally instructive experiments as to the influence of variations in the hours of labour on output : but international studies on the subject seem to be specially German. See for instance Bernard, *Höhere Arbeitsinunsität bei Kurzeren Arbeitzeit*, 1909.

allow such a plan to be adopted at once in all the workshops and factories for which it is suited. But some kinds of machinery, when worn out or antiquated, might be replaced on a smaller scale; and, on the other hand, much new machinery that cannot be profitably introduced for a ten hours' day, would be introduced for a sixteen hours' day; and when once introduced it would be improved on. Thus the arts of production would progress more rapidly; the national dividend would increase; working men would be able to earn higher wages without checking the growth of capital, or tempting it to migrate to countries where wages are lower : and all classes of society would reap benefit from the change.

The importance of this consideration is more apparent every year, since the growing expensiveness of machinery, and the quickness with which it is rendered obsolete, are constantly increasing the wastefulness of keeping the untiring iron and steel resting in idleness during sixteen hours out of the twenty-four. In any country, such a change would increase the net produce, and therefore the wages of each worker; because much less than before would have to be deducted from his total output on account of charges for machinery, plant, factory-rent, etc. But Anglo-Saxon artisans, unsurpassed in accuracy of touch, and surpassing all in sustained energy, would more than any others increase their net produce, if they would keep their machinery going at its full speed for sixteen hours a day, even though they themselves worked only eight.[1]

It must however be remembered that this particular plea for a reduction of the hours of labour applies only to those trades which use, or can use, expensive plant; and that in many cases, as for instance in some mines and some branches of railway work, the

---

[1] On the whole of this subject see Prof. Chapman's address at the British Association, 1909, published in the *Economic Journal*, vol. xix.

Double shifts are used more on the Continent than in England. But they have not a fair trial there, for the hours of labour are so long that double shifts involve work nearly all the night through; and night work is never so good as day work, partly because those who work at night do not rest perfectly during the day. No doubt certain practical objections can be urged against the plan; for instance, a machine is not so well cared for when two men share the responsibility of keeping it in order, as when one man has the whole management of it; and there is sometimes a difficulty about fixing responsibility for imperfections in the work done; but these difficulties can be in a great measure overcome by putting the machine and the work in charge of two partners. Again, there would be a little difficulty in readjusting the office arrangements to suit a day of sixteen hours. But employers and their foremen do not regard these difficulties as insuperable; and experience shows that workmen soon overcome the repugnance which they feel at first to double shifts. One set might end its work at noon, and the other begin then; or what would perhaps be better, one shift might work, say, from 5 a.m. to 10 a.m. and from 1.30 p.m. to 4.30 p.m., the second set working from 10.15 a.m. to 1.15 p.m. and from 4.45 p.m. to 9.45 p.m.; the two sets might change places at the end of each week or month. A general adoption of double shifts will be necessary if the extension of the marvellous powers of expensive machinery into every branch of manual work is to exercise the full influence of which it is capable in reducing the hours of labour much below eight.

VI, XIII, 4. system of shifts is already applied so as to keep the plant almost constantly at work.

But in many trades a diminution of the hours of labour would lessen production.

There remain therefore many trades in which a reduction of the hours of labour would certainly lessen the output in the immediate present, and would not certainly bring about at all quickly any such increase of efficiency as would raise the average work done per head up to the old level. In such cases the change would diminish the national dividend; and the greater part of the resulting material loss would fall on the workers whose hours of labour were diminished. It is true that in some trades a scarcity of labour would raise its price for a good long while at the expense of the rest of the community. But as a rule a rise in the real price of labour would cause a diminished demand for the product, partly through the increased use of substitutes; and would also cause an inrush of new labour from less favoured trades.

In considering the influence on wages generally of reducing the hours of labour: it must be remembered that immediate effects are no guide as to ultimate.

§ 4. It may be well to try to explain the great vitality of the common belief that wages could be raised generally by merely making labour scarce. To begin with, it is difficult to realize how different, and often even opposed, are the immediate and permanent effects of a change. People see that when there are competent men waiting for work outside the offices of a tramway company, those already at work think more of keeping their posts than of striving for a rise of wages; and that if these men were away, the employers could not resist a demand for higher wages. They dwell on the fact that, if tramway men work short hours, and there is no diminution in the number of miles run by the cars on existing lines, then more men must be employed; probably at higher wages per hour, and possibly at higher wages per day. They see that when an enterprise is on foot, as for instance the building of a house, or a ship, it must be finished at any cost, since there is nothing to be gained by stopping half way : and the larger the slices of work on it done by any one man, the fewer slices of work on it will be left for other people.

But there are other consequences more important, though less obtrusive, which need to be considered. For instance, if tram workers and building operatives stint their labour artificially, tramway extensions will be checked; fewer men will be employed in making and working tramways; many workpeople and others will walk into town, who might have ridden; many will live closely packed in the cities who might have had gardens and fresher air in the suburbs; the working classes, among others, will be unable to pay for as good housing accommodation as they would otherwise have had; and there will be less building to be done.

In short the argument that wages can be raised permanently by stinting labour rests on the assumption that there is a permanent fixed *work-fund*, i.e. a certain amount of work which has to be done, whatever the price of labour. And for this assumption there is no foundation. On the contrary, the demand for work comes from the national dividend; that is, it comes from work. The less work there is of one kind, the less demand there is for work of other kinds; and if labour were scarce, fewer enterprises would be undertaken. *VI, xiii, 5. and that there is no fixed work-fund;*

Again, constancy of employment is dependent on the organization of industry and trade, and on the success with which those who arrange supply are able to forecast coming movements of demand and of price, and to adjust their actions accordingly. But this would not be better done with a short day's work than with a long one; and indeed the adoption of a short day, not accompanied by double shifts, would discourage the use of that expensive plant, the presence of which makes employers very unwilling to close their works. Almost every artificial stinting of work involves friction, and therefore tends, not to lessen, but to increase the inconstancy of employment.

It is true that, if plasterers or shoemakers could exclude external competition, they would have a fair chance of raising their wages by a mere diminution of the amount of work done by each, whether by shortening the hours of labour or in any other way; but these gains can be got only at the cost of a greater aggregate loss to other sharers in the national dividend; which is the source of wages and profits in all industries in the country. This conclusion is emphasized by the fact, to which experience testifies and which analysis explains, that the strongest instances of a rise in wages attained by trade union strategy are found in branches of industry, the demand for whose labour is not direct, but " derived " from the demand for a product in making which many branches of industry co-operate: for any one branch, which is strong in strategy, can absorb to itself some share of the price of the ultimate product, which might have gone to other branches.[1] *and that every check to the national dividend falls in part on the working classes.*

§ 5. We now come to a second cause of the vitality of the belief that wages can be raised generally and permanently by checking the supply of labour. This cause is an under-estimate of the effects of such a change on the supply of capital. *The limited extent to which capitalists can be made to*

It is a fact—and, so far as it goes, an important fact—that some share of the loss resulting from the lessening of output by (say) plasterers or shoemakers, will fall on those who do not belong to the working classes. Part of it will no doubt fall on employers and *bear the loss resulting from a check to the national dividend.*

[1] See above, V. vi. 2.

VI, xiii, 5. capitalists, whose personal and material capital is sunk in building or shoemaking; and part on well-to-do users, or consumers, of houses or shoes. And further if there were a general attempt by all of the working classes to obtain high wages by restricting the effective supply of their labour, a considerable part of the burden resulting from the shrinkage of the national dividend would doubtless be thrown on other classes of the nation, and especially on the capitalists, for a time : but only for a time. For a considerable diminution in the net return to investments of capital would speedily drive new supplies of it abroad. In regard to this danger it is indeed sometimes urged that the railways and factories of the country cannot be exported. But nearly all of the materials, and a large part of the appliances of production are consumed, or worn out, or become obsolete every year; and they need to be replaced. And a reduction in the scale of this replacement, combined with the exportation of some of the capital thus set free, might probably so lessen the effective demand for labour in the country in a few years, that in the reaction wages generally would be reduced much below their present level.[1]

International wage movements; their limited possibilities.

But though the emigration of capital would not in any case be attended by much difficulty, owners of capital have good business reasons as well as a sentimental preference in favour of investing it at home. And therefore a rise in the standard of life, which makes a country more attractive to live in, is sure to counteract to some extent the tendency of a fall in the net return on investments to cause capital to be exported. On the other hand an attempt to raise wages by anti-social contrivances for stinting output, is certain to drive abroad well-to-do people in general; and especially just that class of capitalists whose enterprise and delight in conquering difficulties is of the most importance to the working classes. For their ceaseless initiative makes for national leadership and enables man's work to raise real wages; while promoting an increased supply of those appliances which make for efficiency, and thus sustain the growth of the national dividend.

---

[1] To take an illustration, let us suppose that shoemakers and hatters are in the same grade, working equal hours, and reciving equal wages, before and after a general reduction in the hours of labour. Then both before and after the change, the hatter could buy, with a month's wages, as many shoes as were the net product of the shoemaker's work for a month (see VI. ii, 7). If the shoemaker worked less hours than before, and in consequence did less work, the net product of his labour for a month would have diminished, unless either by a system of working double shifts the employer and his capital had earned profits on two sets of workers, or his profits could be cut down by the full amount of the diminution in output. The last supposition is inconsistent with what we know of the causes which govern the supply of capital and business power. And therefore the hatter's wages would go less far than before in buying shoes; and so all round for other trades.

It is true also that a general rise in wages however attained, if VI, xiii, 6.
spread over the whole world, could not cause capital to migrate from
any one part of it to another. And it is to be hoped that in time
the wages of manual labour will rise all over the world, mainly
through increased production; but partly also in consequence of a
general fall in the rate of interest, and of a relative—if not absolute—
diminution of incomes larger than are necessary to supply the means
of efficient work and culture even in the highest and broadest senses
of these terms. But methods of raising wages, which make for a
higher standard of comfort by means that lessen rather than promote
efficiency, are so anti-social and shortsighted as to invoke a speedy
retribution; and there is perhaps little chance of their being adopted
over any great part of the world. If several countries adopted such
methods, the others going straight for raising the standards of life
and of efficiency, would speedily attract to themselves much of the
capital and of the best vital force away from those who followed an
ignoble restrictive policy.

§ 6. In this discussion it has been necessary to adhere to general
reasoning : for a direct appeal to experience is difficult; and, if
made lightly, it can but mislead. Whether we watch the statistics
of wages and production immediately after the change or for a long
period following it, the prominent facts are likely to be due chiefly to
causes other than that which we are wishing to study. *Difficulties of the appeal to experience in such cases.*

Thus if a reduction of hours resulted from a successful strike,
the chances are that the occasion chosen for the strike was one when
the strategical position of the workmen was good, and when the
general conditions of trade would have enabled them to obtain a
rise of wages, if there had been no change in the hours of labour :
and therefore the immediate effects of the change on wages are likely
to appear more favourable than they really were. And again many
employers, having entered into contracts which they are bound to
fulfil, may for the time offer higher wages for a short day than
before for a long day. But this is a result of the suddenness of
the change, and is a mere flash in the pan; and, as has just been
observed, the immediate results of such a change are likely to be
in the opposite direction to those which follow later, and are more
enduring.

On the other hand, if men have been overworked, the shortening
of the hours of labour will not at once make them strong : the
physical and moral improvement of the condition of the workers,
with its consequent increase of efficiency and therefore of wages,
cannot show itself at once.

VI, XIII, 7.

Further, the statistics of production and wages several years after the reduction of hours are likely to reflect changes in the prosperity of the country, and especially of the trade in question; of the methods of production; and of the purchasing power of money: and it may be as difficult to isolate the effects of reduction of the hours of labour as it is to isolate the effects on the waves of a noisy sea caused by throwing a stone among them.[1]

We must then be careful not to confuse the two questions whether a cause tends to produce a certain effect and whether that cause is sure to be followed by that effect. Opening the sluice of a reservoir tends to lower the level of the water in it; but if meanwhile larger supplies of water are flowing in at the other end, the opening of the sluice may be followed by a rising of the level of the water in the cistern. And so although a shortening of the hours of labour would tend to diminish output in those trades which are not over-worked, and in which there is no room for double shifts; yet it might very likely be accompanied by an increase of production arising from the general progress of wealth and knowledge. But in that case the rise of wages would have been obtained in spite of, and not in consequence of, a shortening of hours.

We pass to the influence of trade unions on standards of life, work and wages.

§ 7. In modern England nearly all movements of the kind which we have just been discussing are directed by trade unions. A full appreciation of their aims and results lies beyond the scope of the present volume: for it must be based on a study of combinations in general, of industrial fluctuations, and of foreign trade. But a few words may be said here on that part of their policy which is most closely connected with standards of life, and work, and wages.[2]

[1] For instance, when we look at the history of the introduction of the eight hours' day in Australia we find great fluctuations in the prosperity of the mines and the supply of gold, in the prosperity of the sheep farms and the price of wool, in the borrowing from old countries capital with which to employ Australian labour to build railways, etc., in immigration, and in commercial credit. And all these have been such powerful causes of change in the condition of the Australian working man as to completely overlay and hide from view the effects of a reduction of the hours of labour from 10 gross (8¾ net after deducting meal times) to 8 net. Money wages in Australia are much lower than they were before the hours were shortened; and, though it may be true that the purchasing power of money has increased, so that real wages have not fallen, yet there seems no doubt that the real wages of labour in Australia are not nearly as much above those in England as they were before the reduction in the hours of labour: and it has not been proved that they are not lower than they would have been if that change had not taken place. The commercial troubles through which Australia passed shortly after the change were no doubt mainly caused by a series of droughts supervening on a reckless inflation of credit. But a contributory cause appears to have been an over-sanguine estimate of the economic efficiency of short hours of labour, which led to a premature reduction of hours in industries not well adapted for it.

[2] A short provisional description of trade unions is affixed to Vol. I. of my *Elements of Economics*, which is, in other respects, an abridgment of the present volume. And the account of their aims and methods given in the Final Report of the Labour Commission, 1893, has the unique authority derived from the co-operation of employers and trade union leaders of exceptional ability and experience.

The increasing changefulness and mobility of industry obscure VI, xiii, 7.
the influences both for good and for evil which the earnings and
industrial policy of any group of workers in one generation exert on
the efficiency and earning power of the same group in a later generation.[1] The family income, from which the expenses of rearing and
training its younger members must be defrayed, seldom comes now
from a single trade. The sons are less frequently found in their
father's occupation : the stronger and more strenuous of those to
whose nurture the earnings of any occupation have contributed are
likely to seek higher fortunes elsewhere; while the weak and the
dissolute are likely to descend below it. It is therefore becoming
increasingly difficult to bring the test of experience to bear on the
question, whether the efforts, which any particular trade union
has made to raise the wages of its members, have borne rich
fruit in raising the standard of life and work of the generation
reared by aid of those high wages. But some broad facts stand
out clearly.

The original aims of British trade unions were almost as closely *Their*
connected with the standard of life as with the rate of wages. They *earlier*
derived their first great impulse from the fact that the law, partly *in raising*
directly and partly indirectly, sustained combinations among em- *standard*
ployers to regulate wages in their own supposed interest; and pro- *of life and*
hibited under severe penalties similar combinations on the part of *as much*
employees. This law depressed wages a little; but it depressed *wages.*
much more the strength and richness of character of the workman.
His horizon was generally so limited that he could not be fully drawn
out of himself by a keen and intelligent interest in national affairs :
so he thought and cared little about any mundane matters, except
the immediate concerns of himself, his family and his neighbours.
Freedom to combine with others in his own occupation would have
widened his horizon, and given him larger matters to think about :
it would have raised his standard of social duty, even though this
duty might have been tainted with a good deal of class selfishness.
Thus the early struggle for the principle that workmen should be
free to do in combination the counterpart of anything which employers were free to do in combination, was in effect an effort to
obtain conditions of life consistent with true self-respect and broad
social interests, as much as a struggle for higher wages.

On this side of the field victory has been complete. Trade union-
ism has enabled skilled artisans, and even many classes of unskilled
workers, to enter into negotiations with their employers with the

---

[1] Compare above, VI. iii. 7 and v. 2.

VI, XIII, 8. same gravity, self-restraint, dignity and forethought as are observed in the diplomacy of great nations. It has led them generally to recognize that a simply aggressive policy is a foolish policy, and that the chief use of military resources is to preserve an advantageous peace.

This influence on character bears fruit in Boards for adjusting wages, which continue the good work.

In many British industries Boards for the adjustment of wages work steadily, and smoothly, because there is a strong desire to avoid waste of energy on trifles. If an employee disputes the justice of any judgment passed by his employer or foreman on his work or his remuneration for it, the employer in the first instance calls in the trade union secretary as arbiter : his verdict is generally accepted by the employer; and of course it must be accepted by the operative. If beneath this particular personal dispute there is a question of principle on which no clear agreement has been reached by the Board, the matter may be referred for discussion to the secretaries of the employers' association and the trade union in conference : if they cannot agree, it may be passed on to the Board. At last, if the stake at issue is large enough, and neither side will give way, the issue is relegated by a strike or a lock-out to the decision of force. But even then the good services of several generations of organized trade unions are seen in the conduct of the contest; which generally differs in method from the contest waged between employers and employed a century ago, very much as honourable war between modern civilized peoples does from fierce guerilla war among wild peoples. Self-control and moderation of manner overlying resolute purpose distinguish the British delegates above others at an international labour conference.

Noblesse oblige.

But the very greatness of the services which trade unions have rendered imposes on them corresponding obligations. *Noblesse oblige* : and they are bound to look with suspicion on those who exaggerate their power of raising wages by particular devices, especially when such devices contain an anti-social element. There are indeed but few movements which are without reproach : some destructive influence lurks in nearly every great and good effort. But the evil should be stripped of all gloss, and carefully examined, so that it may be kept down.

The Common Rule is the chief instrument of trade unions for good and for evil.

§ 8. The chief instrument by which trade unions have obtained their power of negotiating on even terms with their employers is a " Common Rule " as regards the standard wage to be paid for an hour's work of a given class, or again for piece-work of a given class. Custom and the rather ineffective assessments of wages by Justices of the Peace, while hindering the workman from rising, had also defended him from extreme pressure. But, when competition became free, the isolated workman was at a disadvantage in bargaining with employers. For, even in Adam Smith's time, they were generally in agreement, formal or informal, not to outbid one another in the hire of labour. And when, as time went on, a single firm was often able to employ several thousands of workmen, that firm by itself became a larger as well as a more compact bargaining force than a small trade union.

It is true that the agreements and understandings of employers not to overbid one another were not universal, and were often evaded or broken. It is true that when the net product due to the labour of additional workers was largely in excess of the wages that were being paid to them, a pushing employer would brave the indignation of his peers, and attract workers to him by the offer of higher wages : and it is true that in progressive industrial districts this competition was sufficient to secure that no considerable body of workers should remain for long with wages much below the equivalent of their net product. It is necessary to reassert here the fact that this net product, to which the wages of a worker of normal efficiency approximate, is the net product of a worker of normal efficiency : for a suggestion has indeed been made by some advocates of extreme enforcements of the Common Rule, that competition tends to make the wages of the efficient worker equal to the net product of that worker who is so inefficient that the employer can barely be induced to employ him at all.[1]

But in fact competition does not act in this way. It does not tend to make weekly wages in similar employments equal : it tends to adjust them to the efficiency of the workers. If A will do twice as much work as B, an employer on the margin of doubt as to whether it is worth his while to take on additional workers, will make just as good a bargain by taking on A at four shillings as by taking on B and another at two shillings each. And the causes which govern

The competition of employers tends to adjust the wages of labour to its net product graduated according to efficiency;

it does not adjust wages generally to the net product of inefficient labour.

---

[1] The wholesome influences on social wellbeing, which are exercised by trade union leaders in many directions, are apt to be marred by a misunderstanding on this matter. They commonly give as their authority the very weighty and able treatise on *Industrial Democracy* by Mr. and Mrs. Webb, where the misunderstanding is suggested. Thus they say, p. 710, "It is now theoretically demonstrated, as we saw in our chapter on ' The Verdict of the Economists,' that under ' perfect competition,' and complete mobility between one occupation and another, the common level of wages tends to be no more than ' the net produce due to the labour of the marginal labourer ' who is on the verge of not being employed at all ! " And, p. 787 f. n., they refer to this marginal labourer as an industrial invalid or pauper, saying :—" If the wages of every class of labour under perfect competition tend to be no more than the net produce due to the additional labour of the marginal labourer of that class, who is on the verge of not being employed at all, the abstraction of the paupers, not necessarily from productive labour for themselves, but from the competitive labour market, by raising the capacity of the marginal wage labourer, would seem to increase the wages of the entire labouring class."

VI, xIII, 9. wages are indicated as clearly by watching the marginal case of *A* at four shillings as that of *B* at two.[1]

True standardization is socially beneficial.

§ 9. Speaking broadly then it may be said that trade unions have benefited the nation as well as themselves by such uses of the Common Rule as make for a true standardization of work and wages; especially when combined with a frank endeavour to make the resources of the country go as far as they will, and thus to promote the growth of the national dividend. Any rise of wages or improvement in the conditions of life, and employment, which they may obtain by these reasonable methods, is likely to make for social wellbeing. It is not likely to worry and dishearten business enterprise, nor to throw out of their stride those whose efforts are making most for national leadership : nor will it drive capital abroad to any great extent.

Danger that the Common Rule may work for false standardization.

The case is different with applications of the Common Rule which make for a false standardization; which tend to force employers to put relatively inefficient workers in the same class for payment as more efficient workers; or which prevent anyone from doing work for which he is capable, on the ground that it does not technically belong to him. These uses of the Rule are *primâ facie* anti-social. There may indeed be stronger reasons for such action than appear on the surface : but their importance is apt to be exaggerated by the professional zeal of trade union officials for the technical perfection of the organization, for which they are responsible. The reasons are therefore of a kind for which external criticism may be serviceable, in spite of its aloofness. We may begin with a strong case, on which there is now relatively little difference of opinion.

The case of opposition to improved machinery and methods.

In the days when trade unions had not learnt full self-respect, forms of false standardization were common. Obstacles were put in the way of the use of improved methods and machinery; and attempts were made to fix the standard wage for a task at the

---

[1] It is really an understatement to say that competition tends to make the employer willing to pay twice as high wages to *A* as to *B* under these conditions. For an efficient worker who will make the same factory space and plant and supervision serve for twice as much production as an inefficient worker, is worth more than twice as much wages to the employer : he may really be worth three times as much. (See above, VI. III. 2.) Of course the employer may be afraid to offer to the more efficient worker wages proportionate to his true net product, lest inefficient workers, supported by their unions, should over-estimate his rate of profits, and claim a rise in wages. But in this case the cause which makes the employer pay attention to the net product of the less efficient worker, when considering how much it is worth his while to offer to the more efficient, is not free competition, but that resistance to free competition which is offered by the misapplication of the common rule. Some modern schemes for " gain sharing " aim at raising the wages of efficient workers nearly in proportion to their true net product; that is, more than in proportion to the " piece-work " rate : but trade unions do not always favour such schemes.

equivalent of the labour required to perform it by methods long VI, XIII, 9.
antiquated. This again tended to sustain wages in the particular
branch of industry concerned; but only by so great a check to
production, that the policy, if generally successful, would have
greatly curtailed the national dividend, and lessened employment
at good wages in the country generally. The service which the
leading trade unionists rendered to the country by condemning
this anti-social conduct are never to be forgotten. And though some
partial relapse from its high principles on the part of an enlightened
union led up to the great dispute of 1897 in the engineering trade,
the error was quickly purged of at least its worst features.[1]

Again, false standardization is involved in a practice, still fol- Insistence
lowed by many unions, of refusing to allow an elderly man, who can on full standard
no longer do a full standard day's work, to take something less than wages for
standard wages. This practice slightly restricts the supply of elderly workers.
labour in the trade, and appears to benefit those who enforce it. But
it cannot permanently restrict numbers : it often involves a heavy
burden on the benefit funds of the union, and it is generally shortsighted even from a purely selfish point of view. It lowers the
national dividend considerably : it condemns elderly men to take
their choice between oppressive idleness, and a weary struggle to
work harder than is good for them. It is harsh and anti-social.

To pass to a more doubtful case :—some delimitation of the The more
functions of each industrial group is essential to the working of the doubtful case of de-
Common Rule : and it is certainly in the interests of industrial limitation
progress that every urban artisan should seek to attain high pro- of work.
ficiency in some branch of work. But a good principle is apt to be
pushed to evil excess, when a man is not allowed to do a certain part
of the work on which he is engaged, though it is quite easy to him,
on the pretext that it belongs technically to another department.
Such prohibitions are of relatively little injury in establishments
that make large numbers of similar goods. For in these it is possible
so to arrange the work that there is fairly uniform employment for
an integral number of operatives of each of many different classes :
an *integral number*, *i.e.*, one with no ragged fringe of workers who
earn a part of their living elsewhere. But such prohibitions press

<hr>

[1] A useful history of the opposition to machinery is given in *Industrial Democracy*,
Part II, chapter VIII. It is combined with the advice not generally to resist the
introduction of machinery, but not to accept lower wages for working on the old
methods in order to meet its competition. This is good advice for young men. But
it cannot always be followed by men who have reached their prime : and if the administrative power of Governments should increase faster than the new tasks which
they appropriate from private enterprise, they may do excellent service by grappling
with those social discords that arise, when the skill of middle-aged and elderly men is
rendered almost valueless by improved methods.

VI, XIII,
10.

hardly on small employers; and especially on those who are on the lower rungs of a ladder that may lead in two generations, if not in one, to great achievements that make for national leadership. Even in large establishments, they increase the chance that a man, for whom it is difficult to find work at the time, will be sent to seek employment elsewhere; and thus swell for the time the ranks of the unemployed. Delimitation then, though a social good when applied moderately and with judgment, becomes an evil when pushed to extremes for the sake of the minor tactical advantages which it offers.[1]

Difficulties connected with gradual changes in the purchasing power of money, and fluctuations of commercial credit.

§ 10. Next we may pass to a still subtler and more difficult matter. It is a case in which the Common Rule appears to work badly, not because it is applied harshly : but because the work, to which it is set, requires it to be more perfect technically than it is, or perhaps can be made. The centre of this matter is that the standards of wages are expressed in terms of money : and since the real value of money changes from one decade to another, and fluctuates rapidly from year to year, rigid money standards cannot work out truly. It is difficult, if not impossible, to give them appropriate elasticity : and that is a reason against extreme applications of the Common Rule, which must perforce use so rigid and imperfect an implement.

The urgency of this consideration is increased by the natural tendency of trade unions to press for a rise in standard money wages during inflations of credit, which raise prices and lower the purchasing power of money for the time. At that time employers may be willing to pay high wages, measured in real purchasing power and still higher wages in terms of money, even for labour that falls somewhat short of the standard of full normal efficiency. Thus men of but second-rate efficiency earn the high standard money wages, and make good their claim to be admitted as members of the union. But very soon the inflation of credit subsides, and is followed by a depression; prices fall, and the purchasing power of money rises : the real value of labour falls, and its money value falls faster. The high standard of money wages, attained during the inflation, is now too high to leave a good margin of profits even on the work of fully efficient men; and those, who are below the standard of efficiency, are not worth the standard wages. This false standardization is not an unmixed evil to the efficient members of the trade : for it tends to make their labour more in demand, just as does the com-

---

[1] It may be noted that the great Amalgamated Society of Engineers, to which reference has just been made, led the way to concerted action between kindred branches of industry that softens the hard outlines of delimitation.

pulsory idleness of elderly men. But it does so only by checking VI, xɪɪɪ, 10. production, and therefore checking the demand for the labour of other branches of industry. The more such a policy is persisted in by trade unions generally, the deeper and the more sustained is the injury caused to the national dividend; and the less is the aggregate of employment at good wages throughout the country.

In the long run every branch of industry would prosper better, All would gain in the long run by a broad and generous policy. if each exerted itself more strenuously to set up several standards of efficiency for labour, with corresponding standards for wages; and were more quick to consent to some relaxation of a high standard of money wages when the crest of a wave of high prices, to which it was adapted, had passed away. Such adjustments are full of difficulty : but progress towards them might be hastened if there were a more general and clear appreciation of the fact that high wages, gained by means that hinder production in any branch of industry, necessarily increase unemployment in other branches. For, indeed, the only effective remedy for unemployment is a continuous adjustment of means to ends, in such way that credit can be based on the solid foundation of fairly accurate forecasts; and that reckless inflations of credit—the chief cause of all economic malaise—may be kept within narrower limits.

This matter cannot be argued here : but a few words may be The demand for commodities, of which the ultimate goal is consumption, comes from production. said in further explanation. Mill well observed that " What constitutes the means of payment for commodities is simply commodities. Each person's means of paying for the productions of other people consist of those which he himself possesses. All sellers are inevitably, and by the meaning of the word, buyers. Could we suddenly double the productive powers of the country, we should double the supply of commodities in every market; but we should, by the same stroke, double the purchasing power. Everybody would bring a double demand as well as supply; everybody would be able to buy twice as much, because everyone would have twice as much to offer in exchange."

But though men have the power to purchase they may not choose to use it. For when confidence has been shaken by failures, capital cannot be got to start new companies or extend old ones. Projects for new railways meet with no favour, ships lie idle, and there are no orders for new ships. There is scarcely any demand for the work of navvies, and not much for the work of the building and the engine-making trades. In short there is but little occupation in any of the trades which make fixed capital. Those whose skill and capital is specialized in these trades are earning little, and therefore

VI, xiii,
11.

buying little of the produce of other trades. Other trades, finding a poor market for their goods, produce less; they earn less, and therefore they buy less : the diminution of the demand for their wares makes them demand less of other trades. Thus commercial disorganization spreads : the disorganization of one trade throws others out of gear, and they react on it and increase its disorganization.

The mutual relations of the disorganization of credit, production, and consumption.

The chief cause of the evil is a want of confidence. The greater part of it could be removed almost in an instant if confidence could return, touch all industries with her magic wand, and make them continue their production and their demand for the wares of others. If all trades which make goods for direct consumption agreed to work on, and to buy each other's goods as in ordinary times, they would supply one another with the means of earning a moderate rate of profits and of wages. The trades which make fixed capital might have to wait a little longer : but they too would get employment when confidence had revived so far that those who had capital to invest had made up their minds how to invest it. Confidence by growing would cause itself to grow; credit would give increased means of purchase, and thus prices would recover. Those in trade already would make good profits, new companies would be started, old businesses would be extended; and soon there would be a good demand even for the work of those who make fixed capital. There is of course no formal agreement between the different trades to begin again to work full time, and so make a market for each other's wares. But the revival of industry comes about through the gradual and often simultaneous growth of confidence among many various trades; it begins as soon as traders think that prices will not continue to fall : and with a revival of industry prices rise.[1]

The drift of economic change is so far

§ 11. The main drift of this study of Distribution then suggests that the social and economic forces already at work are changing the distribution of wealth for the better : that they are persistent and

[1] The quotation from Mill and the two paragraphs which follow it are reproduced from *The Economics of Industry*, III. i. 4, published by my wife and myself in 1879. They indicate the attitude which most of those, who follow in the traditions of the classical economists, hold as to the relations between consumption and production. It is true that in times of depression the disorganization of consumption is a contributory cause to the continuance of the disorganization of credit and of production. But a remedy is not to be got by a study of consumption, as has been alleged by some hasty writers. No doubt there is good work to be done by a study of the influence of arbitrary changes in fashion on employment. But the main study needed is that of the organization of production and of credit. And, though economists have not yet succeeded in bringing that study to a successful issue, the cause of their failure lies in the profound obscurity and ever-changing form of the problem; it does not lie in any indifference on their part to its supreme importance. Economics from beginning to end is a study of the mutual adjustments of consumption and production : when the one is under discussion, the other is never out of mind.

increasing in strength; and that their influence is for the greater part cumulative; that the socio-economic organism is more delicate and complex than at first sight appears; and that large ill-considered changes might result in grave disaster. In particular it suggests that the assumption and ownership by Government of all the means of production, even if brought about gradually and slowly, as the more responsible "Collectivists" propose, might cut deeper into the roots of social prosperity than appears at first sight.

Starting from the fact that the growth of the national dividend depends on the continued progress of invention and the accumulation of expensive appliances for production; we are bound to reflect that up to the present time nearly all of the innumerable inventions that have given us our command over nature have been made by independent workers; and that the contributions from Government officials all the world over have been relatively small. Further, nearly all the costly appliances for production which are now in collective ownership by national or local Governments, have been bought with resources borrowed mainly from the savings of business men and other private individuals. Oligarchic Governments have sometimes made great efforts to accumulate collective wealth; and it may be hoped that in the coming time, foresight and patience will become the common property of the main body of the working classes. But, as things are, too great a risk would be involved by entrusting to a pure democracy the accumulation of the resources needed for acquiring yet further command over nature.

There is therefore strong *primâ facie* cause for fearing that the collective ownership of the means of production would deaden the energies of mankind, and arrest economic progress; unless before its introduction the whole people had acquired a power of unselfish devotion to the public good which is now relatively rare. And, though this matter cannot be entered upon here, it might probably destroy much that is most beautiful and joyful in the private and domestic relations of life. These are the main reasons which cause patient students of economics generally to anticipate little good and much evil from schemes for sudden and violent reorganization of the economic, social and political conditions of life.

Further, we are bound to reflect that the distribution of the national dividend, though bad, is not nearly as bad as is commonly supposed. In fact there are many artisan households in England, and even more in the United States in spite of the colossal fortunes that are found there, which would lose by an equal distribution of the national income. Therefore the fortunes of the masses of the

VI, xiii, 11.

beneficial, as to plead for caution in reform.

The economic and social perils of collectivism.

Existing inequalities of wealth are often exaggerated,

VI, xiii,
12.

people, though they would of course be greatly improved *for the time* by the removal of all inequalities, would not be raised even temporarily at all near to the level which is assigned to them in socialistic anticipations of a Golden Age.[1]

but they are needlessly great; and tolerance of them may be excessive.

But this cautious attitude does not imply acquiescence in the present inequalities of wealth. The drift of economic science during many generations has been with increasing force towards the belief that there is no real necessity, and therefore no moral justification for extreme poverty side by side with great wealth. The inequalities of wealth, though less than they are often represented to be, are a serious flaw in our economic organization. Any diminution of them which can be attained by means that would not sap the springs of free initiative and strength of character, and would not therefore materially check the growth of the national dividend, would seem to be a clear social gain. Though arithmetic warns us that it is impossible to raise all earnings beyond the level already reached by specially well-to-do artisan families, it is certainly desirable that those who are below that level should be raised, even at the expense of lowering in some degree those who are above it.

The exceptional case of the Residuum.

§ 12. Prompt action is needed in regard to the large, though it may be hoped, now steadily diminishing, " Residuum " of persons who are physically, mentally, or morally incapable of doing a good days' work with which to earn a good day's wage. This class perhaps includes some others besides those who are absolutely " unemployable." But it is a class that needs exceptional treatment. The system of economic freedom is probably the best from both a moral and material point of view for those who are in fairly good health of mind and body. But the Residuum cannot turn it to good account : and if they are allowed to bring up children in their own pattern, then Anglo-Saxon freedom must work badly through them on the coming generation. It would be better for them and much better for the nation that they should come under a paternal discipline something like that which prevails in Germany.[2]

---

[1] Some years ago the annual income of some 49,000,000 people in the United Kingdom appeared to amount to more than £2,000,000,000. Many leading artisans were earning about £200 a year; and there were a vast number of artisan households in which each of four or five members were earning an income ranging from 18s. to 40s. a week. The expenditure of these households was on as large, if not a larger scale, than would be possible if the total income were divided out equally, so as to yield about £40 annually a head. PS, 1920. No recent statistics are accessible on the matter. But it seems certain that the incomes of the working classes generally are increasing at least as fast as those of other classes. Several of the suggestions made in the present chapter are further developed in an article on " The social possibilities of economic chivalry " in the *Economic Journal* for March 1907.

[2] A beginning might be made with a broader, more educative and more generous administration of public aid to the helpless. The difficulty of discrimination would need to be faced : and in facing it local and central authorities would obtain much of

The evil to be dealt with is so urgent that strong measures against it are eagerly to be desired. And the proposal that a minimum wage should be fixed by authority of Government below which no man may work, and another below which no woman may work, has claimed the attention of students for a long while. If it could be made effective, its benefits would be so great that it might be gladly accepted, in spite of the fear that it would lead to malingering and some other abuses; and that it would be used as a leverage for pressing for a rigid artificial standard of wages, in cases in which there was no exceptional justification for it. But, though great improvements in the details of the scheme have been made recently, and especially in the last two or three years, its central difficulties do not appear to have been fairly faced. There is scarcely any experience to guide us except that of Australasia, where every inhabitant is part owner of a vast landed property; and which has been recently peopled by men and women in full strength and health. And such experience is of but little use in regard to a people whose vitality has been impaired by the old Poor Law, and the old Corn Laws; and by the misuses of the Factory system, when its dangers were not yet understood. A scheme, that has any claim to be ready for practical adoption, must be based on statistical estimates of the numbers of those who under it would be forced to seek the aid of the State, because their work was not worth the minimum wage; with special reference to the question how many of these might have supported life fairly well if it had been possible to work with nature, and to adjust in many cases the minimum wage to the family, instead of to the individual.[1]

VI, XIII, 12.

The claims and the difficulties of the proposal for a minimum wage.

---

the information needed for guiding, and in extreme cases for controlling, those who are weak and especially those whose weakness is a source of grave danger to the coming generation. Elderly people might be helped with a chief regard to economy and to their personal inclinations. But the case of those, who are responsible for young children, would call for a greater expenditure of public funds, and a more strict subordination of personal freedom to public necessity. The most urgent among the first steps towards causing the Residuum to cease from the land, is to insist on regular school attendance in decent clothing, and with bodies clean and fairly well fed. In case of failure the parents should be warned and advised : as a last resource the homes might be closed or regulated with some limitation of the freedom of the parents. The expense would be great : but there is no other so urgent need for bold expenditure. It would remove the great canker that infects the whole body of the nation : and when the work was done the resources that had been absorbed by it would be free for some more pleasant but less pressing social duty.

[1] This last consideration seems to have been pushed on one side largely under the influence of a faulty analysis of the nature of " parasitic " work and of its influence on wages. The family is, in the main, a single unit as regards geographical migration : and therefore the wages of men are relatively high, and those of women and children low where heavy iron or other industries preponderate, while in some other districts less than half the money income of the family is earned by the father, and men's wages are relatively low. This natural adjustment is socially beneficial; and rigid national rules as to minimum wages for men and for women, which ignore or oppose t, are to be deprecated.

VI, XIII,
13.
___

People fit
only for
unskilled
labour are
relatively
diminish-
ing in
numbers.

§ 13. Turning then to those workers who have fairly good moral and physical stamina, it may be estimated roughly that those who are capable only of rather unskilled work constitute about a fourth of the population. And those who, though fit for the lower kinds of skilled work are neither fit for highly skilled work, nor able to act wisely and promptly in responsible positions, constitute about another fourth. If similar estimates had been made in England a century ago, the proportions would have been very different : more than a half would have been found unfit for any skilled labour at all, beyond the ordinary routine of agriculture; and perhaps less than a sixth part would have been fit for highly skilled or responsible work : for the education of the people was not then recognized as a national duty and a national economy. If this had been the only change the urgent demand for unskilled labour would have compelled employers to pay for it nearly the same wage as for skilled : the wages for skilled labour would have fallen a little and those for unskilled would have risen, until the two had nearly met.

But
machinery
has dimin-
ished the
demand for
labour of
those kinds
which used
to be re-
garded as
unskilled.

Even as it is, something like this has happened : the wages of unskilled labour have risen faster than those of any other class, faster even than those of skilled labour. And this movement towards the equalization of earnings would have gone much faster, had not the work of purely unskilled labour been meanwhile annexed by auto- matic and other machinery faster even than that of skilled labour; so that there is less wholly unskilled work to be done now than formerly. It is true that some kinds of work, which traditionally belong to skilled artisans, require now less skill than formerly. But, on the other hand, the so-called " unskilled " labourer has now often to handle appliances too subtle and expensive to have been safely entrusted to the ordinary English labourer a century ago, or to any people at all in some backward countries now.

Thus mechanical progress is a chief cause of the great differences that still exist between the earnings of different kinds of labour; and this may seem at first sight a severe indictment : but it is not. If mechanical progress had been much slower the real wages of unskilled labour would have been lower than they are now, not higher : for the growth of the national dividend would have been so much checked that even the skilled workers would generally have had to content themselves with less real purchasing power for an hour's work than the 6d. of the London bricklayer's labourer : and the unskilled labourers' wages would of course have been lower still. It has been assumed that the happiness of life, in so far as it depends on material conditions, may be said to begin when the income is sufficient to yield the *barest* necessaries of life : and that after that has been attained, an increase by a given percentage of the income will increase that happiness by about the same amount, whatever the income be.   This rough hypothesis leads to the conclusion that an increase by (say) a quarter of the wages of the poorer class of *bonâ fide* workers adds more to the sum total of happiness than an increase by a quarter of the incomes of an equal number of any other class.   And that seems reasonable : for it arrests positive suffering, and active causes of degradation, and it opens the way to hope as no other proportionate increase of incomes does.   From this point of view it may be urged that the poorer classes have derived a greater real benefit from economic progress on its mechanical and other sides, than is suggested by the statistics of their wages.   But all the more is it the duty of society to endeavour to carry yet further an increase of wellbeing which is to be obtained at so low a cost.[1]

VI, xiii, 13.

We have then to strive to keep mechanical progress in full swing : and to diminish the supply of labour, incapable of any but unskilled work; in order that the average income of the country may rise faster even than in the past, and the share of it got by each unskilled labourer may rise faster still.   To that end we need to move in the same direction as in recent years, but more strenuously.   Education must be made more thorough.   The schoolmaster must learn that his main duty is not to impart knowledge, for a few shillings will buy more printed knowledge than a man's brain can hold.   It is to educate character, faculties and activities; so that the children even of those parents who are not thoughtful themselves, may have a better chance of being trained up to become thoughtful parents of the next generation.   To this end public money must flow freely.   And it must flow freely to provide fresh air and space for wholesome play for the children in all working class quarters.[2]

The chief remedy is to fit more of the children of the un-skilled for higher work,

Thus the State seems to be required to contribute generously and even lavishly to that side of the wellbeing of the poorer working class which they cannot easily provide for themselves : and at the same time to insist that the inside of the houses be kept clean, and fit for those who will be needed in after years to act as strong and responsible citizens.   The compulsory standard of cubic feet of air per head needs to be raised steadily though not violently : and this combined with a regulation that no row of high buildings be erected

[1] See above, III. vi. 6; and Note VIII. in the Mathematical Appendix. Compare also Professor Carver on " Machinery and the Laborers " in the *Quarterly Journal of Economics*, 1908.
[2] It is urged below, Appendix G, 8, 9, that the health of the working classes, and especially of their children, has a first claim on rates levied on that special value of urban land which is caused by the concentration of population.

VI, xiii, 13.

without adequate free space in front and behind, will hasten the movement, already in progress, of the working classes from the central districts of large towns, to places in which freer playroom is possible. Meanwhile public aid and control in medical and sanitary matters will work in another direction to lessen the weight that has hitherto pressed on the children of the poorer classes.

and to do the same with the children of the skilled.

The children of unskilled workers need to be made capable of earning the wages of skilled work : and the children of skilled workers need by similar means to be made capable of doing still more responsible work. They will not gain much, they are indeed more likely to lose, by pushing themselves into the ranks of the lower middle class : for, as has already been observed, the mere power of writing and keeping accounts belongs really to a lower grade than skilled manual work; and has ranked above it in past times, merely because popular education had been neglected. There is often a social loss as well as a social gain when the children of any grade press into the grade above them. But the existence of our present lowest class is an almost unmixed evil : nothing should be done to promote the increase of its numbers, and children once born into it should be helped to rise out of it.

The constructive imagination on which material progress mainly depends.

There is plenty of room in the upper ranks of the artisans; and there is abundant room for new comers in the upper ranks of the middle class. It is to the activity and resource of the leading minds in this class that most of those inventions and improvements are due, which enable the working man of to-day to have comforts and luxuries that were rare or unknown among the richest of a few generations ago : and without which indeed England could not supply her present population with a sufficiency even of common food. And it is a vast and wholly unmixed gain when the children of any class press within the relatively small charmed circle of those who create new ideas, and who embody those new ideas in solid constructions. Their profits are sometimes large : but taking one with another they have probably earned for the world a hundred times or more as much as they have earned for themselves.

Malignant forms of speculation are a grievous hindrance to progress.

It is true that many of the largest fortunes are made by speculation rather than by truly constructive work : and much of this speculation is associated with anti-social strategy, and even with evil manipulation of the sources from which ordinary investors derive their guidance. A remedy is not easy, and may never be perfect. Hasty attempts to control speculation by simple enactments have invariably proved either futile or mischievous : but this is one of those matters in which the rapidly increasing force of economic studies may be expected to render great service to the world in the course of this century.

VI, XIII, 14.

In many other ways evil may be lessened by a wider understanding of the social possibilities of economic chivalry. A devotion to public wellbeing on the part of the rich may do much, as enlightenment spreads, to help the tax-gatherer in turning the resources of the rich to high account in the service of the poor, and may remove the worst evils of poverty from the land.

Social possibilities of economic chivalry.

§ 14. The inequalities of wealth, and especially the very low earnings of the poorest classes, have just been discussed with reference to their effects in dwarfing activities as well as in curtailing the satisfaction of wants. But here, as everywhere, the economist is brought up against the fact that the power of rightly using such income and opportunities, as a family has, is in itself wealth of the highest order, and of a kind that is rare in all classes. Perhaps £100,000,000 annually are spent even by the working classes, and £400,000,000 by the rest of the population of England, in ways that do little or nothing towards making life nobler or truly happier. And, though it is true that a shortening of the hours of labour would in many cases lessen the national dividend and lower wages : yet it would probably be well that most people should work rather less; provided that the consequent loss of material income could be met exclusively by the abandonment by all classes of the least worthy methods of consumption; and that they could learn to spend leisure well.

It is easier to work well than to use wealth well, and much easier than to use leisure well.

But unfortunately human nature improves slowly, and in nothing more slowly than in the hard task of learning to use leisure well. In every age, in every nation, and in every rank of society, those who have known how to work well, have been far more numerous than those who have known how to use leisure well. But on the other hand it is only through freedom to use leisure as they will, that people can learn to use leisure well : and no class of manual workers, who are devoid of leisure, can have much self-respect and become full citizens. Some time free from the fatigue of work that tires without educating, is a necessary condition of a high standard of life.

In this, as in all similar cases, it is the young whose faculties and activities are of the highest importance both to the moralist and the economist. The most imperative duty of this generation is to provide for the young such opportunities as will both develop their higher nature, and make them efficient producers. And an essential condition to this end is long-continued freedom from mechanical

Leisure for the young.

VI, xiii, 15.

toil; together with abundant leisure for school and for such kinds of play as strengthen and develop the character.

The interest of the rising generation in the hours of labour of their parents.

Even if we took account only of the injury done to the young by living in a home in which the father and the mother lead joyless lives, it would be in the interest of society to afford some relief to them also. Able workers and good citizens are not likely to come from homes, from which the mother is absent during a great part of the day; nor from homes, to which the father seldom returns till his children are asleep : and therefore society as a whole has a direct interest in the curtailment of extravagantly long hours of duty away from home, even for mineral-train-guards and others, whose work is not in itself very hard.

Industrial adjustment is hindered by the length of human life, and by the still longer life of inherited traits of character.

§ 15. In discussing the difficulty of adjusting the supply of industrial skill of various kinds to the demand for it, attention was called to the fact that the adjustment could not be nearly accurate, because the methods of industry change rapidly, and the skill of a worker needs to be used for some forty or even fifty years after he has set himself to acquire it.[1] The difficulties which we have just discussed turn largely on the long life of inherited habits and tones of thought and feeling. If the organization of our joint-stock companies, of our railways or our canals is bad, we can set it right in a decade or two. But those elements of human nature which have been developed during centuries of war and violence, and of sordid and gross pleasures, cannot be greatly changed in the course of a single generation.

If human nature could be ideally transformed private property would be unnecessary and harmless.

Now, as always, noble and eager schemers for the reorganization of society have painted beautiful pictures of life, as it might be under institutions which their imagination constructs easily. But it is an irresponsible imagination, in that it proceeds on the suppressed assumption that human nature will, under the new institutions, quickly undergo changes such as cannot reasonably be expected in the course of a century, even under favourable conditions. If human nature could be thus ideally transformed, economic chivalry would dominate life even under the existing institutions of private property. And private property, the necessity for which doubtless reaches no deeper than the qualities of human nature, would become harmless at the same time that it became unnecessary.

There is evil in extreme impatience as well as

There is then need to guard against the temptation to overstate the economic evils of our own age, and to ignore the existence of similar and worse evils in earlier ages; even though some exaggeration may for the time stimulate others, as well as ourselves, to a more

[1] See VI. v. 1, 2.

intense resolve that the present evils shall no longer be allowed to exist. But it is not less wrong, and generally it is much more foolish, to palter with truth for a good than for a selfish cause. And the pessimist descriptions of our own age, combined with romantic exaggerations of the happiness of past ages, must tend to the setting aside of methods of progress, the work of which if slow is yet solid; and to the hasty adoption of others of greater promise, but which resemble the potent medicines of a charlatan, and while quickly effecting a little good, sow the seeds of widespread and lasting decay. This impatient insincerity is an evil only less great than that moral torpor which can endure that we, with our modern resources and knowledge, should look on contentedly at the continued destruction of all that is worth having in multitudes of human lives, and solace ourselves with the reflection that anyhow the evils of our own age are less than those of the past.

And now we must conclude this part of our study. We have reached very few practical conclusions; because it is generally necessary to look at the whole of the economic, to say nothing of the moral and other aspects of a practical problem before attempting to deal with it at all : and in real life nearly very economic issue depends, more or less directly, on some complex actions and reactions of credit, of foreign trade, and of modern developments of combination and monopoly. But the ground which we have traversed in Books V and VI is, in some respects, the most difficult of the whole province of economics; and it commands, and gives access to, the remainder.

VI, xiii, 15.

in extreme patience, with social ills.

APPENDIX A

THE GROWTH OF FREE INDUSTRY AND ENTERPRISE

APP. A, 1.

§ 1. The last section of the first chapter of Book I describes the purpose of Appendices A and B; and may be taken as an introduction to them.

Individual action and race character act and react on one another: both are much influenced by physical causes.

Although the proximate causes of the chief events in history are to be found in the actions of individuals, yet most of the conditions which have made these events possible are traceable to the influence of inherited institutions and race qualities and of physical nature. Race qualities themselves are, however, mainly caused by the action of individuals and physical causes in more or less remote time. A strong race has often sprung, in fact as well as in name, from some progenitor of singular strength of body and character. The usages which make a race strong in peace and war are often due to the wisdom of a few great thinkers who have interpreted and developed its customs and rules, perhaps by formal precepts, perhaps by a quiet and almost unperceived influence. But none of these things are of any permanent avail if the climate is unfavourable to vigour : the gifts of nature, her land, her waters, and her skies, determine the character of the race's work, and thus give a tone to social and political institutions.

Savage life is ruled by custom and impulse.

These differences do not show themselves clearly so long as man is still savage. Scanty and untrustworthy as is our information about the habits of savage tribes, we know enough of them to be sure that they show a strange uniformity of general character, amid great variety of detail. Whatever be their climate and whatever their ancestry, we find savages living under the dominion of custom and impulse; scarcely ever striking out new lines for themselves; never forecasting the distant future, and seldom making provision even for the near future; fitful in spite of their servitude to custom, governed by the fancy of the moment; ready at times for the most arduous exertions, but incapable of keeping themselves long to steady work. Laborious and tedious tasks are avoided as far as possible; those which are inevitable are done by the compulsory labour of women.

Physical causes act most powerfully in the early stages of civilization

It is when we pass from savage life to the early forms of civilization that the influence of physical surroundings forces itself most on our notice. This is partly because early history is meagre, and tells us but little of the particular events and of the influences of strong individual characters by which the course of national progress has been guided and controlled, hastened onwards or turned backwards. But it is chiefly because in this stage of his progress man's power of contending with nature is small, and he can do nothing without her generous help. Nature has marked out a few places on the earth's surface as specially favourable to man's first attempts to raise himself from the savage state; and the first growth of culture and the industrial arts was directed and controlled by the physical conditions of these favoured spots.[1]

which have necessarily

Even the simplest civilization is impossible unless man's efforts are more than sufficient to supply him with the necessaries of life; some surplus over

---

[1] On the general question of the influence of physical surroundings on race character, both directly and indirectly, by determining the nature of the dominant occupations, see Knies, *Politsche Œkonomie*, Hegel's *Philosophy of History*, and Buckle's *History of Civilization*. Compare also Aristotle's *Politics*, and Montesquieu's *Esprit des Lois*.

them is required to support that mental effort in which progress takes its rise. APP. A, 1.
And therefore nearly all early civilizations have been in warm climates where ——
the necessaries of life are small, and where nature makes bountiful returns even taken place
to the rudest cultivation. They have often gathered around a great river in warm
which has lent moisture to the soil and afforded an easy means of communica- climates.
tion. The rulers have generally belonged to a race that has recently come from Ruling
a cooler climate in a distant country or in neighbouring mountain lands; for a castes have
warm climate is destructive of energy, and the force which enabled them to rule given their
has almost in every case been the product of the more temperate climate of energies to
their early homes. They have indeed retained much of their energy in their war and
new homes for several generations, living meanwhile in luxury on the surplus politics,
products of the labour of the subject races; and have found scope for their not to
abilities in the work of rulers, warriors, and priests. Originally ignorant, they industry.
have quickly learnt all that their subjects had to teach, and have gone beyond
them. But in this stage of civilization an enterprising intellectual character
has almost always been confined to the ruling few, it has scarcely ever been
found in those who have borne the main burden of industry.

The reason of this is that the climate which has rendered an early civilization The
possible has also doomed it to weakness.[1] In colder climates nature provides influence
an invigorating atmosphere; and though man has a hard struggle at first, yet of a warm
as his knowledge and riches increase he is able to gain plentiful food and warm climate.
clothing; and at a later stage he provides himself with those large and substantial buildings which are the most expensive requisites of a cultured life
in places in which the severity of the weather makes it necessary that nearly
all domestic services and meetings for social intercourse should have the
protection of a roof. But the fresh invigorating air which is necessary to the
fulness of life cannot be obtained at all when nature does not freely give it.[2]
The labourer may indeed be found doing hard physical work under a tropical
sun; the handicraftsman may have artistic instincts; the sage, the statesman
or the banker may be acute and subtle : but high temperature makes hard and
sustained physical work inconsistent with a high intellectual activity. Under
the combined influence of climate and luxury the ruling class gradually lose
their strength; fewer and fewer of them are capable of great things : and at
last they are overthrown by a stronger race which has come most probably
from a cooler climate. Sometimes they form an intermediate caste between
those whom they have hitherto ruled and their new rulers; but more often
they sink down among the spiritless mass of the people.

Such a civilization has often much that is interesting to the philosophical In an early
historian. Its whole life is pervaded almost unconsciously by a few simple civilization
ideas which are interwoven in that pleasant harmony that gives their charm to movement
Oriental carpets. There is much to be learnt from tracing these ideas to their is slow, but
origin in the combined influence of race, of physical surroundings, of religion, there is
philosophy and poetry; of the incidents of warfare and the dominating in- movement.
fluence of strong individual characters. All this is instructive to the economist
in many ways; but it does not throw a very direct light on the motives, which
it is his special province to study. For in such a civilization the ablest men
look down on work; there are no bold free enterprising workmen, and no

---

[1] Montesquieu says quaintly (Bk. XIV. ch. II.) that the superiority of strength
caused by a cold climate produces among other effects " a greater sense of superiority—
that is, less desire of revenge; and a greater opinion of security—that is, more frankness, less suspicion, policy, and cunning." These virtues are eminently helpful to
economic progress.

[2] This may have to be modified a little, but only a little, if F. Galton should prove
to be right in thinking that small numbers of a ruling race in a hot country, as for
instance the English in India, will be able to sustain their constitutional vigour unimpaired for many generations by a liberal use of artificial ice, or of the cooling effects
of the forcible expansion of compressed air. See his Presidential Address to the
Anthropological Institute in 1881.

APP. A, 2. adventurous capitalists; despised industry is regulated by custom, and even looks to custom as its sole protector from arbitrary tyranny.

Custom is never altogether on the side of the strong,
The greater part of custom is doubtless but a crystallized form of oppression and suppression. But a body of custom which did nothing but grind down the weak could not long survive. For the strong rest on the support of the weak, their own strength cannot sustain them without that support; and if they organize social arrangements which burden the weak wantonly and beyond measure, they thereby destroy themselves. Consequently every body of custom that endures, contains provisions that protect the weak from the most reckless forms of injury.[1]

and is indeed a necessary protection when the means of communication are small.
In fact when there is little enterprise and no scope for effective competition custom is a necessary shield to defend people not only from others who are stronger than themselves, but even from their neighbours in the same rank of life. If the village smith can sell his ploughshares to none but the village, and if the village can buy their shares from no one but him, it is to the interest of all that the price should be fixed at a moderate level by custom. By such means custom earns sanctity: and there is nothing in the first steps of progress that tends to break down the primitive habit of regarding the innovator as impious, and an enemy. Thus the influence of economic causes is pressed below the surface, where they work surely and slowly. They take generations instead of years to produce their effect: their action is so subtle as easily to escape observation altogether, and they can indeed hardly be traced except by those who have learnt where to look for them by watching the more conspicuous and rapid workings of similar causes in modern times.[2]

Divided ownership strengthens the force of custom and resists changes.
§ 2. This force of custom in early civilizations is partly a cause and partly a consequence of the limitations of individual rights in property. As regards all property more or less, but especially as regards land, the rights of the individual are generally derived from and limited by, and in every way subordinate to those of the household and the family in the narrower sense of the term. The rights of the household are in like manner subordinate to those of the village; which is often only an expanded and developed family, according to traditional fiction if not in fact.

It is true that in an early stage of civilization few would have had much desire to depart far from the practices that were prevalent around them. However complete and sharply defined had been the rights of individuals over their own property, they would have been unwilling to face the anger with which their neighbours would regard any innovation, and the ridicule which would be poured on any one who should set himself up to be wiser than his ancestors. But many little changes would occur to the bolder spirits; and if they had been free to try experiments on their own account, changes might have grown by small and almost imperceptible stages, until sufficient variation of practice had been established to blur the clear outline of customary regulations, and to give considerable freedom to individual choice. When however each head of a household was regarded as only senior partner and trustee for the family property, the smallest divergence from ancestral routine met with the opposition of people who had a right to be consulted on every detail.

And further in the background behind the authoritative resistance of the

---

[1] Comp. Bagehot's *Physics and Politics*, also the writings of Herbert Spencer and Maine.

[2] Thus the "moderate level" at which custom fixes the price of a ploughshare will be found when analysed to mean that which gives the smith in the long run about an equal remuneration (account being taken of all his privileges and perquisites) with that of his neighbours who do equally difficult work; or in other words, that which under the régime of free enterprise, of easy communications and effective competition, we should call a normal rate of pay. If a change of circumstances makes the pay of smiths, including all indirect allowances, either less or more than this, there almost always sets in a change in the substance of the custom, often almost unrecognized and generally without any change in form, which will bring it back to this level.

family was that of the village. For though each family had sole use for a time APP. A, 3. of its cultivated ground, yet many operations were generally conducted in common, so that each had to do the same things as the others at the same time. Each field when its turn came to be fallow, became part of the common pasture land; and the whole land of the village was subject to redistribution from time to time.[1] Therefore the village had a clear right to prohibit any innovation; for it might interfere with their plans for the collective cultivation; and it might ultimately impair the value of the land, and thus injure them when the time came for the next redistribution. In consequence there often grew up a complex network of rules, by which every cultivator was so rigidly bound, that he could not use his own judgment and discretion even in the most trivial details.[2] It is probable that this has been the most important of all the causes which have delayed the growth of the spirit of free enterprise among mankind. It may be noticed that the collective ownership of property was in harmony with that spirit of quietism which pervades many Eastern religions; and that its long survival among the Hindoos has been partly due to the repose which is inculcated in their religious writings.

It is probable that while the influence of custom over prices, wages and rent has been overrated, its influence over the forms of production and the general economic arrangements of society has been underrated. In the one case its effects are obvious, but they are not cumulative; and in the other they are not obvious, but they are cumulative. And it is an almost universal rule that when the effects of a cause, though small at any one time, are constantly working in the same direction, their influence is much greater than at first sight appears possible. *The influence of custom on the methods of industry is cumulative.*

But however great was the influence of custom in early civilization the spirit of Greeks and Romans was full of enterprise, and more interest attaches to the inquiry why they knew and cared so little for those social aspects of economic problems which are of so great interest to us.

§ 3. The homes of most of the earlier civilizations had been in great river-basins, whose well-watered plains were seldom visited by famine; for in a climate in which heat is never lacking, the fertility of the soil varies almost directly with its moisture : the rivers also offered means of easy communication that were favourable to simple forms of trade and division of labour, and did not hinder the movements of the large armies by which the despotic force of the central government was maintained. It is true that the Phœnicians lived on the sea. This great Semitic race did good service by preparing the way for free intercourse among many peoples, and by spreading the knowledge of writing, of arithmetic, and of weights and measures : but they gave their chief energies to commerce and manufacture. *The older civilizations had been chiefly inland.*

It was left for the genial sympathies and the fresh spirit of the Greeks to breathe in the full breath of freedom over the sea : and to absorb into their own free lives the best thoughts and the highest art of the Old World. Their numberless settlements in Asia Minor, Magna Græcia, and in Hellas proper, developed freely their own ideals under the influence of the new thoughts that *The sea gave the Greeks knowledge,*

---

[1] The Teutonic Mark system is indeed now known to have been much less general than some historians had supposed. But where it was fully developed one small part, the home mark, was set aside permanently for living on, and each family retained its share in that for ever. The second part or arable mark was divided into three large fields, in each of which each family had generally several scattered acre strips. Two of these were cultivated every year, and one left fallow. The third and largest part was used as grazing land by the whole village in common; as was also the fallow field in the arable mark. In some cases the arable mark was from time to time abandoned to pasture, and land to make a new arable mark was cut out of the common mark, and this involved a redistribution. Thus the treatment of its land by every family affected for good or ill all the members of the village.

[2] Compare the Duke of Argyll's account of Runrig cultivation in *Unseen Foundations of Society*, ch. IX.

APP. A, 4.
———
freedom,
and the
power of
variation.

Their
climate
made
culture in-
expensive,
and yet did
not quicky
relax their
strength.

Modern
in many
respects,
they did
not antici-
pate the
economic
problems
which have
grown up
with the
sense of
the dignity
of labour.

Their
impatience
of the
discipline
of steady
industry
led to
their fall.

The
strength of
character

burst upon them; having constant intercourse with one another, as well as with those who held the keys of the older learning; sharing one another's experiences, but fettered by no authority. Energy and enterprise, instead of being repressed by the weight of traditional usage, were encouraged to found a new colony and work out new ideas without restraint.

Their climate absolved them from the need of exhausting work; they left to their slaves what drudgery had to be done, and gave themselves up to the free play of their fancy. House-room, clothing and firing cost but little; their genial sky invited them to out-of-door life, making intercourse for social and political purposes easy and without expense. And yet the cool breezes of the Mediterranean so far refreshed their vigour, that they did not for many generations lose the spring and elasticity of temper which they had brought from their homes in the North. Under these conditions were matured a sense of beauty in all its forms, a subtle fancy and an originality of speculation, an energy of political life, and a delight in subordinating the individual to the State, such as the world has never again known.[1]

The Greeks were more modern in many respects than the peoples of Mediæval Europe, and in some respects were even in advance of our own time. But they did not attain to the conception of the dignity of man as man; they regarded slavery as an ordinance of Nature, they tolerated agriculture, but they looked on all other industries as involving degradation; and they knew little or nothing of those economic problems, which are of absorbing interest to our own age.[2]

They had never felt the extreme pressure of poverty. Earth and sea, and sun and sky had combined to make it easy for them to obtain the material requisites for a perfect life. Even their slaves had considerable opportunities of culture: and had it been otherwise, there was nothing in the Greek temper, and nothing in the lessons that the world had up to that time learnt, to make them seriously concerned. The excellence of Greek thought has made it a touchstone by which many of the leading thinkers of after ages have tried every new inquiry: and the impatience with which the academic mind has often regarded the study of economics is in a great measure due to the impatience which the Greeks felt for the anxious cares and plodding work of business.

And yet a lesson might have been learnt from the decadence of Greece; which was brought about by the want of that solid earnestness of purpose which no race has ever maintained for many generations without the discipline of steady industry. Socially and intellectually they were free: but they had not learnt to use their freedom well; they had no self-mastery, no steady persistent resolution. They had all the quickness of perception and readiness for new suggestions which are elements of business enterprise; but they had not its fixity of purpose and patient endurance. A genial climate slowly relaxed their physical energies; they were without that safeguard to strength of character which comes from resolute and steadfast persistence in hard work; and at last they sank into frivolity.

§ 4. Civilization still moving westwards had its next centre in Rome. The Romans were a great army, rather than a great nation. They resembled the Greeks in leaving business as much as possible to slaves; but in most

---

[1] Compare Neumann and Partsch, *Physikalische Geographie von Griechenland*, ch. I., and Grote's *History of Greece*, Part II. ch. I.

[2] See above, p. 4. Thus even Plato says :—" Nature has made neither boot-makers nor blacksmiths; such occupations degrade the people engaged in them, miserable mercenaries excluded by their very position from political rights." (*Laws*, XII.) And Aristotle continues :—" In the state which is best governed the citizens . . . must not lead the life of mechanics or tradesmen, for such a life is ignoble and inimical to virtue." (*Politics*, VII. 9; see also III. 5.) These passages give the key-note of Greek thought with regard to business. But as there were few independent fortunes in ancient Greece, many of her best thinkers were compelled to take some share in business.

other respects were a contrast to them. In opposition to the fresh fulness of
the life of the Athenians, to the youthful joy with which they gave free play to
all their faculties and developed their own idiosyncrasy, the Romans showed
the firm will, the iron resolution, the absorption in definite serious aims of the
mature man.[1]

Singularly free from the restraints of custom, they shaped their own lives
for themselves with a deliberate choice that had never been known before.
They were strong and daring, steady of purpose and abundant in resource,
orderly in habit, and clearsighted in judgment; and thus, though they preferred war and politics, they had in constant use all the faculties required for
business enterprise.

Nor was the principle of association inactive. Trade gilds had some
vigour in spite of the paucity of artisans who were free. Those methods of
combined action for business purposes, and of production on a large scale by
slave labour in factories, in which Greece had been the pupil of the East,
gained new strength when imported into Rome. The faculties and the temper
of the Romans fitted them especially well for the management of joint-stock
companies; and a comparatively small number of very wealthy men, with no
middle class, were able, with the aid of trained slaves and freedmen, to undertake large contracts by land and by sea at home and abroad. They made
capital hateful; but they made it powerful and efficient; they developed the
appliances of money-lending with great energy; and partly in consequence of
the unity of the imperial power, and the wide extent of the Roman language,
there was in some important respects more freedom of commerce and of movement throughout the civilized world in the days of the Roman Empire than
even now.

When, then, we recollect how great a centre of wealth Rome was; how
monstrous the fortunes of individual Romans (and they have only recently
been surpassed); and how vast the scale of her military and civil affairs, of
the provision needed for them and of the machinery of her traffic; we cannot
wonder that many writers have thought they found much resemblance between
her economic problems and our own. But the resemblance is superficial and
illusory. It extends only to forms, and not to the living spirit of national life.
It does not extend to the recognition of the worth of the life of the common
people, which in our own time is giving to economic science its highest interest.[2]

In ancient Rome industry and commerce lacked the vital strength which
they have attained in more recent times. Her imports were won by the
sword; they were not bought with the products of skilled work in which the
citizens took a worthy pride, as were those of Venice or Florence or Bruges.
Traffic and industry alike were pursued almost with a sole eye to the money
gains to be derived from them; and the tone of business life was degraded by

(margin notes:) APP. A, 4. — of the Romans fitted them for business, but they generally preferred war and politics. Roman economic conditions were in some respects modern in form; but not at all in substance.

---

[1] This fundamental opposition between the Greek and Roman tempers was made
clear by Hegel in his *Philosophy of History*. " Of the Greeks in the first genuine form
of their freedom we may assert that they had no conscience; the habit of living for
their country without further analysis or reflection was the principle dominant
among them. . . . Subjectivity plunged the Greek world into ruin "; and the
harmonious poetry of the Greeks made way for " the prose life of the Romans,"
which was full of subjectivity, and " a hard dry contemplation of certain voluntary
aims." A generous, though discriminating, tribute to the services which Hegel
indirectly rendered to Historical Economics is given by Roscher, *Gesch. der Nat. Œk.
in Deutschland*, § 188. Compare also the chapters on Religion in Mommsen's *History*,
which seem to have been much influenced by Hegel; also Kautz, *Entwickelung der
National-Œkonomie*, Bk. I.

[2] See above, ch. I. § 2. The misunderstanding is in some measure attributable to
the influence of the generally acute and well-balanced Roscher. He took a special
delight in pointing out analogies between ancient and modern problems; and though
he also pointed out differences, yet the general influence of his writings tended to mislead. (His position is well criticized by Knies, *Politische Œkonomie vom geschichtlichen
Standpunkte* : especially p. 391 of the second edition.)

APP. A, 4.   the public disdain which showed itself in the " legal and practically effective restriction "[1] of the Senators from all forms of business except those connected with the land.   The Equites found their richest gains in farming the taxes, in the plunder of provinces, and, in later times, in the personal favour of the Emperors, and did not cherish that spirit of probity and thorough work which are needed for the making of a great national trade; and at length private enterprise was stifled by the ever-growing shadow of the State.[2]

But they founded the modern law of property. The Stoic philosophy and the cosmopolitan experience of the later Roman lawyers

But though the Romans contributed but little directly to the progress of economic science, yet indirectly they exerted a profound influence over it, for good and evil, by laying the foundations of modern jurisprudence.   What philosophic thought there was in Rome was chiefly Stoic; and most of the great Roman Stoics were of Oriental origin.   Their philosophy when transplanted to Rome developed a great practical power without losing its intensity of feeling; and in spite of its severity, it had in it much that is kindred to the suggestions of modern social science.   Most of the great lawyers of the Empire were among its adherents, and thus it set the tone of the later Roman Law, and through it of all modern European Law.   Now the strength of the Roman State had caused State rights to extinguish those of the Clan and the Tribe in Rome at an earlier stage than in Greece.   But many of the primitive Aryan habits of thought as to property lingered on for a long while even in Rome. Great as was the power of the head of the family over its members, the property which he controlled was for a long time regarded as vested in him as the representative of the family rather than as an individual.   But when Rome had become imperial, her lawyers became the ultimate interpreters of the legal rights of many nations : and under Stoic influence they set themselves to discover the fundamental Laws of Nature, which they believed to lie in concealment at the foundation of all particular codes.   This search for the universal, as opposed to the accidental elements of justice, acted as a powerful solvent on rights of common holding, for which no other reason than that of

led them gradually to enlarge the sphere of contract

local usage could be given.   The later Roman Law therefore gradually but steadily enlarged the sphere of contract; gave it greater precision, greater elasticity, and greater strength.   At last almost all social arrangements had come under its dominion; the property of the individual was clearly marked out, and he could deal with it as he pleased.   From the breadth and nobility of the Stoic character modern lawyers have inherited a high standard of duty : and from its austere self-determination they have derived a tendency to define

[1] Friedländer, *Sittengeschichte Roms*, p. 225. Mommsen goes so far as to say (*History*, Book IV. ch. XI.) :—" Of trades and manufactures there is nothing to be said, except that the Italian nation in this respect persevered in an inactivity bordering on barbarism. . . . The only brilliant side of Roman private economics was money dealing and commerce." Many passages in Cairnes' *Slave Power* read like modern versions of Mommsen's *History*. Even in the towns the lot of the poor free Roman resembled that of the " mean white " of the Southern Slave States. *Latifundia perdidere Italiam*; but they were farms like those of the Southern States, not of England.   The weakness of free labour at Rome is shown in Liebenam's *Geschichte des römischen Vereinswesens.*

[2] One aspect of this is described by Schmoller in his short but excellent account of the Trading Companies of Antiquity.   After showing how trading groups of which all the members belong to one family may thrive even among primitive peoples, he argues (*Jahrbuch für Gesetzgebung*, XVI. pp. 740–2) that no form of business association of the modern type could flourish long in such conditions as those of ancient Rome unless it had some exceptional privileges or advantages as the *Societates Publicanorum* had. The reason why we moderns succeed in bringing and keeping many people " under the same hat " to work together, which Antiquity failed in doing, " is to be sought exclusively in the higher level of intellectual and moral strength, and the greater possibility now than then of binding together men's egoistic commercial energies by the bonds of social sympathy." See also Deloume, *Les Manieurs d'Argent à Rome*; an article on *State control of Industry in the fourth century* by W. A. Brown in the *Political Science Quarterly*, Vol. II.; Blanqui's *History of Political Economy*, chs. V. and VI.; and Ingram's *History*, ch. II.

sharply individual rights in property.   And therefore to Roman and especially APP. A, 5, 6. Stoic influence we may trace indirectly much of the good and evil of our present economic system : on the one hand much of the untrammelled vigour of the individual in managing his own affairs; and on the other not a little harsh wrong done under the cover of rights established by a system of law, which has held its ground because its main principles are wise and just.

The strong sense of duty which Stoicism brought with it from its Oriental But a new spirit was needed. home had in it something also of Eastern quietism.   The Stoic, though active in well-being, was proud of being superior to the troubles of the world : he took his share in the turmoil of life because it was his duty to do so, but he never reconciled himself to it : his life remained sad and stern, oppressed by the consciousness of its own failures.   This inner contradiction, as Hegel says, could not pass away till inward perfection was recognized as an object that could be attained only through self-renunciation;   and thus its pursuit was reconciled with those failures which necessarily accompany all social work. For this great change the intense religious feeling of the Jews prepared the way.   But the world was not ready to enter into the fulness of the Christian spirit, till a new tone had been given to it by the deep personal affections of the German race.   Even among the German peoples true Christianity made its way slowly : and for a long time after the fall of Rome there was chaos in Western Europe.

§ 5. The Teuton, strong and resolute as he was, found it very difficult to The Teuton slow to learn from those whom he had conquered. free himself from the bonds of custom and of ignorance.   The heartiness and fidelity [1] which gave him his special strength, inclined him to cherish overmuch the institutions and customs of his family and his tribe.   No other great conquering race has shown so little capacity as the Teutons have done for adopting new ideas from the more cultured, though weaker, people whom they conquered.   They prided themselves on their rude strength and energy; and cared little for knowledge and the arts.   But these found a temporary refuge on the Eastern coasts of the Mediterranean; until another conquering race coming from the south was ready to give them new life and vigour.

The Saracens learnt eagerly the best lessons that the conquered had to Our debt to the Saracens. teach.   They nurtured the arts and sciences, and kept alive the torch of learning at a time when the Christian world cared little whether it went out or not; and for this we must ever owe them gratitude.   But their moral nature was not so full as that of the Teutons.   The warm climate and the sensuality of their religion caused their vigour rapidly to decay; and they have exercised very little direct influence on the problems of modern civilization.[2]

The education of the Teutons made slower but surer progress.   They carried Later on civilization moved northwards and westwards, civilization northwards to a climate in which sustained hard work has gone hand in hand with the slow growth of sturdy forms of culture; and they carried it westwards to the Atlantic.   Civilization, which had long ago left the shores of the rivers for those of the great inland sea, was ultimately to travel over the vast ocean.

But these changes worked themselves out slowly.   The first point of and the old contest between town and country revived. interest to us in the new age is the re-opening of the old conflict between town and nation that had been suspended by the universal dominion of Rome; which was indeed an army with head-quarters in a town, but drawing its power from the broad land.

§ 6. Until a few years ago complete and direct self-government by the Without the tele- people was impossible in a great nation : it could exist only in towns or very

[1] Hegel (*Philosophy of History*, Part IV.) goes to the root of the matter when he speak of their energy, their free spirit, their absolute self-determination (Eigensinn), their heartiness (Gemüth), and adds, " Fidelity is their second watchword, as Freedom is the first."

[2] A brilliant eulogy of their work is given by Draper, *Intellectual Development of Europe*, ch. XIII.

X

APP. A, 7.

graph and printing press, freedom in a large country was confined to the aristocracy.

small territories.. Government was necessarily in the hands of the few, who looked upon themselves as privileged upper classes, and who treated the workers as lower classes. Consequently the workers, even when permitted to manage their own local affairs, were often wanting in the courage, the self-reliance, and the habits of mental activity, which are required as the basis of business enterprise. And as a matter of fact both the central Government and the local magnates did interfere directly with the freedom of industry; prohibiting migration, and levying taxes and tolls of the most burdensome and vexatious character. Even those of the lower classes who were nominally free, were plundered by arbitrary fines and dues levied under all manner of excuses, by the partial administration of justice, and often by direct violence and open pillage. These burdens fell chiefly on just those people who were more industrious and more thrifty than their neighbours—those among whom, if the country had been free, the spirit of bold enterprise would gradually have arisen to shake off the bonds of tradition and custom.

But self-government by the people was possible in the towns.

Far different was the state of people in the towns. There the industrial classes found strength in their numbers; and even when unable to gain the upper hand altogether, they were not, like their brethren in the country, treated as though they belonged to a different order of beings from their rulers. In Florence and in Bruges, as in ancient Athens, the whole people could hear, and sometimes did hear, from the leaders of public policy a statement of their plans and the reasons for them, and could signify their approval or disapproval before the next step was taken. The whole people could on occasion discuss together the social and industrial problems of the time, knowing each other's counsel, profiting by each other's experience, working out in common a definite resolution and bringing it into effect by their own action. But nothing of this kind could be done over a wide area till the invention of the telegraph, the railway and the cheap press.

And it is now for the first time possible in a large country.

By their aid a nation can now read in the morning what its leaders have said on the evening before; and, ere another day has passed, the judgment of the nation on it is pretty well known. By their aid the council of a large trades union can at a trifling cost submit a difficult question to the judgment of their members in every part of the country and get their decision within a few days. Even a large country can now be ruled by its people; but till now what was called "popular Government" was of physical necessity the government by a more or less wide oligarchy. Only those few who could themselves go frequently to the centre of Government, or at least receive constant communication from it, could take part directly in government. And though a much larger number of people would know enough of what was going on to make their will broadly effective through their choice of representatives, yet even they were a small minority of the nation till a few years ago; and the representative system itself is only of recent date.

The Mediæval towns were the direct precursors of modern industrial civilization.

§ 7. In the Middle Ages the history of the rise and fall of towns is the history of the rise and fall of successive waves on the tide of progress. The mediæval towns as a rule owed their origin to trade and industry, and did not despise them. And though the wealthier citizens were sometimes able to set up a close government in which the workers had no part, they seldom retained their power long : the great body of the inhabitants frequently had the full rights of citizens, deciding for themselves the foreign and domestic policy of their city, and at the same time workng with their hands and taking pride in their work. They organized themselves into Gilds, thus increasing their cohesion and educating themselves in self-government; and though the Gilds were often exclusive, and their trade-regulations ultimately retarded progress, yet they did excellent work before this deadening influence had shown itself.[1]

---

[1] What is true of the great free towns, that were practically autonomous, is true in a less degree of the so-called free boroughs of England. Their constitutions were even

The citizens gained culture without losing energy; without neglecting App. a, 8. their business, they learnt to take an intelligent interest in many things besides their business. They led the way in the fine arts, and they were not backward in those of war. They took pride in magnificent expenditure for public purposes; and they took equal pride in a careful husbanding of the public resources, in clear and clean State budgets, and in systems of taxes levied equitably and based on sound business principles. Thus they led the way towards modern industrial civilization; and if they had gone on their course undisturbed, and retained their first love of liberty and social equality, they would probably long ago have worked out the solutions of many social and economic problems which we are only now beginning to face. But after being long troubled by tumults and war, they at last succumbed to the growing power of the countries by which they were surrounded; and indeed when they had obtained dominion over their neighbours, their own rule had often been harsh and oppressive, so that their ultimate overthrow by the country was in some degree the result of a just retribution. They have suffered for their wrong-doings : but the fruit of their good work remains, and is the source of much that is best in the social and economic traditions that our age has inherited from its predecessors.

§ 8. Feudalism was perhaps a necessary stage in the development of the Chivalry Teutonic race. It gave scope to the political ability of the dominant class, did not and educated the common people in habits of discipline and order. But it protect concealed under forms of some outward beauty much cruelty and uncleanness, the poor. physical and moral. The practices of chivalry combined extreme deference to women in public with domestic tyranny : elaborate rules of courtesy towards combatants of the knightly order were maintained by the side of cruelty and extortion in dealing with the lower classes. The ruling classes were expected to discharge their obligations towards one another with frankness and generosity.[1] They had ideals of life which were not devoid of nobility; and therefore their characters will always have some attractiveness to the thoughtful historian, as well as to the chronicler of wars, of splendid shows and of romantic incidents. But their consciences were satisfied when they had acted up to the code of duty which their own class required of them : and one article of that code was to keep the lower classes in their place; though indeed they were often kind and even affectionate towards those retainers with whom they lived in daily contact.

So far as cases of individual hardship went, the Church strove to defend The the weak and to diminish the sufferings of the poor. Perhaps those finer Church natures who were attracted to its service might often have exercised a wider helped the and a better influence, if they had been free from the vow of celibacy, and growth of able to mingle with the world. But this is no reason for rating lightly the economic benefit which the clergy, and still more the monks, rendered to the poorer freedom classes. The monasteries were the homes of industry, and in particular of the in some scientific treatment of agriculture : they were secure colleges for the learned, ways, and they were hospitals and alms-houses for the suffering. The Church acted

---

more various than the origins of their liberties; but it now seems probable that they were generally more democratic and less oligarchic than was at one time supposed. See especially Gross, *The Gild Merchant*, ch. VII.

[1] But treachery was common in Italian cities, and was not very rare in northern castles. People compassed the death of their acquaintances by assassination and poison : the host was often expected to taste the food and drink which he offered to his guest. As a painter rightly fills his canvas with the noblest faces he can find, and keeps as much in the background as possible what is ignoble, so the popular historian may be justified in exciting the emulation of the young by historical pictures in which the lives of noble men and women stand out in bold relief, while a veil is drawn over much of the surrounding depravity. But when we want to take stock of the world's progress, we must reckon the evil of past times as it really was. To be more than just to our ancestors is to be less than just to the best hopes of our race.

APP. A. 8. as a peace-maker in great matters and in small : the festivals and the markets held under its authority gave freedom and safety to trade.[1]

Again, the Church was a standing protest against caste exclusiveness. It was democratic in its organization, as was the army of ancient Rome. It was always willing to raise to the highest posts the ablest men, in whatever rank they were born; its clergy and monastic orders did much for the physical and moral wellbeing of the people; and it sometimes even led them in open resistance to the tyranny of their rulers.[2]

but hindered it in others.

But, on the other hand, it did not set itself to help them to develop their faculties of self-reliance and self-determination, and to attain true inner freedom. While willing that those individuals who had exceptional natural talents should rise through its own offices to the highest posts, it helped rather than hindered the forces of feudalism in their endeavour to keep the working classes as a body ignorant, devoid of enterprise, and in every way dependent on those above them. Teutonic feudalism was more kindly in its instincts than the military dominion of ancient Rome; and the laity as well as clergy were influenced by the teachings, imperfectly understood as they were, of the Christian religion with regard to the dignity of man as man. Nevertheless the rulers of the country districts during the early middle ages united all that was most powerful in the Oriental subtlety of theocratic caste and in the Roman force of discipline and resolution; and they used their combined strength in such a manner as on the whole to retard the growth of strength and independence of character among the lower orders of the people.

Overthrow of the cities.

The military force of feudalism was however for a long time weakened by local jealousies. It was admirably adapted for welding into one living whole the government of a vast area under the genius of a Charles the Great : but it was equally prone to dissipate itself into its constituent elements as soon as its guiding genius was gone. Italy was for a long time ruled by its towns, one of which indeed, of Roman descent, with Roman ambition and hard fixity of purpose held its water-ways against all attack till quite modern times. And in the Netherlands and other parts of the Continent the free towns were long able to defy the hostility of kings and barons around them. But at length stable monarchies were established in Austria, Spain and France. A despotic monarchy, served by a few able men, drilled and organized the military forces of vast multitudes of ignorant but sturdy country folk; and the enterprise of the free towns, that noble combination of industry and culture, was cut short before they had had time to outgrow their early mistakes.

The invention of printing,

Then the world might have gone backwards if it had not happened that just at that time new forces were rising to break up the bonds of constraint, and spread freedom over the broad land. Within a very short period came

[1] We are perhaps apt to lay too much stress on the condemnation by the Church of " usury " and some kinds of trade. There was then very little scope for lending capital to be used in business, and when there was, the prohibition could be evaded by many devices, some of which were indeed sanctioned by the Church itself. Though St. Chrysostom said that " he who procures an article to make profit by disposing of it entire and unaltered, is ejected from the temple of God "; yet the Church encouraged merchants to buy and sell goods unaltered at fairs and elsewhere. The authority of Church and State and the prejudices of the people combined to put difficulties in the way of those who bought up large quantities of goods in order to sell them retail at a profit. But though much of the business of these people was legitimate trade, some of it was certainly analogous to the " rings " and " corners " in modern produce markets. Compare the excellent chapter on the Canonist Doctrine in Ashley's *History* and the notice of it by Hewins in the *Economic Review*, Vol. IV.

[2] Indirectly it aided progress by promoting the Crusades; of which Ingram well says (*History*, ch.) II. that they " produced a powerful economic effect by transferring in many cases the possessions of the feudal chiefs to the industrial classes, whilst by bringing different nations and races into contact, by enlarging the horizon and widening the conceptions of the populations, as well as by affording a special stimulus to navigation, they tended to give a new activity to international trade."

the invention of printing, the Revival of Learning, the Reformation, and the APP. A, 9.
discovery of the ocean routes to the New World and to India. Any one of 10.
these events alone would have been sufficient to make an epoch in history; the Refor-
but coming together as they did, and working all in the same direction, they mation,
effected a complete revolution. and the
    Thought became comparatively free, and knowledge ceased to be altogether discovery
inaccessible to the people. The free temper of the Greeks revived; the of the New
strong self-determining spirits gained new strength, and were able to extend World.
their influence over others. And a new continent suggested new problems to
the thoughtful, at the same time that it offered a new scope to the enterprise
of bold adventurers.
    § **9.** The countries which took the lead in the new maritime adventure The first
were those of the Spanish Peninsula. It seemed for a time as though the benefit
leadership of the world, having settled first in the most easterly peninsula of of the
the Mediterranean, and thence moved to the middle peninsula, would settle discoveries
again in that westerly peninsula which belonged both to the Mediterranean went to the
and the Atlantic. But the power of industry had by this time become sufficient Spanish
to sustain wealth and civilization in a northern climate. Spain and Portugal Peninsula.
could not hold their own for long against the more sustained energy and the
more generous spirit of the northern people.
    The early history of the people of the Netherlands is indeed a brilliant But soon
romance. Founding themselves on fishing and weaving, they built up a noble moved
fabric of art and literature, of science and government. But Spain set herself further
to crush out the rising spirit of freedom, as Persia had done before. And as Holland;
Persia strangled Ionia, but only raised yet higher the spirit of Greece proper,
so the Austro-Spanish Empire subdued the Belgian Netherlands, but only
intensified the patriotism and energy of the Dutch Netherlands and England.
    Holland suffered from England's jealousy of her commerce, but still more
from the restless military ambition of France. It soon became clear that
Holland was defending the freedom of Europe against French aggression. But
at a critical time in her history she was deprived of the aid she might reasonably have expected from Protestant England; and though from 1688 onwards
that aid was liberally given, her bravest and most generous sons had then
already perished on the battle-field, and she was overburdened with debt.
She has fallen into the background: but Englishmen above all others are
bound to acknowledge what she did, and what more she might have done for
freedom and enterprise.
    France and England were thus left to contend for the empire of the ocean. to France;
France had greater natural resources than any other northern country, and
more of the spirit of the new age than any southern country; and she was for
some time the greatest power of the world. But she squandered in perpetual
wars her wealth, and the blood of the best of those citizens whom she had not
already driven away by religious persecution. The progress of enlightenment
brought with it no generosity on the part of the ruling class towards the ruled,
and no wisdom in expenditure.
    From revolutionary America came the chief impulse towards a rising of
the oppressed French people against their rulers. But the French were
strikingly wanting in that self-controlling freedom which had distinguished
the American colonists. Their energy and courage was manifested again in
the great Napoleonic wars. But their ambition overleaped itself, and ultimately left to England the leadership of enterprise on the ocean. Thus the and to
industrial problems of the New World are being worked out under the direct England.
influence, as to some extent those of the Old World are under the indirect
influence, of the English character. We may then return to trace with somewhat more detail the growth of free enterprise in England.
    § **10.** England's geographical position caused her to be peopled by the The
strongest members of the strongest races of northern Europe; a process of character

APP. A, 10. natural selection brought to her shores those members of each successive
——— migratory wave who were most daring and self-reliant. Her climate is better
of English- adapted to sustain energy than any other in the northern hemisphere. She is
men. divided by no high hills, and no part of her territory is more than twenty miles
from navigable water, and thus there was no material hindrance to freedom
of intercourse between her different parts; while the strength and wise policy
of the Normans and Plantagenet kings prevented artificial barriers from being
raised by local magnates.

As the part which Rome played in history is chiefly due to her having
combined the military strength of a great empire with the enterprise and
fixedness of purpose of an oligarchy residing in one city, so England owes her
greatness to her combining, as Holland had done on a smaller scale before,
much of the free temper of the mediæval city with the strength and broad basis
of a nation. The towns of England had been less distinguished than those of
other lands; but she assimilated them more easily than any other country
did, and so gained in the long run most from them.

The custom of primogeniture inclined the younger sons of noble families
to seek their own fortunes; and having no special caste privileges they mixed
readily with the common people. This fusion of different ranks tended to
make politics business-like; while it warmed the veins of business adventure
with the generous daring and romantic aspirations of noble blood. Resolute
on the one hand in resistance to tyranny, and on the other in submission to
authority when it is justified by their reason, the English have made many
revolutions; but none without a definite purpose. While reforming the constitution they have abided by the law; they alone, unless we except the
Dutch, have known how to combine order and freedom; they alone have
united a thorough reverence for the past with the power of living for the future
rather than in the past. But the strength of character which in later times
made England the leader of manufacturing progress, showed itself at first
chiefly in politics, in war, and in agriculture.

While they   The English archer was the forerunner of the English artisan. He had the
were still   same pride in the superiority of his food and his physique over those of his
an agri-   Continental rivals; he had the same indomitable perseverance in acquiring
cultural   perfect command over the use of his hands, the same free independence and
nation   the same power of self-control and of rising to emergencies; the same habit of
they   indulging his humours when the occasion was fit, but, when a crisis arose, of
showed   preserving discipline even in the face of hardship and misfortune.[1]
signs of   But the industrial faculties of Englishmen remained latent for a long time.
their   They had not inherited much acquaintance with nor much care for the com-
modern   forts and luxuries of civilization. In manufactures of all kinds they lagged
faculty for   behind the Latin countries, Italy, France and Spain, as well as the free cities
organized   of northern Europe. Gradually the wealthier classes got some taste for
action.   imported luxuries, and England's trade slowly increased.

Their   But there was for a long time no sign on the surface of her future com-
trade has   merce. That indeed is the product of her special circumstances as much as, if
been a con-   not more than, of any natural bias of her people. They had not originally,
sequence   and they have not now, that special liking for dealing and bargaining, nor for
of their   the more abstract side of financial business, which is found among the Jews,
activity in   the Italians, the Greeks and the Armenians; trade with them has always taken
production   the form of action rather than of manœuvring and speculative combination.
and in   Even now the subtlest financial speculation on the London Stock Exchange is
navi-   done chiefly by those races which have inherited the same aptitude for trading
gation.   which the English have for action.

---

[1] For the purposes of statistical comparison the well-to-do yeoman must be ranked
with the middle classes of to-day, not with the artisans. For those who were better
off than he were very few in number; while the great mass of the people were far
below him; and were worse off in almost every respect than they are now.

The qualities which have caused England in later times under different APP. A, 11.
circumstances to explore the world, and to make goods and carry them for ——
other countries, caused her even in the Middle Ages to pioneer the modern The
capitalist
organization of agriculture, and thus to set the model after which most other organiza-
modern business is being moulded. She took the lead in converting labour tion of
dues into money payments, a change which must increased the power of agriculture
everyone to steer his course in life according to his own free choice. For pioneered
good and for evil the people were set free to exchange away their rights in the for that
land and their obligations to it. The relaxation of the bonds of custom was of manu-
hastened alike by the great rise of real wages which followed the Black Death facture.
in the fourteenth century; and by the great fall of real wages which, in the
sixteenth century, resulted from the depreciation of silver, the debasement of
coin, the appropriation of the revenues of the monasteries to the purposes of
court extravagance; and lastly by the extension of sheep-farming, which set
many workers adrift from their old homes, and lowered the real incomes and
altered the mode of life of those who remained. The movement was further
extended by the growth of the royal power in the hands of the Tudors, which
put an end to private war, and rendered useless the bands of retainers which
the barons and landed gentry had kept together. The habit of leaving real
property to the eldest son, and distributing personal property among all the
members of the family, on the one hand increased the size of landed properties,
and on the other narrowed the capital which the owners of land had at their
own command for working it.[1]

These causes tended to establish the relation of landlord and tenant in
England : while the foreign demand for English work and the English demand
for foreign luxuries led, especially in the sixteenth century, to the concentration
of many holdings into large sheep-runs worked by capitalist farmers. That
is, there was a great increase in the number of farmers who undertook the
management and the risks of agriculture, supplying some capital of their own,
but borrowing the land for a definite yearly payment, and hiring labour for
wages : in like manner as, later on, the new order of English business men undertook the management and the risks of manufacture, supplying some capital of
their own, but borrowing the rest on interest, and hiring labour for wages. Free
enterprise grew fast and fiercely, it was one-sided in its action and cruel to the
poor. But it remains true that the English large farm, arable and pastoral, worked
with borrowed capital, was the forerunner of the English factory, in the same
way as English archery was the forerunner of the skill of the English artisan.[2]

§ 11. Meanwhile the English character was deepening. The natural England's
gravity and intrepidity of the stern races that had settled on the shores of industry
England inclined them to embrace the doctrines of the Reformation; and these was much
influenced
reacted on their habits of life, and gave a tone to their industry. Man was, as by the
it were, ushered straight into the presence of his Creator, with no human spirit that
intermediary; and now for the first time large numbers of rude and uncultured underlay
people yearned towards the mysteries of absolute spiritual freedom. The iso- the Refor-
lation of each person's religious responsibility from that of his fellows, rightly mation,
understood, was a necessary condition for the highest spiritual progress.[3]

---

[1] Rogers says that in the thirteenth century the value of arable land was only a
third of the capital required to work it; and he believes that so long as the owner of
the land was in the habit of cultivating it himself, the eldest son often used various
devices for alienating a part of his land to his younger brothers in exchange for some
of their capital. *Six Centuries of Work and Wages*, pp. 51, 2.
[2] This parallelism is further developed in Book VI.; see especially ch. IX. § 5.
[3] The Reformation " was the affirmation . . . of Individuality. . . . Individuality
is not the sum of life, but it is an essential part of life in every region of our nature and
our work, in our work for the part and for the whole. It is true, though it is not the
whole truth, that we must live and die alone, alone with God." Westcott's *Social
Aspects of Christianity*, p. 121. Comp. also Hegel's *Philosophy of History*, Part IV.
section iii. ch. 2.

APP. A, 12.
———

But the notion was new to the world, it was bare and naked, not yet over-grown with pleasant instincts; and even in kindly natures individuality showed itself with a hard sharpness of outline, while the coarser natures became self-conscious and egotistic.   Among the Puritans especially, the eagerness to give logical definiteness and precision to their religious creed was an absorbing passion, hostile to all lighter thoughts and lighter amusements.   When occasion arose they could take combined action, which was made irresistible by their resolute will.   But they took little joy in society; they shunned public amuse-ments, and preferred the quieter relaxations of home life; and, it must be confessed, some of them took an attitude hostile to art.[1]

which sup-plied the strength necessary for the next stage of social life.

The first growth of strength had then something in it that was rude and ill-mannered; but that strength was required for the next stage upwards.   It needed to be purified and softened by much tribulation; it needed to become less self-assertive without becoming weaker, before new instincts could grow up around it to revive in a higher form what was most beautiful and most solid in the old collective tendencies.   It intensified the affections of the family, the richest and fullest of earthly feelings : perhaps there never has been before any material of texture at once so strong and so fine, with which to build up a noble fabric of social life.

Holland and other countries shared with England the great ordeal which was thus opened by the spiritual upheaval that closed the middle ages.   But from many points of view, and especially from that of the economist, England's experiences were the most instructive and the most thorough; and were typical of all the rest.   England led the way in the modern evolution of industry and enterprise by free and self-determining energy and will.

The seriousness of the character of the English people was in-tensified through her at-tracting refugee artisans from the Continent.

§ 12.   England's industrial and commercial characteristics were intensified by the fact that many of those who had adopted the new doctrines in other countries sought on her shores a safe asylum from religious persecution.   By a sort of natural selection, those of the French and Flemings, and others whose character was most akin to the English, and who had been led by that character to study thoroughness of work in the manufacturing arts, came to mingle with them, and to teach them those arts for which their character had all along fitted them.[2]   During the seventeenth and eighteenth centuries, the court and the upper classes remained more or less frivolous and licentious; but the middle class and some parts of the working class adopted a severe view of life; they took little delight in amusements that interrupted work, and they had a high standard as to those material comforts which could be obtained only by unremitting, hard work.   They strove to produce things that had a solid and lasting utility, rather than those suited only for the pur-pose of festivities and ostentation.   The tendency, when once it had set in, was promoted by the climate; for, though not very severe, it is specially unsuited to the lighter amusements; and the clothing, house-room and other requisites for a comfortable existence in it, are of a specially expensive character.

These were the conditions under which the modern industrial life of Eng-land was developed : the desire for material comforts tends towards a ceaseless straining to extract from every week the greatest amount of work that can be got out of it.   The firm resolution to submit every action to the deliberate

---

[1] The licentiousness of some forms of art created in serious but narrow minds a prejudice against all art; and in revenge socialists now rail at the Reformation as having injured both the social and the artistic instincts of man.   But it may be questioned whether the intensity of the feelings which were engendered by the Re-formation has not enriched art more than their austerity has injured it.   They have developed a literature and a music of their own; and if they have led man to think slightingly of the beauty of the works of his own hands, they have certainly increased his power of appreciating the beauties of nature.   It is no accident that landscape painting owes most to lands in which the Reformed religion has prevailed.

[2] Smiles has shown that the debt which England owes to these immigrants is greater than historians have supposed, though they have always rated it highly.

judgment of the reason tends to make everyone constantly ask himself APP. A, 13. whether he could not improve his position by changing his business, or by changing his method of doing it. And, lastly, complete political freedom and security enables everyone to adjust his conduct as he has decided that it is his interest to do, and fearlessly to commit his person and his property to new and distant undertakings.

In short, the same causes which have enabled England and her colonies to set the tone of modern politics, have made them also set the tone of modern business. The same qualities which gave them political freedom gave them also free enterprise in industry and commerce.

§ 13. Freedom of industry and enterprise, so far as its action reaches, tends to cause everyone to seek that employment of his labour and capital in which he can turn them to best advantage; and this again leads him to try to obtain a special skill and facility in some particular task, by which he may earn the means of purchasing what he himself wants. And hence results a complex industrial organization, with much subtle division of labour. English free enterprise naturally tended towards division of labour,

Some sort of division of labour is indeed sure to grow up in any civilization that has held together for a long while, however primitive its form. Even in very backward countries we find highly specialized trades; but we do not find the work within each trade so divided up that the planning and arrangement of the business, its management and its risks, are borne by one set of people, while the manual work required for it is done by hired labour. This form of division of labour is at once characteristic of the modern world generally, and of the English race in particular. It may be merely a passing phase in man's development; it may be swept away by the further growth of that free enterprise which has called it into existence. But for the present it stands out for good and for evil as the chief fact in the form of modern civilization, the kernel of the modern economic problem.

The most vital changes hitherto introduced into industrial life centre around this growth of business *Undertakers*.[1] We have already seen how the undertaker made his appearance at an early stage in England's agriculture. The farmer borrowed land from his landlord, and hired the necessary labour, being himself responsible for the management and risks of the business. The selection of farmers has not indeed been governed by perfectly free competition, but has been restricted to a certain extent by inheritance and by other influences, which have often caused the leadership of agricultural industry to fall into the hands of people who have had no special talents for it. But England is the only country in which any considerable play has been given to natural selection : the agricultural systems of the Continent have allowed the accident of birth to determine the part which every man should take in cultivating land or controlling its cultivation. The greater energy and elasticity obtained by even this narrow play of selection in England, has been sufficient to put English agriculture in advance of all others, and has enabled it to obtain a much larger produce than is got by an equal amount of labour from similar soils in any other country of Europe.[2] especially in the management of business,

[1] This term, which has the authority of Adam Smith and is habitually used on the Continent, seems to be the best to indicate those who take the risks and the management of business as their share in the work of organized industry.

[2] In the latter half of the eighteenth century, especially, the improvements in agriculture moved very fast. Implements of all kinds were improved, draining was carried out on scientific principles, the breeding of farm animals was revolutionized by Bakewell's genius; turnips, clover, rye-grass, etc. came into general use, and enabled the plan of refreshing land by letting it lie fallow to be superseded by that of "alternating husbandry." These and other changes constantly increased the capital required for the cultivation of land; while the growth of fortunes made in trade increased the number of those who were able and willing to purchase their way into country society by buying large properties. And thus in every way the modern commercial spirit spread in agriculture.

APP. A, 13.

and the
localiza-
tion of
industry.

But the natural selection of the fittest to undertake, to organize, and to manage has much greater scope in manufacture. The tendency to the growth of undertakers in manufactures had set in before the great development of England's foreign trade; in fact traces of it are to be found in the woollen manufacture in the fifteenth century. But the opening up of large markets in new countries gave a great stimulus to the movement, both directly and through its influence on the localization of industry, that is, the concentration of particular branches of production in certain localities.

These
tendencies
promoted
by the
growth of
consumers
beyond the
seas, who
wanted
goods of
simple
patterns.

The records of mediæval fairs and wandering merchants show that there were many things each of which was made in only one or two places, and thence distributed north and south, east and west, over the whole of Europe. But the wares whose production was localized and which travelled far, were almost always of high price and small bulk : the cheaper and heavier goods were supplied by each district for itself. In the colonies of the new world, however, people had not always the leisure to provide manufactures for themselves : and they were often not allowed to make even those which they could have made; for though England's treatment of her colonies was more liberal than that of any other country, she thought that the expense which she incurred on their behalf justified her in compelling them to buy nearly all kinds of manufactures from herself. There was also a large demand for simple goods to be sold in India and to savage races.

These causes led to the localization of much of the heavier manufacturing work. In work which requires the highly trained skill and delicate fancy of the operative, organization is sometimes of secondary importance. But the power of organizing great numbers of people gives an irresistible advantage when there is a demand for whole ship cargoes of goods of a few simple patterns. Thus localization and the growth of the system of capitalist undertakers were two parallel movements, due to the same general cause, and each of them promoting the advance of the other.

The under-
takers at
first
merely
organized
supply
without
super-
vising
industry :
that was
still done
by small
masters.

The factory system, and the use of expensive appliances in manufacture, came at a later stage. They are commonly supposed to be the origin of the power which undertakers wield in English industry; and no doubt they increased it. But it had shown itself clearly before their influence was felt. At the time of the French Revolution there was not a very great deal of capital invested in machinery whether driven by water or steam power; the factories were not large, and there were not many of them. But nearly all the textile work of the country was then done on a system of contracts. This industry was controlled by a comparatively small number of undertakers who set themselves to find out what, where and when it was most advantageous to buy and to sell, and what things it was most profitable to have made. They then let out contracts for making these things to a great number of people scattered over the country. The undertakers generally supplied the raw material, and sometimes even the simple implements that were used; those who took the contract executed it by the labour of themselves and their families, and sometimes but not always by that of a few assistants.

As time went on, the progress of mechanical invention caused the workers to be gathered more and more into small factories in the neighbourhood of water power; and when steam came to be substituted for water power, then into larger factories in great towns. Thus the great undertakers who bore the chief risks of manufacturing, without directly managing and superintending, began to give way to wealthy employers, who conducted the whole business of manufacturing on a large scale. The new factories attracted the attention of the most careless observer; and this last movement was not liable to be overlooked by those who were not actually engaged in the trade, as the preceding movement had been.[1]

---

[1] The quarter of a century beginning with 1760 saw improvements follow one another in manufacture even more rapidly than in agriculture. During that period the

Thus at length general attention was called to the great change in the APP. A, 14, 15.
organization of industry which had long been going on; and it was seen that
the system of small businesses controlled by the workers themselves was being But the under-takers collected into factories large bodies of workers. Hence-forth man-ufacturing labour was hired wholesale.
displaced by the system of large businesses controlled by the specialized ability
of capitalist undertakers. The change would have worked itself out very much
as it has done, even if there had been no factories : and it will go on working
itself out even if the retail distribution of force by electric or other agencies
should cause part of the work that is now done in factories to be taken to the
home of the workers.[1]

§ 14. The new movement, both in its earlier and later forms, has tended
constantly to relax the bonds that used to bind nearly everyone to live in the
parish in which he was born; and it developed free markets for labour, which
invited people to come and take their chance of finding employment. And in
consequence of this change the causes that determine the value of labour
began to take a new character. Up to the eighteenth century manufacturing
labour had been hired, as a rule, retail; though a large and fluid labour class,
which could be hired wholesale, had played a considerable part in the industrial
history of particular places on the Continent and in England before then. In
that century the rule was reversed, at least for England; and the price of
labour ceased to be dominated by custom, or by bargaining in small markets.
During the last hundred years it has ever more and more been determined
by the circumstances of supply and demand over a large area—a town, a
country, or the whole world.

The new organization of industry added vastly to the efficiency of pro- The new organiza-tion was accom-panied by great evils; many of which were due to other causes.
duction; for it went far towards securing that each man's labour should be
devoted to just the highest kind of work which he was capable of performing
well, and that his work should be ably directed and supplied with the best
mechanical and other assistance that wealth and the knowledge of the age
could afford. But it brought with it great evils. Which of these evils was
unavoidable we cannot tell. For just when the change was moving most
quickly, England was stricken by a combination of calamities almost un-
paralleled in history. They were the cause of a great part—it is impossible to
say of how great a part—of the sufferings that are commonly ascribed to the
sudden outbreak of unrestrained competition. The loss of her great colonies
was quickly followed by the great French war, which cost her more than the
total value of the accumulated wealth she had at its commencement. An
unprecedented series of bad harvests made bread fearfully dear. And worse
than all, a method of administration of the poor law was adopted which undermined the independence and vigour of the people.

The first part of last century therefore saw free enterprise establishing itself
in England under favourable circumstances, its evils being intensified and its
beneficial influences being hindered by external misfortunes.

§ 15. The trade customs and the gild regulations, by which the weak had There were some futile
been defended in past times, were unsuitable to the new industry. In some

---

transport of heavy goods was cheapened by Brindley's canals, the production of
power by Watt's steam-engine, and that of iron by Cort's processes of puddling and
rolling, and by Roebuck's method of smelting it by coal in lieu of the charcoal that
had now become scarce; Hargreaves, Crompton, Arkwright, Cartwright and others
invented, or at least made economically serviceable, the spinning-jenny, the mule, the
carding machine, and the power-loom; Wedgwood gave a great impetus to the pottery
trade that was already growing rapidly; and there were important inventions in
printing from cylinders, in bleaching by chemical agents, and in other processes. A
cotton factory was for the first time driven directly by steam power in 1785, the last
year of the period. The beginning of the nineteenth century saw steam-ships and
steam printing-presses, and the use of gas for lighting towns. Railway locomotion,
telegraphy and photography came a little later. See for further details a brilliant
chapter by Professor Clapham in the *Cambridge Modern History*, Vol. x.
[1] See Held's *Sociale Geschichte Englands*, Bk. II. ch. III.

APP. A, 15.
———
attempts
to
revive old
ordinances
regulating
labour,

which had
done both
good and
evil in
their time,
but were
unfitted
for the
modern
era of rapid
change.
The manu-
facturers
were
chiefly
strong self-
made men,
who saw
only the
good side
of com-
petition.
The
pressure of
war taxes
and the
scarcity of
food forced
down real
wages,

and
induced
unhealthy
and exces-
sive work,
which
lowered
the wage-
earning
power.

But
the new
system

places they were abandoned by common consent : in others they were successfully upheld for a time. But it was a fatal success; for the new industry,
incapable of flourishing under the old bonds, left those places for others where
it could be more free.[1] Then the workers turned to Government for the en-
forcement of old laws of Parliament prescribing the way in which the trade
should be carried on, and even for the revival of the regulation of prices and
wages by justices of the peace.

These efforts could not but fail. The old regulations had been the expression of the social, moral and economic ideas of the time; they had been
felt out, rather than thought out; they were the almost instinctive results of
the experience of generations of men who had lived and died under almost
unchanged economic conditions. In the new age changes came so rapidly that
there was no time for this. Each man had to do what was right in his own
eyes, with but little guidance from the experience of past times : those who
endeavoured to cling to old traditions were quickly supplanted.

The new race of undertakers consisted chiefly of those who had made their
own fortunes, strong, ready, enterprising men : who, looking at the success
obtained by their own energies, were apt to assume that the poor and the
weak were to be blamed rather than to be pitied for their misfortunes. Impressed with the folly of those who tried to bolster up economic arrangements
which the stream of progress had undermined, they were apt to think that
nothing more was wanted than to make competition perfectly free and to let
the strongest have their way. They glorified individuality of character, and
were in no hurry to find a modern substitute for the social and industrial bonds
which had kept men together in earlier times.

Meanwhile misfortune had reduced the total net income of the people of
England. In 1820 a tenth of it was absorbed in paying the mere interest on
the National Debt. The goods that were cheapened by the new inventions
were chiefly manufactured commodities of which the working man was but a
small consumer. As England had then almost a monopoly of manufactures,
he might indeed have got his food cheaply if manufacturers had been allowed
to change their wares freely for corn grown abroad; but this was prohibited
by the landlords who ruled in Parliament. The labourer's wages, so far as
they were spent on ordinary food, were the equivalent of what his labour would
produce on the very poor soil which was forced into cultivation to eke out the
insufficient supplies raised from the richer grounds. He had to sell his labour
in a market in which the forces of supply and demand would have given him a
poor pittance even if they had worked freely. But he had not the full advantage of economic freedom; he had no efficient union with his fellows; he had
neither the knowledge of the market, nor the power of holding out for a reserve
price, which the seller of commodities has, and he was urged on to work and
to let his family work during long hours, and under unhealthy conditions.
This reacted on the efficiency of the working population, and therefore on the
net value of their work, and therefore it kept down their wages. The employment of very young children for long hours was no new thing : it had been common in Norwich and elsewhere even in the seventeenth century. But the
moral and physical misery and disease caused by excessive work under bad
conditions reached their highest point among the factory population in the
first quarter of the century. They diminished slowly during the second quarter, and more rapidly since then.

After the workmen had recognized the folly of attempts to revive the old
rules regulating industry, there was no longer any wish to curtail the freedom
of enterprise. The sufferings of the English people at their worst were never

---

[1] The tendency of industries to flee away from places where they were over-
regulated by the gilds was of old standing, and had shown itself in the thirteenth
century, though it was then comparatively feeble. See Gross's *Gild Merchant*, Vol.
I. pp. 43 and 52.

comparable to those which had been caused by the want of freedom in France APP. A, 16.
before the Revolution; and it was argued that, had it not been for the strength
which England derived from her new industries, she would probably have had saved England from French armies, and the workmen accepted it.
succumbed to a foreign military despotism, as the free cities had done before
her. Small as her population was she at some times bore almost alone the
burden of war against a conqueror in control of nearly all the resources of the
Continent; and at other times subsidized larger, but poorer countries in the
struggle against him. Rightly or wrongly, it was thought at the time that
Europe might have fallen permanently under the dominion of France, as she
had fallen in an earlier age under that of Rome, had not the free energy of
English industries supplied the sinews of war against the common foe. Little
was therefore heard in complaint against the excess of free enterprise, but much
against that limitation of it which prevented Englishmen from obtaining food
from abroad in return for the manufactures which they could now so easily
produce.

And even trades-unions, which were then beginning that brilliant though Change in the policy of Trades-Unions.
chequered career which has been more full of interest and instruction than
almost anything else in English history, passed into the phase of seeking little
from authority except to be left alone. They had learnt by bitter experience
the folly of attempting to enforce the old rules by which Government had
directed the course of industry; and they had as yet got no far-reaching views
as to the regulation of trade by their own action: their chief anxiety was to
increase their own economic freedom by the removal of the laws against combinations of workmen.

§ 16. It has been left for our own generation to perceive all the evils which People could not see, as we can, how great are the evils of economic freedom when it degener- ates into license.
arose from the suddenness of this increase of economic freedom. Now first are
we getting to understand the extent to which the capitalist employer, untrained to his new duties, was tempted to subordinate the wellbeing of his
workpeople to his own desire for gain; now first are we learning the importance
of insisting that the rich have duties as well as rights in their individual and in
their collective capacity; now first is the economic problem of the new age
showing itself to us as it really is. This is partly due to a wider knowledge
and a growing earnestness. But however wise and virtuous our grandfathers
had been, they could not have seen things as we do; for they were hurried
along by urgent necessities and terrible disasters.[1]

We must judge ourselves by a severer standard. For, though England We now have greater means and must aim higher.
has recently been called on to struggle once more for national existence, her
powers of production have been immensely increased; free trade and the
growth of steam communication have enabled a largely increased population
to obtain sufficient supplies of food on easy terms. The average money income
of the people has more than doubled; while the price of almost all important
commodities except animal food and house-room has fallen by one-half or
even further. It is true that even now, if wealth were distributed equally, the
total production of the country would only suffice to provide necessaries and
the more urgent comforts for the people, and that as things are, many have
barely the necessaries of life. But the nation has grown in wealth, in health,
in education and in morality; and we are no longer compelled to subordinate
almost every other consideration to the need of increasing the total produce of
industry.

In particular this increased prosperity has made us rich and strong enough The new restraints
to impose new restraints on free enterprise; some temporary material loss

---

[1] In times of peace no one ventures openly to rank money as of high importance in
comparison with human lives; but in the crisis of an expensive war money can always
be used so as to save them. A general who at a critical time sacrifices lives in order
to protect material, the loss of which would cause the loss of many men, is held to have
acted rightly, though no one would openly defend a sacrifice of soldiers' lives in order
to save a few army stores in time of peace.

APP. A, 17.

on freedom are chiefly in the interests of women and children.

being submitted to for the sake of a higher and ultimate greater gain. But these new restraints are different from the old. They are imposed not as a means of class domination; but with the purpose of defending the weak, and especially children and the mothers of children, in matters in which they are not able to use the forces of competition in their own defence. The aim is to devise, deliberately and promptly, remedies adapted to the quickly changing circumstances of modern industry; and thus to obtain the good, without the evil, of the old defence of the weak that in other ages was gradually evolved by custom.

The telegraph and print-ing-press enable the people now to decide on their own remedies for their evils.

Even when industry remained almost unchanged in character for many generations together, custom was too slow in its growth and too blind to be able to apply pressure only when pressure was beneficial: and in this later stage custom can do but little good, and much harm. But by the aid of the telegraph and the printing press, of representative government and trade associations, it is possible for the people to think out for themselves the solution of their own problems. The growth of knowledge and self-reliance has given them that true self-controlling freedom, which enables them to impose of their own free will restraints on their own actions; and the problems of collective production, collective ownership and collective consumption are entering on a new phase.

And we are gradually moving towards forms of collective action, higher than the old, because based on strong self-disciplined individual-ity.

Projects for great and sudden changes are now, as ever, foredoomed to fail, and to cause reaction; we cannot move safely, if we move so fast that our new plans of life altogether outrun our instincts. It is true that human nature can be modified: new ideals, new opportunities and new methods of action may, as history shows, alter it very much even in a few generations; and this change in human nature has perhaps never covered so wide an area and moved so fast as in the present generation. But still it is a growth, and therefore gradual; and changes of our social organization must wait on it, and therefore they must be gradual too.

But though they wait on it, they may always keep a little in advance of it, promoting the growth of our higher social nature by giving it always some new and higher work to do, some practical ideal towards which to strive. Thus gradually we may attain to an order of social life, in which the common good overrules individual caprice, even more than it did in the early ages before the sway of individualism had begun. But unselfishness then will be the offspring of deliberate will; and, though added by instinct, individual freedom will then develop itself in collective freedom :—a happy contrast to the old order of life, in which individual slavery to custom caused collective slavery and stagna-tion, broken only by the caprice of despotism or the caprice of revolution.

America is throwing much light on certain economic problems.

§ 17. We have been looking at this movement from the British point of view. But other nations are hastening in the same direction. America faces new practical difficulties with such intrepidity and directness that she has already attained leadership in some economic affairs; she supplies many of the most instructive instances of the latest economic tendencies of the age, such as the development of speculation and trade combination in every form, and she will probably before long take the chief part in pioneering the way for the rest of the world.

Australia.

Australia also shows signs of vigour, and she has indeed some advantage over the United States in the greater homogeneity of her people. For, though the Australians—and nearly the same may be said of the Canadians—come from many lands, and thus stimulate one another to thought and enterprise by the variety of their experiences and their habits of thought, yet nearly all of them belong to one race : and the development of social institutions can proceed in some respects more easily, and faster than if they had to be adjusted to the capacities, the temperaments, the tastes, and the wants of peoples who have little affinity with one another.

On the Continent the power of obtaining important results by free association is less than in English-speaking countries; and in consequence there is APP. A, 17. less resource and less thoroughness in dealing with industrial problems. But their treatment is not quite the same in any two nations: and there is something characteristic and instructive in the methods adopted by each of them; particularly in relation to the sphere of governmental action. In this matter Germany is taking the lead. It has been a great gain to her that her manufacturing industries developed later than those of England; and she has been able to profit by England's experience and to avoid many of her mistakes.[1]

In Germany an exceptionally large part of the best intellect in the nation seeks for employment under Government, and there is probably no other Government which contains within itself so much trained ability of the highest order. On the other hand the energy, the originality and the daring which make the best men of business in England and America have but recently been fully developed in Germany; while the German people have a great faculty of obedience. They thus differ from the English; whose strength of will makes them capable of thorough discipline when strong occasion arises but who are not naturally docile. The control of industry by Government is seen in its best and most attractive forms in Germany; and at the same time the special virtues of private industry, its vigour, its elasticity and its resource, are beginning to be seen in full development there. In consequence the problems of the economic functions of Government have been studied in Germany with great care, and with results that may be very instructive to English-speaking people; provided they recollect that the arrangements best suited for the German character are perhaps not quite the best for them; since they could not, if they would, rival the Germans in their steadfast docility, and in their easy contentment with inexpensive kinds of food, clothing, house-room and amusements.

Germany has special facilities for experimenting in the management of business by the Government for the people.

And Germany contains a larger number than any other country of the most cultivated members of that wonderful race who have been leaders of the world in intensity of religious feeling and in keenness of business speculation. In every country, but especially in Germany, much of what is most brilliant and suggestive in economic practice and in economic thought is of Jewish origin. And in particular to German Jews we owe many daring speculations as to the conflict of interests between the individual and society, and as to their ultimate economic causes and their possible socialistic remedies.

But we are trenching on the subject of Appendix B. Here we have seen how recent is the growth of economic freedom, and how new is the substance of the problem with which economic science has now to deal; we have next to inquire how the form of that problem has been fashioned by the progress of events and the personal peculiarities of great thinkers.

[1] List worked out with much suggestiveness the notion that a backward nation must learn its lessons not from the contemporary conduct of more forward nations, but from their conduct when they were in the same state in which it is now. But, as Knies well shows (*Politische Œkonomie*, II. 5), the growth of trade and the improvement of the means of communication are making the developments of different nations tend to synchronize.

APPENDIX B[1]

THE GROWTH OF ECONOMIC SCIENCE

APP, B, 1.

Modern economic science owes much to ancient thought indirectly, but little directly.

§ **1.** We have seen how economic freedom has its roots in the past, but is in the main a product of quite recent times; we have next to trace the parallel growth of economic science. The social conditions of the present day have been developed from early Aryan and Semitic institutions by the aid of Greek thought and Roman law; but modern economic speculations have been very little under the direct influence of the theories of the ancients.

It is true that modern economics had its origin in common with other sciences at the time when the study of classic writers was reviving. But an industrial system which was based on slavery, and a philosophy which regarded manufacture and commerce with contempt, had little that was congenial to the hardy burghers who were as proud of their handicrafts and their trade as they were of their share in governing the State. These strong but uncultured men might have gained much from the philosophic temper and the broad interests of the great thinkers of past times. But, as it was, they set themselves to work out their own problems for themselves; and modern economics had at its origin a certain rudeness and limitation of scope, and a bias towards regarding wealth as an end rather than a means of man's life. Its immediate concern was generally with the public revenue, and the effects and yield of taxes; and here the statesmen of the free cities and the great empires alike found their economic problems more urgent and more difficult, as trade became broader and war more expensive.

Influence of trade with the New World.

In all ages, but especially in the early middle ages, statesmen and merchants had busied themselves with endeavours to enrich the State by regulating trade. One chief object of their concern had been the supply of the precious metals, which they thought the best indication if not the chief cause of material prosperity, whether of the individual or the nation. But the voyages of Vasco da Gama and Columbus raised commercial questions from a secondary to a dominating position among the nations of Western Europe. Theories with regard to the importance of the precious metals, and the best means of obtaining supplies of them, became in some measure the arbiters of public policy, dictating peace and war, and determining alliances that issued in the rise and fall of nations : and at times they largely influenced the migration of peoples over the face of the globe.

The early regulation of trade.

Regulations as to trade in the precious metals were but one group of a vast body of ordinances, which undertook, with varying degrees of minuteness and severity, to arrange for each individual what he should produce and how he should produce it, what he should earn and how he should spend his earnings. The natural adhesiveness of the Teutons had given custom an exceptional strength in the early middle ages. And this strength told on the side of trade gilds, of local authorities and of national Governments when they set themselves to cope with the restless tendency to change that sprang directly or indirectly from the trade with the New World. In France this Teutonic bias was directed by the Roman genius for system, and paternal government reached its zenith; the trade regulations of Colbert have become a proverb.

---

[1] See I. I. 5.

It was just at this time that economic theory first took shape, the so-called APP. B, 2.
Mercantile system became prominent; and regulation was pursued with a
masterful rigour that had not been known before.

As years went on there set in a tendency towards economic freedom, and The
those who were opposed to the new ideas claimed on their side the authority mercantile
of the Mercantilists of a past generation. But the spirit of regulation and theory
restriction which is found in their systems belonged to the age; many of the tended to
loosen the
changes which they set themselves to bring about were in the direction of the fetters of
freedom of enterprise. In particular they argued, in opposition to those who trade.
wished to prohibit absolutely the exportation of the precious metals, that it
should be permitted in all cases in which the trade would in the long run bring
more gold and silver into the country than it took out. By thus raising the
question whether the State would not benefit by allowing the trader to manage
his business as he liked in one particular case, they had started a new tendency
of thought; and this moved on by imperceptible steps in the direction of
economic freedom, being assisted on its way by the circumstances of the time,
no less than by the tone and temper of men's minds in Western Europe. The
broadening movement did go on till, in the latter half of the eighteenth century,
the time was ripe for the doctrine that the wellbeing of the community almost
always suffers when the State attempts to oppose its own artificial regulations
to the "natural" liberty of every man to manage his own affairs in his own
way.[1]

§ 2. The first systematic attempt to form an economic science on a broad The Physi-
basis was made in France about the middle of the eighteenth century by a ocrats in-
group of statesmen and philosophers under the leadership of Quesnay, the sisted that
restriction
noble-minded physician to Louis XV.[2] The corner-stone of their policy was is artificial
obedience to Nature.[3]   and liberty
They were the first to proclaim the doctrine of free trade as a broad principle is natural.
of action, going in this respect beyond even such advanced English writers as

[1] Meanwhile "Cameralistic" studies were developing the scientific analysis of
public business, at first on the financial side alone; but from 1750 onwards increasingly
in regard to the material, as distinguished from the human, conditions of the wealth
of nations.

[2] Cantillon's essay *Sur la Nature de Commerce*, written in 1755, and covering a
wide range, has indeed some claims to be called systematic. It is acute and in some
respects ahead of his time; though it now appears that he had been anticipated on
several important points by Nicholas Barbon, who wrote sixty years earlier. Kautz
was the first to recognize the importance of Cantillon's work; and Jevons declared he
was the true founder of Political Economy. For a well-balanced estimate of his place
in economics, see an article by Higgs in the *Quarterly Journal of Economics*, Vol. VI.

[3] In the two preceding centuries writers on economic questions had continually
appealed to Nature; each disputant claiming that his scheme was more natural than
that of others, and the philosophers of the eighteenth century, some of whom exercised
a great influence on economics, were wont to find the standard of right in conformity
to Nature. In particular Locke anticipated much of the work of the French economists
in the general tone of his appeals to Nature, and in some important details of his
theory. But Quesnay, and the other French economists who worked with him, were
drawn to the pursuit of natural laws of social life by several forces in addition to those
which were at work in England.

The luxury of the French court, and the privileges of the upper classes which were
ruining France, showed the worst side of an artificial civilization, and made thoughtful
men yearn for a return to a more natural state of society. The lawyers, among whom
much of the best mental and moral strength of the country was to be found, were
full of the Law of Nature which had been developed by the Stoic lawyers of the later
Roman Empire, and as the century wore on, the sentimental admiration for the
"natural" life of the American Indians, which Rousseau had kindled into flame,
began to influence the economists. Before long they were called Physiocrats or
adherents of the rule of Nature; this name being derived from the title of Dupont de
Nemours' *Physiocratie ou Constitution Naturelle du Gouvernement le plus avantageux au
Genre Humain* published in 1768. It may be mentioned that their enthusiasm for
agriculture and for the naturalness and simplicity of rural life was in part derived from
their Stoic masters.

626 THE GROWTH OF ECONOMIC SCIENCE

APP. B, 3. Sir Dudley North; and there was much in the tone and temper of their treatment of political and social questions which was prophetic of a later age. They fell however into a confusion of thought which was common even among scientific men of their time, but which has been banished after a long struggle from the physical sciences. They confused the ethical principle of conformity to Nature, which is expressed in the imperative mood, and prescribes certain laws of action, with those causal laws which science discovers by interrogating Nature, and which are expressed in the indicative mood. For this and other reasons their work has but little direct value.

They gave to economics its modern philanthropic tone.

But its indirect influence on the present position of economics has been very great. For, firstly, the clearness and logical consistency of their arguments have caused them to exercise a great influence on later thought. And, secondly, the chief motive of their study was not, as it had been with most of their predecessors, to increase the riches of merchants and fill the exchequers of kings; it was to diminish the suffering and degradation which was caused by extreme poverty. They thus gave to economics its modern aim of seeking after such knowledge as may help to raise the quality of human life.[1]

Adam Smith's genius.

§ 3. The next great step in advance, the greatest step that economics has ever taken, was the work, not of a school but of an individual. Adam Smith was not indeed the only great English economist of his time. Shortly before he wrote, important additions to economic theory had been made by Hume and Steuart, and excellent studies of economic facts had been published by Anderson and Young, But Adam Smith's breadth was sufficient to include all that was best in all his contemporaries, French and English; and, though he undoubtedly borrowed much from others, yet the more one compares him with those who went before and those who came after him, the finer does his genius appear, the broader his knowledge and the more well-balanced his judgment. He resided a long time in France in personal converse with the Physiocrats; he made a careful study of the English and French philosophy of his time, and he got to know the world practically by wide travel and by intimate association with Scotch men of business. To these advantages he added unsurpassed powers of observation, judgment and reasoning. The result is that wherever he differs from his predecessors, he is more nearly right than they; while there is scarcely any economic truth now known of which he did not get some glimpse. And since he was the first to write a treatise on wealth in all its chief social respects, he might on this ground alone have a claim to be regarded as the founder of modern economics.[2]

[1] Even the generous Vauban (writing in 1717) had to apologize for his interest in the wellbeing of the people, arguing that to enrich them was the only way to enrich the king—Pauvres paysans, pauvre Royaume, pauvre Royaume, pauvre Roi. On the other hand Locke, who exercised a great influence over Adam Smith, anticipated the ardent philanthropy of the Physiocrats as he did also some of their peculiar economic opinions. Their favourite phrase *Laisser faire, laisser aller*, is commonly misapplied now. *Laissez faire* means that anyone should be allowed to make what things he likes, and as he likes; that all trades should be open to everybody; that Government should not, as the Colbertists insisted, prescribe to manufacturers the fashions of their cloth. *Laisser aller* (or *passer*) means that persons and goods should be allowed to travel freely from one place to another, and especially from one district of France to another, without being subject to tolls and taxes and vexatious regulations. It may be noticed that *laisser aller* was the signal used in the Middle Ages by the Marshals to slip the leash from the combatants at a tournament.

[2] Compare the short but weighty statement of Adam Smith's claims to supremacy in Wagner's *Grundlegung*, Ed. 3, pp. 6, etc.; also Hasbach's *Untersuchungen über Adam Smith* (in which the notice of the influence of Dutch thought on both English and French is of special interest); and L. L. Price's *Adam Smith and his relations to Recent Economics* in the *Economic Journal*, Vol. III. Cunningham, *History*, § 306, argues forcibly that "his great achievement lay in isolating the conception of national wealth, while previous writers had treated it in conscious subordination to national power"; but perhaps each half of this contrast is drawn with too sharp outlines. Cannan in his Introduction to the *Lectures of Adam Smith*, shows the importance of Hutcheson's influence on him

But the area which he opened up was too vast to be thoroughly surveyed App. b, 3. by one man; and many truths of which at times he caught sight escaped from his view at other times. It is therefore possible to quote his authority in support of many errors; though, on examination, he is always found to be working his way towards the truth.[1]

He developed the Physiocratic doctrine of Free Trade with so much practical He greatly wisdom, and with so much knowledge of the actual conditions of business, as developed to make it a great force in real life; and he is most widely known both here the doc- and abroad for his argument that Government generally does harm by inter- free trade, fering in trade. While giving many instances of the ways in which self-interest may lead the individual trader to act injuriously to the community, he contended that even when Government acted with the best intentions, it nearly always served the public worse than the enterprise of the individual trader, however selfish he might happen to be. So great an impression did he make on the world by his defence of this doctrine that most German writers have it chiefly in view when they speak of *Smithianisus*.[2]

But after all, this was not his chief work. His chief work was to combine but his and develop the speculations of his French and English contemporaries and chief work predecessors as to value. His highest claim to have made an epoch in thought was to is that he was the first to make a careful and scientific inquiry into the manner theory of in which value measures human motive, on the one side measuring the desire value a of purchasers to obtain wealth, and on the other the efforts and sacrifices (or common " Real Cost of Production ") undergone by its producers.[3] centre

Possibly the full drift of what he was doing was not seen by him, certainly that gave it was not perceived by many of his followers. But for all that, the best economic economic work which came after the *Wealth of Nations* is distinguished from science. that which went before, by a clearer insight into the balancing and weighing, by means of money, of the desire for the possession of a thing on the one hand, and on the other of all the various efforts and self-denials which directly and indirectly contribute towards making it. Important as had been the steps that others had taken in this direction, the advance made by him was so great that he really opened out this new point of view, and by so doing made an epoch. In this he and the economists, who went before and came after him, were not inventing a new academic notion; they were merely giving definiteness and precision to notions that are familiar in common life. In fact the

[1] For instance, he had not quite got rid of the confusion prevalent in his time between the laws of economic science and the ethical precept of conformity to nature. " Natural " with him sometimes means that which the existing forces actually produce or tend to produce, sometimes that which his own human nature makes him wish that they should produce. In the same way, he sometimes regards it as the province of the economist to expound a science, and at others to set forth a part of the art of government. But loose as his language often is, we find on closer study that he himself knows pretty well what he is about. When he is seeking for causal laws, that is, for laws of nature in the modern use of the term, he uses scientific methods; and when he utters practical precepts he generally know that he is only expressing his own views of what ought to be, even when he seems to claim the authority of nature for them.

[2] The popular use of this term in Germany implies not only that Adam Smith thought that free play of individual interests would do more for the public weal than Government interference could, but further that it almost always acted in the ideally best way. But the leading German economists are well aware that he steadily insisted on the frequent opposition that there is between private interests and the public good : and the old use of the term *Smithianismus* is becoming discredited. See for instance a long list of such conflicts quoted from the *Wealth of Nations* by Knies, *Politische Œkonomie*, ch. III. § 3. See also Feilbogen, *Smith und Turgot*, and Zeyss, *Smith und der Eigennutz*.

[3] The relations of Value to Cost of Production had been indicated by the Physiocrats and by many earlier writers, among whom may be mentioned Harris, Cantillon, Locke, Barbon, Petty; and even Hobbes who hinted, though vaguely, that plenty depends on labour and abstinence applied by man to working up and accumulating the gifts of nature by land and by sea—*proventus terræ et aquæ, labor et parsimonia*.

APP. B, 4. ordinary man, without analytical habits of mind, is apt to regard money as measuring motive and happiness more closely and exactly than it actually does; and this is partly because he does not think out the manner in which the measurement is effected. Economic language seems technical and less real than that of common life. But in truth it is more real, because it is more careful and takes more account of differences and difficulties.[1]

The study of facts.
§ 4. None of Adam Smith's contemporaries and immediate successors had a mind as broad and well balanced as his. But they did excellent work, each giving himself up to some class of problems to which he was attracted by the natural bent of his genius, or the special events of the time in which he wrote. During the remainder of the eighteenth century the chief economic writings were historical and descriptive, and bore upon the condition of the working classes, especially in the agricultural districts. Arthur Young continued the inimitable records of his tour, Eden wrote a history of the poor which has served both as a basis and as a model for all succeeding historians of industry; while Malthus showed by a careful investigation of history what were the forces which had as a matter of fact controlled the growth of population in different countries and at different times.

Bentham's opposition to customary restrictions on trade for which no valid reason could be given, greatly influenced English economists early in last century.
But on the whole the most influential of the immediate successors of Adam Smith was Bentham. He wrote little on economics himself, but he went far towards setting the tone of the rising school of English economists at the beginning of the nineteenth century. He was an uncompromising logician, and averse to all restrictions and regulations for which no clear reason could be given; and his pitiless demands that they should justify their existence received support from the circumstances of the age. England had won her unique position in the world by her quickness in adapting herself to every new economic movement; while by their adherence to old-fashioned ways the nations of Central Europe had been prevented from turning to account their great natural resources. The business men of England therefore were inclined to think that the influence of custom and sentiment in business affairs was harmful, that in England at least it had diminished, was diminishing, and would soon vanish away: and the disciples of Bentham were not slow to conclude that they need not concern themselves much about custom. It was enough for them to discuss the tendencies of man's action on the supposition that everyone was always on the alert to find out what course would best promote his own interest, and was free and quick to follow it.[2]

There is then some justice in the charges frequently brought against the

---

[1] Adam Smith saw clearly that while economic science must be based on a study of facts, the facts are so complex, that they generally can teach nothing directly; they must be interpreted by careful reasoning and analysis. And as Hume said, the *Wealth of Nations* "is so much illustrated with curious facts that it must take the public attention." This is exactly what Adam Smith did: he did not very often prove a conclusion by detailed induction. The data of his proofs were chiefly facts that were within everyone's knowledge, facts physical, mental and moral. But he illustrated his proofs by curious and instructive facts; he thus gave them life and force, and made his readers feel that they were dealing with problems of the real world, and not with abstraction; and his book, though not well arranged, is a model of method. The supremacy of Adam Smith and of Ricardo, each in his own way, is well set forth by Prof. Nicholson in *The Cambridge Modern History*, Vol. x. ch. xxiv.

[2] Another way in which he influenced the young economists around him was through his passionate desire for security. He was indeed an ardent reformer. He was an enemy of all artificial distinctions between different classes of men; he declared with emphasis that any one man's happiness was as important as any other's, and that the aim of all action should be to increase the sum total of happiness; he admitted that other things being equal this sum total would be the greater, the more equally wealth was distributed. Nevertheless so full was his mind of the terror of the French revolution, and so great were the evils which he attributed to the smallest attack on security that, daring analyst as he was, he felt himself and he fostered in his disciples an almost superstitious reverence for the existing institutions of private property.

English economists of the beginning of last century, that they neglected to App. b, 5. inquire with sufficient care whether a greater range might not be given to collective as opposed to individual action in social and economic affairs, and that they exaggerated the strength of competition and its rapidity of action : and there is some ground, though a very slight one, for the charge that their work is marred by a certain hardness of outline and even harshness of temper. These faults were partly due to Bentham's direct influence, partly to the spirit of the age of which he was an exponent. But they were partly also due to the fact that economic study had again got a good deal into the hands of men whose strength lay in vigorous action rather than in philosophical thought.

§ 5. Statesmen and merchants again threw themselves into problems of money and foreign trade with even more energy than they used to do when these questions were first started in the earlier period of the great economic change at the end of the Middle Ages. It might at first sight seem probable that their contact with real life, their wide experience, and their vast knowledge of facts would have led them to take a wide survey of human nature and to found their reasonings on a broad basis. But the training of practical life often leads to a too rapid generalization from personal experience. Many of whom had a bias towards rapid generalization.

So long as they were well within their own province their work was excellent. The theory of currency is just that part of economic science in which but little harm is done by neglecting to take much account of any human motives except the desire for wealth; and the brilliant school of deductive reasoning, which Ricardo led, was here on safe ground.[1] Their work was excellent so long as they treated of money

The economists next addressed themselves to the theory of foreign trade and cleared away many of the flaws which Adam Smith had left in it. There is no other part of economics, except the theory of money, which so nearly falls within the range of pure deductive reasoning. It is true that a full discussion of a free trade policy must take account of many considerations that are not strictly economic; but most of these, though important for agricultural countries, and especially for new countries, had little bearing in the case of England. and foreign trade,

During all this time the study of economic facts was not neglected in England. The statistical studies of Petty, Arthur Young, Eden, and others were ably continued by Tooke, McCulloch and Porter. And though it may be true that an undue prominence is given in their writings to those facts which were of direct interest to merchants and other capitalists, the same cannot be said of the admirable series of Parliamentary inquiries into the condition of the working classes, which were brought about by the influence of the economists. In fact, the public and private collections of statistics and the economic nor did they neglect statistics and inquiries into the

---

[1] He is often spoken of as a representative Englishman : but this is just what he was not. His strong constructive originality is the mark of the highest genius in all nations. But his aversion to inductions and his delight in abstract reasonings are due, not to his English education, but, as Bagehot points out, to his Semitic origin. Nearly every branch of the Semitic race has had some special genius for dealing with abstractions, and several of them have had a bias towards the abstract calculations connected with the trade of money dealing, and its modern developments; and Ricardo's power of threading his way without slip through intricate paths to new and unexpected results has never been surpassed. But it is difficult even for an Englishman to follow his track; and his foreign critics have, as a rule, failed to detect the real drift and purpose of his work. For he never explains himself : he never shows what his purpose is in working first on one hypothesis and then on another, nor how by properly combining the results of his different hypothesis it is possible to cover a great variety of practical questions. He wrote originally not for publication, but to clear away the doubts of himself, and perhaps a few friends, on points of special difficulty. They, like himself, were men of affairs with a vast knowledge of the facts of life : and this is one cause of his preferring broad principles, consonant with general experience, to particular inductions from select groups of facts. But his knowledge was one-sided : he understood the merchant, but not the working man. His sympathies however were with the working man; and he supported his friend Hume in the defence of the right of the working men to combine for mutual aid in the same way as their employers were able to do. Compare Appendix I below.

APP. B, 6.

condition
of the
working
classes.
But they
lacked a
knowledge
of the Com-
parative
Method.
histories that were produced in England at the end of the eighteenth century
and the beginning of the nineteenth, may fairly be regarded as the origin of
systematic historical and statistical studies in economics.

Nevertheless there was a certain narrowness in their work : it was truly
historical; but for the greater part it was not " comparative." Hume, Adam
Smith, Arthur Young and others had been led by their own instinctive genius
and the example of Montesquieu occasionally to compare social facts of different
ages and different countries, and to draw lessons from the comparison. But
no one had grasped the notion of the comparative study of history on a systematic plan. In consequence the writers of that time, able and earnest as
they were in their search for the actual facts of life, worked rather at haphazard. They overlooked whole groups of facts which we now see to be of vital
importance, and they often failed to make the best use of those which they
collected. And this narrowness was intensified when they passed from the
collection of facts to general reasonings about them.

Their
desire for
simplicity
led them
sometimes
to argue as
though all
mankind
had the
same
habits of
mind as
city men.
§ 6. For the sake of simplicity of argument, Ricardo and his followers often
spoke as though they regarded man as a constant quantity, and they never
gave themselves enough trouble to study his variations. The people whom
they knew most intimately were city men; and they sometimes expressed
themselves so carelessly as almost to imply that other Englishmen were very
much like those whom they knew in the city.

They were aware that the inhabitants of other countries had peculiarities
of their own that deserved study; but they seemed to regard such differences
as superficial and sure to be removed, as soon as other nations had got to know
that better way which Englishmen were ready to teach them. The same bent
of mind that led our lawyers to impose English civil law on the Hindoos, led
our economists to work out their theories on the tacit supposition that the
world was made up of city men. And though this did little harm so long as
they were treating of money and foreign trade, it led them astray as to the
relations between the different industrial classes. It caused them to speak of
labour as a commodity without staying to throw themselves into the point of
view of the workman; and without dwelling upon the allowances to be made
for his human passions, his instincts and habits, his sympathies and antipathies,
his class jealousies and class adhesiveness, his want of knowledge and of the
opportunities for free and vigorous action. They therefore attributed to the
forces of supply and demand a much more mechanical and regular action than
is to be found in real life : and they laid down laws with regard to profits and
wages that did not really hold even for England in their own time.[1]

But their most vital fault was that they did not see how liable to change
are the habits and institutions of industry. In particular they did not see

[1] As regards wages there were even some logical errors in the conclusions they
deduced from their own premisses. These errors when traced back to their origin are
little more than careless modes of expression. But they were seized upon eagerly
by those who cared little for the scientific study of economics, and cared only to quote
its doctrines for the purpose of keeping the working classes in their place; and perhaps
no other great school of thinkers has ever suffered so much from the way in which
its " parasites " (to use a term that is commonly applied to them in Germany), pro-
fessing to simplify economic doctrines, really enunciated them without the conditions
required to make them true. Miss Martineau gave some colour to these statements by
her vehement writings against the Factory Acts : and Senior also wrote on the same
side. But Miss Martineau was not an economist in the proper sense of the word :
she confessed that she never read more than one chapter of an economic book at a
time before writing a story to illustrate economic principles, for fear the pressure on
her mind should be too great : and before her death she expressed a just doubt whether
the principles of economics (as understood by her) had any validity. Senior wrote
against the Acts when he had only just begun to study economics : a few years later
he formally recanted his opinions. It has sometimes been said that McCulloch was an
opponent of the Acts; but in fact he heartily supported them. Tooke was the chief
of the sub-Commissioners, whose report on the employment of women and children
in the mines, roused public opinion to decisive action against it.

that the poverty of the poor is the chief cause of that weakness and ineffi- APP. B, 7.
ciency which are the causes of their poverty : they had not the faith that
modern economists have in the possibility of a vast improvement in the They did
condition of the working classes. not allow
enough

The perfectibility of man had indeed been asserted by the socialists. But for the de-
their views were based on little historic and scientific study; and were ex- pendence
pressed with an extravagance that moved the contempt of the business-like of man's
economists of the age. The socialists did not study the doctrines which they character
attacked; and there was no difficulty in showing that they had not understood on his
the nature and efficiency of the existing economic organization of society. stances.
The economists therefore did not trouble themselves to examine carefully any The
of their doctrines, and least of all their speculations as to human nature.[1] Socialists.

But the socialists were men who had felt intensely, and who knew something
about the hidden springs of human action of which the economists took no
account. Buried among their wild rhapsodies there were shrewd observations
and pregnant suggestions from which philosophers and economists had much
to learn. And gradually their influence began to tell. Comte's debts to
them were very great; and the crisis of John Stuart Mill's life, as he tells us
in his autobiography, came to him from reading them.

§ 7. When comparing the modern view of the vital problem of the Distribu- The
tion of wealth with that which prevailed at the beginning of last century we growing
have found that, over and above all changes in detail and all improvements in tendency
scientific accuracy of reasoning. there is a fundamental change in treatment; of
economists
for, while the earlier economists argued as though man's character and effi- to take
ciency were to be regarded as a fixed quantity, modern economists keep con- account
stantly in mind the fact that it is a product of the circumstances under which of the
he has lived. This change in the point of view of economics is partly due to pliability
the fact that the changes in human nature during the last fifty years have been of human
so rapid as to force themselves on the attention; partly to the direct influence nature
of individual writers, socialists and others; and partly to the indirect influence
of a similar change in some branches of natural science.

At the beginning of last century the mathematico-physical group of is partly
sciences were in the ascendant; and these sciences, widely as they differ from due to the
one another, have this point in common, that their subject-matter is constant influence of
and unchanged in all countries and in all ages. The progress of science was biological
studies.
familiar to men's minds but the development of the subject-matter of science
was strange to them. As the century wore on, the biological group of sciences
were slowly making way, and people were getting clearer ideas as to the nature
of organic growth. They were learning that if the subject-matter of a science
passes through different stages of development, the laws which apply to one
stage will seldom apply without modification to others; the laws of the science
must have a development corresponding to that of the things of which they treat.
The influence of this new notion gradually spread to the sciences which relate
to man; and showed itself in the works of Goethe, Hegel, Comte and others.

At last the speculations of biology made a great stride forwards: its
discoveries fascinated the attention of the world as those of physics had
done in earlier years; and there was a marked change in the tone of the
moral and historical sciences. Economics has shared in the general movement;
and is getting to pay every year a greater attention to the pliability of human
nature, and to the way in which the character of man affects and is affected
by the prevalent methods of the production, distribution and consumption

---

[1] A partial exception must be made for Malthus, whose studies of population were
suggested by Godwin's essay. But he did not properly belong to the Ricardian school
and he was not a man of business. Half a century later Bastiat, a lucid writer but
not a profound thinker, maintained the extravagant doctrine that the natural organization of society under the influence of competition is the best not only that can be
practically effected, but even that can be theoretically conceived.

APP. B, 7.

John Stuart Mill. Recent English economists.

Characteristics of modern English work.

The abandonment of dogma, the development of analysis.

of wealth. The first important indication of the new movement was seen in John Stuart Mill's admirable *Principles of Political Economy*.[1]

Mill's followers have continued his movement away from the position taken up by the immediate followers of Ricardo; and the human as distinguished from the mechanical element is taking a more and more prominent place in economics. Not to mention writers yet living, the new temper is shown in Cliffe Leslie's historical inquiries, and in the many-sided work of Bagehot, Cairnes, Toynbee and others : but above all in that of Jevons, which has secured a permanent and notable place in economic history by its rare combination of many various qualities of the highest order.

A higher notion of social duty is spreading everywhere. In Parliament, in the press and in the pulpit, the spirit of humanity speaks more distinctly and more earnestly. Mill and the economists who have followed him have helped onwards this general movement, and they in their turn have been helped onwards by it. Partly for this reason, partly in consequence of the modern growth of historical science, their study of facts has been broader and more philosophic. It is true that the historical and statistical work of some of the earlier economists has seldom if ever been surpassed. But much information, which was beyond their reach, is now accessible to everyone; and economists who have neither McCulloch's familiarity with practical business, nor his vast historical learning, are enabled to get a view of the relations of economic doctrine to the true facts of life which is both broader and clearer than his. In this they have been helped by the general improvement which has taken place in the methods of all sciences, including that of history.

Thus in every way economic reasoning is now more exact than it was : the premises assumed in any inquiry are stated with more rigid precision than formerly. But this greater exactness of thought is partly destructive in its action; it is showing that many of the older applications of general reasoning were invalid, because no care had been taken to think out all the assumptions that were implied and to see whether they could fairly be made in the special cases under discussion. As a result, many dogmas have been destroyed which appeared to be simple only because they were loosely expressed; but which, for that very reason, served as an armoury with which partisan disputants (chiefly of the capitalist class) have equipped themselves for the fray. This destructive work might appear at first sight to have diminished the value of processes of general reasoning in economics : but really it has had the opposite result. It has cleared the ground for newer and stronger machinery, which is being steadily and patiently built up. It has enabled us to take broader views of life, to proceed more surely though more slowly, to be more scientific and much less dogmatic than those good and great men who bore the first brunt of the battle with the difficulties of economic problems; and to whose pioneering work we owe our own more easy course.

The change may, perhaps, be regarded as a passing onward from that early

---

[1] James Mill had educated his son in the straitest tenets of Bentham and Ricardo, and had implanted in his mind a zeal for clearness and definiteness. And in 1830 John Mill wrote an essay on economic method in which he proposed to give increased sharpness of outlines to the abstractions of the science. He faced Ricardo's tacit assumption that no motive of action except the desire for wealth need be much considered by the economist; he held that it was dangerous so long as it was not distinctly stated, but no longer; and he half promised a treatise which should be deliberately and openly based on it. But he did not redeem the promise. A change had come over his tone of thought and of feeling before he published in 1848 his great economic work. He called it *Principles of Political Economy, with some of their Applications to Social Philosophy* [it is significant that he did not say *to other branches of Social Philosophy*; comp. Ingram's *History*, p. 154], and he made in it no attempt to mark off by a rigid line those reasonings which assume that man's sole motive is the pursuit of wealth from those which do not. The change in his attitude was a part of the great changes that were going on in the world around him, though he was not fully aware of their influence on himself.

stage in the development of scientific method, in which the operations of Nature are represented as conventionally simplified for the purpose of enabling them to be described in short and easy sentences, to that higher stage in which they are studied more carefully, and represented more nearly as they are, even at the expense of some loss of simplicity and definiteness, and even apparent lucidity. And in consequence general reasoning in economics has made more rapid progress, and established a firmer position in this generation in which it is subject to hostile criticism at every step, than when it was at the height of its popularity and its authority was seldom challenged.

So far we have looked at recent progress from the point of view of England only : but progress in England has been only one side of a broader movement which has extended over the whole western world.

§ 8. English economists have had many followers and many critics in French foreign countries. The French school has had a continuous development econo-from its own great thinkers in the eighteenth century, and has avoided many mists. errors and confusions, particularly with regard to wages, which have been common among the second rank of English economists. From the time of Say downwards it has done a great deal of useful work. In Cournot it has had a constructive thinker of the highest genius ; while Fourier, St. Simon, Proud-hon and Louis Blanc have made many of the most valuable, as well as many of the wildest suggestions of Socialism.

The greatest relative advance during recent years is perhaps that which American has been made by America. A generation ago, the " American school " of School. economists was supposed to consist of the group of Protectionists who followed Carey's lead. But new schools of vigorous thinkers are now growing up ; and there are signs that America is on the way to take the same leading posi-tion in economic thought, that she has already taken in economic practice.

Economic science is showing signs of renewed vigour in two of its old homes, Holland and Italy. And more especially is the vigorous analytical work of the Austrian economists attracting much attention in all countries.

But on the whole the most important economic work that has been done German on the Continent in recent times is that of Germany. While recognizing the econo-leadership of Adam Smith, the German economists have been irritated more mists. than any others by what they have regarded as the insular narrowness and self-confidence of the Ricardian school. In particular they resented the way in which the English advocates of free trade tacitly assumed that a proposition which had been established with regard to a manufacturing country, such as England was, could be carried over without modification to agricultural countries. The brilliant genius and national enthusiasm of List overthrew List. this presumption ; and showed that the Ricardians had taken but little account of the indirect effects of free trade. No great harm might be done in neglecting them so far as England was concerned ; because there they were in the main beneficial and thus added to the strength of its direct effects. But he showed that in Germany, and still more in America, many of its in-direct effects were evil ; and he contended that these evils outweighed its direct benefits. Many of his arguments were invalid, but some of them were not ; and as the English economists scornfully refused them a patient discussion, able and public-spirited men, impressed by the force of those which were sound, acquiesced in the use for the purposes of popular agitation of other arguments which were unscientific, but which appealed with greater force to the working classes.

American manufacturers adopted List as their advocate : and the be-ginning of his fame, as well as of the systematic advocacy of protectionist doctrines in America, was in the wide circulation by them of a popular treatise which he wrote for them.[1]

[1] It has already been observed that List overlooked the tendency of modern inter-communication to make the development of different nations synchronize. His

APP. B, 8.

The Germans press the claims of nationalism against those of individualism on the one hand and cosmopolitanism on the other.

The Germans are fond of saying that the Physiocrats and the school of Adam Smith underrated the importance of national life; that they tended to sacrifice it on the one hand to a selfish individualism and on the other to a limp philanthropic cosmopolitanism. They urge that List did great service in stimulating a feeling of patriotism, which is more generous than that of individualism, and more sturdy and definite than that of cosmopolitanism. It may be doubted whether the cosmopolitan sympathies of the Physiocrats and of the English economists have been as strong as the Germans think. But there is no question that the recent political history of Germany has influenced the tone of her economists in the direction of nationalism. Surrounded by powerful and aggressive armies Germany can exist only by the aid of an ardent national feeling; and German writers have insisted eagerly, perhaps too eagerly, that altruistic feelings have a more limited scope in the economic relations between countries than in those between individuals.

Their great work in the study of economic history by the comparative method, and in relation to general history and jurisprudence.

But though national in their sympathies, the Germans are nobly international in their studies. They have taken the lead in the " comparative " [1] study of economic, as well as of general history. They have brought side by side the social and industrial phenomena of different countries and of different ages; have so arranged them that they throw light upon and interpret one another, and have studied them all in connection with the suggestive history of jurisprudence.[1] The work of a few members of this school is tainted by exaggeration, and even by a narrow contempt for the reasonings of the Ricardian school, the drift and purpose of which they have themselves failed to understand : and this has led to much bitter and dreary controversy. But with scarcely an exception, the leaders of the school have been free from this narrowness. It would be difficult to overrate the value of the work which they and their fellow-workers in other countries have done in tracing and explaining the history of economic habits and institutions. It is one of the great achievements of our age; and an important addition to our real wealth. It has done more than almost anything else to broaden our ideas, to increase our knowledge of ourselves, and to help us to understand the evolution of man's moral and social life, and of the Divine Principle of which it is an embodiment.

Their work in economic theory and analysis.

They have given their chief attention to the historical treatment of the science, and to its application to the conditions of German social and political life, especially to the economic duties of the German bureaucracy. But led by the billiant genius of Hermann they have made careful and profound analyses which add much to our knowledge, and they have greatly extended the boundaries of economic theory.[2]

---

patriotic fervour perverted in many ways his scientific judgment : but Germans listened eagerly to his argument that every country had to go through the same stages of development that England had gone through, and that she had protected her manufacturers when she was in transition from the agricultural to the manufacturing stage. He had a genuine desire for truth; his method was in harmony with the comparative method of inquiry which is being pursued with vigour by all classes of students in Germany, but especially by her historians and lawyers; and the direct and indirect influence of his thought has been very great. His *Outlines of a New System of Political Economy* appeared in Philadelphia in 1827, and his *Das nationale System der Politischen Œkonomie* in 1840. It is a disputed point whether Carey owed much to List; see Miss Hirst's *Life of List*, ch. IV. As to the general relations between their doctrines, see Knies, *Pol. Œk.*, 2nd edition, pp. 440, etc.

[1] The excellence of this work may perhaps partly be attributed to the union of legal and economic studies in the avenues to many careers in Germany as in other countries of the Continent. A splendid instance is to be found in Wagner's contributions to economics.

[2] In such matters, the English, the Germans, the Austrians, and indeed every nation claim for themselves more than others are willing to allow them. This is partly because each nation has its own intellectual virtues, and misses them in the writings of foreigners; while it does not quite understand the complaints which others make as to its shortcomings. But the chief reason is that, since a new idea is generally of gradual growth, and is often worked out by more than one nation at the same time,

German thought has also given an impetus to the study of socialism and the functions of the State. It is from German writers, some of whom have been of Jewish origin, that the world has received the greater part of the most thoroughgoing of recent propositions for utilizing the property of the world for the benefit of the community with but little reference to the existing incidents of ownership. It is true that on closer investigation their work turns out to be less original as well as less profound than at first sight appears : but it derives great power from its dialectic ingenuity, its brilliant style, and in some cases from its wide-reaching though distorted historical learning.

Besides the revolutionary socialists, there is a large body of thinkers in Germany who are setting themselves to insist on the scantiness of the authority which the institution of private property in its present form can derive from history; and to urge on broad scientific and philosophic grounds a reconsideration of the rights of society as against the individual. The political and military institutions of the German people have recently increased their natural tendency to rely more on Government and less on individual enterprise than Englishmen do. And in all questions bearing on social reforms the English and German nations have much to learn from one another.

But amid all the historical learning and reforming enthusiasm of the age there is danger that a difficult but important part of the work of economic science may be neglected. The popularity of economics has tended in some measure to the neglect of careful and rigorous reasoning. The growing prominence of what has been called the biological view of the science has tended to throw the notions of economic law and measurement into the background; as though such nations were too hard and rigid to be applied to the living and ever-changing economic organism. But biology itself teaches us that the vertebrate organisms are the most highly developed. The modern economic organism is vertebrate; and the science which deals with it should not be invertebrate. It should have that delicacy and sensitiveness of touch which are required for enabling it to adapt itself closely to the real phenomena of the world; but none the less must it have a firm backbone of careful reasoning and analysis.

APP. B, 8.
——
German Socialism.

There is some danger that the severe and less popular task of careful scientific reasoning may be neglected.

each of those nations is likely to claim it ; and thus each is apt to under-estimate the originality of the others.

APPENDIX C[1]

THE SCOPE AND METHOD OF ECONOMICS

APP. C, 1.

A unified Social Science, however desirable, is unattainable, as is shown by experience,

§ **1.** There are some who hold, with Comte, that the scope of any profitable study of man's action in society must be coextensive with the whole of social science. They argue that all the aspects of social life are so closely connected, that a special study of any one of them must be futile; and they urge on economists to abandon their distinctive *rôle* and to devote themselves to the general advancement of a unified and all embracing social science. But the whole range of man's actions in society is too wide and too various to be analysed and explained by a single intellectual effort. Comte himself and Herbert Spencer have brought to the task unsurpassed knowledge and great genius; they have made epochs in thought by their broad surveys and their suggestive hints; but they can hardly be said even to have made a commencement with the construction of a unified social science.

and as may be inferred from the history of Physical Science.

The physical sciences made slow progress so long as the brilliant but impatient Greek genius insisted on searching after a single basis for the explanation of all physical phenomena; and their rapid progress in the modern age is due to a breaking up of broad problems into their component parts. Doubtless there is a unity underlying all the forces of nature; but whatever progress has been made towards discovering it, has depended on knowledge obtained by persistent specialized study, no less than on occasional broad surveys of the field of nature as a whole. And similar patient detailed work is required to supply the materials which may enable future ages to understand better than we can the forces that govern the development of the social organism.

Comte showed well the evils of extreme specialization,

But on the other hand it must be fully conceded to Comte that, even in the physical sciences, it is the duty of those who are giving their chief work to a limited field, to keep up close and constant correspondence with those who are engaged in neighbouring fields. Specialists who never look beyond their own domain are apt to see things out of true proportion; much of the knowledge they get together is of comparatively little use; they work away at the details of old problems which have lost most of their significance and have been supplanted by new questions rising out of new points of view; and they fail to gain that large illumination which the progress of every science throws by comparison and analogy on those around it. Comte did good service therefore by insisting that the solidarity of social phenomena must render the work of exclusive specialists even more futile in social than in physical science. Mill

but failed to prove that there should be none.

conceding this continues :—" A person is not likely to be a good economist who is nothing else. Social phenomena acting and reacting on one another, they cannot rightly be understood apart; but this by no means proves that the material and industrial phenomena of society are not themselves susceptible of useful generalizations, but only that these generalizations must necessarily be relative to a given form of civilization and a given stage of social advancement." [2]

---

[1] See I. II.

[2] Mill, *On Comte*, p. 82. Comte's attack on Mill illustrates the general rule that in discussions on method and scope, a man is nearly sure to be right when affirming the usefulness of his own procedure, and wrong when denying that of others. The present

§ 2. It is true that the forces with which economics deals have one advantage for deductive treatment in the fact that their method of combination is, as Mill observed, that of mechanics rather than of chemistry. That is to say, when we know the action of two economic forces separately—as for instance the influences which an increase in the rate of wages and a diminution in the difficulty of the work in a trade will severally exert on the supply of labour in it—we can predict fairly well their conjoint action, without waiting for specific experience of it.[1]

APP. C, 2.

——

Economic forces combine mechanically rather than chemically.

But even in mechanics long chains of deductive reasoning are directly applicable only to the occurrences of the laboratory. By themselves they are seldom a sufficient guide for dealing with the heterogeneous materials and the complex and uncertain combination of the forces of the real world. For that purpose they need to be supplemented by specific experience, and applied in harmony with, and often in subordination to, a ceaseless study of new facts, a ceaseless search for new inductions. For instance, the engineer can calculate with fair precision the angle at which an ironclad will lose her stability in still water; but before he predicts how she would behave in a storm, he will avail himself of the observations of experienced sailors who have watched her movements in an ordinary sea; and the forces of which economics has to take account are more numerous, less definite, less well known, and more diverse in character than those of mechanics; while the material on which they act is more uncertain and less homogeneous. Again the cases in which economic forces combine with more of the apparent arbitrariness of chemistry than of the simple regularity of pure mechanics, are neither rare nor unimportant. For instance a small addition to a man's income will generally increase his purchases a little in every direction : but a large addition may alter his habits, perhaps increase his self-respect and make him cease to care for some things altogether. The spread of a fashion from a higher social grade to a lower may destroy the fashion among the higher grade. And again increased earnestness in our care for the poor may make charity more lavish, or may destroy the need for some of its forms altogether.

But economics has no near kinship with any physical science.

Lastly, the matter with which the chemist deals is the same always : but economics, like biology, deals with a matter, of which the inner nature and constitution, as well as the outer form, are constantly changing. The chemist's predictions all rest on the latent hypothesis that the specimen operated upon is what it is supposed to be, or at least that the impurities in it are only such as may be neglected. But even he, when dealing with living beings, can seldom sail safely any considerable way out of sight of the firm land of specific experience : he must rely mainly on that to tell him how a new drug will affect a person in health, and again how it will affect a person with a certain disease; and even after some general experience he may find unexpected results in its action on persons of different constitutions or in a new combination with other drugs.

It is a branch of biology broadly interpreted.

---

movement towards Sociology in America, England and other countries recognizes the need for the intensive study of economics and other branches of social science. But perhaps the use of the term Sociology is premature. For it seems to claim that a unification of social sciences is already in sight : and though some excellent intensive studies have been published under the name of Sociology, it is doubtful whether those efforts at unification which have been made so far have achieved any great success beyond that of preparing the way and erecting danger posts at its pitfalls for the guidance of later generations, whose resources will be less inadequate for the giant task than our own.

[1] Mill exaggerated the extent to which this can be done; and he was thereby led to make excessive claims for the deductive methods in economics. See the last of his *Essays*; Book VI. of his *Logic*, and especially its ninth chapter; also pp. 157–161 of his *Autobiography*. His practice, like that of many other writers on economic method of all shades of opinion, was less extreme than his profession.

APP. C, 3. If however we look at the history of such strictly economic relations as those of business credit and banking, of trade-unionism or co-operation, we see that modes of working, that have been generally successful at some times and places, have uniformly failed at others. The difference may sometimes be explained simply as the result of variations in general enlightenment, or of moral strength of character and habits of mutual trust. But often the explanation is more difficult. At one time or place men will go far in trust of one another and in sacrifice of themselves for the common wellbeing, but only in certain directions; and at another time or place there will be a similar limitation, but the directions will be different; and every variation of this kind limits the range of deduction in economics.

For our present purpose the pliability of the race is more important than the pliability of the individual. It is true that individual character changes, partly in an apparently arbitrary way, and partly according to well-known rules. It is true for instance that the average age of the workmen engaged in a labour dispute is an important element in any forecast of the lines on which it will run. But as, generally speaking, young and old, people of a sanguine and a despondent temperament are found in about like proportions at one place as at another, and at one time as at another, individual peculiarities of character and changes of character are a less hindrance to the general application of the deductive method, than at first sight appears. Thus by patient interrogation of nature and the progress of analysis, the reign of law is being made to invade new fields in both therapeutics and economics : and some sort of prediction, independent of specific experience, is becoming possible as to the separate and combined action of an ever-increasing variety of agencies.

The work of analysis and deduction. Explanation and prediction are the same operation in opposite directions. § 3. The function then of analysis and deduction in economics is not to forge a few long chains of reasoning, but to forge rightly many short chains and single connecting links. This however is no trivial task. If the economist reasons rapidly and with a light heart, he is apt to make bad connections at every turn of his work. He needs to make careful use of analysis and deduction, because only by their aid can he select the right facts, group them rightly, and make them serviceable for suggestions in thought and guidance in practice; and because, as surely as every deduction must rest on the basis of inductions, so surely does every inductive process involve and include analysis and deduction. Or to put the same thing in another way the explanation of the past and the prediction of the future are not different operations, but the same worked in opposite directions, the one from effect to cause, the other from cause to effect. As Schmoller well says, to obtain " a knowledge of individual causes " we need " induction ; the final conclusion of which is indeed nothing but the inversion of the syllogism which is employed in deduction. . . . Induction and deduction rest on the same tendencies, the same beliefs, the same needs of our reason."[1]

We can explain an event completely only by first discovering all the events which can have affected it, and the ways in which they can severally have done so. In so far as our analysis of any of these facts or relations is imperfect, in so far is our explanation liable to error; and the inference latent in it is already on its way to build up an induction which, though probably plausible, is false. While in so far as our knowledge and analysis are complete, we are able by merely inverting our mental process to deduce and predict the future almost as certainly as we could have explained the past on a similar basis of knowledge. It is only when we go beyond a first step that a great difference arises between the certainty of prediction and the certainty of explanation : for any error made in the first step of prediction, will be accumulated and intensified in the second; while in interpreting the past, error is not so likely to be accumulated; for observation or recorded history will probably bring a fresh check at each step. The same processes, both inductive and deductive, are used in nearly the same way in the explanation of a known fact in the history APP. c, 4. of the tides, and in the prediction of an unknown fact.[1]

It must then always be remembered that though observation or history may tell us that one event happened at the same time as another, or after it, they cannot tell us whether the first was the cause of the second. That can be done only by reason acting on the facts. When it is said that a certain event in history teaches this or that, formal reckoning is never made for all the conditions which were present when the event happened; some are tacitly, if not unconsciously, assumed to be irrelevant. This assumption may be justifiable in any particular case; but it may not. Wider experience, more careful inquiry, may show that the causes to which the event is attributed could not have produced it unaided; perhaps even that they hindered the event, which was brought about in spite of them by other causes that have escaped notice.

The difficulty of interpreting facts.

This difficulty has been made prominent by recent controversies as to contemporary events in our own country. Whenever a conclusion is drawn from them that meets with opposition, it has to stand a sort of trial; rival explanations are offered; new facts are brought to light; the old facts are tested and rearranged, and in some cases shown to support the opposite conclusion from that on behalf of which they were at first invoked.

Both the difficulty of analysis and the need for it are increased by the fact that no two economic events are exactly alike in all respects. Of course there may be a close resemblance between two simple incidents : the terms of the leases of two farms may be governed by nearly the same causes : two references of wages questions to Boards of Arbitration may raise substantially the same question. But there is no exact repetition even on a small scale. However nearly two cases correspond, we have to decide whether the difference between the two may be neglected as practically unimportant; and this may not be very easy, even if the two cases refer to the same place and time.

And if we are dealing with the facts of remote times we must allow for the changes that have meanwhile come over the whole character of economic life : however closely a problem of to-day may resemble in its outward incidents another recorded in history, it is probable that a closer examination will detect a fundamental difference between their real characters. Till this has been made, no valid argument can be drawn from one case to the other.

The untrustworthiness of primâ facie evidence drawn from the distant past.

§ 4. This brings us to consider the relation in which economics stands to the facts of distant times.

The study of economic history may have various aims, and correspondingly various methods. Regarded as a branch of general history it may aim at helping us to understand " what has been the institutional framework of society at the several periods, what has been the constitution of the various social classes and their relation to one another "[1] : it may " ask what has been the material basis of social existence; how have the necessities and conveniences of life been produced; by what organization has labour been provided and directed; how have the commodities thus produced been distributed; what have been the institutions resting on this direction and distribution " ; and so on.[2]

The work of the economic historian is various.

And for this work, interesting and important as it is on its own account, not very much analysis is essential; and most of what is needed may be supplied for himself by a man of active and inquiring mind. Saturated with a knowledge of the religious and moral, the intellectual and æsthetic, the political and social environment, the economic historian may extend the boundaries of our knowledge and may suggest new and valuable ideas, even though he may have contented himself with observing those affinities and those causal relations which lie near the surface.

The aid of subtle analysis is not needed for all :

---

[1] Compare Mill, *Logic*, Book VI. ch. III.
[2] Ashley, *On the Study of Economic History.*

but it is
needed for
deriving
guidance
from the
past for the
present.

But even in spite of himself, his aims will surely run beyond these limits; and will include some attempt to discover the inner meaning of economic history, to unveil the mysteries of the growth and decay of custom, and other phenomena which we are not any longer contented to take as ultimate and insoluble facts given by nature : nor is he likely altogether to withhold himself from suggesting inferences from the events of the past for guidance in the present. And indeed the human mind abhors a vacuum in its notions of the causal relations between the events that are presented vividly to it. By merely placing things together in a certain order, and consciously or unconsciously suggesting *post hoc ergo propter hoc*, the historian takes on himself some responsibility as a guide.

For example :—the introduction of long leases at fixed money rents in North Britain was followed by a great improvement in agriculture, and in the general condition of the people there; but before inferring that it was the sole, or even the chief cause of the improvement, we must inquire what other changes were taking place at the same time, and how much of the improvement is to be referred to each of them. We must, for instance, allow for the effects of changes in the prices of agricultural produce, and of the establishment of civil order in the border provinces. To do this requires care and scientific method; and till it has been done, no trustworthy inference can be drawn as to the general tendency of the system of long leases. And even when it has been done, we cannot argue from this experience to a proposal for a system of long leases in, say, Ireland now, without allowing for differences in the character of local and world markets for various kinds of agricultural produce, for probable changes in the production and consumption of gold and silver, and so on. The history of Land Tenures is full of antiquarian interest; but until carefully analysed and interpreted by the aid of economic theory it throws no trustworthy light on the question what is the best form of land tenure to be adopted now in any country. Thus some argue that since primitive societies usually held their land in common, private property in land must be an unnatural and transitional institution. Others with equal confidence contend that, since private property in land has extended its range with the progress of civilization, it is a necessary condition for further progress. But to wrest from history her true teaching on the subject requires the effects of the common holding of land in the past to be analysed so as to discover how far each of them is likely to act always in the same way, how far to be modified by changes in the habits, the knowledge, the wealth, and the social organization of mankind.

Even more interesting and instructive is the history of the professions, made by Gilds and other Corporations and Combinations in industry and in domestic and foreign trade, that they used their privileges on the whole for the benefit of the public. But to bring in a complete verdict on the question, and still more to deduce from it sound guidance for our own time, needs not only the wide general knowledge and subtle instincts of the practised historian, but also a grasp of many of the most difficult analyses and reasonings relating to monopolies, to foreign trade, to the incidence of taxation, etc.

If then the economic historian aims at discovering the hidden springs of the economic order of the world, and at obtaining light from the past for guidance in the present, he should avail himself of every resource that may help him to detect real differences that are disguised by a similarity of name or outward appearance, and real similarities that are obscured by a superficial difference. He should strive to select the true causes of each event and assign to each its proper weight; and above all to detect the remoter causes of change.

An analogy may be borrowed from naval affairs. The details of a battle with appliances that have passed away may be of great interest to the student of the general history of those times; but they may afford little useful guidance for the naval commander of to-day, who has to deal with a wholly different material of war. And therefore, as Captain Mahan has admirably shown, the naval commander of to-day will give more attention to the *strategy* than to the tactics of past times.   He will concern himself not so much with the incidents of particular combats, as with practical illustrations of those leading principles of action which will enable him to hold his whole force in hand, and yet give to each part of it adequate initiative; to keep up wide communication, and yet be able to concentrate quickly, and select a point of attack at which he can bring an overwhelming force.

Similarly a man saturated with the general history of a period may give a vivid picture of the tactics of battle, which will be true in its main outlines, and almost harmless even if occasionally wrong : for no one is likely to copy tactics, the appliances of which have passed away.   But to comprehend the strategy of a campaign, to separate the real from the apparent motives of a great general of past times, a man must be a strategist himself.   And if he is to make himself responsible for suggesting, however unobtrusively, the lessons which the strategists of to-day have to learn from the story which he records; then he is bound to have analysed thoroughly the naval conditions of to-day, as well as those of the time about which he is writing; and he must neglect no aid for this end that is to be had from the work of many minds in many countries studying the difficult problem of strategy.   As it is with naval history, so it is with economic.

It is only recently, and to a great extent through the wholesome influence of the criticisms of the historical school, that prominence has been given to that distinction in economics which corresponds to the distinction between strategy and tactics in warfare.   Corresponding to tactics are those outward forms and accidents of economic organization which depend on temporary or local aptitudes, customs and relations of classes; on the influence of individuals; or on the changing appliances and needs of production.   While to strategy corresponds that more fundamental substance of economic organization, which depends mainly on such wants and activities, such preferences and aversions as are found in man everywhere : they are not indeed always the same in form, nor even quite the same in substance; but yet they have a sufficient element of permanence and universality to enable them to be brought in some measure under general statements, whereby the experiences of one time and one age may throw light on the difficulties of another.

This distinction is akin to the distinction between the uses of mechanical and of biological analogies in economics.   It was not sufficiently recognized by economists at the beginning of last century.   It is markedly absent from Ricardo's writings : and when attention is paid, not to the principles which are embodied in his method of working, but to particular conclusions which he reaches; when these are converted into dogmas and applied crudely to the conditions of times or places other than his own, then no doubt they are almost unmixed evils.   His thoughts are like sharp chisels with which it is specially easy to cut one's fingers, because they have such awkward handles.

But modern economists distilling his crude expressions; extracting their essence, and adding to it; rejecting dogmas, but developing principles of analysis and reasoning, are finding the Many in the One and the One in the Many.   They are learning for instance that the principle of his analysis of rent is inapplicable to much that commonly goes by the name of rent to-day; as well as to a much larger part of those things which are commonly, but incorrectly, described as rent by historians of the Middle Ages.   But yet the application of the principle is being extended, and not contracted.   For economists are also learning that it is applicable with proper care to a great variety of things in every stage of civilization which do not appear at first sight to be of the nature of rent at all.

The Many in the One, the One in the Many.

But of course no student of strategy can ignore tactics.   And, though no one life will reach out to a study in detail of the tactics of every fight which man has waged with his economic difficulties; yet no study of the broad prob-

Y

APP. C, 5. lems of economic strategy is likely to be worth much unless it is combined with an intimate knowledge of the tactics as well as the strategy of man's struggles against his difficulties in some particular age and country. And further every student should make by personal observation a minute study of some particular set of details, not necessarily for publication, but for his own training; and this will help him much to interpret and weigh the evidence which he obtains in print or writing, whether with regard to present or past times. Of course every thoughtful and observant man is always obtaining, from conversation and current literature, a knowledge of the economic facts of his own time, and especially in his own neighbourhood; and the store of facts which he thus imperceptibly gets is sometimes more full and thorough in certain special regards than is to be distilled from all the records in existence as to some classes of facts in remote places and times. But independently of this, the direct and formal study of facts, perhaps mainly those of his own age, will much exceed the study of mere analysis and " theory," in its demands on the time of any serious economist; even though he may be one of those who rank most highly the importance of ideas relatively to facts, even though he may think that it is not so much the collection of new facts as the better study of those already collected, that is our most urgent need now, or that will help us most in improving the tactics as well as the strategy of man's contests with his difficulties.

Common sense and mother-wit can go far in analysis,   § 5. It is doubtless true that much of this work has less need of elaborate scientific methods, than of a shrewd mother-wit, of a sound sense of proportion, and of a large experience of life. But on the other hand there is much work that is not easily to be done without such machinery. Natural instinct will select rapidly, and combine justly, considerations which are relevant to the issue in hand; but it will select chiefly from those which are familiar; it will seldom lead a man far below the surface, or far beyond the limits of his personal experience.

but not far enough for all purposes.   And it happens that in economics, neither those effects of known causes, nor those causes of known effects which are most patent, are generally the most important. " That which is not seen " is often better worth studying than that " which is seen." Especially is this the case if we are not dealing with some question of merely local or temporary interest, but are seeking guidance in the construction of a far-reaching policy for the public good; or if, for any other reason, we are concerned less with immediate causes, than with causes of causes,—*causæ causantes*. For experience shows, as might have been anticipated, that common sense, and instinct, are inadequate for this work; that even a business training does not always lead a man to search far for those causes of causes, which lie beyond his immediate experience; and that it does not always direct that search well, even when he makes the attempt. For help in doing that, everyone must perforce rely on the powerful machinery of thought and knowledge that has been gradually built up by past generations. For indeed the part which systematic scientific reasoning plays in the production of knowledge resembles that which machinery plays in the production of goods.

Analogy between the machinery of science and that of material production   When the same operation has to be performed over and over again in the same way, it generally pays to make a machine to do the work; though when there is so much changing variety of detail that it is unprofitable to use machines, the goods must be made by hand. Similarly in knowledge, when there are any processes of investigation or reasoning in which the same kind of work has to be done over and over again in the same kind of way; then it is worth while to reduce the processes to system, to organize methods of reasoning and to formulate general propositions to be used as machinery for working on the facts and as vices for holding them firmly in position for the work. And though it be true that economic causes are intermingled with others in so many different ways, that exact scientific reasoning will seldom bring us very far on the way to the conclusion for which we are seeking, yet it would be foolish to refuse to avail ourselves of its aid, so far as it will reach :—just as foolish as APP. C, 6. would be the opposite extreme of supposing that science alone can do all the work, and that nothing will remain to be done by practical instinct and trained common sense. An architect whose practical wisdom and æsthetic instincts are undeveloped will build but a poor house however thorough his knowledge of mechanics : but one, who is ignorant of mechanics, will build insecurely or wastefully. A Brindley, without academic instruction, may do some engineering work better than a man of inferior mother-wit, however well he may have been trained. A wise nurse, who reads her patients by instinctive sympathy, may give better counsel on some points than a learned physician. But yet the study of analytical mechanics should not be neglected by the engineer, nor that of physiology by the medical man.

For mental faculties, like manual dexterity, die with those who possess them : but the improvement which each generation contributes to the machinery of manufacture or to the organon of science is handed down to the next. There may be no abler sculptors now than those who worked on the Parthenon, no thinker with more mother-wit than Aristotle. But the appliances of thought develop cumulatively as do those of material production.

Ideas, whether those of art and science, or those embodied in practical appliances, are the most " real " of the gifts that each generation receives from its predecessors. The world's material wealth would quickly be replaced if it were destroyed, but the ideas by which it was made were retained. If however the ideas were lost, but not the material wealth, then that would dwindle and the world would go back to poverty. And most of our knowledge of mere facts could quickly be recovered if it were lost, but the constructive ideas of thought remained; while if the ideas perished, the world would enter again on the Dark Ages. Thus the pursuit of ideas is not less " real " work in the highest sense of the word than is the collection of facts; though the latter may in some cases properly be called in German a *Realstudium*, that is, a study specially appropriate to *Realschulen*. In the highest use of the word, that study of any field of the wide realm of economics is most " real " in which the collection of facts, and the analysis and construction of ideas connecting them are combined in those proportions which are best calculated to increase knowledge and promote progress in that particular field. And what this is, cannot be settled offhand, but only by careful study and by specific experience.

§ 6. Economics has made greater advances than any other branch of the Every social sciences, because it is more definite and exact than any other. But widening every widening of its scope involves some loss of this scientific precision; and of the the question whether that loss is greater or less than the gain resulting from scope of economics its greater breadth of outlook, is not to be decided by any hard and fast rule. brings

There is a large debateable ground in which economic considerations are of good considerable but not dominant importance; and each economist may reason- and evil. ably decide for himself how far he will extend his labours over that ground. It is best He will be able to speak with less and less confidence the further he gets away that each from his central stronghold, and the more he concerns himself with conditions should work as of life and with motives of action which cannot be brought to some extent at he is least within the grasp of scientific method. Whenever he occupies himself inclined, largely with conditions and motives, the manifestations of which are not never for- reducible to any definite standard, he must forego nearly all aid and support getting his from the observations and the thought of others at home and abroad, in this limitations and earlier generations; he must depend mainly on his own instincts and conjectures; he must speak with all the diffidence that belongs to an individual judgment. But if when straying far into less known and less knowable regions of social study he does his work carefully, and with a full consciousness of its limitations, he will have done excellent service.[1]

---

[1] As the imitators of Michael Angelo copied only his faults, so Carlyle, Ruskin and Morris find to-day ready imitators, who lack their fine inspirations and intuitions.

APPENDIX D[1]

USES OF ABSTRACT REASONING IN ECONOMICS

§ 1. Induction, aided by analysis and deduction, brings together appropriate classes of facts, arranges them, analyses them and infers from them general statements or laws. Then for a while deduction plays the chief *rôle* : it brings some of these generalizations into association with one another, works from them tentatively to new and broader generalizations or laws and then calls on induction again to do the main share of the work in collecting, sifting and arranging these facts so as to test and " verify " the new law.

It is obvious that there is no room in economics for long trains of deductive reasoning; no economist, not even Ricardo, attempted them. It may indeed appear at first sight that the contrary is suggested by the frequent use of mathematical formulæ in economic studies. But on investigation it will be found that this suggestion is illusory, except perhaps when a pure mathematician uses economic hypotheses for the purpose of mathematical diversions; for then his concern is to show the potentialities of mathematical methods on the supposition that material appropriate to their use had been supplied by economic study. He takes no technical responsibility for the material, and is often unaware how inadequate the material is to bear the strains of his powerful machinery. But a training in mathematics is helpful by giving command over a marvellously terse and exact language for expressing clearly some general relations and some short processes of economic reasoning; which can indeed be expressed in ordinary language, but not with equal sharpness of outline. And, what is of far greater importance, experience in handling physical problems by mathematical methods gives a grasp, that cannot be obtained equally well in any other way, of the mutual interaction of economic changes. The direct application of mathematical reasoning to the discovery of economic truths has recently rendered great services in the hands of master mathematicians to the study of statistical averages and probabilities and in measuring the degree of consilience between correlated statistical tables.

§ 2. If we shut our eyes to realities we may construct an edifice of pure crystal by imaginations, that will throw side lights on real problems; and might conceivably be of interest to beings who had no economic problems at all like our own. Such playful excursions are often suggestive in unexpected ways : they afford good training to the mind : and seem to be productive only of good, so long as their purpose is clearly understood.

For instance, the statement that the dominant position which money holds in economics, results rather from its being a measure of motive than an aim of endeavour, may be illustrated by the reflection that the almost exclusive use of money as a measure of motive is, so to speak, an accident, and perhaps an accident that is not found in other worlds than ours. When we want to induce a man to do anything for us we generally offer him money. It is true that we might appeal to his generosity or sense of duty; but this would be calling into action latent motives that are already in existence, rather than supplying new motives. If we have to supply a new motive we generally consider how much money will just make it worth his while to do it. Sometimes indeed the gratitude, or esteem, or honour which is held out as an inducement to the

[1] See I, III.

APP. D, 3.

action may appear as a new motive : particularly if it can be crystallized in some definite outward manifestation; as for instance in the right to make use of the letters C.B., or to wear a star or a garter. Such distinctions are comparatively rare and connected with but few transactions; and they would not serve as a measure of the ordinary motives that govern men in the acts of every-day life. But political services are more frequently rewarded by such honours than in any other way : so we have got into the habit of measuring them not in money but in honours. We say, for instance, that A's exertions for the benefit of his party or of the State, as the case may be, were fairly paid for by knighthood; while knighthood was but shabby pay for B, he had earned a baronetcy.

It is quite possible that there may be worlds in which no one ever heard of private property in material things, or wealth as it is generally understood; but public honours are meted out by graduated tables as rewards for every action that is done for others' good. If these honours can be transferred from one to another without the intervention of any external authority they may serve to measure the strength of motives just as conveniently and exactly as money does with us. In such a world there may be a treatise on economic theory very similar to the present, even though there be little mention in it of material things, and no mention at all of money.

It may seem almost trivial to insist on this, but it is not so. For a misleading association has grown up in people's minds between that measurement of motives which is prominent in economic science, and an exclusive regard for material wealth to the neglect of other and higher objects of desire. The only conditions required in a measure for economic purposes are that it should be something definite and transferable. Its taking a material form is practically convenient, but is not essential.

§ 3. The pursuit of abstractions is a good thing, when confined to its proper place. But the breadth of those strains of human character with which economics is concerned has been underrated by some writers on economics in England and other countries; and German economists have done good service by emphasizing it. They seem however to be mistaken in supposing that it was overlooked by the founders of British economics. It is a British habit to leave much to be supplied by the common sense of the reader; in this case reticence has been carried too far, and has led to frequent misunderstanding at home as well as abroad. It has led people to suppose the foundations of economics to be narrower and less closely in touch with the actual conditions of life than they really are.

But in serious work realities must be closely followed.

Thus prominence has been given to Mill's statement, that "Political Economy considers man as occupied solely in acquiring and consuming wealth" (*Essays*, p. 138, and again, *Logic*, Bk. VI. ch. IX. § 3). But it is forgotten that he is there referring to an abstract treatment of economic questions, which he once indeed contemplated; but which he never executed, preferring to write on "Political Economy, with some of its applications to Social Philosophy." It is forgotten also that he goes on to say, "There is, perhaps, no action of a man's life in which he is neither under the immediate nor under the remote influence of any impulse but the mere desire of wealth"; and it is forgotten that his treatment of economic questions took constant account of many motives besides the desire for wealth (see above, Appendix B, 7). His discussions of economic motives are, however, inferior both in substance and in method to those of his German contemporaries, and notably Hermann. An instructive argument that non-purchasable, non-measurable pleasures vary at different times and tend to increase with the progress of civilization is to be found in Knies' *Politische Œkonomie*, III. 3 ; and the English reader may be referred to Syme's *Outlines of an Industrial Science*.

Germans have done good service by insisting on the breadth of economic motives.

It may be well to give here the chief heads of the analysis of economic motives (*Motive im wirthschaftlichen Handeln*) in the third edition of Wagner's

Wagner's classifica-

APP. D, 3.
tion of
motives.

monumental treatise. He divides them into Egoistic and Altruistic. The former are four in number. The first and least intermittent in its action is the striving for one's own economic advantage, and the fear of one's own economic need. Next comes the fear of punishment, and the hope of reward. The third group consists of the feeling of honour, and the striving for recognition (*Geltungsstreben*), including the desire for the moral approbation of others, and the fear of shame and contempt. And the last of the egoistic motives is the craving for occupation, the pleasure of activity; and the pleasure of the work itself and its surroundings, including the "pleasures of the chase." The altruistic motive is " the impelling force (*Trieb*) of the inward command to moral action, the pressure of the feeling of duty, and the fear of one's own inward blame, that is, of the gnawings of conscience. In its pure form this motive appears as the ' Categorical Imperative,' which one follows because one feels in one's soul the command to act in this or that manner, and feels the command to be right. . . . The following of the command is no doubt regularly bound up with feelings of pleasure (*Lustgefühle*), and the not following it with feelings of pain. Now it may be, and often is, that these feelings act as strongly as the Categorical Imperative, or even more strongly, in driving us, or in taking part in driving us on to do or to leave undone. And in so far as this is the case this motive also has in it an egoistic element, or at least itself merges into one."[1]

APPENDIX E[1]

DEFINITIONS OF CAPITAL

§ 1. It was observed in Book II. chapter IV. that economists have no choice but to follow well-established customs as regards the use of the term capital in ordinary business, *i.e.* trade-capital. The disadvantages of this use are however great and obvious. For instance it compels us to regard as capital the yachts, but not the carriage, belonging to a yacht builder. If therefore he had been hiring a carriage by the year, and instead of continuing to do so, sold a yacht to a carriage builder who had been hiring it, and bought a carriage for his own use; the result would be that the total stock of capital in the country would be diminished by a yacht and a carriage. And this, though nothing had been destroyed; and though there remained the same products of saving, themselves productive of as great benefits to the individuals concerned and to the community as before, and probably even of greater benefits.

Nor can we avail ourselves here of the notion that capital is distinguished from other forms of wealth by its superior power of giving employment to labour. For in fact, when yachts and carriages are in the hands of dealers and are thus counted as capital, less employment is given to labour by a given amount of yachting or carriage driving than when the yachts or carriages are in private hands and are not counted as capital. The employment of labour would not be increased but lessened by the substitution of professional cook-shops and bakeries (where all the appliances are reckoned as capital) for private kitchens (where nothing is reckoned as capital). Under a professional employer, the workers may possibly have more personal freedom : but they almost certainly have less material comfort, and lower wages in proportion to the work they do than under the laxer régime of a private employer.

But these disadvantages have been generally overlooked; and several causes have combined to give vogue to this use of the term. One of these causes is that the relations between private employers and their employees seldom enter into the strategical and tactical movements of the conflicts between employers and employed; or, as is commonly said, between capital and labour. This point has been emphasized by Karl Marx and his followers. They have avowedly made the definition of capital turn on it; they assert that only that is capital which is a means of production owned by one person (or group of persons) and used to produce things for the benefit of another, generally by means of the hired labour of a third; in such wise that the first has the opportunity of plundering or exploiting the others.

Secondly this use of the term Capital is convenient in the money market as well as in the labour market. Trade-capital is habitually connected with loans. No one hesitates to borrow in order to increase the trade-capital at his command, when he can see a good opening for its use; and for doing this he can pledge his own trade-capital more easily and more regularly in the ordinary course of business transactions, than he could his furniture or his private carriage. Lastly, a man makes up the accounts of his trade-capital carefully; he allows for depreciation as a matter of course : and thus he keeps his stock intact. Of course a man who has been hiring a carriage by the year, can buy it with the produce of the sale of railway stock that yields very much less

APP. E, 1.

Note has already been made of difficulties in the use of the term Trade-capital.

It does not include all wealth that promotes the employment of labour.

Causes that have given vogue to this use of the term.

[1] See above, p. 69.

APP. E, 2. interest than he has paid as hire. If he lets the annual income accumulate till the carriage is worn out, it will more than suffice to buy him a new one : and thus his total stock of capital will have been increased by the change. But there is a chance that he will not do this : whereas, so long as the carriage was owned by the dealer, he provided for replacing it in the ordinary course of his business.

Differences as to the delimitation of social capital cause less confusion than might be expected.

§ 2. Let us pass to definitions of capital from the social point of view. It has already been indicated that the only strictly logical position is that which has been adopted by most writers on mathematical versions of economics, and which regards " social capital " and " social wealth " as coextensive; though this course deprives them of a useful term. But whatever definition a writer takes at starting, he finds that the various elements which he includes in it, enter in different ways into the successive problems with which he has to deal. If therefore his definition pretended to precision, he is compelled to supplement it by an explanation of the bearing of each several element of capital on the point at issue; and this explanation is in substance very much like those of other writers. Thus ultimately there is a general convergence; and readers are brought to very much the same conclusion by whatever route they travel; though it may indeed require a little trouble to discern the unity in substance, underlying differences in form and in words. The divergence at starting turns out to be a less evil than it seemed.

We adhere to tradition in using the term Capital when regarding wealth as an agent of production.

Further, in spite of these differences in words there is a continuity of tone in the definition of capital by the economists of several generations and many countries. It is true that some have laid greater stress on the " productivity " of capital, some on its " prospectiveness "; and that neither of these terms is perfectly precise, or points to any hard and fast line of division. But though these defects are fatal to precise classification, that is a matter of secondary importance. Things relating to man's actions never can be classified with precision on any scientific principle. Exact lists may be made of things which are to be placed in certain classes for the guidance of the police officer, or the collector of import duties : but such lists are frankly artificial. It is the spirit and not the letter of economic tradition, which we should be most careful to preserve. And, as was suggested at the end of Book II. chapter IV., no intelligent writer has ever left out of account either the side of prospectiveness or that of productiveness : but some have enlarged more on the one side and others on the other; while on either side difficulty has been found in drawing a definite line of demarcation.

Social capital regarded as a provision for the future.

Let us then look at the notion of capital as a store of things, the result of human efforts and sacrifices, devoted mainly to securing benefits in the future rather than in the present. The notion itself is definite, but it does not lead to a definite classification; just as the notion of length is definite, but yet does not enable us to divide off long walls from short walls save by an arbitrary rule. The savage shows some prospectiveness when he puts together branches of trees to protect him for a night; he shows more when he makes a tent of poles and skins, and yet more when he builds a wooden hut : the civilized man shows increasing prospectiveness when he substitutes solid houses of brick or stone for wooden shanties. A line could be drawn anywhere to mark off those things the production of which shows a great desire for future satisfactions rather than present : but it would be artificial and unstable. Those who have sought one, have found themselves on an inclined plane : and have not reached a stable resting-place till they have included all accumulated wealth as capital.

This logical result was faced by many French economists; who, following in the lines laid down by the Physiocrats, used the term Capital very much in the sense in which Adam Smith and his immediate followers used the word Stock, to include all accumulated wealth (*valeurs accumulées*); *i.e.* all the result of the excess of production over consumption. And although in recent

years they have shown a decided tendency to use the term in the narrower
English sense, there is at the same time a considerable movement on the part
of some of the profoundest thinkers in Germany and England in the direction
of the older and broader French definition. Especially has this been remarkable in writers who, like Turgot, have been inclined towards mathematical
modes of thought; among whom Hermann, Jevons, Walras, and Professors
Pareto and Fisher are conspicuous. The writings of Professor Fisher contain
a masterly argument, rich in fertile suggestion, in favour of a comprehensive
use of the term. Regarded from the abstract and mathematical point of
view, his position is incontestable. But he seems to take too little account of
the necessity for keeping realistic discussions in touch with the language of
the market-place; and to ignore Bagehot's caution against trying " to express
various meanings on complex things with a scanty vocabulary of fastened
uses." [1]

§ 3. Most of the attempts to define capital rigidly, whether in England or <u>Social</u>
other countries, have turned mainly on its productivity, to the comparative <u>capital</u>
neglect of its prospectivity. They have regarded social capital as a means for <u>regarded</u>
acquisition (*Erwerbskapital*) or as a stock of the requisites of production <u>as a means</u>
(*Productions-mittel Vorrath*). But this general notion has been treated in <u>duction,</u>
different ways. <u>and first</u>

According to the older English traditions capital consists of those things <u>as both</u>
which *aid or support* labour in production : or, as has been said more recently, <u>supporting</u>
it consists of those things without which production could not be carried on <u>labour;</u>
with equal efficiency, but which are not free gifts of nature. It is from this
point of view that the distinction already noticed between consumption capital
and auxiliary capital, has been made.

This view of capital has been suggested by the affairs of the labour market;
but it has never been perfectly consistent. For it has been made to include
as capital everything which employers directly or indirectly provide in payment for the work of their employees—*wage capital* or *remuneratory capital*, as
it is called; but yet not to include any of the things needed for their own
support, or that of architects, engineers, and other professional men. But to
be consistent it should have included the necessaries for efficiency of all classes
of workers; and it should have excluded the luxuries of the manual labour
classes as well as of other workers. If, however, it had been pushed to this
logical conclusion, it would have played a less prominent part in the discussion
of the relations of employers and employed.[2]

---

[1] See above, footnote on p. 43.
Hermann said (*Staatswirthschaftliche Untersuchungen*, chs. III. and v.) that capital
consists of goods " which are a lasting source of satisfaction that has exchange value."
Walras (*Éléments d'Économie Politique*, p. 197) defines capital as " every kind of
social wealth which is not consumed at all, or is consumed but slowly; every utility
limited in quantity, that survives the first use which is made of it; in one word, which
can be used more than once; a house, a piece of furniture."
Knies defined capital as the existing stock of goods " which is ready to be applied
to the satisfaction of demand in the future." And Prof. Nicholson says :—" The
line of thought suggested by Adam Smith and developed by Knies is found to lead to
this result : Capital is wealth set aside for the satisfaction—directly or indirectly—of
future needs." But the whole phrase, and especially the words " set aside," seem to
lack definiteness, and to evade rather than overcome the difficulties of the problem.

[2] The following are among the chief definitions of capital by Adam Smith's English
followers :—Ricardo said :—" Capital is that part of the wealth of a country which is
employed in production and consists of food, clothing, tools, raw materials, machinery,
etc. necessary to give effect to labour." Malthus said :—" Capital is that portion of
the stock of a country which is kept or employed with a view to profit in the production
and distribution of wealth." Senior said :—" Capital is an article of wealth, the result
of human exertion, employed in the production or distribution of wealth." John
Stuart Mill said :—" What capital does for production, is to afford the shelter, protection, tools and materials which the work requires, and to feed and otherwise maintain the labourers during the process. Whatever things are destined for this use are

In some countries however, and especially in Germany and Austria, there has been some tendency to confine capital (from the social point of view) to auxiliary or instrumental capital. It is argued that in order to keep clear the contrast between production and consumption, nothing which enters directly into consumption should be regarded as a means to production. But there appears no good reason why a thing should not be regarded in a twofold capacity.[1]

It is further argued that those things which render their services to man not directly, but through the part which they play in preparing other things for his use, form a compact class; because their value is derived from that of the things which they help to produce. There is much to be said for having a name for this group. But there is room for doubt whether capital is a good name for it; and also for doubt whether the group is as compact as it appears at first sight.

Thus we may define instrumental goods so as to include tramways and other things which derive their value from the personal services which they render; or we may follow the example of the old use of the phrase productive labour, and insist that those things only are properly to be regarded as instrumental goods the work of which is directly embodied in a material product. The former definition brings this use of the term rather close to that discussed in the last section and shares with it the demerit of vagueness. The latter is a little more definite : but seems to make an artificial distinction where nature has made none, and to be as unsuitable for scientific purposes as the old definitions of productive labour.

To conclude :—From the abstract point of view the French definition, advocated by Professor Fisher and others, holds the field without a rival. A man's coat is a stored up product of past efforts and sacrifices destined as a means to provide him with future gratifications, just as much as a factory is : while both yield immediate shelter from the weather. And if we are seeking a definition that will keep realistic economics in touch with the market-place, then careful account needs to be taken of the aggregate volume of those things which are regarded as capital in the market-place and do not fall within the limits assigned to " intermediate " products. In case of doubt, that course is to be preferred which is most in accordance with tradition. These were the considerations which led to the adoption of the twofold definition of capital, from the business and the social point of view, given above.[2]

---

capital." We shall have to return to this conception of capital in connection with the so-called Wages Fund doctrine; see Appendix J.

As Held remarked, the practical problems which were prominent early in the last century suggested some such conception of capital as this. People were anxious to insist that the welfare of the working classes depended on a provision of the means of employment and sustenance made beforehand : and to emphasize the dangers of attempting to make employment for them artificially under the extravagance of the Protective system and the old Poor-law. Held's point of view has been developed with great acumen in Cannan's suggestive and interesting *Production and Distribution,* 1776–1848 : though some of the utterances of the earlier economists seem capable of other and more reasonable interpretations than those which he assigns to them.

[1] For an argument to this effect, and an excellent discussion of the difficulties of the whole subject, see Wagner, *Grundlegung,* Ed. 3, pp. 315–6.

[2] See II. IV, 1. 5. The connection of the productiveness of capital with the demand for it, and of its prospectiveness with the supply of it has long been latent in men's minds; though it has been much overlaid by other considerations, many of which appear now to be based on misconceptions. Some writers have laid more stress on the supply side and others on the demand side : but the difference between them has often been little more than a difference of emphasis. Those who have laid stress on the productivity of capital, have not been ignorant of man's unwillingness to save and sacrifice the present for the future. And on the other hand, those who have given their thought mainly to the nature and extent of the sacrifice involved in this postponement, have regarded as obvious such facts as that a store of the implements of production gives mankind a largely increased power of satisfying their wants. In

short there is no reason to believe that the accounts which Prof. Böhm-Bawerk has
given of the "naive productivity theories," the "use theories" etc. of capital and
interest would have been accepted by the older writers themselves as well-balanced
and complete presentations of their several positions.   Nor does he seem to have
succeeded in finding a definition that is clear and consistent.   He says that "Social
capital is a group of products destined to serve towards further production ; or briefly
a group of Intermediate products."   He formally excludes (Book I. ch. VI.) " dwelling
houses and other kinds of buildings such as serve immediately for any purpose of
enjoyment or education or culture."   To be consistent, he must exclude hotels, tramways, passenger ships and trains, etc. ; and perhaps even plant for supplying the
electric light for private dwellings ; but that would seem to deprive the notion of
capital of all practical interest.   There seems no good ground for excluding the public
theatre while including the tramcar, which would not justify the inclusion of mills
engaged in making home-spun and the exclusion of those engaged in making lace.
In answer to this objection he urges, with perfect reason, that every economic classification must allow for the existence of border lines between any two classes, to contain
things which belong in part to each of the two.   But the objections submitted to his
definition are that its border lines are too broad relatively to the area which they
inclose ; that it conflicts violently with the uses of the market-place, and that yet it
does not embody, as the French definition does, a perfectly consistent and coherent
abstract idea.

APPENDIX F

BARTER [1]

APP. F.

The rate of barter between two individuals is governed by accident.

Let us consider the case of two individuals engaged in barter. A has, say, a basket of apples, B a basket of nuts; A wants some nuts, B wants some apples. The satisfaction which B would get from one apple would perhaps outweigh that which he would lose by parting with 12 nuts; while the satisfaction which A would get from perhaps three nuts would outweigh that which he would lose by parting with one apple. The exchange will be started somewhere between these two rates: but if it goes on gradually, every apple that A loses will increase the marginal utility of apples to him and make him more unwilling to part with any more : while every additional nut that he gets will lower the marginal utility of nuts to him and diminish his eagerness for more : and *vice versâ* with B. At last A's eagerness for nuts relatively to apples will no longer exceed B's; and exchange will cease because any terms that the one is willing to propose would be disadvantageous to the other. Up to this point exchange has increased the satisfaction on both sides, but it can do so no further. Equilibrium has been attained; but really it is not *the* equilibrium, it is *an* accidental equilibrium.

There is a rate which may be called the true rate;

There is, however, one equilibrium rate of exchange which has some sort of right to be called the true equilibrium rate, because if once hit upon it would be adhered to throughout. It is clear that if very many nuts were to be given throughout for an apple, B would be willing to do but little business; while if but very few were to be given, A would be willing to do but little. There must be some intermediate rate at which they would be willing to do business to the same extent. Suppose that this rate is six nuts for an apple; and that A is willing to give eight apples for 48 nuts, while B is willing to receive eight apples at that rate; but that A would not be willing to give a ninth apple for another six nuts while B would not be willing to give another six nuts for a ninth apple. This is then the true position of equilibrium; but there is no reason to suppose that it will be reached in practice.

but it is not likely to be attained in practice.

Suppose, for instance, that A's basket had originally 20 apples in it and B's 100 nuts, and that A at starting induced B to believe that he does not care much to have any nuts; and so manages to barter four apples for 40 nuts, and afterwards two more for 17 nuts, and afterwards one more for eight. Equilibrium may now have been reached, there may be no further exchange which is advantageous to both. A has 65 nuts and does not care to give another apple even for eight; while B, having only 35 nuts, sets a high value on them, and will not give as many as eight for another apple.

On the other hand, if B had been the more skilful in bargaining he might have perhaps induced A to give six apples for 15 nuts, and then two more for seven. A has now given up eight apples and got 22 nuts; if the terms at starting had been six nuts for an apple and he had got 48 nuts for his eight apples, he would not have given up another apple for even seven nuts; but having so few nuts he is anxious to get more and is willing to give two more apples in exchange for eight nuts, and then two more for nine nuts, and then one more for five; and then again equilibrium may be reached; for B, having 13 apples and 56 nuts, does not perhaps care to give more than five nuts for an

[1] See p. 280.

apple, and A may be unwilling to give up one of his few remaining apples for less than six.

In both these cases the exchange would have increased the satisfaction of both as far as it went; and when it ceased, no further exchange would have been possible which would not have diminished the satisfaction of at least one of them. In each case an equilibrium rate would have been reached; but it would be an arbitrary equilibrium.

Next suppose that there are a hundred people in a similar position to that of A, each with about 20 apples, and the same desire for nuts as A; and an equal number on the other side similarly situated to the original B. Then the acutest bargainers in the market would probably be some of them on A's side, some of them on B's; and whether there was free communication throughout the market or not, the mean of the bargains would not be so likely to differ very widely from the rate of six nuts for an apple as in the case of barter between two people. But yet there would be no such strong probability of its adhering very closely to that rate, as we saw was the case in the corn-market. In would be quite possible for those on the A side to get in varying degrees the better of those on the B side in bargaining, so that after a time 6500 nuts might have been exchanged for 700 apples; and then those on the A side, having so many nuts, might be unwilling to do any more trade except at the rate of at least eight nuts for an apple, while those on the B side, having only 35 nuts apiece left on the average, might probably refuse to part with any more at that rate. On the other hand, the B's might have got in various degrees the better of the A's in bargaining, with the result that after a time 1300 apples had been exchanged for only 4400 nuts : the B's having then 1300 apples and 5600 nuts, might be unwilling to offer more than five nuts for an apple, while the A's, having only seven apples apiece left on the average, might decline that rate. In the one case equilibrium would be found at a rate of eight nuts for an apple, and in the other at the rate of five nuts. In each case *an* equilibrium would be attained, but not *the* equilibrium.

This uncertainty of the rate at which equilibrium is reached depends indirectly on the fact that one commodity is being bartered for another instead of being sold for money. For, since money is a general purchasing medium, there are likely to be many dealers who can conveniently take in, or give out, large supplies of it; and this tends to steady the market. But where barter prevails apples are likely to be exchanged for nuts in one case, for fish in another, for arrows in another, and so on; the steadying influences which hold together a market in which values are set in money are absent; and we are obliged to regard the marginal utilities of all commodities as varying. It is however true that, if nut-growing had been a chief industry of our barter-district, and all the traders on both sides had large stores of nuts, while only the A's had apples; then the exchange of a few handfuls of nuts would not have visibly affected their stores, or changed appreciably the marginal utility of nuts. In that case the bargaining would have resembled in all fundamentals the buying and selling in an ordinary corn-market.

Thus, for instance, let a single A with 20 apples, bargain with a single B. Let A be willing to sell 5 apples for 15 nuts, a sixth for 4 nuts, a seventh for 5, an eighth for 6, a ninth for 7 and so on; the marginal utility of nuts being always constant to him, so that he is just willing to sell the eighth for 6 and so on, whether in the earlier part of the trade he has got the better of the bargaining with B or not. Meanwhile let B be willing to pay 50 nuts for the first five apples rather than go without them, 9 for a sixth, 7 for a seventh, 6 for an eighth, and only 5 for a ninth; the marginal utility of nuts being constant to him, so that he will just give 6 nuts for the eighth apple whether he has bought the earlier apples cheaply or not. In this case the bargaining *must* issue in the transfer of eight apples, the eighth apple being given for six nuts. But of course if A had got the better of the bargaining at first, he might have got 50 or 60 nuts for the first seven apples; while if *B* had got the better of the bargaining at first, he might have got the first seven apples for 30 or 40 nuts. This corresponds to the fact that in the corn-market dicusssed in the text, about 700 quarters would be sold with a final rate of 36*s.*; but if the sellers had got the best of the bargaining at first, the aggregate price paid might be a good deal more than 700 times 36*s.*; while if the buyers had got the better of the bargaining at first, the aggregate price would be a good deal less than 700 times 36*s.* The real distinction then between the theory of buying and selling and that of barter is that in the former it generally is, and in the latter it generally is not, right to assume that the stock of one of the things which is in the market and ready to be exchanged for the other is very large and in many hands; and that therefore its marginal utility is practically constant. See Note XII. *bis* in the Mathematical Appendix.

APPENDIX G[1]

THE INCIDENCE OF LOCAL RATES, WITH SOME SUGGESTIONS AS TO POLICY

§ 1. We have seen [2] that the incidence of a new local tax on printing would differ from that of a national tax mainly by causing such parts of the local printing industry as could conveniently migrate beyond the boundaries of the local tax to do so. Those customers who needed their printing to be done in the locality would pay rather higher for it. Compositors would migrate till only enough remained to find employment locally at about the same wages as before; and some printing offices would be transferred to other industries. The incidence of general local rates on immovable property follows different lines in some respects. The power of migration beyond the boundaries of the rates is a very important factor here, as in the case of a local tax on printing. But of perhaps even greater importance is the fact that a large part of the local rates is spent in ways that conduce directly to the comfort of those very residents and workers in the locality, who might otherwise be driven away. Here two technical terms are needed. *Onerous* rates are those which yield no compensating benefit to the persons who pay them. An extreme case is that of rates devoted to paying interest on a loan incurred by a municipality for an enterprise which failed and has been abandoned. A more representative case is that of a poor-rate levied mainly from the well-to-do. Onerous rates tend of course to drive away those persons on whom they would fall.

On the other hand *beneficial* or *remunerative* rates are those spent on lighting, draining, and other purposes; so as to supply the people who pay the rates with certain necessaries, comforts and luxuries of life, which can be provided by the local authority more cheaply than in any other way. Such rates, ably and honestly administered, may confer a net benefit on those who pay them; and an increase in them may attract population and industry instead of repelling it. Of course a rate may be onerous to one class of the population and beneficial to another. A high rate spent on providing good primary and secondary schools may attract artisan residents, while repelling the well-to-do. "Services which are preponderantly National in character" are "generally onerous"; while "those which are preponderantly Local in character generally confer upon rate-payers a direct and peculiar benefit more or less commensurate with the burden." [3]

But the term "rate-payer" needs to be interpreted differently in regard to different kinds of local expenditure. Rates spent on watering the streets are remunerative to the occupier; but of course those spent on permanent improvements yield only a part of their return to him : the greater part accrues in the long run to the landlord.

The occupier generally regards the rates which are collected from him as forming a single aggregate with his rent; but he makes his reckoning also for the amenities of life which are secured by remunerative local expenditure of rates : that is he tends, other things equal, to select districts in which the

The incidence of all local taxes is influenced by the migration of the population and by the manner in which the rates are expended. *Onerous* rates.

Beneficial or *remunerative* rates.

Extent to which it may be assumed

---

[1] See pp. 375 and 548.
[2] Above V. ix. 1. This Appendix is largely based on the Memorandum there mentioned.
[3] *Final Report of Royal Commission on Local Taxation*, 1901, p. 12.

that the
occupier
is mobile.

aggregate of rents and onerous rates is low. But there is great difficulty in estimating the extent to which migration is actually governed by this consideration. It is probably hindered less than is commonly supposed by ignorance and indifference. But it is much hindered by the special requirements of each individual. Low rates in Devonshire will not draw there people who prefer London life; and certain classes of manufacturers have practically little choice as to the place in which they settle. To say nothing of personal and business ties, the tenant is further hindered by the expense and trouble of moving : and, if that were the equivalent of two years' rent, he would lose by moving unless the advantage which he secured in rates amounted to two shillings in the pound for thirty years. When, however, a person is changing his abode for any reason, he is likely to allow their full weight to all considerations as to the present and prospective rates in different localities, which may be suitable for his purpose.

The mobility of the working classes is, in some respects, greater than that of the well-to-do; but, when rates are compounded, friction sometimes acts on the side of the tenant, and delays the transference to him of his share of new burdens. The manufacturer is often affected as much by the rates on his workmen's dwellings as by those on his own premises : and though high rates may be among the causes which have driven some manufacturers out of large towns, it is doubtful whether, when economically administered, they have had much net effect in this direction. For most new expenditure from the rates, when under able and upright management, materially increases local comforts or lessens local discomforts from the point of view of the workpeople, if not of the manufacturer himself. Further, although the balance of evidence goes to show that lessees consider carefully the present and probable immediate future of local rates, yet they cannot see far ahead, and they seldom even try to do so.[1]

Difficulties
of pre-
diction
when
changes
are rapid,
and adjust-
ments are
slow.

Any analysis that is offered of the incidence of rates, must be taken to refer to general tendencies rather than actual facts. The causes which prevent these tendencies from being applied in prediction resemble those which prevent mathematical reasonings from being applied to the course of a ball on the deck of a ship that is rolling and pitching in cross seas. If the ship would but stay at one inclination, the movement of the ball could be calculated. But before any one tendency has had time to produce much result it will have ceased to exist, and its successor cannot be predicted. Just so, though economists settled once for all, nearly a century ago, the general tendencies of the shifting of taxation; yet the relative weight of onerous rates in different places often changes so rapidly that a tendency may make but little headway before it is stopped off, or even reversed, by changes which cannot be predicted.

The term
*building
value.*

§ 2. We have already seen that the ground rent which a builder is willing to pay for any site is governed by his estimate of the additional value which that site will give to the buildings erected on it. Before taking the lease his capital and that which he will borrow for the purpose is " free " and expressed in terms of money. The anticipated income from his investment is expressed also in money. He sets on the one side his outlay for building; and on the other side, the excess of the rental value of the building with its site over the ground rent to which he is about to commit himself. He works out—perhaps roughly and by instinct rather than definite arithmetical calculations—the present (discounted) value of this excess for the (say) 99 years of his lease. Finally he takes the lease if he sees his way to a good margin of profit; and no better opening for his enterprise is at hand.[2]

---

[1] A good deal of evidence on these points was taken by the Commission just named (p. 655, n. 3).

[2] See above, V. XI. 3 and 8. The builder generally looks to sell his lease before much of it has run out. But the price which he expects to get is the (discounted) excess of the rental value of the property over the ground rent for the remaining years : and therefore the substance of his calculations is nearly the same as it would be if he intended to keep the property in his own hands.

He contrives to the best of his ability that the site and the house (or other APP. G,
building), which he puts upon it, shall be permanently appropriate the one to 3, 4.
the other. In so far as he succeeds, the rent of the property at any future
time is the sum of its annual site value and the annual value of the building :
and this he expects to yield him full profits on his outlay, allowing for insurance
against the risks of a rather hazardous industry. This second part of the rent
is commonly, though perhaps not with strict propriety, called the (annual)
building value, or the building rent of the house.

As time goes on, the purchasing power of money may change; the class of If a
house for which that site is suitable is likely to change; and the technique of building
building is certain to be improved. Consequently the total annual value of has become
the property at a later date consists of its annual site value, together with inappro-
profits on the cost of building a house giving accommodation equally desirable its site,
at that date with the existing house. But all this is subject to the dominant the whole
condition that the general character of the house has remained appropriate to value may
its site : if it has not, no precise statement as to the relation between total be only
value, site value and building value can be made. If for instance a warehouse site.
or a dwelling house of quite a different character is needed to develop the full
resources of the site, the total value of the property as it stands may be less
than its site value alone. For the site value cannot be developed without
pulling down those buildings and erecting new. And the value of the old
material in those buildings may be less than the cost of pulling them down,
allowance being made for the obstruction and loss of time incident thereto.

§ 3. As between two buildings equally eligible in other respects, the Onerous
occupier will pay for that which has the better situation an annual sum equiva- taxes on
lent to its special advantages : but he does not care what part of this sum site values,
goes as rent and what as taxes. Therefore *onerous* taxes on site values tend as fore-
to be deducted from the rental which the owner, or lessee receives : and they seen, are
are accordingly deducted, in so far as they can be foreseen, from the ground deducted
rent which a builder, or anyone else, is willing to pay for a building lease. Such from
local rates as are remunerative, are in the long run paid by the occupier, but ground
are no real burden to him. The condition " in the long run " is essential : for new leases.
instance, rates levied on account of interest and sinking fund on a town improvement, which will for several years to come disturb the public thorough-
fares, and yield none of its good fruit, will be onerous to the occupier, if he pays
it. In strict justice it should be deducted from his rent; because when the
improvement is in full working order and especially when the debt has been
paid off, so that the rate in question lapses, the owner of the property will reap
the benefit of the onerous rates levied on account of it from the first.[1]

§ 4. Taxes on building values are on a different footing. If uniform all Taxes on
over the country, they do not alter the differential advantages of favoured sites; building
and therefore do not—directly at least—make the builder or anyone else less values, if
willing to pay a high ground rent for a good site. If they are so heavy as uniform all
materially to narrow the area of ground built upon, they will indeed lower the country,
value of all building ground : and special site values will fall with the rest. cannot be
But their effect in this direction is so small, that no great error is made by say- evaded by
ing that uniform taxes on building values do not fall on the ground owner. the oc-
The builder, in so far as he anticipates such taxes, adjust his plans to them : cupier, ex-
he aims at putting up buildings of only such expense as can be let to tenants far as he

---

[1] This assumes that the land is assessed to the tax at the same amount, whatever
the use to which it is put.   The case of an extra tax for a special use can be treated as
in V. x. 6. If agricultural land were exempt from the tax, then the tenant of a house
or factory in the country would escape that part of the site tax which is assessed on
the excess of the value of the land for building uses over its value for agriculture.
This might slightly increase concentration in towns, and thus take a little from the
burden on site owners in them : but it would not materially affect the values of sites
in the centre of towns. See also below § 6.

selects a less expensive building.

at rents that will yield him normal profits; while the tenant pays the rates. He may of course miscalculate. But in the long run builders as a class, like all other able business men, are nearly right in their calculations. And in the long run, uniform taxes on building values fall upon the occupier; or at the last on his customers if he uses the building for trade purposes, and his competitors are subject to similar rates.

Remunerative rates are of course no net burden.

But the case is quite different in regard to special high onerous local rates on building values : and here comes in the chief difference between the incidence of national taxes on immovable property and local rates on it. Remunerative expenditure from the rates, which adds more to the conveniences of life than the equivalent of its cost, do not of course repel the occupier; that part of them which is assessed on building values is paid by him, but is no real burden on him; as we have seen in the case of remunerative rates on site values.

Exceptionally onerous rates on building values tend to be shifted on to owners, in the same way as if assessed on site values.

But that part of the rates on building values which is onerous, and in excess of corresponding charges in other localities, does *not* fall mainly on the occupiers. Any exceptional pressure will cause them to migrate beyond its reach in sufficient numbers to reduce the demand for houses and other buildings in the locality, till the burden of these exceptional rates falls upon the lessees or owners. Builders therefore, in so far as they can foresee the future, deduct the equivalent of these exceptional onerous rates on building values, together with all rates and taxes on site values from the ground rent which they are willing to pay.

Grave inequalities of onerous rates seldom last long.

But the cases, in which great deductions of this kind are made, are not numerous and important. For permanent inequalities of onerous rates, though considerable, are less than is commonly thought : and many of them are due to accidents which cannot easily be foreseen, such as mismanagement by a particular group of local administrators. There is indeed one broad and perhaps permanent cause, which throws its shadow before, namely the tendency of the well-to-do to move away from crowded districts to roomy and fashionable suburbs : thus leaving the working classes to bear an undue share of the national duties towards the very poor. But no sooner does this evil become conspicuous, than legislation is invoked to remedy it, by widening the areas of rating for some purposes, so as to include poor and rich districts under the same budget; and in other ways.

Specially onerous rates in one district are a bounty to ground landlords in others.

It is of greater importance to remember that exceptional onerous rates on building values, while tending to lower site rents, and to lower the ground rents on new leases in the districts to which they apply, are not as great a burden on the whole body of owners of land as seems at first sight. For much of the building enterprise, which is checked by such rates, is not destroyed but directed to other districts, and raises the competition for new building leases there.

Old rates and taxes established before the sale of a property are no burden to the purchaser.

§ 5. The incidence of a long-established rate is little affected by its being collected from the tenant, and not from the owners; though it is vitally affected by the proportions in which the rate is assessed on site and building values respectively. On the other hand, the incidence for the first few years of an increase in onerous rates is much affected by the mode of collection. The occupier bears more of the new burden than he would if part of the rates were collected from the owners, or he were allowed to deduct a part of them from his rent. This applies only to neighbourhoods that are making progress. Where the population is receding, and building has ceased, onerous rates tend to press upon owners. But in such places economic friction is generally strong.

The evils of sudden great changes in rates.

It seems probable that the total pressure of onerous rates on the enterprise of building speculators and other interim owners is not very great; and that many rates, of which they have complained, have really enriched them. But vicissitudes of the rates increase slightly the great risks of the building trade, and inevitably the community pays for such risks more than their actuarial

equivalent. All this points to the grievous evils which arise from great and APP. G, 6.
sudden increases in the rates, especially in regard to premises the rateable value
of which is high relatively to the net income of the occupier.

The trader, especially if a shopkeeper, is often able to throw some part of The
the burden of his rates on his customers, at all events if he deals in things which case of
cannot be easily got from a distance. But the shopkeeper's rates are very the shop-
large relatively to his income; and some of that expenditure from the rates, keeper.
which is remunerative from the point of view of well-to-do residents, appears
onerous to him. His work belongs to that group in which economic progress
is raising supply relatively to demand. A little while ago his remuneration
was artificially high, at the expense of society : but now it is falling to a lower
and perhaps more equitable level, and he is slow to recognize the new conditions.
His mind fastens on the real injustice which he suffers when rates are suddenly
raised much; and he attributes to that some of the pressure on him which is
really due to deeper causes. His sense of injustice is sharpened by the fact
that he does not always bargain on quite even terms with his landlord; for,
to say nothing of the cost of fixtures and the general expense of a change, he
might lose a great part of his custom by moving to equally good premises even
a little way off. It must however be remembered that the shopkeeper does
migrate sometimes, that his mind is alert, and he takes full account of the rates;
and thus, after a few years, he shifts the burden of onerous rates on to the
owners and customers more fully than a man of almost any other class does.
(The hotel and lodging-house keeper may rank here with the shopkeeper.)

§ 6. Land near to a growing town, which is still used for agriculture, may The
yield very little net rent : and yet be a valuable property. For its future assessment
ground rents are anticipated in its capital value; and further its ownership of vacant
is likely to yield an income of satisfaction outside of the money rent received building
for it. In this case, it is apt to be under-assessed even when rated at its full land on its
rental value; and the question arises whether it should not be assessed at a value,
percentage on its capital value instead of at a percentage on its rent.

Such a plan would hasten on building, and thus tend to glut the market for
buildings. Therefore rents would tend to fall, and builders would be unable
to take building leases on high ground rents. The change would therefore
transfer to the people at large some part of " the public value " of land which
now goes to owners of land, that is built upon or is likely to be built upon.
But unless accompanied by energetic action on the part of urban authorities in
planning out the lines on which towns should grow, it would result in hasty and
inappropriate building; a mistake for which coming generations would pay a
high price in the loss of beauty and perhaps of health.

The principle which lies at the base of this scheme is capable of larger and a par-
application : and something may be said as to one suggestion of an extreme tial trans-
character, which has recently attracted some attention, to the effect that in ference of
future rates should be assessed mainly or even wholly on site values, with little assess-
or no reference to the value of the buildings. Its immediate effect would be ments
an addition to the value of some properties at the expense of others. In generally
particular it would raise the value of high and expensive buildings in districts from build-
in which the rates were heavy, even more than those in which they were low; ing values
because it would afford relief from a greater burden. But it would lower the to site
the value of low obsolete buildings on large sites in heavily rated districts. values,
After a time, the amount of building put upon a site would vary generally, might
subject to the bylaws, with its advantages of situation; instead of as now partly work well.
in proportion to these advantages, and partly inversely as the rates. This
would increase concentration and tend to raise gross site values in advantageous districts : but it would also increase the aggregate expenditure from the
rates; and, as this would fall on site values, the net site values might be very
low. Whether on the whole the concentration of population would be
increased, it is difficult to say : for the most active building would probably

be in the suburbs, where vacant land no longer escaped heavy rating. Much would depend on the building bylaws : the concentration might be much lessened by a rigorous rule that there should be a large free space at the back as well as in front of all high buildings.[1]

Rural rates.

§ 7. Reference has already been made to the latent partnership between tenant and landlord in British agriculture generally.[2] Competition is less effective in rural than in urban districts. But on the other hand the contributions which the landlord makes to the effective capital of the farm are elastic, and liable to variation according to the stress of circumstances. These adjustments obscure the incidence of agricultural rates, as the eddies of wind rushing past a house will often carry snow-flakes upwards, overbearing, but not destroying, the tendency of gravitation ; and hence arises the common saying that the farmer will pay both his and the landlord's share of new rates, if the competition for farms is strong ; while the landlord will pay all, if he has reason to fear that farms will be thrown on his hands.

However, rural populations probably bear less onerous rates than is commonly supposed. They have gained by improved police service and the abolition of turnpikes, and they have increasing access to advantages purchased by rates in the neighbouring towns, to which they do not contribute, and which are generally much higher than their own rates. In so far as the rates are remunerative in the immediate present, they are no net burden to the occupier, though he pays them. But rates are a considerable percentage on the farmer's net income ; and the burden on him is apt to be heavy in those very rare cases in which onerous rural rates are increased greatly. As already indicated, an onerous rate confined to one district is likely to press more heavily on the local landlords and farmers than if general throughout the country.[3]

Reasons for departing from the general plan of the volume and applying these considerations to some practical issues.

§ 8. This volume is mainly occupied with scientific inquiries ; but yet not without some glances at the practical issues, which supply a motive to economic studies.[4] And here some consideration of policy seems desirable in regard to rates. For all economists are agreed that land in an old country resembles other forms of wealth in many respects, and that it differs in others : and in some recent controversial writings there has appeared a tendency to relegate the points of difference to a secondary place, and to give almost exclusive prominence to those of similarity. A moderate tendency in that direction might be judicious, if the points of similarity alone were of high importance in urgent practical issues. But the contrary is the fact. And therefore it may be well to consider some great issues of administrative finance, in which a leading part is played by those attributes of land which are not largely shared by other forms of wealth. But first a little must be said as to equity.

Particular remunerative rates to be judged separately, onerous

When a special tax is levied for a particular purpose and the case is not one for any interference by public authority with existing rights of ownership— as, for instance, when an arterial system of land drainage is created—the owners of the properties to be benefited may fitly be assessed on the "joint stock principle,"[1] according to which calls are made from shareholders in proportion to their stake in the common venture. The equity of every such charge must be judged separately. But on the other hand all onerous taxes

---

[1] For instance suppose an area of a million square feet to be covered with rows of parallel buildings 40 feet high and 40 feet deep ; a bylaw, that the sky must subtend half a right angle at the ground looking straight back as well as front, will cause the distance between each row and the next to be 40 feet : and the aggregate volume of building will be 40 feet multiplied into half the total area, *i.e.* 20,000,000 cubic feet. Now suppose the height of the buildings to be trebled. Under the same bylaw, the distances between the rows must be 120 feet : and, on the supposition that it is not convenient to increase the depth of the houses beyond 40 feet the aggregate volume of building will be 120 feet multiplied into a quarter of the total area, that is, 30,000,000 cubic feet. Thus the total accommodation will be increased by only one half ; instead of being trebled, as would have been the case if the old distances of 40 feet between the rows had been maintained.

[2] See VI. x. 10.　　　[3] See above, p. 363.　　　[4] See I. iv. 2–4.

and rates must be judged in equity as a whole. Almost every onerous tax APP. G, 8.
taken by itself presses with undue weight on some class or other; but this is
of no moment so long as the inequalities of each are compensated by those of taxation to
others, and variations in the several parts synchronize. If that difficult con- be judged
as a whole.
dition is satisfied, the system may be equitable, though any part of it regarded
alone would be inequitable.

Secondly, there is a general agreement that a system of taxation should be Taxes on
adjusted, in more or less steep graduation, to people's incomes : or better still houses are
to their expenditures. For that part of a man's income, which he saves, con- roughly
tributes again to the Exchequer until it is consumed by expenditure. Conse- proportionate to ex-
quently, when considering the fact that our present system of taxation, general penditure
and local, bears heavily on houses, it should be remembered that large expen- and equi-
diture generally requires large house-room : and that while taxes, and especi- table in
ally graduated taxes on expenditure in general, present great technical diffi- themselves.
culties to the tax collector; and further cost much more to the consumer
directly and indirectly than they bring into the revenue; taxes on houses are
technically simple, cheap in collection, not liable to evasion, and easy of
graduation.[1]

But, thirdly, this argument does not apply to buildings other than houses. But heavy
And for that reason it may be equitable to tax shops, warehouses, factories, taxes on
etc. on a lower scale than houses, at all events as far as new rates are concerned : trade pre-
the burden of old rates is already shifted from the occupiers of business mises are
premises partly on to their landlords and partly on to their customers. This equitable
only in so
process of shifting is constantly going on; and therefore no great hardship far as
would be inflicted on the trading classes in urban districts if they were charged they are
at once with a farthing for every penny of new rates; while a part, or the whole, shifted :
of the remaining three farthings were left to be added to their burden gradually and new
taxes
by small annual percentages. It may be that some such plan will be necessary, cannot be
if the expenses of urban local government continue to increase fast. shifted

These considerations lead us to repeat that, whether in an old or a new quickly.
country, a far-seeing statesman will feel a greater responsibility to future The
generations when legislating as to land than as to other forms of wealth; statesman
and that, from the economic and from the ethical point of view, land must has heavy
and many-
everywhere and always be classed as a thing by itself. If from the first the sided
State had retained true rents in its own hands, the vigour of industry and responsi-
accumulation need not have been impaired, though in a very few cases the bilities in
settlement of new countries might have been delayed a little. Nothing at all relation to
like this can be said of the incomes derived from property made by man. But the land.
the very greatness of the public interests concerned makes it specially necessary
to bear in mind, when discussing the equities of the public value of land, that
a sudden appropriation by the State of any incomes from property, the private
ownership of which had once been recognized by it, would destroy security and
shake the foundations of society. Sudden and extreme measures would be
inequitable; and partly, but not solely for that reason, they would be unbusiness-like and even foolish.

Caution is necessary. But the cause of high site values is that concentration of population, which is threatening a scarcity of fresh air and light and

---

[1] In old times the windows of a house were taken as representative of the house,
and were taxed heavily : but the tax did not strike, and was not intended to strike,
persons as owners and users of windows only ; it was intended to strike them, and did
strike them, as owners and users of houses. And, just as the window is a more or less
good representative of the house; so the house is a representative, perhaps a better
representative, of a certain scale and style of household expenditure in general;
and when houses are taxed, the tax is, and is intended to be, a tax upon the ownership
and use of the means of living in certain general conditions of comfort and social
position. If part of the tax assessed on houses were removed, and the deficit made up
by taxes assessed on furniture and indoor servants, the true incidence of the taxes
would be nearly the same as now.

APP. G, 9. playroom so grievous as to lower the vigour and the joyousness of the rising
generation. Thus rich private gains accrue, not merely through causes which
are public rather than private in their character, but also at the expense of one
of the chief forms of public wealth. Large expenditure is needed to secure air
and light and playroom. And the most appropriate source from which that
expense can be defrayed seems to be those extreme rights of private property
in land, which have grown up almost imperceptibly from the time when the
king, representing the State, was the sole *landowner*. Private persons were
but *landholders* subject to the obligation to work for the public wellbeing :
they have no equitable right to mar that wellbeing by congested building.

Sudden
disturb-
ances of
old rates
are to be
avoided.

§ 9. Accordingly the following practical suggestions seem to emerge :—
As regards old rates a sudden change in the person from whom they are collected seems unadvisable : but additional rates should, as far as may be convenient, be collected from the person on whom they are ultimately to fall;
unless, like the income tax under Schedule A, they are collected from the tenant
with the instruction that they are to be deducted from his rent.

New rates
should be
imposed as
far as may
be on those
by whom
they are
ultimately
to be paid.

The reasons for this are that nearly the whole of that part of old rates,
which is assessed on public or site value of land, is already borne by owners
(including lessees, so far as those rates go, which, though old, were not anticipated when their leases were taken); and nearly all the remainder of it is borne
by tenants or their customers. This result would not be very greatly disturbed
by allowing the tenant to deduct a half or even the whole of his rates from
his rent : though such a law would run some risk of handing over some of the
property of the owners to lessees, who had reckoned for paying those old rates
when taking their leases. On the other hand, a provision for the division of
new, that is additional, rates would have great advantages : the occupier
whether of a farm, of business premises or a house would deduct one half of
the new rates from his rent ; his immediate landlord would deduct in proportion
from his payments to the superior holder next to him ; and so on. And in
addition new local taxes on business premises of all kinds might be assessed,
as has just been suggested, at less than full rates in the first instance ; and
gradually increased. By these provisions farmers, shopkeepers and other
traders would be relieved from the occasional injustice, and the constant fear
of injustice, which are now associated with sudden, disproportionate additions
to the public burdens thrown upon particular classes.

Urban land
might be
charged
with a
general
site rate
and a
special
"fresh
air rate."

In regard to site values, it would seem well to rule that all land, whether
technically urban or not, should be regarded as having a special site value if
when cleared of buildings it could be sold at even a moderately high price, say
£200 an acre. It might then be subjected to a general rate assessed on its
capital value ; and, in addition, to a " fresh air rate " to be spent by local
authority under full central control for the purposes indicated above. This
fresh air rate would not be a very heavy burden on owners, for a good deal of it
would be returned to them in the form of higher values for those building sites
which remained. As it is, the expenditure of such private societies as the
Metropolitan Public Gardens Association, and much of the rates raised on
building values for public improvements, is really a free gift of wealth to owners
who are already fortunate.

Rates
should be
graduated
but no one
wholly
exempted.

For rural and urban districts alike, after reckoning for the initial rates on
land, the remainder of the necessary funds would perhaps best be obtained by
rates on immovable property, supplemented by some minor local taxes at the
discretion of the local authorities. The Inhabited House Duty might be
suppressed, unless it was needed for any great new expenditure such as old age
pensions : and the main rates might be graduated as the present Inhabited
House Duty is ; but more gently for houses of moderate size, and more severely
for very large houses. But no one should be exempted altogether : for so
long as a person retains the right of voting on the levying and expenditure of
rates, it is not safe that he should wholly escape their pressure. It may however

be safe and reasonable to return to him or his children the equivalent of his APP. G, 9.
payments in such benefits as will increase physical and mental health and ——
vigour, and will not tend towards political corruption.[1]

[1] The recent Commission on Local Taxation was much occupied with the difficulty
of assessing site values; and with the even greater difficulty of making *ad interim*
arrangements by which an equitable share (whether more or less) of the rates, which
were designed in the long run to be paid by the ultimate land-owners, might be transferred from the occupiers to lessees.   (See especially pp. 153–176 of the *Final Report.*)
The difficulty of assessment, though undoubtedly very great, is of a kind to be diminished rapidly by experience; the first thousand such assessments might probably give
more trouble, and yet be less accurately made than the next twenty thousand.

LIMITATIONS OF THE USE OF STATICAL ASSUMPTIONS IN
REGARD TO INCREASING RETURN

APP. H,
1, 2.
———
Nature
of the
difficulty
to be
considered.

§ 1. Some hints have already been given of the difficulties which beset the theory of equilibrium in regard to commodities which obey the law of increasing return. Those hints are now to be developed a little.

The central point is that the term " margin of production " has no significance for long periods in relation to commodities the cost of production of which diminishes with a gradual increase in the output : and a tendency to increasing return does not exist generally for short periods. Therefore, when we are discussing the special conditions of value of those commodities which conform to that tendency, the term " margin " should be avoided. It may be used of course for these commodities as for all others, with regard to a short and quick fluctuation in demand ; because in relation to such fluctuations the production of those commodities, as well as others, conforms to the law of diminishing and not increasing return. But in problems in which the tendency to increasing return is in effective force, there is no clearly defined marginal product. In such problems our units have to be larger, we have to consider the conditions of the representative firm rather than a given individual firm : and above all we have to consider the cost of a whole process of production, without any attempt to isolate that of a single commodity, such as a single rifle or yard of cloth. It is true that when nearly the whole of any branch of industry is in the hands of a few giant businesses, none of them can be fairly described as " representative." If these businesses are fused in a trust, or even closely combined with one another, the term " normal expenses of production " ceases to have a precise meaning. And, as will be argued fully in a later volume, it must be regarded as *primâ facie* a monopoly : and its procedure must be analysed on the lines of Book V. chapter XIV. ; though the last years of the nineteenth century and the early years of this have shown that even in such cases competition has a much greater force, and the use of the term " normal " is less inappropriate than seemed probable *a priori*.

An illustration.

§ 2. Let us return to the instance of an increased demand for aneroid barometers, caused by a movement of fashion, which after a while had led to improved organization and to a lower supply price.[2] When at last the force of fashion died away, and the demand for aneroids was again based solely on their real utility ; this price might be either greater or less than the normal demand price for the corresponding scale of production. In the former case capital and labour would avoid that trade. Of the firms already started some might pursue their course, though with less net gains than they had hoped ; but others would try to edge their way into some nearly related branch of production that was more prosperous : and as old firms dwindled, there would be few new ones to take their place. The scale of production would dwindle again ; and the old position of equilibrium would have shown itself fairly stable against assaults.

But now let us turn to the other case, in which the long-period supply price for the increased output fell so far that the demand price remained above it.

In that case undertakers, looking forward to the life of a firm started in that APP. H, 2. trade, considering its chances of prosperity and decay, discounting its future outlays and its future incomings, would conclude that the latter showed a good balance over the former. Capital and labour would stream rapidly into the trade; and the production might perhaps be increased tenfold before the fall in the demand price became as great as the fall in the long-period supply price, and a position of stable equilibrium had been found.

For indeed, though in the account of the oscillations of demand and supply *Two positions of stable equilibrium* about a position of stable equilibrium, which was given in the third chapter, it was tacitly implied, as is commonly done, that there could be only one position of stable equilibrium in a market : yet in fact under certain conceivable, though rare, conditions there can be two or more positions of real equilibrium *are theoretically possible.* of demand and supply, any one of which is equally consistent with the general circumstances of the market, and any one of which if once reached would be stable, until some great disturbance occurred.[1]

---

[1] Besides positions of stable equilibrium, there are theoretically at least positions of unstable equilibrium : they are the dividing boundaries between two positions of stable equilibria, the watersheds, so to speak, dividing two river basins, and the price tends to flow away from them in either direction.

When demand and supply are in unstable equilibrium, then, if the scale of production be disturbed ever so little from its equilibrium position, it will move rapidly away to one of its positions of stable equilibrium; as an egg if balanced on one of its ends would at the smallest shake fall down, and lie lengthways. Just as it is theoretically possible, but practically impossible, that an egg should stand balanced on its end, so it is theoretically possible, but practically impossible, that the scale of production should stay balanced in unstable equilibrium.

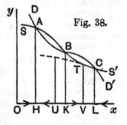

Fig. 38.

Thus in fig. 38 the curves intersect several times and the arrow heads on *Ox* show the directions in which, according to its situation, R tends to move along *Ox*. This shows that if R is at H or at L and is displaced slightly in either direction, it will, as soon as the disturbing cause is over, return to the equilibrium position from which it was displaced : but that if it is at K and is displaced towards the right, it will continue, even after the cessation of the disturbing cause, to move to the right till it reaches L, and if displaced towards the left it will continue to move to the left till it reaches H. That is to say, H and L are points of stable equilibrium and K is a point of unstable equilibrium. We are thus brought to the result that :—

The equilibrium of demand and supply corresponding to the point of intersection of the demand and supply curves is stable or unstable according as the demand curve lies above or below the supply curve just to the left of that point; or, which is the same thing, according as it lies below or above the supply curve just to the right of that point.

We have seen that the demand curve is inclined throughout negatively. From this it follows that, if just to the right of any point of intersection the supply curve lies above the demand curve; then, if we move along the supply curve to the right, we must necessarily keep above the demand curve till the next point of intersection is reached : that is to say, the point of equilibrium next on the right-hand side of a point of stable equilibrium, must be a point of unstable equilibrium; and, it may be proved in like manner, that so must the adjacent point of intersection on the left-hand side. In other words, in cases in which the curves cut each other more than once, points of stable and unstable equilibrium alternate.

Also the last point of intersection reached, as we move to the right, must be a point of stable equilibrium. For if the amount produced were increased indefinitely, the price at which it could be sold would necessarily fall almost to zero; but the price required to cover the expense of producing it would not so fall. Therefore, if the supply curve be produced sufficiently far towards the right, it must at last lie above the demand curve.

The first point of intersection arrived at as we proceed from left to right may be a point either of stable or of unstable equilibrium. If it be a point of unstable equilibrium, this fact will indicate that the production of the commodity in question on a small scale will not remunerate the producers; so that its production cannot be commenced at all unless some passing accident has caused temporarily an urgent demand

APP. H, 3.

§ 3. It must however be admitted that this theory is out of touch with real conditions of life, in so far as it assumes that, if the normal production of a commodity increases and afterwards again diminishes to its old amount, the demand price and the supply price will return to their old positions for that amount.[1]

No great violence is involved in the assumption that the list of demand prices is rigid;

Whether a commodity conforms to the law of diminishing or increasing return, the increase in consumption arising from a fall in price is gradual :[2] and, further, habits which have once grown up around the use of a commodity while its price is low, are not quickly abandoned when its price rises again. If therefore after the supply has gradually increased, some of the sources from which it is derived should be closed, or any other cause should occur to make the commodity scarce, many consumers will be reluctant to depart from their wonted ways. For instance, the price of cotton during the American war was higher than it would have been if the previous low price had not brought cotton into common use to meet wants, many of which had been created by the low price. Thus then the list of demand prices which holds for the forward movement of the production of a commodity will seldom hold for the return movement, but will in general require to be raised.[3]

but the assumption that the list of supply prices is rigid is inappropriate to increasing return.

Again, the list of supply prices may have fairly represented the actual fall in the supply price of the thing that takes place when the supply is being increased; but if the demand should fall off, or if for any other reason, the supply should have to be diminished, the supply price would not move back by the course by which it had come, but would take a lower course. The list of supply prices which had held for the forward movement would not hold for the backward movement, but would have to be replaced by a lower schedule. This is true whether the production of the commodity obeys the law of diminishing or increasing return; but it is of special importance in the latter case, because the fact that the production does obey this law, proves that its increase leads to great improvements in organization.

For, when any casual disturbance has caused a great increase in the production of any commodity, and thereby has led to the introduction of extensive economies, these economies are not readily lost, Developments of mechanical appliances, of division of labour and of the means of transport, and improved organization of all kinds, when they have been once obtained are not readily abandoned. Capital and labour, when they have once been devoted to any particular industry, may indeed become depreciated in value, if there is a falling off in the demand for the wares which they produce : but they cannot quickly be converted to other occupations; and their competition will for a time prevent a diminished demand from causing an increased price of the wares.[4]

---

for the commodity, or has temporarily lowered the expenses of producing it; or unless some enterprising firm is prepared to sink much capital in overcoming the initial difficulties of the production, and bringing out the commodity at a price which will ensure large sales.

[1] See V. III. 6.   [2] See III. IV. 6.

[3] That is, for any backward movement of the amount offered for sale, the left end of the demand curve would probably need to be raised in order to make it represent the new conditions of demand.

[4] For instance, the shape of the supply curve in fig. 38 implies that if the ware in question were produced on the scale OV annually, the economies introduced into its production would be so extensive as to enable it to be sold at a price TV. If these economies were once effected the shape of the curve SS' would probably cease to represent accurately the circumstances of supply. The expenses of production, for instance, of an amount OU would no longer be much greater proportionately than those of an amount OV. Thus in order that the curve might again represent the circumstances of supply it would be necessary to draw it lower down, as the dotted curve in the figure. Professor Bullock, *Quarterly Journal of Economics*, Aug. 1902, p. 508, argues that this dotted curve should not slope upward from T however gently : but should slope downward, to indicate that the diminished production will lower marginal cost, " by forcing out of business the weakest producers," so that the marginal cost will in future be that of more competent producers than before. This result is possible.

Partly for this reason, there are not many cases in which two positions of
stable equilibrium would stand out as possible alternatives at one and the
same moment, even if all the facts of the market could be ascertained by the
dealers concerned. But when the conditions of a branch of manufacture are
such that the supply price would fall very rapidly, if there should be any great
increase in the scale of production; then a passing disturbance, by which the
demand for the commodity was increased, might cause a very great fall in the
stable equilibrium price; a very much larger amount than before being henceforward produced for sale at a very much lower price. This is always possible
when, if we could trace the lists of demand and supply prices far ahead, we
should find them keeping close together.[1] For if the supply prices for largely
increased amounts are but very little above the corresponding demand prices,
a moderate increase in demand, or a comparatively slight new invention or
other cheapening of production may bring supply and demand prices together
and make a new equilibrium. Such a change resembles in some respects a
movement from one alternative position of stable equilibrium to another, but
differs from the latter in that it cannot occur except when there is some change
in the conditions of normal demand or normal supply.

The unsatisfactory character of these results is partly due to the imperfections of our analytical methods, and may conceivably be much diminished
in a later age by the gradual improvement of our scientific machinery. We
should have made a great advance if we could represent the normal demand
price and supply price as functions both of the amount normally produced and
of the time at which that amount became normal.[2]

§ 4. Next let us revert to the distinction between average values and normal values.[3] In a stationary state the income earned by every appliance of
production being truly anticipated beforehand, would represent the normal
measure of the efforts and sacrifices required to call it into existence.

But it must be remembered that the marginal cost of the weakest producer does not
govern value, but only indicates the force of the causes which govern it. In so far as
the economies of production on a large scale are " internal," *i.e.* belonging to the
internal organization of individual firms, the weaker firms must speedily be driven out
of existence by the stronger. The continued existence of weaker firms is an evidence
that a strong firm cannot indefinitely increase its output; partly because of the difficulty of extending its market, and partly because the strength of a firm is not permanent. The strong firm of to-day was probably weak, because young, some time
back; and will be weak, because old, some time hence. With a smaller output there
will still be weak firms at the margin; and they will probably in the course of time be
weaker than if the scale of total production had been maintained. Also the external
economies will be less. In other words the representative firm will probably be smaller,
weaker, and with less access to external economies. See Prof. Flux in the same
Journal for Feb. 1904.
    [1] That is, when at a good distance to the right of the equilibrium point, the supply
curve is but little above the demand curve.
    [2] One difficulty arises from the fact that a suitable time to allow for the intro-
duction of the economies appertaining to one increase in the scale of production is
not long enough for another and larger increase, so we must fix on some fairly long time
ahead, which is likely to be indicated by the special problem in hand, and adjust the
whole series of supply prices to it.
    We could get much nearer to nature if we allowed ourselves a more complex illus-
tration. We might take a series of curves, of which the first allowed for the economies
likely to be introduced as the result of each increase in the scale of production during
one year, a second curve doing the same for two years, a third for three years, and so
on. Cutting them out of cardboard and standing them up side by side, we should
obtain a *surface*, of which the three dimensions represented amount, price, and time
respectively. If we had marked on each curve the point corresponding to that amount
which, so far as can be foreseen, seems likely to be the normal amount for the year to
which that curve related, then these points would form a curve on the surface, and
that curve would be a fairly true long-period normal supply curve for a commodity
obeying the law of increasing return. Compare an article by Mr. Cunynghame, in the
Economic Journal for 1892.
    [3] See above V. III. 6; v. 4; and IX. 6.

verage
xpenses
e equal to
aarginal
.nd to
ıormal
xpenses.

The aggregate expenses of production might then be found either by multiplying these marginal expenses by the number of units of the commodity; or by adding together all the actual expenses of production of its several parts, and adding in all the rents earned by differential advantages for production. The aggregate expenses of production being determined by either of these routes, the average expenses could be deduced by dividing out by the amount of the commodity; and the result would be the normal supply price, whether for long periods or for short.

But in the world in which we live, the term " average " expenses of production is somewhat misleading. For most of the appliances of production, material and personal, by which a commodity was made, came into existence long before. Their values are therefore not likely to be just what the producers expected them to be originally; but some of their values will be greater, and others less. Thus present incomes earned by them will be governed by the general relations between the demand for, and the supply of, their products; and their values will be arrived at by capitalizing these incomes. And therefore, when making out a list of normal supply prices, which, in conjunction with the list of normal demand prices, is to determine the equilibrium position of normal value, we cannot take for granted the values of these appliances for production without reasoning in a circle.

This caution, which is of special importance with regard to industries that tend to increasing return, may be emphasized by a diagrammatic presentation of the relations of demand and supply which are possible in a stationary state, but only there. There every particular thing bears its proper share of supplementary costs; and it would not ever be worth while for a producer to accept a particular order at a price other than the total cost, in which is to be reckoned a charge for the task of building up the trade connection and external organization of a representative firm. The illustration has no positive value : it merely guards against a possible error in abstract reasoning.[1]

[1] In the adjoining diagram, SS' is not a true supply curve adapted to the conditions of the world in which we live; but it has properties, which are often erroneously attributed to such a curve. We will call it the *particular expenses curve.* As usual the amount of a commodity is measured along Ox, and its price along Oy. OH is the amount of the commodity produced annually, AH is the equilibrium price of a unit of it. The producer of the OHth unit is supposed to have no differential advantages; but the producer of the OMth unit has differential advantages which enable him to produce with an outlay PM, a unit which it would have cost him an outlay AH to produce without those advantages. The locus of P is our particular expenses curve; and it is such that any point P being taken on it, and PM being drawn perpendicular to Ox, PM represents the particular expenses of production incurred for the production of the OMth unit. The excess of AH over $PM = QP$, and is a producer's surplus or rent. For convenience the owners of differential advantages may be arranged in descending order from left to right; and thus SS' becomes a curve sloping upwards to the right.

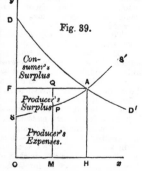

Fig. 39.

Proceeding as in the case of consumer's surplus or rent (III. VI. 3), we may regard MQ as a thin parallelogram or as a thick straight line. And as M takes consecutive positions along OH, we get a number of thick straight lines cut in two by the curve SA, the lower part of each representing the expenses of production of a unit of the commodity, and the upper the contribution which that unit affords towards rent. The lower set of thick lines taken together fill up the whole space $SOHA$; which therefore represents the aggregate of the expenses of propuction of an amount OH. The upper set of thick lines taken together fill up the space FSA, which therefore represents producer's surplus or rent in the ordinary sense of the term. Subject to the corrections mentioned above (III. VI. 3), DFA represents the surplus satisfaction which consumers get from an amount OH over that, the value of which is represented to them by a sum of money equal to $OH \times HA$.

Now the difference between the particular expenses curve and a normal supply curve lies in this, that in the former we do, and in the latter we do not, take the general economies of production as fixed and uniform throughout. The particular expenses curve is based throughout on the assumption that the aggregate production is OH, and that all the producers have access to the internal and external economies which belong to this scale of production; and, these assumptions being carefully borne in mind, the curve may be used to represent a particular phase of any industry, whether agricultural or manufacturing : but they cannot be taken to represent its general conditions of production.

That can be done only by the normal supply curve, in which PM represents the normal expenses of production of the OMth unit on the supposition that OM units (not any other amount, as OH) are being produced; and that the available economies of production external and internal are those which belong to a representative firm where the aggregate volume of production is OM. These economies will generally be less than if the aggregate volume of production were the larger quantity OH; and therefore, M being to the left of H, the ordinate at M for the supply curve will be greater than for a particular expenses curve drawn for an aggregate production OH.

It follows that the area SAF which represents aggregate rent in our present diagram would have represented something less than the aggregate rent, if SS' had been a normal supply curve even for agricultural produce (DD' being the normal demand curve). For even in agriculture the general economies of production increase with an increase in the aggregate scale of production.

If however we choose to ignore this fact for the sake of any particular argument; that is, if we choose to assume that MP being the expenses of production of that part of the produce which was raised under the most difficult circumstances (so as to pay no rent) when OM units were produced, it remains also the expenses of production (other than rent) of the OMth unit even when OH is produced; or, in other words, if we assume that the increase in production from the amount OM to the amount OH did not alter the expenses of production of the OMth unit, then we may regard SAF as representing the aggregate rent even when SS' is the normal supply curve. It may be occasionally convenient to do this, attention being of course called every time to the nature of the special assumption made.

But no assumption of the kind can be made with regard to the supply curve of a commodity that obeys the laws of increasing return. To do so would be a contradiction in terms. The fact that the production of the commodity obeys that law, implies that the general economies available when the aggregate volume of production is large, are so much greater than when it is small, as to override the increasing resistance that nature offers to an increased production of the raw materials of which the industry makes use. In the case of a particular expenses curve, MP will always be less than AH (M being to the left of H) whether the commodity obeys the law of increasing or diminishing return; but on the other hand in the case of a supply curve, for a commodity that obeys the law of increasing return, MP would generally be greater than AH.

It remains to say that if we are dealing with a problem in which some even of those appliances for production which were made by man, have to be taken as a given quantity for the time, so that their earnings will be of the nature of a quasi-rent; we may then draw a particular expenses curve, in which MP stands for the expenses of production in the narrower sense in which such quasi-rents are excluded; and the area SAF would thus represent the aggregate of rents proper and of these quasi-rents. This method of treating short-period normal value problems has attractions, and may perhaps ultimately be of service : but it requires careful handling, for the assumptions on which it rests are very slippery.

APP. I, 1.

Ricardo had practical experience, but was abstract and un-systematic as a writer.

§ 1. When Ricardo · was addressing a general audience, he drew largely upon his wide and intimate knowledge of the facts of life, using them " for illustration, verification, or the premises of argument." But in his *Principles of Political Economy* " the same questions are treated with a singular exclusion of all reference to the actual world around him." [2] And he wrote to Malthus in May, 1820 (the same year in which Malthus published his *Principles of Political Economy considered with a view to their practical application*), " Our differences may in some respects, I think, be ascribed to your considering my book as more practical than I intended it to be. My object was to elucidate principles, and to do this I imagined strong cases, that I might show the operation of those principles." His book makes no pretence to be systematic. He was with difficulty induced to publish it; and if in writing it he had in view any readers at all, they were chiefly those statesmen and business men with whom he associated. So he purposely omitted many things which were necessary for the logical completeness of his argument, but which they would regard as obvious. And further, as he told Malthus in the following October, he was " but a poor master of language." His exposition is as confused as his thought is profound; he uses words in artificial senses which he does not explain, and to which he does not adhere; and he changes from one hypothesis to another without giving notice.

If then we seek to understand him rightly, we must interpret him generously, more generously than he himself interpreted Adam Smith. When his words are ambiguous, we must give them that interpretation which other passages in his writings indicate that he would have wished us to give them. If we do this with the desire to ascertain what he really meant, his doctrines, though very far from complete, are free from many of the errors that are commonly attributed to them.

He took utility for granted, because its influence is relatively simple;

He considers, for instance (*Principles*, Ch. I. § 1), that utility is " absolutely essential " to (normal) value though not its measure; while the value of things " of which there is a very limited quantity . . . varies with the wealth and inclinations of those who are desirous to possess them." And elsewhere (*Ib.* Ch. IV.) he insists on the way in which the market fluctuations of prices are determined by the amount available for sale on the one hand and " the wants and wishes of mankind " on the other.

Again, in a profound, though very incomplete, discussion of the difference between " Value and Riches " he seems to be feeling his way towards the distinction between marginal and total utility. For by Riches he means total utility, and he seems to be always on the point of stating that value corresponds to the increment of riches which results from that part of the commodity which it is only just worth the while of purchasers to buy; and that when the supply runs short, whether temporarily in consequence of a passing accident, or permanently in consequence of an increase in cost of production, there is a rise in that marginal increment of riches which is measured by value, at the same time that there is a diminution in the aggregate

---

[1] Compare the concluding remarks of Book V. : and Appendix B, 5.

[2] See an admirable article on *Ricardo's Use of Facts* in the first volume of the Harvard *Quarterly Journal of Economics*, by the late Professor Dunbar.

riches, the total utility, derived from the commodity. Throughout the whole discussion he is trying to say, though (being ignorant of the terse language of the differential calculus) he did not get hold of the right words in which to say it neatly, that marginal utility is raised and total utility is lessened by any check to supply.

App. i, 2

§ 2. But while not thinking that he had much to say that was of great importance on the subject of utility, he believed that the connection between cost of production and value was imperfectly understood; and that erroneous views on this subject were likely to lead the country astray in practical problems of taxation and finance; and so he addressed himself specially to this subject. But here also he made short cuts.

and he analysed cost of production because its influence is less obvious.

For, though he was aware that commodities fall into three classes according as they obey the law of diminishing, of constant, or of increasing return; yet he thought it best to ignore this distinction in a theory of value applicable to all kinds of commodities. A commodity chosen at random was just as likely to obey one as the other of the two laws of diminishing and of increasing return; and therefore he thought himself justified in assuming provisionally that they all obeyed the law of constant return. In this perhaps he was justified, but he made a mistake in not stating explicitly what he was doing.

He argued in the first Section of his first Chapter that " in the early stages of society " where there is scarcely any use of capital, and where any one man's labour has nearly the same price as any other man's, it is, broadly speaking, true that " the value of a commodity, or the quantity of a commodity for which it will exchange, depends on the relative quantity of labour which is necessary for its production." That is, if two things are made by twelve and four men's labour for a year, all the men being of the same grade, the normal value of the former will be three times that of the latter. For if ten per cent. has to be added for profits on the capital invested in the one case, ten per cent. will need to be added in the other also. [If w be a year's wages of a worker of this class, the costs of production will be $4w.\frac{110}{100}$, and $12w.\frac{110}{100}$: and the ratio of these is 4 : 12, or 1 : 3.]

1. Cost of production dependent on quantity of labour used directly;

But he went on to show that these assumptions cannot be properly made in later stages of civilization, and that the relation of value to cost of production is more complex than that with which he started; and his next step was to introduce in Section ii. the consideration that " labour of different qualities is differently rewarded." If the wages of a jeweller are twice as great as those of a working labourer, an hour's work of the one must count for two hours' work of the other. Should there be a change in their relative wages, there will of course be a corresponding change in the relative values of things made by them. But instead of analysing, as economists of this generation do, the causes which make (say) jewellers' wages change from one generation to another relatively to those of ordinary labourers, be contented himself with stating that such variations cannot be great.

2, also on quality of that labour;

Next in Section iii. he urged that in reckoning the cost of production of a commodity, account must be taken not only of the labour applied immediately to it, but also of that which is bestowed on the implements, tools and buildings with which such labour is assisted; and here the element of time, which he had carefully kept in the background at starting, was necessarily introduced.

3, on labour spent previously on implements;

Accordingly in Section iv. he discusses more fully the different influences exerted on the value of " a set of commodities " [he uses this simple method sometimes to evade the difficulties of the distinctions between prime cost and total cost]: and especially he takes account of the different effects of the application of circulating capital which is consumed in a single use, and of fixed capital; and again of the time for which labour must be invested in making machinery to make commodities. If that be long, they will have a greater cost of production and be " more valuable to compensate for the greater length of time, which must elapse before they can be brought to market."[1]

4, on the length of time which must elapse before the goods can be brought to market;

APP. I, 2.
5, on the
consequent
influence
of the rate
of profits
on relative
value.

And lastly in Section V. he sums up the influence which different lengths of investment, whether direct or indirect, will have upon relative values; arguing correctly that if wages all rise and fall together the change will have no permanent effect on the relative values of different commodities. But he argues if the rate of profits falls it will lower the relative values of those commodities the production of which requires capital to be invested a long while before they can be brought to market. For if in one case the average investment is for a year and requires ten per cent. to be added to the wages bill for profits; and in another is for two years and requires twenty per cent. to be added; then a fall of profits by one-fifth will reduce the addition in the latter case from 20 to 16, and in the former only from 10 to 8. [If their direct labour cost is equal the ratio of their values before the change will be $\frac{120}{110}$ or 1·091; and after the change $\frac{116}{108}$ or 1·074; a fall of nearly two per cent.] His argument is avowedly only provisional; in later chapters he takes account of other causes of differences in profits in different industries, besides the period of investment. But it seems difficult to imagine how he could more strongly have emphasized the fact that Time or Waiting as well as Labour is an element of cost of production than by occupying his first chapter with this discussion. Unfortunately however he delighted in short phrases, and he thought that his readers would always supply for themselves the explanations of which he had given them a hint.

He
corrects
Malthus'
anticipa-
tion of
Marx's
misunder-
standing.

Once indeed, in a note at the end of the sixth Section of his first Chapter, he says :—" Mr. Malthus appears to think that it is a part of my doctrine that the cost and value of a thing should be the same; it is, if he means by cost, ' cost of production ' including profits. In the above passage, this is what he does not mean, and therefore he has not clearly understood me.'¹ And yet Rodbertus and Karl Marx claim Ricardo's authority for the statement that the natural value of things consists solely of the labour spent on them; and even those German economists who most strenuously combat the conclusions of these writers, are often found to admit that they have interpreted Ricardo rightly, and that their conclusions follow logically from his.

This and other facts of a similar kind show that Ricardo's reticence was an error of judgment. It would have been better if he had occasionally repeated the statement that the values of two commodities are to be regarded as in the long run proportionate to the amount of labour required for making them, only on the condition that other things are equal : i.e., that the labour employed in the two cases is equally skilled, and therefore equally highly paid; that it is assisted by proportionate amounts of capital, account being taken of the period of its investment; and that the rates of profits are equal. He does not state clearly, and in some cases he perhaps did not fully and clearly perceive how, in the problem of normal value, the various elements govern one another *mutually*, and not *successively* in a long chain of causation. And he was more guilty than almost anyone else of the bad habit of endeavouring to express great economic doctrines in short sentences.¹

¹ Prof. Ashley in a suggestive criticism of this Note, as part of an attempted " Rehabilitation of Ricardo " (*Economic Journal*, Vol. I.), insists that it has been commonly believed that Ricardo did in fact habitually think of mere quantities of labour as constituting cost of production, and governing value, subject only to " slight modifications "; and that this interpretation of him is the most consistent with his writings as a whole. It is not disputed that this interpretation has been accepted by many able writers : otherwise there would have been little need for rehabilitating, *i.e.* clothing more fully his somewhat too naked doctrine. But the question whether Ricardo is to be supposed to have meant nothing by the first chapter of his book, merely because he did not constantly repeat the interpretation clauses contained in it, is one which each reader must decide for himself according to his temperament : it does not lend itself to be solved by argument. It is here claimed not that his doctrines contained a complete theory of value : but only that they were in the main true as far as they went. Rodbertus and Marx interpreted Ricardo's doctrine, to mean that interest does not enter into that cost of production which governs (or rather takes part

§ 3. There are few writers of modern times who have approached as near
to the brilliant originality of Ricardo as Jevons has done. But he appears
to have judged both Ricardo and Mill harshly, and to have attributed to them
doctrines narrower and less scientific than those which they really held. And
his desire to emphasize an aspect of value to which they had given insufficient
prominence, was probably in some measure accountable for his saying, " Repeated reflection and inquiry have led me to the somewhat novel opinion
that *value depends entirely upon utility* " (*Theory*, p. 1). This statement seems
to be no less one-sided and fragmentary, and much more misleading, than that
into which Ricardo often glided with careless brevity, as to the dependence
of value on cost of production; but which he never regarded as more than a
part of a larger doctrine, the rest of which he had tried to explain.

Jevons continues :—" We have only to trace out carefully the natural laws
of variation of utility as depending upon the quantity of commodity in our
possession, in order to arrive at a satisfactory theory of exchange, of which the
ordinary laws of supply and demand are a necessary consequence. . . . Labour
is found often to determine value, but only in an indirect manner by varying
the degree of utility of the commodity through an increase or limitation of the
supply." As we shall presently see, the latter of these two statements had
been made before in almost the same form, loose and inaccurate as it is, by
Ricardo and Mill; but they would not have accepted the former statement.
For while they regarded the natural laws of variation of utility as too obvious
to require detailed explanation, and while they admitted that cost of production
could have no effect upon exchange value if it could have none upon the
amount which producers brought forward for sale; their doctrines imply that
what is true of supply, is true *mutatis mutandis* of demand, and that the utility
of a commodity could have no effect upon its exchange value if it could have
none on the amount which purchasers took off the market. Let us then turn
to examine the chain of causation in which Jevons' central position is for-
mulated in his Second Edition, and compare it with the position taken up by
Ricardo and Mill. He says (p. 179) :—

" Cost of production determines supply.   Jevons'
Supply determines final degree of utility.   central
Final degree of utility determines value."   position.

Now if this series of causations really existed, there could be no great harm in
omitting the intermediate stages and saying that cost of production determines
value. For if A is the cause of B, which is the cause of C, which is the cause
of D; then A is the cause of D. But in fact there is no such series.

A preliminary objection might be taken to the ambiguity of the terms
" cost of production " and " supply "; which Jevons ought to have avoided,
by the aid of that technical apparatus of semi-mathematical phrases, which was
at his disposal, but not at Ricardo's. A graver objection lies against his third
statement. For the price which the various purchasers in a market will pay
for a thing, is determined not solely by the final degrees of its utility to them,
but by these in conjunction with the amounts of purchasing power severally
at their disposal. The exchange value of a thing is the same all over a market;
but the final degrees of utility to which it corresponds are not equal at any
two parts. Jevons supposed himself to be getting nearer the foundations of
exchange value when in his account of the causes which determine it, he substituted the phrase " final degree of utility," for " the price which consumers
are only just willing to pay,"—the phrase which in the present treatise is con-
densed into " marginal demand price." When for instance describing (Second

---

in governing) value : and as regards this Prof. Ashley appears to concede all that is
claimed here when (p. 480) he takes it as beyond question that Ricardo " regarded the
payment of interest, that is, of something more than the mere replacement of capital,
as a matter of course."

APP. I, 3. Edition, p. 105) the settlement of exchange between "one trading body possessing only corn, and another possessing only beef," he makes his diagram represent "a person" as gaining a "utility" measured along one line and losing a "utility" measured along another. But that is not what really happens; a trading body is not "a person," it gives up things which represent equal purchasing power to all of its members, but very different utilities. It is true that Jevons was himself aware of this; and that his account can be made consistent with the facts of life by a series of interpretations, which in effect substitute "demand-price" and "supply-price" for "utility" and "disutility" : but, when so amended, they lose much of their aggressive force against the older doctrines, and if both are to be held severely to a strictly literal interpretation, then the older method of speaking, though not perfectly accurate, appears to be nearer the truth than that which Jevons and some of his followers have endeavoured to substitute for it.

He sub-
stitutes
a catena
of causes
for mutual
causation.

But the greatest objection of all to his formal statement of his central doctrine is that it does not represent supply price, demand price and amount produced as mutually determining one another (subject to certain other conditions), but as determined one by another in a series. It is as though when three balls A, B, and C rest against one another in a bowl, instead of saying that the position of the three mutually determines one another under the action of gravity, he had said that A determines B, and B determines C. Someone else however with equal justice might say that C determines B and B determines A. And in reply to Jevons a catena rather less untrue than his can be made by inverting his order and saying :—

Utility determines the amount that has to be supplied,
The amount that has to be supplied determines cost of production,
Cost of production determines value,

because it determines the supply price which is required to make the producers keep to their work.

Ricardo's
correct
though
inadequate
treatment
of utility,
took some
account
of the
element
of time.

Let us then turn to Ricardo's doctrine which, though unsystematic and open to many objections, seems to be more philosophic in principle and closer to the actual facts of life. He says, in the letter to Malthus already quoted :— " M. Say has not a correct notion of what is meant by value when he contends that a commodity is valuable in proportion to its utility. This would be true if buyers only regulated the value of commodities; then indeed we might expect that all men would be willing to give a price for things in proportion to the estimation in which they held them; but the fact appears to me to be that the buyers have the least in the world to do in regulating price; it is all done by the competition of the sellers, and, however really willing the buyers might be to give more for iron than for gold, they could not, because the supply would be regulated by cost of production. . . . You say demand and supply regulates value [*sic*]; this I think is saying nothing, and for the reason I have given in the beginning of this letter : it is supply which regulates value, and supply is itself controlled by comparative cost of production. Cost of production, in money, means the value of labour as well as of profits." (See pp. 17–36 of Dr. Bonar's excellent edition of these letters.) And again in his next letter, " I do not dispute either the influence of demand on the price of corn or on the price of all other things : but supply follows close at its heels and soon takes the power of regulating price in his [*sic*] own hands, and in regulating it he is determined by cost of production."

These letters were not indeed published when Jevons wrote, but there are very similar statements in Ricardo's *Principles*. Mill also, when discussing the value of money (Book III. ch. IX. § 3), speaks of " the law of demand and supply which is acknowledged to be applicable to all commodities, and which in the case of money as of most other things, is controlled but not set aside by the law of cost of production, since cost of production would have no effect on

value if it could have none on supply." And again, when summing up his APP. I, 3.
theory of value (Book III. ch. XVI. § 1), he says :—" From this it appears that
demand and supply govern the fluctuations of prices in all cases, and the permanent values of all things of which the supply is determined by any agency
other than that of free competition : but that, under the régime of free competition, things are, on the average, exchanged for each other at such values
and sold for such prices as afford equal expectation of advantage to all classes
of producers; which can only be when things exchange for one another in the
ratio of their cost of production." And, on the next page, speaking of commodities which have a joint cost of production, he says, " since cost of production here fails us we must resort to a law of value anterior to cost of production and more fundamental, the law of demand and supply."

Jevons (p. 215), referring to this last passage, speaks of " the fallacy Jevons'
involved in Mill's idea that he is reverting to *an anterior law of value*, the law position
of supply and demand, the fact being that in introducing the cost of production less
principle, he has never quitted the law of supply and demand at all. The cost different
of production is only one circumstance which governs supply and thus in- appears,
directly influences values."

This criticism seems to contain an important truth; though the wording
of the last part is open to objection. If it had been made in Mill's time he
would probably have accepted it; and would have withdrawn the word
" anterior " as not expressing his real meaning. The " cost of production
principle " and the " final utility " principle are undoubtedly component
parts of the one all-ruling law of supply and demand; each may be compared
to one blade of a pair of scissors. When one blade is held still, and the cutting
is effected by moving the other, we may say with careless brevity that the
cutting is done by the second; but the statement is not one to be made
formally, and defended deliberately.[1]

Perhaps Jevons' antagonism to Ricardo and Mill would have been less if and he
he had not himself fallen into the habit of speaking of relations which really underrated
exist only between demand price and value as though they held between the broad
utility and value; and if he had emphasized as Cournot had done, and as the symmetry
use of mathematical forms might have been expected to lead him to do, that of demand
fundamental symmetry of the general relations in which demand and supply and
stand to value, which coexists with striking differences in the details of those supply.
relations. We must not indeed forget that, at the time at which he wrote,
the demand side of the theory of value had been much neglected; and that
he did excellent service by calling attention to it and developing it. There
are few thinkers whose claims on our gratitude are as high and as various as
those of Jevons : but that must not lead us to accept hastily his criticisms
on his great predecessors.[2]

It seemed right to select Jevons' attack for reply, because, in England at

---

[1] See V. III. 7.

[2] See an article on Jevons' *Theory* by the present writer in the *Academy* for April
1, 1872. The edition of his *Theory* brought out by his son in 1911, contains an Appendix on his account of interest, with special reference to that article (see also above
VI. I. 8). He contends that his father's theory is " true as far as it goes " though he
" followed the unfortunate practice of the Ricardian school by abstracting for treatment certain ideas, and assuming that his readers are familiar with their relations and
taking his point of view." The son may be accepted as the true interpreter of the
father : and the debts of economics to the father are no doubt as great as to be comparable with its transcendent obligations to Ricardo. But Jevons' *Theory* had a
combative side, as well as a constructive. In great part it was an attack on what he
called in his Preface, " that able but wrong-headed man, David Ricardo " who
" shunted the car of Economic science on to a wrong line." His criticisms on Ricardo
achieved some apparently unfair dialectical triumphs, by assuming that Ricardo
thought of value as governed by cost of production without reference to demand.
This misconception of Ricardo was doing great harm in 1872 : and it seemed necessary
to show that Jevons' Theory of Interest, if interpreted as he interpreted Ricardo, is
untenable.

APP. I, 3.

Other
critics

have
imitated
Ricardo's
careless-
ness in
exposition
as to the
element of
time, and
have failed
to subvert
his central
doctrine.

all events, it has attracted more attention than any other. But somewhat similar attacks on Ricardo's theory of value had been made by many other writers. Among them may specially be mentioned Mr. Macleod, whose writings before 1870 anticipated much both of the form and substance of recent criticisms on the classical doctrines of value in relation to cost, by Profs. Walras and Carl Menger, who were contemporary with Jevons, and Profs. v. Böhm-Bawerk and Wieser, who were later.

The carelessness of Ricardo with regard to the element of Time has been imitated by his critics, and has thus been a source of twofold misunderstanding. For they attempt to disprove doctrines as to the ultimate tendencies, the causes of causes, the *causæ causantes*, of the relations between cost of production and value, by means of arguments based on the causes of temporary changes, and short-period fluctuations of value. Doubtless nearly everything they say when expressing their own opinions is true in the sense in which they mean it; some of it is new and much of it is improved in form. But they do not appear to make any progress towards establishing their claim to have discovered a new doctrine of value which is in sharp contrast to the old; or which calls for any considerable demolition, as distinguished from development and extension of the old doctrine.

Ricardo's first chapter has been discussed here with sole reference to the causes which govern the relative exchange values of different things; because its chief influence on subsequent thought has been in this direction. But it was originally associated with a controversy as to the extent to which the price of labour affords a good standard for measuring the general purchasing power of money. In this connection its interest is mainly historical: but reference may be made to an illuminating article on it by Prof. Hollander in the *Quarterly Journal of Economics*, 1904.

APPENDIX J[1]

THE DOCTRINE OF THE WAGES-FUND

§ 1. At the beginning of last century, great as was the poverty of the English people, the peoples of the Continent were poorer still. In most of them population was sparse, and therefore food was cheap; but for all that they were underfed, and could not provide themselves with the sinews of war. France, after her first victories, helped herself along by the forced contributions of others. But the countries of Central Europe could not support their own armies without England's aid. Even America, with all her energy and national resources, was not rich; she could not have subsidized Continental armies. The economists looked for the explanation; and they found it chiefly in England's accumulated capital, which, though small when judged by our present standard, was very much greater than that of any other country. Other nations were envious of England, and wanted to follow in her steps; but they were unable to do so, partly indeed for other reasons, but chiefly because they had not capital enough. Their annual income was required for immediate consumption. There was not in them a large class of people who had a good store of wealth set by, which they did not need to consume at once, and which they could devote to making machines and other things that would aid labour, and would enable it to produce a larger store of things for future consumption. A special tone was given to their arguments by the scarcity of capital everywhere, even in England; by the growing dependence of labour on the aid of machinery; and lastly, by the folly of some followers of Rousseau, who were telling the working classes that they would be better off without any capital at all.

In consequence, the economists gave extreme prominence to the statements; first, that labour requires the support of capital, *i.e.* of good clothes, etc., that have been already produced; and secondly, that labour requires the aid of capital in the form of factories, stores of raw material, etc. Of course the workman might have supplied his own capital, but in fact he seldom had more than a little store of clothes and furniture, and perhaps a few simple tools of his own—he was dependent for everything else on the savings of others. The labourer received clothes ready to wear, bread ready to eat, or the money with which he could purchase them. The capitalist received a spinning of wool into yarn, a weaving of yarn into cloth, or a ploughing of land, and only in a few cases commodities ready for use, coats ready to be worn, or bread ready to be eaten. There are, no doubt, important exceptions, but the ordinary bargain between employers and employed is that the latter receives things ready for immediate use and the former receives help towards making things that will be of use hereafter. These facts the economists expressed by saying that all labour requires the support of capital, whether owned by the labourer or by someone else; and that when anyone works for hire, his wages are, as a rule, advanced to him out of his employer's capital—advanced, that is, without waiting till the things which he is engaged in making are ready for use. These simple statements have been a good deal criticized, but they have never been denied by anyone who has taken them in the sense in which they were meant.

The older economists, however, went on to say that the amount of wages

APP. J, 1.
Early in last century special causes emphasized the dependence on the aid of capital,

[1] See above, p. 452.

678 THE DOCTRINE OF THE WAGES-FUND

APP. J, 2.

but this dependence was exaggerated by some careless expressions.

was limited by the amount of capital, and this statement cannot be defended; at best it is but a slovenly way of talking. It has suggested to some people the notion that the total amount of wages that could be paid in a country in the course of, say a year, was a fixed sum. If by the threat of a strike, or in any other way, one body of workmen got an increase of wages, they would be told that in consequence other bodies of workmen must lose an amount exactly equal in the aggregate to what they had gained. Those who have said this have perhaps thought of agricultural produce, which has but one harvest in the year. If all the wheat raised at one harvest is sure to be eaten before the next, and if none can be imported, then it is true that if anyone's share of the wheat is increased, there will be just so much less for others to have. But this does not justify the statement that the amount of wages payable in a country is fixed by the capital in it, a doctrine which has been called "the vulgar form of the Wages-fund theory." [1]

Mill attempted to discuss wages before he had reached the theory of value.

§ 2. It has already been noticed (Book I. ch. IV. § 7) that Mill in his later years under the combined influence of Comte, of the Socialists, and of the general tendencies of public sentiment, set himself to bring into prominence the human, as opposed to the mechanical, element in economics. He desired to call attention to the influences which are exerted on human conduct by custom and usage, by the ever-shifting arrangements of society, and by the constant changes in human nature; the pliability of which he agreed with Comte in thinking that the earlier economists had underrated. It was this desire which gave the chief impulse to his economic work in the latter half of his life, as distinguished from that in which he wrote his *Essays on Unsettled Questions*; and which induced him to separate distribution from exchange, and to argue that the laws of distribution are dependent on "particular human institutions," and liable to be perpetually modified as man's habits of feeling, and thought, and action pass from one phase to another. He thus contrasted the laws of distribution with those of production, which he regarded as resting on the immutable basis of physical nature; and again with the laws of exchange, to which he attributed something very much like the universality of mathematics. It is true that he sometimes spoke as though economic science consisted chiefly of discussions of the production and distribution of wealth, and thus seemed to imply that he regarded the theory of exchange as a part of the theory of distribution. But yet he kept the two separate from one another; he treated of distribution in his second and fourth Books, and gave his third Book to the "Machinery of Exchange" (compare his *Principles of Political Economy*, Book II. ch. 1. § 1 and ch. XVI. § 6).

He was thus drawn on to an incomplete statement; and the correction of it in his fourth Book has not been generally noticed;

In doing this he allowed his zeal for giving a more human tone to economics to get the better of his judgment, and to hurry him on to work with an incomplete analysis. For, by putting his main theory of wages before his account of supply and demand, he cut himself off from all chance of treating that theory in a satisfactory way; and in fact he was led on to say (*Principles*, Book II. ch. XI. § 1), that "Wages depend mainly upon . . . the proportion between population and capital"; or rather, as he explains later on, between "the number of the labouring class . . . who work for hire," and "the aggregate of what may be called the Wages-fund which consists of that part of circulating capital . . . which is expended in the direct hire of labour."

The fact is that the theories of Distribution and Exchange are so intimately connected as to be little more than two sides of the same problem; that in each of them there is an element of "mechanical" precision and universality, and that in each of them there is an element, dependent on "particular human institutions," which has varied, and which probably will vary, from place to

---

[1] These three paragraphs are reproduced from a paper written for the *Co-operative Annual*, and reprinted in the *Report of the Industrial Remuneration Conference*, 1885, which contained the outlines of the central argument of the first two chapters of Book VI.

place and from age to age. And if Mill had recognized this great truth, he APP. J, 3.
would not have been drawn on to appear to substitute, as he did in his second
Book, the statement of the problem of wages for its solution : but would have
combined the description and analysis in his second Book, with the short but
profound study of the causes that govern the distribution of the national
dividend, given in his fourth Book; and the progress of economics would have
been much hastened.

As it was, when his friend Thornton, following in the wake of Longe, Cliffe partly
Leslie, Jevons and others, convinced him that the phrases in his second Book because he
were untenable, he yielded too much; and overstated the extent of his own took a less
past error and of the concessions which he was bound to make to his assailants. scientific position
He said (*Dissertations*, Vol. IV. p. 46) : " There is no law of nature making it in his
inherently impossible for wages to rise to the point of absorbing not only the answers to
funds which he (the employer) had intended to devote to carrying on his busi- Thornton.
ness, but the whole of what he allows for his private expenses beyond the
necessaries of life. The real limit to the rise is the practical consideration how
much would ruin him, or drive him to abandon the business, not the inexorable
limits of the Wages-fund." He did not make it clear whether this statement
refers to immediate or ultimate effects, to short periods or long : but in either
case it appears untenable.

As regards long periods the limit is put too high : for wages could not rise The
permanently so as to absorb nearly as large a share of the national dividend bearing of
as is here indicated. And for short periods, it is not put high enough : for a the theory
well-organized strike at a critical juncture may force from the employer for a of wages on the
short time more than the whole value of his output, after paying for raw issue of
material during that time; and thus make his gross profits for the time a particular
negative quantity. And indeed the theory of wages whether in its older or trade
newer form has no direct bearing on the issue of any particular struggle in the conflicts
labour market : that depends on the relative strength of the competing parties. is indirect
But it has much bearing on the general policy of the relation of capital to and remote.
labour; for it indicates what policies do, and what do not, carry in themselves
the seeds of their ultimate defeat; what policies can be maintained, aided by
suitable organizations; and what policies will ultimately render either side
weak, however well organized.

After a while Cairnes, in his *Leading Principles*, endeavoured to resuscitate Cairnes
the Wages-fund theory by expounding it in a form, which he thought would explained
evade the attacks that had been made on it. But, though in the greater part away the
of his exposition, he succeeded in avoiding the old pitfalls, he did so only by crudities of the
explaining away so much which is characteristic of the doctrine, that there is wages-fund
very little left in it to justify its title. He states however (p. 203) that " the doctrine in
rates of wage, other things being equal, varies inversely with the supply of its extreme
labour." His argument is valid in regard to the immediate result of a *sudden* forms;
great increase in the supply of labour. But in the ordinary course of the
growth of population there results simultaneously, not only some increase in
the supply of capital, but also greater subdivision of labour, and more efficiency.
His use of the term " varies inversely" is misleading. He should have said
" varies for the time at least in the opposite direction." He goes on to derive but his
an " unexpected consequence," that an increase in the supply of labour, when position is
it is of a kind to be used in conjunction with fixed capital and raw material, not clear.
would cause the Wages-fund to undergo " diminution as the number who are
to share it is increased." But that result would follow only if the aggregate
of wages were not influenced by the aggregate of production; and in fact this
last cause is the most powerful of all those which influence wages.

§ 3. It may be noticed that the extreme forms of the Wages-fund theory The wages-
represent wages as governed entirely by demand; though the demand is fund
represented crudely as dependent on the stock of capital But some popular doctrine
expositors of economics appear to have held at the same time both this doctrine relates

APP. J, 3.
———
only to the
demand
side of the
question.

It was
applied in
support of
some
important
truths,

but they
can be
defended
without it

Symmetry
of some
of the
relations
between
capital and
labour.

The re-
sources of
individual
employers
are
returned
to them
through
sales to
customers.

But in a
broad view
all are
consumers;
and to say
that the
resources
of pro-

and the iron law of wages, which represents wages as governed rigidly by the cost of rearing human beings. They might of course have softened each of them and then worked the two into a more or less harmonious whole; as Cairnes did later. But it does not appear that they did so.

The proposition that *Industry is limited by capital*, was often interpreted so as to make it practically convertible with the Wages-fund theory. It can be explained so as to be true : but a similar explanation would make the statement that " capital is limited by industry " equally true. It was however used by Mill chiefly in connection with the argument that the aggregate employment of labour cannot generally be increased by preventing people, by protective duties or in other ways, from satisfying their wants in that manner which they would prefer. The effects of protective duties are very complex and cannot be discussed here ; but Mill is clearly right in saying that in general the capital, that is applied to support and aid labour in any new industry created by such duties, " must have been withdrawn or withheld from some other, in which it gave, or would have given, employment to probably about the same quantity of labour which it employs in its new occupation." Or, to put the argument in a more modern form, such legislation does not *primâ facie* increase either the national dividend or the share of that dividend which goes to labour. For it does not increase the supply of capital ; nor does it, in any other way, cause the marginal efficiency of labour to rise relatively to that of capital. The rate that has to be paid for the use of capital is therefore not lowered ; the national dividend is not increased (in fact it is almost sure to be diminished) ; and as neither labour nor capital gets any new advantage over the other in bargaining for the distribution of the dividend, neither can benefit by such legislation.

This doctrine may be inverted ; so as to assert that the labour required to give effect to capital in a new industry created by protective duties must have been withdrawn or withheld from some other, in which it gave, or would have given, effect to probably about the same quantity of capital as in his new occupation. But this statement though equally true would not appeal with equal force to the minds of ordinary people. For as the buyer of goods is commonly regarded as conferring a special benefit on the seller, though in fact the services which buyers and sellers render to one another are in the long run co-ordinate ; so the employer is commonly regarded as conferring a special benefit on the worker, whose labour he buys, though in the long run the services which the employers and employees render to one another are co-ordinate. The causes and consequences of this pair of facts will occupy us much at later stages of our inquiry.

Some German economists have argued that the resources with which the employer pays wages come from consumers. But this appears to involve a misapprehension. It might be true of an individual employer if the consumer paid him in advance for what he produced : but in fact the rule goes the other way ; the consumer's payments are more often in arrear, and merely give deferred command over ready commodities in return for ready commodities. It may be admitted that if the producer could not sell his goods he might not be able for the time to hire labour ; but that would only mean that the organization of production was partially out of gear : a machine may stop if one of its connecting rods gets out of order, but that does not mean that the driving force of the machine is to be found in the rod.

Nor again is the amount which the employer pays as wages at any time governed by the price which consumers *do* pay him for his wares ; though it generally is largely influenced by his expectations of the price they *will* pay him. It is indeed true that in the long run and under normal conditions, the prices which consumers do pay him and those which they will pay him are practically the same. But when we pass from the particular payments of an individual employer to the normal payments of employers generally—and it is really only with these latter that we are now concerned—consumers cease to form a separate class, for every one is a consumer. The national dividend goes exclusively to consumers in the broad sense in which wool or a printing press is said to go into consumption when it is transferred from the warehouse or engineering works in which it has rested, to a woollen manufacturer or a printer, and these consumers are also the producers, that is, the owners of the agents of production, labour, capital and land. Children and others who are supported by them, and the Government which levies taxes on them,[1] do but expend part of their incomes for them. To say therefore that the resources of employers generally are ultimately drawn from those of consumers generally, is undoubtedly true. But it is only another way of saying that all resources have been parts of the national dividend, which have been directed into forms suitable for deferred, instead of immediate use ; and if any of them are now applied to any other purpose than immediate consumption, it is in the expectation that their place will be taken (with increment or profit) by the incoming flow of the national dividend.[2]

[margin: APP. J, 4. —— ducers come from consumers is but to say that they come from the national dividend.]

The first Fundamental Proposition of Mill's is closely connected with his fourth, viz. that *Demand for commodities is not demand for labour* : and this again expresses his meaning badly. It is true that those who purchase any particular commodities do not generally supply the capital that is required to aid and support the labour which produces those commodities : they merely divert capital and employment from other trades to that for the products of which they make increased demand. But Mill, not contented with proving this, seems to imply that to spend money on the direct hire of labour is more beneficial to the labourer than to spend it on buying commodities. Now there is a sense in which this contains a little truth. For the price of the commodities includes profits of manufacturer and middleman ; and if the purchaser acts as employer, he slightly diminishes the demand for the services of the employing class, and increases the demand for labour as he might have done by buying, say, hand-made lace instead of machine-made lace. But this argument assumes that the wages of labour will be paid, as in practice they commonly are, while the work is proceeding ; and that the price of the commodities will be paid, as in practice it commonly is, after the commodities are made : and it will be found that in every case which Mill has chosen to illustrate the doctrine, his arguments imply, though he does not seem to be aware of it, that the consumer when passing from purchasing commodities to hiring labour, postpones the date of his own consumption of the fruits of labour. And the same postponement would have resulted in the same benefit to labour if the purchaser had made no change in the mode of his expenditure.[3]

[margin: Demand for commodities is generally demand for labour.]

§ 4. Throughout the whole discussion of the national dividend the relations in which the kitchen apparatus of a hotel and those of a private house stand to the employment of cooks have been implicitly treated as on a like footing. That is to say the capital has been regarded broadly : it has not been limited to mere " trade capital."[1] But a little more may be said on this subject.

It is indeed often thought that, though those workers who have little or no accumulated wealth of their own, have much to gain by an increase of the capital in that narrower sense of the term in which it is nearly convertible

[margin: The benefits which wage-earners derive from the increase of wealth]

<hr>

[1] Unless indeed we reckon the security and other benefits which Government provides as separate items of the national income.

[2] Considerable light has been thrown on the subject of the Wages-fund by Walker's writings, and the controversies connected with them. The instances which he has collected of employees rendering their services in advance of payment bear effectively on some turns of the controversy, but not on its main issue. Cannan's *Production and Distribution*, 1776–1848, contains much acute, if sometimes too severe, criticism of the earlier wage theories. A more conservative attitude is taken in Taussig's weighty *Capital and Wages* ; to which the English reader may be specially referred for a fuller account and criticism of the German doctrines mentioned in the text.

[3] See the Appendix to Book IV. of Newcomb's *Political Economy*.

APP. J, 4.

not owned
by them
and not in
the form
of trade
capital.

with trade capital that supports and aids them in their work; yet they have little to gain from an increase of other forms of wealth not in their own hands. No doubt there are a few kinds of wealth the existence of which scarcely affects the working classes; while they are directly affected by almost every increase of (trade) capital. For the greater part of it passes through their hands as implements or materials of their work; while a considerable part is directly used or even consumed by them.[1] It seems therefore that the working classes must necessarily gain when other forms of wealth become trade capital and *vice versâ*. But it is not so. If private people generally gave up keeping carriages and yachts, and hired them out from capitalist undertakers, there would result a smaller demand for hired labour. For part of what would have been paid as wages would go as profits to a middleman.[2]

It may be objected that if other forms of wealth take the place of trade capital on a large scale, there may be a scarcity of the things needed to aid labour in its work and even of those needed to support it. This may be a real danger in some Oriental countries. But in the western world, and especially in England, the total stock of capital is equal in value to the aggregate of the commodities consumed by the working classes during many years : and a very small increase in the demand for those forms of capital that minister directly to labour's needs, relatively to other forms, would quickly bring forward an increased supply of them, either imported from some other part of the world, or specially produced to meet the new demand. There is therefore no necessity to trouble ourselves much on this score. If the marginal efficiency of labour is kept high, its net product will be high; and so will therefore its earnings : and the constantly flowing stream of the national dividend will divide itself up in corresponding proportions, giving always an adequate supply of commodities for immediate consumption by the workers, and assigning to the production of those commodities an adequate stock of implements. When the general conditions of demand and supply have decided what part of the national dividend the other classes of society are free to spend as they will; and when the inclinations of those classes have decided the mode in which they will distribute their expenditure between present and deferred gratifications, etc., it matters not to the working classes whether orchids come from the private conservatories, or from the glass houses which belong to professional florists, and which are therefore trade capital.

---

[1] At all events according to most definitions. There are some indeed who confine capital to "intermediate goods," and must therefore exclude hotels, and lodging-houses, and workmen's cottages, at all events as soon as they are used. But grave objections to the adoption of this definition have already been indicated in Appendix E, 4.

[2] See above, p. 647. Again, an increased use of brass furniture that needs much cleaning, and generally of modes of living that require the assistance of many indoor and outdoor servants, operates on the demand for labour in the same way as the use of hand-made goods in place of goods made by expensive machinery and other fixed capital. It may be true that the employment of a great number of domestic servants is an ignoble and wasteful use of a large income : but there is no other equally selfish method of spending it which tends so directly to increase the share of the national dividend which goes to the working classes.

APPENDIX K

CERTAIN KINDS OF SURPLUS

§ 1. We have next to make some study of the relations in which different kinds of surplus stand to one another, and to the national income. The study is difficult, and it has little practical bearing; but it has some attractions from the academic point of view.

While the national income or dividend is completely absorbed in remunerating the owner of each agent of production at its marginal rate, it yet generally yields him a surplus which has two distinct, though not independent sides. It yields to him, as consumer, a surplus consisting of the excess of the total utility to him of the commodity over the real value to him of what he paid for it. For his marginal purchases, those which he is only just induced to buy, the two are equal : but those parts of his purchases for which he would gladly have paid a higher price rather than go without them, yield him a surplus of satisfaction : a true net benefit which he, as consumer, derives from the facilities offered to him by his surroundings or conjuncture. He would lose this surplus, if his surroundings were so altered as to prevent him from obtaining any supplies of that commodity, and to compel him to divert the means which he spends on that to other commodities (one of which might be increased leisure) of which at present he does not care to have further supplies at their respective prices.

Another side of the surplus which a man derives from his surroundings is better seen when he is regarded as producer, whether by direct labour, or by the accumulated, that is acquired and saved, material resources in his possession. As a worker, he derives a *worker's surplus*, through being remunerated for all his work at the same rate as for that last part, which he is only just willing to render for its reward ; though much of the work may have given him positive pleasure. As capitalist (or generally as owner of accumulated wealth in any form) he derives a *saver's surplus* through being remunerated for all his saving, that is waiting, at the same rate as for that part which he is only just induced to undergo by the reward to be got for it. And he generally is remunerated at that rate even though he would still have made some savings if he had been compelled to pay for their safe keeping, and had reaped a negative interest from them.[1]

These two sets of surpluses are not independent : and it would be easy to reckon them up so as to count the same thing twice. For when we have reckoned the producer's surplus at the value of the general purchasing power which he derives from his labour or saving, we have reckoned implicitly his consumer's surplus too, provided his character and the circumstances of his environment are given. This difficulty might be avoided analytically; but in no case would it be practically possible to estimate and add up the two series. The consumer's surplus, the worker's surplus, and the saver's surplus, which anyone is capable of deriving from his surroundings, depend on his individual character. They depend in part on his general sensibility to the satisfactions and dissatisfactions of consumption and of working and waiting severally ; and in part also on the elasticity of his sensibilities, that is, on the

---

[1] This point was emphasized by Gossen and Jevons. See also Clark's *Surplus Gains of Labour.*

Marginal notes: The nation's income is completely distributed ; but yet everyone gets a surplus of satisfaction as consumer over the worth to him of his payments, and other surpluses accrue generally to workers, and to savers,

rates at which they change with an increase of consumption, of work and of waiting respectively. Consumer's surplus has relation in the first instance to individual commodities, and each part of it responds directly to changes in the conjuncture affecting the terms on which that commodity is to be had : while the two kinds of producer's surplus appear always in terms of the general return that the conjuncture gives to a certain amount of purchasing power. The two kinds of producer's surplus are independent and cumulative, and they stand out distinct from one another in the case of a man working and saving things for his own use. The intimate connection between both of them and consumer's surplus is shown by the fact that, in estimating the weal and woe in the life of a Robinson Crusoe, it would be simplest to reckon his producer's surpluses on such a plan as to include the whole of his consumer's surplus.

A great part of a worker's earnings are of the nature of a deferred return to the trouble and expense of preparing him for his work; and there is therefore a great difficulty in estimating his surplus. Nearly all his work may be pleasurable; and he may be earning a good wage for the whole of it : but in reckoning up the balance of human weal and endurance we must set off against this much effort and sacrifice endured by his parents and by himself in past time : but we cannot say clearly how much. In a few lives there may be a balance of evil : but there is reason to think that there is a balance of good in most lives, and a large balance in some. The problem is as much philosophical as economic; it is complicated by the fact that man's activities are ends in themselves as well as means of production, and also by the difficulty of dividing clearly the immediate and direct (or prime) cost of human effort from its total cost; and it must be left imperfectly solved.[1]

§ 2. The case is in some respects simpler when we pass to consider the earnings of material appliances for production. The work and the waiting by which they have been provided, yield their own worker's and waiter's surplus just mentioned, and in addition a surplus (or quasi-rent) of the excess of total money returns over direct outlay ; provided we confine our attention to short periods only. But for long periods, that is, in all the more important problems of economic science, and especially in the problems discussed in this chapter, there is no distinction between immediate outlay and total outlay. And in the long run the earnings of each agent are, as a rule, sufficient only to recompense at their marginal rates the sum total of the efforts and sacrifices required to produce them. If less than these marginal rates had been forthcoming the supplies would have been diminished; and on the whole therefore there is in general no extra surplus in this direction.

This last statement applies in a sense to land which has been but recently taken up; and possibly it might apply to much land in old countries, if we could trace its records back to their earliest origins. But the attempt would raise controversial questions in history and ethics, as well as in economics; and the aims of our present inquiry are prospective rather than retrospective. Looking forward rather than backward, and not concerning ourselves with the equity and the proper limits of the present private property in land, we see that that part of the national dividend which goes as earnings of land is a surplus in a sense in which the earnings from other agents are not a surplus.

To state from the point of view of this chapter a doctrine which has been discussed at length in V. VIII.-XI. :—All appliances of production, whether machinery, or factories with the land on which they are built, or farms, are alike in yielding large surpluses over the prime costs of particular acts of production to a man who owns and works them : also in yielding him normally no special surplus in the long run above what is required to remunerate him for his trouble and sacrifice and outlay in purchasing and working them (no special surplus, as contrasted with his general worker's and waiter's surplus). But there is this difference between land and other agents of production, that

[1] See VI. v.

from a social point of view land yields a permanent surplus, while perishable
things made by man do not. The more nearly it is true that the earnings of
any agent of production are required to keep up the supply of it, the more
closely will its supply so vary that the share which it is able to draw from the
national dividend conforms to the cost of maintaining the supply : and in an
old country land stands in an exceptional position, because its earnings are
not affected by this cause. The difference between land and other durable
agents is however mainly one of degree : and a great part of the interest of the
study of the rent of land arises from the illustrations which it affords of a great
principle that permeates every part of economics.

RICARDO'S DOCTRINE AS TO TAXES AND IMPROVEMENTS IN AGRICULTURE

APP. L.
———
Malthus
ustly com-
plains of
Ricardo's
nconsis-
istency
n paying
nore at-
ention to
proximate
han
ltimate
esults as
egards
ent and
mprove-
nents in
agri-
ulture.
Much has already been said about the excellence of Ricardo's thought and the imperfections of his expression of it, and in particular notice has been taken of the causes which led him to lay down the law of diminishing return without proper qualifications. Similar remarks apply to his treatment of the influence of improvements and the incidence of taxes in agriculture. He was especially careless in his criticisms of Adam Smith; and as Malthus justly said (Summary of Section x. of his *Political Economy*), " Mr. Ricardo, who generally looks to permanent and final results, has always pursued an opposite policy in reference to the rents of land. It is only by looking to temporary results, that he could object to Adam Smith's statement, that the cultivation of rice or of potatoes would yield higher rent than corn."[1] And Malthus was perhaps not far wrong when he added :—" Practically, there is reason to believe that, as a change from corn to rice must be gradual, not even a temporary fall of rent would take place."[1]

Nevertheless, in Ricardo's time it was of great practical importance to insist, and it is of much scientific interest even now to know, that in a country which cannot import much corn, it is very easy so to adjust taxes on cultivation and so to hinder improvements as to enrich the landlords for a time and to impoverish the rest of the people. No doubt when the people had been thinned by want, the landlords would suffer in pocket : but that fact took little of the force from Ricardo's contention that the enormous rise of agricultural prices and rents which occurred during his life was an indication of an injury to the nation beyond all comparison greater than the benefits received by the landlords. But let us now pass in review some of those arguments in which Ricardo delighted to start from sharply defined assumptions, so as to get clear net results, which would strike the attention; and which the reader might combine for himself so as to make them applicable to the actual facts of life.

Let us first suppose that the " Corn " raised in a country is absolutely necessary; *i.e.* that the demand for it has no elasticity, and that any change in its marginal cost of production would affect only the price that people paid for it, and not the amount of it consumed. And let us suppose that no Corn is ut let
s follow
Licardo
nd as-
ame the
emand
or Corn
o be
xed;
nen a
ax on it
ould not
ffect
ents. imported. Then the effect of a tax of one-tenth on Corn would be to cause its real value to rise till nine-tenths as much as before would suffice to remunerate the marginal dose, and therefore every dose. The gross Corn surplus on every piece of land would therefore remain the same as before; but one-tenth being taken away as a tax, the remainder would be nine-tenths of the old Corn surplus. Since, however, each part of it would have risen in real value in the ratio of ten to nine, the real surplus would remain unchanged.

But the assumption that the demand for produce is absolutely inelastic is a very violent one. The rise in price would in fact be sure to cause an immediate falling-off in the demand for some kinds of produce, if not for the staple cereals : and therefore the value of Corn, *i.e.* produce in general, would never rise in full proportion to the tax, and less capital and labour would be applied

[1] Compare VI. ix. 4.

in the cultivation of all lands. There would thus be a diminution in the
Corn surplus from all lands, but not in the same proportion from all; and
since a tenth of the Corn surplus would be taken by the tax, while the value
of each part of it would have risen in less than the ratio of ten to nine, there
would be a double fall in the real surplus. (The diagrams on page 132 suggest
at once translations of those reasonings into the language of geometry.)

The immediate fall would be very great under modern conditions in which
free importation of Corn prevents its real value from being much raised by
the tax; and the same result would follow gradually, even in the absence of
importation, if the rise in its real value diminished the numbers of the people;
or, what is at least as probable, if it had the effect of lowering the standard of
living, and the efficiency of the working population. These two effects would
operate very much in the same way on the producer's surplus; both would
make labour dear to the employer, while the latter would also make real
time wages low to the worker.

Ricardo's reasonings on all these questions are rather difficult to follow :
because he often gives no hint when he ceases to deal with results which are
" immediate," and belong to a " short period " relatively to the growth of
population; and passes to those which are " ultimate," and belong to a
" long period " in which the labour value of raw produce would have time
materially to affect the numbers of the people and therefore the demand for
raw produce. When such interpreting clauses are supplied, very few of his
reasonings will be found invalid.

We may now pass to his argument with regard to the influence of improvements in the arts of agriculture, which he divides into two classes. A special
scientific interest attaches to his treatment of the first, which consists of those
improvements that " I can obtain the same produce with less capital, and
without disturbing the difference between the productive powers of the
successive portions of capital "; [1] of course neglecting for the purpose of his
general argument the fact that any given improvement may be of greater
service to one particular piece of land than another. (See above, Book IV.
ch. III. § 4.) Assuming as before that the demand for Corn has no elasticity,
he proved that capital would be withdrawn from the poorer lands (and from
the more intensive cultivation of the richer lands), and therefore the surplus
measured in Corn, the Corn surplus—as we may say—obtained by applications
of capital under the most favourable circumstances, will be a surplus relatively
to lands not so poor as those which were on the margin of cultivation before;
and the differential productiveness of any two applications of capital remaining,
by hypothesis, unchanged, the Corn surplus must necessarily fall, and of course
the real value and the labour value of the surplus will fall much more than in
proportion.

On the same assumption improvements which increase the return to each dose of capital by equal amounts will cause a double fall of real rents.

This may be made clear by the adjoining figure; in which curve AC
represents the return which the land of the whole
country, regarded as one farm, makes to doses of capital
and labour applied to it, these doses being arranged
not in the order of their application, but in that of
their productiveness. In equilibrium OD doses are
applied, the price of the Corn being such that a return
DC is just sufficient to remunerate a dose; the whole
amount of Corn raised being represented by the area
AODC, of which AHC represents the aggregate Corn
surplus. [We may pause to notice that the only change
in the interpretation of this diagram which is required by our making it refer to

Fig. 40.

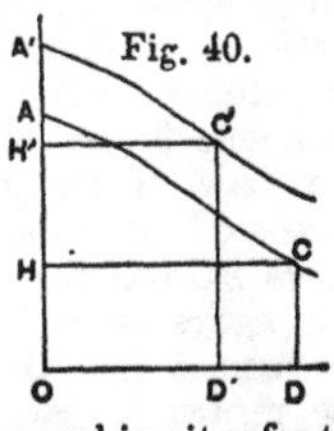

[1] Ch. II. *Collected Works*, p. 42. Comp. Cannan's *Production and Distribution,
1776–1848*, pp. 325–6. Ricardo's distinction between his two classes of improvements is not altogether happy, and need not be considered here.

the whole country instead of a single farm, arises from our not being able now, as we could then, to suppose that all the several doses of capital are applied in the same neighbourhood, and that therefore the values of equal portions (of the same kind) of produce are equal. We may however get over this difficulty by reckoning the expenses of transporting the produce to a common market as part of its expenses of production; a certain part of every dose of capital and labour being assigned to the expenses of transport.]

Now an improvement of Ricardo's first class will increase the return to the dose applied under the most favourable conditions from OA to OA', and the returns to other doses, not in like *proportion*, but by equal *amounts*. The result is that the new produce curve $A'C'$ will be a repetition of the old produce curve AC, but raised higher than it by the distance AA'. If, therefore, there were an unlimited demand for corn, so that the old number of doses, OD, could be profitably applied, the aggregate Corn surplus would remain the same as before the change. But in fact such an immediate increase of production could not be profitable; and therefore an improvement of this kind must necessarily lessen the aggregate Corn surplus. And on the assumption made here by Ricardo that the aggregate produce is not increased at all, only OD' doses will be applied, OD' being determined by the condition that $A'OD'C'$ is equal to $AODC$; and the aggregate Corn surplus will shrink down to $A'H'C'$. This result is independent of the shape of AC; and, which is the same thing, of the particular figures selected for the numerical illustration which Ricardo used in proof of his argument.

Mill sub-
stituted
equal pro-
portions
for equal
amounts,
and then
tried to
establish
the same
result,
but in-
correctly.And here we may take the occasion to remark that numerical instances can as a rule be safely used only as illustrations and not as proofs: for it is generally more difficult to know whether the result has been implicitly assumed in the numbers shown for the special case than it is to determine independently whether the result is true or not. Ricardo himself had no mathematical training. But his instincts were unique; and very few trained mathematicians could tread as safely as he over the most perilous courses of reasoning. Even the acute logical mind of Mill was unequal to the task.

Mill characteristically observed that it is much more probable that an improvement would increase the returns to capital applied to different classes of land in equal proportions than by equal amounts. (See his second case, *Political Economy*, Book IV. ch. III. § 4.) He did not notice that by so doing he cut away the basis of Ricardo's sharply defined argument, which was that the change did not alter the differential advantages of different applications of capital. And though he arrived at the same result as Ricardo, it was only because his result was implicitly contained in the numbers he chose for his illustration.

The adjoining figure tends to show that there is a class of economic problems which cannot be safely treated by anyone of less genius than Ricardo without the aid of some apparatus, either of mathematics or of diagrams, that present as a continuous whole the schedules of economic forces, whether with regard to the Law of Diminishing Return or to those of Demand and Supply. The curve AC has the same interpretation in this figure as in the last; but the improvement has the effect of increasing the return to each dose of capital and labour by one-third, *i.e.* in an equal proportion and not by an equal amount: and the new produce curve $A'C'$ stands much higher above AC at its left end

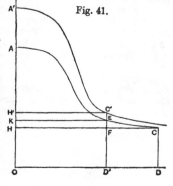

Fig. 41.

APP. L.

than at its right. Cultivation is restricted to OD' doses, where the area
$A'GD'C'$, representing the new aggregate product, is as before equal to $AODC$;
and $A'H'C'$ is as before the new aggregate Corn surplus.   Now it can be easily
proved that $A'H'C'$ is four-thirds of AKE, and whether this is greater or less
than AHC depends upon the particular shape assigned to AC.   If AC be a
straight line or nearly a straight line (both Mill's and Ricardo's numbers represented points on a straight Produce line) $A'H'C'$ would be less than AHC;
but with the shape assigned to AC in our figure $A'H'C'$ is greater than AHC.
And thus Mill's argument is, while Ricardo's is not, dependent for its conclusion on the particular shape assumed by them for the gross produce curve.

(Mill assumes that the cultivated part of a country consists of three
quantities of land, yielding at an equal expense 60, 80, and 100 bushels; and
he then shows that an improvement which increased the return to each dose
of capital by one-third, would lower corn rents in the ratio of 60 to 26⅔.   But
if he had taken the distribution of fertility in a country to be such that the
land consisted of three qualities yielding at an equal expense 60, 65, and 115
bushels, as is done roughly in our figure, he would have found in that case the
improvement would raise corn rents in the ratio 60 to 66⅔.)

Finally it may be noticed that Ricardo's paradox as to the possible effects
of improvements on the rent of land is applicable to urban as well as agricultural
land.   For instance, the American plan of building stores sixteen stories high
with steel frames, and served with elevators, may be supposed suddenly to
become very efficient, economical and convenient in consequence of improvements in the arts of building, lighting, ventilation and the making of elevators.
In that case the trading part of each town would occupy a less area than now;
a good deal of land would have to revert to less remunerative uses; and the
net result might possibly be a fall in the aggregate site values of the town.

Ricardo's paradox applies to urban land.

MATHEMATICAL APPENDIX

NOTE I. (p. 79). The law of diminution of marginal utility may be expressed thus :—If u be the total utility of an amount x of a commodity to a given person at a given time, then marginal utility is measured by $\frac{du}{dx}.\delta x$; while $\frac{du}{dx}$ measures the *marginal degree* of utility. Jevons and some other writers use " Final utility " to indicate what Jevons elsewhere calls Final degree of utility. There is room for doubt as to which mode of expression is the more convenient : no question of principle is involved in the decision. Subject to the qualifications mentioned in the text $\frac{d^2u}{dx^2}$ is always negative.

NOTE II. (p. 81). If m is the amount of money or general purchasing power at a person's disposal at any time, and μ represents its total utility to him, then $\frac{d\mu}{dm}$ represents the marginal degree of utility of money to him.

If p is the price which he is just willing to pay for an amount x of the commodity which gives him a total pleasure u, then

$$\frac{d\mu}{dm}\Delta p = \Delta u; \quad \text{and} \quad \frac{d\mu}{dm}\frac{dp}{dx} = \frac{du}{dx}.$$

If p' is the price which he is just willing to pay for an amount x' of another commodity, which affords him a total pleasure u', then

$$\frac{d\mu}{dm}\cdot\frac{dp'}{dx'} = \frac{du'}{dx'};$$

and therefore

$$\frac{dp}{dx}:\frac{dp'}{dx'} = \frac{du}{dx}:\frac{du'}{dx'}.$$

(Compare Jevons' chapter on the *Theory of Exchange*, p. 151.)

Every increase in his means diminishes the marginal degree of utility of money to him; that is, $\frac{d^2\mu}{dm^2}$ is always negative.

Therefore, the marginal utility to him of an amount x of a commodity remaining unchanged, an increase in his means increases $\frac{du}{dx}\div\frac{d\mu}{dm}$; i.e. it increases $\frac{dp}{dx}$, that is, the rate at which he is willing to pay for further supplies of it. We may regard $\frac{dp}{dx}$ as a function of m, u, and x; and then we have $\frac{d^2p}{dm\,dx}$ always positive. Of course $\frac{d^2p}{du\,dx}$ is always positive.

NOTE III. (pp. 86–7). Let P, P' be consecutive points on the demand curve; let PRM be drawn perpendicular to Ox, and let PP' cut Ox and Oy in T and t respectively; so that $P'R$ is that increment in the amount demanded which corresponds to a diminution PR in the price per unit of the commodity.

Then the elasticity of demand at P is measured by

$$\frac{P'R}{OM}\div\frac{PR}{PM}, \text{ i.e. by } \frac{P'R}{PR}\times\frac{PM}{OM};$$

$$\text{i.e. by } \frac{TM}{PM}\times\frac{PM}{OM},$$

$$\text{i.e. by } \frac{TM}{OM}\times \text{ or by } \frac{PT}{Pt}.$$

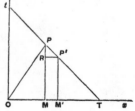

When the distance between P and P' is diminished indefinitely, PP' becomes the tangent; and thus the proposition stated on pp. 86–7 is proved.

It is obvious à priori that the measure of elasticity cannot be altered by altering relatively to one another the scales on which distances parallel to Ox and Oy are measured. But a geometrical proof of this result can be got easily by the method of projections: while analytically it is clear that $\dfrac{dx}{x} \div \dfrac{-dy}{y}$, which is the analytical expression for the measure of elasticity, does not change its value if the curve $y = f(x)$ be drawn to new scales, so that its equation becomes $qy = f(px)$; where p and q are constants.

If the elasticity of demand be equal to unity for all prices of the commodity, any fall in price will cause a proportionate increase in the amount bought, and therefore will make no change in the total outlay which purchasers make for the commodity. Such a demand may therefore be called a *constant outlay demand*. The curve which represents it, a *constant outlay curve*, as it may be called, is a rectangular hyperbola with Ox and Oy as asymptotes; and a series of such curves are represented by the dotted curves in the following figure.

There is some advantage in accustoming the eye to the shape of these curves; so that when looking at a demand curve one can tell at once whether it is inclined to the vertical at any point at a greater or less angle than the part of a constant outlay curve, which would pass through that point. Greater accuracy may be obtained by tracing constant outlay curves on thin paper, and then laying the paper over the demand curve. By this means it may, for instance, be seen at once that the demand curve in the figure represents at each of the points A, B, C, and D an elasticity about equal to one; between A and B, and again between C and D, it represents an elasticity greater than one; while between B and C it represents an elasticity less than one. It will be found that practice of this kind makes it easy to detect the nature of the assumptions with regard to the character

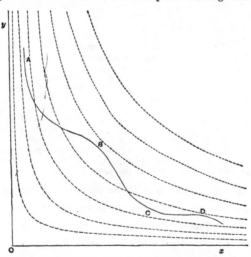

of the demand for a commodity, which are implicitly made in drawing a demand curve of any particular shape; and is a safeguard against the unconscious introduction of improbable assumptions.

The general equation to demand curves representing at every point an elasticity equal to n is $\dfrac{dx}{x} + n\dfrac{dy}{y} = 0$, i.e. $xy^n = C$.

It is worth noting that in such a curve $\dfrac{dx}{dy} = -\dfrac{C}{y^{n+1}}$; that is, the proportion in which the amount demanded increases in consequence of a small fall in the price varies inversely as the $(n + 1)^{th}$ power of the price. In the case of the constant outlay curves it varies inversely as the square of the price; or, which is the same thing in this case, directly as the square of the amount.

NOTE IV. (pp. 92–3). The lapse of time being measured downwards along Oy; and the amounts, of which record is being made, being measured by distances from Oy; then P' and P being adjacent points on the curve which traces the growth of the amount, the rate of increase in a small unit of time $N'N$ is

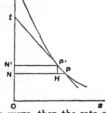

$$\frac{PH}{P'N'} = \frac{PH}{P'H} \cdot \frac{P'H}{P'N'} = \frac{PN}{Nt} \cdot \frac{P'H}{P'N'} = \frac{P'H}{Nt};$$

since PN and $P'N'$ are equal in the limit.

If we take a year as the unit of time we find the annual rate of increase represented by the inverse of the number of years in Nt.

If Nt were equal to c, a constant for all points of the curve, then the rate of increase would be constant and equal to $\frac{1}{c}$. In this case $-x\frac{dy}{dx} = c$ for all values of x; that is, the equation to the curve is $y = a - c \log x$.

NOTE V. (p. 102). We have seen in the text that the rate at which future pleasures are discounted varies greatly from one individual to another. Let r be the rate of interest per annum, which must be added to a present pleasure in order to make it just balance a future pleasure, that will be of equal amount to its recipient, when it comes; then r may be 50 or even 200 per cent. to one person, while for his neighbour it is a negative quantity. Moreover some pleasures are more urgent than others; and it is conceivable even that a person may discount future pleasures in an irregular random way; he may be almost as willing to postpone a pleasure for two years as for one; or, on the other hand, he may object very strongly indeed to a long postponement, but scarcely at all to a short one. There is some difference of opinion as to whether such irregularities are frequent; and the question cannot easily be decided; for since the estimate of a pleasure is purely subjective, it would be difficult to detect them if they did occur. In a case in which there are no such irregularities, the rate of discount will be the same for each element of time; or, to state the same thing in other words, it will obey the exponential law. And if h be the future amount of a pleasure of which the probability is p, and which will occur, if at all, at time t; and if $R = 1 + r$; then the present value of the pleasure is phR^{-t}. It must, however, be borne in mind that this result belongs to Hedonics, and not properly to Economics.

Arguing still on the same hypothesis we may say that, if ω be the probability that a person will derive an element of happiness, Δh, from the possession of, say, a piano in the element of time Δt, then the present value of the piano to him is

$$\int_0^T \omega R^{-t} \frac{dh}{dt} dt.$$ If we are to include all the happiness that results from the event at whatever distance of time we must take $T = \infty$. If the source of pleasure is in Bentham's phrase " impure," $\frac{dh}{dt}$ will probably be negative for some values of t; and of course the whole value of the integral may be negative.

NOTE VI. (pp. 109–10). If y be the price at which an amount x of a commodity can find purchasers in a given market, and $y = f(x)$ be the equation to the demand curve, then the total utility of the commodity is measured by $\int_0^a f(x) dx$, where a is the amount consumed.

If however an amount b of the commodity is necessary for existence, $f(x)$ will be infinite, or at least indefinitely great, for values of x less than b. We must therefore take life for granted, and estimate separately the total utility of that

part of the supply of the commodity which is in excess of absolute necessaries :
it is of course $\int_b^a f(x)\,dx$.

If there are several commodities which will satisfy the same imperative want, as e.g. water and milk, either of which will quench thirst, we shall find that, under the ordinary conditions of life, no great error is introduced by adopting the simple plan of assuming that the necessary supply comes exclusively from that one which is cheapest.

It should be noted that, in the discussion of consumers' surplus, we assume that the marginal utility of money to the individual purchaser is the same throughout. Strictly speaking we ought to take account of the fact that if he spent less on tea, the marginal utility of money to him would be less than it is, and he would get an element of consumers' surplus from buying other things at prices which now yield him no such rent. But these changes of consumers' rent (being of the second order of smallness) may be neglected, on the assumption, which underlies our whole reasoning, that his expenditure on any one thing, as, for instance, tea, is only a small part of his whole expenditure. (Compare Book V. ch.III. § 3.) If, for any reason, it be desirable to take account of the influence which his expenditure on tea exerts on the value of money to him, it is only necessary to multiply $f(x)$ within the integral given above by that function of $xf(x)$ (i.e. of the amount which he has already spent on tea) which represents the marginal utility to him of money when his stock of it has been diminished by that amount.

NOTE VII. (p. 111). Thus if a_1, a_2, a_3, ... be the amounts consumed of the several commodities of which b_1, b_2, b_3, ... are necessary for existence, if $y = f_1(x)$, $y = f_2(x)$, $y = f_3(x)$, ... be the equations to their demand curves and if we may neglect all inequalities in the distribution of wealth; then the total utility of income, subsistence being taken for granted, might be represented by $\Sigma \int_b^a f(x)\,dx$, if we could find a plan for grouping together in one common demand curve all those things which satisfy the same wants, and are rivals; and also for every group of things of which the services are complementary (see Book V. ch. VI.). But we cannot do this : and therefore the formula remains a mere general expression, having no practical application. See n.[1] on p. 109; also the latter part of Note XIV.

NOTE VIII. (p. 111). If y be the happiness which a person derives from an income x; and if, after Bernoulli, we assume that the increased happiness which he derives from the addition of one per cent. to his income is the same whatever his income be, we have $x\dfrac{dy}{dx} = K$, and $\therefore$ $y = K \log x + C$ when K and C are constants. Further with Bernoulli let us assume that, a being the income which affords the barest necessaries of life, pain exceeds pleasure when the income is less than a, and balances it when the income equals a; then our equation becomes $y = K \log \dfrac{x}{a}$. Of course both K and a vary with the temperament, the health, the habits, and the social surroundings of each individual. Laplace gives to x the name fortune physique, and to y the name fortune morale.

Bernoulli himself seems to have thought of x and a as representing certain amounts of property rather than of income; but we cannot estimate the property necessary for life without some understanding as to the length of time during which it is to support life, that is, without really treating it as income.

Perhaps the guess which has attracted most attention after Bernoulli's is Cramer's suggestion that the pleasure afforded by wealth may be taken to vary as the square root of its amount.

NOTE IX. (p. 112). The argument that fair gambling is an economic blunder is generally based on Bernoulli's or some other definite hypothesis. But it requires no further assumption than that, firstly the pleasure of gambling may be neglected; and, secondly, $\phi''(x)$ is negative for all values of x, where $\phi(x)$ is the pleasure derived from wealth equal to x.

For suppose that the chance that a particular event will happen is p, and a man makes a fair bet of py against $(1 - p)\, y$ that it will happen. By so doing he changes his expectation of happiness from

$$\phi(x) \text{ to } p\phi\{x + (1 - p)\, y\} + (1 - p)\, \phi(x - py).$$

This when expanded by Taylor's Theorem becomes

$$\phi(x) + \tfrac{1}{2}p\,(1 - p)^2 y^2 \phi'' \{x + \theta(1 - p)\, y\} + \tfrac{1}{2}p^2\,(1 - p)\, y^2\phi''(x - \Theta py);$$

assuming $\phi''(x)$ to be negative for all values of x, this is always less than $\phi(x)$.

It is true that this loss of probable happiness need not be greater than the pleasure derived from the excitement of gambling, and we are then thrown back upon the induction that pleasures of gambling are in Bentham's phrase "impure"; since experience shows that they are likely to engender a restless, feverish character, unsuited for steady work as well as for the higher and more solid pleasures of life.

NOTE X. (p. 118). Following on the same lines as in Note I., let us take v to represent the disutility or discommodity of an amount of labour l, then $\dfrac{dv}{dl}$ measures the marginal degree of disutility if labour; and, subject to the qualifications mentioned in the text, $\dfrac{d^2v}{dl^2}$ is positive.

Let m be the amount of money or general purchasing power at a person's disposal, μ its total utility to him, and therefore $\dfrac{d\mu}{dm}$ its marginal utility. Thus if Δw be the wages that must be paid him to induce him to do labour Δl, then $\Delta w \dfrac{d\mu}{dm} = \Delta v$, and $\dfrac{dw}{dl} \cdot \dfrac{d\mu}{dm} = \dfrac{dv}{dl}.$

If we assume that his dislike to labour is not a fixed, but a fluctuating quantity, we may regard $\dfrac{dw}{dl}$ as a function of m, v, and l; and then both $\dfrac{d^2w}{dm\,dl}, \dfrac{d^2w}{dv\,dl}$ are always positive.

NOTE XI. (p. 206). If members of any species of bird begin to adopt aquatic habits, every increase in the webs between the toes—whether coming about gradually by the operation of natural selection, or suddenly as a sport—will cause them to find their advantage more in aquatic life, and will make their chance of leaving offspring depend more on the increase of the web. So that, if $f(t)$ be the average area of the web at time t, then the rate of increase of the web increases (within certain limits) with every increase in the web, and therefore $f''(t)$ is positive. Now we know by Taylor's Theorem that

$$f(t + h) = f(t) + hf'(t) + \frac{h^2}{1 \cdot 2} f''(t + \theta h);$$

and if h be large, so that h^2 is very large, then $f(t + h)$ will be much greater than $f(t)$ even though $f'(t)$ be small and $f''(t)$ is never large. There is more than a superficial connection between the advance made by the applications of the differential calculus to physics at the end of the eighteenth century and the beginning of the nineteenth, and the rise of the theory of evolution. In sociology as well as in biology we are learning to watch the accumulated effects of forces which, though weak at first, get greater strength from the growth of their own effects; and the universal form, of which every such fact is a special embodiment, is Taylor's Theorem; or, if the action of more than one cause at a time is to be taken account of, the corresponding expression of a function of several variables. This conclusion will remain valid even if further investigation confirms the suggestion, made by some Mendelians, that gradual changes in the race are originated by large divergences of individuals from the prevailing type. For economics is a study of mankind, of particular nations, of particular social strata; and it is only indirectly concerned with the lives of men of exceptional genius or exceptional wickedness and violence.

NOTE XII. (p. 276). If, as in Note X., v be the discommodity of the amount of labour which a person has to exert in order to obtain an amount x of a commodity from which he derives a pleasure u, then the pleasure of having further supplies will be equal to the pain of getting them when $\dfrac{du}{dx} = \dfrac{dv}{dx}$.

If the pain of labour be regarded as a negative pleasure; and we write $U \equiv -v$; then $\dfrac{du}{dx} + \dfrac{dU}{dx} = 0$, i.e. $u + U = $ a maximum at the point at which his labour ceases.

NOTE XII. *bis* (p. 654). In an article in the *Giornale degli Economisti* for February, 1891, Prof. Edgeworth draws the adjoining diagram, which represents the cases of barter of apples for nuts described on pp. 652-4. Apples are measured along Ox, and nuts along Oy; $Op = 4$, $pa = 40$; and a represents the termination of the first bargain in which 4 apples have been exchanged for 40 nuts, in the case in which A gets the advantage at starting: b represents the second, and c the final stage of that case. On the other hand, a' represents the first, and b', c', d' the second, third, and final stages of the set of bargains in which B gets the advantage at starting. QP, the locus on which c and d' must both necessarily lie, is called by Prof. Edgeworth the *Contract Curve*.

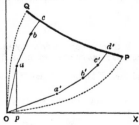

Following a method adopted in his *Mathematical Psychics* (1881), he takes U to represent the total utility to A of apples and nuts when he has given up x apples and received y nuts, V the total utility to B of apples and nuts when he has received x apples and given up y nuts. If an additional Δx apples are exchanged for Δy nuts, the exchange will be indifferent to A if

$$\frac{dU}{dx}\Delta x + \frac{dU}{dy}\Delta y = 0;$$

and it will be indifferent to B if $\dfrac{dV}{dx}\Delta x + \dfrac{dV}{dy}\Delta y = 0$. These, therefore, are the equations to the indifference curves OP and OQ of the figure respectively; and the contract curve which is the locus of points at which the terms of exchange that are indifferent to A are also indifferent to B has the elegant equation $\dfrac{dU}{dx} \div \dfrac{dU}{dy} = \dfrac{dV}{dx} \div \dfrac{dV}{dy}.$

If the marginal utility of nuts be constant for A and also for B, $\dfrac{dU}{dy}$ and $\dfrac{dV}{dy}$ become constant; U becomes $\Phi(a - x) + ay$, and V becomes $\Psi(a - x) + \beta y$; and the contract curve becomes $F(x) = 0$; or $x = C$; that is, it is a straight line parallel to Oy, and the value of $\Delta y : \Delta x$ given by either of the indifference curves, a function of C; thus showing that by whatever route the barter may have started, equilibrium will have been found at a point at which C apples have been exchanged, and the final rate of exchange is a function of C; that is, it is a constant also. This last application of Prof. Edgeworth's mathematical version of the theory of barter, to confirm the results reached in the text, was first made by Mr. Berry, and is published in the *Giornale degli Economisti* for June, 1891.

Prof. Edgeworth's plan of representing U and V as general functions of x and y has great attractions to the mathematician; but it seems less adapted to express the every-day facts of economic life than that of regarding, as Jevons did, the marginal utilities of apples as functions of x simply. In that case, if A had no nuts at starting, as is assumed in the particular case under discussion, U takes the form

$$\int_{u}^{x}\phi_1(a - x)\,dx + \int_{0}^{y}\psi_1(y)\,dy;$$

similarly for V.   And then the equation to the contract curve is of the form

$$\phi_1 (a - x) \div \psi_1 (y) = \phi_2 (x) \div \psi_2 (b - y);$$

which is one of the Equations of Exchange in Jevons' *Theory*, 2nd Edition, p. 108.

NOTE XIII. (p. 294).   Using the same notation as in Note V., let us take our starting-point as regards time at the date of beginning to build the house, and let T'' be the time occupied in building it.   Then the present value of the pleasures, which he expects to derive from the house, is

$$H = \int_{T'}^{T} \omega R^{-t} \frac{dh}{dt} dt.$$

Let Δv be the element of effort that will be incurred by him in building the house in the interval of time Δt (between the time t and the time $t + \Delta t$), then the present value of the aggregate of effort is

$$V = \int_{0}^{T'} R^{-t} \frac{dv}{dt} dt.$$

If there is any uncertainty as to the labour that will be required, every possible element must be counted in, multiplied by the probability, ω', of its being required; and then V becomes $\int_{0}^{T'} \omega R^{-t} \frac{dv}{dt} dt.$

If we transfer the starting-point to the date of the completion of the house, we have

$$H = \int_{0}^{T_1} \omega R^{-t} \frac{dh}{dt} dt \text{ and } V = \int_{0}^{T'} \omega' R^{t} \frac{dv}{dt} dt,$$

where $T_1 = T - T'$; and this starting-point, though perhaps the less natural from the mathematical point of view, is the more natural from the point of view of ordinary business.   Adopting it, we see V as the aggregate of estimated pains incurred; each bearing on its back, as it were, the accumulated burden of the waitings between the time of its being incurred and the time when it begins to bear fruit.

Jevons' discussion of the investment of capital is somewhat injured by the unnecessary assumption that the function representing it is an expression of the first order; which is the more remarkable as he had himself, when describing Gossen's work, pointed out the objections to the plan followed by him (and Whewell) of substituting straight lines for the multiform curves that represent the true characters of the variations of economic quantities.

NOTE XIV. (p. 297).   Let a_1, a_2, a_3, ... be the several amounts of different kinds of labour, as, for instance, wood-cutting, stone-carrying, earth-digging, etc., on the part of the man in question that would be used in building the house on any given plan; and β, β', β'', etc., the several amounts of accommodation of different kinds such as sitting-rooms, bed-rooms, offices, etc. which the house would afford on that plan.   Then, using V and H as in the previous note, V, β, β', β'' are all functions of a_1, a_2, a_3, ..., and H being a function of β, β', β'', ... is a function also of $a_1, a_2, a_3, \ldots$.   We have, then, to find the marginal investments of each kind of labour for each kind of use.

$$\frac{dV}{da_1} = \frac{dH}{d\beta}\frac{d\beta}{da_1} = \frac{dH}{d\beta'}\frac{d\beta'}{da_1} = \frac{dH}{d\beta''}\frac{d\beta''}{da_1} = - \ldots$$

$$\frac{dV}{da_2} = \frac{dH}{d\beta}\frac{d\beta}{da_2} = \frac{dH}{d\beta'}\frac{d\beta'}{da_2} = \frac{dH}{d\beta''}\frac{d\beta''}{da_2} = \ldots.$$

These equations represent a balance of effort and benefit.   The real cost to him of a little extra labour spent on cutting timber and working it up is just balanced by the benefit of the extra sitting-room or bed-room accommodation that he could get by so doing. If, however, instead of doing the work himself, he pays carpenters to do it, we must take V to represent, not his total effort, but his total outlay of general purchasing power. Then the rate of pay which he is willing to give to carpenters for further labour, his marginal demand price for their labour, is measured by $\dfrac{dV}{da}$; while $\dfrac{dH}{d\beta}, \dfrac{dH}{d\beta'}$ are the money measures to him of the marginal utilities of extra sitting-room and bed-room accommodation respectively, that is, his marginal demand prices for them; and $\dfrac{d\beta}{da}, \dfrac{d\beta'}{da}$ are the marginal efficiencies of carpenters' labour in providing those accommodations. The equations then state that the demand price for carpenters' labour tends to be equal to the demand price for extra sitting-room accommodation, and also for extra bed-room accommodation and so on, multiplied in each case by the marginal efficiency of the work of carpenters in providing that extra accommodation, proper units being chosen for each element.

When this statement is generalized, so as to cover all the varied demand in a market for carpenters' labour, it becomes :—the (marginal) demand price for carpenters' labour is the (marginal) efficiency of carpenters' labour in increasing the supply of any product, multiplied by the (marginal) demand price for that product. Or, to put the same thing in other words, the wages of a unit of carpenters' labour tends to be equal to the value of such part of any of the products, to producing which their labour contributes, as represents the marginal efficiency of a unit of carpenters' labour with regard to that product; or, to use a phrase, with which we shall be much occupied in Book VI. ch. I., it tends to be equal to the value of the " net product " of their labour. This proposition is very important and contains within itself the kernel of the demand side of the theory of distribution.

Let us then suppose a master builder to have it in mind to erect certain buildings, and to be considering what different accommodation he shall provide; as, for instance, dwelling-houses, warehouses, factories, and retail shop-room. There will be two classes of questions for him to decide : how much accommodation of each kind he shall provide, and by what means he shall provide it. Thus, besides deciding whether to erect villa residences, offering a certain amount of accommodation, he has to decide what agents of production he will use, and in what proportions; whether e.g. he will use tile or slate; how much stone he will use; whether he will use steam power for making mortar etc. or only for crane work; and, if he is in a large town, whether he will have his scaffolding put up by men who make that work a speciality or by ordinary labourers; and so on.

Let him then decide to provide an amount β of villa accommodation, an amount β' of warehouse, an amount β'' of factory accommodation, and so on, each of a certain class. But, instead of supposing him to hire simply $a_1, a_2, \ldots$ quantities of different kinds of labour, as before, let us class his expenditure, under the three heads of (1) wages, (2) prices of raw material, and (3) interest on capital : while the value of his own work and enterprise makes a fourth head.

Thus let $x_1, x_2, \ldots$ be the amounts of different classes of labour, including that of superintendence, which he hires; the amount of each kind of labour being made up of its duration and its intensity.

Let $y_1, y_2, \ldots$ be amounts of various kinds of raw materials, which are used up and embodied in the buildings; which may be supposed to be sold freehold. In that case, the pieces of land on which they are severally built are merely particular forms of raw material from the present point of view, which is that of the individual undertaker.

Next let z be the amount of locking up, or appropriation of the employment, of capital for the several purposes. Here we must reckon in all forms of capital reduced to a common money measure, including advances for wages, for the purchase of raw material; also the uses, allowing for wear-and-tear etc. of his plant of all kinds : his workshops themselves and the ground on which they are built being reckoned on the same footing. The periods, during which the various lockings up run, will vary; but they must be reduced, on a " compound rate," i.e. according to geometrical progression, to a standard unit, say a year.

Fourthly, let u represent the money equivalent of his own labour, worry, anxiety, wear-and-tear etc. involved in the several undertakings.

In addition, there are several elements, which might have been entered under separate heads; but which we may suppose combined with those already mentioned. Thus the allowance to be made for risk may be shared between the last two heads. A proper share of the general expenses of working the business ("supplementary costs," see p. 299–300) will be distributed among four heads of wages, raw materials, interest on the capital value of the organization of the business (its goodwill etc.) regarded as a going concern, and remuneration of the builder's own work, enterprise and anxiety.

Under these circumstances V represents his total outlay, and H his total receipts; and his efforts are directed to making $H - V$ a maximum. On this plan, we have equations similar to those already given, viz. :—

$$\frac{dV}{dx_1} = \frac{dH}{d\beta} \cdot \frac{d\beta}{dx_1} = \frac{dH}{d\beta'} \cdot \frac{d\beta'}{dx_1} = \cdots$$

$$\frac{dV}{dx_2} = \frac{dH}{d\beta} \cdot \frac{d\beta}{dx_2} = \frac{dH}{d\beta'} \cdot \frac{d\beta'}{dx_2} = \cdots$$

$$\cdots\cdots$$

$$\frac{dV}{dy_1} = \frac{dH}{d\beta} \cdot \frac{d\beta}{dy_1} = \frac{dH}{d\beta'} \cdot \frac{d\beta'}{dy_1} = \cdots$$

$$\cdots\cdots$$

$$\frac{dV}{dz} = \frac{dH}{d\beta} \cdot \frac{d\beta}{dz} = \frac{dH}{d\beta'} \cdot \frac{d\beta'}{dz} = \cdots$$

$$\frac{dV}{du} = \frac{dH}{d\beta} \cdot \frac{d\beta}{du} = \frac{dH}{d\beta'} \cdot \frac{d\beta'}{du} = \cdots.$$

That is to say, the marginal outlay which the builder is willing to make for an additional small supply, δx_1, of the first class of labour, viz. $\frac{dV}{dx_1} \delta x_1$, is equal to $\frac{dH}{d\beta} \cdot \frac{d\beta}{dx_1} \delta x_1$; i.e. to that increment in his total receipts H, which he will obtain by the increase in the villa accommodation provided by him that will result from the extra small supply of the first class of labour : this will equal a similar sum with regard to warehouse accommodation, and so on. Thus he will have distributed his resources between various uses in such a way that he would gain nothing by diverting any part of any agent of production—labour, raw material, the use of capital—nor his own labour and enterprise from one class of building to another : also he would gain nothing by substituting one agent for another in any branch of his enterprise, nor indeed by any increase or diminution of his use of any agent. From this point of view our equations have a drift very similar to the argument of Book III. ch. v. as to the choice between the different uses of the same thing. (Compare one of the most interesting notes (f) attached to Prof. Edgeworth's brilliant address to the British Association in 1889.)

There is more to be said (see V. XI. 1, and VI. I. 8) on the difficulty of interpreting the phrase the "net product" of any agent of production, whether a particular kind of labour or any other agent; and perhaps the rest of this note, though akin to what has gone before, may more conveniently be read at a later stage. The builder paid $\frac{dV}{dx_1} \delta x_1$ for the last element of the labour of the first group because that was its net product; and, if directed to building villas, it brought him in $\frac{dH}{d\beta} \cdot \frac{d\beta}{dx_1} \delta x_1$, as special receipts. Now if p be the price per unit, which he receives for an amount β of villa accommodation, and therefore $p\beta$ the price which he receives for the whole amount β; and if we put for shortness $\Delta\beta$ in place of $\frac{d\beta}{dx_1} \delta x_1$, the increase of villa accommodation due to the additional element of labour δx_1; then the net product we are seeking is not $p\Delta\beta$, but $p\Delta\beta + \beta\Delta p$; where Δp is a negative quantity, and is the fall in demand price caused by the increase in the amount of villa accommodation offered by the builder. We have to make some study of the relative magnitudes of these two elements $p\Delta\beta$ and $\beta\Delta p$.

If the builder monopolized the supply of villas, β would represent the total supply of them : and, if it happened that the elasticity of the demand for them was less than unity, when the amount β was offered, then, by increasing his supply, he would diminish his total receipts; and $p\Delta\beta + \beta\Delta p$ would be a negative quantity. But of course he would not have allowed the production to go just up to an amount at which the demand would be thus inelastic. The margin which he chose for his production would certainly be one for which the negative quantity $\beta\Delta p$ is less than $p\Delta\beta$, but not necessarily so much less that it may be neglected in comparison. This is a dominant fact in the theory of monopolies discussed in Book V. chapter XIV.

It is dominant also in the case of any producer who has a limited trade connection which he cannot quickly enlarge. If his customers have already as much of his wares as they care for, so that the elasticity of their demand is temporarily less than unity, he might lose by putting on an additional man to work for him, even though that man would work for nothing. This fear of temporarily spoiling a man's special market is a leading influence in many problems of value relating to short periods (see Book V. chs. V. VII. XI.); and especially in those periods of commercial depression, and in those regulations of trade associations, formal and informal, which we shall have to study in the second volume. There is an allied difficulty in the case of commodities of which the expenses of production diminish rapidly with every increase in the amount produced : but here the causes that govern the limits of production are so complex that it seems hardly worth while to attempt to translate them into mathematical language. See V. XII. 2.

When however we are studying the action of an individual undertaker with a view of illustrating the normal action of the causes which govern the general demand for the several agents of production, it seems clear that we should avoid cases of this kind. We should leave their peculiar features to be analysed separately in special discussions, and take our normal illustration from a case in which the individual is only one of many who have efficient, if indirect, access to the market. If $\beta\Delta p$ be numerically equal to $p\Delta\beta$, where β is the whole production in a large market; and an individual undertaker produced β', a thousandth part of β; then the increased receipt from putting on an additional man is $p\Delta\beta'$, which is the same as $p\Delta\beta$; and the deduction to be made from it is only $\beta'\Delta p$, which is a thousandth part of $\beta\Delta p$ and may be neglected. For the purpose therefore of illustrating a part of the general action of the laws of distribution we are justified in speaking of the value of the net product of the marginal work of any agent of production as the amount of that net product taken at the normal selling value of the product, that is, as $p\Delta\beta$.

It may be noticed that none of these difficulties are dependent upon the system of division of labour and work for payment; though they are brought into prominence by the habit of measuring efforts and satisfactions by price, which is associated with it. Robinson Crusoe erecting a building for himself would not find that an addition of a thousandth part to his previous accommodation increased his comfort by a thousandth part. What he added might be of the same character with the rest; but if one counted it in at the same rate of real value to him, one would have to reckon for the fact that the new part made the old of somewhat less urgent need, of somewhat lower real value to him (see note 1 on p. 346). On the other hand, the law of increasing return might render it very difficult for him to assign its true net product to a given half-hour's work. For instance, suppose that some small herbs, grateful as condiment, and easily portable, grow in a part of his island, which it takes half a day to visit; and he has gone there to get small batches at a time. Afterwards he gives a whole day, having no important use to which he can put less than half a day, and comes back with ten times as great a load as before. We cannot then separate the return of the last half-hour from the rest; our only plan is to take the whole day as a unit, and compare its return of satisfaction with those of days in other ways; and in the modern system of industry we have the similar, but more difficult task of taking, for some purposes, the whole of a process of production as a single unit.

It would be possible to extend the scope of such systems of equations as we have been considering, and to increase their detail, until they embraced within themselves the whole of the demand side of the problem of distribution. But while a mathematical illustration of the mode of action of a definite set of causes may be complete in itself, and strictly accurate within its clearly defined limits, it is otherwise with any attempt to grasp the whole of a complex problem of real life, or even any considerable part of it, in a series of equations. For many important considerations, especially those connected with the manifold influences of the element of time, do not lend themselves easily to mathematical expression : they must either be omitted altogether, or clipped and pruned till they resemble the conventional birds and animals of decorative art. And hence arises a tendency towards assigning wrong proportions to economic forces; those elements being most emphasized which lend themselves most easily to analytical methods. No doubt this danger is inherent in every application not only of mathematical analysis, but of analysis of any kind, to the problems of real life. It is a danger which more than any other the economist must have in mind at every turn. But to avoid it altogether, would be to abandon the chief means of scientific progress : and in discussions written specially for mathematical readers it is no doubt right to be very bold in the search for wide generalizations.

In such discussions it may be right, for instance, to regard H as the sum total of satisfactions, and V as the sum total of dissatisfactions (efforts, sacrifices etc.) which accrue to a community from economic causes; to simplify the notion of the action of these causes by assumptions similar to those which are involved, more or less consciously, in the various forms of the doctrine that the constant drift of these causes is towards the attainment of the *Maximum Satisfaction*, in the net aggregate for the community (see above pp. 389–94); or, in other words, that there is a constant tendency to make $H - V$ a maximum for society as a whole. On this plan the resulting differential equations of the same class as those which we have been discussing, will be interpreted to represent value as governed in every field of economics by the balancing of groups of utilities against groups of disutilities, of groups of satisfactions against groups of real costs. Such discussions have their place : but it is not in a treatise such as the present, in which mathematics are used only to express in terse and more precise language those methods of analysis and reasoning which ordinary people adopt, more or less consciously, in the affairs of every-day life.

It may indeed be admitted that such discussions have some points of resemblance to the method of analysis applied in Book III. to the total utility of particular commodities. The difference between the two cases is mainly one of degree : but it is of a degree so great as practically to amount to a difference of kind. For in the former case we take each commodity by itself and with reference to a particular market; and we take careful account of the circumstances of the consumers at the time and place under consideration. Thus we follow, though perhaps with more careful precautions, the practice of ministers of finance, and of the common man when discussing financial policy. We note that a few commodities are consumed mainly by the rich; and that in consequence their real total utilities are less than is suggested by the money measures of those utilities. But we assume, with the rest of the world, that as a rule, and in the absence of special causes to the contrary, the real total utilities of two commodities that are mainly consumed by the rich stand to one another in about the same relation as their money measures do : and that the same is true of commodities the consumption of which is divided out among rich and middle classes and poor in similar proportions. Such estimates are but rough approximations; but each particular difficulty, each source of possible error, is pushed into prominence by the definiteness of our phrases : we introduce no assumptions that are not latent in the practice of ordinary life; while we attempt no task that is not grappled with in a rougher fashion, but yet to good purpose, in the practice of ordinary life : we introduce no new assumptions, and we bring into clear light those which cannot be avoided. But though this is possible when dealing with particular commodities with reference to particular markets, it does not seem possible with regard to the innumerable economic elements that come within the all-embracing net of the doctrine of Maximum Satisfaction. The forces of supply are especially heterogeneous and complex : they include an infinite variety of efforts and sacrifices, direct and indirect, on the part of people in all varieties of industrial grades : and if there were no other hindrance to giving a concrete interpretation to the doctrine, a fatal obstacle would be found in its latent assumption that the cost of rearing children and preparing them for their work can be measured in the same way as the cost of erecting a machine.

For reasons similar to those given in this typical case, our mathematical notes will cover less and less ground as the complexity of the subjects discussed in the text increases. A few of those that follow relate to monopolies, which present some sides singularly open to direct analytical treatment. But the majority of the remainder will be occupied with illustrations of joint and composite demand and supply which have much in common with the substance of this note : while the last of that series Note XXI. goes a little way towards a general survey of the problem of distribution and exchange (without reference to the element of time), but only so far as to make sure that the mathematical illustrations used point towards a system of equations, which are neither more nor less in number than the unknowns introduced into them.

NOTE XIV. *bis* (p. 318). In the diagrams of this chapter (V. VI.) the supply curves are all inclined positively; and in our mathematical versions of them we shall suppose the marginal expenses of production to be determined with a definiteness that does not exist in real life : we shall take no account of the time required for developing a representative business with the internal and external economies of production on a large scale; and we shall ignore all those difficulties connected with the law of increasing return which are discussed in Book V. ch. XII. To adopt any other course would lead us to mathematical complexities, which though perhaps not without their use, would be unsuitable for a treatise of this kind. The discussions therefore in this and the following notes must be regarded as sketches rather than complete studies.

Let the factors of production of a commodity A be a_1, a_2, etc.; and let their supply equations be $y = \phi_1(x)$, $y = \phi_2(x)$, etc. Let the number of units of them required for the production of x units of A be m_1x, m_2x, ... respectively; where m_1, m_2, ... are generally not constants but functions of x. Then the supply equation of A is

$$y = \Phi(x) = m_1\phi_1(m_1x) + m_2\phi_2(m_2x) + \ldots = \Sigma\{m\phi(mx)\}.$$

Let $y = F(x)$ be the demand equation for the finished commodity, then the derived demand equation for a_r the rth factor is

$$y = F(x) - \{\Phi(x) - m_r\phi_r(m_rx)\}.$$

But in this equation y is the price, not of one unit of the factor but of m units; and to get an equation expressed in terms of fixed units let η be the price of one unit, and let $\xi = m_r x$, then $\eta = \dfrac{1}{m_r} \cdot y$ and the equation becomes

$$\eta = f(\xi) = \frac{1}{m_r}\left[F\left(\frac{1}{m_r}\xi\right) - \left\{ \Phi\left(\frac{1}{m_r}\xi\right) m_r\phi_r(\xi)\right\} \right].$$

If m_r is a function of x, say $= \psi_r(x)$; then x must be determined in terms of ξ by the equation $\xi = x\psi_r(x)$, so that m_r can be written $\chi_r(\xi)$; substituting this we have η expressed as a function of ξ. The supply equation for a_r is simply $\eta = \phi_r(\xi)$.

NOTE XV. (p. 320). Let the demand equation for knives be

$$y = F(x) \dots\dots\dots\dots\dots\dots\dots\dots\dots\dots\dots(1),$$
let the supply equation for knives be $y = \Phi(x) \dots\dots\dots\dots\dots\dots\dots\dots\dots\dots(2),$
let that for handles be $\qquad\qquad y = \phi_1(x) \dots\dots\dots\dots\dots\dots\dots\dots\dots(3),$
and that for blades be $\qquad\qquad y = \phi_2(x) \dots\dots\dots\dots\dots\dots\dots\dots\dots(4),$
then the demand equation for handles is

$$y = f_1(x) = F(x) - \phi_2(x) \dots\dots\dots\dots\dots\dots\dots\dots(5).$$

The measure of elasticity for (5) is $-\left\{\dfrac{xf_1'(x)}{f_1(x)}\right\}^{-1}$, that is,

$$-\left\{\frac{xF'(x) - x\phi_2'(x)}{f_1(x)}\right\}^{-1};$$

that is,

$$\left\{-\frac{xF'(x)}{F(x)} \cdot \frac{F(x)}{f_1(x)} + \frac{x\phi_2'(x)}{f_1(x)}\right\}^{-1}$$

This will be the smaller the more fully the following conditions are satisfied : (i) that $-\dfrac{xF'(x)}{F(x)}$, which is necessarily positive, be large, i.e. that the elasticity of the demand for knives be small; (ii) that $\phi_2'(x)$ be positive and large, i.e. that the supply price for blades should increase rapidly with an increase, and diminish rapidly with a diminution of the amount supplied; and (iii) that $\dfrac{F(x)}{f_1(x)}$ should be large; that is, that the price of handles should be but a small part of the price of knives.

A similar, but more complex inquiry, leads to substantially the same results, when the units of the factors of production are not fixed, but vary as in the preceding note.

NOTE XVI. (p. 320). Suppose that m bushels of hops are used in making a gallon of ale of a certain kind, of which in equilibrium x' gallons are sold at a price $y' = F(x')$. Let m be changed into $m + \Delta m$; and, as a result, when x' gallons are still offered for sale let them find purchasers at a price $y' + \Delta y'$; then $\dfrac{\Delta y'}{\Delta m}$ represents the marginal demand price for hops : if it is greater than their supply price, it will be to the interest of the brewers to put more hops into the ale. Or, to put the case more generally, let $y = F(x, m)$, $y = \Phi(x, m)$ be the demand and supply equations for beer, x being the number of gallons and m the number of bushels of hops in each gallon. Then $F(x, m) - \Phi(x, m) =$ excess of demand over supply price. In equilibrium this is of course zero : but if it were possible to make it a positive sum by varying m the change would be effected : therefore (assuming that there is no perceptible change in the expense of making the beer, other than what results from the increased amount of hops) $\dfrac{dF}{dm} = \dfrac{d\Phi}{dm}$: the first represents the marginal demand price, and the second the marginal supply price of hops; and these two are therefore equal.

This method is of course capable of being extended to cases in which there are concurrent variations in two or more factors of production.

NOTE XVII. (p. 321). Suppose that a thing, whether a finished commodity or a factor of production, is distributed between two uses, so that of the total amount x the part devoted to the first use is x_1, and that devoted to the second use is x_2. Let $y = \phi(x)$ be the total supply equation; $y = f_1(x_1)$ and $y = f_2(x_2)$ be the demand equations for its first and second uses. Then in equilibrium the three unknowns x, x_1, and x_2 are determined by the three equations $f_1(x_1) = f_2(x_2) = \phi(x)$; $x_1 + x_2 = x$.

Next suppose that it is desired to obtain separately the relations of demand and supply of the thing in its first use, on the supposition that, whatever perturbations there may be in its first use, its demand and supply for the second use remains in equilibrium; i.e. that its demand price for the second use is equal to its supply price for the total amount that is actually produced, i.e. $f_2(x_2) = \phi(x_1 + x_2)$ always. From this equation we can determine x_2 in terms of x_1, and therefore x in terms of x_1; and therefore we can write $\phi(x) = \psi(x_1)$. Thus the supply equation for the thing in its first use becomes $y = \psi(x_1)$; and this with the already known equation $y = f_1(x_1)$ gives the relations required.

NOTE XVIII. (p. 322). Let $a_1, a_2, \ldots$ be joint products, $m_1x, m_2x, \ldots$ of them severally being produced as the result of x units of their joint process of production, for which the supply equation is $y = \phi(x)$. Let

$$y = f_1(x), \; y = f_2(x), \ldots$$

be their respective demand equations. Then in equilibrium

$$m_1 f_1(m_1x) + m_2 f_2(m_2x) + \cdots\cdots = \phi(x).$$

Let x' be the value of x determined from this equation; then $f_1(m_1x')$, $f_2(m_2x')$ etc. are the equilibrium prices of the several joint products. Of course m_1, m_2 are expressed if necessary in terms of x'.

NOTE XIX. (p. 323). This case corresponds, *mutatis mutandis*, to that discussed in Note XVI. If in equilibrium x' oxen annually are supplied and sold at a price $y' = \phi(x')$; and each ox yields m units of beef: and if breeders find that by modifying the breeding and feeding of oxen they can increase their meat-yielding properties to the extent of Δm units of beef (the hides and other joint products being, on the balance, unaltered), and that the extra expense of doing this is $\Delta y'$, then $\dfrac{\Delta y'}{\Delta m}$ represents the marginal supply price of beef: if this price were less than the selling price, it would be to the interest of breeders to make the change.

NOTE XX. (p. 324). Let a_1, a_2, ... be things which are fitted to subserve exactly the same function. Let their units be so chosen that a unit of any one of them is equivalent to a unit of any others. Let their several supply equations be $y_1 = \phi_1(x_1)$, $y_2 = \phi_2(x_2)$, ...

In these equations let the variable be changed, and let them be written $x_1 = \psi_1(y_1)$, $x_2 = \psi_2(y_2)$, ... Let $y = f(x)$ be the demand equation for the service for which all of them are fitted. Then in equilibrium x and y are determined by the equations $y = f(x)$; $x = x_1 + x_2 + \dots$, $y_1 = y_2 = \dots = y$. (The equations must be such that none of the quantities x_1, x_2, ... can have a negative value. When y_1 has fallen to a certain level x_1 becomes zero; and for lower values x_1 remains zero; it does not become negative.) As was observed in the text, it must be assumed that the supply equations all conform to the law of diminishing return; i.e. that $\phi_1'(x)$, $\phi_2'(x)$, ... are always positive.

NOTE XXI. (p. 326). We may now take a bird's-eye view of the problems of joint demand, composite demand, joint supply and composite supply when they all arise together, with the object of making sure that our abstract theory has just as many equations as it has unknowns, neither more nor less.

In a problem of joint demand we may suppose that there are n commodities A_1, A_2, ... A_n. Let A_1 have a_1 factors of production, let A_2 have a_2 factors, and so on, so that the total number of factors of production is $a_1 + a_2 + a_3 + \dots + a_n$: let this $= m$.

First, suppose that all the factors are different, so that there is no composite demand; that each factor has a separate process of production, so that there are no joint products; and lastly, that no two factors subserve the same use, so that there is no composite supply. We then have $2n + 2m$ unknowns, viz. the amounts and prices of n commodities and of m factors; and to determine them we have $2m + 2n$ equations, viz.—(i) n demand equations, each of which connects the price and amount of a commodity; (ii) n equations, each of which equates the supply price for any amount of a commodity to the sum of the prices of corresponding amounts of its factors; (iii) m supply equations, each of which connects the price of a factor with its amount; and lastly, (iv) m equations, each of which states the amount of a factor which is used in the production of a given amount of the commodity.

Next, let us take account not only of joint demand but also of composite demand. Let β_1 of the factors of production consist of the same thing, say carpenters' work of a certain efficiency; in other words, let carpenters' work be one of the factors of production of β_1 of the n commodities A_1, A_2, ... Then since the carpenters' work is taken to have the same price in whatever production it is used, there is only one price for each of these factors of production, and the number of unknowns is diminished by $\beta_1 - 1$; also the number of supply equations is diminished by $\beta_1 - 1$: and so on for other cases.

Next, let us in addition take account of joint supply. Let γ_1 of the things used in producing the commodities be joint products of one and the same process. Then the number of unknowns is not altered; but the number of supply equations is reduced by $(\gamma_1 - 1)$: this deficiency is however made up by a new set of $(\gamma_1 - 1)$ equations connecting the amounts of these joint products: and so on.

Lastly, let one of the things used have a composite supply made up from δ_1 rival sources: then, reserving the old supply equations for the first of these rivals, we have $2(\delta_1 - 1)$ additional unknowns, consisting of the prices and amounts of the remaining $(\delta_1 - 1)$ rivals. These are covered by $(\delta_1 - 1)$ supply equations for the rivals, and $(\delta_1 - 1)$ equations between the prices of the δ_1 rivals.

Thus, however complex the problem may become, we can see that it is theoretically determinate, because the number of unknowns is always exactly equal to the number of equations which we obtain.

NOTE XXII. (p. 397). If $y = f_1(x)$, $y = f_2(x)$ be the equations to the demand and supply curves respectively, the amount of production which affords the maximum monopoly revenue is found by making $\{xf_1(x) - xf_2(x)\}$ a maximum; that is, it is the root, or one of the roots of the equation

$$\frac{d}{dx}\{xf_1(x) - xf_2(x)\} = 0.$$

The supply function is represented here by $f_1(x)$ instead of as before by $\phi(x)$, partly to emphasize the fact that supply price does not mean exactly the same thing here as it did in the previous notes, partly to fall in with that system of numbering the curves which is wanted to prevent confusion now that their number is being increased.

NOTE XXIII. (p. 398). If a tax be imposed of which the aggregate amount is $F(x)$, then, in order to find the value of x which makes the monopoly revenue a maximum, we have $\frac{d}{dx}\{xf_1(x) - xf_2(x) - F(x)\} = 0$; and it is clear that if $F(x)$ is either constant, as in the case of a license duty, or varies as $xf_1(x) - xf_2(x)$, as in the case of an income-tax, this equation has the same roots as it would have if $F(x)$ were zero.

Treating the problems geometrically, we notice that, if a fixed burden be imposed on a monopoly sufficiently to make the monopoly revenue curve fall altogether below Ox, and q' be the point on the new curve vertically below L in fig. 35, then the new curve at q' will touch one of a series of rectangular hyperbolas drawn with yO produced downwards for one asymptote and Ox for the other. These curves may be called Constant Loss curves.

Again, a tax proportionate to the monopoly revenue, and say m times that revenue (m being less than 1), will substitute for QQ' a curve each ordinate of which is $(1 - m) \times$ the ordinate of the corresponding point on QQ'; i.e. the point which has the same abscissa. The tangents to corresponding points on the old and new positions of QQ' will cut Ox in the same point, as is obvious by the method of projections. But it is a law of rectangular hyperbolas which have the same asymptotes that, if a line be drawn parallel to one asymptote to cut the hyperbolas, and tangents be drawn to them at its points of intersection, they will all cut the other asymptote in the same point. Therefore if q_3' be the point on the new position of QQ' corresponding to q_3, and if we call G the point in which the common tangent to the hyperbola and QQ' cuts Ox, Gq_3' will be a tangent to the hyperbola which passes through q_3'; that is, q_3' is a point of maximum revenue on the new curve.

The geometrical and analytical methods of this note can be applied to cases, such as are discussed in the latter part of § 4 in the text, in which the tax is levied on the produce of the monopoly.

NOTE XXIII. bis (p. 405). These results have easy geometrical proofs by Newton's method, and by the use of well-known properties of the rectangular hyperbola. They may also be proved analytically. As before let $y = f_1(x)$ be the equation to the demand curve; $y = f_2(x)$ that to the supply curve; and that to the monopoly revenue curve is $y = f_3(x)$, where $f_3(x) = f_1(x) - f_2(x)$ the equation to the consumers' surplus curve $y = f_4(x)$; where

$$f_4(x) = \frac{1}{x}\int_0^x f_1(a)\, da - f_1(x).$$

That to the total benefit curve is $y = f_5(x)$; where

$$f_5(x) = f_3(x) + f_4(x) = \frac{1}{x}\int_0^x f_1(a)\, da - f_2(x);$$

a result which may of course be obtained directly. That to the compromise benefit curve is $y = f_6(x)$; where $f_6(x) = f_3(x) + nf_4(x)$; consumers' surplus being reckoned in by the monopolist at n times its actual value.

To find OL (fig. 37), that is, the amount the sale of which will afford the maximum monopoly revenue, we have the equation

$$\frac{d}{dx}\{xf_3(x)\} = 0; \text{ i.e. } f_1(x) - f_2(x) = x\{f_2'(x) - f_1'(x)\};$$

the left-hand side of this equation is necessarily positive, and therefore so is the right-hand side, which shows, what is otherwise obvious, that if Lq_3 be produced to cut the supply and demand curves in q_2 and q_1 respectively, the supply curve at q_2 (if inclined negatively) must make a greater angle with the vertical than is made by the demand curve at q_1.

To find OW, that is, the amount the sale of which will afford the maximum total benefit, we have

$$\frac{d}{dx}\{xf_5(x)\} = 0; \text{ i.e. } f_1(x) - f_2(x) - xf_2'(x) = 0.$$

To find OY, that is, the amount the sale of which will afford the maximum compromise benefit, we have

$$\frac{d}{dx}\{xf_6(x)\} = 0; \text{ i.e. } \frac{d}{dx}\{(1-n)xf_1(x) - xf_2(x) + n\int_0^x f_1(a)\,da\} = 0;$$

$$\text{i.e. } (1-n)xf_1'(x) + f_1(x) - f_2(x) - xf_2'(x) = 0.$$

If $OL = c$, the condition that OY should be greater than ON is that $\frac{d}{dx}\{xf_6(x)\}$ be positive when c is written for x in it; i.e. since $\frac{d}{dx}\{xf_3(x)\} = 0$ when $x = c$,

that $\frac{d}{dx}\{xf_4(x)\}$ be positive when $x = c$; i.e. that $f_1'(c)$ be negative. But this condition is satisfied whatever be the value of c. This proves the first of the two results given at the end of V. xiv. 7; and the proof of the second is similar. (The wording of these results and of their proofs tacitly assumes that there is only one point of maximum monopoly revenue.)

One more result may be added to those in the text. Let us write $OH = a$, then the condition that OY should be greater than OH is that $\frac{d}{dx}\{nf_6(x)\}$ be positive when a is written for x: that is, since $f_1(a) = f_2(a)$, that $(1-n)f_1'(a) - f_2'(a)$ be positive. Now $f_1'(a)$ is always negative, and therefore the condition becomes that $f_2'(x)$ be negative, i.e. that the supply obey the law of increasing return and that $\tan\phi$ be numerically greater than $(1-n)\tan\theta$, where θ and ϕ are the angles which tangents at A to the demand and supply curves respectively make with Ox. When $n = 1$, the sole condition is that $\tan\phi$ be negative: that is, OW is greater than OH provided the supply curve at A be inclined negatively. In other words, if the monopolist regards the interest of consumers as identical with his own, he will carry his production further than the point at which the supply price (in the special sense in which we are here using the term) is equal to the demand price, provided the supply in the neighbourhood of that point obeys the law of increasing return : but he will carry it less far if the supply obeys the law of diminishing return.

NOTE XXIV. (p. 469). Let Δx be the probable amount of his production of wealth in time Δt, and Δy the probable amount of his consumption. Then the discounted value of his future services is $\int_0^T R^{-t}\left(\frac{dx}{dt} - \frac{dy}{dt}\right)dt$; where T is the maximum possible duration of his life. On the like plan the past cost of his rearing and training is $\int_{-T'}^0 R^{-t}\left(\frac{dy}{dt} - \frac{dx}{dt}\right)dt$, where T' is the date of his birth. If we were

A A

to assume that he would neither add to nor take from the material wellbeing of a country in which he stayed all his life, we should have $\int_{-T}^{T} R^{-t}\left(\dfrac{dx}{dt} - \dfrac{dy}{dt}\right) dt = 0$; or, taking the starting-point of time at his birth, and $l = T' + T =$ the maximum possible length of his life, this assumes the simpler form, $\int_{0}^{l} R^{-t}\left(\dfrac{dx}{dt} - \dfrac{dy}{dt}\right) dt = 0.$

To say that Δx is the probable amount of his production in time Δt, is to put shortly what may be more accurately expressed thus :—let $p_1, p_2, \ldots$ be the chances that in time Δt he will produce elements of wealth $\Delta_1 x, \Delta_2 x, \ldots$, where $p_1 + p_2 + \ldots = 1$; and one or more of the series $\Delta_1 x, \Delta x, \ldots$ may be zero; then

$$\Delta x = b_1 \Delta_1 x + p_2 \Delta_2 x + \ldots.$$

COSIMO is a specialty publisher of books and publications that inspire, inform, and engage readers. Our mission is to offer unique books to niche audiences around the world.

COSIMO BOOKS publishes books and publications for innovative authors, nonprofit organizations, and businesses. **COSIMO BOOKS** specializes in bringing books back into print, publishing new books quickly and effectively, and making these publications available to readers around the world.

COSIMO CLASSICS offers a collection of distinctive titles by the great authors and thinkers throughout the ages. At **COSIMO CLASSICS** timeless works find new life as affordable books, covering a variety of subjects including: Business, Economics, History, Personal Development, Philosophy, Religion & Spirituality, and much more!

COSIMO REPORTS publishes public reports that affect your world, from global trends to the economy, and from health to geopolitics.

CPSIA information can be obtained
at www.ICGtesting.com
Printed in the USA
BVHW070838030920
587794BV00001B/2

9 781605 208015